Lecture Notes in Computer Sci

Commenced Publication in 1973
Founding and Former Series Editors:
Gerhard Goos, Juris Hartmanis, and Jan van Leeuwen

Pilar Herrero   Hervé Panetto
Robert Meersman   Tharam Dillon (Eds.)

On the Move to Meaningful Internet Systems: OTM 2012 Workshops

Confederated International Workshops:
OTM Academy, Industry Case Studies Program,
EI2N, INBAST, META4eS, OnToContent, ORM,
SeDeS, SINCOM, and SOMOCO 2012
Rome, Italy, September 10-14, 2012
Proceedings

 Springer

Volume Editors

Pilar Herrero
Universidad Politécnica de Madrid
Boadilla del Monte, Madrid, Spain
E-mail: pherrero@fi.upm.es

Hervé Panetto
University of Lorraine
Vandoeuvre-les-Nancy, France
E-mail: herve.panetto@univ-lorraine.fr

Robert Meersman
Vrije Universiteit Brussel
Brussels, Belgium
E-mail: meersman@vub.ac.be

Tharam Dillon
La Trobe University
Melbourne, VIC, Australia
E-mail: tharam.dillon7@gmail.com

ISSN 0302-9743   e-ISSN 1611-3349
ISBN 978-3-642-33617-1   e-ISBN 978-3-642-33618-8
DOI 10.1007/978-3-642-33618-8
Springer Heidelberg Dordrecht London New York

Library of Congress Control Number: 2012947265

CR Subject Classification (1998): I.2.4, I.2.6, H.3.3-5, J.1, I.6.3-5,
H.5.3, H.4.1-3, C.2, D.2

LNCS Sublibrary: SL 3 – Information Systems and Application,
incl. Internet/Web and HCI

Typesetting: Camera-ready by author, data conversion by Scientific Publishing Services, Chennai, India

Printed on acid-free paper

Springer is part of Springer Science+Business Media (www.springer.com)

General Co-Chairs' Message
for OnTheMove 2012

The OnTheMove 2012 event held in Rome, during September 10–14, further consolidated the importance of the series of annual conferences that was started in 2002 in Irvine, California. It then moved to Catania, Sicily in 2003, to Cyprus in 2004 and 2005, Montpellier in 2006, Vilamoura in 2007 and 2009, in 2008 to Monterrey, Mexico, and was held in Heraklion, Crete, in 2010 and 2011. The event continues to attract a diverse and representative selection of today's worldwide research on the scientific concepts underlying new computing paradigms, which, of necessity, must be distributed, heterogeneous, and autonomous yet meaningfully collaborative. Indeed, as such large, complex, and networked intelligent information systems become the focus and norm for computing, there continues to be an acute and even increasing need to address and discuss face to face in an integrated forum the implied software, system, and enterprise issues as well as methodological, semantic, theoretical, and applicational issues. As we all realize, email, the internet, and even video conferences are not by themselves optimal nor sufficient for effective and efficient scientific exchange.

The OnTheMove (OTM) Federated Conference series was created to cover the scientific exchange needs of the community/ies that work in the broad yet closely connected fundamental technological spectrum of Web-based distributed computing. The OTM program every year covers data and Web semantics, distributed objects, Web services, databases, information systems, enterprise workflow and collaboration, ubiquity, interoperability, mobility, grid, and high-performance computing.

OnTheMove does not consider itself a so-called multi-conference event but instead is proud to give meaning to the "federated" aspect in its full title: it aspires to be a primary scientific meeting place where all aspects of research and development of internet- and intranet-based systems in organizations and for e-business are discussed in a scientifically motivated way, in a forum of loosely interconnected workshops and conferences. This year's OTM Federated Conferences event therefore once more provided an opportunity for researchers and practitioners to understand, discuss, and publish these developments within the broader context of distributed, ubiquitous computing. To further promote synergy and coherence, the main conferences of OTM 2012 were conceived against a background of three interlocking global themes:

- Virtual and Cloud Computing Infrastructures and Security
- Technology and Methodology for an Internet of Things and its Semantic Web
- Collaborative and Social Computing for and in the Enterprise.

Originally the federative structure of OTM was formed by the co-location of three related, complementary, and successful main conference series: DOA (Distributed Objects and Applications, since 1999), covering the relevant infrastructure-enabling technologies; ODBASE (Ontologies, DataBases, and Applications of SEmantics, since 2002), covering Web semantics, XML databases, and ontologies; and CoopIS (Cooperative Information Systems, since 1993), covering the application of these technologies in an enterprise context through, e.g., workflow systems and knowledge management. In 2011 security issues, originally topics of the IS workshop (since 2007), became an integral part of DOA as "Secure Virtual Infrastructures", or DOA-SVI. Each of the main conferences specifically seeks high-quality contributions and encourages researchers to treat their respective topics within a framework that simultaneously incorporates (a) theory, (b) conceptual design and development, (c) methodology and pragmatics, and (d) application in particular case studies and industrial solutions.

As in previous years we again solicited and selected quality workshop proposals to complement the more "archival" nature of the main conferences with research results in a number of selected and emergent areas related to the general area of Web-based distributed computing. We were also glad to see that five of our earlier successful workshops (EI2N, OnToContent, ORM, INBAST, and SeDeS) re-appeared in 2012, in some cases for the fifth or even seventh time, and often in alliance with other older or newly emerging workshops. Three brand-new independent workshops could be selected from proposals and hosted: META4eS, SINCOM, and SOMOCO. The Industry Track, started in 2011 under the auspicious leadership of Hervé Panetto and OMG's Richard Mark Soley, further gained momentum and visibility.

Incidentally, our OTM registration format ("one workshop buys all") actively intends to stimulate workshop audiences to productively mingle with each other and, optionally, with those of the main conferences.

We were most happy to see that once more in 2012 the number of quality submissions for the OnTheMove Academy (OTMA) substantially increased. OTMA implements our unique interactive formula to bring PhD students together, and aims to represent our "vision for the future" in research in the areas covered by OTM. It is managed by a dedicated team of collaborators led by Peter Spyns and Anja Metzner, and of course by the OTMA Dean, Erich Neuhold. In the OTM Academy, PhD research proposals are submitted by students for peer review; selected submissions and their approaches are then presented by the students in front of a wider audience at the conference, and are independently and extensively analyzed and discussed in front of this audience by a panel of senior professors.

As said, all three main conferences and the associated workshops share the distributed aspects of modern computing systems, and the resulting application pull created by the Internet and the so-called Semantic Web. For DOA-SVI 2012, the primary emphasis stayed on the distributed object infrastructure and its virtual and security aspects; for ODBASE 2012, the focus became the knowledge bases and methods required for enabling the use of formal semantics in web-based databases and information systems; for CoopIS 2012, the focus as usual was on the interaction of such technologies and methods with business process issues, such as occur in networked organizations and enterprises. These subject areas overlap in a scientifically natural fashion and many submissions in fact also treated an envisaged mutual impact among them. As in previous years, the organizers wanted to stimulate this cross-pollination by a program of famous keynote speakers, focusing on the chosen themes and shared by all OTM component events. We were quite proud to announce this year

- Ed Parsons, Google Inc, USA;
- Maurizio Lenzerini, U. di Roma La Sapienza, Italy;
- Volkmar Lotz, SAP Research, France;
- Manfred Reichert, U. of Ulm, Germany;
- Guido Vetere, IBM, Italy.

We received a total of 169 submissions for the three main conferences and 127 submissions in total for the workshops, an almost 20% increase compared with those for 2011. Not only may we indeed again claim success in attracting an increasingly representative volume of scientific papers, many from the USA and Asia, but these numbers of course allow the Program Committees to compose a high-quality cross-section of current research in the areas covered by OTM. In fact, the Program Chairs of CoopIS 2012 conferences decided to accept only approximately 1 full paper for every 5 submitted, while the ODBASE 2012 PC accepted less than 1 paper out of 3 submitted, not counting posters. For the workshops and DOA-SVI 2012 the acceptance rate varies but the aim was to stay consistently at about 1 accepted paper for 2-3 submitted, and this as always subordinated to proper peer assessment of scientific quality. As usual we have separated the proceedings into two volumes with their own titles, one for the main conferences and one for the workshops and posters, and we are again most grateful to the Springer LNCS team in Heidelberg for their professional support, suggestions and meticulous collaboration in producing the files ready for downloading on the USB sticks.

The reviewing process by the respective OTM Program Committees was as always performed to professional standards: each paper submitted to the main conferences was reviewed by at least three referees, with arbitrated email discussions in the case of strongly diverging evaluations. It may be worthwhile to emphasize that it is an explicit OnTheMove policy that all conference Program Committees and Chairs make their selections completely autonomously from the OTM organization itself. As in recent years, proceedings on paper were by separate request and order, and incurred an extra charge.

The General Chairs are once more especially grateful to the many people directly or indirectly involved in the setup of these federated conferences. Not everyone realizes the large number of persons that need to be involved, and the huge amount of work, commitment, and in the uncertain economic and funding climate of 2012 certainly also financial risk, that is entailed by the organization of an event like OTM. Apart from the persons in their roles mentioned above, we therefore wish to thank in particular explicitly our 7 main conference PC Chairs:

- CoopIS 2012: Stefanie Rinderle-Ma, Peter Dadam, Xiaofang Zhou;
- ODBASE 2012: Sonia Bergamaschi, Isabel F. Cruz;
- DOA-SVI 2012: Siani Pearson, Alois Ferscha.

And similarly the 2012 OTMA and Workshops PC Chairs (in order of appearance on the website): Hervé Panetto, Michele Dassisti, J. Cecil, Lawrence Whitman, Jinwoo Park, Rafael Valencia García, Thomas Moser, Ricardo Colomo Palacios, Ioana Ciuciu, Anna Fensel, Amanda Hicks, Matteo Palmonari, Terry Halpin, Herman Balsters, Yan Tang, Jan Vanthienen, Wolfgang Prinz, Gregoris Mentzas, Fernando Ferri, Patrizia Grifoni, Arianna D'Ulizia, Maria Chiara Caschera, Irina Kondratova, Peter Spyns, Anja Metzner, Erich J. Neuhold, Alfred Holl, and Maria Esther Vidal. All of them, together with their many PC members, performed a superb and professional job in managing the difficult yet existential process of peer review and selection of the best papers from the harvest of submissions. We all also owe a serious debt of gratitude to our supremely competent and experienced Conference Secretariat and technical support staff in Brussels and Guadalajara, Jan Demey, Daniel Meersman, and Carlos Madariaga.

The General Chairs also thankfully acknowledge the academic freedom, logistic support, and facilities they enjoy from their respective institutions, Vrije Universiteit Brussel (VUB); Université de Lorraine CNRS, Nancy; and Universidad Politécnica de Madrid (UPM), without which such a project quite simply would not be feasible. We do hope that the results of this federated scientific enterprise contribute to your research and your place in the scientific network... We look forward to seeing you again at next year's event!

July 2012

Robert Meersman
Hervé Panetto
Tharam Dillon
Pilar Herrero

Organization

OTM (On The Move) is a federated event involving a series of major international conferences and workshops. These proceedings contain the papers presented at the OTM Academy 2012, the OTM Industry Case Studies Program 2012, the OTM 2012 Federated workshops, and the OTM 2012 Federated conferences poster papers.

Executive Committee

General Co-chairs

Robert Meersman	VU Brussels, Belgium
Tharam Dillon	La Trobe University, Melbourne, Australia
Pilar Herrero	Universidad Politécnica de Madrid, Spain

OnTheMove Academy Dean

Erich Neuhold	University of Vienna, Austria

OnTheMove Academy Organizing Chairs

Peter Spyns	Vrije Universiteit Brussel, Belgium
Anja Metzner	University of Applied Sciences Augsburg, Germany

Industry Case Studies Program Chair

Hervé Panetto	University of Lorraine, France

EI2N 2012 PC Co-Chairs

Hervé Panetto	University of Lorraine, France
Michele Dassisti	Politecnico di Bari, Italy
J. Cecil	Oklahoma State University, USA
Lawrence Whitman	Wichita State University, USA
Jinwoo Park	Seoul National University, Korea

INBAST 2012 PC Co-Chairs

Rafael Valencia García	Universidad de Murcia, Spain
Thomas Moser	Vienna University of Technology, Austria
Ricardo Colomo Palacios	Universidad Carlos III de Madrid, Spain

META4eS 2012 PC Co-Chairs

Ioana Ciuciu	Vrije Universiteit Brussel, Belgium
Anna Fensel	STI Innsbruck, Austria

OnToContent 2012 PC Co-Chairs

Mustafa Jarrar   Birzeit University, Palestine
Amanda Hicks   University of Buffalo, USA
Matteo Palmonarir   Università degli Studi di Milano-Bicocca, Italy

ORM 2012 PC Co-Chairs

Terry Halpin   LogicBlox, Australia and INTI International
     University, Malaysia
Herman Balsters   University of Groningen, The Netherlands

SeDeS 2012 PC Co-Chairs

Yan Tang Demey   STARLab, Vrije Universiteit Brussel, Belgium
Jan Vanthienen   LIRIS, Katholieke Universiteit Leuven,
     Belgium

SINCOM 2012 PC Co-Chairs

Wolfgang Prinz   Fraunhofer FIT, Germany
Gregoris Mentzas   National Technical University of Athens,
     Greece

SOMOCO 2012 PC Co-Chairs

Fernando Ferri   IRPPS, National Research Council, Italy
Patrizia Grifoni   IRPPS, National Research Council, Italy
Arianna D'Ulizia   IRPPS, National Research Council, Italy
Maria Chiara Caschera   IRPPS, National Research Council, Italy
Irina Kondratova   IIT, National Research Council, Canada

Logistics Team

Daniel Meersman
Carlos Madariaga
Jan Demey

OTM Academy 2012 Program Committee

Galia Angelova   Hervé Panetto
Christoph Bussler   Erik Proper
Paolo Ceravolo   Anja Metzner
Philippe Cudré-Mauroux   Fatiha Saïs
Jaime Delgado   Andreas Schmidt
Alfred Holl   Peter Spyns
Frédéric Le Mouël   Maria Esther Vidal
Marcello Leida
Erich J. Neuhold

Industry Case Studies 2012 Program Committee

Sinuhe Arroyo
Frédéric Autran
Arne Berre
Serge Boverie
Christoph Bussler
Francesco Danza
Piero De Sabbata
Marin Dimitrov
Dominique Ernadote
Donald Ferguson
George Fodor
Jean-Luc Garnier
Pascal Gendre
Ted Goranson
Florian Kerschbaum
Juan-Carlos Mendez
Silvana Muscella
Yannick Naudet
Andrea Persidis
Roger Roberts
Ayelet Sapir
François B. Vernadat
Steve Vinoski
Luis Camarinha-Matos

Jorge Cardoso
J. Cecil
Vincent Chapurlat
Yannis Charalabidis
Michele Dassisti
Andres Garcia Higuera
Ricardo Goncalves
Peter Loos
Arturo Molina
Yasuyuki Nishioka
Hervé Panetto
Jin Woo Park
Lawrence Whitman
Milan Zdravkovic
Detlef Zühlke
Peter Benson
Marc Delbaere
Sheron Koshy
Laurent Liscia
Richard Martin
Richard Soley
Martin Zelm

EI2N 2012 Program Committee

Hamideh Afsarmanesh
Alexis Aubry
Giuseppe Berio
Xavier Boucher
Nacer Boudjlida
Luis M. Camarinha-Matos
Vincent Chapurlat
Yannis Charalabidis
David Chen
Michele Dassisti
Claudia Diamantini
Antonio Dourado Correia
Andres Garcia Higuera
Ulrich Jumar
J. Cecil
Ricardo Gonçalves

Ted Goranson
Tran Hoai Linh
Uma Jayaram
Charlotta Johnsson
John Krogstie
Qing Li
Peter Loos
Juan-Carlos Mendez
Istvan Mezgár
Pierre-Alain Millet
Nejib Moalla
Arturo Molina
Yannick Naudet
Shimon Nof
Ovidiu Noran
Angel Ortiz

Hervé Panetto
Erik Proper
Jin Woo Park
Michaël Petit
David Romero
Hubert Roth
Antonio Ruano
Camille Salinesi
Czeslaw Smutnicki
Kamelia Stefanova
Michael Sobolewski
Richard Soley

Kazuhiko Terashima
Miroslav Trajanovic
Bruno Vallespir
François B. Vernadat
Marek Wegrzyn
Georg Weichhart
Agostino Villa
Lawrence Whitman
Milan Zdravkovic
Yun-gui Zhang

INBAST 2012 Program Committee

Giner Alor-Hernández
José María Álvarez-Rodríguez
Ghassand Beydoun
Piotr Bródka
Jordi Conesa Caralt
Sergio de Cesare
Olawande Daramola
Jesualdo Tomás Fernández-Breis
Christian Frühwirth
Roberto García
Achim Hoffmann
Francisco José García Peñalvo
Francisco García Sánchez

Verena Geist
Przemyslaw Kazienko
Olga Kovalenko
José Emilio Labra
Richard Mordinyi
Ana Muñoz
José Luis Ochoa
Inah Omoronyia
Alejandro Rodríguez-González
Vladimir Stantchev
Wikan Danar Sunindyo
Dietmar Winkler

META4eS 2012 Program Committee

Adrian M. P. Brasoveanu
Alberto Messina
Alejandro Vaisman
Alina Dia Miron
Andrea Kő
Andreas Harth
Andres Dominguez Burgos
Andriy Nikolov
Bart Jansen
Christophe Debruyne
Christophe Roche
Constantin Orasan
Cosmin Lazar

Cristian Vasquez
David Chadwick
Davor Meersman
Delia David
Doina Tatar
Dumitru Roman
Efstratios Kontopoulos
Elena Simperl
Erik Mannens
Esteban Zimanyi
Fouad Zablith
Frederik Temmermans
Georgios Meditskos

Irene Celino
John Domingue
Koen Kerremans
Liliana Ibanescu
Magali Séguran
Maria-Esther Vidal
Marin Dimitrov
Marta Sabou
Mike Matton

Mustafa Jarrar
Ozelín Lopez
Peter Spyns
Pieter de Leenheer
Roger Roberts
Stamatia Dasiopoulou
Yan Tang
Yuri Katkov

OnToContent 2012 Program Committee

Alan Ruttenberg
Albert Goldfain
Aldo Gangemi
Alex Borgida
Andreas Schmidt
Anna Fensel
Armando Stellato
Axel-Cyrille Ngonga Ngomo
Barry Smith
Boris Villazon-Terrazas
Christiane Fellbaum
Christophe Roche
David Osumi-Sutherland
Fabian Neuhaus
Francky Trichet
German Rigau
Giancarlo Guizzardi

Irene Celino
Jacek Kopecky
Jouni Tuominen
Luigi Selmi
Luis Manuel Vilches Blázquez
Marcello Leida
Marco Rospocher
Mathias Brochhausen
Miguel-Angel Sicilia
Nikos Loutas
Patrice Seyed
Richard Cyganiak
Roberta Cuel
Stefan Schulz
William Hogan
Zoltan Miklos

ORM 2012 Program Committee

Herman Balsters
Linda Bird
Anthony Bloesch
Peter Bollen
Andy Carver
Matthew Curland
Dave Cuyler
Necito Dela Cruz
Ken Evans
Pat Hallock
Terry Halpin
Clifford Heath
Stijn Hoppenbrouwers
Mike Jackson

Mustafa Jarrar
Inge Lemmens
Dirk van der Linden
Tony Morgan
Maurice Nijssen
Baba Piprani
Erik Proper
Gerhard Skagestein
Peter Spyns
Serge Valera
Theo van der Weide
Jos Vos
Jan Pieter Wijbenga

SeDeS 2012 Program Committee

Frode Eika Sandnes
Kazuya Haraguchi
Olegas Vasilecas
Ying Liu
Dimitris Askounis
Weihua Li
Seunghyun Im
José Fernán Martínez
Piotr Paszek
Yue Liu
Saiful Akbar

Jiehan Zhou
Peter Spyns
Zhiwen Yu
Johan Criel
Bin Guo
Dean Vucinic
Luke Chen
Antonia Albani
Stijn Hoppenbrouwers
Damien Trog

SINCOM 2012 Program Committee

Steffen Budweg
Ernesto Damiani
Stefan Decker
Schahram Dustdar
Sean Goggins
Sergio Gusmeroli
Nils Jeners
Epaminondas Kapetanios
Ralf Klamma
Michael Koch

Yiannis Kompatsiaris
Stefanie Lindstaedt
Giorgio de Michelis
Marc Pallot
Markus Strohmaier
Klaus-Dieter Thoben
Christian Timmerer
Alessandra Toninelli
Wolfgang Wörndl

SOMOCO 2012 Program Committee

Kevin C. Almeroth
Frederic Andres
Richard Chbeir
Karin Coninx
Juan De Lara
Anna Formica
Rajkumar Kannan
Nikos Komninos
Stephen Marsh

Rebecca Montanari
Nitendra Rajput
Tommo Reti
Nicola Santoro
Thanassis Tiropanis
Riccardo Torlone
Adam Wojciechowski

The Coming Age of Ambient Information

Ed Parsons

Google Inc, USA

Short Bio

Ed Parsons is the Geospatial Technologist of Google, with responsibility for evangelising Google's mission to organise the world's information using geography, and tools including Google Earth, Google Maps and Google Maps for Mobile. In his role he also maintains links with Universities, Research and Standards Organisations which are involved in the development of Geospatial Technology.

Ed is based in Google's London office, and anywhere else he can plug in his laptop.

Ed was the first Chief Technology Officer in the 200-year-old history of Ordnance Survey, and was instrumental in moving the focus of the organisation from mapping to Geographical Information.

Ed came to the Ordnance Survey from Autodesk, where he was EMEA Applications Manager for the Geographical Information Systems (GIS) Division.

He earned a Masters degree in Applied Remote Sensing from Cranfield Institute of Technology and holds a Honorary Doctorate in Science from Kingston University, London.

Ed is a fellow of the Royal Geographical Society and is the author of numerous articles, professional papers and presentations to International Conferences and he developed one of the first weblogs in the Geospatial Industry at www.edparsons.com.

Ed is married with two children and lives in South West London.

Talk

"The coming age of ambient information"

With the growing adoption of Internet Protocol Version 6 (IPv6) applications and services will be able to communicate with devices attached to virtually all human-made objects, and these devices will be able to communicate with each other. The Internet of Things could become an information infrastructure a number of orders of magnitude larger than the internet today, and one which although similar may offer opportunities for radically new consumer applications. What are some of the opportunities and challenges presented by ambient information.

Inconsistency Tolerance in Ontology-Based Data Management

Maurizio Lenzerini

Università di Roma La Sapienza, Italy

Short Bio

Maurizio Lenzerini is a professor in Computer Science and Engineering at the Università di Roma La Sapienza, Italy, where he is currently leading a research group on Artificial Intelligence and Databases. His main research interests are in Knowledge Representation and Reasoning, Ontology languages, Semantic Data Integration, and Service Modeling. His recent work is mainly oriented towards the use of Knowledge Representation and Automated Reasoning principles and techniques in Information System management, and in particular in information integration and service composition. He has authored over 250 papers published in leading international journals and conferences. He has served on the editorial boards of several international journals, and on the program committees of the most prestigious conferences in the areas of interest. He is currently the Chair of the Executive Committee of the ACM Symposium of Principles of Database Systems, a Fellow of the European Coordinating Committee for Artificial Intelligence (ECCAI), a Fellow of the Association for Computing Machinery (ACM), and a member of The Academia Europaea - The Academy of Europe.

Talk

"Inconsistency tolerance in ontology-based data management"

Ontology-based data management aims at accessing, using, and maintaining a set of data sources by means of an ontology, i.e., a conceptual representation of the domain of interest in the underlying information system. Since the ontology describes the domain, and not simply the data at the sources, it frequently happens that data are inconsistent with respect to the ontology. Inconsistency tolerance is therefore a crucial feature of an in the operation of ontology-based data management systems. In this talk we first illustrate the main ideas and techniques for using an ontology to access the data layer of an information system, and then we discuss several issues related to inconsistency tolerance in ontology-based data management.

Towards Accountable Services in the Cloud

Volkmar Lotz

SAP Research, France

Short Bio

Volkmar Lotz has more than 20 years experience in industrial research on Security and Software Engineering. He is heading the Security & Trust practice of SAP Research, a group of 40+ researchers investigating into applied research and innovative security solutions for modern software platforms, networked enterprises and Future Internet applications. The Security & Trust practice defines and executes SAP's security research agenda in alignment with SAP's business strategy and global research trends.

Volkmar's current research interests include Business Process Security, Service Security, Authorisation, Security Engineering, Formal Methods and Compliance. Volkmar has published numerous scientific papers in his area of interest and is regularly serving on Programme Committees of internationally renowned conferences. He has been supervising various European projects, including large-scale integrated projects. Volkmar holds a diploma in Computer Science from the University of Kaiserslautern.

Talk

"Towards Accountable Services in the Cloud"

Accountability is a principle well suited to overcome trust concerns when operating sensitive business applications over the cloud. We argue that accountability builds upon transparency and control, and investigate in control of services in service-oriented architectures. Control needs to reach out to different layers of a SOA, both horizontally and vertically.

We introduce an aspect model for services that enables control on these layers by invasive modification of platform components and upon service orchestration. This is seen as a major constituent of an accountability framework for the cloud, which is the objective of an upcoming collaborative research project.

Process and Data: Two Sides of the Same Coin?

Manfred Reichert

University of Ulm, Germany

Short Bio

Manfred holds a PhD in Computer Science and a Diploma in Mathematics. Since January 2008 he has been appointed as full professor at Ulm University, Germany. Before, he was working in the Netherlands as associate professor at the University of Twente. There, he was also leader of the strategic research orientations on "E-health" and "Applied Science of Services", and member of the Management Board of the Centre for Telematics and Information Technology - the largest ICT research institute in the Netherlands.

His major research interests include next generation process management technology, adaptive processes, process lifecycle management, data-driven process management, mobile processes, process model abstraction, and advanced process-aware applications (e.g., e-health, automotive engineering). Together with Peter Dadam he pioneered the work on the ADEPT process management technology and co-founded the AristaFlow GmbH. Manfred has been participating in numerous BPM research projects and made outstanding contributions in the BPMfield. His new Springer book on "Enabling Flexibility in Process-aware Information Systems" will be published in September 2012. Manfred was PC Co-chair of the BPM'08 and CoopIS'11 conferences and General Chair of the BPM'09 conference.

Talk

"Process and Data: Two Sides of the Same Coin?"

Companies increasingly adopt process management technology which offers promising perspectives for realizing flexible information systems. However, there still exist numerous process scenarios not adequately covered by contemporary information systems. One major reason for this deficiency is the insufficient understanding of the inherent relationships existing between business processes on the one side and business data on the other. Consequently, these two perspectives are not well integrated in existing process management systems.

This keynote emphasizes the need for both object- and process-awareness in future information systems, and illustrates it along several case studies. Especially, the relation between these two fundamental perspectives will be discussed, and the role of business objects and data as drivers for both process modeling and process enactment be emphasized. In general, any business process support should consider object behavior as well as object interactions, and therefore be based on two levels of granularity. In addition, data-driven process execution and integrated user access to processes and data are needed. Besides giving insights into these fundamental properties, an advanced framework supporting them in an integrated manner will be presented and its application to complex process scenarios be shown. Overall, a holistic and generic framework integrating processes, data, and users will contribute to overcome many of the limitations of existing process management technology.

Experiences with IBM Watson Question Answering System

Guido Vetere

Center for Advanced Studies, IBM, Italy

Short Bio

Guido Vetere has attained a degree in Philosophy of Language at the University of Rome 'Sapienza' with a thesis in computational linguistics. He joined IBM Scientific Center in 1989, to work in many research and development projects on knowledge representation, automated reasoning, information integration, and language technologies. Since 2005, he leads the IBM Italy Center for Advanced Studies. He is member of Program Committees of various international conferences on Web Services, Ontologies, Semantic Web. Also, he represents IBM in several joint research programs and standardization activities. He is the author of many scientific publications and regularly collaborates with major Italian newspapers on scientific divulgation. He is co-founder and VP of 'Senso Comune', a no-profit organization for building a collaborative knowledge base of Italian.

Talk

"Experience with IBM Watson Question Answering System"

The IBM "Watson" Question Answering system, which won the Jeopardy! contest against human champions last year, is now being applied to real business. Watson integrates Natural Language Processing, Evidence-based Reasoning and Machine Learning in a way that makes it possible to deal with a great variety of information sources and to move beyond some of the most compelling constraints of current IT systems. By developing Watson, IBM Research is focusing on various topics, including language understanding, evidence evaluation, and knowledge acquisition, facing some of the fundamental problems of semantic technologies, which ultimately root in open theoretical questions about linguistic practices and the construction of human knowledge. Experiences with Watson show how it is possible to effectively use a variety of different approaches to such open questions, from exploiting ontologies and encyclopedic knowledge to learning from texts by statistical methods, within a development process that allows evaluating the best heuristics for the use case at hand.

Table of Contents

OnTheMove 2012 Keynotes

On The Move Academy (OTMA) 2012

OTM Industry Case Studies Program 2012

Industrial Session

Workshop on Enterprise Integration, Interoperability and Networking (EI2N) 2012

Enterprise Services and Sustainability

Semantic Issues in Enterprise Engineering

Workshop on Industrial and Business Applications of Semantic Web Technologies (INBAST) 2012

Workshop on Methods, Evaluation, Tools and Applications for the Creation and Consumption of Structured Data for the e-Society (META4eS) 2012

Workshop on Fact-Oriented Modeling (ORM) 2012

Workshop on Ontology Content (OnToContent) 2012

Workshop on Semantics and Decision Making (SeDeS) 2012

Workshop on Socially Intelligent Computing (SINCOM) 2012

Workshop on SOcial and MObile COmputing for Collaborative Environments (SOMOCO) 2012

Cooperative Information Systems (CoopIS) 2012 Posters

Ontologies, DataBases, and Applications of Semantics (ODBASE) 2012 Posters

The 9th OnTheMove Academy Chairs' Message

The term 'academy', originating from Greek antiquity, implies a strong mark of *quality and excellence in higher education and research* that is upheld by its members. This label is equally valid in our context. OTMA Ph.D. students get the opportunity of publishing in a highly reputed publication channel, namely the Springer LNCS OTM workshops proceedings. The OTMA faculty members, who are well-respected researchers and practitioners, critically reflect on the students work in a highly positive and inspiring atmosphere, so that the students can improve not only their research capacities but also their presentation and writing skills. OTMA participants also learn how to review scientific papers. And they enjoy ample possibilities to build and expand their professional network. This includes personal feedback and exclusive time of prominent experts on-site. In addition, thanks to an OTMA LinkedIn-group the students can stay in touch with all OTMA participants and interested researchers. And last but not least, an ECTS credit certificate rewards their hard work.

Crucial for the success of OTM Academy is the commitment of our other OTMA faculty members whom we sincerely thank:

- Erich J. Neuhold (University of Vienna, Austria), OTMA Dean
- Alfred Holl (University of Applied Sciences, Nuremberg, Germany)
- Maria Esther Vidal (Universidad Simon Bolivar, Caracas, Venezuela)
- Josefa Kumpfmller (Vienna, Austria), OTM Integrated Communications Chair

The OTMA submissions were reviewed by an international programme committee of well-respected experts. We gratefully thank them for their effort and time:

- Galia Angelova (Bulgarian Academy of Science, Sofia, Bulgary)
- Christoph Bussler (XTime Inc., USA)
- Paolo Ceravolo (Universit degli Studi di Milano, Milan, Italy)
- Philippe Cudr-Mauroux (Massachusetts Institute of Technology, USA)
- Marcello Leida (Khalifa University, Abu Dhabi, United Arabic Emirates)
- Frdric Le Moul (University of Lyon, Lyon, France)
- Herv Panetto (Nancy University, Nancy, France)
- Erik Proper (Public Research Centre - Henri Tudor, Luxembourg)
- Fatiha Sas (Universit Paris-Sud XI, France)
- Andreas Schmidt (Karlsruhe University of Applied Sciences, Germany)

We also express our thanks to Christophe Debruyne (Vrije Universiteit Brussel) who again volunteered to be the OTMA 2012 social media master and to Zhivko Angelov and Stoyan Mihov (Bulgarian Academy of Science) as additional reviewers.

This year, nine papers were submitted by Ph.D. students from nine different countries. Five submissions have been accepted as regular papers, one as a short

P. Herrero et al. (Eds.): OTM 2012 Workshops, LNCS 7567, pp. 1–2, 2012.

paper and one as a poster paper for inclusion in the proceedings. We hope that you find the papers of these upcoming researchers promising and inspiring for your own research.

July 2012   Peter Spyns
                                                                         Anja Metzner

Improving Efficiency of Data Intensive Applications on GPU Using Lightweight Compression

Piotr Przymus[1] and Krzysztof Kaczmarski[2]

[1] Nicolaus Copernicus University, Chopina 12/18, Toruń, Poland
eror@umk.mat.pl
[2] Warsaw University of Technology, Plac Politechniki 1, 00-661 Warszawa, Poland
k.kaczmarski@mini.pw.edu.pl

Abstract. In many scientific and industrial applications GPGPU (General-Purpose Computing on Graphics Processing Units) programming reported excellent speed-up when compared to traditional CPU (central processing unit) based libraries. However, for data intensive applications this benefit may be much smaller or may completely disappear due to time consuming memory transfers. Up to now, gain from processing on the GPU was noticeable only for problems where data transfer could be compensated by calculations, which usually mean large data sets and complex computations. This paper evaluates a new method of data decompression directly in GPU shared memory which minimizes data transfers on the path from disk, through main memory, global GPU device memory, to GPU processor. The method is successfully applied to pattern matching problems. Results of experiments show considerable speed improvement for large and small data volumes which is a significant step forward in GPGPU computing.

Keywords: lightweight compression, data-intensive computations, GPU, CUDA.

1 Introduction

In all branches of science and industry amount of data which needs to be processed increase every year with enormous speed. Often this analysis involve uncomplicated algorithms but working on large data sets which in most cases cannot be efficiently reduced. This kind of applications are called data-intensive and are characterized by the following properties:

1. data itself, its size, complexity or rate of acquisition is the biggest problem;
2. require fast data access and minimization of data movement;
3. expects high, preferably linear, scalability of both hardware and software platform.

One of the most typical solutions to process large volumes of data is the map-reduce algorithm which gained huge popularity due to its simplicity, scalability and distributed nature. It is designed to perform large scale computations which may last from seconds to weeks or longer and involve from several to hundreds or thousands of machines processing together peta-bytes of data.

P. Herrero et al. (Eds.): OTM 2012 Workshops, LNCS 7567, pp. 3–12, 2012.

On the opposite side we can find problems which reside in a single machine but are large enough to require high processing power to get results within milliseconds. GPU programming offers tremendous processing power and excellent scalability with increasing number of parallel threads but with several other limitations. One of them is obligatory data transfer between RAM (random-access memory) and the computing GPU processor which generates additional cost of computations when compared to a pure CPU-based solution. This barrier can make all GPU computations unsatisfactory especially for smaller problems.

Time series matching is a popular example of this kind of data intensive applications in which a user may expect ultra fast results. Therefore in the rest of this work we use this example as a proof of concept application.

1.1 Motivation

Goal of this work is to improve efficiency of data transfer between disk, through RAM, global GPU memory and processing unit, which is often a bottleneck of many algorithms and gain noticeable higher speed up of algorithms when compared to classical CPU programming. We focus on memory bound data intensive applications since many computation intensive applications already proved to be much faster when properly implemented in parallel GPU algorithms.

Let us consider a problem of matching whole patterns in time series. As a distance function we can use the Hamming distance. Due to the lack of complex calculations main limitation of this problem is data transfer. To facilitate the transfer of data we can use either hardware solutions or try to reduce the data size by compressing or eliminating data. Since the hardware is expensive and the elimination of data is not always possible, data compression is usually the only option. Classic compression algorithms are computationally expensive (gain from the transfer data does not compensate the calculations [1]) and difficult to implement on the GPU [2]. Alternatives such as lightweight compression algorithms which are successfully used for the CPU are therefore very attractive.

1.2 Related Works

Lossless data compression is a common technique for reducing data transfers. In the context of SIMD (Single Instruction Multiple Data) computations data compression was successfully utilized by [3] in tree searching to increase efficiency of cache line transfer between memory and processor. The authors indicate that GPU implementation of the same search algorithm is computational bound and cannot be improved by compression. In [4] authors present interesting study of different compression techniques for WWW data in order to achieve querying speed up. A general solution for data intensive applications by cache compression is discussed in [1]. Obviously efficiency may be increased only if decompression speed is higher than I/O operation. In our case we show that decoding is really much faster and eliminates this memory bottleneck. The compression schemes proposed by Zukowski et al. [1] offer good trade-off between compression time and encoded data size and what is more important are designed especially for super scalar processors which means also very good properties for GPU. Delbru et al. [5] develop a new Adaptive Frame of Reference compression algorithm in order to achieve significant speed up of compression time, which in turn allows for effective updates of data.

All these works are in fact entry points to our solution. Our contribution is that the compression methods have been redesigned for GPU architecture and may offer excellent encoding and decoding speed for all compression ratios. Our solution may be utilised in any data intensive algorithms involving integer or fixed-decimal number data. We also explain how this method may be extended to other algorithms.

As the preliminary work we checked if lightweight compression algorithms can be used for different kinds of common time series databases. We collected data from various data sets covering: star light curve (TR1, TR2 – [6]), CFD (contract for difference) and stock quotations for AUDJPY, EURUSD, Shenzen Development Bank respectively (IN1, IN2, TS1 – [7,8]), radioactivity in the ground at 2 hourly intervals over one year (TS2 – [8]) and sample ECG (electrocardiogram) data (PH1,PH2 – [9]). The data used in this experiment is the data with fixed decimal precision that can be stored as integers, which allows to use lightweight compression. Efficiency of conventional compression algorithms (gzip, bzip2 - with default settings) compared to the lightweight compression methods (PFOR, PFOR-DIFF) is presented in figure 1. We can notice that lightweight compression, although not achieving as high compression ratio as gzip, may also obtain similar results, bzip2 is always much better but also significantly slower. This is also proved by L. Wu et al. [2] who showed that conventional compression is too slow to increase overall algorithm efficiency for GPU.

Due to its specificity, time series usually have a good compression ratio (Fig. 1). The most important benefits of compression can be summarized as follows:

- shorter time to load data from disk
- shorter time to copy data from RAM to device
- possibility to fit larger set of data directly on the GPU (GPU DRAM is often limited)
- reduced data size in storage

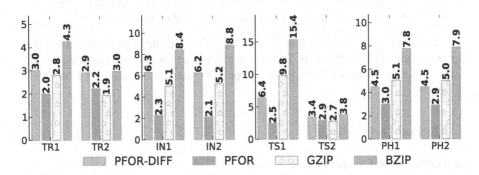

Fig. 1. Achieved compression level of lightweight compression and conventional compression methods for various datasets (higher is better). Data sets: TR1, TR2 – star light curve; IN1, IN2, TS1 – CFD and stock quotations; TS2 – radioactivity in the ground; PH1, PH2 – ECG data.

We conclude that lightweight compression may be used in time series data intensive applications achieving compression ratio from 2 to 7. This initial investigation lets us to predict that data transfer cost accompanied with decompression time may be noticeably decreased.

1.3 Research Hypothesis and Methodology

The main research hypothesis for this project is as follows.

- Data-intensive applications may increase their efficiency by utilization of lightweight compression methods in GPU global and shared memory.
- Cost of data decompression can be amortised by fewer global memory reads.
- Additional benefit may be obtained by proper utilisation of shared memory decompression.
- Data-intensive applications may benefit from GPU computing when applied for smaller data sets than without the method.

In order to verify the hypotheses we implement a prototype which will be used as a proof of concept equipped with several real-time and real-data measurements performed by fine grained timers and memory access analysis done by a professional profiler. Checking the hypotheses will involve a few kinds of experiments including data intensive application using:

1. GPU algorithm without decompression compared to CPU algorithm without decompression. This will allow to estimate possible general speed up of an algorithm when run on a GPU and also will be a starting point for other experiments by registering time necessary to perform pure computations without any decompression overhead.
2. GPU algorithm with decompression in global memory compared to CPU algorithm with decompression. This will show potential speed up when data transfer is minimised by data compression.
3. GPU algorithms with decompression in shared memory compared to GPU with decompression in global memory and CPU algorithm with decompression. This will show the speed up when minimising GPU global memory reads.

As an initial set up for this research we use time series matching problems as an exemplar of data intensive applications. Because of efficiency requirements mentioned in the previous section we utilise lightweight compression methods: PFOR and FOR-DIFF algorithms.

2   Method Description

2.1 Lightweight Compression

In this section we discuss the algorithm FOR and FOR-DIFF in different variations, as well as discuss problems and solutions when using this approach on the GPU. FOR determines range of values for the frame, and then maps the values in this interval using a minimum number of bits needed to distinguish the data [10]. A common practice is to convert the data in the frame to the interval $\{0, \ldots, max - min\}$. In this situation, we need exactly $\lceil log_2(max - min + 1) \rceil$ bits to encode each value in the frame.

The main advantage of the FOR algorithm is the fact that compression and decompression are highly effective on GPU because these routines contain no branching-conditions, which decrease parallelism of SIMD operations. Additionally functions are loop-unrolled and use only shift and mask operations. This implies that there are dedicated compression and decompression routines prepared for every bit encoding length.

The compression algorithm works as follows, for the data frame of length n loop is performed each m values (where m is a multiple of 8) and compressed using the same function at each iteration step. Decompression is similar to compression. We iterate through the m-coded values, and we use a function that decodes m values.

FOR-DIFF algorithm is similar to FOR, however, stores the differences between successive data points in frame. Compression needs to calculate the difference, then compresses them using the FOR compression scheme. Decompression begins by decompressing and then reconstructs the original data from the differences. This approach can significantly improve the compression ratio for certain types of data.

The main drawback of FOR is that it is prone to outliers in the data frame. For example, for the frame $\{1,2,3,3,2,2,2,3,3,1,1,64,2,3,1,1\}$, if not the value 64 we could use the $\lceil log_2(3 - 1 + 1) \rceil = 2$ bits to encode the frame, but due to the outlier we have to use 6-bit encoding ($\lceil log_2(64 - 1 + 1) \rceil$) thus wasting 4 bits for each element.

Solution to the problem of outliers has been proposed in the work [1] in the modified version of the algorithm, called Patched FOR or PFOR. In this version of the algorithm outliers are stored as exceptions. PFOR first selects a new range mapping for the data in order to minimise the size of compressed data frames taking into account the space needed to store exceptions. Therefore, compressed block consists of two sections, within the first section the compressed data are kept and in the second exceptions are stored (encoded using 8, 16 or 32 bits). Unused slots for exceptions in the first section are used to hold the offset of the following exception in the data in order to create linked list, when there is no space to store the offset of the next exception, a *compulsive exception* is created [1]. For large blocks of data, the linked lists approach may fail because the exceptions may appear sparse thus generate a large number of compulsory exceptions. To minimise the problem of various solutions have been proposed, such as reducing the frame size [1], or algorithms that do not generate compulsive exceptions, such as Adaptive FOR [5] or modified version of PFOR [4]. Our publication is based on PFOR algorithm presented in [4]. Compressed block consists of three parts: the first in which compressed data are kept, second section where exceptions offsets are stored, and the last section which holds remainders of exceptions. When the outlier is processed, its position is preserved in an offset array, and the value divided into bits that are stored in the first section and the remainder to be retained in the third. Second and third section are then compressed using FOR(separately).

Decompression proceeds as follows: first decompresses the data section. Then decompresses the offset and exceptions array. Then iterates over the array offset, and restore the value of by applying patch from exception array.

2.2   GPU Implementation

To be able to decompress a data frame, decompression functions must be specified (for block of values, positions and supplements). In the case of the CPU one can use function pointers. On GPU this is dependent on the GPU computation capabilities (cc). For cc lower than the 2.x is not possible to use function pointers, which were introduced in version 2.x and higher. So far we used solution compatible with both architectures. In future work a version that uses features introduced in 2.x cards may simplify the code and make it more flexible.

Our current implementation is based on macros and requires information about the compressed data at compile time. This is not a serious limitation in the case of data that we analysed, as the optimum compression parameters were found to be constant within particular sets of data. Usual practice is to determine the optimal compression parameters based on sample data [1] and use them for the rest of the data set.

Another challenge was the issue of optimal reads of global memory during decompression: first decompression threads do not form coalesced reads leading to a drop in performance, and secondly the CUDA architecture can not cope well with the types of readings less than 32 bits in length. Our solution involves packaging data in texture memory, which solves the first problem. The second problem is solved by casting compressed data (char array) to array of integers. Decompression requires the reverse conversion. Texture, however, introduces some limitations, the maximum size is 2^{27} elements in case of one dimensional array. In future we plan to abolish the need for packaging data in the texture by modifying the compression and decompression algorithm. In this way readings of compressed data will allow for coalesced reads.

We prepared two versions of the experiments for GPU. In the first one we decompresses into the shared memory and in the second one into global memory. Algorithm based on global memory, as expected, is considerably slower than the algorithm based on shared memory (global memory is hundreds of times slower than shared), but this is still good choice for the considered experiment. On the other hand using shared memory is not always possible, so the algorithm based on global memory is still an alternative.

In the case of PFOR-DIFF algorithm we still need to perform reconstruction step, which involves iterating over decompressed buffer. In our opinion the best solution for this step, is to use properly implemented parallel prefix sum.

To decompress m (where m is a multiple of 8) values, we use $m/8$ threads. Each of the threads decompresses 8 values. Assuming that we have k exceptions (where k is a multiple of 8) we use the $k/8$ threads to decompress the offset and exception array. Then we patch 8 values as indicated in offset array using exceptions. This scheme is easily customisable when we have fewer threads. For performance reasons, we still need an array of 24 integers (safely located within threads registers) - ensuring best performance. After the decompression phase, array can be safely used for other purposes. For the convenience we have a macro that entered at the beginning of the kernel will prepare the appropriate code for uncompressing data, making use of decompression in other solutions easy.

We prepared uncompressing data code for both algorithms, ie. PFOR and PFOR-DIFF. In the experimental part we used the PFOR-DIFF algorithm as it is computationally more complex.

3 Preliminary Results

3.1 Experiment Results

Experiment Settings. In our experiment we used the following equipment: two Nvidia cards - Tesla C2050 / C2070 with 2687 MB and GeForce 2800 GTX with 896 MB (from CUDA Capability Major 2.0 and 1.3) - 2 x Six-Core processor AMD Opteron (tm) Processor with 31 GB RAM, Intel (R) RAID Controller RS2BL040 set in RAID5, 4 drives Seagate Constellation ES ST2000NM0011 2000 GB. We used the Linux operating system kernel 2.6.38-11 with the CUDA driver version 4.0.

Based on the observations that we made when analysis of example time series, we generated test data sets to ensure equal sizes of test data at different compression ratios. Each data set consists of 5% of outliers (which is consistent with the analysed data).

Experiments were conducted on different sizes of data ($2MB$, $4MB$, $10MB$, $50MB$, $100MB$, $250MB$, $500MB$, $750MB$, $1GB$). For each size, 10 iterations were performed and the results were averaged. In addition, to ensure the same disk read times for the same size of data we averaged disk read times for each data size. For the experiment with 1GB of data we present detailed results in table 1 which is visualised in figure 2. For the remaining data sizes we present average speed up in figures 3b and 3a.

Table 1. Measured times in seconds for 1GB of data. **Level** – compression level of input data. **IO** – time of disk IO operations. **Mem** – time of RAM to GPU Device data copying. **Computation** – algorithm computation time including data decompression.

Method type	Level	IO	Mem	Computation	Summarized
No compr. CPU	1	67.295	0.0	2.410	69.705
No compr. GPU	1	67.330	0.581	0.010	67.922
Compr. GPU shar.	2	33.448	0.286	0.085	33.821
Compr. GPU glob.	2	33.495	0.286	0.426	34.208
Compr. CPU	2	33.949	0.0	7.690	41.640
Compr. GPU shar.	4	16.778	0.104	0.083	16.966
Compr. GPU glob.	4	16.785	0.105	0.427	17.318
Compr. CPU	4	17.009	0.0	7.203	24.213
Comp. GPU shar.	6	11.192	0.095	0.082	11.369
Comp. GPU glob.	6	11.178	0.095	0.428	11.701
Comp. CPU	6	11.345	0.0	6.961	18.307

3.2 Discussion

Figure 2 presents final results of our experiments which were run on whole pattern matching algorithm. The bars are grouped by levels of compression, from 2 to 6, plus no compression. On the left we may compare efficiency of global and shared memory decompression. The right side shows CPU performance.

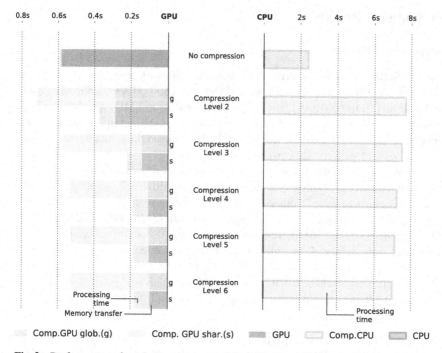

Fig. 2. Performance of a whole pattern matching algorithm with and without compression for 1GB of data, excluding IO times (lower is better). g – global memory decompression, s – shared memory decompression.

CPU performance is highly influenced by data decompression time. We can see that decompression takes from 4 to almost 6 seconds which is about 200% to 300% of the algorithm without decompression. The only possible improvement can be then observed on IO operations.

Thanks to ultra fast decompression GPU implementation of the algorithm performs much better. We can observe that for compression level 2 decompression in shared memory improved overall execution time by almost 2 times. For level 6 it is almost 3 times better. Decompression in global memory although also very fast can be slower for lower levels.

We must point out here that architecture of GPU shared memory limits possible number of algorithms which may use shared memory decompression method. Currently, subsequent kernel calls is the only method for global synchronisation. However, GPU cannot store shared memory state between kernel calls. As the consequence data decompression and algorithm execution must be done in single kernel. We are conscious that this may be improved by more complex kernels and data decompression strategy which will be addressed in our future research.

Figures 3a and 3b show interesting results concerning our shared memory decompression method. First we must notice that data compression alone increases application speed by reducing necessary data transfer. Fig. 3a demonstrates that pure IO operation speed up corresponds data compression ratio, which is an obvious result.

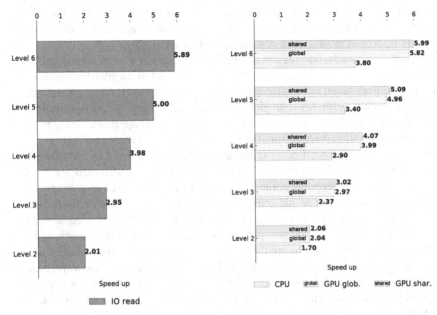

(a) Speed up on IO read time (higher is better)

(b) Computations speed up when using lightweight decompression compared to single threaded CPU version without decompression. This includes IO. (higher is better)

Fig. 3. Performance improvments when using lightweight compression

However, fig. 3b shows that this speed up may be significantly better if decompression is performed in shared memory. We achieved speed up improvement from 2% with compression ratio 2 up to 10% with compression ratio 6. These results prove our hypothesis that shared memory decompression increases efficiency of data intensive applications.

4   Conclusions and Future Work

In this paper we presented research devoted to improvement of GPU algorithms by utilisation of shared memory decompression. The hypothesis was evaluated and proved in many experiments. The contribution of our work may be summarised as follows.

We developed two highly optimised GPU parallel decompression methods: one dedicated for global and one for shared memory. We improved original algorithms by adding ability to deal with time series data, include negative values and fixed point values. We have no information about any other GPU implementations of lightweight compression with similar abilities.

We tested lightweight compression for time series and applied our novel methods to data intensive pattern matching mechanism. Our evaluation proved that the method significantly improved results when compared to other methods.

We showed that data decompression in GPU shared memory may generally improve performance of other data intensive applications due to ultra fast parallel decompression procedure since time saved by smaller data transfer is not wasted for decompression.

We analysed relationship between global and shared memory decompression showing that although shared memory may limit number of possible applications due to lack of global synchronisation mechanism, it significantly improves performance.

We plan to design a general purpose library which could be used in a similar way to CUDA Thrust library. Utilisation of common iterator pattern with memory blocks overlapping may offer interesting abilities breaking barrier of inter block threads communication. Such an iterator would require to define size of a shared memory buffer which would be common for more than one block in parallel threads execution. Description of such an extended iterator pattern for overlapping shared memory will be the next step of this research. During the preparation of this work, we managed to locate several problems of the current solution. In the future we also plan to prepare a new version of the algorithm which will allow for better use of CUDA 2.x computation capabilities and remove the constraints which we mentioned in the implementation description.

This work is a part of a larger project which aims to create a GPU based database for scientific data (such as time series, array, etc.).

References

1. Zukowski, M., Heman, S., Nes, N., Boncz, P.: Super-scalar ram-cpu cache compression. In: Proc. of the 22nd Intern. Conf. on Data Engineering, ICDE 2006, pp. 59–59. IEEE (2006)
2. Wu, L., Storus, M., Cross, D.: Cs315a: Final project cuda wuda shuda: Cuda compression project. Technical report. Stanford University (March 2009)
3. Kim, C., Chhugani, J., Satish, N., Sedlar, E., Nguyen, A.D., Kaldewey, T., Lee, V.W., Brandt, S.A., Dubey, P.: Fast: fast architecture sensitive tree search on modern cpus and gpus. In: Proc. of the 2010 Intern. Conf. on Management of Data, pp. 339–350. ACM (2010)
4. Yan, H., Ding, S., Suel, T.: Inverted index compression and query processing with optimized document ordering. In: Proc. of the 18th Intern. Conf. on World Wide Web, pp. 401–410. ACM (2009)
5. Delbru, R., Campinas, S., Samp, K., Tummarello, G.: Adaptive frame of reference for compressing inverted lists. Technical report. DERI – Digital Enterprise Research Institute (December 2010)
6. Harvard IIC. Data and search interface, time sries center (2012), http://timemachine.iic.harvard.edu/
7. Integral. Truefx (2012), http://www.truefx.com/
8. Hyndman, R.J.: Time series data library (2012), http://robjhyndman.com/tsdl
9. Goldberger, A.L., et al.: Physiobank, physiotoolkit, and physionet: Components of a new research resource for complex physiologic signals. Circulation 101(23), e215-e220
10. Goldstein, J., Ramakrishnan, R., Shaft, U.: Compressing relations and indexes. In: Proc. of the 14th Intern. Conf. on Data Engineering, pp. 370–379. IEEE (1998)

Towards a Trust and Reputation Framework for Social Web Platforms

Thao Nguyen[1,2,*], Luigi Liquori[1], Bruno Martin[2], and Karl Hanks

[1] Institut National de Recherche en Informatique et Automatique, France
[2] Université Nice Sophia Antipolis, France
{Thao.Nguyen,Luigi.Liquori}@inria.fr,
Bruno.Martin@unice.fr,
Karl.Hanks@cantab.net

Abstract. Trust and Reputation Systems (TRSs) represent a significant trend in decision support for Internet-based interactions. They help users to decide whom to trust and how much to trust a transaction. They are also an effective mechanism to encourage honesty and cooperation among users, resulting in healthy online markets or communities. The basic idea is to let parties rate each other so that new public knowledge can be created from personal experiences. The major difficulty in designing a reputation system is making it robust against malicious attacks. Our contribution in this paper is twofold. Firstly, we combine multiple research agendas into a holistic approach to building a robust TRS. Secondly, we focus on one TRS component which is the reputation computing engine and provide a novel investigation into an implementation of the engine proposed in [7].

1 Introduction

Information concerning the reputation of individuals has always been spread by word-of-mouth and has been used as an enabler of numerous economic and social activities. Especially now, with the development of technology and, in particular, the Internet, reputation information can be broadcast more easily and faster than ever before. Trust and Reputation Systems (TRSs) have gained the attention of many information and computer scientists since the early 2000s. TRSs have a wide range of applications and are domain specific. The multiple areas where they are applied, include social web platforms, e-commerce, peer-to-peer networks, sensor networks, ad-hoc network routing, and so on [5]. Among these, we are most interested in social web platforms. We observe that trust and reputation is used in many online systems, such as online auction and shopping websites, including eBay [1], where people buy and sell a broad variety of goods and services, and Amazon [2], which is a world famous online retailer. Online services with TRSs provide a better safety to their users. A good TRS can also create incentives for good behavior and penalize damaging actions. As noted by

---

* Corresponding author.

P. Herrero et al. (Eds.): OTM 2012 Workshops, LNCS 7567, pp. 13–22, 2012.

Resnick et al. [10], markets with the support of TRSs will be healthier, with a variety of prices and quality of service. TRSs are very important for an online community, with respect to the safety of participants, robustness of the network against malicious behavior and for fostering a healthy market.

From a functional point of view, a TRS can be split into three components, as justified in [9]. The first component gathers feedback on participants' past behavior from the transactions that they were involved in. This component includes storing feedback from users after each transaction they take part in. The second component computes reputation scores for participants through a Reputation Computing Engine (RCE), based on the gathered information. The third component processes the reputation scores, implementing appropriate reward and punishment policies if needed, and representing reputation scores in a way which gives as much support as possible to users' decision-making. A TRS can be centralized or distributed. In centralized TRSs, there is a central authority responsible for collecting ratings and computing reputation scores for users. Most of the TRSs currently on the Internet are centralized, for example the feedback system on eBay [1] and customer reviews on Amazon [2]. On the other hand, a distributed TRS has no central authority. Each user has to collect ratings and compute reputation scores for other users himself. Almost all proposed TRSs in the literature are distributed [7,9,5].

Some of the main unwanted behaviors of users that might appear in TRSs are: *free riding* (people are usually not willing to give feedback if they are not given an incentive to do so [10]), *untruthful rating* (users give incorrect feedback either because of malicious intent or because of unintended and uncontrolled variables), *colluding* (a group of users coordinate their behavior to inflate each other's reputation scores or bad-mouth other competitors. Colluding motives are only clear in a specific application), *whitewashing* (a user creates a new identity in the system to replace his old one when the reputation of the old one has gone bad), *milking reputation* (at first, a participant behaves correctly to get a high reputation and then turns bad to make a profit from their high reputation score). The milking reputation behavior is more harmful to social network services and e-commerce than to the others. More types of attacks can be found in [4,5].

In this section, we provide readers with a brief overview of TRSs with respect to their applications, components, classification and potential attacks. The rest of the paper is organized as follows. Sect. 2 introduces readers to our research methodology and gives an agenda for building a TRS which is robust against attacks. Sect. 3 details the implemented RCE. Sect. 4 reports the results from a thorough simulation on the engine. Sect. 5 and 6 discuss related work and our future areas of study respectively.

2   Trust and Reputation System Design Agenda

The design of a robust TRS is already partially addressed in several academic papers [5,4,3]. In this section, we aim to build on these studies and systematize the process of designing a TRS in general as in Fig. 1. First, we characterize the application system into which we want to integrate a TRS, and find and identify new elements of information which substitute for traditional signs of trust and reputation in the physical world [5]. Second, based on the characteristics of the application, we find suitable working mechanisms and processes for each component of the TRS, as already introduced in Sect. 1. This step should answer the following questions: "What kind of information do we need to collect and how?", "How should the reputation scores be computed using the collected information?", and "How should they be represented and processed to lead users to a correct decision?". To answer the first question, which corresponds to the information gathering component, we should take advantage of information technology to collect the vast amounts of necessary data [5]. According to [5], a RCE should meet these criteria: *accuracy* for long-term performance (distinguishing a newcomer with unknown quality from a low-quality participant who has stayed in the system for a long time), *weighting* towards recent behavior, *smoothness* (adding any single rating should not change the score significantly), and *robustness* against attacks. The work in [3] is an effective guide for social web applications. It is applicable directly to the tasks of designing the information gathering and decision support components. Third, we study the tentative design obtained after the second step in the presence of selfish behaviors. During the third step, we can repeatedly return to Step 2 whenever appropriate until the system reaches a desired performance. The fourth step will refine the TRS and make it more robust against malicious attacks, some of which are listed in Sect. 1. If a modification is made, we should return to Step 2 and check all the conditions in steps 2 and 3 before accepting the modification (Fig. 1).

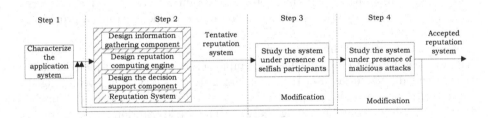

Fig. 1. Process of designing a robust trust and reputation system

In different applications, there are different kinds of available information and activities, hence different ways of computing reputation scores and different types of attacks. Accordingly, designing a TRS must be put in the specific context of an application. Most of the challenges for a TRS are induced by selfish and malicious behaviors. The problems arising from malicious behaviors are usually more complicated and difficult to cope with than those caused by normal selfish users. Therefore, the logic of our methodology is to first design a TRS that works for a community where all the members are obedient, and then increase the sophistication of the system to cope with selfish members and finally with malicious ones. After having a TRS which is robust against some kinds of attacks, we can continue testing its robustness, using the approaches proposed in [4]. These are: implementing the system in reality, performing a theoretical test by third parties so that the evaluation is more credible, and defining a comprehensive set of robustness evaluation methods and criteria.

3   Reputation Computing Engine

Among the three components of a TRS, information gathering is most dependent on the application system, followed by the decision support component and then by the RCE. Accordingly, the next step in our research will be building a robust RCE, which will be as general as possible so that the engine is applicable to a variety of applications. In the following part of this section, we will elaborate on our assumptions, concepts and the implementation of a preliminary computing engine which is a specification and a simplification of the framework proposed in [5].

3.1   Assumptions and Notations

There is a large group of systems where the transactions are bilateral. In these systems, for each transaction there are two parties that we call *consumer* and *provider*. The consumer is the one who requests the service, while the provider is the one who is capable of providing the service. When we add a TRS to this kind of system, a user can have an additional role as a rater who has interacted with the provider before and therefore has an opinion about the provider's service. When a consumer needs a service, he collects ratings on the candidate providers and computes reputation scores for them. The consumer then ranks the providers according to their reputation scores and chooses one of the top ranked providers to interact with.

Without losing generality, we consider the RCE within the context of a service having one criterion to be judged. An example of service with multiple criteria is that provided by an eBay user [1]. As of May 2012, this service has been judged by four criteria, including "Item as described", "Communication", "Shipping time", and "Shipping and handling charges". The single criterion in our example is called "Quality of Service" (QoS), whose value is normalized to the interval $[0,1]$, where 1 is the optimal value. Correspondingly, the rating value is in the range $[0,1]$ and the optimal value is also 1. The following are the main variables that a consumer will use for his computation. They are private information and accessible only to the owner.

Rater Credibility (C_r): reputation of a user in giving accurate feedback. It reflects how much the consumer should trust the rater r's ratings. The value range is $[0,1]$ and it is initiated at 0.5.

Usefulness Factor (U_r): $U_r = N_{useful}/S$, where N_{useful} is the number of times that the rater r submits useful ratings, S is the total number of submissions. After a transaction, if the difference between a rating and the outcome observed by the consumer is under a predefined threshold then the rating is useful. We set the threshold at 0.2 and the initial value of U_r at 0.5.

Personal Evaluation (E_p): the consumer's first-hand experience with the provider p. $E_p \in [0,1]$. We set E_p as the experience of the last transaction with the provider. It might not be available if the consumer has never done any transactions with this provider.

Previously Assessed Reputation Score (A): the last computed reputation score of a provider when the consumer interacted with him. If the consumer has never interacted with this provider, then A will be initiated as 0.5.

3.2   Adjusting Raters' Credibility

After collecting ratings on a provider's service, the consumer will adjust raters' credibility which will be used to calculate weights for the ratings. The two main criteria which adjust a rater's credibility are the consistency of his rating to other raters and to the previous reputation score A of the provider. We use a modification of the K-means clustering algorithm in [6] to find the majority rating value among the raters. The main idea of this algorithm is to divide the rating set into clusters, so that similar ratings are grouped into the same cluster, while different ones are separated into different clusters. The most crowded cluster is then labeled as the majority and its mean is the majority rating M. The values used to decide if ratings belong to the same or different clusters are affected by coarsening and refinement distances, C and R respectively: $0 \leq C \leq R \leq 1$. The three parameters of the algorithm are C, R, and the initial number of clusters. After having M, the consumer computes factor $M_r^f \in [0,1]$, which has the effect of changing rater r's credibility, due to the closeness of its rating R_r to M.

$$
M_r^f = \begin{cases} 1 - \dfrac{|R_r - M|}{\sigma_M} & \text{if } |R_r - M| < \sigma_M \\[2mm] 1 - \dfrac{\sigma_M}{|R_r - M|} & \text{otherwise} \end{cases}
$$

where σ_M is the standard deviation of the received rating set, i.e.:

$$
\sigma_M = \sqrt{\frac{\sum_{r=1}^{N_R} R_r^2}{N_R} - (\sum_{r=1}^{N_R} \frac{R_r}{N_R})^2}
$$

with N_R is the total number of collected ratings. Factor $A^f = 1$ has an effect on the change of a rater's credibility, due to the closeness of its rating to A. We denote $\aleph = C_r \times (1 - |R_r - M|)$, and ρ the consumer's pessimism factor which has a suggested minimum value of 2 ($\rho \geq 2$). The credibility C_r of rater r is adjusted as follows:

1. If rating R_r is similar to both M and A, i.e., $(|R_r - M| < 0.1)$ and $(|R_r - A| < 0.1)$, then: $C_r = \min(1, C_r + \aleph \times \dfrac{M_r^f + A^f}{\rho})$.

2. If $(|R_r - M| < 0.1)$ and $(|R_r - A| \geq 0.1)$, then C_r is still increased, but less than the first case: $C_r = \min(1, C_r + \aleph \times \dfrac{M_r^f}{\rho})$.

3. If $(|R_r - M| \geq 0.1)$ and $(|R_r - A| < 0.1)$, then C_r is decreased a little bit:
$C_r = \max(0, C_r - \aleph \times \dfrac{A^f}{\rho})$.

4. If $(|R_r - M| \geq 0.1)$ and $(|R_r - A| \geq 0.1)$, then C_r is decreased the most:
$C_r = \max(0, C_r - \aleph \times \dfrac{M_r^f + A^f}{\rho})$.

According to the above formulas, a pessimistic consumer with high ρ will increase C_r slowly for a rating consistent with M and A. Finally, $C_r = C_r \times U_r$.

3.3   Computing Assessed Reputation Score

To prepare weights for collected ratings, in addition to the credibility of raters, we also need to calculate *temporal factors* (f^t) for ratings and E_p. The reason for using f^t is to give more weight to the more recent information. Depending on the characteristics of the service and the discretion of the designers, f^t can be calculated in different ways. We propose one example here. Ratings and E_p are arranged into chronological order and then a f_r^t corresponding to each rating R_r or f_E^t for E_p is calculated, which is the inverse of the number of ratings (S) counted between R_r and the latest rating inclusively: $f_r^t = 1/S$. Then the assessed reputation score of provider p is computed as in the following formula:

$$Rep_p = \frac{(\sum_{r=1}^{N_R} (R_r \times C_r \times f_r^t) + E_p \times f_E^t)}{(\sum_{r=1}^{N_R} C_r + 1)}$$

Where N_R is the total number of collected ratings and E_p is the consumer's first-hand experience (if available) with the provider.

4   Simulation Results

We have implemented the RCE described above and tested it under different user behaviors. The details of our simulation in Java language are the following.

4.1   Simulation Settings

We set up a population of N_u users, providing the same service, and undertaking N_t transactions. In each transaction, a random consumer is assigned to request the service. Other users will then be candidate providers for this request. When a user plays the role of a consumer, his behavior is modeled in *raterType* attribute. Three types of raters include HONEST, DISHONEST and COLLUSIVE. HONEST raters share their personal experience honestly, i.e. $R_r = E_p$. DISHONEST raters provide ratings 0.5 different from their true estimation, i.e. $R_r = E_p \pm 0.5$. COLLUSIVE raters give the highest ratings $(R_r = 1)$ to users in their collusion and the lowest ratings $(R_r = 0)$ to the rest. Similarly, when a user acts as a provider, he can be one of the following types of providers: GOOD, NORMAL, BAD, or GOODTURNBAD. This type is denoted in *providerType* attribute.

The QoS of the service provided by a BAD, NORMAL, or GOOD provider has a value in the interval $(0, 0.4]$, $(0.4, 0.7]$, or $(0.7, 1]$ respectively. A GOODTURNBAD provider will change the QoS of his service when 50% of N_t transactions have been done in the simulation. To get a transaction done, a consumer obtains a list of providers, computes reputation scores for them, chooses a provider to perform the transaction, updates his private information, and publishes his rating for the provider. The quality of service that the consumer will experience depends on the $providerType$ of the chosen provider. The difference between the consumer's rating for the provider and his observation depends on the consumer's $raterType$. In our simulation, $providerType$ and $raterType$ of a user are independent.

For each user, we have two measures: p_p which is the percentage of N_t transactions, in which the user has performed as the provider; and $a_d = \overline{|Rep_p - E_p|}$ which is an average of absolute difference between the Rep_p before a transaction and the E_p after the transaction. Apparently, p_p should be proportional to the user's QoS and can be referred to as the user's "Market Share". a_d reflects the correctness of the system in assessing a provider's QoS and is captured when a user plays the role of a consumer. We repeat a simulation at least five times before taking the average values to analyze. A simulation run is denoted:

$$Simulation(N_u, N_t, \%G, \%N, \%B, \%GTB, \%H, \%D, \%C, \%dataLost).$$

Where $\%G$, $\%N$, $\%B$, $\%GTB$ are the percentage of GOOD, NORMAL, BAD, and GOODTURNBAD providers in the population respectively, so that $\%G + \%N + \%B + \%GTB = 100\%$. $\%H$, $\%D$, $\%C$ are the percentage of HONEST, DISHONEST, and COLLUSIVE raters respectively, so that $\%H + \%D + \%C = 100\%$. $\%dataLost$ is the percentage of ratings on a specific provider which are not available for the consumer at the moment he computes the reputation score for the provider.

4.2   User Decision Simulation

We observe that, in reality, a user might not always choose a provider with the highest reputation score. This is due to the complexity of human decision-making, which is based not only on reputation and personal experience but also on many other factors, such as *aversion*, *bias*, *antecedents* and *mood*. For the purpose of examining a TRS, we model a user's decision-making in the following selection strategy. The consumer ranks candidate providers based on their reputation scores and makes a cut-off, removing those having scores lower than $(Top - 0.5)$, where Top is the score of the first ranked provider. He then uses a Gaussian distribution having standard deviation $\sigma = \sqrt{N_{Size}}$ and mean $a = 0$ to calculate Gaussian random values (G_p)s for providers in the short list of size N_{Size}. Accordingly, the G_p of a provider depends on N_{Size} and its rank in the list but not on its absolute reputation score Rep_p. Finally, the consumer opts for a provider randomly, with a probability proportional to the provider's G_p. The intuition of this strategy is that the providers with higher Rep_p, therefore higher rank, will have higher chance to be chosen.

4.3   Simulation Scenarios and Analysis

In this section, we are going to apply the methodology mentioned in Sect. 2 to study the implemented RCE. We examine the engine to see firstly, if it works correctly when all users are obedient, secondly if it is robust against selfish users and thirdly, if it is robust against malicious users.

Obedient Users. We consider obedient users to be those who provide a service correctly, as stated, to the best of their ability, and share their personal experience honestly with the community. Applying this concept to our simulation model, they are GOOD, NORMAL, or BAD providers and HONEST raters. Simulation on obedient users with parameters:

$$Simulation(200, 10000, 10, 20, 70, 0, 100, 0, 0, 0).$$

shows that BAD providers are avoided always.

Selfish Users. A selfish behavior in generic TRSs can be named as *free riding*. The consumer does not give feedback to the system after a transaction. We simulated that behavior in an approximate manner using the parameter %*dataLost*:

$$Simulation(200, 10000, 10, 20, 70, 0, 100, 0, 0, 60).$$

The result obtained is almost the same as the one when all the users are obedient. It proves that the engine still functions even when 60% of the ratings which are supposed to be supplied are not available.

Malicious Raters. As raters, malicious users can be categorized as DISHONEST or COLLUSIVE. DISHONEST raters act individually, while COLLUSIVE ones act in groups. It is difficult to identify COLLUSIVE users, especially when they form a large group. The simulation with the presence of DISHONEST raters:

$$Simulation(200, 10000, 10, 20, 70, 0, 30, 70, 0, 0).$$

shows that the error in computing (Rep_p)s for BAD providers is 0.39 on average. And this error gives them a chance to acquire $13\% \times N_t$ transactions. Second, we run a simulation with the presence of COLLUSIVE raters, where 60% of users collude as a group against the rest:

$$Simulation(200, 10000, 10, 20, 70, 0, 40, 0, 60, 0).$$

The error in computing (Rep_p)s are now increased for all types of providers (Fig. 2). Especially, for BAD users, the error reaches 0.57, which is quite high. However, the market share of these BAD providers is only 7%, which is acceptable compared to their population percentage of 60%.

Malicious Providers. A provider displaying malicious behavior and *milking reputation* can be modeled by GOODTURNBAD users:

$$Simulation(200, 10000, 10, 10, 70, 10, 100, 0, 0, 0).$$

We observe that when the users change the QoS of their service from high to low, they continue to get high reputation scores and have a high chance of being

Fig. 2. Simulation results for a scenario with COLLUSIVE raters forming a group

selected for many transactions later. Even a consumer who has experienced the bad service of a GOODTURNBAD provider, can still choose the provider again. From these results, we conclude that the current engine is robust against a population displaying dishonest behavior of up to 70% and colluding behavior of up to 60% of the population, but still vulnerable to *milking reputation* attack.

5   Related Work

After a thorough survey of the current research, we find the model proposed in [7] the most interesting. The service oriented environment analyzed in the paper fits into the bilateral transaction environment we are aiming at. The experimental results that are provided are appealing. However, the disadvantage of this model is that it is complicated to implement. Furthermore, it is not clear which specific formulas and parameter values were used by the authors to get the results presented in the paper. In their proposed framework, a number of formulas are left open to readers. Such formulas include the one for updating personal evaluations and the one for aggregating the provider's assessed reputations at previous time instances. Some other points that are unclear in the paper, are the thresholds used to estimate if a rating is useful, to decide if a rating is similar to the majority rating and if it is similar to previously assessed reputations. In our opinion, the variance of these formulas and thresholds all affect the precision of assessed reputations and this concern has forced us to re-implement their model but using a simpler form. From a technical point of view, we have adopted the credibility update algorithm from the RateWeb framework [7]. Then we apply our methodology to study the robustness of the implemented engine. For the simulation, we propose a new measure which is the percentage of market share that a user gains. In terms of the accuracy of the reputation values, the results in our simulation are not as good as in [7] due to the modification we made to the engine and the simulation/experimental settings. The critical difference between the experimental settings in [7] and our simulation settings is the existence of bootstrapping. We assign a neutral default value to newcomers (initiating A, C_r, and U_r to 0.5) as a simple bootstrapping mechanism integrated into the computing engine and let every user start from scratch. On the other hand, [7] assumes that the bootstrapping has been done and that the system is running with correct reputation scores and credibilities.

6 Conclusions and Future Work

In this paper, we have presented our preliminary work on building a trust and reputation framework for social web platforms which will be robust against attacks. We propose a research methodology which can be used to study the robustness of many TRSs, and also implement a model which is a simplified and modified version of the RateWeb engine [7]. Since the experimental results in [7] were no longer correct for the implemented engine, we applied our methodology to study it. The results of the simulation showed a flaw in the engine, which is vulnerable to *milking reputation* attack. For that reason, we have decided to design a new RCE. During the course of studying the implemented engine, we realized that we needed a common tool and measuring system to compare the performance of multiple engines. Unfortunately, there is very little work in the literature on simulation tools and TRS performance measures. We have found only one implemented simulator for TRSs in sensor networks [8], whose measuring system is not applicable to our context. Therefore, another branch of our research in the future will be building a simulator with measures suitable for social web applications, as we have introduced partly in Sect. 4. We are interested not only in the accuracy of the TRSs, but also in how they shape the community.

References

1. http://www.ebay.com/
2. http://www.amazon.com/
3. Dellarocas, C.: Online reputation systems: How to design one that does what you need. MIT Sloan Management Review 51(3) (spring 2010)
4. Josang, A., Golbeck, J.: Challenges for robust trust and reputation systems. In: Proceedings of the 5th International Workshop on Security and Trust Management, Saint Malo, France (September 2009)
5. Josang, A., Ismail, R., Boyd, C.: A survey of trust and reputation systems for online service provision. Decision Support Systems 43(2), 618–644 (2007)
6. MacQueen, J.B.: Some methods for classification and analysis of multivariate observations. In: Proceedings of the Fifth Berkeley Symposium on Mathematical Statistics and Probability, pp. 281–297 (1967)
7. Malik, Z., Bouguettaya, A.: Rateweb: Reputation assessment for trust establishment among web services. The International Journal on Very Large Data Bases 18(4), 885–911 (2009)
8. Marmol, F.G., Perez, G.M.: Trmsim-wsn, trust and reputation models simulator for wireless sensor networks. In: IEEE International Conference on Communications (IEEE ICC 2009), Communication and Information Systems Security Symposium (June 2009)
9. Marti, S.: Trust and Reputation in Peer-to-Peer Networks. PhD thesis, Stanford University. Stanford InfoLab (May 2005)
10. Resnick, P., Zeckhauser, R., Friedman, E., Kuwabara, K.: Reputation systems. Communications of the ACM, pp. 45–48 (December 2000)

Social Emergent Semantics
for Personal Data Management

Cristian Vasquez

Semantics Technology and Applications Research Lab,
Vrije Universiteit Brussel, Brussels, Belgium
cvasquez@vub.ac.be

Abstract. In order use our personal data within our day to day activities, we need to manage it in a way that is easy to consume, which currently is not an easy task. People have found their own ways to organize their personal data, such as categorizing files in folders, labeling emails etc. This is acceptable to a certain degree, since we have to deal with have some (human) difficulties such as our limited capacity of categorization and our incapacity of maintaining highly structured artifacts for long periods of time. We believe that to organize this great amount of personal data, we need the help of our communities. In this work, we apply the emergent semantics field to personal data management, aiming to decrease our cognitive efforts spent in simple tasks, handling semantic evolution in conjunction with our close peers.

Keywords: Personal data management, Social Annotation, Distributed ontology evolution, Emergent semantics.

1 Introduction

Lots of effort has been put into improving our personal data management capabilities through a computer. One of the most common approaches is to distill structures from our resources, or just add or "attach" metadata to them. It is commonly agreed that we can use these structures to answer complex and precise questions, which incentives resource annotation. Some estimations says that more than the 12% of the Web is structured to some degree[14][12], corpus that is currently exploited by the most popular search engines.

These web resources have been "annotated" with meta-data expressed using published vocabularies, which have been constructed via standardization committees and other organized groups, or just driven by the market. This is useful, but in some cases it is not sufficient since we live in a heterogeneous world, where differences exist and can be observed. We can easily agree that we will use coordinates to individualize a geographic region, but is not easy to agree the political nature of that region. Regarding some topics, global interoperability just cannot be reached. In these cases we need to reach local agreements between communities of limited size, essentially constructing specific vocabularies for a certain world view. This is usually archived via agreement processes that multiple individuals and communities reach following a *bottom up* approach to support their

P. Herrero et al. (Eds.): OTM 2012 Workshops, LNCS 7567, pp. 23–32, 2012.
© Springer-Verlag Berlin Heidelberg 2012

tasks, such as information sharing. This interplay have been studied in the field of emerging semantics [1], but haven't been widely exploited yet.

Within this work, we want to exploit local and global semantics to improve our personal data management capabilities. In this context, we will refer to personal data as all kind of digital information that is gathered by an individual over (long) periods of time, and stored in a Personal space of information (PSI) which "includes all the information items that are, at least nominally, under that person's control (but not necessarily exclusively so)" [7]. This data includes for example emails, files, image recordings, URLs of resources of the web, etc. We know that managing this kind of information cannot be addressed only by means of global vocabularies, since users have their own ways of categorizations, which can be completely different from person to person [6]. The main focus of this work will be to improve our personal data managing capabilities, taking into account the social discourses with our close peers. This will be reflected in individual and collaborative mechanisms that will be used together to improve our long term retrieval capabilities with the help of *semantics* .

The idea of using semantics to manage personal data is not new, we can find interesting research in the field of Semantic Desktops [22]. A semantic desktop is a collection of tools that allows us to store personal information using flexible data models, usually graphs that represent and relate digital information. A Semantic Desktop is built on top of the ontological knowledge that is generated starting from user observations and his own behavior. Some may think about a single user's Semantic Desktop as a building block of a global Semantic Web [21], while others will see it as some formal and semi-formal complement of the user's mental models, where a user stores its own "interpretations" of their observed world. Additionally, one common tool that allow users to build representations of their own mental models is the personal wiki. A wiki is essentially a collection of documents which is connected via hyperlinks, making use of simple syntax for editing content. Wikis are used in many areas, such as online encyclopedias, collaborative learning environments, personal and group knowledge management systems [26]

Through this study we will focus on how we can represent our digital data in order to be shared, and how we can profit from our social interactions to build and link dynamic artifacts that will represent our shared "understanding", which we believe, would be useful for long term retrieval. In order to study possible benefits of combining (i) our local context with (ii) the emergent semantics of our close communities, we have designed a preliminary experiment in order to observe how the distinct contributions of our communities can be used to improve our data management capabilities. We know that the more structure the users contribute to their descriptions, the better are the shared artifacts to find information efficiently, to promote re-usage and sharing with other users [24]. In order to provide structure, we incur into costs. Within this experiment, we aim to perform a cost-benefit analysis about the total modeling efforts which are spent for the construction of those shared artifacts.

This document is organized as follows: Section 2 describes how annotations are interpreted in this work. Section 3 will explore the notion of description. Section 4 will explore the notion of personal context. Section 5 will describe the role of emergent semantics in this experiment. Section 6 will describe the experiment. Section 7 presents our conclusions and future work.

2   The Notion of Annotation

Currently, there is no consensus about what an annotation is. One of the most common definitions is that an annotation is an object that describes or says something about other object of information, constituting descriptive information of any type about objects. Usually this is understood as a piece "attached" to other piece of information, but an annotation is not limited to that interpretation. We can also see the process of annotating as the process of building *relationships* between descriptions. We can note that this last interpretation of annotation is plausible since the annotations are objects of information which can be seen as equivalent[1] to the objects being annotated; since they are both descriptions.

To focus on relationships rather than in "attached data" is a convenient interpretation for some cases. Particularly in this work we refer to descriptions and relations between information objects as the same.

Annotations can be hard to capture, yet worth to keep. It is unclear to a person creating an annotation, when and in which context that particular annotation will be relevant again. Because of this uncertainty, we want to keep contextual information in form of meta-data about the relationships between the descriptions. Which contextual information is the best to use, remains an open question, the most used are the five "who, what, when, where, how" or the "who, what, when, where, why" dimensions [19]. We will treat these "associations" as first class citizens, used to discover, understand and manage our stored objects, exploiting annotation processes as the association of things, complementing categorization or selecting resources to "attach" meta-data such as descriptions, properties, type etc. We expect that focusing on the representation of "associations" instead of the attached descriptions potentially will leverage the complexity of our underlying models that focus on personal data management. For example, metadata about relationships can directly support associative browsing, where we can analyze and cluster the information to find related items.

3   The Notion of Description

But how we describe our reality through a computer? People naturally refer to their "reality" using distinct languages and notations. Those languages allow them to say things about their perceived world and finally share information with others. When multiple persons want to agree about some observed

---

[1] Although the annotated object and the annotation itself may be represented in a different way.

subject, they may decide to interact sharing descriptions collectively, trying to converge into useful representations, which can improve their communication means. Within the Web, multiple artifacts (documents) are currently used to "hold" those descriptions, which are used to incrementally convey into shared concept definitions or vocabularies. These artifacts can vary from wikipedia web pages to web ontologies, depending on the degree of formalization or "precision" required to describe the observation subjects. It is important to note that these artifacts are constructed gradually and usually are based on the combination of previous description artifacts.

When we talk about describing our perceived world we frequently refer to semantics. Semantics classically concerns a triadic structure comprising a symbol (how some idea is expressed), a conceptualization (what is abstracted by someone from reality) and a referent (the observed thing or concept) [13]. According to Peirce, this triadic structure is indivisible, meaning that people cannot be left out of this process.

In the web domain, sophisticated systems have been constructed aiming to capture and represent the "semantics" that are relevant to a web community. To better describe our observation subjects we choose distinct mechanisms, just to name a few we can make use of multimedia content, tagging or formal models, which allow us to reach distinct degrees of expressiveness or "precision". Additionally we can refer to the observation subjects using universal identification schemes such as URLs, which we use to retrieve documents from the web in a decentralized environment. This is a powerful and unique mechanism that allows us to get distinct representation variants starting from a symbol, and probably it is one of the most important steps towards the semantic web. We can say that today we count with symbols and identified referents which allows us to share concept descriptions across the Web.

However, we still have difficulties to model simplifications of the third component of peirce's triadic structure, which refer to the conceptualizations. Usually, in computer science literature the importance of human interpretation is left out, which is natural since we don't count yet with logic systems capable of characterizing the interpretation made by a human. However, interpretivist research [4][27] can work together with the predominantly positivist research tradition in information systems, which is not necessarily sufficient to deal with data from one individual.

4   The Notion of Context

But how we can characterize a conceptualization? how can we represent our interpretations in a way that a computer can make use of them?. In this work we don't aim to answer those questions, instead we will experiment with models which make use of the notion of *personal context*, in order to model artifacts which can be used and observed to reach efficient retrieval of our personal data, using knowledge representations that make sense to us.

We can observe in the work of Santini et al. [20] that we cannot encode the semantics of a document independently of the act of human interpretation, which is a major limitation. As an alternative, the notion of context is introduced as an essential ingredient to determine the meaning[2] of a document. Santini et al. proposes to observe and measure how certain document *changes the context* of the user, and use that information to archive personal context-based retrieval. Here, context is formalized to a certain degree using a similar technique to the semantic maps WEBSOM [8]. The semantic maps represent a context by means of self organizing maps in the euclidean space of words, which are used to reformulate user queries by means of deforming the queries according to this context. After the query is transformed, it can be "projected" in traditional information retrieval representations. This approach was tested with promising results [20] showing an approach that will be tested in the early stages of this work, in conjunction with emerging semantics.

5   The Notion of Emergent Semantics

If we are not isolated from the online world, to more or less degree, we can influence and we are influenced by others. We can say that many of the distinct terminologies or categorizations that we use to organize our objects are learned in community. Moreover, we copy, transform and combine things that we get from others. It seems convenient to use those organic and common ways of organization to manage our own personal data. One problem is that to follow the dynamics of online communities is not inherently simple, specially when we see these online communities as groups of people determined by their own interactions. In this work we don't want to address explicitly the dynamic nature of those interactions, instead we want to capture to certain degree the terminology or "semantics" used within our interplay by means of incrementally trade knowledge within our communities. Interesting work have been found in the field of *emergent semantics*, where Cudr-Maurux [2] presents several techniques to allow observation and capture of semantics from interacting agents in the wild. In this approach, global interoperability is seen as emerging from collections of dynamic agreements between autonomous self-interested agents. Those agents interact following a Peer-to-Peer paradigm, where agents are allowed to create mappings in order to interact. These mappings are the ones that determine the formation of semantic neighborhoods of agents.

In our experiment, instead of simulating an interaction network of agents, we will make use of simple artifacts, which we call web *semantic blackboards* [23], which are freely used by users as main interface. These blackboards are extensions of a semantic wiki web page, which is used as a playgrounds where the participants are allowed describe some observation subject collaboratively, making use of distinct description mechanisms and formalisms. We aim to

---

[2] According to Santini et al, it is only possible to formalize meaning only in the extent that is possible to formalize context.

exploit this description diversity to improve custom query results and exploratory search, using structured descriptions in conjunction with others more suitable for result recognition (i.e photograph). In general terms, a participant is allowed to subscribe to multiple blackboards and contribute content, aiming to converge into acceptable conceptualizations "agreed" by his peers. A user can "collect" distinct blackboards, constructing a network that he can he bind directly with his own personal data in form of folders, files, mails etc. Participants of each blackboard are allowed to (i) contribute content from their own private spaces, building implicit relationships. In the same way, participants can (ii) borrow descriptions from others or (iii) relate external descriptions to their own descriptions (iv) or relate blackboards using relationships such as causality, location, function etc.

Within this interplay, we expect to count with a increasing number of relationships between observation subjects, forming a network of blackboards. Having a considerable amount of transitive or symmetric relationships such as "part of", "is a", "same as" etc, can be beneficial in order to observe emerging semantics. In early stages of this work we will experiment with some of the techniques presented in [3], which include cycle analysis and probabilistic message passing. We expect that analysis of transitive closures between blackboards would be a valuable tool to provide feedback to the communities, increasing their awareness. For example, if some path of multiple "is a" relations forms a cycle within a network of blackboards, we can suspect that the involved blackboards are sharing similar semantics. We can mark these blackboards for semantic reconciliation, potentially leading to agreed inter-blackboard meaning convergence. This can result into *merging* multiple blackboards into one, or *branching* a new observation subject(blackboard) to be described, for example an "abstraction" of the blackboards of the cycle. In the same way, failed convergence processes can give us clues about sub-optimal relations or conflicting descriptions within "semantic neighborhood" which can result in blackboards that diverge(or branch) into new ones. Other example could be the generation of "composite blackboards" for blackboards with multiple incoming "part of" relationships.

This mechanism of diverging and converging, provides a strong support for non-linear development which is already used widely in large scale scenarios such as collaborative software coding sites, benefited by distributed version control systems (DVCS[3]). Divergence of blackboards allows to follow an "organic" approach which doesn't rely principally in agreements. For example, it is useful when a group of participants have irreconcilable conceptualization (interpretations) conflict about some description subject (i.e. unicorns doesn't exist vs they exist), or having categorizations that are just not convenient for some participants. In these cases of divergence and convergence, participants may choose to keep a complete traceability, which is a valuable tool to improve management, measure formalization costs and understanding our own neighborhood evolutions.

---

[3] http://en.wikipedia.org/wiki/Distributed_revision_control

6 Preliminar Experiment

In order to study possible the benefits of combining (i) our local context with (ii) the observed emergent semantics of our close communities, we have designed an architecture which will allow us to perform a cost-benefit analysis about the total description formalization efforts within the blackboards. The configuration of this experiment is in early stages, although we have distinguished and constructed some of its main components.

The applicability and effectiveness of the experiment will depend largely on how we represent our information artifacts. We can represent them using a variety of technologies, but for the sake of simplicity we will limit this experiment to use only RDF[4] as data model, with a limited set of representations. We can categorize these representations in families according to their intended use and level of precision. These preliminary families are: (i) pragmatical representation family, which include vocabularies that support communication between users, such as the representation of dialogues (ii) empirical representations, that refer to vocabularies that constitute high precision artifacts to observe subjects, for example a photograph or geographical coordinates (iii) semantic level, which refer to the models or schemes created via human abstraction, such as a personal folder structures, or public "ontologies".

On the early stages we intend to support subject descriptions via structured note taking. The core process from notes to a document can be described as steps in a knowledge maturing process [10]. These activities will be integrated into a classical semantic wiki, because of its three defining characteristics: "easy contribution", "easy editing", and "easy linking" [26]. The tool itself needs to be extended in order to sort items, manage subscribed blackboards and link them to personal data items. In the same way we have to provide notification systems to increase user's awareness regarding detected semantic patterns. The overview about the "collected" blackboards of a user can be provided using a spatial layout. A good example of these layouts are IMaps [5], that can be seen as a large blackboard where smaller blackboards are positioned like post-its but also nested in each other. The preliminary technologies used include (i) DVCS implementations such as JGIT[5] to keep the traceability of the blackboard dynamics and to directly support divergence and convergence capabilities, (ii) RDF triplifiers[6] to extract structure from containers such as files or web pages and (iii) the nepomuk[7] framework to keep track of user digital "residues" within their desktops. With the use the nepomuk framework we benefit from a (iv) Personal Information Model Ontology (PIMO) editor component like in [18], where each user augments his own PIMO manually or by means of implicitly infering metadata from his resources, according to his own context. We can

---

[4] http://www.w3.org/TR/rdf-syntax-grammar
[5] http://eclipse.org/jgit
[6] http://code.google.com/p/any23/
[7] http://nepomuk.kde.org/

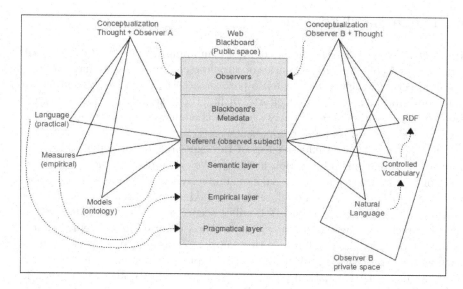

Fig. 1. Example of inter-subjective space between two participants, regarding some observation subject. "Conceptualizations" try to converge into a shared space, through a pragmatic, empirical and semantic levels. These levels can be seen as language, examples and models respectively. Fuzzy representations can also mutate into more formal ones, handling a continuous spectrum of description mechanisms which follow distinct degrees of structure.

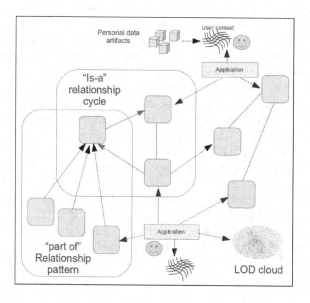

Fig. 2. Setup of an experiment where distinct observers commit to a set of interconnected blackboards. Patterns such as cycles are used to provide feedback to the users. Each application instance interact with blackboards, a personal context and external sources such as Linked Open Data.

automatically associate selected blackboards with the user PIMO concepts and the conceptual data structures [25] used in the nepomuk framework, in order to share distinct degrees of structuredness and formalization within a community.

7   Conclusions

Through this document, we explored notions such as personal context and emergent semantics, describing artifacts such as blackboards that can diverge and converge in order to support meaning evolution. We have presented the preliminary setup of a experiment which aims to measure possible benefits of using our (i) personal data context and (ii) the emergent semantics of our close peers, in order to retrieve our personal data. We can see this setup as a set of "semantic bridges", where our own semantics are "hooked" with the semantics of others. We expect that this mechanism facilitates the retrieval of personal data segments, since it will be organized in terms of the semantics of our communities.

Additionally we track the evolution of our shared descriptions, constituting artifacts which may provide significant insight about the evolution of our semantics, which is a valuable asset for the study of this approach.

In this work we don't aim to distill global semantics. Instead we want our own semantics, taking as hypothesis that they are incrementally constructed within our close communities. We will benefit from local schemes to reflect our "ideologies" or "realities". This approach can be considered as a single particular step within a wider production chain of knowledge, starting from the individual to its society and viceversa.

Acknowledgments. The research described in this paper was partially sponsored by the INNOViris Open Semantic Cloud for Brussels (OSCB) project.

References

1. Aberer, K., Ouksel, A.: Emergent semantics principles and issues. Database Systems for 2 (2004)
2. Philippe cudr E-mauroux. Emergent Semantics: Rethinking interoperability for large scale descentralized information systems (2006)
3. Cudré-Mauroux, P., Aberer, K.: Belief Propagation on Uncertain Schema Mappings in Peer Data Management Systems 1 (001935) (2003)
4. Falkenberg, E.D., Hesse, W., Lindgreen, P., Nilsson, B.E., Han Oei, J.L., Rolland, C., Stamper, R.K., Van Assche, F.J.M., Verrijn-Stuart, A.A., Voss, K.: A Framework of Information System Concepts - The FRISCO Report. International Federation for Information Processing WG 8.1 4 (1998)
5. Haller, H., Abecker, A.: iMapping A Zooming User Interface Approach for Personal and Semantic Knowledge Management. Knowledge Creation Diffusion Utilization 119–128 (Autumn 2010)
6. Hearst, M.A.: Clustering versus faceted categories for information exploration. Communications of the ACM 49(4), 59 (2006)

7. Jones, W., Phuwanartnurak, A.J., Gill, R.: Phuwanartnurak, and Rajdeep Gill. Don't take my folders away!: organizing personal information to get ghings done. In: CHI 2005 Extended Abstracts, pp. 1–4 (2005)
8. Kaski, S.: Computationally efficient approximation of a probabilistic model for document representation in the WEBSOM full-text analysis method. Neural Processing Letters, 139–151 (1997)
9. De Leenheer, P.: On Community-based Ontology Evolution. PhD thesis (2009)
10. Maier, R.: Characterizing knowledge maturing: A conceptual process model for integrating e-learning and knowledge management. In: Professional Knowledge Management, Wm 2007 (2007)
11. Marshall, C.C.: How people manage personal information over a lifetime. Personal Information Management (2007)
12. Mika, P., Potter, T.: Metadata Statistics for a Large Web Corpus, pp. 1–4 (2012)
13. Moore, E.C.: Writings of Charles S. Peirce: A Chronological Edition. University Press, Bloomington (1982)
14. Mühleisen, H., Bizer, C.: Web Data Commons Extracting Structured Data from Two Large Web Corpora. Distribution, 2–5 (2012)
15. Nadeem, D.: From Philosophy and Mental-Models to Semantic Desktop Research: Theoretical Overview. Proc. I-Sematics (2007)
16. Nonaka, I.: The Knowledge-Creating Company. Research Policy 26(4-5), 598–600 (1997)
17. Oren, E., Völkel, M., Breslin, J.G., Decker, S.: Semantic Wikis for Personal Knowledge Management. In: Bressan, S., Küng, J., Wagner, R. (eds.) DEXA 2006. LNCS, vol. 4080, pp. 509–518. Springer, Heidelberg (2006)
18. Papailiou, N., Apostolou, D., Panagiotou, D., Mentzas, G.: Exploring Knowledge Management with a Social Semantic Desktop Architecture. In: Wagner, R., Revell, N., Pernul, G. (eds.) DEXA 2007. LNCS, vol. 4653, pp. 213–222. Springer, Heidelberg (2007)
19. Ranganathan, S.R.: Elements of Library Classification. Asia Publi. (1945)
20. Santini, S., Dumitrescu, A.: Context as a non-ontological determinant of semantics
21. Sauermann, L.: The Gnowsis Semantic Desktop for Information Integration
22. Sauermann, L., Bernardi, A., Dengel, A.: Overview and Outlook on the Semantic Desktop
23. Vasquez, C.: Blackboard Data Spaces for the Elicitation of Community-based Lightweight ontologies. In: IEEE/ACM ASONAM 2012 (2012)
24. Völkel, M., Abecker, A.: Cost-benefit analysis for the design of personal knowledge management systems. In: ICEIS, pp. 95–105 (2008)
25. Völkel, M., Haller, H.: Conceptual data structures for personal knowledge management. Online Information Review 33(2), 298–315 (2009)
26. Völkel, M., Schaffert, S.: Personal Knowledge Management with Semantic Technologies. Technologies for Semantic Work, 1–20 (2008)
27. Walsam, G.: ISR emergence of interpretivism in IS research.pdf (1995)

Extracting a Causal Network of News Topics

Eduardo Jacobo Miranda Ackerman

Computer Networks, Dresden University of Technology,
Nöthnitzer Str. 46, Dresden, Germany
eduardo.miranda@inf.tu-dresden.de

Abstract. Because of the abundance of online news, it is impossible for users to process all the available information. Tools are needed to help process this information. To mitigate this challenge we propose generating a network of causally related news topics to help the user understand and navigate throughout the news. We assume that by providing the causes or effects of a news topics, the user will be able to relate current news to past news topics that the user knows about, or that the user will discover past news topics as currently relevant. Also, the additional context will facilitate the understanding of the current news topic.

To generate the causal network, information is extracted from several distributed news sources while maintaining important journalistic features such as source referencing and author attribution. We propose ranking different causes of an event, to provide a more intuitive summary of multiple causal relations.

To make the network easily understandable, news topics must be represented in a format that can be causally related therefore, a news topic model is proposed. The model is based on the phrases used by online news sources to describe an event or activities, during a limited time-frame. To maintain usability the results must be provided in a timely manner from streaming sources and in an easy to understand format.

Keywords: Topic Detection, Causal Relation Extraction, Information Overload, Automatic News Organization.

1 Introduction

The overwhelming amount of online news presents a challenge called news information overload, to mitigate this challenge we propose a system to generate a causal network of news topics. The causal network has some advantages over term-overlap clustering techniques. First, the news topics are put into a context the user may already know, thus facilitating understanding. If the causally related topics are unknown to the user, these novel topic may now be of interest, therefore novel interesting material may be presented. Also, it may be easier for a user to navigate the news on a causally related network instead of a traditional list-column layout.

To generate the aforementioned network several components are necessary. These include a component to extract causal relations from news article text and defining a news topic in a way that can be discovered in causally-related

P. Herrero et al. (Eds.): OTM 2012 Workshops, LNCS 7567, pp. 33–42, 2012.

text. All this while maintaining journalistic features such as source reference and author attribution, to allow the user to verify the information.

To illustrate the proposed system, consider a user interested in reading the news. The user finds a novel news topic, namely *The Dodd-Frank Act*. To get a quick intuition about the topic the user generated a causal network, with the proposed system, for *The Dodd-Frank Act*. The generated causal network shows that *The Dodd-Frank Act* was created in response to *The Late-2000s Financial Crisis*, that was in turn a cause by *The Subprime Mortgage Crisis*. Because the user already knows about some of the causally related topics beforehand, the novel topic gets an interesting context. The causally related topics the user does not know about have already past, but now they become newly interesting, because of the novel context. For the above illustration the causal chain of news topics is as follows: *The Subprime Mortgage Crisis* caused *The Late-2000s Financial Crisis* caused *The Dodd-Frank Act*.

2   Related Works

To generate a causal chain we need to extract this information from natural text such as news articles. To present this information in a clear and understandable format it is necessary to find a topic representation that is coherent within a causal relation, a topic such as *Sports* is often too coarse grained to provide a coherent causal relation. Other topic representations, such as term vectors, are also not well suited because a causal relation between vectors is not readily understandable. In this section we present three types of works: Works that mitigate news information overload by generating a network of news, works that extract causal relations from natural text, and works that generate topic models.

2.1   Network of News

Incident Threading for News Passages [1], is a work that builds upon Topic Detection and Tracking [21]. In it they present a method of generating a network of events about a single news topic. The network is generated by clustering passages at different thresholds, one threshold for clustering passages and a lower one for linking clusters. The links are based on term overlap, though they are given a direction based on temporal features. A work that focuses on causal relations is Causal Network Construction to Support Understanding of News [2]. In this work causal relations are extracted based on "clue phrases" in Japanese such as "Tame" (translated: for the sake of), and the topics are represented by keywords extracted from the title or body of news article. A dictionary of Japanese case frames is used to extract the keywords and causal phrases, a relevance metric is given to the keyword vector that represents a topic, this metric is used to discard causal relations thus reducing the complexity of the resulting graph. The keyword vector that represents a topic is not intuitively coherent therefore the results may hinder understanding. To find a focus on coherence we review Connecting the Dots Between News Articles [3]. It presents a system that generates a coherent chain of stories given an initial and final story. The system is compared to a baseline system as well as Google Timeline and Event Threading [4], a precursor of Incident Treading [1]. The system does not generate a network per se, but it does link news articles as though they were news topics. Another work that generates chains of news topics is Topic Chains for Understanding a News Corpus [5], in this work Latent Dirichlet Allocation (LDA) [6] is used to generate topics and several techniques are used to cluster topics, clusters are segregated into different time periods and links are generated between similar clusters from consecutive time periods, the result is a sequence of news topics that change over time. Other systems such as Unified Analysis of Streaming News [7] focus on scalability aspects of generating links between news topics.

2.2   Causal Relation Extraction

To better explain causal relation extraction, we classify the works into two types: explicitly causal and implicitly causal. Explicit causation is characterized by a causal marker in the phrase, for example "because" in the sentence "he fell because it was wet". An implicit causal relation may not have the causal markers for example "he fell and went to the hospital". We focus on explicit causation because it is less ambiguous therefore easier to understand. An example of explicit causal relation extraction is given [2], another example is given in [13], where causal taxonomies [14,15] are used to define causal markers and patterns, to extract causal relations.

There are several approaches to finding implicit causal relations. In [12] verb pairs are assigned a probability of being causally related, for example a sentence that contains the verbs "slip-fall" is likely a causal sentence. Noun pairs can also be used to extract causation, in [16] the noun pair "HIV-AIDS" is used to extract causal markers. There are explicit-implicit hybrid approaches [17], and there are also methods that extract several types of semantic relations, such as [18,19]. We propose to rank causal relation between news topics, by comparing occurrence probabilities similar to [12], using the temporal order features of news topics instead of screenplays. The proposed approach would be comparable to the method presented in [20]. And the results would be useful for a user to asses the validity of the extracted information.

2.3   Topic Models

Many works represent a topic as a weighted term vector, a popular model is Latent Dirichlet Allocation (LDA) [6], this method is useful to classify a large collection of documents into a set of topics. The top ranking words in a topic vector provide an intuition about the topic concept, but the vector format is not well suited for causal relations. A more comprehensive topic model has been proposed for the task of automatic multi-document summarization. In Topic Themes for Multi-document Summarization [8] phrases are selected based on LDA and part-of-speech-patterns, the phrases are used to represent a topic and key information about the topic. One drawback of this approach is that it does not consider multiple phrases referring to the same topic. Having a collection of phrases that represent a single news topic makes it possible to reduce the result set of a network of news topics, thus making it easier for the user to understand.

3   Research Hypotheses

The proposed system is based on several hypotheses:

Hypothesis 1. Causal relations between news topics help the user understand the news. We know that clustering news articles into topics reduces the result set thus reducing the cognitive load for selecting a news topic and we know that other semantic relations, such as temporal order, also known as a timeline, add information but still facilitate understanding, we must evaluate if the additional information from causal relations also facilitates understanding.

Hypothesis 2. Causal relations between news topics can be coherently extracted from a single phrase or sentence. This is important to provide understandable results to the user, to be able to directly reference the source of the information and to reduce processing requirements.

Hypothesis 3. Because of the abundance of online news sources, causal relation information is available for almost all popular news topics. Although we know there is an increasing amount of online news, we need to define the scope of news topics for which causal relation information is generated, namely news topics for which there is an abundance of information.

In order to evaluate these hypotheses, a system is proposed that will automatically generate a causal network of news topics. For the system to function properly the gaps presented in the related works section need to be filled, these are: The development of a topic model that is well suited for establishing causal relation and a method to rank explicit causal relations between news topics. The technical contributions of this work will be the methods to fill the aforementioned gaps and the proposed system to mitigate information overload.

4   Material

Currently an experimental prototype is under development, it uses the Palladian toolkit[1], to extract information from online news article accessed trough a web search engine. The system can use a static collection of documents as a corpus, for example the Reuters corpus[2] with access via a search engine such as Lucene[3]. The online version is preferred because it reduces local processing requirements.

---

[1] http://palladian.ws/ accessed 1.6.2012

[2] http://about.reuters.com/researchandstandards/corpus/ accessed 1.6.2012

[3] http://lucene.apache.org/core/ accessed 1.6.2012

Redirect link information is extracted from Wikipedia with the help of JWPL[4] a library that provides structured access to Wikipedia.

To better understand the system architecture we first introduce the notion of news topic references (NTR). These are the phrases used to refer to a news topic, for example in a Wikipedia article about a news topic such as *"The Arab Spring"*, the title of that article is a NTR. News topic references are often found in the title of news articles or in the initial part of the body where a summary is provided, for example the title "After the Arab spring" or in the body "...As the Arab Spring remakes the...". We can also find multiple NTR that refer to the same news topic. For example the article titled "Tunisia Effect" in Wikipedia is a redirect page to the "Arab Spring", we can assume that both "Tunisia Effect" and "Arab Spring" refer to the same news topic. A feature of NTRs is that they are coherent in a causal relation, for example in the title "Arab Spring Causes Bankruptcy of Russia's Top Fruit Importer", two NTRs are causally related "Arab Spring" and "Bankruptcy of Russia's Top Fruit Importer", this example shows how different news topics can be causally related. Because most of the information is extracted from online sources, there are limitations to the information the system can provide, namely information for poorly documented news topics and distinction between opinion and fact.

5   Methods

To illustrate how the prototype system works we present Figure 1 and explain each step. In the figure the term "Alias", found in **Step 2, 8 and 9**, is used to refer to the collection of NTRs that refer to the same news topic, so the NTR "Arab Spring" is an alias of "Tunisia Effect" because both refer to the same news topic.

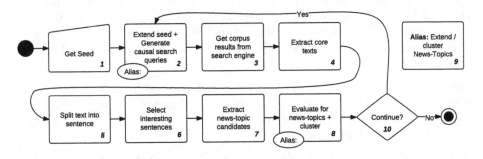

Fig. 1. Experimental prototype process flow

Step 1. The process begins by getting a seed NTR from the user, this will be the first node of the causal network. The heuristics used to validate the seed as an NTR are as follows:

---

[4] http://www.ukp.tu-darmstadt.de/software/jwpl/ accessed 1.6.2012

Heuristics 1. The seed phrase is the title for a Wikipedia article that is classified as an event. We classify a Wikipedia article as event type article when it present several markers such as a time and place of happening, or the article contains section titles including timeline, aftermath, impacts, reaction, reponse; negative markers are also used such as title including the phrases "list of", "disambiguation", "band", "film" or "country"[5].

Heuristics 2. The seed phrase is found with semantic markers, such as "The", in the title of multiple news articles.

Heuristics 3. A collection of similar news articles is generated by using the seed phrase as a query. The search engine used may semantically enhance the query by normalizing the phrase, for example with stop word removal, word stemming and synonyms addition. The similarity metric used can be term vector based such as Jaccard's Coefficient or KL divergence [9], where the terms are entities referenced in the news articles. These heuristics are still under development.

Step 2. The initial seed is extended with causal markers such as "caused" and "led to" in a method similar to Hearst's in [10] to generate a query for retrieving relevant documents. The query is also extended with NTR aliases when they are available. We propose two methods to discover NTR aliases: First, when the seed NTR is the title of a Wikipedia article classified as an event, then the titles of the redirect pages are considered NTR aliases. Second, an experimental approach is based on the assumption that alias NTRs are used as search terms with correlated patterns, this is to say an NTR will be used as a search term with a similar popularity distribution to an alias of that NTR. Thus, by analyzing query patterns, like in Google Correlate[6], potential NTR aliases can be discovered.

Step 3. The extended query is used to retrieve relevant documents through the search engine. The top ranked results are selected for further processing. In this step the search engine can be based on a local corpus indexed by Lucene with additional libraries such as Mahout and WordNet, to discover semantically related results. For simplicity Google online search engine was used in the implementation.

Step 4. The next step is to obtain relevant information from the top ranked results, this includes the human readable text and metadata such as creation time and source information. This information can later be used to refine the results in the causal network.

Step 5. The readable text is split into sentences, this facilitates processing the results and allows a summary results to be presented in the causal graph.

Step 6. Validating phrases to be NTR is resource intensive, therefore only selected phrases that contain the seed NTR or an alias, and a causal marker are further processed.

---

[5] The system for *Heuristics 1* is available upon request, please contact the author.
[6] http://www.google.com/trends/correlate

Step 7. The causal marker and pattern approach is used to define the causally related items, if one of the items is the seed NTR or an alias the counterpart is marked as a NTR candidate, to be evaluated in the next step.

Step 8. The NTR candidates are evaluated, all the validated NTRs are collected and alias matching is performed in **Step 9**, to reduce the result set. The causally related news topics can then be used as new seed NTR to continue expanding the network.

Step 10. At the end of the process we have a seed NTR and causally related NTRs, and the user is able to review the sources of the information at a sentence level. Additional information such as temporal sorting and ranking of causal relations may also be presented.

6 Results

From the process flow in 1 there is a series of intermediate results, such as generating the query in **Step 2** and extracting causal relations from sentences in **Step 7**, then evaluating the cause and effect as valid references to news topics in **Step 8**. The final result to the initial query from the user is a collection of phrases that are references to a news topics, clustered for simplification. The phrases are provided with additional information such as the document source and sentence from which the phrase were extracted. This information can be presented in a graphical interface to make the information more intuitive, similar to a Bayesian network.

7 Evaluation

Several components of the system have been evaluated, for the evaluation of the proposed hypotheses the complete system is required and under development. The evaluated components demonstrate the viability of the approach, these are: event classification from Wikipedia articles, NTR validation, NTR alias discovery and causal relation extraction between NTRs.

We conducted an empirical test to evaluate the efficiency of our event classification algorithm. For this, we randomly selected a Wikipedia article from the database and let the system try to identify it as an event. This process was repeated till one hundred events were found. The algorithmically identified events were then manually rechecked, to see if they were correctly identified or if they are false positives. We also rechecked the Wikipedia articles which did *not* pass the algorithm to find false negatives. The Table 1 shows the results.

Table 1. Wikipedia event article classification

	Positive (predicted)	Negative (predicted)	Recall
Positive (actual)	81	138	37%
Negative (actual)	19	3686	
Precision	**81%**		**Accuracy 82%**

An analysis of the results shows that the performance is highly affected by the quantity of information in articles, for example articles that contain many sections or articles that do not contain an infobox were in many cases misclassified. In future work we consider information quantity as a feature for classification.

The NTR validation was evaluated on a collection of 60 phrases extracted by the prototype system. To extract the phrases the system was initialized with 20 distinct seed NTR. The seed NTRs were not expanded with alias NTR to facilitate the evaluation. From the resulting 215 phrases the system classified as causally related news topic, a random selection of 60 were selected for evaluation. The evaluation by human annotators was done via an online survey system[7]. Annotators were given the NTR that is causally related to the seed NTR and the phrase from which the NTR was extracted, then the users were asked if the NTR refers to an event or activities in the given phrase. The possible annotations were true, false or unknown, the latter option is to consider phrases that are unclear or incorrectly parsed from the original source. Results show that from the phrases that could be classified by the annotators close to 64% were correctly classified by the system.

In future work a collection of phrases composed of known NTRs and additional phrases will be used to test if the system can sort them correctly. The performance of this component is comparable to the keyword extraction accuracy of 24% to 60% in [2].

To evaluate causal relation extraction between NTRs, human annotators were provided information that was extracted by the prototype. The information consisted of a seed NTR, a phrase that the system classified as causally relating the seed NTR to an another NTR, and the additional NTR extracted from the causal phrase. Because the system is intended to causally relate NTR it follows that the performance of the causal relation extraction is dependent on the performance of NTR validation. The triplets of seed NTR, causal phrase and additional NTR were generated based on 20 seed NTR, 40 generated triplets were randomly selected for evaluation. Annotators were asked to confirm if the seed NTR and the additional NTR were causally related in the given phrase. The system showed an accuracy of around 24%, an analysis of the results show that many of the extracted NTR were incorrect and that question phrases were wrongly classified as causal. The performance of causal relation extraction between news topic references is similar to causal relation extraction systems trained in one domain and evaluated in a different domain [11]. In future work causal relation extraction will be evaluated separately from NTR validation.

To evaluate NTR aliases annotators were provided 40 pairs of phrases the system classified as aliases, these aliases were generated based on eight seed NTRs. Annotators were given the phrase pairs and asked if they refer to the same event or activity. Annotators could answer yes, no or unknown, the latter option was given to consider terminology that may be obscure or unknown to the user. The overall accuracy was 65%. The results are an improvement over 36% accuracy in [2] for linking similar topic event pairs.

---

[7] https://crowdflower.com/jobs/65074/

8 Discussion

Much research in causal relation extraction and topic modeling has already been completed, but there are still gaps to be filled, in order to complete the system as proposed here. Though the experimental prototype performs better than state of the art only in very narrow aspects of the preliminary evaluation, it does function as a proof-of-concept system and provides an intuition of the overall architecture of the system. Because the proposed method for causal relation extraction is based on a novel topic model and vice versa, these two must be developed in parallel. These technical contributions will allow a more general contribution of a useful tool to aid in understanding current news, a novel approach to navigating between news topics and a method to potentially present past news topics as newly relevant.

9 Future Work

In [11] the probability of verb pairs being in a causal relation was estimated based on temporally ordered text, it follows that news topic references, that are also temporally ordered, can also be used to calculate causal relation probability. News topic references for past event can be extracted from knowledge bases such as Wikipedia, a greater challenge is discovering news topic references for current events that are not yet in knowledge bases, by using known news topic references and explicit causal relations it is possible to extract novel news topic references, this process will be developed in future work. Based on the aforementioned future works a system that automatically generates a network of causally related news topics to facilitate used understanding will be presented, this system will be used to evaluate the hypotheses presented above.

10 Conclusion

In this paper we propose a system to reduce news information overflow by automatically generating a network of causally related news topics. To generate the network, information is extracted from distributed news sources and presented in a simplified format. To causally related news topics, a topic model called "News Topic Reference" is presented. This topic model is suitable for extracting causal relations from natural language, it is semantically comprehensive and it can be used to cluster results from the causal relation extraction, this model is one of the contributions of this work. Using features found in news topics such as occurrence count and temporal order, it is possible to aggregate information to causal relations in order to provide more comprehensive results.

The proposed system is based on several assumptions that will be fully evaluated once the system is past the prototype stage. These assumptions focus on the usability of the system and the availability of information for the system to function. A preliminary evaluation provides a proof-of-concept for the viability of the proposed system.

References

1. Feng, A., Allan, J.: Incident threading for news passages. In: Proc. of the 18th ACM Conference on Information and Knowledge Management, pp. 1307–1316 (2009)
2. Ishii, H., et al.: Causal Network Construction to Support Understanding of News. In: Proceedings of HICSS 2010, pp. 1–10 (2010)
3. Shahaf, D., Guestrin, C.: Connecting the dots between news articles. In: Proc. of the 16th ACM SIGKDD Conference on Knowledge Discovery and Data Mining, pp. 623–632 (2010)
4. Nallapati, R., et al.: Event threading within news topics. In: ACM International Conference on Information and Knowledge Management, pp. 446–453 (2012)
5. Kim, D., Oh, A.: Topic chains for understanding a news corpus. In: Computational Linguistics and Intelligent Text Processing, pp. 163–176 (2011)
6. Blei, D.M., Ng, A.Y., Jordan, M.I.: Latent Dirichlet Allocation. Journal of Machine Learning Research 3, 993–1022 (2003)
7. Ahmed, A., et al.: Unified Analysis of Streaming News. In: Proc. 20th International Conference on World Wide Web, pp. 267–276 (2011)
8. Harabagiu, S., Lacatusu, F.: Topic themes for multi-document summarization. In: Proc. 28th Annual International ACM SIGIR Conference on Research and Development in Information Retrieval (2005)
9. Huang, A.: Similarity Measures for Text Document Clustering. In: Proc. 6th New Zealand Computer Science Research Student Conference, pp. 49–56 (2008)
10. Girju, R., Moldovan, D.: Text mining for causal relations. In: Proceedings FLAIRS Conference, pp. 360–364 (2002)
11. Rink, B., et al.: Learning Textual Graph Patterns to Detect Causal Event Relations. In: Proc. 23rd Florida Artificial Intelligence Research Society International Conference, Applied Natural Language Processing Track, pp. 265–270 (2010)
12. Beamer, B., Girju, R.: Using a Bigram Event Model to Predict Causal Potential. In: Gelbukh, A. (ed.) CICLing 2009. LNCS, vol. 5449, pp. 430–441. Springer, Heidelberg (2009)
13. Radinsky, K., Davidovich, S.: Learning Causality from Textual Data. In: NLU 21 (2011)
14. Wolff, P., et al.: Models of causation and causal verbs. In: The Meeting of the Chicago Linguistics Society, pp. 607–622 (2002)
15. Joshi, S., et al.: Lexico-syntactic causal pattern text mining. In: Proc. 14th WSEAS International Conference on Computers, pp. 446–451 (2010)
16. Chang, D.-S., Choi, K.-S.: Incremental cue phrase learning and bootstrapping method for causality extraction using cue phrase and word pair probabilities. Information Processing & Management 42(3), 662–678 (2006)
17. Ittoo, A., Bouma, G.: Extracting Explicit and Implicit Causal Relations from Sparse, Domain-Specific Texts. In: Muñoz, R., Montoyo, A., Métais, E. (eds.) NLDB 2011. LNCS, vol. 6716, pp. 52–63. Springer, Heidelberg (2011)
18. Butnariu, C., et al.: SemEval-2010 Task 9: The Interpretation of Noun Compounds Using Paraphrasing Verbs and Prepositions. In: Proc. 5th International Workshop on Semantic Evaluation, pp. 39–44 (2010)
19. Chan, Y.S.: Minimally Supervised Event Causality Identification. In: Proc. Conference on Empirical Methods in Natural Language Processing, pp. 294–303 (2011)
20. Riaz, M., Girju, R.: Another Look at Causality: Discovering Scenario-Specific Contingency Relationships with No Supervision. In: IEEE 4th International Conference on Semantic Computing, pp. 361–368 (2010)
21. Allan, J., et al.: Topic detection and tracking pilot study final report (1998)

Towards Model-Driven Requirements Analysis for Context-Aware Well-Being Systems

Steven Bosems

University of Twente,
Department of Electrical Engineering, Mathematics and Computer Science,
Enschede, The Netherlands
s.bosems@utwente.nl

Abstract. Over the years, the interest in the field of pervasive computing has increased. A specific class of applications in this domain is that of context-aware applications. These programs utilize context information to adapt to their current environment. This quality can be used, among others, when dealing with health care and well-being situations. However, as the user requirements for these specific applications are almost never well-specified, there is a real risk that the resulting application does not offer the right set of features to the user. In order to mitigate this risk, we propose a model-driven method of requirements engineering for systems in the domain of context-aware well-being applications. This method will result in an explicit specification of requirements, and an improved alignment of user requirements and system features. Furthermore, due to the model-driven character of the method, the artifacts created during the requirements engineering phase of the development process can directly be incorporated in the subsequent development steps.

Keywords: requirements, architecture, model-driven development, pervasive, context-aware.

1 Introduction

According to Scopus [2], the field of pervasive computing has increased drastically over the last 15 years, the number of published research papers increasing from less than 500 to over 3,000 per year. In order to make pervasive systems adaptive to their environment, we add context information to them. In these context-aware applications, sensors are used to monitor the user's environment such that the experience the user has when using the application can be improved. By analyzing the data collected by the sensors and reasoning about this information, the program can adapt itself in order to better suit the current situation the user is in, provide relevant information to the user, or offer services that are deemed useful. One domain in which this type of application can be particularly useful, is that of health care and well-being. In this PhD research, we will be focusing on this specific field of application.

This research will be performed as part of the COMMIT SWELL project [1]. The focus of this project is the well-being of knowledge workers. Over the years,

P. Herrero et al. (Eds.): OTM 2012 Workshops, LNCS 7567, pp. 43–50, 2012.
© Springer-Verlag Berlin Heidelberg 2012

this group has seen a decline in their well-being [9]. SWELL aims to improve both the physical and the mental well-being of knowledge workers by providing the users with a context-aware well-being system. However, the features offered by this system have to be aligned with the demands of the user. If this is not the case, the system will be disregarded. As such, the process of requirements engineering and alignment in context-aware applications is of key importance. During this PhD research, we aim to improve this process.

Our contribution to the field of requirements engineering is a model-driven method of requirements elicitation in the domain of context-aware well-being applications, which can be used to increase user involvement in the software development process, resulting in higher user satisfaction in the resulting application. It is to be noted that the planned method is to be used while designing and developing a context-aware well-being system. We do not intend to utilize it for runtime alteration of the system's behavior; we deem a model-driven method using model transformations unsuitable for runtime adaptation of these systems.

The rest of this paper is structured as follows: Section 2 discusses the work done in the domain of context-aware applications and model-driven development, Section 3 introduces the hypothesis for our research, Section 4 outlines the planning for the rest of this thesis, Section 5 looks at some possible drawbacks of the proposed method and Section 6 provides concluding remarks.

2   Related Work

In 1991, [19] explored the idea of ubiquitous computing systems, interconnected by wired and wireless technology, that would be invisible to the users. The author predicted the rise of small computing devices that could be used and combined in order to provide the best possible user experience. The inclusion of context information and the term context-awareness, however, were not used until 1994. [16] was the first to define the term context-aware computing. The authors identify the location, people, hosts, accessible devices, and changes of these over time as relevant contexts for mobile distributed computing systems.

[6] defines context information in a broader way as "any information that can be used to characterize the situation of an entity" and defines an entity as "a person, place or object that is considered relevant to the interaction between a user and an application, including the user and applications themselves." The authors deem a system context-aware, if this context is used in order to "provide relevant information and/or services to the user." They note that this relevancy is dependent on the task of the user. Context-aware applications can be categorized according to three features: presentation of information, execution of services and tagging of context to information. Four context types are recognized: activity, identity, location and time. It is noted that "activity" describes the environment and everything that happens in it at the given time. The authors further describe that these context types are primary context types. Using this information, secondary context types can be derived from other sources.

The authors of [7] distinguish between intrinsic and relational context, the former inhering in a single entity and the latter being defined as a property of an entity in relationship to one or more other entities. They also introduce the concept of situation, which represents a state of affairs of interest to the application, defined in terms of temporal constraints on context value.

In the field of requirements engineering, multiple methods exist in order to model goals and requirements. Modeling goals of the users and stakeholders is part of the requirements engineering process. KAOS [11], use case models [15], and i* [20] are some examples of such methods and languages. When looking at these, however, we find that the level of abstraction at which the goals are specified is too high to be directly usable for model transformations into system architectures; for this additional information is required. [4] uses a Model-Driven Architecture-based approach to transform business rules, located at the Computational Independent Model (CIM) level, into Platform Independent Models (PSMs), however, they do not supply us with the additional step of generating Platform Specific Models (PSMs), i.e. system architectures.

Introduced in 2001 by the Object Management Group (OMG), the Model-Driven Architecture (MDA) [12] explains how OMG standards may be used together. MDA focuses on the relation between the concepts of Platform Independent Models (PIMs) and Platform Specific Models (PSMs). Model-Driven Engineering (MDE) [10] incorporates these techniques, and adds tool support to aid developers in maintaining models, the primary artifacts in this process, at different levels of abstraction. Model transformations are used to translate between these levels. We shall use the term "model-driven" for any process using these transformation techniques, having models as primary development artifact. [3] argues that model-driven development should not be structured as the OMG proposes it in MDA. The author calls this "Generative MDD." Rather, he suggests that MDD techniques are to be used in an agile fashion, "Agile MDD", iteratively creating models and writing code. MDD techniques are then used to keep these artifacts synchronized.

[8] defines a way to model the context of pervasive systems. The method proposed allows for the description of the concept of a 'Person', who is authorized to use, or is located near a certain 'Device'. The Person also has a (communication) 'Channel', which in turn requires a Device. 'Location Coordinates' are used to locate the Person and the Device. The authors allow for the use of different association types in the models, including 'Static associations', 'Derived associations', and 'Sensed associations'. Dependencies can be added between associations in order to guarantee a stable system. Furthermore, associations can be annotated with quality parameters, indicating accuracy and certainty of these connections between entities.

In [13], the authors introduce the Pervasive Modeling Language (PervML). This Platform Independent Modeling (PIM) language allows the user to define the pervasive system in an abstract way that does not rely on the underlying implementation technology. The authors propose to use model transformations in order to obtain Open Services Gateway initiative (OSGi) models. These

Platform Specific Models (PSMs) can then be used to generate OSGi-based Java programming code. A PervML model specifies a *ServiceModel*, which in turn has zero or more *Services*. These model the way different parts of the system inter-operate, defining triggers, pre- and postconditions, and service aggregation. According to [14], a model that will facilitate the description of requirements for a context-aware system, is to capture the characteristics of the physical environment, a description of tasks and a description of the system behavior. Using this information, a PervML model can be generated. [17] uses PervML and the PervML Generative Tool (PervGT) [5] to develop a context-aware system in a model-driven way. Their conclusions are that MDD of these systems decreases development time, increases reusability and increases software quality. For our purpose, however, PervML is too low level, as the language requires training in systems architecture for a user of the final product to understand it, thus hindering direct user involvement in the development process.

3   Research Hypothesis

As experience shows, a discrepancy often exists between user demands and features offered by the final version of the system that is being developed. It is the task of the requirements engineer, the systems architect and the system developer to minimize this gap between what is expected, and what is offered. In pervasive computing, even more so than in regular software applications, the system must do exactly as the user anticipates it will do. If this is not the case, the system becomes a hindrance and is no longer pervasive.

In current requirements elicitation practices, the link between the user requirements and the technical implementation is often neglected. As such, the requirements have to be reinterpreted and re-elicited in subsequent development steps. Furthermore, current tools and practices do not deal with the specific challenges the well-being domain poses.

Because of the importance of proper requirements engineering in the field of pervasive systems, our research results in the definition of a domain specific modeling language for the specification of requirements of context-aware applications, along with model transformations that will allow us to transform between user requirements and system architectures. Through the use of this technique, the requirements and the architecture of the system that is to satisfy them can be kept synchronized.

The method envisioned is structured as follows: a user provides requirements, which are captured in a model. The requirements engineer can use this model to continue the requirements elicitation process. The completed model is then to be transferred to the system architect, who makes sure the architecture fits the requirements. This step is to be performed in a model-driven fashion, using model transformations. The completed architectural model can then be used by the developer of the system. However, during this process, feedback is continuously provided to people working on the project: alterations in the architecture will have to be reflected in the requirements. For this flow to be supported, model transformations can also be used. Figure 1 illustrates this process.

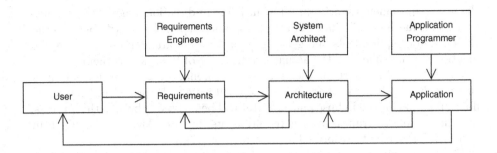

Fig. 1. Conceptual framework

In this PhD project, we will be researching the validity of the following hypothesis:

> *Through the use of model-driven engineering techniques, the process of creating user requirements for context-aware well-being applications can be improved, resulting in programs that better suit the demands of the users, than those that were created using general purpose requirements engineering techniques.*

4   Work Plan

In order to prove that the use of model-driven techniques involving the user requirements of context-aware applications is beneficiary to the process of the creation of well-being applications, several steps will have to be taken.

Firstly, we will have to identify the methods currently used in the field of requirements engineering for pervasive systems. A distinction shall be made between general purpose software requirements engineering methods, and methods tailored specifically to pervasive systems. Both model-driven and non-model-driven techniques shall be evaluated. This research shall be performed as a structured literary survey.

Secondly, research will be conducted to get a full overview of the domain in order to create meta-models for the model-driven process. These meta-models will be used to define models of the user requirements and system architectures, and should contain all elements that could be present in the field of pervasive systems: the requirements of the user toward the system itself, the specification and requirements of the context, and a profile of the user. The validity of these models shall be tested through interviews with domain experts.

Thirdly, a model-driven method will be created that uses the meta-models described in the previous step. This method will aim to involve the intended users of the system under development in the process of creating requirements. By using model-driven techniques, we will allow these users to express themselves in a non-technical way, while still creating artifacts that are used throughout the rest of the design process. Also, we aim to keep these resulting artifacts and the used requirements synchronized by utilizing bi-directional model transformations. This method will differ from [13], [14], and [17], in that it will focus on the elicitation of requirements and generation of a system architecture, whereas the mentioned sources aim at the actual development of the systems themselves.

Fourthly, tool support for the creation, maintenance, and transformation of the models mentioned in the previous step will have to be provided. In order to do so, plug-ins for the Eclipse platform [18] will be created. Through this process, we will be able to transform user requirements into PervML models, which in turn can further be transformed as described in [17].

Finally, we will verify that the proposed method, supported by the tool, does indeed result in an improvement of the developed applications. For this, case studies and interviews with the intended product users shall be conducted. One of these case studies will be in the COMMIT SWELL project, researching whether direct transformation from requirements into an architecture yields better results, than when requiring interpretation of requirements by domain experts and manual translation of these into an overall system architecture, as is currently the case.

5   Discussion

As the proposed model-driven process is likely to involve additional work from developers and architects when compared to traditional methods of working, it is likely that the overhead of this process might be counterproductive for small-scale projects. Due to this possible problem, it is important to gain knowledge on the estimated size of the project at hand before choosing to use our method.

As we are involving users in the design process of software, we have to create a tool to aid us with this. The design of the tool is to be adapted with regard to the intended audience: traditional design tools are used by software developers that work with these tools on a regular basis. As such, they gain knowledge into the workings of the tool and structure their work flow around them. However, as the users of these tools will be non-experts, the workings of the tool will have to be clear to them when using it for the first time. Experts in the field of human-computer interaction and interface design might have to be consulted.

6   Conclusion

Over the years, the well-being of knowledge workers has been degrading. The COMMIT SWELL project aims to improve this using pervasive, context-aware applications. In order to improve the alignment of user requirements and features offered by the system envisioned, we propose to use model-driven techniques during the process of requirements engineering of these well-being applications. We hypothesized that this will result in programs that better suit the user's requirements, then when using general purpose requirements engineering techniques. A work plan has been illustrated, and a discussion was provided with regard to potential problems when implementing our methodology.

Acknowledgments. We would like to thank Marten van Sinderen for his insights and comments.

This publication was supported by the Dutch national program COMMIT (project P7 SWELL).

References

[1] Commit: A public-private research community (2011), http://commit-nl.nl/

[2] Scopus (March 2012), http://www.scopus.com

[3] Ambler, S.: Agile model driven development is good enough. IEEE Software 20(5), 71–73 (2003)

[4] Castro, V.D., Marcos, E., Vara, J.M.: Applying CIM-to-PIM model transformations for the service-oriented development of information systems. Information and Software Technology 53(1), 87–105 (2011), http://www.sciencedirect.com/science/article/pii/S0950584910001588

[5] Cetina, C., Serral, E., Muñoz, J., Pelechano, V.: Tool support for model driven development of pervasive systems. In: Fernandes, J.M., Machado, R.J., Khedri, R., Clarke, S. (eds.) Proceedings of 4th International Workshop on Model-based Methodologies for Pervasive and Embedded Software, pp. 33–41. IEEE Computer Society Press (March 2007)

[6] Dey, A.K., Abowd, G.D.: Towards a better understanding of context and context-awareness. In: Computer Human Intraction 2000 Workshop on the What, Who, Where, When, Why and How of Context-Awareness (2000), ftp://ftp.cc.gatech.edu/pub/gvu/tr/1999/99-22.pdf

[7] Dockhorn Costa, P., Almeida, J.P.A., Ferreira Pires, L., van Sinderen, M.: Situation Specification and Realization in Rule-Based Context-Aware Applications. In: Indulska, J., Raymond, K. (eds.) DAIS 2007. LNCS, vol. 4531, pp. 32–47. Springer, Heidelberg (2007), http://doc.utwente.nl/61762/

[8] Henricksen, K., Indulska, J., Rakotonirainy, A.: Modeling Context Information in Pervasive Computing Systems. In: Mattern, F., Naghshineh, M. (eds.) PERVASIVE 2002. LNCS, vol. 2414, pp. 167–180. Springer, Heidelberg (2002), http://dx.doi.org/10.1007/3-540-45866-2_14

[9] Hooftman, W., Hesselink, J.K., van Genabook, J., Wiezer, N., Willems, D.: Arbobalans 2010: Kwaliteit van de arbeid, effecten en maatregelen in nederland. Tech. rep., TNO (2011)

[10] Kent, S.: Model Driven Engineering. In: Butler, M., Petre, L., Sere, K. (eds.) IFM 2002. LNCS, vol. 2335, pp. 286–298. Springer, Heidelberg (2002)

[11] Lamsweerde, A., Dardenne, A., Belcourt, F.D.: The KAOS project: knowledgeacquisition in automated specification of software. In: Design of Composite Systems. Proceedings of AAAI Spring Symposium Series, pp. 59–62 (1991)

[12] Miller, J., Mukerji, J.: MDA guide version 1.0.1. OMG document. Object Management Group (2001), http://www.omg.org/cgi-bin/doc?omg/03-06-01

[13] Muñoz, J., Pelechano, V., Fons, J.: Model driven development of pervasive systems. In: Intl. Workshop on Model-Based Methodologies for Pervasive and Embedded Software (MOMPES), pp. 3–14 (2004)

[14] Muñoz, J., Valderas, P., Pelechano, V., Pastor, O.: Requirements engineering for pervasive systems. a transformational approach. In: Requirements Engineering, 14th IEEE International Conference, pp. 351–352 (September 2006)

[15] Object Management Group: OMG Unified Modeling Language (OMG UML), infrastructure, v2.1.2 (2007), http://www.omg.org/spec/UML/2.1.2/Infrastructure/PDF

[16] Schilit, B., Adams, N., Want, R.: Context-aware computing applications. In: Proceedings of the 1994 First Workshop on Mobile Computing Systems and Applications, WMCSA 1994, pp. 85–90. IEEE Computer Society, Washington, DC (1994), http://dx.doi.org/10.1109/WMCSA.1994.16

[17] Serral, E., Valderas, P., Pelechano, V.: Towards the model driven development of context-aware pervasive systems. Pervasive and Mobile Computing 6, 254–280 (2009)

[18] The Eclipse Foundation: Eclipse (2012), http://eclipse.org/

[19] Weiser, M.: The computer for the 21st century. Scientific American 265(3), 94–104 (September 1991), http://doi.acm.org/10.1145/329124.329126

[20] Yu, E.: Towards modelling and reasoning support for early-phase requirements engineering. In: Proceedings of the Third IEEE International Symposium on Requirements Engineering, pp. 226–235 (January 1997)

OWL 2: Towards Support for Context Uncertainty, Fuzziness and Temporal Reasoning

Wilbard Nyamwihula and Burchard Bagile

Department of Computer Science and Engineering,
University of Dar es Salaam,
Tanzania
{wbilungi,bbagile}@yahoo.com

1 Introduction

Context-awareness plays a vital role in pervasive computing. Context-aware applications relay on context information in order to provide appropriate and consistent adaptive services by integrating sensor data from a diverse range of sources with varying degree of accuracy, precision, dynamism, and are failure prone. Therefore, context information are inherently imperfect, they exhibit various types of uncertainties: incomplete, imprecise. vague, inconsistency, and/or temporal. Therefore context-aware applications must be supported by an adequate context information modeling and reasoning formalism.

There have been several efforts in modeling context information with uncertainty, but still there is a lack of a hybrid context modeling framework capable of modeling and support reasoning for all various types of uncertainties and temporal characteristics. The web ontology language (OWL) has been recommended as standard language for Semantic web by World Wide Web Consortium (W3C) [1]. Unfortunately, OWL1 and its predecessor OWL2 are not sufficient for handling context imperfections: Imprecise, vague, incomplete, inconsistency, inaccurate, and temporal information that is commonly found in applications and domains [2].

To address these problems, this PhD research focuses on extending OWL 2 framework to support context uncertainty, fuzziness and temporal modeling and reasoning.

2 Related Work

Over a decade, some efforts have been made in representing and reasoning with uncertainty in the Semantic Web. These works are mainly focused on how to extend the classical description logics (SHOIN(D) for OWL1 & SROIQ(D) for OWL2) behind Semantic Web ontology languages to the probabilistic and possibilistic logics [,3,4,5,6,7,8,9.10.11], fuzzy logics {12,13,14,15,16}, and temporal description logics[17,18,19]

P. Herrero et al. (Eds.): OTM 2012 Workshops, LNCS 7567, pp. 51–53, 2012.

3   Research Hypotheses/Questions

- What extension for OWL 2 able handle contextual uncertainty, fuzziness and temporal information?
- What are optimization and reasoning techniques for an extended Description Logic (i.e., SROIQ a logical model for OWL2) able to support reasoning with uncertainty, fuzziness and temporal information for extended OWL2?

4   Methods / Work Plan

Different approaches for contextual uncertain and temporal information modeling and reasoning will be reviewed and analyzed for possible extension of Web Ontology Language OWL2 with theories (i.e., probabilistic/possibilistic logics, fuzzy logics, and temporal description logic theories) able to handle contextual uncertainty, fuzziness and temporal information. The description logic (SROIQ) [1], underlying logic model for OWL2 will be extended to support reasoning with uncertainty, fuzziness, and temporal information taking into account the balance between expressiveness, tractability, soundness and completeness.

5   Conclusion

This PhD research, will contribute to knowledge by providing formalism on extending the OWL 2 framework to handle contextual uncertainty, fuzziness and temporal information as well as extending underlying description logic (SROIQ) for OWL2 to support reasoning with uncertainty, fuzziness, and temporal information; taking into account the balance between expressiveness, tractability, soundness and completeness.

References

1. W3C OWLWorking Group, OWL 2Web Ontology Language: Document Overview (2009), http://www.w3.org/TR/owl2-overview
2. URW3, Uncertainty reasoning for the world wide web incubator group report, Technical report. W3C Incubator Group Final Report, 3 (2008),
   http://www.w3.org/2005/Incubator/urw3/XGR-urw3
3. Lukasiewicz, T., Straccia, U.: Managing uncertainty and vagueness in description logics for the semantic web. Journal ofWeb Semantics 6(4), 291–308 (2008)
4. da Costa, P.C.G.: Bayesian semantics for the Semantic Web. PhD thesis. George Mason University, Fairfax, VA, USA (2005)
5. da Costa, P.C.G., Laskey, K.B.: PR-OWL: A framework for probabilistic ontologies. In: Proceedings FOIS 2006, pp. 237–249. IOS Press (2006)
6. da Costa, P.C.G., Laskey, K.B., Laskey, K.J.: PR-OWL: A Bayesian ontology lan-guage for the Semantic Web. In: Proceedings URSW 2005, pp. 23–33 (2005)
7. Ding, Z., Peng, Y.: A probabilistic extension to ontology language OWL. In: Proceedings HICSS 2004 (2004)

8. Ding, Z., Peng, Y., Pan, R.: BayesOWL: Uncertainty modeling in Semantic Web ontologies. In: Ma, Z. (ed.) Soft Computing in Ontologies and Semantic Web. SFSC, vol. 204. Springer (2006)
9. Predoiu, L., Stuckenschmidt, H.: A probabilistic framework for information integra-tion and retrieval on the semantic web ABSTRACT. In: Proceedings of the 3rd International Workshop on Database Interoperability, InterDB (2007)
10. Pan, R., Ding, Z., Yu, Y., Peng, Y.: A Bayesian Network Approach to Ontology Mapping. In: Gil, Y., Motta, E., Benjamins, V.R., Musen, M.A. (eds.) ISWC 2005. LNCS, vol. 3729, pp. 563–577. Springer, Heidelberg (2005)
11. Yang, Y., Calmet, J.: OntoBayes: An ontology-driven uncertainty model. In: Proceedings IAWTIC 2005, pp. 457–463. IEEE Press (2005)
12. Nottelmann, H., Fuhr, N.: Adding probabilities and rules to OWL Lite subsets based on probabilistic Datalog. International Journal of Uncertainty, Fuzziness and Knowledge-Based Systems 14(1), 17–42 (2006)
13. Gao, M., Liu, C.: Extending OWL by fuzzy description logic. In: Proceedings of the 17th IEEE International Conference on Tools with Artificial Intelligence (ICTAI 2005). IEEE (2005)
14. Stoilos, G., Stamou, G., Pan, J.Z.: Fuzzy extensions of OWL: logical properties and reduc-tion to fuzzy description logics. International Journal of Approximate Reasoning 51, 656–679 (2010) Computer Society, 562–567 (2005)
15. Stoilos, G., Stamou, G.: Extending fuzzy description logics for the semantic web. In: Proceedings of the 3rd International Workshop on OWL: Experiences and Directions (OWLED 2007). CEURWorkshop Proceedings, vol. 258 (2007)
16. Bobillo, F., Straccia, U.: An OWL Ontology for Fuzzy OWL 2. In: Rauch, J., Raś, Z.W., Berka, P., Elomaa, T. (eds.) ISMIS 2009. LNCS, vol. 5722, pp. 151–160. Springer, Heidelberg (2009)
17. Milea, V., Frasincar, F., Kaymak, U.: Knowledge Engineering in a Temporal Semantic Web Context. In: The Eighth International Conference on Web Engineering, ICWE 2008 (2008)
18. Batsakis, S., Petrakis, E.G.M.: SOWL: Spatio-temporal Representation, Reasoning and Querying over the SemanticWeb. In: 6th International Conference on Semantic Systems, Graz, Austria, September 1–3, pp. 1–3 (2010)
19. Tao, C., Wei, W.Q., Solbrig, H.R., Savova, G., Chute, C.G.: CNTRO: A Semantic Web Ontology for Temporal Relation Inferencing in Clinical Narratives. In: AMIA Annual Symp. Proc. 2010, pp. 787–791 (2010)

Semantic Web Technologies' Role in Smart Environments

Faisal Razzak

Department of Control and Computer Engineering
Politecnico di Torino, Italy
faisal.razzak@polito.it

Abstract. Today semantic web technologies and Linked Data principles are providing formalism, standards, shared data semantics and data integration for unstructured data over the web. The result is a transformation from the Web of Interaction to the Web of Data and actionable information. On the crossroad lies our daily lives, containing plethora of unstructured data which is originating from low cost sensors and appliances to every computational element used in our modern lives, including computers, interactive watches, mobile phones, GPS devices etc. These facts accentuate an opportunity for system designers to combine these islands of data into a large actionable information space which can be utilized by automated and intelligent agents. As a result, this phenomenon is likely to institute a space that is smart enough to provide humans with comfort of living and to build an efficient society. Thus, in this context, the focus of my research has been to propose solutions to the problems in the domains of smart environment and energy management, under the umbrella of ambient intelligence. The potential role of semantic web technologies in these proposed solutions has been analyzed and architectures for these solutions were designed, implemented and tested.

Keywords: ambient intelligence, Domotic Effects, LO(D)D, SEIPF, semantic web technologies' role, smart environments.

1 Introduction

The emergence of economically viable and efficient sensor technology has enabled system designers to build smart environments [6] that measure different features across environment, i.e., proximity, temperature, luminosity. Consequently, it gives rise to computational models in which networks of appliances or sensors interact with each other and with their corresponding environments to provide residents, a better living and comfortable experience. The requirement is to model different artifacts of the environment and then processing these models in combination with other computer technologies to reach some environment specific goals, i.e., ubiquitous access to appliances and their information, fulfilling user goals. Semantic web technologies can act as a modeling tool, as they support the representation of structured data, explicit context representation, expressive

P. Herrero et al. (Eds.): OTM 2012 Workshops, LNCS 7567, pp. 54–58, 2012.

context querying, and flexible context reasoning [8]. Since architectural and device modeling deals with the artifacts that are described for each environment and varies across different vendors, their modeling was identified as *Lower Level Modeling (LLM)*. By contrast, the abstract modeling to achieve intelligence and innovative interaction management techniques were identified as *Higher Level Modeling (HLM)* as they deal with generic human centric expression.

This paper very briefly outlines the research contribution and perspective of the author in addressing the issues of ubiquitous access to smart environment, enabling users to program their own environments, achieving user goals, minimizing energy usage in the domains of smart environment and energy management, and the potential role of semantic web technologies. The architectures for these contributions were designed, implemented and tested.

2   Research Methodology

The research methodology was to design, develop and test frameworks addressing different issues related to the fields of smart environments and energy management. These issues tackled were providing a ubiquitous access to smart environment, enabling users to program their own environments, achieving user goals, minimizing energy consumption. In addition, the frameworks were designed to be modular so that they can be integrated with an existing IDE (in our case Dog [1]). The following three steps were iterated to address different problems.

1. The first step was to identify artifacts or concepts and their interrelationships (at LLM or HLM level), and to model them using the ontologies. An ontology represents a specific perspective of the environment that is device modeling, energy modeling, therefore during ontology development the modularity pattern was followed [2,5]. W3C's *Ontology Web Language (OWL)*[1] was chosen to encode the ontology.
2. The second step was to design and develop ontology-powered frameworks. These frameworks build their knowledge base from the ontologies but the processing, reasoning and decisions over the knowledge base depend upon application specific requirements
3. The third step was more like a principle. If a framework intends to share its output on a large-scale or communicate with other frameworks, Linked Data (LD) principles were followed.

Table 1 highlights different frameworks and the combination of ontologies (HLM/LLM) powering them.

3   Research Activities

3.1   Web of Domotics (WoD) [7]

WoD is an amalgam of Smart Environments and the Internet of Things. It represents an Internet architecture enabling mobile users to access information

---

[1] www.w3.org/2004/OWL

Table 1. Development relationship between the ontologies and frameworks

HLM \ LLM	None	Publisher	DogOnt	DogPower
None	X	LO(D)D	Web of Domotics	SEIPF
DogEffects	X	X	Domotic Effects	I.E.O

regarding devices and to operate on those devices in a ubiquitous manner, independent from location constraints. It considers the home and office environments and go beyond the "simple" adoption of real objects as web service proxies [3] by transforming such objects into actionable environment entities. WoD is open and interoperable, network agnostic and location aware. The adoption of standard technologies and protocols, users should be able to interact and operate any smart environment through their "normal" mobile terminals, and without requiring any prior user registration or environment set-up. WoD provides (i) identification of devices by proximity, i.e., through tags (ii) discovery of device access points, through standard DNS aliases (iii) single-sign-on authentication based on OpenID (iv) policy-based authorization for granting different operation possibilities to different users (v) LD information exchange to support interoperability with semantic web technologies. (vi) REST based interaction for querying status and triggering actions on physical devices.

3.2 Domotic Effects

The "Domotic Effects" is a high level modeling approach (Fig. 1), which provides AmI designers with an abstract layer that enables the definition of generic goals in a smart environment, in a declarative way, which can be used to design and develop intelligent applications. The high-level nature of Domotic Effects allows the residents to program their personal space as they see fit: they can define different achievement criteria for a particular generic goal. For example, a user may describe a Domotic Effect (DE) corresponding to the generic goal of lighting up a room, and this goal may be reached by acting, in different ways, on lamps, curtains, and shutters in that room, possibly by taking into account external conditions. Given the state of these devices, the AmI system may determine whether the lighting goal is actually reached (Domotic Effects Evaluation); conversely, if the user asks for this DE to take place, then the AmI system will bring the home devices into a state that satisfies the request (Domotic Effects Enforcement). A "DogEffects" ontology has been developed to provide a formal knowledge base for the modeling framework and is organized in a structure that corresponds to the architecture shown in Fig. 1. The Core layer contains the basic class definitions for expressing DEs. Each DE is expressed as a function of device states or sensor values. Such function is expressed using a set of operators that can be defined by the AmI designer. The AmI layer encodes the set of operators depending on the application domain. Finally, the Instance layer represents the specific DEs being defined in a specific environment.

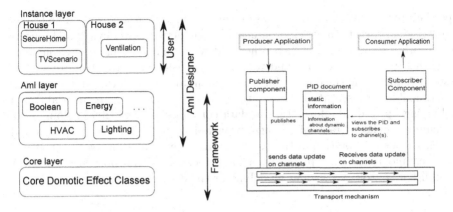

Fig. 1. Domotic Effect Modeling Framework

Fig. 2. Architecture of LO(D)D

3.3 Energy Management: SEIPF [2]

A Semantic Energy Information Publishing Framework (SEIPF) was proposed to address the issue of energy management. It publishes, for different appliances in the environment, their power consumption information and other appliance properties, in a machine understandable format following LD principles. While appliance properties are exposed according to the DogOnt ontology [1], power consumption is modeled by introducing a new modular DogPower ontology (previously Energy Profile ontology). The DogPower ontology was designed to model nominal, typical and real power consumptions for each appliance in achievable states. It can be plugged with another ontology (having the notions of device and states), as it follows modularity pattern.

SEIPF is consistent with publication of information at different granularity levels (e.g., by aggregating over device groups) and respecting different authorization levels. The ability to collect and share instantaneous power consumed by different devices in a house can enable the creation of many applications that can lead towards a more energy efficient society. In the future, intelligent negotiation and consumption coordination based on open and semantic representation will allow third-party service providers to build intelligent and automated services that use the energy consumption information to build dynamic services. An example is the optimization of energy inside the smart environment(I.E.O [4]). Based on the Domotic Effects modeling and the power consumption details provided by the DogPower ontology, minimization of energy usage of an environment is achieved along with fulfilling users' goals.

3.4 Publishing Linked Open (Dynamic) Data [5]

It is a distributed framework that provides a systematic way to publish environment data which is being updated continuously; such updates might be issued at specific time intervals or bound to some environment specific event. The framework (Fig. 2) targets smart environments having networks of devices and sensors which are interacting with each other and with their respective environments to gather and generate data and willing to publish this data. It addresses the issues of supporting the data publishers to maintain up-to-date and machine understandable representations, separation of views (static or dynamic data) and delivering up-to-date information to data consumers in real time, helping data consumers to keep track of changes triggered from diverse environments and keeping track of evolution of the smart environment. The framework consists of three components, i.e., a publisher, a subscriber and a transport mechanism. A "Publisher" ontology provides modeling for the different elements of the framework.

4   Conclusion

This paper briefly highlighted the activities undertaken during my research to address problems in the domains of smart environment and energy management. The role of semantic web technologies as a knowledge base was also outlined. In the future, the focus will be to devise developmental guidelines (based on the author's experience) for the use of semantic web technologies, in solving the issues of smart environments.

References

1. Bonino, D., Castellina, E., Corno, F.: The dog gateway: enabling ontology-based intelligent domotic environments. IEEE Transactions on Consumer Electronics 54(4), 1656–1664 (2008)
2. Bonino, D., Corno, F., Razzak, F.: Enabling machine understandable exchange of energy consumption information in intelligent domotic environments. Energy and Buildings 43(6), 1392–1402 (2011)
3. Broll, G., Rukzio, E., Paolucci, M., Wagner, M., Schmidt, A., Hussmann, H.: Perci: Pervasive service interaction with the internet of things. IEEE Internet Computing 13(6), 74–81 (2009)
4. Corno, F., Razzak, F.: Intelligent energy optimization for user intelligible goals in smart environments. IEEE Transactions on Smart Grid (submitted, 2012)
5. Corno, F., Razzak, F.: Publishing LO(D)D: Linked open (dynamic) data for smart sensing and measuring environments. In: The 3rd International Conference on Ambient Systems, Networks and Technologies, Niagara Falls, Ontario, Canada, August 27-29 (accepted, 2012)
6. Diane, C., Sajal, D.: Smart environments: Technology, protocols and applications. Wiley-Interscience (2004)
7. Razzak, F., Bonino, D., Corno, F.: Mobile interaction with smart environments through linked data. In: 2010 IEEE International Conference on Systems Man and Cybernetics (SMC), pp. 2922–2929. IEEE (2010)
8. Wang, X., Dong, J.S., Chin, C.Y., Hettiarachchi, S.R., Zhang, D.: Semantic space: an infrastructure for smart spaces. IEEE Pervasive Computing 3(3), 32–39 (2004)

OTM Industry Program 2012
PC Co-chairs Message

Cloud computing, service-oriented architecture, business process modelling, enterprise architecture, enterprise integration, semantic interoperabilitywhat is an enterprise systems administrator to do with the constant stream of industry hype surrounding him, constantly bathing him with (apparently) new ideas and new technologies? It is nearly impossible, and the academic literature does not help solving the problem, with hyped technologies catching on in the academic world just as easily as the industrial world. The most unfortunate thing is that these technologies are actually useful, and the press hype only hides that value.

What the enterprise information manager really cares about is integrated, interoperable infrastructures that support cooperative information systems, so he can deliver valuable information to management in time to make correct decisions about the use and delivery of enterprise resources, whether those are raw materials for manufacturing, people to carry out key business processes, or the management of shipping choices for correct delivery to customers. Cooperative Information Systems provide enterprises and communities of computing application users with flexible, scalable and intelligent services in large-scale networking environments typical of industrial enterprises.

The OTM conference series have established itself as a major international forum for exchanging ideas and results on scientific research for practitioners in fields such as computer supported cooperative work (CSCW), middleware, Internet/Web data management, electronic commerce, workflow management, knowledge flow, agent technologies and software architectures, to name a few. The recent popularity and interest in service-oriented architectures & domains require capabilities for on-demand composition of services. Furthermore, cloud computing environments are becoming more prevalent, in which information technology resources must be configured to meet user-driven needs. These emerging technologies represent a significant need for highly interoperable systems. As a part of OnTheMove 2012, the Industry Case Studies Program on Industry Applications and Standard initiatives for Cooperative Information Systems for Interoperable Infrastructures emphasized Research/Industry cooperation on these future trends. The focus of the program is on a discussion of ideas where research areas address interoperable information systems and infrastructure. Industry leaders, standardization initiatives, European and international projects consortiums were invited to submit position papers discussing how projects within their organizations addressed software, systems and architecture interoperability.

An international Programme Committee composed of representatives of Academia, Industry and Standardisation initiatives reviewed proposals. We hope that you find this industry-focused part of the program valuable as feedback from industry practitioners, and we thank the authors for the time and effort taken to contribute to the program.

July 2012

Herv Panetto

P. Herrero et al. (Eds.): OTM 2012 Workshops, LNCS 7567, p. 59, 2012.
© Springer-Verlag Berlin Heidelberg 2012

A Toolkit for Choreographies of Services: Modeling, Enactment and Monitoring

Amira Ben Hamida, Julien Lesbegueries,
Nicolas Salatgé, and Jean-Pierre Lorré

Linagora R&D
3 Avenue Didier Daurat 31400 France
name.surname@linagora.com

Abstract. The support of the business community has considerably urged the advancement of the SOA by bringing useful supporting standards, for instance for Web Services description and collaboration design. Nevertheless, as the platforms are getting wider over geographically distant locations, there is a real need of keeping the link between the design time and the runtime. Model to model approaches ensure this kind of link, and in this context, choreography models help answering such issues. We bring our know how as ESB and BPM experts and propose an open source toolkit for services choreography. This toolkit provides a way to design a choreography, execute it on an Enterprise Service Bus and finally to monitor it. A Model to Model (M2M) top-down approach is implemented. We illustrate our purpose thanks to a business use case inspired from the CHOReOS European Project.

Keywords: Choreography, Service, SOA, EDA, Monitoring, ESB.

1 Motivations and Proposal

Large scale SOAs need complex design phases in order to be enacted. In particular, businesses interactions composing workflows executions are hot and risky points prone to failures. Moreover, they are hard to manage since the failure can come from one side, other side, or both ones. The OMG BPMN2.0 specification [1] answers to such issues by proposing a formal model to control these interactions: the Choreography conformance. We rely on a M2M transformation process that is composed of the following: (i) the choreography is designed thanks to BPMN2.0, (ii) a first transformation of the choreography specification leads to a set of executable processes, (iii) then a second transformation is operated from the choreography specification to a workflow monitoring model, and finally, (iv) finally, the choreography is enacted and monitored on the ESB. In the following, we present a standard-based approach implementing the aforementioned choreography-centric process. We provide a toolkit based on Business Process Modeling (BPM), and supporting functionality for choreography transformation

---

[1] http://www.bpmn.org/

P. Herrero et al. (Eds.): OTM 2012 Workshops, LNCS 7567, pp. 60–63, 2012.

and enactment on an Enterprise Service Bus (ESB), namely the Petals ESB. Furthermore, we implement an event-based monitoring based on Web Service Distributed Management[2].

2   Choreography Design

Very recently, the OMG BPMN2.0 specification rises as the de facto notation for modeling services collaborations and workflows. BPMN2.0 comes with new patterns facing the new challenges brought by the highly distributed and heterogeneous services. Indeed, it provides a means of modeling in a graphical and synthetic way complex collaborations between participants. Collaboration patterns such as the Choreography Tasks encapsulating the activity between 2 partners or Specific Gateways expressing the different possible paths in a large collaboration, are supported.

Most of the commonly used workflow designers either open source or proprietary such as Oryx[3], Intalio[4], Bonita[5], etc. start adopting the BPMN2.0 trend in their products. However, most of them do not provide a complete suite that handles the entire choreography lifecycle from its modeling to its deployment on a middleware. We argue that the choreography abstractions raise new challenges precisely in the M2M transformation, enactment and monitoring issues.

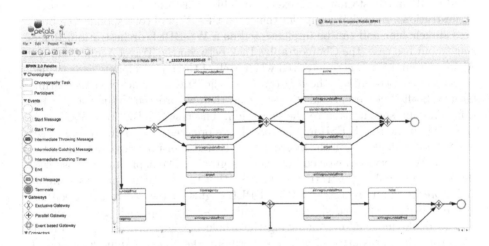

Fig. 1. Petals BPM Snapshot

The designed use case represents the case of managing an *unexpected arrival of a flight to an airport*. In this case, several participants take part to the scenario to ensure the passengers are transferred to the right places and hosted in

---

[2] https://www.oasis-open.org/committees/tc_home.php?wg_abbrev=wsdm

[3] http://bpt.hpi.uni-potsdam.de/Oryx/BPMN

[4] http://www.intalio.com/bpm/

[5] http://fr.bonitasoft.com/

hotels while waiting for the storm to pass. Thanks to the Petals BPM toolbar, a choreography designer can drag and drop the needed patterns to represent the participants collaborating. For instance, the airline ground staff contacts the travel agency to ask for handling the passengers arrival. Then, the airline ground staff needs to communicate to the airport the arrival of the flight and the troubles they are encountering. Each 2 communicating participants are expressed as doing a common activity into a Choreography Task. Though distinct, these participants take part in a wide choreography that acts for a final objective. In Figure 1, we show the aspect of this GWT Web tool as well as a snapshot of the scenario. We can see the Choreography Tasks involving each time 2 or more partners within a given activity, Inclusive and Exclusive Gateways showing the possible branches as well as the choreography Starting and Ending events.

The next section is dedicated to the transformation from the specification to the execution, and the enactment of the choreography over the middleware.

3   Choreography Deployment and Enactment

Once the choreography is designed, Petals BPM offers a mean to connect to a registry of services, and provides a matching utility to find services corresponding to the model tasks. When the choreography is fully concretized, the BPMN2BPEL transformation is executed. This transformation results in a set of orchestrations. Indeed, we consider that each BPMN pool corresponds to a business stakeholder and can be implemented as a WS-BPEL orchestration. Referring to our use case, the Choreography Task between the Travel Agency and the Airline Ground Staff, is concretized when each of these participants are satisfied by a service discovered in the registry. Once the Travel Agency and the Airline Ground Staff Roles are provided by services, then we proceed to the transformation from the specification to the execution. The resulted BPEL processes are deployed on the Petals ESB middleware. More precisely, the middleware is a set of ESB nodes deployed on the internet, distributed over the neighborhood of the different Web Services involved in the choreography. The deployment phase uses the Web Service Administration of the ESB that takes a BPEL process as input and stores it in an orchestrator (EasyBPEL engine) dedicated to the execution of the WS-BPEL 2.0-based processes. This top-down approach from specification to deployment allows managing the whole business process execution, in an automatic and controlled way. Furthermore, the choreography definition at design time enables the management of non-functional needs for monitoring the activity (See section 4).

4   Choreography Monitoring

We exploit our top-down approach for realizing an exhaustive choreography monitoring. More precisely, once deployed and enacted, a choreography is quite difficult to follow, by default, contrary to well structured orchestration processes. However, elements involved in it, such as services and orchestrations, are prone to failures, and supervision needs to introspect them. Moreover, it is important for the supervision to know which partners of the choreography need to be warned, which ones are responsible for the failure, which parts can be replaced, etc. For that purpose, we implement a monitoring tool (EasierBSM), ensuring the monitoring of services, orchestrations and choreographies. Actually, the EasierBSM is a service bus, with a particular profile dedicated to monitoring. Its additional components provide an event-based mechanism based on the WS-BrokeredNotification[6]. Once an EasierBSM node subscribes to an ESB node, it receives its activity reports that are used by EasierBSM components to compute the 3 layers of monitoring. As Petals ESB, EasierBSM is a distributed bus that scales up dynamically by adding nodes to its topology. At the service level, specific components gather information about Quality of Service (QoS) and the Web Services SLAs [7] violations. This low-level monitoring allows the detection of the failing and non efficient services. At the orchestration level, processes status is given, allowing to know which branch of a process is executed. This allows to warn a particular stakeholder where its SOA application has failed. Finally, at the choreography level, a global workflow status is given, detailing which relationships have been successfully executed. In particular for this level, a top-down transformation is also operated. The original choreography model is passed to a component called EasierCOS, that compiles it and produces a monitoring model, executed in one or distributed way. This monitoring model is a graph onto which each node corresponds to a relationship of the choreography. Referring to our use case, the Choreography Task between the Travel Agency and Airline Ground Staff is expressed as a specific monitoring graph-based structure. The graph is updated as the choreography evolves and the services are invoking each other. If the Travel Agency stated in its SLA for a 3 minutes time response, then in case of any delay the Airline Ground Staff is notified. This way, we are able to detect within the whole choreography where is the failing task.

5   Conclusion

The toolkit we propose tries to face design issues related to large scale SOAs, and in particular, focuses on the monitoring part of choreographies they compose. Indeed, in addition of generating business execution of these SOAs, it provides a choreography monitoring engine able to detect stakeholders and operations involved in high level failures.

Acknowledgments. We present the result of the collective efforts deployed within our involvement in research projects. It was partially supported by the EC framework by the Play FP7-258659 and the CHOReOS FP7-257178 projects, and the French ANR project Soceda. The work reflects only the author's views. The community is not liable for any use that may be made of the information contained therein.

---

[6] https://www.oasis-open.org/committees/tc_home.php?wg_abbrev=wsn
[7] http://www.research.ibm.com/wsla/

Requirements towards Effective Process Mining

Matthias Lohrmann and Alexander Riedel

KPMG AG Wirtschaftsprüfungsgesellschaft,
IT Advisory,
{mlohrmann,ariedel}@kpmg.com

Abstract. Process mining is prominent contemporary research topic. This paper describes requirements to be fulfilled for effective practical adoption on the basis of application scenarios and a sample project.

1 Introduction

Business process management (BPM) methods have achieved broad acceptance to support cooperation requirements within and between organizations [1]. In this context, process mining has been a prominent research issue in recent years [2,3]. From our perspective, its purpose lies in complementing or even substituting *a-priori design models* with *ex-post enactment models* of business processes. In terms of practical application, this is very promising considering the following issues:

- Design models are subject to an "enactment bias", i.e. deviations between to-be model and as-is instantiations, or not available at all.
- As opposed to design models, enactment models can be enriched with actual enactment statistics covering, e.g., the prevalence of certain enactment patterns or process variants, cycle times, or actually contributing individuals or roles. Note that this leads to a "wider" view of process mining than what is adopted in parts of related literature – respective tools, however, generally integrate these aspects.

This position paper aims at illustrating potentials of and requirements for process mining techniques and tools from the perspective of an audit and advisory firm. Its contribution lies in highlighting topics of practical relevance for future research. In the following sections, we thus describe general application scenarios (cf. Section 2) and more specific findings from a real-world pilot project executed with an industrial client (cf. Section 3). Both lead to requirements for further development as discussed in Section 4.

Note that our affiliation with an audit firm requires us to refrain from citing concrete tools and suppliers in this paper.

2 Application Scenarios

This section describes application scenarios for process mining enabling to deduct functional requirements. The scenarios have been selected on the basis of the topics that have emerged as the most relevant from discussions with our clients.

P. Herrero et al. (Eds.): OTM 2012 Workshops, LNCS 7567, pp. 64–68, 2012.

Application Scenario 1 (Process Optimization in Functionally Structured Organizations). In most organizations, function-oriented organizational structures (e.g., the procurement, logistics, and accounting functions) are still prevalent in comparison to process-oriented structures (e.g., purchase-to-pay). In this context, end-to-end (E2E) process optimization is a very important, but challenging issue. As an example, consider the capturing of supplier order data. This is often seen as tedious work by the procurement function, which, however, leads to huge additional workload in accounting. Process mining can make these issues transparent by analyzing process patterns independently of organizational borders. Thus, continuous end-to-end process improvement can be fostered.

Application Scenario 2 (Compliance Management and Identification of Deficiencies). For many real-world processes, compliance deficiencies cannot be rigorously precluded through appropriate process design. Moreover, the capability to clearly retrace process execution often constitutes a compliance requirement in itself (e.g., §238 of the German *Handelsgesetzbuch*). Process mining techniques allow to analyze execution logs with respect to non-compliant characteristics (e.g., occurrence of non-approved payment instances). Here, their particular advantage lies in the automated analysis of large numbers of process instances. Compared to the "traditional" risk-oriented audit approach, they allow to execute continuous or even full-scope audits [4]. In some cases, even the systematic circumvention of compliance requirements through certain process patterns can be uncovered (cf. Section 3).

Application Scenario 3 (Internal Benchmarking). Benchmarking refers to the comparison of good practices and performance indicator values (e.g., cycle times, unit costs, and transaction volumes per unit of capacity) between peer organizations [5]. From our experience, the so-called *internal* benchmarking, i.e. the comparison within one group, for instance between business units or production plants, has emerged as particularly useful since it reduces the issue of (perceived or real) limitations to the comparability of peers. In this context, process mining can play an important role. Typical tools combine the assessment of practices (i.e., enactment patterns or process variants) with performance indicators. It is particularly suited for internal benchmarking because in that case the probability of equal process-aware information systems (PAISs) is higher. As an additional advantage with regard to implementation, it makes use of readily available process log data instead of additional surveys, thus reducing the cost of benchmarking.

Application Scenario 4 (Capacity Management). Process mining allows to identify "bottlenecks" in transactional processing. This is achieved by identifying roles or users with particular high transactional volumes or cycle times in terms of time lag between "receipt" and "completion" events. The respective capacities can then be subject to specific management.

3 Pilot Application and Findings

This section shortly discusses findings from a pilot project conducted with a client. The objectives of the project primarily corresponded to Application Scenario 1 as described above, although aspects of other scenarios were addressed as well. Example 1 describes the sample process.

Example 1 (Sample Process: Purchase-to-Pay). The purchase-to-pay process covers process steps that are briefly summarized in Business Process Model and Notation (BPMN, [6]) in Figure 1. The model has been simplified for reasons of space, but amended with reference numbers we use to allocate findings. The total mining sample covered 28,345 process instances with ca. 400 event types incurred at a foreign subsidiary in a timeframe of three months after data cleansing. Data cleansing involved removing all instances that were not started and completed (with defined start and end events) within the given timeframe.[1]

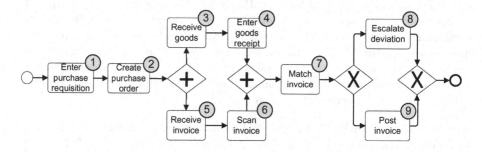

Fig. 1. Sample Process: Purchase-to-Pay

Due to its transactional character, its well-understood semantic content with a high degree of standardization, its occurrence in basically all industries, and its broad support in PAISs, the purchase-to-pay process is particularly well-suited to illustrate the potentials of process mining. The application of two exemplary process mining tools enabled comparing a broader range of functionality. Major findings described in the following illustrate which topics should be covered (i.e., *discoverable*) by effective process mining techniques and tools:

1. Up to two thirds of total project effort can be incurred in data integration and cleansing.
2. 72% of invoices are below the threshold value for mandatory purchase order creation, leading to missing purchasing data.
3. Missing purchasing data (Ref. 2 in Figure 1) leads to an 88% failure rate in automated invoice matching (Ref. 7).
4. 86% of postings (Ref. 9) occur on five out of a total of 116 accounts.

---

[1] Note that this constitutes an inherent weakness since issues leading to pending instances (e.g., "deadlocks") are systematically hidden from further analysis.

5. Transactional volume shifts significantly between months, which leads to issues with capacity management.
6. There have been more than 60,000 segregation of duty violations (e.g. one user entering both purchase order and payment approval).
7. In ca. 3% of cases, purchase orders have been created (Ref. 2) immediately before or after an invoice became overdue, which might point to a compliance violation.

4 Conclusion

Based on the application scenarios and the sample case discussed, we conclude that the following requirements are of particular relevance to the effective practical application of process mining:

Requirement 1 (Data Integration). To enable broad application, the integration of (process log) data from various sources is of critical importance. This issue is currently cumbersome with most tools and includes recurring and automated data staging as well as cleansing (e.g. Finding 1).

Requirement 2 (Compliance Rules Modeling). Tools should include a modeling facility for compliance rules such as the segregation of duties [7]. Automated analysis with respect to violations should be feasible (e.g. Application Scenario 2, Findings 6/7).

Requirement 3 (Pattern Analysis). The analysis of process variants including their cumulative frequency has emerged as the most useful aspect for management discussions. Tools should support this analysis including enrichment of patterns with performance indicators (e.g. Application Scenario 1, Finding 2).

Requirement 4 (Approximation of Manual Effort). Manual effort incurred in process activities cannot be measured by mining execution events, but approximation facilities should be provided by tools (e.g. Application Scenario 3, Finding 5).

Requirement 5 (Automated Regression Analysis). Statistical regression analysis, i.e. the analysis of relations between dependent and independent variables should be automated. This would, for instance, be useful to identify bottlenecks or for lower level internal benchmarking (e.g. between cost centers, Finding 4).

Requirement 6 (Sample Delineation). A methodical solution for delineating a sample of process instances is still missing. For instance, delineation on the basis of completed instances can result in blanking out precisely critical cases (e.g. Finding 1).

Requirement 7 (Visualization of Variants). For management discussions, process variants should be visualized effectively (e.g. regarding the difference between two patterns) using innovative solutions (e.g. Application Scenarios 1-4).

References

1. van der Aalst, W.M.P., ter Hofstede, A.H.M., Weske, M.: Business Process Management: A Survey. In: van der Aalst, W.M.P., ter Hofstede, A.H.M., Weske, M. (eds.) BPM 2003. LNCS, vol. 2678, pp. 1–12. Springer, Heidelberg (2003)
2. van der Aalst, W.M.P., Weijters, A.J.M.M.: Process mining: a research agenda. Computers in Industry 53(3), 231–244 (2004)
3. Li, C., Reichert, M., Wombacher, A.: Mining business process variants: Challenges, scenarios, algorithms. Data & Knowledge Engineering 70(5), 409–434 (2011)
4. Rezaee, Z., Sharbatoghlie, A., Elam, R., McMickle, P.L.: Continuous auditing: Building automated auditing capability. Auditing 21(1), 147–163 (2002)
5. Camp, R.C.: Benchmarking: The search for industry best practices that lead to superior performance. Quality Press (1989)
6. The Object Management Group: Business Process Model and Notation: Version 2.0 (2011), http://www.omg.org/spec/BPMN/2.0
7. Ly, L.T., Knuplesch, D., Rinderle-Ma, S., Göser, K., Pfeifer, H., Reichert, M., Dadam, P.: SeaFlows Toolset – Compliance Verification Made Easy for Process-Aware Information Systems. In: Soffer, P., Proper, E. (eds.) CAiSE Forum 2010. LNBIP, vol. 72, pp. 76–91. Springer, Heidelberg (2011)

Specialization of a Fundamental Ontology for Manufacturing Product Lifecycle Applications: A Case Study for Lifecycle Cost Assessment

Ana Milicic[1], Apostolos Perdikakis[1], Soumaya El Kadiri[1], Dimitris Kiritsis[1], Sergio Terzi[2], Paolo Fiordi[2], and Silvia Sadocco[3]

[1] Ecole Polytechnique Fédérale de Lausanne, Lausanne, Switzerland
{ana.milicic,apostolos.perdikakis,soumaya.elkadiri,
dimitris.kiritsis}@epfl.ch
[2] Polytechnico di Milano, Milano, Italy
{sergio.terzi,paolo.fiordi}@polimi.it
[3] COMAU, Turin, Italy
silvia.sadocco@comau.it

Abstract. This paper aims to study the specialization of a fundamental ontology describing manufacturing product lifecycle applications. This specialization is conducted through a case study of an Italian company. On the one hand this specialization is meant to define a specific ontology for LCC applications and on the other hand it aims to validate the mapping with the fundamental ontology implemented for manufacturing product lifecycle applications.

Keywords: Ontology, Specialization, Product Lifecycle Applications, Lifecycle Cost Assessment.

1 Introduction

In today's world of fast manufacturing, high quality demands and highly competitive markets, it has became vital for companies to be able to extract knowledge from their operating data, to manage and to reuse this knowledge in efficient and automated manner. Ontology has proven to be one of the most successful methods in fulfilling this demand. The most appealing features of the ontology are well-defined structure of the knowledge organization; being machine understandable enables automatic reasoning and inference and finally, well defined semantics enables easy interoperability. However, designing an ontology requires highly specialized knowledge experts working closely with the domain experts for, sometimes, significant period of time [1]. Within the context of a FP7[1] European project named LinkedDesign, a fundamental ontology has been designed to be easily adjusted and adopted for different product engineering systems [1]. Being generalized, this ontology needs to be specialized for each specific application. This paper aims to study the case of product lifecycle assessment. A specific ontology has been implemented and aligned with the fundamental ontology.

---

[1] Seventh Framework Programme.

P. Herrero et al. (Eds.): OTM 2012 Workshops, LNCS 7567, pp. 69–72, 2012.

2   A Fundamental Ontology for Product Lifecycle Management Applications

2.1   LinkedDesign Fundamental Ontology

LinkedDesign[2] is a FP7 European Project within the context of Digital factories. It aims at providing an integrated and holistic view on data, persons and processes across the product lifecycle as a vital resource for the design of novel products and manufacturing processes. LinkedDesign Ontology – LDO is being designed to utilize knowledge extraction, structuring, exchange and reuse for 3 application scenarios with highly diverse products and activities. Such challenging task, resolved in a generalized solution which is applicable for almost every design and manufacturing business, after very light adjustment and installation. This significaly reduces the resources needed for design of ontology from the beginning. The LDO conceptualization follows an iterative-incremental process based on the "NeOn" methodology [2], and it is implemented using Protégé[3]; the graph representation of the ontology is given in figure 1. Further details can be found in [3].

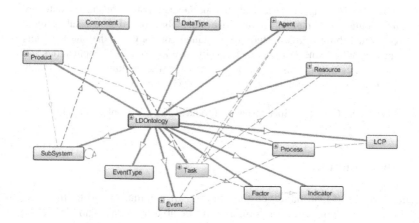

Fig. 1. The fundamental ontology

3   Specialization of the fundamental ontology: Lifecycle Cost Assessment Case Study

3.1   Lifecycle Cost Assessment

Lifecycle Cost Assessment – LCA applies to new products and do not necessary apply to those that are well developed. The lifecycle goes from the system concept definition up to the final disposal and it is divided into 5 phases as described in figure 2.

---

[2] www.linkeddesign.eu
[3] http://protege.stanford.edu/

Fig. 2. Lifecycle phases

Lifecycle Cost - LCC is the total cost of ownership of a system during its whole operational life. LCC analysis and assessment is a key factor in product's early design phase.

3.2   Ontology Specialization for LCC Assessment

LCA is performed based on several information related to the lifecycle phases. Exploiting knowledge on LCC from previous projects is a key element to support this process. This requires exploring several projects documents and inputs. Providing access to the several existing data sources to analyze LCC can be enabled through a single entry point. This requires an integration of all data sources. Ontologies enable such integration through the usage of semantics and offer a global model for schema matching enabling therefore the integration of several data sources. The detail discussion on schema and ontology matching is beyond the scope of this paper and please refer to [4] and [5] for extended discussions.

Specialization for LCC Assessment. One of the high-level concepts in the fundamental ontology is "Factor" that groups relevant issues related to a product. One of these factors is the "LCC".

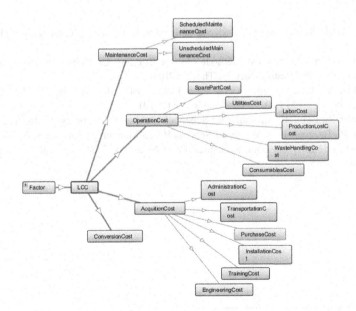

Fig. 3. The LCC specific ontology

The specialization process has been performed in two steps. The first consisted in defining the specific concepts related to LCC based on ORSD[4]. The second consisted in mapping the fundamental ontology and the specific ontology for LCC through the concept "Factor". The graph representation of the specific ontology is given in figure 3. This work is not an attempt at a complete representation and it is still on-going as it follows an incremental-iterative approach.

4   Conclusion and Perspectives

In this research we have experimented the specialization of a fundamental ontology for manufacturing product lifecycle applications. The concepts presented in the ontology covered the needs for the case of LCC Assessment specialization. Beyond the usage of a fundamental ontology and its specialization as a basis for knowledge representation, the future research will encompass the implementation of an LCA Design Support System for evaluating design approaches alternatives. Using ontologies has several benefits: (1) it represents a global model for schema matching through the usage of semantic mediation; (2) it provides several benefits by: (a) embedding additional and complex knowledge through the usage of rules; and (b) performing automatic reasoning and inference for extraction of embedded knowledge.

Acknowledgement. The authors thank the collaborative efforts and the support from Comau Company in different phases of this research work.

References

1. Staab, S., et al.: Knowledge processes and ontologies. IEEE Intelligent Systems 16(1), 26–34 (2001)
2. Suárez-Figueroa, M.C.: NeOn Methodology for Building Ontology Networks: Specification, Scheduling and Reuse, Doctoral Thesis (2010)
3. Perdikakis, A., et al.: Design of Generalized Ontology for Manufacturing Product Lifecycle Applications. In: APMS 2012, Rhodes, Greece (2012)
4. Bellahsene, Z., Bonifati, A., Rahm, E.: Schema Matching and Mapping. Springer (2011)
5. Shvaiko, P., Euzenat, J.: A Survey of Schema-Based Matching Approaches. In: Spaccapietra, S. (ed.) Journal on Data Semantics IV. LNCS, vol. 3730, pp. 146–171. Springer, Heidelberg (2005)

---

[4] Ontology Requirements Specification Document defined within the NeOn methodology [2].

Information Infrastructures for Utilities Management in the Brewing Industry

Michael Lees[1,2], Robert Ellen[3], Marc Steffens[4], Paul Brodie[2], Iven Mareels[1], and Rob Evans[5]

[1] The Department of Electrical & Electronic Engineering,
The University of Melbourne, Parkville, Australia
{leesmj,i.mareels}@unimelb.edu.au
[2] Carlton & United Breweries, Yatala, Australia
{Michael.Lees,Paul.Brodie}@cub.com.au
[3] EGA Technologies, Brisbane, Australia
rellen@ieee.org
[4] Daesim Technologies, Brisbane, Australia
msteffens@daesim.com
[5] NICTA Victoria Research Laboratory,
The Department of Electrical & Electronic Engineering,
The University of Melbourne, Parkville, Australia
rob.evans@nicta.com.au

Abstract. There is an increasing focus on sustainability in manufacturing industries. Operations management and plant/process control have a significant impact on production efficiency and hence environmental footprint. Information systems are an increasingly important tool for monitoring, managing and optimising production efficiency and resource consumption.

An advanced Utilities Management System (UMS), that operates on the G2® real-time intelligent systems platform, has been developed at the Yatala brewery, Australia. An important characteristic of the UMS is its strong integration with the existing information and automation systems at the plant. The tight integration was required to maximise effectiveness and ease of use as well as to minimise development effort and cost.

Keywords: Green manufacturing, Sustainability, Manufacturing, Interoperability, Industrial informatics.

1 Introduction

There is growing concern about the impact of anthropogenic emissions on the environment. It has been estimated that manufacturing is responsible for around 20% of anthropogenic greenhouse gas emissions [9]. While there is still considerable scope for traditional energy management programs, real-time information systems have the potential to improve the efficiency of operations. The convergence of resource management and plant control is an emerging area of focus. In

P. Herrero et al. (Eds.): OTM 2012 Workshops, LNCS 7567, pp. 73–77, 2012.

general it is not well supported by the existing enterprise-control system integration hierarchy or by the contemporary automation toolkits. The presented information infrastructure has been specifically designed to address this opportunity. It facilitates the operation of existing manufacturing assets in a more efficient manner, presenting a financially appealing pathway to reduced consumption.

2 Utilities Management System

A Utilities Management System (UMS) has been developed at the Carlton & United Breweries plant in Queensland Australia. The purpose-built information system was seen as a way to monitor, manage and further improve the plant's emissions and utilities consumption.

The UMS operates on the G2® real-time intelligent system platform and is tightly integrated into the plant's existing automation infrastructure. It provides an array of modules that both directly and indirectly support various aspects of utilities management [6]. Some of the key modules are listed in Table 1.

Table 1. UMS modules

Modules
Energy management
Clean-In-Place (CIP) management
Operator decision support [5]
Automated assessment & reporting
Alarm notification & escalation
Operations management: brewing and process
Intelligent real-time diagnostics
Support for plant scheduling (automated data feed)

2.1 Information System Integration and Interoperability

While the UMS functionality predominantly presides on level 3 of the *ISA-95 Enterprise-control system hierarchy* [8] (along with Manufacturing Execution Systems) it also provides some of the resource management metrics that have traditionally been hosted by level 4 Enterprise Resource Planning systems. The UMS is based on a centralised client-server architecture that utilises an array of bridges to interface to the existing automation landscape at the brewery. At a functional level system integration is somewhat simplified as the relevant aspects of the plant's automation infrastructure are based on S88 and ISA-95 standards.

Some of the key features that are supported by the tight integration of the UMS with existing systems include:

1. **Data acquisition:** Autonomous access to real-time plant data
2. **Minimise data duplication, maintenance work and error:** (eg recipe information only has to be updated once in its primary application)

3. **Information delivery:** Integration with the Human Machine Interface (HMI) and standard platforms (including web, email and SMS) enables cost-effective and practical information delivery to users. The UMS supports information push: automated reports, real-time notifications and SMS as well as information pull (browsing).
4. **Machine to machine interface:** Wherever possible there should be no requirement for human input into data acquisition or information delivery. Current interface methods include CSV files (UMS to spreadsheet) and SQL (UMS to other databases/systems).
5. **Documentation & training:** Wikis are becoming successful and effective documentation tools in the modern enterprise [3]. Wiki links are embedded throughout the UMS to provide seamless access to documentation for the area/context that is required.

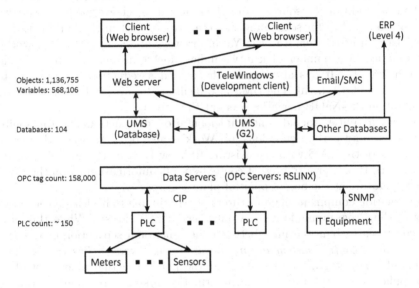

Fig. 1. Topology of the UMS illustrating integration with existing automation infrastructure. The figures on the left provide an indication of scale.

The topology of the UMS is depicted in Fig. 1. Some of the methods and protocols of system integration are illustrated in Table 2.

The UMS is used in a number of ways including: 1) Automated assessment and reporting of plant and process operations - to identify abnormal situations and to reduce the time taken to monitor plant performance, 2) Provision of an automated data-feed (of context-specific plant information) to improve the efficiency and accuracy of stocktaking and scheduling functions, 3) Automated mass/energy balance information with context-specific drill-down to support the user-pays utility consumption program across the plant.

Table 2. System integration

Information source/sink	Function	Method
Documentation	On-line context sensitive	Wiki (MediaWiki)
Sensor/meter	Real-time plant data	OPC, SNMP
Databases	Machine to machine transfer	SQL
Notifications	Information push	Email, SMS
Information presentation	Browsing (information pull)	Web (HTTP, JSP, Javascript)

3   Business Impact and Future Opportunities

The UMS has had a significant impact on the operational efficiency of the plant. Without it, additional resources would be required to achieve the plant's current level of productivity for scheduling, stocktaking and just-in-time production.

It has been instrumental in the Yatala brewery operating at or near world's best practice in a number of utilities indices including mains water at 2.2hl-water/hl-beer [7]. It has also recently facilitated a reduction in service water consumption of 0.14hl/hl. The UMS also facilitated a 57% reduction in caustic consumption (kg-NaOH per hl of beer) at the site [4].

Current activities include the implementation of functionality to monitor product loss and carbon emissions [6]. Work is also progressing on the deeper integration of the UMS with the existing RSView HMI platform. This includes using the HMI platform to present context-specific information (from the UMS) to the operators at the actual point of plant control.

Automation equipment manufacturers are continuing to host higher-level systems in the Programmable Logic Controllers (PLC) chassis. While this practice continues to blur the lines between the functional separation of the *ISA-95 Enterprise-control system integration hierarchy* layers, it has the potential to simplify the integration of systems at the point of actual plant control [2]. The application of the Internet and information systems to manufacturing (e-manufacturing) will also drive (and require) tighter integration between MES and supply chain systems [1].

Acknowledgments. NICTA is funded by the Australian Government as represented by the Department of Broadband, Communications and the Digital Economy and the Australian Research Council through the ICT Centre of Excellence program. The authors would also like to thank the management of *Carlton & United Breweries* for permission to publish this work.

References

1. Cheng, F.-T., Tsai, W.-H., Wang, T.-L., Yung-Cheng, J.C., Su, Y.-C.: Advanced e-manufacturing model: The significance of large-scale, distributed, and object-oriented systems. IEEE Robotics & Automation Magazine 17(1), 71–84 (2010)
2. GE: The changing role of the operator, GFT-791 (2010), http://www.ge-ip.com/hmiscada_operator (accessed: September 21, 2011)
3. Grace, T.P.L.: Wikis as a knowledge management tool. Journal of Knowledge Management 13(4), 64–74 (2009)
4. Lees, M., Ellen, R., Brodie, P., Steffens, M.: A real-time utilities management system for optimising cleaning operations in a brewery. The IEEE International Conference on Industrial Technology, 329–334 (February 2009)
5. Lees, M., Evans, R., Mareels, I.: Autonomous performance monitoring of an on-line real-time decision support system. In: Proceedings of the 18th World Congress of the International Federation of Automatic Control (IFAC), Milano, Italy, pp. 13080–13085 (August 2011), doi:10.3182/20110828-6-IT-1002.00421
6. Lees, M., Evans, R., Mareels, I.: Information infrastructures for on-line measurement of non-productive greenhouse gas emissions in manufacturing: case of the brewing industry. International Journal of Production Research (2012), doi:10.1080/00207543.2012.655864
7. Putman, R.: Down to a water usage of 2.2 to 1. The Brewer & Distiller 2(10), 18–22 (2006)
8. Scholten, B.: A guide to applying the ISA-95 standard in manufacturing. ISA Instrumentation Systems and Automation Society (2007)
9. Stern, N.: The economics of climate change: the Stern review. Cambridge University Press (2006)

Internal Logistics Integration by Automated Storage and Retrieval Systems: A Reengineering Case Study

Michele Dassisti[1], Mariagrazia Dotoli[2], Nicola Epicoco[2], and Marco Falagario[1]

[1] Dip. di Ingegneria Meccanica e Gestionale,
Politecnico di Bari, Viale Japigia 182,
70126 Bari, Italy
{m.dassisti,m.falagario}@poliba.it
[2] Dip. di Elettrotecnica ed Elettronica,
Politecnico di Bari, Via Re David 200,
70125 Bari, Italy
dotoli@poliba.it,
nico.epicoco@gmail.com

1 Introduction

Nowadays, factors like globalization, productivity, and reduction of time-to-market make the impact of logistics on production by far wider than in the past. Such a complex scenario originated considerable interest for the design, planning and control of warehousing systems as new research topics (De Koster et al. 2007). However, in spite of the importance of warehouse design and management, authors agree on the lack of systematic approaches (Baker and Canessa, 2009). Moreover, the existing contributions do not typically consider the problem of warehouse design in a continuous improvement context. On the contrary, with the enhanced customer demand, for most manufacturing industries it has become increasingly important to continuously monitor and progress the internal logistics. This paper presents a preliminary study for the reengineering of the logistics in a Southern Italy firm producing shoes and accessories based on formal modeling. We address a widely used solution for warehouse material handling, i.e., Automated Storage and Retrieval Systems (AS/RSs) (Dotoli and Fanti 2007). These systems are a combination of automatic material handling and storage/retrieval equipments characterized by high accuracy and speed. In order to reengineer the logistic system, a Unified Modelling Language (UML) (Miles and Hamilton, 2006) model is adopted (Dassisti, 2003).

2 The Company Current Internal Logistics

The company logistics is currently organized with a low-tech and low information contents, hence the firm plans to set up an integrated logistics platform to match its needs of growth. By the year 2015 it is expected to reach approximately 5,000,000 moved pieces, almost tripling current flows. The logistics area covers all the activities from procurement to the delivery of products to stores.

P. Herrero et al. (Eds.): OTM 2012 Workshops, LNCS 7567, pp. 78–82, 2012.
© Springer-Verlag Berlin Heidelberg 2012

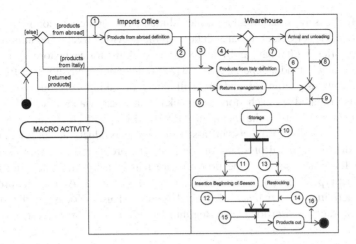

Fig. 1. Macro Activity Diagram of the Current Internal Logistics

Procurements are typically planned a year ahead, based on a statistical analysis of the demand, and according to the expected growth. Once in Italy, products are placed in containers that may stay up to 14 days at the port of arrival. Afterwards products are sent to the firm according to the available warehouse storage space and employees, as well as the priority of a product over another. Products manufactured in Italy, instead, arrive on articulated trucks, according to business needs, and they are delivered and discharged directly in the warehouse, mainly by manual handling. Here the Internal Logistics Manager makes a quantitative and qualitative test of products which, if the test is successful, are placed in the first free warehouse position in the storage area of similar products. Products are stored in packages, each typically containing 8 pairs of shoes (rarely 10 or 12) of the numbered pair sizes 35-40 or 36-41, in which the two central numbers, statistically the most popular and selling ones, are doubled. The mix of different types of packages is determined by the Purchasing Office, based on experience and available space in stores. Accessories also come in packages with dimensions comparable with those containing shoes. Currently, shoes are moved in 8 different types of packages, some of which differ only slightly. The company aims at standardizing types into three main families (large, medium and small), to simplify handling, and likewise it will be agreed with providers to use packages that contain only 8 pairs each. The product is characterized by high seasonality throughout the year, divided into Spring/Summer (S/S) and Fall/Winter (F/W).

Figure 1 depicts the Macro Activity Diagram of the Current Internal Logistics. Supplies to stores are of two kinds: the "Insertion of the beginning of the season", which represents 60% of the overall supplies, and "Restocking", representing the remaining 40%. The Sales Management and the Internal Logistics Manager decide the list of stores to which products are delivered according to their available space and turnover. When the available space for temporary storage is over, a transport document is prepared with an optical reader, one for each store. Merchandising material is handled with the same logic. In case of restocking, the Sales Management sets specific lists of fixed weekly replenishment, taking into account the relative importance of the seller and its sales data from the previous week. The administration provides logistics, with a kanban logic, to issue a pick list for each store. Accordingly, packages are newly made, depending on space optimization, and choosing from boxes that were previously emptied and are still intact or taking new ones. A transport document is prepared for each store and packages are sent via an internal or external service. Another activity is the receipt of "Returned Products" that can be devoted to manage non-complying products, infra-season unsold products or end of the season unsold products. Returned products of the first type are stored in a safe area before being sent for waste, second type products are managed by the restocking activity, while the last type of products are sent to a network of outlets. Among the previously described activities, the analysis of critical issues led us to focus on the stages of "Products Storage", "Insertion of the Beginning of the Season" and "Restocking".

3   The Company Internal Logistics Reengineering

The chosen solution to improve efficiency is an Automated Storage and Retrieval System (AS/RS) serviced by a Rail Guided Vehicle (RGV) system (Dotoli and Fanti, 2007). The reengineering driver was the increase of efficiency in terms of automation, resource utilization, throughput. Hence, the selected AS/RS has to take care of handling operations of packages and to be interfaced with the other logistics operation, such as "Restocking" and "Returned Products Management". The AS/RS ensures a greater speed of operations as well as flexibility. It was decided to discard the possibility of using unit loads, such as pallets or similar, because the currently employed packages have sizes that are not compatible with the standard palletizing units.

The development of the UML model of the To-Be system was a crucial issue because it allowed to understand how to effectively interface the proposed processes and consequently to find the best solutions to ensure the effectiveness and efficiency of the flows. We present in the following the proposed modifications only for the activities interested by changes in the diagram of Fig. 1.

Activity 5 – Products Storage As-Is / To-Be: in the re-designed activity (Fig. 2b) the AS/RS is involved, instead of the warehouse Manager of the As-Is case (Fig. 2a). The flow is divided according to whether products are unpacked or in packages: in the first case they are stored in an area that is specially designed for unpacked products, while in the latter the AS/RS is involved, that operates a fully automated storage in a way described in the following Activity 5b.1.

Activity 5b.1 – Packages Storage Area: in this new stage (Fig. 3), involving the Warehouse Worker and the AS/RS system, the first one stores packages in an input storage station and then the activity is taken over by the AS/RS. A free RGV is waited for and, when this arrives, the package is loaded on the RGV and is brought to the first free storage conveyor. Otherwise, if none of these are free, the RGV turns in circles and retries to make the allocation. When the storage conveyor is free, the package is unloaded and brought into the crane loading position. If the crane is busy, the system waits until it becomes free, hence the crane loads the package and brings it in the storage position to deposit it.

Activity 6 – Insertion of the Beginning of the Season As-Is / To-Be: in this new step the AS/RS, Warehouse Worker and Logistics Administrative Management are involved. The first creates the Insertion Batch, consisting of whole packages, for each store, according to the subsequent Activity 6b.1. Once this batch is defined, an optical reading of the packages code is done by the Warehouse Worker, and according to whether shipments are handled by an external courier or are directly managed by the firm, the Logistics Administrative Management respectively prints the transport document and labels packages, or just prints the transport document.

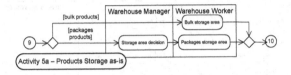

Fig. 2a. Activity 5a – Product Storage As-Is

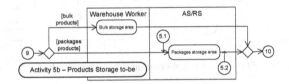

Fig. 2b. Activity 5b – Product Storage To-Be

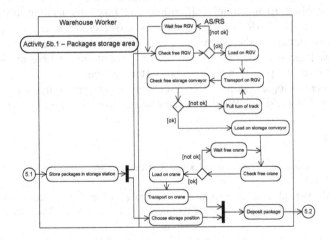

Fig. 3. Activity 5b.1 – Packages Storage Area To-Be

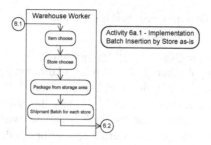

Fig. 4a. Activity 6b.1 – Implementation Batch Insertion by Store As-Is

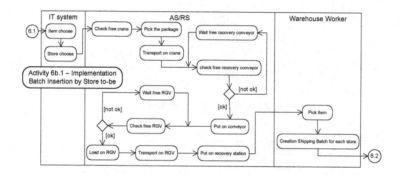

Fig. 4b. Activity 6b.1 – Implementation Batch Insertion by Store To-Be

<u>Activity 6b – Implementation of the Insertion Batch by Store As-is / To-Be</u>: (Figs. 4a and 4b) the IT system chooses the item to send to stores, on the basis of items in stock and according to a suitable algorithm that takes in account priorities and precedence. Then the AS/RS checks if there is a free crane, hence the package is loaded and transported to the conveyor, where it waits for a free RGV; when this arrives, the package is loaded and led to the retrieval station, where the Warehouse Worker picks it up and puts it in the temporary storage area.

With the same logic adopted for Activity 6, we re-engineered Activity 7 concerning the "Restocking". We do not report details for the sake of brevity.

References

[1] Baker, P., Canessa, M.: Warehouse design: A structured approach. Eur. J. Oper. Res. 193, 425–436 (2009)

[2] Dassisti, M.: Formal modelling approaches for integrated quality-management systems in delocalised enterprises: a taxonomy of requirements. Int. J. Autom. Tech. Manag. 3, 202–233 (2003)

[3] De Koster, R., Le-Duc, T., Roodbergen, K.J.: Design and control of warehouse order picking: a literature review. Eur. J. Oper. Res. 182, 481–501 (2007)

[4] Dotoli, M., Fanti, M.P.: Deadlock detection and avoidance strategies for automated storage and retrieval systems. IEEE Trans. Sys., Man Cyb. C 37, 541–552 (2007)

[5] Miles, R., Hamilton, K.: Learning UML 2.0. O'Reilly Media, Sabastopol (2006)

EI2N 2012 PC Co-chairs Message

After the successful Sixth edition in 2011, the seventh edition of the Enterprise Integration, Interoperability and Networking workshop (EI2N2012) has been organised as part of the OTM2012 Federated Conferences and is co-sponsored by the *IFAC Technical Committee 5.3* Enterprise Integration and Networking, the *IFIP TC 8 WG 8.1* Design and Evaluation of Information Systems, the *SIG INTEROP Grande-Rgion* on Enterprise Systems Interoperability, the SIG INTEROP-VLab.IT on Enterprise Interoperability and the *French CNRS National Research Group* GDR MACS.

Collaboration is necessary for enterprises to prosper in the current extreme dynamic and heterogeneous business environment. Enterprise integration, interoperability and networking are the major disciplines that have studied how to do companies to collaborate and communicate in the most effective way. These disciplines are well-established and are supported by international conferences, initiatives, groups, task forces and governmental projects all over the world where different domains of knowledge have been considered from different points of views and a variety of objectives (e.g., technological or managerial). *Enterprise Integration* involves breaking down organizational barriers to improve synergy within the enterprise so that business goals are achieved in a more productive and efficient way. The past decade of enterprise integration research and industrial implementation has seen the emergence of important new areas, such as research into interoperability and networking, which involve breaking down organizational barriers to improve synergy within the enterprise and among enterprises. The ambition to achieve dynamic, efficient and effective cooperation of enterprises within networks of companies, or in an entire industry sector, requires the improvement of existing, or the development of new theories and technologies. Enterprise Modelling, Architectures, and Semantic Interoperability principles are the some of the essential pillars supporting the achievement of Enterprise Integration and Interoperability. The Internet of Things and Cloud Computing now present new opportunities for realising inter-enterprise and intra-enterprise integration. For these reasons, the workshops objective was to foster discussions among researchers active in these related disciplines with a view towards exploring new research paths within the enterprise integration community. After rigorous peer reviews, 8 papers have been accepted out of a total of 19 submissions to this workshop.

This year, our discussions focused around the themes of " Enterprise Interoperability and Sustainability and on the future for Internet-of-Things and Enterprise Sensing as it applies to emerging engineering practices. The outcomes of these respective discussions are reported during a plenary session jointly organized with the CoopIS2012 and the OTM Industry Case Studies Program 2012, in order to share the vision for future research with other conference attendees. The papers published in this volume of proceedings present samples of current research in the enterprise modelling, systems interoperability, services

P. Herrero et al. (Eds.): OTM 2012 Workshops, LNCS 7567, pp. 83–84, 2012.
© Springer-Verlag Berlin Heidelberg 2012

management, cloud integration and, more globally, systems engineering and enterprise architecture domains. Recent frameworks, architectures and principles that have gained currency in the recent past include semantic frameworks, service oriented architectures, virtual engineering and cloud computing principles; they hold the potential to play a vital role in the realization of interoperable, networked and collaborative enterprises.

It has been a great pleasure to work with the members of the international programme committee who played a valuable role in reviewing the submitted papers. We thank them for their dedication and interest.

We would like to take this opportunity to thank all authors for their contributions to the workshop objectives and discussions.

July 2012

Herv Panetto
Lawrence Whitman
Michele Dassisti
J. Cecil
Jinwoo Park

An Ontology-Based Model for SME Network Contracts

Giulia Bruno and Agostino Villa

Politecnico di Torino, Corso Duca degli Abruzzi 24, 10129 Torino, Italy
{giulia.bruno,agostino.villa}@polito.it

Abstract. Even if collaboration is considered an effective solution to improve business strategies, SMEs often lack common principles and common forms of contractual coordination. Several policies implemented by E.U. have addressed the setup of a comprehensive SME policy framework. However, European institutions seem to have focused more on organizational devices to conduct business activities rather than on contractual forms of coordination. In April 2009, Italy adopted a law in network contract to promote the development of inter-firm cooperation strategies to foster enterprises' innovation and growth. Even if this law represents a novelty in Europe and may offer new challenges and hints, it still presents some lacks in its formulation. The current research aims at presenting the Italian law for network contract, by highlighting both its potentialities and its defects. A formal model to support the design of a SME network was proposed, by providing both an ontology-based model to help the definition of the contract in a structured way, and a basic workflow to identify the important phases of the network design, i.e., the feasibility study and the negotiation. In this way, the network rules and criteria for controlling the network members' contributions are defined. Mathematical tools derived from performance optimization were exploited.

Keywords: SME integration, network contract, ontology, UML.

1   Introduction

Collaboration represents an increasing tendency among small and medium enterprises (SMEs) and is considered an effective solution allowing the achievement of development strategies, either to improve production processes or to increase competitiveness based on innovation and quality [5]. However, SMEs usually show a traditional individualistic attitude [2]. This means facing the marketing, technological innovation and purchasing problems alone. On the contrary, being an independent node of a network could lead many advantages to a SME: (i) more complex products can be realized by integrating skills of all the network nodes, (ii) higher manufacturing volumes can be obtained by cumulating node capacities, (iii) fluctuations of market demand volumes can be handled better by sharing workload peaks and shortages among the nodes, and (iv) there is no need of spending resources in hard competitions with the other SMEs [9, 13].

P. Herrero et al. (Eds.): OTM 2012 Workshops, LNCS 7567, pp. 85–92, 2012.

SMEs are the engine of the European economy, being the 99% of all European businesses, and have been the target of several policies implemented by E.U. institutions [12]. For example the "Small Business Act" adopted in June 2008, for the first time puts into place a comprehensive SME policy framework for the E.U. Member States [1]. However, European institutions seem to have focused more on organizational devices to conduct business activities rather than on contractual forms of coordination. The absence of common contractual coordination forms and of common principles of European contract law could negatively affect the functioning of markets and hamper SMEs' growth [5].

In Italy, a recent law defined the "business network contracts" to point out the strategic goals and mutual activities of SMEs that want to build a network. Network contracts can help SMEs overcome limitations due to their dimension without causing them to lose their legal independence, while also enabling them to collaborate with firms of different dimensions. Furthermore, the network contract overcome the limitation of clusters and districts to be composed only by enterprises sited in a specific geographical area.

Even if the Italian law represents a novelty in Europe and may offer new challenges and hints for future discussion at international level, it still presents some lacks in its formulation [8,11]. A fundamental problem is the lack of a formal representation of the ontology of the network contract, being only a descriptive summary of a mode of organization of the market that can be achieved through different negotiation. Another problem is that nothing is said with regard to intellectual property rights, such as the know-how gained during the research and development for technological innovation.

To address these problems we define a formal model to support the design of a SME network, by providing both a formal ontology-based model to help the definition of the contract in a structured way, and a basic workflow which identifies the important phases of the network design, i.e., the feasibility study and the negotiation.

The rest of the paper is organized as follows. Section 2 describes the Italian business network contract, by presenting its weeks and potentialities, and proposes an ontology-based model to highlight the points that are not explicitly addressed by the law. Section 3 focuses on the network contract design phases to correctly set up a SME network. In this way, the network rules and criteria for controlling the network members' contributions are defined. Mathematical tools derived from the performance optimization were exploited. Finally, Section 4 draws conclusions and discusses future works.

2   Italian Business Network Contract

The Italian business network contract of the Law 99 of July 23rd 2009, published under number 136 in the Ordinary supplement of the Gazzetta Ufficiale on July 31st 2009, allows two or more enterprises to jointly perform one or more economic activities falling within their social objects in order to increase their mutual innovation capacity and competitiveness in the market. The law does not force the enterprises to be of the same nationality, thus international networks are allowed.

The essential requirements of the network contract include the statement of the *strategic goal* and *common scopes* to reach the improvement of innovative capacity and competitiveness for the network, the identification of a *network program* that contains the *activities* and *investments* needed for the implementation of the strategic goal, together with the set of *indicators* useful to measure the network performances, and the *rights* and *duties* assumed by each participant, the establishment of a *common fund*, managed by a *management body* composed by SME *representatives*, aimed at pursuing the strategic goal. The firms are also free to establish *entry* and *exit rules*, and *resolutive conditions* for the network.

This bare description can be enriched and structured in an ontology, represented in the form of a UML class diagram [6] in Fig. 1. An ontology formally represents knowledge as a set of concepts, properties and relationships within a domain, and has the aim of both allowing the clear separation of the domain knowledge (the model) from the operational knowledge (the instances) and enabling the reuse of the general model in different applications [7].

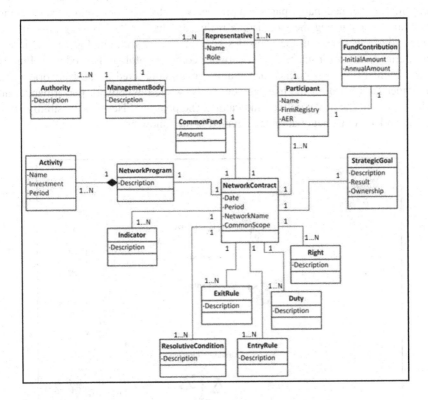

Fig. 1. UML class diagram of the Italian business network contract

The presented model can be exploited by all the firms that want to build a network, to help them in the organization and the filling of the network contract. For each element the relationships with the other elements is formally defined. Furthermore, some additional attribute were explicitly added, even if they are not present in the original law. For example, in the Activity class, the investments and the time period should be specified, while in the Strategic goal class, information about the expected result and its ownership should be provided in addition to its description. Each stipulated network contract can be represented as an instance of the ontology. However, the design of a SME network is not limited to defining the network contract, but it is a process composed by several phases, which are described in the next section.

3   SME Network Design Phases

The basic workflow for SME network design is reported in Fig. 2. Initially, the participants that are to form the network perform a Network feasibility study, with the scope of defining a preliminary sketch to allow the evaluation of the design load as well as their respective involvement. The outputs of this phase are the base of the network, i.e., the strategic goal, the duration of the network, and the initial investments. Once these constraints are defined, participants can proceed with the Network contract negotiation, which aims at balancing the global gain with individual SME financing possibilities. At the end of this phase, all the items described in the network ontology model in Fig. 1 are defined, i.e., an instance of the network contract ontology is produced. Finally, for the defined time period, the participants remain connected in the Network operation, under the control of the management body, while the network performances are evaluated by means of the defined indicators. The phases of Network feasibility study and Network contract negotiation are detailed in the following.

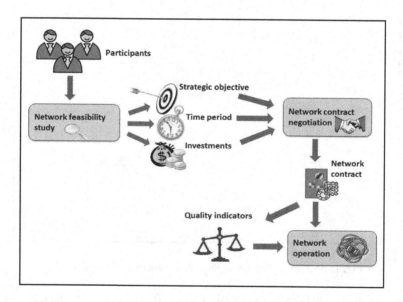

Fig. 2. Phases of the SME network design

3.1   Network Feasibility Study

As above outlined, the feasibility study of the SME network design has the scope of defining a preliminary sketch of the main characters of the network design, such to allow the potential network partners to evaluate the design load as well as their respective involvement [10].

For sake of clarity, the assumption that a given number N of SMEs would be involved in the future network, and that the SMEs are producing similar objects (thus, belonging to the same industrial sector), is adopted. It is also considered that the development of the feasibility study as well as of the whole network design has to be managed by the above mentioned management body, that receives the necessary contributions from the set of N SMEs which would be involved in the future network. A clear distinction between the "n-thSME contribution", i.e., the contribution the SME gives to the common fund in order to compose the finance and resource reserve of the network design, and the "investment in the n-th SME" decided by the management body, will be used in the following.

The feasibility study needs to be supported by a specific formal model that could estimate the network design gain, depending on the investments the management body would plan for each partner SME. Such a formal model is composed by the following objectives and constraints.

Strategic goal of the network design. The SME network is expected to reach a production target $p*$ through an as effective as possible innovation of each n-th SME. Each n-th SME is also expected to reach a quality target q_n* , by applying a specific investment.

Resources to be applied to the design development. The investment to be planned by the management body for application in the n-th SME innovation, denoted by dK_n, is the sum of the two types of investments: the investment for the process innovation (dKP_n) and the investment for the product innovation in term of quality increase (dKQ_n):

$$dK_n = dKP_n + dKQ_n \tag{1}$$

Network design variables. The variables involved in the network design are the process innovation (r_n) and the product innovation in terms of quality increase (dq_n). They are again linearly dependent to the investment dKP_n and dKQ_n respectively.

$$r_n = \mu_n dKP_n \tag{2}$$

$$dq_n = \beta_n dKQ_n \tag{3}$$

where μ_n denotes the rate an investment gives rise to process innovation, and β_n the rate an investment gives rise to a product quality improvement.

Cost of the network design. The sum of all investments planned by the committee for the N SMEs will define the final cost of the network design (i.e., the amount of the common fiund), C, that will be bounded by the sum of contributions provided by the N SMEs, each one denoted by $dK_n°$.

$$C = \sum_n dK_n \leq \sum_n dK_n° \tag{4}$$

where the right-hand-side term specifies the real budget of the network design.

Constraints on the network design results. The expected production level for the whole SME network (P) and the expected quality level to be reached by each SME (q_n) are given by the following formula:

$$P = \sum_n p_n \geq p^*, \quad p_n = p_{0,n} + \varphi_n r_n = p_{0,n} + dp_n \tag{5}$$

$$q_n = q_{0,n} + dq_n \geq q_n^* \tag{6}$$

Gain of the network design. The network design is expected to have a gain, G, resulting from the innovations applied to all SMEs, even if in different forms and amounts according to the initial state of the SME itself. So, each process innovation will generate a gain for the n-th SME, as well as each product quality improvement (respectively measured by the products of the process and quality improvements by two constants, a_n and b_n, that measure the improvements in terms of financial income), whilst the SME contribution will be the real individual cost for participating in the network design.

$$G = \sum_n G_n, \quad G_n = a_n dp_n + b_n dq_n - dK_n° \tag{7}$$

The set of conditions (1) to (7) can be easily recognized as a typical LP problem, where the network gain (7) has to be analyzed by taking into account the set of constraints (1) to (6).

3.2   Network Contract Negotiation

In principle, the LP-stated network design problem should be solved by maximizing the gain (7). This reflects in pushing high innovations for the SMEs where the financial impact is high – according to (7) - as well as their rates of investments – as in (2) and (3). This theoretical solution, indeed, implies some practical defaults. Among them, the main defect is to generate a greatly unbalanced network, with some SMEs, already well organized and with greater quality level, again supported, whilst some others, not so equipped and assessed, not able to receive a good investment. In practice, this means an unsuccessful design. On the other extreme, if a solution of the investment problem is searched by planning a no gain for the network design, then an attribution of investments to SMEs proportional to their respective contributions re₋ sults. In this case, the problem is splitted into N independent sub-problems, and no real meaning of network design remains.

These two considerations suggest that the above stated formal model should be used for clarify the concept of network design, and perhaps to obtain an optimized investment strategy, even if unbalanced, but it must be followed by a "negotiation of contributions and investments", such to balance global increase of innovation with individual SME financing possibilities. To this aim, the negotiation can be viewed as a "game", where each SME representative in the management body tries to have the best possible condition in terms of finance contribution (to be delivered) and of innovation actions to be applied. Looking at the Theory of Games, each participant can bring some influence to bear upon the out-come of a certain event and no single participant by himself can determine the outcome completely [4]. The special feature of the game under consideration is that a "cooperative solution" must be searched, and that some suggestions for an agreement among the SMEs can be given by the solution of the formal model above discussed.

4   Conclusions

Recently, the European Commission has decided to extend the outreach of the *Enterprise Europe Network* - the business and innovation support network for SMEs - to enable more European SMEs to profit from the fast-growing markets in Asia, Latin America and Eastern Europe [3]. With this aim, a contact office has been opened in Japan and the presence in China was doubled. The network was also expanded in southern Mediterranean countries, with further enlargement foreseen in the near future. The network was established to help SMEs to find potential partners in European and world markets and to turn research and innovation into profits. As mentioned in the introductory section, a similar decision has been taken by the Italian government, with the specific goal of promoting agreements among SMEs to create networks.

However, in both these cases and also in regulations adopted in other European countries, the aim of the legislation is mainly to offer support services for commercialization, only in rare instances to give criteria for SMEs cooperation [12]. It seems that cooperation could emerge in an instinctive manner. This is not the case of most of SMEs, whose owners are often jealous of their own enterprise and their knowhow, even they are poor. Owners and managers' individualisms are the first obstacle to cooperation, followed by the lack of practical supports (rules and criteria) to activate effective cooperation.

This paper tries to build a bridge between individualism and the need of SMEs networking, by introducing a new tool for SMEs network designers composed by the following items: (i) an ontology of the network contract for organizing a SME network, (ii) a model for a-priori evaluation of the cost and the gain of the network design, and (iii) some hints for understanding how the potential partners of the network contract can provide financial contributions and human resources for the network design execution.

Looking at the current versions of Italian laws and E.U. recommendations, point (i) will give help to formalize the network design contract, point (ii) will support in estimating how a contract management committee could decide investments, and point (iii) will give suggestions to the network partners about the negotiation of contributions and their utilization for the design development.

An application of these three points is currently under development in cooperation with a Regional Government of North-West Italy and a small group of SMEs used as test subjects.

Acknowledgments. The authors would like to thank Dott. Pietro Massaro (Vecchio Masoero Orlandini Law Firm, Torino, Italy) for his support and fruitful discussion.

References

1. Borbás, L.: A Critical Analysis of the "Small Business Act" for Europe. In: International Conference on Management, Enterprise and Benchmarking, pp. 373–380 (2009)
2. Capelli, F.:: With the crisis of enterprises, a new humanism is necessary. Neo-humanism and human formation in the contemporary society, Università Bicocca, Milano (in Italian, 2012)
3. Corazza, C.: Enterprise Europe Network reinforced in Asia; extended to North Africa (2011), http://portal.enterprise-europe-network.ec.europa.eu/news-media/news/ac-11
4. Dresher, M.: The mathematics of games of strategy - Theory and applications. Dover Publ., N.Y (1981)
5. Ferrari, C.: The Italian "Network contract": a new tool for the growth of enterprises within the framework of the "Small Business Act"? Columbian Journal of European Law Online 16, 77–83 (2010)
6. Fowler, M., Scott, K.: UML distilled. Addison-Wesley (2000)
7. Gaševic, D., Djuric, D., Devedžic, V.:: Model Driven Architecture and Ontology Development, pp. 46–54. Springer (2006)
8. Granieri, M.: The network contract: a solution looking for a problem? I Contratti 10, 934–942 (2009)
9. Mezgár, I., Kovács, G.L., Paganelli, P.: Co-operative production planning for small- and medium-sized enterprises. International Journal of Production Economics 64, 37–48 (2000)
10. Ravazzi, P., Villa, A.: Economic aspects of industrial automation. In: Handbook of Automation, pp. 93–116. Springer (2009)
11. Scognamiglio, C.: The network contract: the problem of the cause. I Contratti 10, 961–965 (2009) (in Italian)
12. Villa, A.: Managing Cooperation in Supply Network Structures and Small or Medium-sized Enterprises: Main criteria and tools for managers. Springer, London (2011)
13. Villa, A., Antonelli, D.: A Road Map to the Development of European SME Networks: Towards Collaborative Innovation. Springer, London (2009)

A Framework for Negotiation-Based Sustainable Interoperability for Space Mission Design

Carlos Coutinho[1], Ricardo Jardim-Goncalves[1], and Adina Cretan[2]

[1] CTS, Departamento de Engenharia Electrotecnica,
Faculdade de Ciencias e Tecnologia, Universidade Nova de Lisboa, Portugal
c.coutinho@campus.fct.unl.pt,
rg@uninova.pt
[2] Computer Science Department, "Nicolae Titulescu" University of Bucharest, Romania
badina20@yahoo.com

Abstract. The need to improve the time spent performing space mission feasibility design studies has led the aerospace industry to the adoption of Concurrent Engineering methods. These high-performance concepts parallelise the design tasks, effectively reducing design time, but at the cost of increasing risk and rework. The fragile interoperability in this design environment depends greatly on the seniority of the space domain engineers and their expertise in the space design engineering area. As design studies get more complex, with an increasing number of new domains, systems and applications, terminologies and data dependability, together with growing pressure and need for adaptation, the design interoperability arena becomes extremely hard to manage and control. This paper presents the concept of developing and maintaining strong interoperability nodes between the design domains by providing a framework of cloud-based services dedicated to negotiating and enforcing a sustainable interoperability between high-performance businesses.

Keywords: Sustainable Enterprise Interoperability, Negotiations, Control, Aerospace.

1 Introduction

The development of conceptual design for space-related missions on the European Space Agency – Concurrent Design Facility (ESA-CDF [1]) is a complex process that involves multiple domains (e.g., Mission analysis, Thermal, Power), which match the different views and interests of the mission. In this process, to increase the performance of the studies duration, the design is fast-tracked into a scenario where multidisciplinary teams perform their activities in parallel, applying the concept of Concurrent Engineering [2]. Although each domain design team models its own view of the mission, the teams need to exchange a large set of mission parameters, required to satisfy the mission and to ensure that all views are fully integrated and fit perfectly. As the heterogeneity grows in the various systems and applications used by each design team and mission, and as studies get larger and more complex, interoperability problems are being reported between the design teams, leading to additional rework.

P. Herrero et al. (Eds.): OTM 2012 Workshops, LNCS 7567, pp. 93–102, 2012.
© Springer-Verlag Berlin Heidelberg 2012

When the involved parties in a study face a detected interoperability problem, they must solve it. Kaddouci et al. [3] state that in any case of divergence, negotiation is the most appropriate method to solve conflicts. Usually these interoperability conflicts are resolved via one party forcing the other to change, or by reaching consensus towards a midway solution. This paper addresses the need for interoperating enterprises to formally negotiate the interoperability solutions towards reaching the most appropriate decision, one that minimises the effort and time spent regaining interoperability. It proposes a collaborative framework to model and support the interoperability negotiations of businesses towards achieving sustainable Enterprise Interoperability (EI) on organisations acting in the same industrial market.

Section 2 of this paper details interoperability problems commonly found in business-to-business activities derived from the example of the ESA-CDF environment. Section 3 presents research questions and hypotheses. Section 4 enumerates requirements towards enforcing interoperability. Section 5 presents the proposed collaborative negotiation framework. Section 6 presents final statements and future work.

2   Problem Description

The rapid evolution and constant improvement that is required towards companies (particularly SMEs) leads to the need to deliver faster, better and cheaper. This typically means the need to fast-track the activities in a company, or otherwise the need to specialise in a particular business area, delegating the other activities to a network of partners and providers. The proposed framework is suitable for enterprises facing the described interoperability problems, and is being validated in a real business-case on the ESA-CDF department.

In the ESA-CDF environment the design of each future space mission is split into a set of engineering domains. Each domain engineering team performs its design using different tools (e.g., CATIA, STK, Matlab) and is provided and supported by a network of partners and suppliers (large companies and SMEs). Therefore interoperability in this case is defined in two levels: i) The interoperability between each domain and its tools, partners, and suppliers towards the target of defining the domain design or vision of the mission, and ii) The interoperability between the various domains of a mission-related study, where all domains compete for their interests into setting the values for mission-related parameters (e.g., Spacecraft dry mass, Electrical power).

These mission parameters are inter-related (e.g., changes in the structure or in the number of instruments naturally affect the total Dry Mass) and their values are kept under control by the mission requirements. The data exchanges between design domains are performed in a set of closed "war-room" sessions [4] where all involved domains and stakeholders are represented and each domain presents its design solutions and corresponding impact on the mission design. Interoperability in this highly-competitive scenario is assured by the study Team Leader which moderates the discussions and the Systems engineer which provides local support to the engineers.

Several interoperability problems were detected and reported in this environment [5]. While some of these relate to problems (e.g., communications, data formats, typos, and syntax) which are frequently discussed in literature and already have some tools for correction (e.g. protocols, check digits, dictionaries and grammars) other less evident grow in abstraction to semantic mismatches, relationships, concepts, method-ologies, strategies and hierarchies. With this growth comes a proportional increase in the difficulty to detect these problems, and a proportional increase of their impact. The fact that each domain has its own set of external dependencies to tools, suppliers and partners makes interoperability on the study life cycle even more difficult, as the number of communicating/interoperating channels increases due to their supply chain.

The proposed framework aims to provide support in reaching a sustainable EI (SEI) by providing mechanisms that allow businesses to model and formalise their knowledge (e.g., questionnaires and surveys, modelling of business activities and data), providing services that are dedicated to assisting the interoperation, particularly a mechanism to model and formalise the interoperability negotiations (Fig. 1).

Fig. 1. Application of the proposed framework to the ESA-CDF business

This research worked together with the ESA-CDF team to develop questionnaires and gather information on issues regarding interoperability. The outcomes of this analysis can be mapped into most common problems reported by companies when dealing with business-to-business interactions.

Each domain interoperates with the others and with its supply chain using a het-erogeneous set of interfaces which include shared data and tool interfaces, shared workspaces (e.g., shared databases) and shared tools. Heterogeneity in this environ-ment grows with new trends, concepts, platforms, technologies and development methods.

The main difficulty regarding interoperability is related to the lack of a deeper common knowledge of the business concepts, which then leads to misunderstandings and errors caused by simple mistakes e.g., on data meaning, data units, or methods.

The tools that are used to perform the design activities (e.g., Domain-specific tools, STK, CATIA) are standard and not customised to the specific design business needs, which means their concepts and terminology may not be aligned with the business.

Despite its high-performance target, the ESA-CDF environment manages to incor-porate several knowledge management tools for capture of design study knowledge like decisions and lessons-learned recording. However the knowledge management on the scope of each domain is very limited. The reuse of each domain's tools and knowledge of these tools itself is very scarce as each study carries its own context, dependability, together with limited available time on the domain engineers' side. This is mostly a habit and cultural problem, as several methodologies like CMMI [6] and six-sigma enforce the benefits of corporate knowledge capture and reuse [7].

This paper enforces that interoperability must comprise a dynamic, recurring and adaptable effort for tackling changes, supported by a strong business knowledge [8]. However, flexibility to submit to all changes is not always desirable. Complying with a new concept may alter the delicate balance of the whole interoperating network. Therefore, it is essential to have a formal negotiation mechanism to deal with interoperability changes and factually support decisions on the best solution for compliance, to state that the benefit/cost ratio needs to support higher investment on a stronger interoperability, or even that interoperability in this case is not feasible or worthy.

3   Research Questions and Hypotheses

Following the performed research, the authors advance the following key open research question addressing the interoperability problems described previously:

- How can negotiations improve business towards achieving a sustainable EI?

Under this consideration, a set of hypotheses is enumerated:

- If businesses are served by dedicated entities that formalise decisions regarding interoperability, it will be easier to detect and correct divergences earlier;
- If business parties detect that changes need to be performed to be able to reach interoperability, negotiation is a good way to ensure success and the adoption of the best solution.

4   Requirements for Interoperability in the Work Environment

Driven by the outcomes of this research, the authors proceed to enumerate requirements considered essential for improving the interoperability between partners in a business-to-business relationship:

- Req#1: Interoperability should be taken into consideration from the very foundations of any business application;
- Req#2: Interoperability regards three logical layers (middleware, coordination and business logic), and all these should be covered;
- Req#3: Each party should clearly define and model its core business so that other interoperating parties can understand it;
- Req#4: The interaction between interoperating parties should be clearly defined and modelled;
- Req#5: Data models for each party should be clearly defined and available to the interoperating parties. These models should be standardised as well as the procedures to access data;

- Req#6: Each party should model its definitions and knowledge into one or more business-related ontologies and share it with the other operating parties;
- Req#7: Systems and applications should be adaptable to accommodate interoperability in businesses.

5   Framework towards Sustainability of the EI Environment

This paper proposes a collaborative framework for achieving a sustainable interoperability in a distributed environment, together with a methodology, in this case as it was submitted to the ESA-CDF business case (see Fig. 1). This framework is supported by a set of service tools that enhance collaboration and promote negotiations.

Literature refers several examples of methodologies to enhance interoperability, most focusing on the development of adapters, translators, even also using MDI [9]. While this approach is valid as it pertains acting solely in translating the interaction between two different entities, there are times the changes are too many and too profound, leading to the inability of maintaining interoperability.

The proposed approach aims to work in an earlier stage, determining the best solution to handle the existing problems, which means analysing and formalising the required changes, determining the pros and cons of each solution and then maturely and factually selecting the solution that best suits the purpose. Negotiations favour the analysis of alternative solutions, the adoption of new methodologies, models, semantics, or instead the creation of adaptors and translators, but especially, they motivate decisions supported by consensus of the involved parties.

The framework bases its interaction in the definition of a set of negotiation rules, supported by a negotiation model to formalise and register the negotiation interactions in a set of declarative rules, implemented in Java Expert System Shell (JESS, [10]).

5.1   Negotiation Model

Negotiations are sets of complex actions, some of which may occur in parallel, where multiple participants exchange and take decisions in multiple phases over a set of multiple attributes [11], [12]. The participants to a negotiation may define proposals, and each participant can decide autonomously to end a negotiation, either by accepting or rejecting the received proposal. Depending on its role in a negotiation, a participant may invite new participants to the negotiation. The negotiation services make use of negotiation techniques and negotiation model to determine the best alternatives for the negotiation.

The Negotiation Model is defined as a quintuplet $M = <T, P, N, R, O>$ where:

- T represents the time of the system, assumed to be discrete, linear, and uniform;
- P denotes the set of participants in the negotiation framework. The participants may be involved in one or many negotiations;
- N is the set of negotiations that take place within the negotiation framework;

- *R* characterises the set of coordination rules among negotiations that take place within the negotiation framework;
- *O* represents the common reference ontology. This ontology consists on the set of definitions of the attributes that are used in a negotiation.

A negotiation is defined at a determined time instance through a set of sequences: Let Sq = {si | i ∈ ℕ} represent the set of sequences, such that ∀si , sj ∈ Sq, i ≠ j implies si ≠ sj. A negotiation sequence si ∈ Sq where si ∈ N(t) is a succession of negotiation graphs that describe the negotiation *N* from its initiation up to the time instance *t*. The negotiation graph produced at a time instance is an oriented graph where the nodes describe negotiation phases present at that time instance (i.e., the negotiation proposals sent until that moment in terms of status and negotiated attributes) and edges express precedence relationships between negotiation phases.

This model covers formal and non-formal aspects of the interoperability, as they may be qualified and hence modelled in the framework in order to be able to be included in the negotiation.

5.2   Framework Architecture

The architecture that supports the negotiation framework performs the actions described on Fig. 2, satisfying Req#2. These actions, described as negotiation levels, are implemented by services as described on Fig. 4.

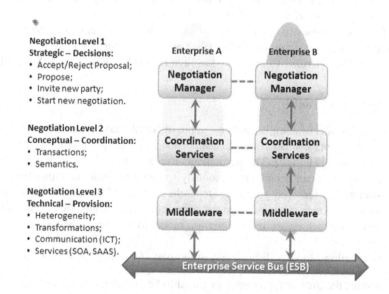

Fig. 2. Negotiation modules of the proposed framework

The proposed methodology started by filling a set of questionnaires that defined a qualitative classification of the business, as well as conducting interviews with stakeholders, to capture the business knowledge of each engineering domain. This knowledge was then modelled into a Model Driven Architecture (MDA) Computation-Independent Model (CIM), describing the business strategies, objectives and visions of each domain. This CIM layer can be split into two layers [13]: a Top CIM layer handles the strategic business functionalities, that are stable and conformant to requirements and needs ("as-is"), which include the interoperability needs towards other existing partners. The Bottom CIM layer handles the operational transients and the proposed changes towards new partners, additional self-improvements (due to e.g., adoption of new technologies, supported platforms, lessons learned and best practices) and new interoperability challenges [14]. This satisfies Req#1 and Req#3.

This model was then transformed into a Platform-Independent Model (PIM), which defined the flows and algorithms that rule each domain, while still maintaining platform independence, and defined specific domain ontologies. Finally, the PIM was transformed into a Platform-Specific Model (PSM), rules and code that implement the domain functionalities [15].

Similarly to the vertical transformations that are processed within the MDA approach, Model-Driven Interoperability (MDI [16–18]) operated at each MDA level performing horizontal transformations to allow the interoperability at each level, and where negotiations are settled, which complies with Req#4, as can be seen on Fig. 3.

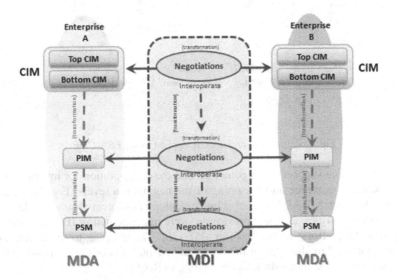

Fig. 3. MDA and MDI including negotiations

At CIM level the purpose was to harmonise the visions of each domain towards the common space mission purpose, defining policies, design strategies and hierarchies.

Then at PIM level, MDI performed black-box test specifications, negotiated and defined the common data model based on standards ISO 10303 STEP [19] and EXPRESS (ESA-SEIM [20]). It also performed negotiations towards the definition of a harmonised reference space ontology (ESA-SERDL [21]), implementing Req#5 and Req#6. These data models and definitions were then implemented in a virtual cloud infrastructure (Infrastructure as a Service – IaaS [22]) to deal with scalability issues regarding the data structure. Finally, at PSM level, negotiations are carried towards setting the middleware convergence and session handling.

The resulting PSM was then implemented as a set of flexible and dynamic services within the governance of a SOA [23], which were deployed as cloud-based services (Software as a Service – SaaS [24]). The whole infrastructure can be seen on Fig. 4.

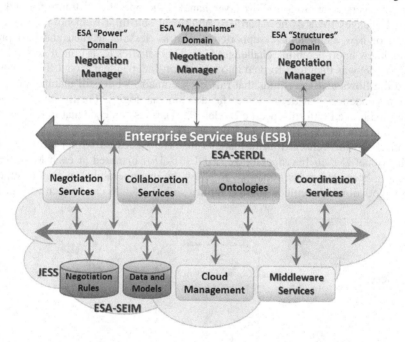

Fig. 4. Framework architecture applied to the ESA-CDF

The services that support the negotiations and the collaboration for interoperability have the same consistence and reasoning of the negotiation levels (Fig. 1), although the support for each MDA/MDI level is implemented in different abstraction levels.

The negotiation rules, as stated previously, were implemented in JESS and were inferred using the platform SWRLJessTab [25], [26]. The decision to implement these in a rule is justified by the need of flexibility and adaptability of the negotiation rules, criteria and evaluation methods, thus responding to Req#7.

6   Final Considerations and Future Work

Driven by the stated research question and the formulated hypotheses, the conclusions are that business interoperability is often developed over tacit knowledge, which in time gets fragile and has a large probability of breaking apart. The integration of a framework that provides formal procedures for modelling, storing and documenting the business activities and data contributed a great deal into achieving a stronger and sustainable interoperability. Furthermore, the adoption of formal methods for capturing corporate knowledge at domain level lead to an increase on the internal knowledge of each domain, and promoted reuse and establishment of best-practices.

Using the proposed framework, the detection of interoperability changes triggers the negotiation services to handle the reestablishment solutions, allowing the selection of the best solution by consensus of all parties. Hence, the authors conclude that negotiations when supported by a knowledge-enabled framework improve SEI. Particularly for ESA-CDF this led to less rework and fewer errors as the data is seamlessly interchanged between domains in a formal well-known and controlled environment.

The development of this framework is still conditioned to the improvement of issues that are still under research on MDI concerning the horizontal transformations in the various abstraction levels, and SOA, with issues still rising against service discovery and service composition and orchestration. Also a step must be taken towards the adoption of Cloud federation and improvements on the negotiation processes to avoid negotiation deadlocks.

Future work regards the assembly of the framework environment in the ESA-CDF facility, the comparison of business metrics before and after the change, and in the negotiation field, provision for each negotiating agent of a library of protocols.

Acknowledgment. The authors wish to acknowledge the support of the European Commission through the funding of the UNITE, MSEE and ENSEMBLE FP7 projects, and the European Space Agency - Concurrent Design Facility (ESA-CDF) for their support, interaction and contribution in the development of the business case that is presented on this paper.

References

[1] ESA-CDF, "ESA-CDF" (2012), http://www.esa.int/esaMI/CDF/ (accessed: January 10, 2012)

[2] Bandecchi, M.: The ESA Concurrent Design Facility (CDF): concurrent engineering applied to space mission assessments. In: 2nd Nordic Systems Engineering Boat Seminar (FinSE 2001), pp. 1–36 (2001)

[3] Kaddouci, A., Zgaya, H., Hammadi, S., Bretaudeau, F.: Multi-agents Based Protocols for Negotiation in a Crisis Management Supply Chain. In: 8th WSEAS International Conference on Computational Intelligence, Man-Machine Systems and Cybernetics (CIMMACS 2009), pp. 143–150 (2009)

[4] Kolfschoten, G., Matthyssen, A., Fijneman, M.: Theoretical foundations for Concurrent Design. In: 4th International Workshop on System & Concurrent Engineering for Space Applications (SECESA 2010), vol. (1) (2010)

[5] Koning, H.P.D., Eisenmann, H., Bandecchi, M.: Evolving Standardization Supporting Model Based Systems Engineering. In: 4th International Workshop on System & Concurrent Engineering for Space Applications (SECESA 2010), vol. (1) (2010)

[6] Chrissis, M.B., Konrad, M., Shrum, S.: CMMI for Development - Version 1.3, 3rd edn., p. 688. Addison Wesley Professional (2011)

[7] Jardim-Goncalves, R., Grilo, A.: SOA4BIM: Putting the building and construction industry in the Single European Information Space. Automation in Construction 19(4), 388–397 (2010)

[8] Grilo, A., Jardim-Goncalves, R.: Value proposition on interoperability of BIM and collaborative working environments. Automation in Construction 19(5), 522–530 (2010)

[9] Jardim-Goncalves, R., Grilo, A., Agostinho, C., Lampathaki, F., Charalabidis, Y.: Syste-
matisation of Interoperability Body of Knowledge: the foundation for Enterprise Interoperability as a science. Enterprise Information Systems 6(3), 1–26 (2012)

[10] JESS Rule Engine, http://www.jessrules.com/jess/index.shtml
(accessed: February 15, 2011)

[11] Cretan, A., Coutinho, C., Bratu, B., Jardim-Goncalves, R.: A Framework for Sustainable
Interoperability of Negotiation Processes. In: 14th IFAC Symposium on Information
Control Problems in Manufacturing, INCOM 2012 (2012)

[12] Jardim-Goncalves, R., Sarraipa, J., Agostinho, C., Panetto, H.: Knowledge Framework
for Intelligent Manufacturing Systems. Journal of Intelligent Manufacturing 22(5), 725–
735 (2009)

[13] Lemrabet, Y., Liu, H., Bourey, J.-P., Bigand, M.: Proposition of Business Process Modelling in Model Driven Interoperability Approach at CIM and PIM Levels. In: Enterprise
Interoperability V, pp. 203–215. Springer (2012)

[14] Nie, L., Xu, X., Chen, D., Zacharewicz, G., Zhan, D.: GRAI-ICE Model Driven Interoperability Architecture for Developing Interoperable ESA. In: Enterprise Interoperability
IV, pp. 111–121. Springer (2010)

[15] Jardim-Goncalves, R., Grilo, A., Steiger-Garcao, A.: Challenging the interoperability between computers in industry with MDA and SOA. Computers in Industry 57(8-9), 679–
689 (2006)

[16] Berre, A.-J., Liu, F., Xu, J., Elvesaeter, B.: Model Driven Service Interoperability through
Use of Semantic Annotations. In: International Conference on Interoperability for Enterprise Software and Applications (IESA 2009), pp. 90–96 (2009)

[17] Lemrabet, Y., Bigand, M., Clin, D., Benkeltoum, N., Bourey, J.-P.: Model Driven Interoperability in practice: preliminary evidences and issues from an industrial project. In:
First International Workshop on Model-Driven Interoperability (MDI 2010), pp. 3–9
(2010)

[18] Athena Consortium, Athena Interoperability Framework (2011),
http://www.modelbased.net/aif (accessed: December 20, 2011)

[19] Jardim-Goncalves, R., Figay, N., Steiger-Garcao, A.: Enabling interoperability of STEP
Application Protocols at metadata and knowledge level. International Journal of Technology Management 36(4), 402–421 (2006)

[20] ESA-SEIM, http://atlas.estec.esa.int/uci_wiki/SEIM
(accessed: January 10, 2012)

[21] ESA-SERDL, http://atlas.estec.esa.int/uci_wiki/SERDL
(accessed: January 10, 2012)

[22] Jeffery, K., Neidecker-Lutz, B.: The Future of Cloud Computing: Opportunities for European Cloud Computing Beyond 2010. Analysis, 71 (2010)

[23] Papazoglou, M.P., Traverso, P., Dustdar, S., Leymann, F.: Service-Oriented Computing:
a Research Roadmap. International Journal of Cooperative Information Systems 17(02),
223 (2008)

[24] Sharma, R., Sood, M.: Cloud SaaS and Model Driven Architecture. In: International Conference on Advanced Computing and Communication Technologies (ACCT 2011), Acct,
pp. 978–981 (2011)

[25] SWRLJessTab (2012), http://protege.cim3.net/cgi-bin/
wiki.pl?SWRLJessTab (accessed: March 20, 2012)

[26] O'Connor, M.F., Knublauch, H., Tu, S., Grosof, B.N., Dean, M., Grosso, W., Musen,
M.A.: Supporting Rule System Interoperability on the Semantic Web with SWRL. In:
Gil, Y., Motta, E., Benjamins, V.R., Musen, M.A. (eds.) ISWC 2005. LNCS, vol. 3729,
pp. 974–986. Springer, Heidelberg (2005)

Service-Oriented Approach for Agile Support
of Product Design Processes

Safa Hachani[1], Hervé Verjus[2], and Lilia Gzara[1]

[1] G-SCOP Laboratory,
Grenoble Institute of Technology,
Grenoble, France
{safa.Hachani,lilia.Gzara}@grenoble-inp.fr
[2] LISTIC Laboratory,
University of Savoie,
Annecy, France
herve.verjus@univ-savoie.fr

Abstract. The need to answer quickly to new market opportunities and the high variability of consumer demands tend industrial companies to review their adopted organisation, so to improve their reactivity and to facilitate the coupling with the business enactment. Therefore, these companies require agility in their information systems to allow business needs scalability and design process flexibility. We propose in this paper, the business activities as a service based on the service paradigm and whereas a design process is made of agile services orchestrations. We discuss the interest to use a service-oriented approach and propose a layered architecture for design process enactment.

Keywords: Design process, agility, PLM, SOA, service orchestration, MDA.

1 Introduction

Traditional business processes (BPs) with a fixed structure are no longer adequate to meet the continuing evolution of the market, enterprises' organization and custumers'expectations. Traditional BPs tend to be inflexible and time consuming to change. In fact, in a context where organizations are in a constant seek of balance facing up to more and more constraints of the competitive environment; working methods cannot be fixed definitively. This is due to product design processes (PDPs) specificities; they are emergent and non deterministic because of the creativity aspect in product design projects. Furthermore, unpredictable events often occur during PDPs due to external constraints (such as sub-contractor or supplier constraints, etc.) and/or internal constraints (such as delay constraints, staff/resources availability, etc.). Some of these factors, such as satisfying suppliers' needs, may only cause temporary changes of PDPs. While others, such as regulation evolution may cause permanent changes. PDPs are thus constantly changing. Reflecting these changes on time represents an ongoing challenge. As a result, companies face some obstacles, including the limited implementation of new working methods. Needs in terms of rapid and

P. Herrero et al. (Eds.): OTM 2012 Workshops, LNCS 7567, pp. 103–112, 2012.

automated support of business operations[1] are necessary to reflect such changes. Service oriented architecture (SOA) can address this issue by facilitating enterprise solutions flexibility and therefore business agility. SOA have different perspectives depending on the user roles (business, architectural or implementation perspective) [1]. Our research focus on the first perspective (*i.e.* business one) and we consider SOA as an architectural style that supports integrating the business as linked services. It can support BP goals and enterprise objectives. So, we can say that a service-oriented approach based on the concept of service[2] can promote a support of flexible PDPs by considering a PDP as a series of services snapped together like building blocks. SOA makes this possible; it allows decomposing processes into independent business services. Then, using the business services cartography, the services can be bands to realize BP.

Several researches have attempted to solve the problem of BP rigidity. Some of them propose to enrich the expression of BP in order to meet flexibility needs. We provide an overview of these related works in second 2 in order to release their limits and disadvantages towards our objectives. Subsequently we present the approach we retained which is based on service oriented approach (section 3). Then, we present our services catalogs (section 4). Section 5 presents the feasibility of the proposed approach. The final chapter concludes this paper.

2   Related Works

Currently, there are scores of BP modeling approaches, which aim to manage flexibility. Bessai proposes a context aware-based approach [2]. The concept of context is used to characterize an activity (designed to operate in a particular state of the world). In this approach the role of the process is to precisely define the order and the context of activities to be performed. The one that should be executed is chosen according to the objects state. Zhao and Liu propose a version-based approach [3]. This work proposes to model versions of BP schemas using graphs: nodes of a graph correspond to activities of a process while arcs between nodes represent the used patterns to link activities. This work also presents a set of operations enabling updates of graphs and defines two strategies to extract versions of BP schemas from these graphs. Lezoche's work proposes a rule-based approach [4]. This approach considers that activities are components reacting to events. Here, the result of one activity represents an initiating event for other ones according to given set of rules. Indeed, an instance of the process model will correspond to one of planned paths. Boukadi resorts to SOA in order to deal with BP flexibility [5]. She focuses on building flexible BP based on service composition and service adaptability. Boukadi's work defines a BP as a sequence of activities. The creation of the BP is essentially based on selecting one or more goal-templates and specifying the flows connecting those goals. The goals-templates

---

[1] We highlight that PDPs are mainly supported by PLM (Product Lifecycle Management) systems. So, in the rest of this paper we are interested on a solution that supports flexible PDPs enactment in PLM.

[2] Services are repeatable business tasks, accessible independently of implementation or transport [1].

correspond to the tasks to be completed. The composition of the different goals-templates leads to an abstract BP model. Based on the goals-templates, services will be selected to replace them and the executable BP will be generated. The offered services are adaptable and have different behaviors depending on the context of their uses.

To sum up, on the one hand, the proposed approaches [2, 3, and 4] allow modeling a BP with maintaining some flexibility in how to meet business objectives by using conditions and/or triggering event to choose between versions of activities. The disadvantage of using these modeling approaches is that they imply having anticipated all scenarios. These approaches are well adapted to representation of process with a limited degree of complexity. However, it is hard to use them in order to design process with emerging structure. On the other hand, Boukadi's work allows modeling reusable activities unlike other works (rule, context-aware and version-based approaches), which make possible to design decoupled activity that can be used by different BPs. Besides, by defining the flows and fixing the goals-templates in advance, this decreases the flexibility of the BP. Her vision of flexibility is limited to the capability to change the manner with which the activities can meet the objectives rather than focusing on the flexibility of the process structure.

Based on the findings outlined above, we conclude that flexible BPs require specific methods for their design and implementation. Thus, the expected approach is the one in which not only the behavior of activities are not defined a priori but also the relations between activities. We resort to service based solution in order to map PDPs to service-oriented solution. The idea is to propose reusable activities as services and evolvable PDPs as services composition. The concept of service defined as providers of reusable functions can be composed and reused to quickly respond to PDP changes. That supposes once changes occur we can add to, delete from or replace one service by another one. Indeed, the generalization of SOA to information systems (and thus, the design and requirements analysis layers) would allow the definition of PDPs and their implementation by reusing existing services.

3   The Proposed Service-Based Approach

3.1   Product Design Process as a Service Orchestration

The aim of a PDP model is to depict interactions between business partners and model their corresponding activities. In past decades, these processes could operate in relatively stable and predictable environments. Now a product design process may not remain steady due to the business environment. That's why we need process flexibility. Process flexibility depends on the easiness to modify PDP model and to set up the new business activities. This perception of process flexibility arises from the need to have a method, which allows composing evolvable PDP models. In other words, flexibility requires processes made of piece of functionalities that can work together and that can be quickly reconfigurable. The challenge here is to address the mechanisms needed for a solid implementation of dynamic PDP change on a real PLM system.

In order to address the problem of PDP rigidity in PLM systems, we propose to resort to SOA and to enrich the formalization of PDP models and open the way for process modeling by dynamic service composition. Thus, we should have a set of product design services (PDSs) that expose the business activities of the industrial engineering domain needed to support PDPs. Afterward, we dynamically compose the necessary identified PDS in order to enact the articulations of PDP. This PDP can be materialized by an orchestration of PDS [6]. In fact, we propose to use service as a means for describing the business operations needed to support the PDPs. These loosely coupled services may be composed in order to enact in a flexible way the articulations of business. This process is called services orchestration [7]. SOA makes this possible; it allows decomposing processes and business activities into independent business services. Dynamic services orchestration stands for assembling and re-assembling these business services while the process is executing. Thus, service can be composed and reused to quickly respond to PDP change and to achieve the new model without needing to replace it completely. Moreover, as services expose operations independently of their real enactment, they can be reused even if the enactment is changing (as consequence, some changes do not affect the services orchestration). This supposes that once a change happens, we can dynamically add to, delete from or replace a service operation with another one. The main characteristic of this service-based approach is that it provides a flexible process structure, which provides the necessary agility to face changing conditions and unpredictable situations.

3.2   Conceptual Architecture

As we have discussed above, business agility is the fundamental business requirement. So, the entire PLM system, starting by IT level, must support business agility. It's important to remember that PDPs are very dependent on the information technology that supports it. So, the business also depends of the IT flexibility. So, we propose the whole system reconsideration and not only a business level reconsideration.

To insure the alignment between technical and business level, there should be a mechanism that allows execution of PDP with the same language chosen for the business level. So, we propose a service type for each level of the organization. The different levels that we consider are justified by the reality of enterprise information system. On the one hand, we find the organizational IS. It consists of information (business objects) and actors whose act on this information through their work methods (business activities). On the other hand, there is the system infrastructure or Computerized IS. The computerized IS consists of an organized set of items, machines and applications. It allows the implementation of the working methods of the companies and the organization of their information. Moreover, the actors of the organizational IS use the computerized IS through the interfaces provided by its tools. Therefore, there are three levels in the enterprise IS: the business level associated with organizational IS, the technical level associated with Computerized IS and the functional level associated with the interfaces of the Computerized IS. Regarding this classification, we propose three layers of services. First, we propose a catalog of Product Design Services (PDS). A PDS is a collection of PDS operations reflecting solutions to some business needs of a product design domain. In fact, each PDS operation partly reflects a business activity typically presented in PDPs. These PDS operations will be used and composed by BP designer to build PDPs. Secondly, we propose a catalog of Functional PLM Services, which (i) ensures alignment between business and technical levels and (ii) aims to be independent of any PLM system. A Functional PLM service is a collection of Functional PLM services operations. The services operations of this layer represent all functions of the PLM as seen by PLM users independently of any existing PLM tool. A set of functional PLM services operations support a PDS operation. They will be used by process performers and composed to achieve the PDS. In other words, once a new business activity is needed to perform a change at the business level (in a PDP), a PDS operation is invoked and added to the orchestration and thus operations of functional PLM services can be solicited from the repository to do it. Finally, we propose a set of technical PLM services that allow the real implementation of functional PLM services. These Technical PLM services cover technical operations carried out in a PLM system and they will be dynamically orchestrated during the enactment of PDPs. They are intended to PLM systems editors. This distinction between functional and technical PLM services allow the reuse of process models, defined only in terms of business and functional PLM services, on different PLM systems. Indeed, once a process deployed on a new PLM system, we have to make correspondence between functional PLM services and technical PLM services.

To make the transition from one level to another one, our conceptual approach is based on a model-driven engineering one (MDE) (Fig. 1). Starting at the top with the business level (Computer Independent Model) it is primarily concerned by the PDPs that comprise the day-to-day activities of the enterprise. It contains also the business services (PDS), which allow composing the PDP. Moving down a level (Platform independent Model), we see the functional PLM services and orchestration fragments that can be predefined or user-defined. Predefined orchestration fragments define the recommended functional PLM services orchestration, which allows fulfilling a given PDS operation.

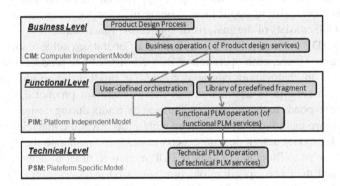

Fig. 1. Conceptual Architecture of the Proposed Approach

Functional PLM services are non-specific to any PLM system. That's why services can be mixed and matched into meaningful combinations without concern for what systems are actually performing the work. Down this, we find the technical level (Platform Specific Model), which contains the technical services. This layer forms the API (core functions) of the PLM system used.

In order to achieve the proposed approach, first we have to propose the services catalogs. Then we have to express PDPs as service orchestration. Finally we should propose alignment techniques that allow moving from business to technical level. In the rest of this paper we concentrate on the two first steps of our approach (services identification and PDP definition as service orchestration).

4   Service Cartography

As we have discussed above, we aim to offer three services catalogs. A PDS catalog, which expresses the business, needs related to PDPs. Functional PLM services catalog enabling the execution of PDS through a functional PLM services orchestration. Finally, technical PLM services catalog enabling the implementation of functional PLM services. The third catalog is dependent on which PLM system we use, that's why we concentrate on the business and functional service catalogs. For the third catalog, we analyzed existing standard in terms of services for PLM systems. In a previous work we defined the appropriate techniques and necessaries steps to achieve our service identification approach [8]. We referred to literature in the domain of SOA development, like Papazoglou [9], Chang [10] and Arsanjani [11] methods, in order to propose our identification method. More precisely, we proposed a top-down method for the identification of PDS. For the derivation of functional PLM services, we proposed a bottom-up method. We note here that the identification approach cannot be the same for high and low level services. Since they don't have the same service consumer and expose different type of information. High-level services expose business needs. That's why we proposed a top-down method, which consists of the analysis of the business domain. Low-level services expose application functionalities. Since most organizations have existing application systems in place we proposed a bottom-up approach, which consists of the analysis of application functionalities.

Regarding PDP context, a PDS is a collection of operations achieved during PDP, by design actors. Hence, each operation of PDS consists of one product design action which operates on one or more business objects (i.e. product design object). A business object is a concept or abstraction that makes sense for product design domain actors and corresponds to the entities manipulated by actors during design. To identify design objects we analyzed interviews done within four French companies, organized meetings with product design domain experts in order to enumerate the shared vocabulary and referred to literature to analyze PDP models in order to determine the different steps and their corresponding outcome (*i.e.* a business objects) [13] and [14]. We identified the following list of product design objects: Delay, Quotation, Quantity, Market analysis sheet, Drawing Assembly, 3D Assembly, Prototype, Validation Report, Design Solution, Bill of Materials, Drawing Part, etc. The product design object is used to describe the entities manipulated by the actors within the description of the job (i.e product design action). A product design action is an act that can be done by an actor in order to achieve a specific outcome. We identified a list of product design actions such as produce solution, produce decision/agreement, request information, request evaluation, etc. Thus, the PDP can be described as a network of product design actions operating on product design objects and iterating continuously to produce a result. As a result, we obtained a set of product design operations for which we have defined meaningful names (eg. Elaborate Test Plan, Create Prototype, etc.) and grouped them together on a PDS. The product design operations are grouped based on service cohesion principle as operation should be grouped together that are functionally related. Other criteria such as business rules and sequence logic were used to decide which operations must be grouped together. In fact, during the analysis of design process model we identified recurring cycle between product design actions. For example, *ElaborateTestPlan*, *TestPlanEvaluationRequest*, and *EvaluateTestPlan* are usually used together. This is justified by the fact that there is a cycle between the formulation of the problem and its resolution. We obtained fifteen PDS. Figure 2 shows an expert of this catalog.

PrototypeRealisation	DesignDepartementDysfonctionnalAnalysis	TestDefinition	BomManagement
CreatePrototype	ElaborateDysfonctionnalAnalysis	ElaborateTestPlan	CreateBOM
LaunchPrototypeCreation	DistributeDysfonctionnalAnalysis	DistributeTestPlan	DistributeBOM
DistributePrototype	EvaluateDysfonctionnalAnalysis	EvaluateTestPlan	EvaluateBOM
AskForThePrototype	ValidateDysfonctionnalAnalysis	ValidateTestPlan	ValidateBOM
	DysfonctionnalAnalysisElaborationRequest	TestPlanElaborationRequest	BOMElaborationRequest
	ConsultDysfonctionnalAnalysis	ConsultTestPlan	ConsultBOM
	DysfonctionnalAnalysisEvaluationRequest	TestPlanEvaluationRequest	BOMEvaluationRequest
	DysfonctionnalAnalysisValidationRequest	TestPlanValidationRequest	BOMValidationRequest

Fig. 2. An expert from product design service catalog

A functional PLM service is a collection of PLM operations which reflect generic PLM functions that should be (at least partially) implemented by PLM systems. Each operation implements the concept of automated business task and exposes a function of PLM that can be reused and composed based on business needs. Thus we have identified three major categories of PLM data: product management, product process management and organization. We then decomposed each category into sub-categories and for each sub-category we have identified a set of operations offered in PLM systems (for instance, "Display product structure" and "Compare BOMs" for the product configuration sub-category).We have classified the identified operations in functional PLM services based on two criteria functional dependencies and process dependencies. As result we obtained nine functional PLM services (Fig. 3).

BOM Management	Compenent Management	Product Management	Document Management	CAD Management
LinkComponentToProduct	DefineComponent	DefineNewProduct	NewDocument (type)	RetreiveASMStructure
LinkComponentToProduct	DefineComponentData	DefinePartData	DefineDocumentData	RetreivePartQuantity
LinkDocumentToProduct	CreateFromComponent	CreateFromProduct	AddDocumentAttachment	VisualizeCAO
LinkDocumentToComponent	UpdateComponentData	UpdateProductData	NewDocumentFromModel	
UpdateLinkCPQuantity	NewComponentVersion	NewProductVersion	EditDocumentAttachment	
UpdateLinkDPQuantity	NewComponentRevision	ChangeProductStatus	CompleteDocumentData	
UpdateLinkDCQuantity	DisplayComponentEditor	DisplayProductAttachment	ExportDocumentToModel	
BrowsingUpDocument	DisplayComponentHistoric	DisplayProductEditor	SearchDocument	
CompareProductStructure	DeleteComponent	DisplayProductHistoric	PrintAttachment	
CompareComponentStructure	GetComponentVersion	DeleteProduct	PrintAttachmentToPDF	
CopyProductStructure	LockComponent	GetProductVersion	ExportDocumentToModel	
CopyComponentstructure	UnlockComponent	LockProduct	DisplayDocumentEditor	
GetComponentTonParent		UnlockProduct	DeleteDocument	
			GetDocumentVersion	

Fig. 3. Expert from Functional PLM service catalog

5   Feasibility of the Proposed Approach

We propose a BP Orchestration meta-model. Figure 4 below presents this meta-model in term of class and relationships between classes. The main concepts of this meta-model are the Business Orchestration, Business Operation, Control Flow, Business Object, Business Actor and Business service. A business process performs business operations, which are associated to business services. A business operation is performed by a business actor and consumes and/or produces business objects. Moreover, it can have pre-conditions or post conditions. The main Control Flows in our meta-model are Sequence, Fork and Join [12]. Modeling PDP as service orchestration is simpler than modeling it using other process modeling approaches that are often ad-hoc and based on complex meta-models.

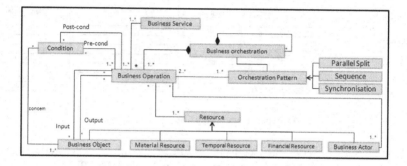

Fig. 4. BP orchestration Meta-model

In order to illustrate the BP orchestration meta-model instantiation, we propose to use the following example. The example describes an Engineering Change Request (ECR). It includes two steps: the elaboration and the validation of the ECR. We modeled this process based on our BP orchestration meta-model and using our PDS (fig. 5-a) to show that we can define all PDP using our PDS catalog and that it's easy to do it using our orchestration meta-model. We used the following PDS operations list; Elaborate Engineering Change Request, Distribute Engineering Change Request and Validate Engineering Change Request. We then mapped it with functional services operations (fig. 5-b) in order to test the articulation between the service levels.

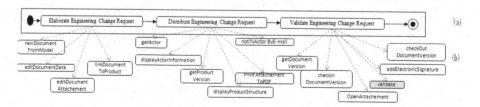

Fig. 5. Engineering Change Request Process

Capturing a business process in a model like this makes it easy for everyone looking at the process model to get a basic understanding of the business process. Each PDS operation is defined by a set of functional PLM services operations that can be executed in turn by invocation of technical PLM services operations. Dotted arrows represent the articulation from one service level to another one. This testing upholds that all business process can be expressed in terms of our identified business services. Moreover it helped us to refine our business service catalog and to ensure that the functional services can meet all PDS.

6 Discussion and Conclusion

In this paper we discussed the problem of PDPs flexibility in PLM system. PDPs are emergent and product design actors cannot deal with existing technical solutions. Existing modeling approaches dealing with BP flexibility were discussed and analyzed. The assumption made is that flexible PDPs require specific methods for their design. Our contributions respond to the limitations and problems described above by providing a methodological approach that aims to provide PDP flexibility by adhering to service orientation. A service-based approach was introduced to address dynamic PDP changes. This approach presents the PDP model as a PDS orchestration. In this case the process refers to business behavior in which all steps are PDS operations. Thus, a PDS can be invoked to perform a given step of a PDP. The challenge here is to react quickly to changes either by replacing some services by other ones or by adding new services to the orchestration. In order to deal with alignment issues between technical and business level, we first proposed a service type for each level. Then, we proposed an orchestration model in each level (business, functional and technical) and a mean that allows transforming the business orchestration model to a functional orchestration model by adhering to MDE techniques. Finally, according to the used PLM system, a mapping between the functional services of the functional orchestration model and the technical services of the PLM system should be done using the same deployment techniques. In this paper we presented the business and functional services catalog. We also defined the meta-model needed to orchestrate PDS.

Techniques that allow moving from one level to another one have not been addressed in this paper. To do so, we proposed a conceptual architecture based on a Model-Driven-Engineering approach [15]. This part of work still under development, we are defining a mapping meta-model between business and functional levels, which we will name business deployment meta-model. According to the business deployment meta-model and the business orchestration model, executing a set of mappings rules can generate the functional orchestration model. As far as, we are defining a mapping meta-model between functional and technical levels that we will name functional deployment meta-model. Using the same deployment techniques, the technical orchestration model can be generated based on the functional orchestration model and the functional deployment meta-model.

The distinction between functional and technical PLM services shows the genericity of the proposed approach. In fact, an enterprise can change her PLM system or even have multiple PLM systems. The advantage of our approach is that the company can uses the same business orchestration model (and the same business deployment model), but execute many functional deployments model according to the used PLM systems. Indeed, once a process model deployed on a new PLM system we have just to execute the right functional deployment. In contrast, the limitation of our approach is that we define the deployment only on a top-down manner and we consider that all functional PLM services operations have a corresponding list of technical PLM service operations.

Acknowledgements. The authors would like to thanks the Region Rhône-Alpes for financial support of this research work.

References

[1] Credle, R., et al.: SOA Approach to entreprise integration for product lifecycle management. In: IBM International Technical Support Organization, pp. 66–80 (2008)

[2] Bessai, K., et al.: Context Aware Business Process Evaluation and Redesign. In: Int. Workshop on Business Process Management, Design and Support, at Int. Conference on Advanced Information Systems, Montpellier, France, pp. 407–414 (2008)

[3] Zhao, X., Liu, C.: Version Management in the Business Process Change Context. In: Alonso, G., Dadam, P., Rosemann, M. (eds.) BPM 2007. LNCS, vol. 4714, pp. 198–213. Springer, Heidelberg (2007)

[4] Lezoche, M., Missikof, M., Tinini, L.: Business Process Evolution: a rule-based Approach. In: Int. Workshop on Business Process Management, Design and Support, at Int. Conference on Advanced Information Systems, Montpelier, France, pp. 407–414 (2008)

[5] Boukadi, K., et al.: CWSC4EC: How to employ context, web service, and community in enterprise collaboration. In: The 8th Int. Conference on New Technologies of Distributed Systems, Lyon, France (2008)

[6] Erl, T.: Service-Oriented Architecture (SOA): Concepts, Technology and Design. Prentice Hall, PTRUpper Saddle River (2005)

[7] Manouvrier, B., Ménard, L.: Intégration applicative EAI, B2B, BPM et SOA. Hermès Science - Lavoisier (2007)

[8] Hachani, S., et al.: Support of Business Processes Flexibility in PLM Systems Using a Services-Based Approach. In: Int. Conference on Industrial Engineering and Systems Management (IESM 2011), Metz, France (2011)

[9] Papazoglou, M.P., Heuvel, W.-J.: Service-oriented design and development methodology. International Journal of Web Engineering and Technology (IJWET) 2, 412–442 (2006)

[10] Chang, S.H., Kim, S.D.: A Service-Oriented Analysis and Design Approach to Developing Adaptable Services. In: The IEEE Int. Conference on Services Computing (SCC 2007), pp. 204–211 (2007)

[11] Arsanjani, A., Allam, A.: Service oriented modeling and architecture for Realization of an SOA. In: The Proceeding of IEEE International Conference on Service Computing (SCC 2006), p. 521. IEEE, Chicago (2006)

[12] Manoloscu, D.A.: Micro-workflow: A Workflow Architecture Supporting Compositional Object-Oriented Development. Phd Thesis. University of Illinois (2001)

[13] Scaravetti, D., et al.: Structuring of embodiment design problem based on the product lifecycle. International Journal of Product Developement, Special Issue on PLM (2004)

[14] Pahl, G., Beitz, W.: Engineering Design; A Systematic Approach. Springer, London (2007)

[15] Schmidt, D.C.: Guest Editor's Introduction: Model-Driven Engineering. Computer Journal 39(2), 25–31 (2006)

Enterprise Integration and Economical Crisis for Mass Craftsmanship: A Case Study of an Italian Furniture Company

Michele Dassisti[*] and Michele De Nicolò

DMMM, Politecnico di Bari, Viale Japigia 182, 70126 - Bari, Italy
{m.dassisti,m.denicolo}@poliba.it

Abstract. The paper presents a real industrial case of an Italian furniture company facing the problem of a strong evolution put by the market-scenario during the economical crisis. The new challenges to face come either for earn margins reduction, increase of customization level, swift of demand fluctuation. The aim of the paper is to provide a clear analysis of the existing problems and constraints, in the light of the project to design the transition toward a new-defined "mass craftsmanship" configuration of the company.

Keywords: Enterprise Interoperability, Information Modeling, Mass craftsmanship.

1 Introduction

The term "mass customization" was first coined by Davis (1987) in his book Future Perfect [1]. Mass customization is presented as one of the ways to deal with the increasingly demanding and turbulent environments. Based on the rapid obtaining of mass customization (MC) demanded information from the consumers, and market changing information, MC product agile manufacture is to develop new products in responding to the consumers' demands and to guide the markets via agile organization management, agile design and manufacturing. Achieving mass customization requires the development of multidimensional strategic capabilities: how to deal with the contradiction between scale production effect and customized demand is the key problem on studying mass customization. Mass personalization is the limiting case of mass customization [2]. Whereas both of these strategies are guided by the criterion of product affordability consistent with mass production efficiencies, the former (mass personalization) aims at a market segment of one while the latter (mass customization) at a market segment of few. Mass Craftsmanship (MCMS) here referred to is an hybrid form between pure mass customization and mass personalization, since it is possible – thanks to the retail chains available at the present in the furniture segment – to address a wide marked but of singular requirements. To a certain extent, the intuition of this new kind of market descending from the crisis times, where customer are still demanding for personalization and fashion but are less available to pay for the

---

[*] Corresponding author.

P. Herrero et al. (Eds.): OTM 2012 Workshops, LNCS 7567, pp. 113–123, 2012.

value added. MCMS should be thus an opportunity to respond to this changed customer demand while maintaining good profit margins. Products are deeply customized according to the single customer but, at the same time, manufacturing and assembly schedules should try to see it as a standard product, to gain advantage of efficiencies proper of a mass production. Different than a do-it-yourself setting (i.e., autonomous creation activities of consumers), this is done in a mode of interaction with the manufacturer who is responsible for providing the custom solution ("co-creation,") [3].

This is, shortly, the position of the problem the Italian furniture company here addressed, facing the strong transition from a quite stable market situation toward an unstable situation due to the economical crisis experienced in the Euro-zone. We will concentrate on the software part of the solution of the business-process reengineering process. The most of the approaches presented above share the same features, which can be easily recognized as critical to the present study: the need to integrate information, to reduce loss of it and efficiency – as well as efficacy – in its use. Fragmentation of information, interoperability of different IT applications as well as univocal semantic interpretation of knowledge are critical in the mass customization paradigm. The stronger thus it criticality for the new mass craftsmanship paradigm, which increases the demand for a clear view of job assignments. These points will be further developed in the following paragraphs.

2   The Case Study

The sector of furniture, at least in Italy, is characterized by a relative product complexity with an high changing of the demand pattern either in volume and/or in product models over time. This leads to an extremely volatile market, which is also affected by the ever-decreasing profit-margin problems. Competition is thus based on anticipating the customer desires as well as in challenging appealing prices to customers which are even less available to spend their money, due to true or perceived crisis time. The challenge for any company is to increase the worthiness of money spent by customer, by providing the tacit benefit of fashion while maintaining an high levelof quality and service. The mass craftsmanship paradigm (MCMS) is here addressed as the natural business strategy to simultaneously compete on these rival competitive priorities, descending from Mass Customization [4].

The Italian furniture company under analysis lives in the situation above described. It produces kitchens for the private sector since 1987. It has grown from a small company up to a medium-large company in the south of Italy, with around 2 weeks delivery time, mainly for the Italian market. Approximately, the company works with more than 30.000 component variants (which is not unusual for a modern mass customization manufacturing process (see, e.g. [5]).

In the last years it has experienced a strong increase in its production volumes, leading to a threshold situation where all the inefficiencies and criticalities in the managerial decision became evident. The call for a change management derived from this situation.

Amongst all, the two most critical issues recognized by the management are: i) stratification over time of a mass of different IT applications that, despite coming from the same supplier, presents significant inefficiencies in integration and data synchronization; ii) difficulties in maintaining the adequate degree of operational flexibility of the small artisan size with the increased demand in terms of volumes and variety.

These two strong challenges unfortunately, but obviously, negatively impact with the presence of consolidated craftsmanship habits from the organizational point of view. This last attitude, on the other hand, is also a success factor of the company, since furniture market – at least in Italy – is mainly a "market of one", where personalization is critical to the customer. It it thus mandatory for the company to maintain his craftsmanship behavior; this is thus the true challenge to face at the present time of analysis of the system.

3   The Enterprise Integration Analysis

The key step to find an enterprise integration solution is to follow a structured path. To this aim, in the present study we adopted the HY-CHANGE© methodology [6]. The choice descends from a comparison with other approaches (as presented in [1]) where, despite the similarity in the structured approach, the HY-CHANGE structured hybrid methodology for Continuous Performance Improvement provides multiple perspectives of analysis.

3.1   Push Event (WHY)

The present market scenario of furniture industry in Italy shows a increase in fragmentation of orders, characterized by an rapid changing variety of modular components - at the same time with swift change in customer's demands for aesthetics and excitements such as domotic applications. At the same time, profit margins are continuously reducing with also a potential reduction of overall selling volumes. This evolution, which belongs also to the multicultural evolution of society with respect to the previous decades, is partially interpreted by a growing phenomenon of big selling centers, collecting single customer demands while trying to influence the market orientation with a selected offer of models and varieties. Nevertheless, customers demand is fragmented for cultural and social reasons, highly customized but at the same time – by the nature of this market – it is the same customer the "designer" of the product (co-creation). This is essentially the main issue to face: how to take into account the variety of customer requirements - from higher quality to high fashion products - even though there is not an design expert when issuing an order. The most of the problems, in fact, typically born in the product specification phase, which is coincident with the order collection from the vendors collecting personalization desire but with few experience of production and/or assembly. To make this furniture scenario more complex, is the 'lower cost economy' where customers are extremely exigent but at the cheapest price: this is the true challenge for manufacturers and assemblers to win the present crisis competition. Italian furniture scenario is thus urging – much more now than ever- new answers, asking for a significant reshaping of the organization endeavoring the mass craftsmanship paradigm, which can be sometime a critical demand for most of the players. Reengineering business processes thus is a must to be pursued, do readapt to this changing reality.

It happens quite often that, due to the fragmented customer demand profile, a constant dynamical rearrangements of orders is required, urging sometimes for rush orders that requires a flexible but effective dynamical adjustment of the scheduling. Information management is thus vital in this process, since availability, forecasts as well as technical information should be perfectly integrated as it was for the craftsman in the past.

This picture represent the "push event" that motivated the company to ask for a business process re-engineering action to be designed and implemented. The feeling that "something was going wrong" pervaded the company in the last years, either in the disorganization evidences or in the overall profit lowering. To summarize, the push event was a psychological feeling of confusion in the organization, that brought the employees to distrust the management actions.

3.2   Preliminary Study (WHAT)

According to interviews and brainstorming, it emerged the need to define a new "mass craftsmanship" paradigm, to produce personalized products to meet each individual customers needs but with mass production efficiency. Expected results from these were recognized into an higher flexibility to adapt customer's demand patterns as well as maintaining a reasonable level of remuneration by cutting non-value added activities and inefficiencies. An implicit goal, that may result from implementing changes according to the above mentioned goals, can be the proneness to innovate product anticipating customer tendencies: reorganization of company may in fact release resources of creativity.

Information and its correct flows play a critical role for controlling either order, production planning, manufacturing as well as delivery operations. The implications derived from the drastic increase of varieties, very small batch size, random arrival of orders, and wide spread of due dates are really impressive into the organization and operation of the company.

Existing strategies and solutions for facing enterprise integration are at the present time rarely implementable tout-court, provided the specific history of the company and its operating constraints. The organizational functional areas involved into this change process are commercial one, technical/design one, production planning and control and finally logistic. Production, in the very first phases of change are not directly involved, if a proper policy of push of orders and pull of expedition is set up in the other areas.

3.3   Analysis of the Existing Situation (WHERE)

For the sake of the present paper, we will focus only on the software aspect of change; we will thus concentrate on information flows. The information can be in fact viewed as an organizational resource [7]. Each task within an organization, has a management content and, as such, manages information [8]. Therefore the information is a cross-function resource. It is an intangible asset and is the root of all other intangible organizational resources such as knowledge and individual and organizational experience. Unlike other resources that tend to run out, the information is self-regenerating and its use often increases its value [7].

Actually, the computer system adopted throughout the company can be said to be tied to the history of the company; i.e., the IS that makes use of technological HW/ SW resources has different approaches depending on the functional area of pertinence Our case study is characterized by the presence of a legacy computer system that consists of a fairly diverse set of applications that have been layering over time as a set of solutions to particular problems and, despite being largely supplied by a single software provider, show high levels of inefficiency resulting from low levels of integration and interoperability. For this reason the level of integration doesn't allow us to say that we have a real IS for the integrated management of business processes. The IS structure looks like what is depicted in the following figure 1:

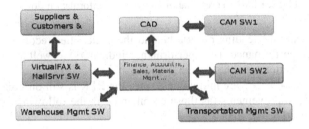

Fig. 1. Schemata of the IS in the Italian furniture company

The approach that has been followed to analyze the existing situation is to represent information flows using a standard tool (see, e.g. figure 2). The main goal was to appreciate the functioning of the legacy system with the aim of appreciating interoperability features of the set of IT applications represented in fig.1.

Lying behind this picture there is a major obstacles to a correct interoperability in our case study, represented by existing SW solutions poorly adapted to interoperability because of their stratification over time. This is a major problem recognized, since the design of SW solutions rarely is able to cope with future interoperability requirements, coming from new SW solutions or applications. In this cases, SW provider is often a strategic asset to work with, since it can maintain the memory of the IT solutions adopted and can guarantee the co-design or co-evolution of the IS.

Externalization of IT solution means to realize the strategic importance of cooperation with the IT provider over time. In the present paper we present an example of the order flow analysis. The chosen notation to represent the order process is BPMN that is an OMG standard described, for example, in [9] and [10]. Figure 2 presents a high level order fulfillment diagram.

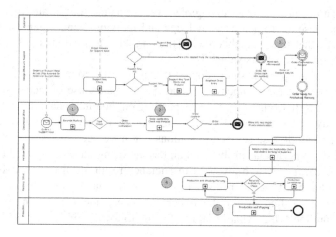

Fig. 2. BPMN representation of the As-Is information flows

It is evident that the leading criteria behind the criticalities recognised are mainly improvement of performances (key-performance indicators) as well as the efficacy of the management action over the system.

Solutions here proposed are initial ones, since the BPR is still on-going and the effect of potential improvements (as those commented in the following paragraph) are still far to be raised on the field.

4   Plan of Improvement (WHEN)

The solution here initially proposed was to synchronize the technical solutions here listed, for managing the production and the information, with a correct organizational approach aiming at integrating the company view and its supply chain. Basically, these analyses were performed according to the IS alignment approach proposed in [11], namely: alignments with the strategy, with the environment and with the uncertain evolutions. We considered the IT strategy into account as a standalone domain required to align IS.

The temporal dimension is taken into account by considering the pattern of "Past / As-Is + Next-Step / To-Be" scenarios that constitute the temporal evolution of the IS as a function of the remaining variables.

The approach developed to face the existing organizative/IS problems is similar to the "classical" alignment path in which the business strategy is the anchor domain and drives both the design of the organizational infrastructure and processes and the design of the IT infrastructure and processes.

The alignment path could be assimilated to a sort of a blend of the approaches MIT90s and BALES [36] and is described by the following figure:

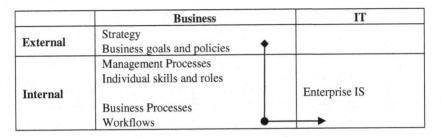

	Business	IT
External	Strategy Business goals and policies	
Internal	Management Processes Individual skills and roles Business Processes Workflows	Enterprise IS

Fig. 3. Graphical representation of the "involved domains" and "alignment sequences" for the developed alignment approach

The key factor for the change is represented by the strategy and the pivotal domains are the Structure, the Management Processes, the Individual skills and roles and the Workflows. The impacted domain is the Enterprise IS.

To achieve the business change the idea is to adapt the existing enterprise model to reflect the new business reality and to determine a new mapping between the enterprise model and the legacy system.

4.1   Integration Model of Information

Customer co-creation is the central theme of mass craftsmanship. Quite often, through an interactive website, but also through telephone, the customer chooses a product configuration based on the offerings of a company. This seems to be the new challenge of the next years to come, at least in the Italian furniture sector. A very simplified version of the re-designed order fulfillment process is shown in the following diagram (see figure 4). The aims of the five introduced modifications are:

1. To partially automate the order arrival process
2. To simplify and rationalize the order entry process
3. To partially outsource the design process to the sales network provided that a CAD configurator is simply to use and the ability to configure kitchens following the final customer expectations is a typical task of the sales network
4. To simplify the task of the Planning Office letting it to concentrate on the container loading and transportation planning problems also moving downstream the issuing of the production and picking lists
5. To give the necessary flexibility to the production process by managing in the last-possible-stage the always up-to-date production and picking lists

The indicated numbers are respectively correspondent in the diagrams of fig. 2 and fig. 4, in the table 1 and in the above list.

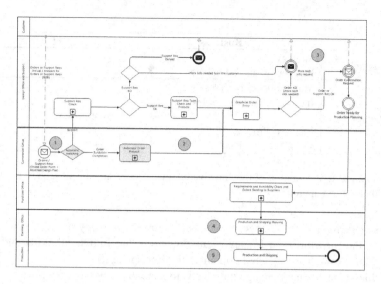

Fig. 4. BPMN representation of the proposed To-Be information flows

4.2   Merging Postponement and Push

Postponed manufacturing is where product components are standardized into generics and mass produced for global markets. The big challenge for the Italian company under study to react swiftly to market demand is a proper balance between good level of stock of standard components, while providing a really fast response to customization for only a small part of customized components.

A clear analysis of the customer order decoupling point was made (see definition in [[12]]), then realizing the critical situation of a mixed push-pull production due to order collection system. CODP is mainly at vendor chain level, i.e. far from the true action radius of the company. The idea of a Virtual Customer Decoupling Point (VCDP) was thus initially explored. The aim was to see if it was possible anticipating the market orientation, on the basis of an effective and well connected chain of vendors and in-house retailer. VCDP can be the good idea of creating a virtual stock holding point that separates the part of the supply chain that responds directly to the customer from the part of the supply chain that uses forecast planning.

This idea will be explored in practice in the course of the project. To this regard, we wish to highlight two fundamental issues concerning the IS, which allow to achieve the described purposes. The IS must first present the highest possible level of inner integration and cohesion, and moreover the boundary that defines the separation between what is well integrated and what's not has to coincide with the boundary of the enterprise. This means that the "legacy" issues must address the relationship of the enterprise with its customers and suppliers rather than the relationship between the various departments / functions of the enterprise itself as it occurs now.

Table 1. Detailed description of the proposed modifications

N	Office	As-Is	To-Be
1	Commercial Office	Receives oders in a virtual fax/mail server. Both fax and emails (and their attachments) are barcoded. Barcoded documents are then passed into the management system	The order (management data) is filled in online (B2B) and the design file (graphical data) is correspondingly attached. All the information are immediately recorded into the management system.
2	Commercial Office	Order protocol Commercial conformity check of the order: - OK: furniture design development by the Design Office - KO: communications with the customer to correct the order	Commercial conformity check of the order (B2B): - OK: Order protocol and furniture design development by the Design Office - KO: the customer must re-send the complete, correct order
3	Design Office	Develops the furniture with the CAD configurator and sends the confirmation / more info needed request to the customer	Technical conformity check of the order: - OK: Order Confirmation Request and Order Ready for Production Planning - KO: more tech info needed. The customer must re-send the complete, correct order
4	Planning Office	Generates the production plan based on the carrier cargo volume, geographic area and availability of products. Print the production and picking lists and the packaging labels	Process the production plan based on container loading constraints and geographical constraints of transport.
5	Production	Production based on production planning	Production based on production planning Print the production and picking lists and the packaging labels

4.3   Community of Practice

In today's competitive environment, the ability to transition to an improved enterprise is a critical discriminator. The reference model of social learning systems will benefit and shorten the training time to equip novice knowledge managers and personnel with the required knowledge to practice the construction of an effective social learning system. This is a very critical point that will be addressed in the next phases of the project, according to the model presented in [12]. Implementing a model of social learning within the company reality is a challenge, due to non favorable structural as well as social context. Mass craftsmanship production processes require substantially higher worker skills compared to homogeneous mass production processes: the social process is thus much more important than ever in this context.

4.4   Lean-Manufacturing

Lean manufacturing principles can be easily applied to situations with low levels of MC. However, as the degree of customization increases and customer involvement occurs earlier in the design and fabrication stages, the direct application of lean principles to maintain flow and low levels of inventory becomes difficult. It is clear that lean production provides a base for mass customization: this is one of the key merging points between technical solutions and organizational one. Without a strong commitment of the company to the zero-defects culture no chance at all is possible to perform an effective transition toward mass customization.

5   Discussion and Conclusion

The paper presents the first outcomes of a project under development for supporting the transition of an Italian furniture company toward a new equilibrium of mass customization. The analysis show that it is not easy at all to merge technical and organizational aspects in the current hybrid situation, due also to the need of change of mentality and practices.

At the root of the metamorphosis required also in the furniture sector, as well as in many others sectors, is the customer of today who is itching to express his or her personality through personalized products, but is restricted by the size of the purse.
This is not yet the case of furniture sector, but software product line will result a very clear and interesting idea to explore in order to bring a true innovation for the Italian furniture segment.

As a final remark, mass craftsmanship is a new paradigm here introduced is a strategy susceptible also for a possible relocation of production processes through extremely low worker wages. Particularly, mass production processes seem to be highly appropriate for a relocation, provided an adequate IT structure is working.

Aknowledgements. This paper is partially funded within the frame of the research project called "Turinnova", co-funded by Italian Government ("*Credito d'imposta per la ricerca scientifica*") and by the Mobilturi S.r.l. company.

References

[1] Davis, S.M.: From 'future perfect': Mass customizing. Strategy & Leadership 17(2), 16–21 (1989)
[2] Kumar, A.: From mass customization to mass personalization: a strategic transformation. International Journal of Flexible Manufacturing Systems 19(4), 533–547 (2007)

[3] Piller, F.: Mass Customization: Reflections on the State of the Concept. International Journal of Flexible Manufacturing Systems 16(4), 313–334 (2004)

[4] Kumar, A., Gattoufi, S., Reisman, A.: Mass customization research: trends, directions, diffusion intensity, and taxonomic frameworks. International Journal of Flexible Manufacturing Systems 19(4), 637–665 (2007)

[5] Bock, S.: Supporting offshoring and nearshoring decisions for mass customization manufacturing processes. European Journal of Operational Research 184(2), 490–508 (2008)

[6] Dassisti, M.: HY-CHANGE\copyright methodology: an industrial application for tool management systems. International Journal of Automotive Technology and Management 9(4), 438–453 (2009)

[7] Glazer, R.: Measuring the value of information: The information-intensive organization. IBM Systems Journal 32(1), 99–110 (1993)

[8] Huber, G.P.: The nature and design of post-industrial organizations. Management Science, 928–951 (1984)

[9] BPMN, http://www.omg.org/spec/BPMN/2.0/

[10] White, S.A.: Process Modeling Notations and Workflow Patterns (2006)

[11] Avila, O., Goepp, V., Kiefer, F.: Understanding and classifying information system alignment approaches. Journal of Computer Information Systems 50(1), 2 (2010)

[12] Schunk, P.P., Malzahn, D.E., Whitman, L.E.: Social Learning System: A Reference Model. In: 14th IFAC Symposium "Information Control Problems in Manufacturing, INCOM 2012" (May 2012)

Towards a Benchmark for Ontology Merging

Salvatore Raunich and Erhard Rahm

University of Leipzig, Germany

Abstract. Benchmarking approaches for ontology merging is challenging and has received little attention so far. A key problem is that there is in general no single best solution for a merge task and that merging may either be performed symmetrically or asymmetrically. As a first step to evaluate the quality of ontology merging solutions we propose the use of general metrics such as the relative coverage of the input ontologies, the compactness of the merge result as well as the degree of introduced redundancy. We use these metrics to evaluate three merge approaches for different merge scenarios.

1 Motivation

Ontologies and taxonomies are increasingly used to semantically categorize or annotate information, e.g., for e-commerce or e-science. For example, product catalogs of online shops or comparison portals categorize products to help users and applications finding relevant information. Since many ontologies refer to the same domain and to the same objects, there is a growing need to integrate or merge such related ontologies. The goal is to create a merged ontology providing a unified view on two or more input ontologies.

Ontology merging is a challenging problem especially for large and heterogeneous ontologies and require semi-automatic approaches to reduce the manual effort. Several such merge approaches have already been proposed, however their relative quality is largely unknown. One increasingly adopted and promising idea is to decompose the complex integration problem into match and merge subtasks and leverage the advances made for automatic ontology and schema matching [13] to solve the first subproblem. The merge subtask can then utilize a match mapping identifying corresponding concepts in the input ontologies that should be merged. Such a *match-based merging* is followed in [11] [17] [16] [12] [15]. In general, merging can be symmetric or asymmetric with respect to the input ontologies. *Symmetric solutions* (e.g., [10], [9], [8] [7]) are most common and aim at completely integrating all input ontologies with the same priority. *Asymmetric approaches*, by contrast, take one of the input ontologies as the target and merge the other input ontologies into this target [11] [15] [6] thereby giving preference to the target ontology.

Given the different merge approaches we see an increasing need to quantitatively evaluate their quality and performance. For the subproblem of ontology matching such evaluations are now quite common [1] [3] and there is also a benchmark for determining schema mappings [2]. Typically the quality of a match algorithm is determined by evaluating it on some match problems for which a manually defined perfect match result is provided for comparison. While a similar approach for evaluating merge approaches

P. Herrero et al. (Eds.): OTM 2012 Workshops, LNCS 7567, pp. 124–133, 2012.

has been advocated for in [4] we argue that there is in general no single perfect merge result but that there can be several similarly valid solutions. Also the quality of a merged ontology likely depends on the domain and its intended use making it difficult to define a general benchmark for ontology merging.

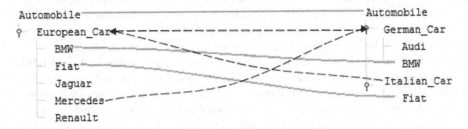

Fig. 1. Running Example

For illustration let us consider two sample taxonomies (also referred to as source and target taxonomies) in Figure 1 that classify European cars in different ways. The first (source) taxonomy uses a single concept *European_Car* while the target distinguishes between *German* and *Italian* cars. Let us suppose that a match mapping is already given as input (solid lines), automatically generated by a matching tool or manually designed by an expert user. Figure 2 shows four possible solutions that a merging tool or human expert can produce. Merged concepts present in both inputs are marked with a star in the solutions. For example, the concept *BMW** is a combined concept covered by an equivalence correspondence in the match mapping. The problem is to evaluate the quality of the different solutions, e.g., to find the best merge result.

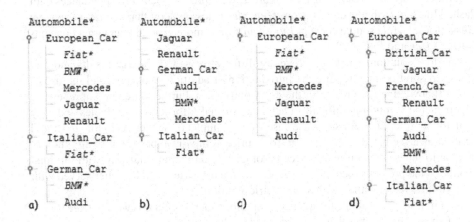

Fig. 2. a) Full Merge - b) Target-driven - c) Source-driven - d) Expert Result

Two of the solutions (a,d) are the result of a symmetric and two the result of an asymmetric merging (b,c). Solution (a) is the output of a straight-forward *Full Merge* approach that takes the union of the input ontologies and combines equivalent (matching) concepts. It is easy to see that such a Full Merge preserves all input concepts and relationships. However, the example shows that such a solution is not always desirable since it can introduce a semantic overlap (e.g., between *Italian_Car*, *German_Car* and *European_Car*) by redundantly representing the same information and introducing multiple inheritance for some concepts (*Fiat* and *BMW*). Furthermore, the concept *Mercedes* should be better placed under the more specific concept *German_Car*.

Such problems may be avoided by asymmetric merge approaches such as ATOM [15] that preserve only the concepts and relationships of one input and integrate only non-redundant concepts of the other ontology. Solutions (b) and (c) show the ATOM results when the target input and source input ontology is chosen as the preferred ontology, respectively. In both cases, the result is more compact than for the Full Merge and has no multiple inheritance. In solution (b) the concepts Jaguar and Renault could not be well placed since they are directly under root concept *Automobile* as opposed to the other leaf concepts. Solution (c) is more homogeneous but has dropped inner target concepts (such as *German_Car*, *Italian_Car*) to conform to the structure of the source input ontology. Note that both asymmetric solutions preserve all leaf concepts and can thus maintain all information of the input ontologies.

Finally, (d) shows the most complex merge solution that may be manually generated by an expert user. Like (a) it retains all concepts and relationships of the input ontologies but it introduces new inner concepts for British and French cars. Furthermore, all leaf concepts (e.g. Mercedes) are perfectly placed without multiple inheritance. Such an improved placement and minimization of redundancy is difficult to achieve automatically. However, it can be supported by providing enhanced match mappings containing not only equivalence correspondences but also semantic relationships *less general* or *more general* correspondences [5] [15]. In Figure 1, we represent such correspondences with dashed lines, e.g., that source concept *Mercedes* is less general than the target concept *German_Car* while source concept *European_Car* is more general than target concepts *German_Car* and *Italian_Car*.

The four solutions show that there are different reasonable merge results and that an expert solution may require the introduction of additional concepts and the use of further knowledge not present in the input ontologies. Furthermore, a comprehensive expert merge solution is difficult to achieve especially for larger ontologies and may actually be suboptimal for some use cases. For example, if the merged ontology should be used as a mediated ontology (e.g. for a price comparison portal) it is important to be able to integrate additional source ontologies in an incremental way with minimal change to the previous mediated ontology. Such a use case could be better served with an asymmetric merge than with a symmetric solution.

As a first step to evaluate the quality of ontology merge solutions we advocate for the use of simple approaches that do not depend on the provision of a perfect merge result. We rather focus on general criteria such as the input coverage and compactness of the merge result as well as the degree of redundancy. Before we introduce our benchmark metrics in Section 3, we first discuss the general desiderata of a merge solution in more detail (Section 2). In Section 4, we present first evaluation results using the introduced metrics for different merge scenarios and merge approaches.

2 Desiderata of a Merge Solution

Before one can determine the quality of an ontology merging algorithm it is necessary to define the requirements or desiderata for (semi-)automatic merging. Several research papers have defined such requirements [11] [17] [14] albeit for different kinds of ontologies and schemas and mostly without considering requirements imposed by specific use cases. Since we do not want to limit ourselves to the evaluation of a specific algorithm we merely discuss general requirements that we consider as especially significant for the quality of a merge solution, namely the preservation of information of the input ontologies and the understandability (and thus usability) of the merged ontology.

In this paper we focus on the wide-spread class of is-a-based ontologies (taxonomies) that may or may not include multiple inheritance. Ontologies consist of a set of concepts and a set of relationships of type "is-a" ("subclass") between concepts forming a rooted, acyclic graph structure. Additional kinds of relationships such as "part-of" are possible. A concept represents a collection of objects with similar properties; each concept has a name (or label) and optionally further attributes. Concepts may also have associated instances, e.g. product offers of a certain product category. We further focus on merging two ontologies at a time and assume the existence of an equality-based match mapping indicating pairs of corresponding concepts.

A key requirement for ontology merging is a high degree of *information preservation* so that the information represented in the input ontologies is preserved in the merge result. In this respect, we differentiate between symmetric and asymmetric merge approaches. For symmetric approaches, we require that all concepts, attributes, and relationships of both input ontologies are preserved in the merge result. In particular, for every concept in any input ontology there must be a corresponding concept in the merged ontology. Relationships may also implicitly be preserved via newly introduced intermediate concepts. For example, the input relationship "*BMW* is-a *European_Car*" of Figure 1 is implicitly preserved by "*BMW* is-a *German_Car* is-a *European_Car*". It is easy to see that solutions (a) and (d) in Figure 2 satisfy the information preservation properties.

For asymmetric merge approaches, we demand the preservation of all concepts, attributes and relationships only for the preferred input ontology into which the other ontology is merged in. Information from the non-preferred input ontology should also be retained but without introducing redundant or conflicting information presentation (see below). For both, symmetric and asymmetric merge we demand that all instance objects of both input ontologies - if present - should be preserved, i.e. every object needs to be assigned (migrated) to a proper concept in the merge result.

Another important requirement is that the merge algorithm should support a good *understandability* and usability of the merge result. This is by necessity a subjective and thus vague requirement. The understandability of the merge result is also strongly dependent on the understandability of the input ontologies, e.g. their size and whether good modeling practices such as the avoidance of unnecessary redundancy have been followed. In general we believe that it is beneficial for understandability to have compact ontologies and to avoid conflicting or redundant representations of the same information. In particular, we must ensure the property of *equality preservation*, i.e. matching concepts from both input ontologies (as represented in the input mapping) need to be merged to the same concept in the result ontology so that they are represented only once. The merge result thus becomes more compact and less redundant than a simple union of the input ontologies (if there is at least one matching concept). All solutions in Figure 2 satisfy the equality preservation property.

The discussion and example in the introductory section has shown that providing equality preservation and information preservation is not sufficient to achieve a well understandable merge result. In particular, the Full Merge solution (a) in Figure 2 suffers from a redundant and conflicting representation of several concepts that is avoided by symmetric solution (d) as well as the asymmetric solutions (b) and (c). We thus view it as desirable to reduce semantic overlap and redundant / conflicting concept placements. A frequent cause of redundancy is the assignment of a merged concept under several parent concepts leading to multiple root paths to the merged concept (e.g. for concepts *Fiat* and *BMW* in Figure 2(a)). [14] proposes a property to control the semantic overlap in the merge result by requiring that the merge must not lead to additional (is-a) root paths for leaf concepts. This criterion implies that no multiple inheritance is introduced for merging tree-structured input ontologies. The semantic overlap property is not satisfied by the Full Merge result (a) but for solutions (b), (c) and (d) in Figure 2.

3   Quality Measures for Ontology Merging

A benchmark for ontology merging should mainly be able to fairly evaluate the quality of different merge tools by defining appropriate quality metrics and providing suitable test scenarios. It would also be of interest to measure the runtime performance (efficiency) of different algorithms and to evaluate the manual user effort to determine the final merge result. In this section we mainly discuss the first point, metrics for assessing the merge quality. In the next section, we present a series of test scenarios that have been used to evaluate different merge algorithms. We will briefly discuss the user effort involved in the considered tools but leave its quantitative evaluation for future work.

Evaluating the quality of an ontology merging approach is a difficult task for reasons that we have already discussed to some extent. First, it implies measuring the quality of the output ontology which is at least partially subjective, e.g. regarding its understandability. Furthermore, there is a strong dependency on the quality of the input ontologies, e.g. whether they contain errors, whether they are well modelled with little redundancy, how complete they cover a given domain, etc. To keep the evaluation tractable, we only aim at evaluating the quality of the merge result relative to the input ontologies. Ideally, the input ontologies are correct and exhibit no or only little overlap between concepts. We assume that the given input match mapping/alignment is correct although obtaining such a mapping is non-trivial for larger ontologies.

Another main problem to evaluate the quality of a merge approach is that there is generally no unique perfect merge result for comparison (as assumed in [4]). As already discussed there are often several equally suited merge results that can still differ substantially. Especially for larger ontologies it is also very laborsome (and subjective) to specify expert solutions.

To overcome these problems we propose the use of the following simple criteria to evaluate the quality of merge results and thus merge approaches: *coverage*, *compactness* and *redundancy*.

Coverage. The coverage of a merge solution is related to the degree of information preservation and measures the share of input concepts preserved in the result. We can differentiate various sub-cases such as *source coverage* and *target coverage* for the degree to which concepts of the source and target input ontologies are preserved. We may also consider the *leaf coverage* as the degree to which input leaf concepts are preserved. This can be of interest when only leaf concepts carry instance objects so that it becomes important to preserve all leaf concepts to avoid information loss. The *overall coverage* is defined as the arithmetic average of source and target coverage. Coverage values range between 0 and 1 (or 0-100%). Symmetric merge approaches should achieve a coverage of 1, i.e. cover all input concepts. Smaller values than 1 do not necessarily imply an information loss but may be a consequence of avoiding redundancy in the merge result.

In our running example, the symmetric solutions (a) and (d) achieve a source and target coverage of 1. By contrast, the asymmetric, target-driven solution (b) achieves a source coverage of 0.86 (concept *European_Car* is not preserved) and the source-driven solution (c) achieves a target coverage of only 0.67 (2 of 6 concepts are missing: *German_Car* and *Italian_Car*). All solutions have a leaf coverage of 1.

Compactness. This measure checks the size or compactness of the generated merge result which is related to its understandability since a merge solution should not be unnecessarily large. In addition to the *absolute result size* (number of concepts in the result ontology) we determine the *relative result size* compared to the Full Merge result. The size of the Full Merge result can be approximated as the sum of the number of concepts of both input ontologies minus the number of merged concepts (i.e. the number of equality match correspondences in the input mapping). By definition, the relative result size of the Full Merge is 1. Values smaller than 1 indicate an improved compactness, e.g. if some input concepts are dropped to avoid redundancy in the merge result. Values larger than 1 are also possible when the result ontology contains newly introduced concepts, e.g. added by an expert to consolidate differences in the input ontology.

The absolute result size of our running example is 10, 9, 8 and 12 respectively for (a), (b), (c) and (d); the relative result size w.r.t. the full merge solution is 1.0, 0.9, 0.8 and 1.2.

Redundancy. As discussed in Section 2, it is desirable to reduce the degree of redundancy or semantic overlap in an integrated ontology for improved understandability. This can be supported by avoiding the introduction of additional paths from the ontology root to leaf concepts. In addition to the absolute number of leaf paths we use a relative measure to evaluate the degree of semantic redundancy. Let LP_S and LP_T be the number of leaf paths in the source and target input ontology, respectively, and M_L the number of matching leaf concepts in the input match mapping. Then $LP_B = LP_S + LP_T - M_L$ is the least possible number of leaf paths that does not introduce any redundancy. We define the *relative redundancy* in a merge result as the ratio between the number of leaf paths in the result and LP_B. Values larger than 1 indicate the introduction of redundant paths for merged concepts and thus leaves. This is considered harmful to the understandability of the merge result. A value of 1 is typically optimal as it indicates the successful avoidance of redundant paths. Values smaller than 1 imply that some leaf concepts are not covered in the merge result referring to an information loss and reduced (leaf) coverage.

For our running example, we count 8 different leaf paths in the full merge result (a) and 6 for the other solutions (b), (c) and (d), leading to a relative redundancy of 1.33 for solution (a) and of 1.0 for (b), (c) and (d).

The introduced metrics reflect some of the tradeoffs in achieving the contradicting goals of information preservation and good understandability. While we consider a relative redundancy of 1 as optimal, the best values for coverage and compactness are less clear, i.e. they may be smaller than 1 or (for compactness) even larger than 1. We discuss these issues further in the next section when we present the evaluation results.

4 Experimental Results

We first sketch the algorithms we were able to evaluate and then introduce our test scenarios. We then use the proposed quality measures to evaluate the algorithms for the different scenarios.

4.1 Merge Algorithms

While many systems for schema and ontology merging have been proposed and implemented during the last years, we could only find two tools (providing three algorithms) for conducting our evaluation: PROMPT [10] and ATOM [15]. We briefly discuss their characteristics.

PROMPT provides an algorithm for both aligning and merging ontologies. The merging algorithm is semi-automatic since it can perform some tasks automatically, while the other tasks are suggested to the user as a list of possible operations to execute. The main merge approach is symmetric. However, in case of conflicts the system also provides the possibility to manually give preference to one input resulting in a partially asymmetric solution. PROMPT is available as a plug-in for Protègè, an open-source ontology design and editor.

ATOM provides a fully automatic ontology merging based on a given match mapping between the input taxonomies. Two algorithms are provided. First, a symmetric Full Merge as introduced in Section 1 is offered. The main approach is an asymmetric algorithm that preserves one input ontology as the merge target and incrementally extends it with concepts and relationships from the other input ontology. It can either use an equivalence-based match mapping as input or an enhanced match mapping containing equivalence, is-a and inverse is-a relationships between concepts of the input taxonomies.

4.2 Test Scenarios for Ontology Merging

For our evaluation, we use five test cases of different size and complexity. We consider three hand-crafted small-sized scenarios for which we can also manually provide a merge solution. We additionally evaluate two larger real-life merge problems.

– **Cars:** This test case is our running example presented in Section 1. This scenario merges two taxonomies classifying European cars in different ways.
– **Computers:** Two small product catalogs of different computer and hardware shops are to be merged. One input ontology classifies products first by manufacturer (e.g., *Dell* or *HP*) and then by product type (e.g., *Laptops*, *Accessories*, etc.) while the second input uses the opposite order.
– **Anatomy Subset:** This is a small subset of the fourth scenario (Anatomy) and includes multiple inheritance. It merges part of the subgraph describing *"Eye Muscle"* in the Mouse Anatomy to the subgraph describing an equivalent concept in the NCI Thesaurus.
– **Anatomy:** Anatomy is the full match scenario with multiple inheritance proposed by the OAEI [1] that merges the Adult-Mouse Anatomy (over 2,700 concepts) with the anatomical part of the NCI Thesaurus (NCIT) (about 3,300 concepts).
– **EBay:** eBay scenario merges different versions of the eBay product catalog containing on average more than 22,000 concepts organized in a tree structure.

4.3 Evaluation of Test Scenarios

We used PROMPT and ATOM to solve the introduced test scenarios. Since ATOM is fully automatic while PROMPT strongly requires user interaction to generate the integrated ontology, we have not compared the user effort needed to build the final result and we simulate an automatic algorithm with PROMPT manually discarding all wrong suggestions. Except for large size scenarios we were able to generate a full merge solution using PROMPT. On the other side, ATOM implements both a full merge and an asymmetric target-driven algorithm; a source-driven merge solution can be easily generated by changing the source and the target in the input of the algorithm. In addition to the full merge solution we will also evaluate the source-driven and target-driven solutions produced by ATOM. For the three small-sized scenarios we also determined manually an expert solution for comparison.

We summarize the coverage, compactness and redundancy results of our experiments in Table 1. We show results for three mentioned automatic merge approaches; an expert solution could only be evaluated for the first three scenarios. We observe that the symmetric full merge and the expert solutions always achieve a complete coverage of 1. The asymmetric solutions achieve a complete coverage only for their preferred input ontology but do not include some concepts from the other ontology to avoid introducing redundancy. As a result their overall coverage is somewhat reduced, albeit merely by 1-2% for the real-life scenarios *Anatomy* and *eBay*. All determined merge solutions preserve all leaf concepts that typically carry instance objects.

About the compactness, we note that the symmetric merge solutions determine the largest result ontology in all scenarios. In particular, for our *Cars* scenario we had additional concepts in the merge result leading to a compactness of 1.2. Similar than for

Table 1. Summary of Experiments

		Coverage				Compactness		Redundancy	
		Source	Target	Leaf	Overall	Abs. Size	Rel. Size	# Leaf Paths	Relative
Cars	Full Merge	1	1	1	1	10	(1)	8	1.33
	Source-driven	1	0.67	1	0.83	9	0.9	6	1
	Target-driven	0.86	1	1	0.93	8	0.8	6	1
	Expert Result	1	1	1	1	12	1.2	6	1
Computers	Full Merge	1	1	1	1	20	(1)	13	1.3
	Source-driven	1	0.86	1	0.93	18	0.9	10	1
	Target-driven	0.9	1	1	0.95	19	0.95	10	1
	Expert Result	1	1	1	1	20	1	10	1
AnatomySubset	Full Merge	1	1	1	1	9	(1)	7	2.33
	Source-driven	1	0.83	1	0.91	8	0.89	3	1
	Target-driven	0.33	1	1	0.66	8	0.89	3	1
	Expert Result	1	1	1	1	9	1	3	1
Anatomy	Full Merge	1	1	1	1	4.5K	(1)	14K	1.94
	Source-driven	1	0.97	1	0.98	4.4K	0.98	7.2K	1
	Target-driven	0.96	1	1	0.98	4.4K	0.98	7.2K	1
eBay	Full Merge	1	1	1	1	23.3K	(1)	21.5K	1.05
	Source-driven	1	0.99	1	0.99	23.2K	0.99	20.4K	1
	Target-driven	0.99	1	1	0.99	23.2K	0.99	20.4K	1

coverage, the asymmetric solutions achieve smaller values than 1 albeit merely by 1-2% for the real-life scenarios *Anatomy* and *eBay*.

More significant differences result for the redundancy evaluation which is primarily influenced by the number of paths to leafs and thus to how concepts are organized and connected within ontologies. In Table 1 we report both the absolute number of leaf paths for the merge solutions as well as their relative redundancy. We observe that the Full Merge approach produces a substantial amount of redundancy and semantic overlap even for the real-life test cases. The relative redundancy is especially severe (factor 1.94 and 2.33) for the two anatomy scenarios exhibiting multiple inheritance. By contrast, the manually determined expert solutions avoid redundancy altogether although they cover both input ontologies completely and may include additional concepts (as for the first scenario). The asymmetric solutions of ATOM are also able to achieve the optimal relative redundancy of 1, but in a fully automatic way and even for the large real-life scenarios.

5 Conclusions

We proposed the use of general metrics to evaluate the quality of ontology merging solutions such as the relative coverage of the input ontologies, the compactness of the merge result and the degree of introduced redundancy. We found these metrics useful to evaluate different symmetric and asymmetric merge approaches for diverse test cases of different size and complexity. We observed that straight-forward symmetric merge approaches can achieve a complete coverage (information preservation) of the input ontologies but are generally too large due to the introduction of a significant semantic overlap and redundant paths, e.g. when compared to manually specified expert solutions. We thus see a need for improved symmetric merge approaches that achieve automatically a reduced degree of redundancy. Asymmetric merge approaches completely cover (preserve) only one of the input ontologies as useful for many applications. The evaluation showed that these approaches only miss 1-2% of the input concepts in real-life scenarios but achieve a perfect relative redundancy. This means that they successfully avoid introducing semantic overlap in the merge result and thus improve its understandability.

References

1. The Ontology Alignment Evaluation Initiative,
   http://oaei.ontologymatching.org
2. Alexe, B., Tan, W., Velegrakis, Y.: STBenchmark: Towards a Benchmark for Mapping Systems. Proc. of the VLDB Endowment 1(1), 230–244 (2008)
3. Bellahsene, Z., Bonifati, A., Rahm, E. (eds.): Schema Matching and Mapping. Springer (2011)
4. Duchateau, F., Bellahsene, Z.: Measuring the Quality of an Integrated Schema. In: Parsons, J., Saeki, M., Shoval, P., Woo, C., Wand, Y. (eds.) ER 2010. LNCS, vol. 6412, pp. 261–273. Springer, Heidelberg (2010)
5. Giunchiglia, F., Shvaiko, P., Yatskevich, M.: S-Match: an Algorithm and an Implementation of Semantic Matching. In: Bussler, C.J., Davies, J., Fensel, D., Studer, R. (eds.) ESWS 2004. LNCS, vol. 3053, pp. 61–75. Springer, Heidelberg (2004)
6. Guzmán-Arenas, A., Cuevas-Rasgado, A.-D.: Knowledge Accumulation through Automatic Merging of Ontologies. Expert Syst. Appl. 37(3), 1991–2005 (2010)
7. Kotis, K., Vouros, G.A.: The HCONE Approach to Ontology Merging. In: Bussler, C.J., Davies, J., Fensel, D., Studer, R. (eds.) ESWS 2004. LNCS, vol. 3053, pp. 137–151. Springer, Heidelberg (2004)
8. Lambrix, P., Tan, H.: SAMBO-A System for Aligning and Merging Biomedical Ontologies. Journal of Web Semantics 4, 196–206 (2006)
9. McGuinness, D.L., Fikes, R., Rice, J., Wilder, S.: An Environment for Merging and Testing Large Ontologies. In: KR, pp. 483–493 (2000)
10. Noy, N.F., Musen, M.A.: PROMPT: Algorithm and Tool for Automated Ontology Merging and Alignment. In: AAAI/IAAI, pp. 450–455 (2000)
11. Pottinger, R.A., Bernstein, P.A.: Merging Models Based on Given Correspondences. In: VLDB, pp. 862–873 (2003)
12. Radwan, A., Popa, L., Stanoi, I.R., Younis, A.A.: Top-K Generation of Integrated Schemas Based on Directed and Weighted Correspondences. In: SIGMOD, pp. 641–654 (2009)
13. Rahm, E.: Towards Large Scale Schema and Ontology Matching. In: Schema Matching and Mapping, ch. 1, pp. 3–27. Springer (2011)
14. Raunich, S., Rahm, E.: Target-driven Merging of Taxonomies. Technical report. University of Leipzig (2010)
15. Raunich, S., Rahm, E.: ATOM: Automatic Target-driven Ontology Merging. In: Proc. of ICDE (2011)
16. Saleem, K., Bellahsene, Z., Hunt, E.: PORSCHE: Performance ORiented SCHEma mediation. Inf. Syst. 33(7-8), 637–657 (2008)
17. Thau, D., Bowers, S., Ludäscher, B.: Merging Taxonomies under RCC-5 Algebraic Articulations. In: ONISW, pp. 47–54 (2008)

System Definition
of the Business/Enterprise Model

Nataliya Pankratova[1], Oleksandr Maistrenko[2], and Pavlo Maslianko[2]

[1] Institute for Applied System Analysis,
National Technical University of Ukraine "KPI"
natalidmp@gmail.com
[2] Applied Mathematics Faculty, National Technical University of Ukraine "KPI"
{o.maistrenko,p.maslianko}@selab.kpi.ua

Abstract. Business and enterprise modeling has gained its momentum. Today, there are various approaches that allow describing an enterprise from different points of view. However, it is not possible to cope with the growing variety of the heterogeneous models without a clear and well-defined approach. This paper proposes the system definition of the business/enterprise models based on the systems analysis and the general system theory. This definition is verified by four examples of the existing business/enterprise models given by different authors and widely used both in academia and industry.

1 Introduction

Business modeling is considered to be a "managerial equivalent of the scientific method" [1]. A scientific method requires a sound foundation, however, there is no single definition of the business/enterprise model that is accepted by the research community and industry as a standard [2–5]. It is often the case that the business/enterprise model is defined in terms of some domain where this model emerges, and, thus, it cannot be understood by all the stakeholders of the enterprise. It is commonly agreed that the business model describes the enterprises' nature and might show a way to gain a competitive advantage [6]. The lack of such information on the managerial's table doesn't lead to a failure, but rather to an inefficient use of the existing enterprises' resources. Moreover, the business/enterprise model plays an important role in different projects executed in the enterprise, such as enterprise engineering and enterprise integration [7].

This paper shows how the business/enterprise model can be defined using the systems analysis [8] and the general system theory [9]. We propose to represent a business/enterprise model as the system of interconnected views (representations) [10]. The features selected by the stakeholders determine these views. Such multi-view implementation of the business/enterprise model is driven by a necessity to show a single enterprise-object from multiple points of view. Our definition of the business/enterprise model could be regarded as a meta-definition in the sense of meta-modeling. We show examples of the enterprise features that

P. Herrero et al. (Eds.): OTM 2012 Workshops, LNCS 7567, pp. 134–143, 2012.

might have been chosen in the existing definitions of the business/enterprise model [2, 11–13].

This paper is structured as follows. Section 2 revisits the basics of the systems analysis and the systems theory. Section 3 presents a system theory based definition of the business/enterprise model. Section 4 provides an evaluation of the proposed definition on four examples. Section 5 gives an overview on the state of the art in the business/enterprise modeling, while Section 6 concludes the paper.

2   What Is a System and Systems Analysis?

Systems analysis [8] is an applied scientific methodology that is based on a variety of mathematical methods and procedures, and provides guidance on how to study the object under research by developing an interdisciplinary knowledge about it. The systems analysis takes into consideration conflicting goals, existing risks, and the incompleteness of the information about the object under research and its environment. The core idea of this methodology is to create a new "dimension" when doing research or solving a problem by adding the systems aspect [14]. This aspect unifies the knowledge about the properties of the object, the information about its relations with other objects within some environment, and the internal relations between the parts of the object.

The main concept in the systems analysis is the notion of a system. This paper uses the following definition [10]: *system* $S = (E, R)$ is a structure containing a set of *entities* E and a set of *relations* $R \subseteq E^n$ between these entities. The system is more than just a set of its entities, because of the *synergy* effect. This effect causes the system to have some new features that are not provided by the set of disjoint entities [15].

The system, its entities and relations have some *features* (*properties*). The feature is a pair $f = (k, v)$, where k is a definition of the feature, and v is its value for a given system, entity or relation. The values of k and v are not limited to a particular notion or domain, and depend purely on the system under consideration and the problem being solved.

Consider an enterprise represented as a system, then one of the features of its entities is a function of the entity within the enterprise $f_F = (k_F, v_F)$. So, k_F is defined as "the function of the entity within the enterprise". The value can be given in a textual form (e.g., "production", "marketing", "finance"), or in a form of a process showing how the inputs are transformed into the outputs (e.g., a business process diagram [16]). However, a good practice would be using a single modeling notion to express the values of each feature. The values of different features might be expressed in different notions. Such practice arises due to the need to compare the system's entities based on the selected features. Therefore the values should be comparable, preferably in a single notion to avoid a comparison of apples and oranges.

Based on the features of the system, we define a *view* on the system S as a transition function $P : (S, F) \rightarrow (E, R)$, where F is a set of features [10].

The system is split into entities based on the selected features, and all the entities have pairwise different values of these features. Splitting a system into smaller parts, and working with a partial system's representation (view) is one of the systems analysis foundations [8]. The views of the same system can be ordered. The ordering allows discovering a set of features defining the smallest entities of the system, i.e., the essence of the system in a classical way [9]. Moreover, the ordering also allows determining the smallest set of features required to represent the system under analysis given the setup of the problem.

Using an already described feature f_F, we can define a view $P(S, \{f_F\})$ for an enterprise S. Having chosen a textual notion for the value of the feature, we create a functional structure of the enterprise [17]. When choosing a business process description as a value of the feature, we create a process based organizational structure [18]. This example shows a need for the precise definition of the used features, and a proper selection of the notion for their values.

The features of the system and the feature-based views on the system are the fundamentals of the business/enterprise model definition presented in the next Section.

3   The Business/Enterprise Model

There is no single definition of the business/enterprise model [2–5]. However, there is a common understanding that such model should present the enterprise to its stakeholders by means of showing some particular aspects or dimensions of the enterprise. These aspects can be expressed based on the features of the enterprise and its entities.

The business model and the enterprise model can be regarded as synonyms [19] or different terms [5], and the relation between them requires a separate research that is beyond the scope of this paper. However, recently the term "business model" is more frequently used in the literature. Therefore, this paper uses the term "business model" to refer to both business and enterprise models.

The business model can be defined as a system derived from the enterprise. The entities of this system are the views on the enterprise that are defined by the selected features.

Definition 1. *Business model $BM(S)$ for the enterprise S is a system, whose entities p_i are the views on the enterprise based on the subset $F_{BM}^{(i)}$ of the enterprise's features F_S.*

$$BM(S) = \left(\left\{ p_i = P\left(S, F_{BM}^{(i)}\right) | F_{BM}^{(i)} \subseteq F_S \right\}, R_{BM} \right)$$

Definition 1 could be regarded as a meta-definition of the business model in the sense of meta-modeling. It allows defining a specific business model by choosing a set of features required for analysis of the enterprise in the specific situation. The views of the business model in Definition 1 are conceptualizations. They only define enterprise's entities and relations between them in a formal way, but don't show their essence. Therefore, the views should be implemented using some modeling tool before they can be used in the discussion with the stakeholders (e.g., by means of mathematical, graphical, or descriptional models). For example, UML can be used as a modeling tool for implementation of the views. The result will be UML class diagrams with the organizational entities being classes, and associations being relations between them. Another possibility to implement the views is to use a kind of descriptional model (i.e., textual description containing non-standardized block diagrams). The latter is better accepted and often used by the management.

Figure 1 summarizes the previous discussion around the given definition of the business model. For the sake of simplicity, we have shown only one business model, but there might be multiple depending on the set of selected features. For each view there might be also different implementations. Note that we distinguish between two types of relations among the entities in Figure 1: dependency and realization.

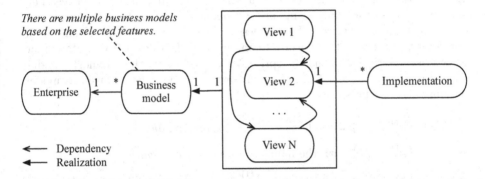

Fig. 1. Relations between the enterprise and its business model

Let's show an example of a business model for the enterprise. Every enterprise has an organizational structure [17], and we can select a structural feature $f_S = (k_S, v_S)$ to build the business model. The business model is $BM(S) = (\{p_S\}, R_{BM})$, where $p_S = P(S, \{f_S\})$. The definition k_S is "the organizational role of the entity in the enterprise". The view p_S contains the organizational entities of the enterprise and the relations between them (e.g., the values v_S for the entities will be "an institute", "a faculty", and "a chair" in a university, when a university is regarded as an enterprise).

4   Evaluation

Definition 1 allows inspecting the features that have been possibly selected to create existing definitions of the business model. We have selected four examples of the business model definitions described in the literature [2, 11–13]. The models have been chosen for the following reasons. The definition given in [2] is popular in the scientific community, and at the moment of writing this paper has been cited more than 430 times. Schief and Buxmann [11] apply this model to the software engineering domain, and make an empirical verification of their definition. Osterwalder and Pigneur [12] have proposed another definition of the business model that has been co-created by 470 members of the Business Model Innovation Hub. And the last selected definition is a "classical" enterprise architecture work by Zachman [13]. As discussed in [5], the enterprise architecture is a business model, though it is not referred to as such.

The evaluation goes as follows. First, we describe the definition of the business model. After that, we give a possible set of features that might have been used for the definition, and show the correspondence between the definition in the business model and Definition 1.

Example 1. The unified perspective on the business model [2] consists of six "components". Each component is defined in a form of a question to an enterprise, and the answer could be given it terms of component's properties. The relations between the components are not defined, though the components describe the same enterprise. The business model has three levels (foundation, proprietary, and rules) that form a hierarchy, and drill down from an abstract to a precise description of the enterprise. We consider only the top most foundation level. A possible set of features that drove creation of this business model contains three features:

- $f_1^{(1)} = \left(k_1^{(1)}, v_1^{(1)}\right)$ with the name $k_1^{(1)}$ *"customers/outputs"*
- $f_2^{(1)} = \left(k_2^{(1)}, v_2^{(1)}\right)$ with the name $k_2^{(1)}$ *"competitors/market"*
- $f_3^{(1)} = \left(k_3^{(1)}, v_3^{(1)}\right)$ with the name $k_3^{(1)}$ *"internal processes of the enterprise"*

In terms of our approach, the "component" can be mapped to a view, and the business model is defined as $BM(S) = (\{p_i\}, R_{BM})$, where $p_i = (S, F_i)$, and $i = \overline{1,6}$. The relations between the views p_i should be captured in the set R_{BM}. So, the views-components are built using the following features:

1. Component "how do we create value?":$F_1 = \left\{f_1^{(1)}, f_3^{(1)}\right\}$

2. Component "who do we create value for?": $F_2 = \left\{f_1^{(1)}\right\}$

3. Component "what is our source of competence?": $F_3 = \left\{f_3^{(1)}\right\}$

4. Component "how do we competitively position ourselves?": $F_4 = \left\{f_2^{(1)}\right\}$

5. Component "how we make money?": $F_5 = \left\{f_1^{(1)}, f_2^{(1)}\right\}$

6. Component "what are our time, scope and size ambitions?": $F_6 = \left\{f_1^{(1)}, f_2^{(1)}\right\}$

This business model provides quite interesting insights on the enterprise by using various combinations of features when building the views.

Example 2. In [11], authors propose a software industry specific business model containing 5 groups and 20 elements. The business model is specific for the software industry, and it is based on multiple other definitions, including [2]. This business model definition is similar to Example 1 in its descriptive approach, and also doesn't specify the relations between its groups. A possible set of features to characterize the groups contains three features:

- $f_1^{(2)} = \left(k_1^{(2)}, v_1^{(2)} \right)$ with the name $k_1^{(2)}$ *"technical?"*
- $f_2^{(2)} = \left(k_2^{(2)}, v_2^{(2)} \right)$ with the name $k_2^{(2)}$ *"enterprise or software related?"*
- $f_3^{(2)} = \left(k_3^{(2)}, v_3^{(2)} \right)$ with the name $k_3^{(2)}$ *"strategical or operational?"*

The groups can be mapped to the views, and the elements are the entities of these views in terms of our approach. So, the business model is $BM(S) = \left(P \left(S, \left\{ f_1^{(2)}, f_2^{(2)}, f_3^{(2)} \right\} \right), R_{BM} \right)$. Each view has been created using all the features, and they have the following values $(f_1^{(2)}; f_2^{(2)}; f_3^{(2)})$:

1. Group "strategy": non technical; enterprise and software related; strategical
2. Group "revenue": non technical; enterprise and software related; operational
3. Group "upstream': technical; software related; operational
4. Group "downstream": non technical; enterprise related; operational
5. Group "usage": non technical; software related; operational

This business model definition could be regarded as a set of views on the enterprise along three different axes identified by the selected features.

Example 3. The business model proposed by Osterwalder and Pigneur [12] gives an insight into the nature of the business model. It consists of nine building blocks that are organized on a so called canvas: customer segments (CS), value propositions (VP), channels (CH), customer relationships (CR), revenue streams (RS), key resources (KR), key activities (KA), key partnerships (KP), and cost structure (CS). These building blocks are connected in a complicated way. The relations between these blocks are implicitly defined in the business model. Such specification qualitatively improves the business model, and positively distinguishes it from Examples 1 and 2. The blocks and the structure of the business model are shown in Figure 2.

A possible set of features that inspired the creation of this business model definition is:

- $f_1^{(3)} = \left(k_1^{(3)}, v_1^{(3)} \right)$ with the name $k_1^{(3)}$ *"does the view reflect financial sides of the enterprise?"* and possible values $v_1^{(3)} \in \{yes, no\}$
- $f_2^{(3)} = \left(k_2^{(3)}, v_2^{(3)} \right)$ with the name $k_2^{(3)}$ *"what is the target of the view?"* and possible values $v_2^{(3)} \in \{company, customer, both\}$
- $f_3^{(3)} = \left(k_3^{(3)}, v_3^{(3)} \right)$ with the name $k_3^{(3)}$ *"does it belong to an enterprise (is it managed by an enterprise)?"* and possible values $v_3^{(3)} \in \{yes, no\}$

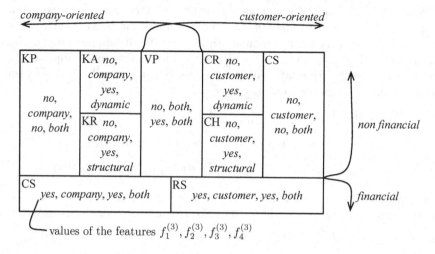

Fig. 2. The entities of the business model proposed in [12] with the values of the features $f_1^{(3)}$, $f_2^{(3)}$, $f_3^{(3)}$, and $f_4^{(3)}$

- $f_4^{(3)} = \left(k_4^{(3)}, v_4^{(3)} \right)$ with the name $k_4^{(3)}$ "*type of the view?*" and possible values $v_3^{(3)} \in \{structural, dynamic, both\}$

The building blocks of the business model can be mapped to the view in our approach, so $BM(S) = \left(P \left(S, \left\{ f_1^{(3)}, f_2^{(3)}, f_3^{(3)}, f_4^{(3)} \right\} \right), R_{BM} \right)$. The values of these features for each entity are shown in Figure 2.

Example 4. Zachman [13] proposes a set of views on the enterprise in a form of a table that is called the Zachman framework. This is a 6 times 6 table formed by an intersection of communication questions (what, how, when, who, where, and why) and reification transformations (identification, definition, representation, specification, configuration, and instantiation). Lately, the reification transformations have been mapped to the audience perspectives [20].

The business model according to this framework contains six views corresponding to the audience perspective, and they can be also considered as views in our approach, so $BM(S) = (\{p_i\}, R_{BM})$, where $i = \overline{1,6}$. The feature that has been chosen to define this set of views is a "*level of detalization*" with the values ranging from *a high-level perspective* to *a very detailed* one. Each view consists of six entities that correspond to the communication questions, namely $p_i = \left(\left\{ e_{what}^i, e_{how}^i, e_{when}^i, e_{who}^i, e_{where}^i, e_{why}^i \right\}, R_{p_i} \right)$. The relations between the entities inside the view differ depending on the view.

Evaluation Summary. We have selected four business models that are coming from different backgrounds. We have given examples of the features that might have been used to define these business models, and, thus, these definitions can be formalized using Definition 1. Note that there might exist other ways to identify the features of the presented business models.

The examples have shown that it is possible to formalize the business model as a system of views or components of an enterprise. However, in practice, these views are often isolated, and the relations between them are not defined at all, though they target the same enterprise.

After the analysis of the features that might have driven to the creation of the business model, it is possible to reveal the necessity of using the ideas from UML, systems analysis [8] and the system theory of technology [21] in order to separate the identified features into groups. The examples of such groups are static, dynamic, use case, and control features. These groups allow to pre-define a set of possible features that can be used when defining a specific business model, and, thus, provide a possible guidance to the unified definition of the business/enterprise model.

5   Related Work

The definition of the business model has been widely discussed both in academia and industry [2–5]. Recent literature review [3, 4] has revealed the rise and the growing importance of the business modeling domain since early 1990s. However, there is no single definition of the business model, possibly due to the fact that this field is relatively young, and still in a rapid evolution phase.

The variety of the business models tries to cover the variety of the existing enterprises. This is typically achieved by a definition of the industry specific models, e.g., software industry [11], e-commerce [22], and utility services [23]. Such models are created as a result of the detailed analysis of the selected industry, and it is not easy to reapply them in a different context (i.e., in a different industry). Moreover, these models are empirical, and, hence, don't take into consideration the knowledge from the theory of the firm [17]. To build an adequate business model, it is required to integrate this knowledge into the business model definition. In our approach this can be done by a proper selection of the features when building the business model.

In [5], authors make first steps towards a unified definition of the business model by defining two levels: a metamodel and a model of the enterprise. The metamodel shows the elements belonging to a business model, and the model is an instance of the business model for the specific enterprise. However, the methodology for definition of such metamodel hasn't been described. We cover this gap by using the meta-modeling mechanisms and the system theory [24].

Another possible tooling for creating a concept and an instance of the business model is an ontology [25]. Ontology is a very powerful tool because it accepts the object under research as an open system, and allows defining the missing elements. However, the core of the ontology is defined empirically, as in the other works discussed previously.

There is a common tendency to define the business models using two notions [4]: a component [26] as a building block of the business model, and a point of view [27] that represents the enterprise from different perspectives. However, these concepts haven't been formalized to form a crisp and generic business model definition. Our work extensively uses these concepts having formalized them by means of the system theory [8, 9, 21].

In [28], authors apply the general system theory to the enterprise in order to analyze the enterprise architecture. The enterprise is interpreted as a socio-technical system, and the elements of the enterprise architecture are mapped to the concepts of the socio-technical system. The authors describe the motivation of application of the systems theory to the enterprise. However, their work is limited to the enterprise architecture.

In summary, the definition of the business model has been given from different perspectives and in various contexts. The idea of separating the business model into multiple conceptual layers has been discussed. However, to the best of the authors' knowledge there is no in-depth analysis of the business model with regards to the general system theory from a scientific perspective.

6   Conclusion

This paper proposes an application of the systems analysis and the general system theory to the business modeling domain. It presents a (meta-)definition of the business model, and shows its correlation with the existing definitions of the business model. Such feature-based definition allows a system representation of the enterprise that can be plugged into various enterprise frameworks. The roles of the features are manifold: they are the levels of the enterprise's formalization process, and can be also used for model validation. The evaluation has shown the rationality of such approach and has identified missing points in some definitions. It is often the case that the business model definitions represent the business model as a set of views, but don't consider the relations between them. Our future work will focus on the deep analysis of the features that drive creation of the business model definitions. Such set of features could be a possible way to the unified definition of the business/enterprise model.

References

1. Magretta, J.: Why business models matter. Harvard Business Review 80(5), 86–92 (2002)
2. Morris, M., Schindehutte, M., Allen, J.: The entrepreneur's business model: toward a unified perspective. Journal of Business Research 58(6), 726–735 (2005)
3. Zott, C., Amit, R., Massa, L.: The business model: Recent developments and future research. Journal of Management 37(4), 1019–1042 (2011)
4. Burkhart, T., Krumeich, J., Werth, D., Loos, P.: Analyzing the business model concept — a comprehensive classification of literature. In: Proceedings of the International Conference on Information Systems, ICIS 2011, Association for Information Systems (2011)
5. Osterwalder, A., Pigneur, Y., Tucci, C.L.: Clarifying business models: Origins, present and future of the concept. CAIS 15, 751–775 (2005)

6. Pohle, G., Chapman, M.: IBM's global CEO report 2006: business model innovation matters. Strategy & Leadership 34(5), 34–40 (2006)
7. Panetto, H., Molina, A.: Enterprise integration and interoperability in manufacturing systems: Trends and issues. Computers in Industry 59(7), 641–646 (2008)
8. Zgurovsky, M.Z., Pankratova, N.D.: System Analysis: Theory and Applications (Data and Knowledge in a Changing World). Springer (2007)
9. Bertalanffy, L.: General System Theory: Foundations, Development, Applications, Revised edn. George Braziller, Inc. (1969)
10. Maslianko, P., Maistrenko, O.: Enterprise business engineering. Research Bulletin of the National Technical University of Ukraine "Kyiv Polytechnic Institute" 75(1), 69–78 (2011)
11. Schief, M., Buxmann, P.: Business models in the software industry. In: Proceedings of 45th Hawaii International International Conference on Systems Science (HICSS-45 2012), pp. 3328–3337. IEEE Computer Society (2012)
12. Osterwalder, A., Pigneur, Y.: Business Model Generation: A Handbook for Visionaries, Game Changers, and Challengers, 1st edn. Wiley (2010)
13. Zachman, J.A.: A framework for information systems architecture. IBM Syst. J. 38(2-3), 454–470 (1999)
14. Klir, G.J.: The emergence of two-dimensional science in the information society. Systems Research 2(1), 33–41 (1985)
15. Anderson, P.W.: More is different. Science 177(4047), 393–396 (1972)
16. Weske, M.: Business process management concepts, languages, architectures. 1 edn. Springer (2007)
17. Daft, R.L.: Organization Theory and Design, 10th edn. South-Western College Pub. (2009)
18. Hammer, M., Stanton, S.: How process enterprises really work. Harvard Businsess Review 77(6), 108–118 (1999)
19. Katz, R.L.: Business/enterprise modeling. IBM Systems Journal 29(4), 509–525 (1990)
20. Zachman, J.A.: John Zachman's Concise Definition of The Zachman Framework (2008), http://www.zachman.com/about-the-zachman-framework
21. Ropohl, G.: Allgemeine Technologie. Eine Systemtheorie der Technik, 3rd edn. Universitätsverlag Karlsruhe. München, Wien (2009)
22. Timmers, P.: Business models for electronic markets. Electronic Markets 8, 3–8 (1998)
23. Rappa, M.A.: The utility business model and the future of computing services. IBM Systems Journal 43(1), 32–42 (2004)
24. Maslianko, P.P., Maistrenko, A.S.: A system of entities for enterprise business models. Cybernetics and Systems Analysis 48(1), 99–107 (2012)
25. Dietz, J.L.G., Hoogervorst, J.A.P.: Enterprise ontology in enterprise engineering. In: Proceedings of the 2008 ACM Symposium on Applied Computing, SAC 2008, pp. 572–579. ACM (2008)
26. Onetti, A., Zucchella, A., Jones, M., McDougall-Covin, P.: Internationalization, innovation and entrepreneurship: business models for new technology-based firms. Journal of Management and Governance, 1–32 (2010)
27. Samavi, R., Yu, E., Topaloglou, T.: Strategic reasoning about business models: a conceptual modeling approach. Information Systems and E-Business Management 7(2), 171–198 (2009)
28. Kloeckner, S., Birkmeier, D.: Something Is Missing: Enterprise Architecture from a Systems Theory Perspective. In: Dan, A., Gittler, F., Toumani, F. (eds.) ICSOC/ServiceWave 2009. LNCS, vol. 6275, pp. 22–34. Springer, Heidelberg (2010)

Semantic and Structural Annotations
for Comprehensive Model Analysis

Axel Hahn and Sabina El Haoum

University of Oldenburg, 26111 Oldenburg, Germany
{hahn,elhaoum}@wi-ol.de

Abstract. Nowadays enterprise models exist in a variety of types and are based mostly on graphical modeling languages, prominent examples being UML and BPMN. Model relations oftentimes are not made explicit and are hard to analyze. As a consequence, the information integration and interoperability potential of existing enterprise models cannot be exploited efficiently. This paper presents an approach, where based on annotations the model-contained information is made accessible for further processing. Multiple dimensions of the model (i.e. semantic and structural) are considered, allowing a comprehensive view on the model-contained information. Based on that, inter-model relations can be discovered and analyzed.

Keywords: enterprise modeling, inter-model links, semantic annotation.

1 Introduction

Enterprise modeling is concerned with the creation of conceptual models representing the structure and behavior of the fundamental elements of an enterprise or organization. Examples of such fundamental elements are processes, products, humans, applications, goals, policies. The aims of enterprise modeling are [1]:

- To externalize the enterprise knowledge and gain insight into its structure and behavior.
- To support change management and the applicability of enterprise engineering methods.
- To control and monitor enterprise operations.

While the first aim can be generalized as description of the enterprise, the second targets the design of the enterprise and the third its management.

Zikra et al. argue that enterprise models (EM) lay the cornerstone to model driven development (MDD) of information systems, namely "EM provides the context for high level requirements, which in turn are the input to MDD" [2].

As conceptual models in general also enterprise models facilitate the human communication about complex systems [3]. Additionally, the model creation process has an impact on organizations and their commitment to the modeling results. Therefore some authors advocate the participative enterprise modeling approach, i.e. modeling in facilitated group sessions [4].

P. Herrero et al. (Eds.): OTM 2012 Workshops, LNCS 7567, pp. 144–153, 2012.
© Springer-Verlag Berlin Heidelberg 2012

Consistent and inter-related enterprise models are an important driver for integration and interoperability; their essential role in this respect has long been acknowledged [5], [6], [1]. In practice, this potential cannot be exploited efficiently as:

- The existing enterprise models exist in a variety of types
- The inter-model relations oftentimes are not made explicit.

Due to economic pressure the trend for agile and lean enterprises prevails. This requires *intra-integration* (i.e. process integration within enterprises to ensure "consistent overall operations of the enterprise with respect to its business objectives" [6] p.7) and *inter-integration* (i.e. integration of processes among different enterprises along the supply chain or in virtual enterprises).

This paper presents an approach, where based on annotations the model-contained information is made accessible for further processing. The aim is to explicitly state the information captured in enterprise models by considering its multiple dimensions (i.e. semantic and structural). Based on that, inter-model relations can be discovered and analyzed in a systematic way. The results are used to support model alignment and serve enterprise integration.

The next section gives an overview of the related work. Section 3 defines some basic terminology and describes how a comprehensive explication of model-contained information can benefit from meta models and ontologies. The proposed approach is presented in section 4. Section 5 provides a use case demonstration. Finally, section 6 draws a conclusion.

2   Related Work

Semantic technologies in the context of modeling have been subject of intensive research in recent years. Beyond model annotations for the purpose of information system integration, Liao et al. [7] identify several applications of semantic annotations in different domains (e.g. XML Schema annotations for XML documents transformation, annotation of Web Service descriptions for the purpose of service discovery and composition). Agt et al. [8] focus in their work on the semantic conflict analysis of different models at different abstraction levels (business process, interfaces, respectively CIM, PSM/PIM) of the Model Driven Architecture (MDA) approach. Bräuer and Lochmann [9], [10] investigate the benefit of semantic technologies in the Model Driven Software Development (MDSD) with multiple domain-specific languages.

Several works concentrate specifically on business process models. Belonging to this group, in his ongoing work Fellmann [11] examines the annotation of process model semantics and structure. Missikoff et al. [12], [13] also focus on process models, which they represent in terms of the BPAL (Business Process Abstract Language). In contrast to this work, the process oriented approaches do not allow the broader perspective on all aspects of the enterprise.

The work described in [14] and [15] emphasizes interoperability of enterprise models for the purpose of model exchange and formulates the need for effective tool support of the annotation process. The Astar (sometimes also written as A*) annotation tool [16] represents one tool for model annotation.

Meta model integration of enterprise models has also been described in the literature. In [17] an object oriented meta model is used as integration vehicle for heterogeneous modeling languages. This type of work however does not include the domain semantic perspective.

A further line of research related to this work is the field of model comparison. In this context Gerke et al. investigate the compliance of process models with reference models [18]. One of the issues identified by them is the difficulty to overcome different levels of detail in the compared models. In this respect, the work presented here takes advantage of the semantic methods applied to alleviate this problem.

3   Meta Models and Ontologies in Externalization of Models

After introducing the basic terminology, this section explains the different dimension of model-contained information as well as the role of meta models and ontologies in externalization of models.

3.1   Basic Terminology

Conceptual Models, Modeling Language, Meta Model. As stated in the introduction enterprise models are *conceptual models*, i.e. models of cognitive artifacts. The cognitive artifacts are in particular the domain concepts shaping the enterprise as well as descriptions of certain aspects of the enterprise (e.g. business processes), which already exist (descriptive mode) or have to be implemented (prescriptive mode). The models are created using a *modeling language*, which defines a set of modeling artifacts, the valid combinations of these artifacts and their semantics. A *meta model* is a model of a modeling language [19].

Enterprise Interoperability and Integration. Enterprise interoperability and integration are both related terms. In general, interoperability refers to the ability of two systems to function jointly. In the context of networked enterprises, *enterprise interoperability* means the ability of organizations to interact (i.e. exchange information and services) on different levels, like data, services and processes [20]. On the other hand, *enterprise integration* is defined as "process of ensuring the interaction between enterprise entities necessary to achieve enterprise domain objectives"[21]. When relating the terms *enterprise interoperability* and *enterprise integration,* it can be said that components of fully integrated systems are highly interdependent (i.e. not separable) whereas interoperability equates to a loose integration [20].

3.2   Dimensions of Model-Contained Information

The information contained in a conceptual model relates to different dimensions. Also in enterprise modeling it is important to recognize the following dimensions of model-contained information:

1. Modeling artifacts: Which modeling artifacts are used?
2. Type semantics: What is the meaning of these artifacts?
3. Model structure: How are the artifacts arranged?
4. Domain semantics: Which application domain terms are used to label the artifacts?

To illustrate this, the different dimensions are explicated for the example Entity Relationship Model (ERM) shown in Fig. 1.

Fig. 1. Example ERM

Firstly, let us consider the dimension related to the modeling artifacts. In this respect, the example model presents two entities (E1, E2) and a relationship (R1) with associated cardinality (C1, C2). Hence, *entity*, *relationship* and *cardinality* are the modeling artifacts being used. This dimension is illustrated in Fig. 2.

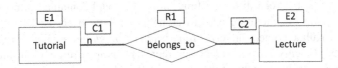

Fig. 2. ERM modeling artifacts used in the example

Secondly, the fact that the two concepts "Tutorial" and "Lecture" are of type *entity* whereas "belongs_to" is of type *relationship* means something. This meaning is referred to as *type semantics*. The type semantics explication for the ERM example is shown in Fig. 3.

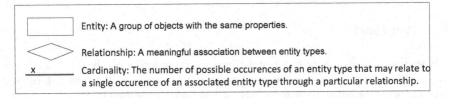

Fig. 3. Type semantics of the ERM example

With respect to the model structure (point number 3), what we learn from the model is that the entities E1 and E2 are related with each other by the relation R1. Further, the cardinality C1 and C2 belong to relation R1.

Finally, the dimension dealing with the domain semantics holds the information about the meaning of the natural language terms used as labels of the model elements. One important piece of information is that both concepts "Tutorial" and "Lecture" are some kinds of university courses, see Fig. 4.

Tutorial: Session of intensive instruction given by a tutor to a small number of students. A specialization of university course.

belongs_to: is attributed to, depends on

Lecture: Teaching form based on a sequence of oral presentations. A specialization of a university course.

Fig. 4. Domain semantics of the labels in the ERM example

3.3   Comprehensive Externalization of Model-Contained Information

The first three dimensions (modeling artifacts, type semantics, and model structure) of model-contained information can be made explicit through the link between the model and its meta model. However, the domain semantics cannot be captured by means of the meta model only. Here ontologies are helpful. A so called *semantic annotation* (i.e. a machine readable link between some domain term and its representation in the domain ontology [15], [22]) allows for adequate explication of the domain semantics dimension of the model.

The distinction between different dimensions of model-contained information has been described in the literature and different terms have been used to describe it. Atkinson and Kühne coined the terms *linguistic metamodeling* and *ontological metamodeling* [23]. *Linguistic metamodeling* in their terminology refers to all information that can be expressed by means of the meta modeling language of a model. What they call *ontological metamodeling* denotes the domain semantics related dimension. Karagiannis and Höfferer use the term *inherent semantics* to refer to the domain semantics dimension of a model [24].

The benefit of using the combination of meta models and ontologies as basis for externalization of model-contained information is argued for in the literature. Karagiannis and Höfferer describe how meta models and ontologies can facilitate the integration of models [24],[25].

4   Approach

This section describes how the model-contained information can be made machine processable by means of semantic and structural annotations. First, high level requirements are formulated. Then the general procedure is presented.

4.1   High Level Requirements

First, the following high level requirements are formulated:

- Req 1: In order to achieve a comprehensive externalization of model-contained information, all dimensions of model-contained information (see section 3.2) have to be taken into account.

- Req. 2: Enterprise models cover different aspects of the enterprise and hence come in a variety of model types; therefore the solution must consider different modeling languages / meta models and be easily extensible with respect to additional modelling languages / meta models.
- Req: 3: The system must be able to process ontologies in some standard ontology language (e.g. OWL[1])
- Req. 4: The system must enable the user to create new annotations, and to view and/or edit already existing ones.
- Req. 5: Based on a reasoning process, the system discovers inter-model relations and realizes their visualization.

4.2   Proposed Solution

The line of action of the proposed solution is the following

1. The meta models of all modeling languages under consideration are formulated in terms of an ontology. For each modeling language the system holds a so called *meta model ontology*.
2. The enterprise models to be analyzed are stored as individuals of their respective meta model ontology.
3. The represented models are subject to a semi-automatic semantic annotation. Based on the state of the art methods (see survey in [26]) annotation candidates are presented to the user, who can accept, modify or reject the proposed annotations and add manual annotations as well. The result of this process are annotations documenting some kind of relation (like equivalence, subsumption) between the artifact labels and concept(s) in a domain ontology. The annotations are stored according to a predefined way determined by the so called *annotation scheme* [14], [15] or *annotation (structure) model* [7],[22].
4. Now the reasoning process is executed. The result is presented in a Matrix Browser [27], where for each pair of models their relations are visualized in a user-friendly way.

5   Use Case Demonstration

To demonstrate a possible use case of the proposed approach, this section presents a simple example from the university domain. In the example setting, based on the model annotations the relation of two models is analyzed in terms of their semantic relation. The first model is the ERM introduced in section 3.2 and the second a process model expressed as Event-driven Process Chain (EPC) [28]. Let the ERM be a portion of the data in a Campus Management Software and the EPC a process description of a reporting procedure.

Following the steps introduced in section 4.2, first the meta model information is considered. For an ERM this means storing it as instantiation of the ERM meta model

---

[1] See http://www.w3.org/TR/owl2-overview/

ontology displayed in Fig. 5. This ontology is composed of the core concepts of the ERM meta model and is based upon the ERM meta model as defined in [29]. For the sake of simplicity more advanced concepts like cardinality, roles and weak entities are omitted here.

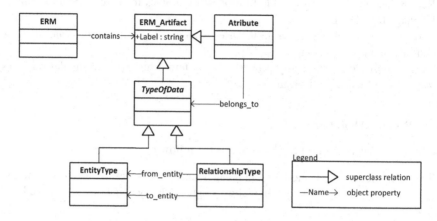

Fig. 5. The core ERM Meta Model Ontology

The instantiation would result in the following representation of the model[2]:

```
1: ClassAssertion ( :ERM :ERMExample)
2: ClassAssertion ( :EntityType :Tutorial)
3: ClassAssertion ( :EntityType :Lecture)
4: ClassAssertion ( :RelationshipType :belongs_to)
5: ObjectPropertyAssertion ( :contains : ERMExample :Tutorial)
6: ObjectPropertyAssertion ( :contains : ERMExample :Lecture)
7: ObjectPropertyAssertion ( :contains : ERMExample :belongs_to)
8: ObjectPropertyAssertion ( :from_entity : belongs_to :Tutorial)
9: ObjectPropertyAssertion ( :to_entity : belongs_to :Lecture)
```

These statements explicate the information related to the first three dimensions:

- modeling artifacts and type semantics (line 1 to line 4)
- model structure (line 5 to line 9).

In the next step the missing domain semantics perspective is added. This process relies on the domain knowledge being modeled in an ontology. In our example this could be an ontology about the university domain. In the simplest case the domain terms used as labels in the ERM ("Lecture" and "Tutorial") can directly be found in the domain ontology, where it also says that both concepts are subclasses of the concept "Course".

---

[2] The notation corresponds to the Functional-Style Syntax of OWL, see
http://www.w3.org/TR/2009/REC-owl2-primer-20091027/

Two semantic annotations candidates are presented to the user: from the label "Tutorial" of the ERM to the concept "Tutorial" in the domain ontology and from the "Lecture" label to the ontology concept "Lecture". The user confirms these annotations.

After executing the reasoning process the inferred inter-model relations are displayed to the user. In our example (see Fig. 6) a semantic relation between the ERM and a process model is discovered. The process model describes how a lecturer reports his teaching activities. The process steps for a lecturer are: (1) "Determine courses taught" and (2) "Determine theses supervised" in the period under report. The process is documented in the system and its elements appear under the abbreviation EPC (Event-driven Process Chain).

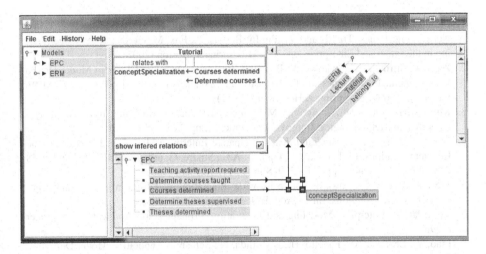

Fig. 6. Visualization of inferred inter- model relations

The model analysis results reveal the relations between the process model and the data model (portion) of the Campus Management Software. In detail, the results disclose that relevant data for the process are located in the Campus Management Software data schema (namely about the lectures and tutorials). At the same time, other process parts are not covered there, as in the ERM fragment presented there is no information about the theses supervision activities.

6   Conclusion

In this paper the basic principle of an approach for comprehensive model analysis has been introduced. The approach relies on semantic and structural model annotations which are used to deduce information about model relations. The expected benefits are

- Explicit model documentation and improved readability
- Enhanced model analysis possibility e.g. with respect to enterprise wide consistency of models

- Inter-model navigation possibility
- Model comparison possibility. Beyond qualitative comparison also quantitative considerations (e.g. which percentage of one model is covered by another model) are relevant.

An exemplary use case has been provided to demonstrate the potential use of the approach. As the work presented here is ongoing, concluding evaluation has to be performed yet.

References

1. Molina, A., Chen, D., Panetto, H., Vernadat, F., Whitman, L.: Enterprise Integration and Networking: Issues, Trends and Vision. In: Bernus, P., Fox, M.S. (eds.) Knowledge Sharing in the Integrated Enterprise, pp. 303–313. Springer, Boston (2005)
2. Zikra, I., Stirna, J., Zdravkovic, J.: Bringing Enterprise Modeling Closer to Model-Driven Development. In: Johannesson, P., Krogstie, J., Opdahl, A.L. (eds.) PoEM 2011. LNBIP, vol. 92, pp. 268–282. Springer, Heidelberg (2011)
3. Kung, C.H., Sølvberg, A.: Activity Modeling and Behavior Modeling. Information Systems Design Methodologies: Improving the Practice. pp. 145–171 (1986)
4. Stirna, J., Persson, A., Sandkuhl, K.: Participative Enterprise Modeling: Experiences and Recommendations. In: Krogstie, J., Opdahl, A.L., Sindre, G. (eds.) CAiSE 2007 and WES 2007. LNCS, vol. 4495, pp. 546–560. Springer, Heidelberg (2007)
5. Weston, R.H.: Steps towards enterprise-wide integration: a definition of need and first-generation open solutions. Int. J. Prod. Res. 31, 2235–2254 (1993)
6. Vernadat, F.: Enterprise Modeling and Integration: Principles and Applications. Springer (1996)
7. Liao, Y., Lezoche, M., Panetto, H., Boudjlida, N.: Semantic Annotation Model Definition for Systems Interoperability. In: OTM 2011 Workshops 2011 - 6th International Workshop on Enterprise Integration, Interoperability and Networking (EI2N), pp. 61–67. Springer, Hersonissos (2011)
8. Agt, H., Bauhoff, G., Kutsche, R.-D., Milanovic, N., Widiker, J.: Semantic Annotation and Conflict Analysis for Information System Integration. In: Hein, C., Wagner, M., Mader, R., Kreis, A., Armengaud, E. (eds.) Model Driven Tool and Process Integration, Proceedings of the Third Workshop on Model-Driven Tool and Process Integration (MDTPI), Paris, France, June 16, pp. 7–18. Fraunhofer FOKUS, Berlin (2011)
9. Lochmann, H.: HybridMDSD: Multi-Domain Engineering with Model-Driven Software Development using Ontological Foundations (2010), http://nbn-resolving.de/urn:nbn:de:bsz:14-qucosa-27380
10. Bräuer, M., Lochmann, H.: An Ontology for Software Models and Its Practical Implications for Semantic Web Reasoning. In: Bechhofer, S., Hauswirth, M., Hoffmann, J., Koubarakis, M. (eds.) ESWC 2008. LNCS, vol. 5021, pp. 34–48. Springer, Heidelberg (2008)
11. Fellmann, M.: Konzeption und Anwendung einer ontologiebasierten Geschäftsprozessmodellierung. In: Eymann, T. (ed.) Tagungsband zum Doctoral Consortium der WI 2011, pp. 40–49 (2011)
12. Missikoff, M., Proietti, M., Smith, F.: Linking ontologies to Business Process Schemas. Consiglio Nazionale Delle Ricerche (CNR), Roma, Italy (2010)

13. Missikoff, M., Proietti, M., Smith, F.: Querying Semantically Enriched Business Processes. In: Hameurlain, A., Liddle, S.W., Schewe, K.-D., Zhou, X. (eds.) DEXA 2011, Part II. LNCS, vol. 6861, pp. 294–302. Springer, Heidelberg (2011)
14. Boudjlida, N., Panetto, H.: Enterprise Semantic Modelling for Interoperability. In: IEEE (eds.) 12th IEEE Conference on Emerging Technologies and Factory Automation, ETFA 2007, pp. 847–854. IEEE, Patras (2007)
15. Boudjlida, N., Panetto, H.: Annotation of Enterprise Models for Interoperability Purposes. In: International Workshop on Advanced Information Systems for Enterprises, pp. 11–17 (2008)
16. Vujasinovic, M., Ivezic, N., Kulvatunyou, B., Barkmeyer, E., Missikoff, M., Taglino, F., Marjanovic, Z., Miletic, I.: Semantic Mediation for Standard-Based B2B Interoperability (2010)
17. Kühn, H., Bayer, F., Junginger, S., Karagiannis, D.: Enterprise Model Integration. In: Bauknecht, K., Tjoa, A.M., Quirchmayr, G. (eds.) E-Commerce and Web Technologies, pp. 379–392. Springer, Heidelberg (2003)
18. Gerke, K., Cardoso, J., Claus, A.: Measuring the Compliance of Processes with Reference Models. In: Meersman, R., Dillon, T., Herrero, P. (eds.) OTM 2009, Part I. LNCS, vol. 5870, pp. 76–93. Springer, Heidelberg (2009)
19. Favre, J.-M.: Megamodelling and Etymology. In: Transformation Techniques in Software Engineering. IBFI, Dagstuhl (2006)
20. Chen, D., Doumeingts, G., Vernadat, F.: Architectures for enterprise integration and interoperability: Past, present and future. Computers in Industry 59, 647–659 (2008)
21. CEN European Committee for Standardization eds.: Enterprise integration - Framework for enterprise modelling (ISO 19439:2006), (2006).
22. Liao, Y., Lezoche, M., Panetto, H., Boudjlida, N.: Why, Where and How to use Semantic Annotation for Systems Interoperability. In: 1st UNITE Doctoral Symposium, Bucarest, Roumanie, pp. 71–78 (2011)
23. Atkinson, C., Kühne, T.: Model-Driven Development: A Metamodeling Foundation. IEEE Software 20, 36–41 (2003)
24. Karagiannis, D., Höfferer, P.: Metamodels in action: An overview. In: Proceedings of the First International Conference on Software and Data Technologies. INSTICC Press (2006)
25. Karagiannis, D., Höfferer, P.: Metamodeling as an Integration Concept. In: Filipe, J., Shishkov, B., Helfert, M. (eds.) Software and Data Technologies, pp. 37–50. Springer (2008)
26. Kalfoglou, Y., Schorlemmer, M.: Ontology Mapping: The State of the Art. In: Kalfoglou, Y., Schorlemmer, M., Sheth, A., Staab, S., Uschold, M. (eds.) Semantic Interoperability and Integration. Internationales Begegnungs- und Forschungszentrum für Informatik (IBFI). Schloss Dagstuhl, Germany (2005)
27. Ziegler, J., Kunz, C., Botsch, V.: Matrix browser: visualizing and exploring large networked information spaces. In: CHI 2002 Extended Abstracts on Human Factors in Computing Systems, pp. 602–603. ACM, New York (2002)
28. Scheer, A.-W.: Aris - Business Process Modeling. Springer (2000)
29. Chen, P.P.-S.: The entity-relationship model - toward a unified view of data. ACM Trans. Database Syst. 1, 9–36 (1976)

On the Data Interoperability Issues
in SCOR-Based Supply Chains

Milan Zdravković and Miroslav Trajanović

Laboratory for Intelligent Production Systems,
Faculty of Mechanical Engineering in Niš, University of Niš, Serbia
{milan.zdravkovic,traja}@masfak.ni.ac.rs

Abstract. Supply Chain Operations Reference (SCOR) is a reference model
which can be used to design and implement inter-organizational processes of a
supply chain. Its implementation assumes a high level of integration between
the supply chain partners which reduces their flexibility. The problem of integration requirements may be addressed by enabling the supply chain partners to
use their enterprise information systems (instead of specialized software tools)
in the implementation and facilitation of SCOR processes. The performance of
these processes can be significantly improved if the enterprise information systems of the supply chain actors are interoperable. In this paper, we are using
semantic SCOR models to highlight data interoperability requirements for
cross-enterprise SCOR processes and to make this data explicit, by relating it to
the corresponding domain ontology concepts.

Keywords: Systems Interoperability, Ontology, Supply Chain, SCOR.

1   Introduction

Supply Chain Operations Reference (SCOR) [1] is a standard approach for analysis,
design and implementation of five core processes in supply chains: plan, source,
make, deliver and return. SCOR defines a framework which considers business processes, metrics, best practices and technologies with the objective to improve collaboration between partners. The SCOR model is implemented from the perspective of the
single enterprise and it considers all interactions two levels ahead from the enterprise,
towards its supply and customer directions. So, it assumes a significant level of cross-
enterprise collaboration. This collaboration can be enabled by the specialized software
tools or Enterprise Information Systems (EIS).

Implementation of SCOR reference model can be facilitated by the specialized
software systems, such as ARIS EasySCOR [2] or e-SCOR [3]. However, the use of
all of these systems implies a significant level of technical commitments of the enterprise and thus, it has a negative effect on their flexibility. Systems integration assumes
fixed agreements on the message formats, interfaces and other types of commitments
which implementation is costly and time consuming. In contrast to system integration,
which basically deals with formats, protocols and processes of information exchange,

P. Herrero et al. (Eds.): OTM 2012 Workshops, LNCS 7567, pp. 154–161, 2012.
© Springer-Verlag Berlin Heidelberg 2012

the objective of interoperability is to have two systems exchanging information with the consideration that they are not aware of each other's internal workings [4]. The main conditions for achievement of systems interoperability are: 1) to maximize the amount of semantics which can be utilized and 2) to make it increasingly explicit [5]. Then, this semantics can facilitate the interoperability at the different levels, such as data, processes and systems [6].

In this paper, we attempt to show how the above arguments can be used to resolve the data interoperability issues for the implementation of cross-enterprise SCOR processes. For this purpose, we are using implicit OWL representation of the SCOR model – SCOR-KOS OWL and its semantic enrichment – SCOR-Full [7], a micro theory which identifies and classifies common enterprise concepts in the context of supply chain operations. While they are explained in detail in the cited work, these representations are shortly described in Section 2 of this paper. In the Section 3, a main contribution of this paper is presented. The above mentioned formal models are used to infer about the data interoperability requirements in SCOR inter-organizational processes and to make this data explicit. The resulting formal representation can be used to facilitate the interoperability of two heterogeneous systems in context of the SCOR processes' requirements.

2   Formal Model of Supply Chain Operations

Although reference models reflect a common consensus of the industrial community about the specific domain, in most of the cases, they are developed by using a free form natural language. In such way, they are easily communicated throughout the community. However, the implicit definitions of the reference models entities make them difficult to exchange among EISs.

In our previous work [7], we made an attempt to address the problem of the required balance between implicit and explicit knowledge about the SCOR reference model. As a result, two logically related OWL formalizations of SCOR have been developed. First, implicit SCOR-KOS (Knowledge Organization System) OWL model is developed (see Figure 1). It directly translates the natural language form of SCOR entities to OWL language.

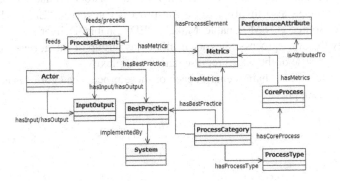

Fig. 1. Partial representation of SCOR-KOS OWL model

Second, a semantic analysis of SCOR entities is performed and SCOR-Full ontology is developed. SCOR-Full is a micro theory which formalizes knowledge about supply chain operations, by identifying and aggregating common enterprise notions. All concepts are classified into the generalizations, such as: Course, Setting, Quality, Function and Resource.

The implicit and explicit concepts of two models are then inter-related by using SWRL rules. Thus, it became possible to combine SCOR tools with other domain ontologies to make a formal reasoning about the process configuration [7], supply chain performance or database schemas [8] in context of SCOR reference model.

3   Data Interoperability Issues in SCOR Cross-Organizational Processes

SCOR reference model describes the key processes of supply chain operations (plan, source, make, deliver, return, enable) and their categories, according to the choice of the manufacturing strategy for a product (make-to-stock, make-to-order or engineer-to-order). These categories are then configured into cross-organizational processes.

For example, in the simple scenario, the relevant processes of the customer are plan source, source and return of the product or part. In this scenario, supplier plans manufacturing and delivery and subsequently make and deliver this product. Process categories can be decomposed into ordered set of process elements, each of which can exchange information with other process elements, within the same process category or externally.

SCOR-KOS OWL enables the inference of the relationships between individual process elements, namely, the flows of the tangible and intangible assets between activities of the processes. Hence, a direct reasoning about the data interoperability issues in SCOR cross-organizational processes can be carried out.

Figure 2 illustrates the exchange of the SCOR assets in the case of engineered-to-order manufacturing, between the customer and supplier (dashed lines). According to SCOR, the above mentioned manufacturing strategy assumes the exchange between "P2. Plan Source", "S3. Source Engineered-to-Order Product", "M3. Make Engineering-to-Order product" and "D3. Deliver Engineered-to-Order product" process categories. This process also involves following process categories: "EP. Enable Plan", "ES. Enable Source", "EM. Enable Make", "ED. Enable Deliver" and "P3. Plan Make". Only the latter process category from the last group of categories is illustrated on Figure 2, because of the visual representation complexity.

In the simple supply chain scenario, each of these process categories is assigned to a customer or a supplier.

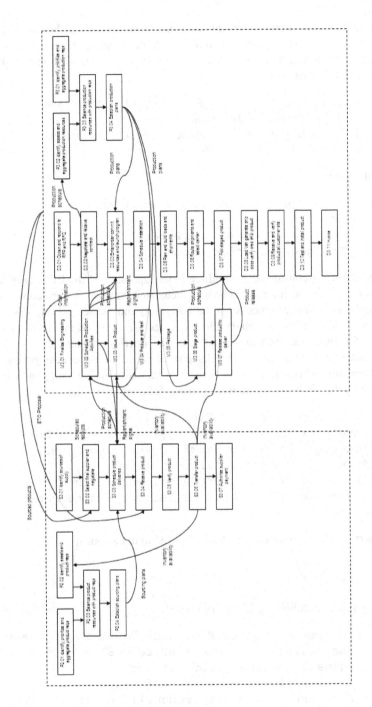

Fig. 2. Assets flows between process elements for engineered-to-order production type

If we assume that both partners are using the EISs, these systems can be considered as interoperable (in context of exchange information between SCOR processes), if they are capable to transmit and understand the information which is exchanged between following process categories:

— `S3_Source_Engineer-to-Order_Product` of the customer and `M3_Engineer-to-Order` of the supplier
— `S3_Source_Engineer-to-Order_Product` of the customer and `D3_Deliver_Engineered-to-Order_Product` of the supplier,

and in opposite direction:

— `M3_Engineer-to-Order` and `S3_Source_Engineer-to-Order_Product`
— `D3_Deliver_Engineered-to-Order_Product` and `S3_Source_Engineer-to-Order_Product`

Since interoperability is considered as unidirectional capability of the EISs, two different queries are needed to infer the concepts exchanged between two systems. The first query implements Source process (of the customer) and the second one – Make and Deliver processes (of the supplier). Both queries are using SCOR-KOS OWL ontology to infer about the exchanged entities. The queries consider the flow of SCOR Input/Output elements between the elements of the given process categories.

Hence, information which needs to be sent from the customer's to supplier's EIS and interpreted by the latter can be inferred by using following DL query:

```
(isOutputFrom some (isProcessElementOf value
S3_Source_Engineer-to-Order_Product)) and (isInputFor
some (isProcessElementOf value M3_Engineer-to-Order)) or
(isOutputFrom some (isProcessElementOf value
S3_Source_Engineer-to-Order_Product)) and (isInputFor
some (isProcessElementOf value D3_Deliver_Engineered-to-
Order_Product))
```

The above query results with following SCOR Input-Output elements:

```
Scheduled_Receipts
Inventory_Availability
```

In the opposite direction, following DL query is used:

```
(isOutputFrom some (isProcessElementOf value M3_Engineer-
to-Order)) and (isInputFor some (isProcessElementOf value
S3_Source_Engineer-to-Order_Product)) or
(isOutputFrom some (isProcessElementOf value
D3_Deliver_Engineered-to-Order_Product)) and (isInputFor
some (isProcessElementOf value S3_Source_Engineer-to-
Order_Product))
```

The above query results with following SCOR Input-Output elements:

```
Replenishment_Signal
Production_Schedule
```

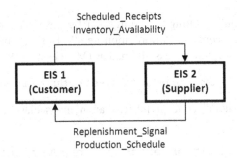

Fig. 3. The example of interoperability requirements

The illustration at Figure 3 shows the data interoperability requirements for two EISs which implement the corresponding SCOR processes, related to the exchange of assets between those. It is very important to emphasize that inferred assets are relevant only when above mentioned SCOR processes environment is considered. In other words, according to SCOR reference, it is sufficient to exchange only the above information between systems to facilitate the customer-supplier collaboration cross-organizational processes, relevant for engineer-to-order manufacturing strategy.

3.1 Explication of the Exchanged Information

In the previous section, the SCOR Input-Output elements which need to be exchanged between the customer's and supplier's EISs in the engineer-to-order collaboration scenario are identified. In order to make the SCOR data interoperable, it is now made explicit by logically relating the resulting SCOR Input-Output elements to the concepts of SCOR-Full ontology. This task is illustrated on the case of one of the exchanged assets – a production schedule.

According to SCORs semantic enrichment - the SCOR-Full ontology, production schedule is considered as sub-concept of "setting" notion and is represented explicitly by the concept "production-schedule", sub-concept of "function-schedule"->"schedule". Thus, the sameness of the instances of "production-schedule" concept of SCOR-Full and "Production_Schedule" instance of SCOR-KOS OWL (of SCOR_Input_Output type) is inferred by the following simple SWRL rule:

```
production-schedule(?x) ⇒ SameAs (?x, Production_Schedule)
```

In SCOR-Full, a setting is defined as a circumstance of any type which affects some course of actions. It is associated with some state or configuration of the tangible (physical-item) or intangible (information-item) resources, namely, with an instance of "configured-item":

```
∀s (setting(s)) ∃ci (configured-item(ci) ∧ has-
realization(s,ci))
```

The production schedule "setting" is configured by the realization of "production-schedule-item" sub-concept of "information-item". Hence, "production-schedule" concept inherits the anonymous class, defined as (Manchester OWL syntax):

```
has-realization some production-schedule-item
```

"Production-schedule-item" concept inherits anonymous classes, defined as (Manchester OWL syntax):

```
has-product-information exactly 1 product-information
has-production-end-date exactly 1 dateTime
has-production-start-date exactly 1 dateTime
has-product-quantity exactly 1 float
```

where "has-production-end-date" and "has-production-start-date" data properties are sub-properties of "has-date-value" data property, and "has-product-quantity" is sub-property of has-numerical-value data property. "Has-product-information" is a sub-property of "has-realization property". Hence, necessary conditions for having one production schedule item are: 1) to have exactly one product associated; 2) to have a production start date for this product; and 3) to have a production end date for this product.

Similarly, "product-information" information item is configured (hence, its realization is used in the range of first necessary condition above) by having exactly one product id associated:

```
has-product-id exactly 1 string
```

In addition, "function-schedule" concept also inherits the anonymous class:

```
∀fs (function-schedule(fs)) ∃f (function(f) ∧ sched-
ules(fs,f))
```

For the concept of "production-schedule", this condition is specialized to:

```
schedules some production
```

As shown above, the SCOR-Full ontology semantically describes the concept of production schedule. This description is mapped to the corresponding instance of the SCOR-KOS OWL model, so it can be used in the context of SCOR processes. When the SCOR-Full ontology is correlated to the EIS (for example, by the logical correspondences between SCOR-Full and EIS's local ontology), then this EIS can be used as facilitator of the SCOR processes in the collaboration environment. Hence, there is no need for specialized software applications.

4   Conclusions

Like other reference models, SCOR framework can be considered as an interoperability tool, since it formalizes the common agreements on the collaboration processes in the supply chain. However, it uses very weak structural formalism to only aggregate enterprise entities in the specific categories and it does this in the context of the supply chain. It does not provide syntactic nor semantic view which can help to express and interpret the model by the computer systems. SCOR-KOS OWL and SCOR-Full aim at closing this gap by providing the semantic model and correspondences of this model with a native one (actually, with the OWL representation of the native model).

In this paper, the above-mentioned OWL models (or ontologies) are used to identify and to make explicit the data interoperability issues related to exchange of the information between the arbitrary systems of customer and supplier in the engineer-to-order scenario. The simplistic process definition of the SCOR model, emphasizes the flow of data throughout the supply chain. This data can be considered as interoperable when its different representations (e.g. in SCOR reference and/or in number of EISs) logically correspond to a single concept of the domain ontology which is a formal description of its meaning. These logical correspondences enable all the systems in a supply chain to correctly interpret all representations of this data. Thus, it becomes possible to make the individual systems, and consequently, processes (SCOR process categories) interoperable, at least within the scope, prescribed by SCOR reference model.

References

1. Stewart, G.: Supply-chain operations reference model (SCOR): the first cross-industry framework for integrated supply-chain management. Logistics Information Management 10(2), 62–67 (1997)
2. Poluha, R.G.: Application of the SCOR model in Supply Chain Management. Cambria Press, New York (2007)
3. Barnett, M.W., Miller, C.J.: Analysis of the virtual enterprise using distributed supply chain modeling and simulation: an application of e-SCOR. In: The Proceedings of the 32nd Conference on Winter Simulation, pp. 352–355 (2000)
4. Chen, D., Vernadat, F.: Standards on enterprise integration and engineering - a state of the art. International Journal of Computer Integrated Manufacturing 17(3), 235–253 (2004)
5. Obrst, L.: Ontologies for semantically interoperable systems. In: 12th International Conference on Information and Knowledge Management. ACM, New York (2003)
6. Berre, A.J., Elvesæter, B., Figay, N., Guglielmina, C.J.: The ATHENA Interoperability Framework. In: The ATHENA Interoperability Framework, Proceedings of the 3rd International Conference on Interoperability for Enterprise Software and Applications (I-ESA 2007), pp. 569–580. Springer (2007)
7. Zdravković, M., Panetto, H., Trajanović, M., Aubrey, A.: An approach for formalising the supply chain operations. Enterprise Information Systems 5(4), 401–421 (2011)
8. Zdravković, M., Trajanović, M., Panetto, H.: Local ontologies for semantic interoperability in supply chain networks. In: 13th International Conference on Enterprise Information Systems. SciTePress (2011)

INBAST 2012 PC Co-chairs Message

The Semantic Web was planned as a web of data that enables machines to understand the meaning of information on the WWW. Many of the Semantic Web technologies proposed by the W3C already exist and are used in various contexts where sharing data is a common necessity, such as scientific research or data exchange among businesses. However, the Semantic Web as originally envisioned, a system that enables machines to understand and respond to complex human requests based on their meaning, has remained largely unrealized and its critics have questioned its feasibility. Semantic Web technologies have found a greater degree of practical adoption among specialized communities and organizations for intra-company projects. The practical constraints toward adoption have appeared less challenging where domain and scope is more limited than that of the general public and the WWW.

The goal of the workshop was the feasibility investigation of advanced Semantic Web methods and techniques and their application in different domains such as in the run time of safety-critical live systems or in design time engineering disciplines like software and systems engineering.

The workshop attracted a number of submissions, of which 5 papers were accepted for presentation. During the review process, a total of 21 reviewers were involved with an average of 3 reviews per paper. The topics of the accepted paper cover a wide range of interesting application areas of semantic web technologies, such as Information Retrieval, Requirement Specification, Business Process Modeling, Tourist Services and Product Lifecycle Management. Selected papers will be considered for publication in a special issue of the Journal of Universal Computer Science (J.UCS). Authors of these selected papers presented at the workshop with papers published in the workshop proceedings are invited to submit their extended papers.

July 2012

Rafael Valencia Garca
Thomas Moser
Ricardo Colomo Palacios

P. Herrero et al. (Eds.): OTM 2012 Workshops, LNCS 7567, p. 162, 2012.
© Springer-Verlag Berlin Heidelberg 2012

An Ontology Evolution-Based Framework for Semantic Information Retrieval

Miguel Ángel Rodríguez-García, Rafael Valencia-García,
and Francisco García-Sánchez

Departamento de Informtica y Sistemas,
Universidad de Murcia, Campus de Espinardo 30100 Murcia, Spain
{miguelangel.rodriguez,valencia,frgarcia}@um.es
http://www.um.es

Abstract. Ontologies evolve continuously during their life cycle to adapt to new requirements and necessities. Ontology-based information retrieval systems use semantic annotations that are also regularly updated to reflect new points of view. In order to provide a general solution and to minimize the users' effort in the ontology enriching process, a methodology for extracting terms and evolve the domain ontology from Wikipedia is proposed in this work. The framework presented here combines an ontology-based information retrieval system with an ontology evolution approach in such a way that it simplifies the tasks of updating concepts and relations in domain ontologies. This framework has been validated in a scenario where ICT-related cloud services matching the user needs are to be found.

1 Introduction

Ontologies constitute the standard knowledge representation mechanism for the Semantic Web [1]. The formal semantics underlying ontology languages enables the automatic processing of the information and allows the use of semantic reasoners to infer new, non-explicit knowledge. In this work, an ontology is seen as "a formal and explicit specification of a shared conceptualization" [2]. Ontologies provide a formal, structured knowledge representation, and have the advantage of being reusable and shareable. They also provide a common vocabulary for a domain and define, with different levels of formality, the meaning of the terms and the relations between them. Ontologies have proven their value in various fields such as information retrieval [3], semantic search [4], service discovery [5] and question answering [6]

Ontology evolution can be defined as the timely adaptation of an ontology to changed business requirements, as well as the consistent management/ propagation of these changes to dependent elements [7]. In fact, the evolution and modification in one part of the domain ontology can produce inconsistencies in the whole ontology [8]. In this context, it is important to distinguish between ontology evolution and ontology versioning. While ontology evolution allows access to all data only through the newest ontology, the ontology versioning allows

P. Herrero et al. (Eds.): OTM 2012 Workshops, LNCS 7567, pp. 163–172, 2012.
© Springer-Verlag Berlin Heidelberg 2012

access to data through different versions of the ontology [7]. The use of ontology versioning in platforms is gaining success and some platforms such as SHOE [9] and KAON [10] support multiple versions of ontologies and enable to declare whether the new version is backward-compatible with an old version.

In this work, an ontology-based information retrieval system supported by an ontology evolution approach is presented. The proposed framework is capable of simplifying the tasks of updating the concepts and relations that form part of the domain ontologies that comprise the core of the system. The framework has been tested in a scenario where ICT-related cloud services matching the user needs are to be found. The rest of this paper is organized as follows. In Section 2, a detailed description of the whole platform is given. The use case scenario for retrieving services in the cloud is presented in Section 3. Finally, conclusions and future work are put forward in Section 4.

2   Platform Architecture

The architecture of the proposed framework is shown in figure 1. The system is composed of five main modules: (1) the semantic representation and annotation module, (2) the semantic indexing module, (3) the term extractor module, (4) the ontology evolution module and (5) the semantic search engine. In a nutshell the system works as follows. First, natural-language, non-structured texts are

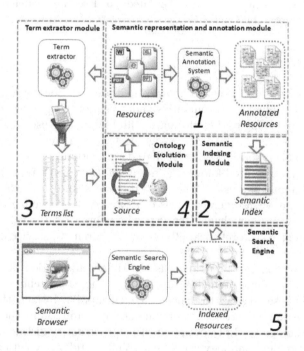

Fig. 1. Platform architecture

semantically represented and annotated by using the domain ontologies. From these annotations a semantic index is then created using the classic vector space model. At the same time, the term extractor obtains the terms appearing in the texts that are not present in the domain ontologies. The ontology evolution module then checks whether the most important new terms previously gathered can be added to the domain ontologies. Finally, a semantic search engine permits to retrieve the matching text from keyword-based searches.

2.1   Semantic Annotation Module (1)

This module receives both the domain ontologies and the natural-language, non-structured texts as inputs. Using a set of natural language processing (NLP) tools, it then obtains a semantic annotation for the analyzed texts in accordance with the domain ontologies. This module is based on the methodology presented in [3] and is composed of two main phases, namely, the NLP phase and the semantic annotation phase.

The main aim of the NLP stage is the extraction of the morphosyntactic structure of each sentence. For this purpose, a set of NLP software tools, including a sentence detection component, a tokenizer, a set of POS taggers, a set of lemmatizers and a set of syntactic parsers, have been developed. Besides, the GATE framework [1] has been employed. GATE is an infrastructure for developing and deploying software components that process human language. GATE helps scientists and developers in three ways: (i) by specifying an architecture, or organizational structure, for language processing software; (ii) by providing a framework, or class library, that implements the architecture and can be used to embed language processing capabilities in diverse applications; (iii) by providing a development environment built on top of the framework made up of convenient graphical tools for developing components. As a result of this first phase, a set of annotations rep-resenting the syntactic structure of the text is obtained.

During the semantic annotation phase texts are annotated with the classes and instances of the domain ontologies by following the process described next. First, the most important linguistic expressions are identified by means of linguistic approaches based on the syntactic structure of the text. For each linguistic expression the system tries to determine whether such expression is an individual or a class of any of the domain ontologies by searching through the hierarchy categories of Wikipedia. If so, the linguistic expression is related with the URI (Uniform Resource Identifier) of the class or instance of such domain ontology.

2.2   Semantic Indexing Module (2)

In this module, the system retrieves all the annotated knowledge from the previous module and tries to create fully-filled annotations with this knowledge. This step is based on the work presented in [11]. Each annotation of each document is stored in a database and is assigned a weight, which reflects how relevant

---

[1] http://gate.ac.uk/

the ontological entity is for the document meaning. Weights are calculated by using the TF-IDF algorithm [12], which satisfies the following equation (see equation 1).

$$(tf - idf)_{i,d} = \frac{n_{i,d}}{\sum_k n_{k,d}} * \log \frac{|D|}{N_i} \qquad (1)$$

where $n_{i,d}$ is the number of occurrences of the ontological entity i in the document d, $\sum_k n_{k,d}$ is the sum of the occurrences of all the ontological entities identified in the document d, $|D|$ is the set of all documents and N_i is the number of all documents annotated with i.

In this scenario, the content descriptions comprise the documents to be analysed. For each description, an index is calculated based on the adaptation of the classic vector space model presented in [11]. Each description is represented as a vector in which each dimension corresponds to a separate ontological concept of the domain ontology. The value of each ontological concept dimension is calculated as follows (see equation 2).

$$(v_1, v_2, ..., v_n)_d \quad where \quad v_i = \sum_{j=1}^{n} \frac{tf - idf_j d}{e^{dist(i,j)}} n_{k,d} \qquad (2)$$

where $dist(i,j)$ is the semantic distance between the concept i and concept j in the domain ontology. This distance is calculated by using the taxonomic (subclass_of) relationships of concepts in the domain ontology. So, the distance between a concept and itself is 0, the distance between a concepts and its taxonomic parent or child is 1 and so on.

2.3   Term Extractor Module (3)

Through this module, the most significant terms from the text documents are identified. This module is based on previous works of our research group [13]. It is assumed that there exist both multiword and single word terms. By taking into account this assumption, two different methods have been implemented: the NC-Value algorithm [14], which allows to obtain the multiword terms candidates to represent concept, and RIDF [15], which has been employed to obtain terms formed by one word.

The list of the most important terms appearing in the texts that are not part of the domain ontologies, is taken as the input of the ontology evolution module.

2.4   Ontology Evolution Module (4)

The main objective of this module is to maintain and evolve ontologies by using the information available in Wikipedia. The terms list gathered by the term extractor module is used to enrich, enhance and increase the knowledge represented on the domain ontologies. Wikipedia is a free encyclopedia where thousand of concepts are classified in a taxonomy. The main idea of this method is to keep domain ontologies up-to-date by exploiting the structure of Wikipedia, that is, the assignment of articles to categories, the subcategory relation and the cross-language relations linking equivalent articles across languages. The Wikipedia structure is an important and necessary condition since it allows to establish group of terms defining the semantic concepts. This organization is not yet available in DBPedia for all languages. Each relevant term in the list produced by the term extractor module (i.e. terms not currently present in the ontologies) is looked up in Wikipedia. If a Wikipedia article or category is found matching the term, a new concept is created containing all the term's synonyms in both English and Spanish and subsequently added into the domain ontology by using the algorithm described in figure 2.

This algorithm has been implemented by using the OWL API [2] framework and Java Wikipedia API (Bliki engine [3]), which is a parser library for converting Wikipedia wikitext notation to HTML. The module has been designed to allow the access to online wikitext using the Hypertext Transfer Protocol (HTTP), and so the extracted content is always up-to-date since it is gathered from the online version of Wikipedia. Additionally, the tool permits to collect outdated wikitext content if desired.

Figure 2 shows the pseudocode of the algorithm designed to solve the ontology evolution problem. The input of the algorithm is the list of terms produced by the term extractor module. Each term in the list represents a candidate concept that can be used to enrich the ontology knowledge.

The proposed evolution algorithm has been designed to find a path in the Wikipedia hierarchy. This path assists the system to generate relationships between the candidate concepts and the elements already available in the ontology. The process of this algorithm comprises two important phases. In the first phase the system is responsible for extracting all the information about all the classes in the ontology. This information is thus a compact representation of all the concepts in the domain. During the second phase the algorithm attempts to find the shortest path between each term in the list and the ontology concepts based on the Wikipedia categories. An ontology class is defined during the search process for each category that is obtained from the Wikipedia hierarchy. These classes are created by extracting the synonymous terms from Wikipedia, which are used to define the concept. In fact, the algorithm searches for Wikipedia categories that are shared by an ontology concept and one of the relevant terms in the list.

2.5   Semantic Search Engine Module (5)

This module is in charge of finding semantic concepts in different kinds of textual resources from a keyword-based query. This process takes advantage of the semantic content and annotations previously generated by the system.

First, users introduce a number of keywords. Next, the system identifies what concepts in the domain ontology are referred to by those keywords. Each

---

[2] http://owlapi.sourceforge.net/
[3] http://code.google.com/p/gwtwiki/

```
Declare a list of ontology nodes nodesOntology
Obtain all the ontology concepts (classes)from the 'ontology' resource
Declare a list of terms termList
Obtain the list of terms from term extractor module
FOR each term DO
    the next term is obtained
    IF the next term is not already in the ontology THEN
        FOR each node DO
            the node concept is obtained
            the first concept is built from Wikipedia
            IF first concept is null THEN
                //If there is not any concept in the Wikipedia then
                //we have to continue with the next node
                continue;
            ELSE
                the second concept is built from Wikipedia.
                IF second concept is null THEN
                    //If there is not any term in the Wikipedia then
                    //we have to continue to the next term
                    break;
                ELSE
                    joining concepts from Wikipedia
                END IF
            END IF
        END DO
    END IF
END DO
```

Fig. 2. Algorithm for the ontology evolution process

document is represented as a vector in which each dimension corresponds to a separate concept of the domain ontology. The semantic search engine then calculates a similarity value between the query q and each semantic concept. In order to do that, the cosine similarity is used (see equation 3).

$$sim(q, s) = \cos \vartheta = \frac{q \bullet s}{|q| \bullet |s|} \tag{3}$$

A ranking with the most relevant semantic concepts that are related to the topics referenced in the query is then defined by using the similarity function showed in equation 3. In figure 3, the vector space model calculation is shown graphically. The first vector (s) is the vector calculated by equation 2 for each content description and the second vector (q) is the one created from the concepts extracted from search engine query. The ϑ symbol is the angle between both vectors, which represents the similarity degree between two documents.

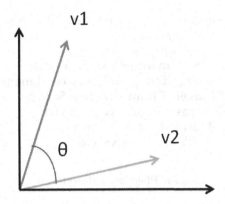

Fig. 3. Platform architecture

3   Use Case Escenario: Retrieving Services in the Cloud

The platform described in the previous section has been implemented and later tested in an ICT domain-based cloud services retrieval use case scenario. For this, in the first place, around 300 different ICT-related cloud services with their description in natural language have been selected to be automatically annotated by the system.

Initially, the ICT ontology was empty. So, no semantic annotation can be obtained during this first stage. The term extractor module is then executed and a list of terms containing the most relevant terms that appear in the cloud services descriptions is generated. Next, the domain ontology is enriched by the ontology evolution module, which takes into account the concepts in Wikipedia that corresponds to each term in the list. As a result, an ontology formed by 10 classes and 40 *"subclass-of"* relationships is produced. In figure 4, an excerpt of the ontology is shown.

Once the initial domain ontology is available, the services descriptions can be semantically annotated and stored in the ontology repository. The Virtuoso repository has been used to implement the ontology repository. A semantic index is then calculated for each service by means of the semantic indexing module. Once the semantic indexes have been created, the system is ready to be queried. The ultimate goal of this experimental evaluation is to elucidate whether the semantic search engine module of the proposed platform is useful. Five topic-based queries were issued. For each query, a set of cloud services was manually selected. At the same time, the semantic search engine was asked to perform the same task, in an automatic way. The outcome of the semantic search engine was then compared against those produced by the manual selection.

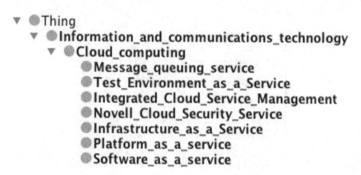

Fig. 4. Platform architecture

The results are shown in Table 1. The system obtained the best results for queries about the topic "Databases", with a precision of 0.85, a recall of 0.77 and a F1 measure of 0.81. In general, the system obtains better results in precision (80% on average) than in recall (76% on average). Anyhow, these results of the proposed system seem very promising.

Table 1. Precision, recall and F1 of the experiment

Topics	Precision	Recall	F1
Databases	0,85	0,77	0,81
Java	0,81	0,76	0,78
Storage	0,75	0,79	0,77
Backup	0,8	0,73	0,76

4   Conclusions and Discussion

Semantic-based information retrieval differs from traditional information retrieval systems because informational resources in the former approach are given formal meaning. Certainly, the added value of semantic information retrieval with respect to traditional keyword-based retrieval relies on the use of ontologies to make explicit the semantics of the resources that are being searched for. However, this novel and powerful approach could be hampered by the changes in the domain in which the system is being used. Therefore, it is of utmost importance to continuously update the ontologies to satisfactorily reflect these changes in the domain. Ontology evolution is the research field concerned with the timely adaptation of ontologies to changing requirements.

In this work, we propose an ontology evolution-based framework for semantic information retrieval. The global resulting platform combines an ontology evolution approach with a semantic-based information retrieval system. This integrated approach allows to automatically keep ontologies up-to-date so that the retrieval tool is constantly accurate during its functioning. In order to evaluate the usefulness of the proposed platform, it has been tested in a real use case scenario. The testing environment consists of the search for ICT-related cloud services from keyword-based queries. The results of the experiments described above show that the value of the system presented here is twofold: (1) it drastically reduces the time-consuming effort of manually extending the ontologies with new concepts and relations to adapt to changing requirements, and (2) it accurately retrieves the services that match a user' query. A further benefit of the approach presented here is the use of Wikipedia as source of information. The structure, organization, dynamism and trustability of Wikipedia's contents enable the system to develop a comprehensive and up-to-date ontology.

The main limitation of the proposed framework is that the "semantic representation and annotation module" only works with unstructured, natural-language text. We plan to extend this module so as to include support for more structured content (e.g. database tables). Additionally, we are currently working on a more ambitious experiment that covers all kinds of cloud services regardless of their application domain. For future work, we aim to improve the approach in a number of ways. First, we intend to broaden the scope of the approach to other application domains such as e-health and e-learning. The ontology evolution process that is supported by our framework can help gathering more up-to-date knowledge to be applied in medical diagnosis or in an e-learning environment. A further enhancement of the framework that is being considered is the use of other information repositories besides Wikipedia. It cannot be expected that all the searched concepts are in Wikipedia. It could be appropriate to consider other trustworthy information sources when a particular concept is not found in Wikipedia.

Acknowledgments. This work has been supported by the Spanish Ministry for Science and Innovation under project SeCloud: TIN2010-18650.

References

1. Shadbolt, N., Berners-Lee, T., Hall, W.: The semantic web revisited. IEEE Intelligent Systems 21(3), 96–101 (2006)
2. Studer, R., Benjamins, V.R., Fensel, D.: Knowledge engineering: Principles and methods. Data Knowledge Engineering 25(1-2), 161–197 (1998)
3. Valencia-García, R., Fernández-Breis, J.T., Ruiz-Martínez, J.M., García-Sánchez, F., Martínez-Bjar, R.: A knowledge acquisition methodology to ontology construction for information retrieval from medical documents. Expert Systems 25(3), 314–334 (2008)
4. Lupiani-Ruiz, E., García-Manotas, I., Valencia-García, R., García-Sánchez, F., Castellanos-Nieves, D., Fernández-Breis, J.T., Camón-Herrero, J.B.: Financial news semantic search engine. Expert Systems with Applications 38(12), 15565–15572 (2011)
5. García-Sánchez, F., Valencia-García, R., Martínez-Béjar, R., Fernández-Breis, J.T.: An ontology, intelligent agent-based framework for the provision of semantic web services. Expert Systems with Applications 36(2), 3167–3187 (2009)

6. Valencia-García, R., García-Sánchez, F., Castellanos-Nieves, D., Fernández-Breis, J.T.: Owlpath: An owl ontology-guided query editor. IEEE Transactions on Systems, Man, and Cybernetics, Part A 41(1), 121–136 (2011)
7. Maedche, A., Motik, B., Stojanovic, L., Stojanovic, N.: User-driven ontology evolution management, pp. 285–300. Springer (2002)
8. Haase, P., Haase, P., Stojanovic, L.: Consistent evolution of owl ontologies, pp. 182–197. Springer (2005)
9. Heflin, J., Hendler, J.A.: Dynamic ontologies on the web. In: Proceedings of the Seventeenth National Conference on Artificial Intelligence and Twelfth Conference on Innovative Applications of Artificial Intelligence, pp. 443–449. AAAI Press (2000)
10. Bozsak, E., Ehrig, M., Handschuh, S., Hotho, A., Maedche, A., Motik, B., Oberle, D., Schmitz, C., Staab, S., Stojanovic, L., Stojanovic, N., Studer, R., Stumme, G., Sure, Y., Tane, J., Volz, R., Zacharias, V.: KAON - Towards a Large Scale Semantic Web. In: Bauknecht, K., Tjoa, A.M., Quirchmayr, G. (eds.) EC-Web 2002. LNCS, vol. 2455, pp. 304–313. Springer, Heidelberg (2002)
11. Castells, P., Fernández, M., Vallet, D.: An adaptation of the vector-space model for ontology-based information retrieval. IEEE Trans. on Knowl. and Data Eng. 19(2), 261–272 (2007)
12. Salton, G., McGill, M.J.: Introduction to Modern Information Retrieval. McGraw-Hill, Inc., New York (1986)
13. Ochoa, J.L., Ángela Almela, M.L.H.A., Valencia-García, R.: Learning morphosyntactic patterns for multiword term extraction. Scientific Research and Essays 6(26), 5563–5578 (2011)
14. Frantzi, K.T., Ananiadou, S., Tsujii, J.: The $C - value/NC - value$ Method of Automatic Recognition for Multi-word Terms. In: Nikolaou, C., Stephanidis, C. (eds.) ECDL 1998. LNCS, vol. 1513, pp. 585–604. Springer, Heidelberg (1998)
15. Church, K., Gale, W.A.: Inverse document frequency (idf): A measure of deviations from poisson. In: Proceedings of the Third Workshop on Very Large Corpora, pp. 121–130 (1995)

Applications for Business Process Repositories Based on Semantic Standardization

Maya Lincoln[1] and Avi Wasser[2]

[1] ProcessGene Ltd
maya.lincoln@processgene.com
[2] University of Haifa, Israel
awasser@haifa.ac.il

Abstract. In recent years, researchers have become increasingly interested in developing frameworks and tools for the generation, customization and utilization of business process model content. One of the enabling central techniques for automated repository standardization is Natural Language Processing (NLP). This work reviews previous works on NLP standardization, and presents a set of derived Business Process Management (BPM) applications. We then discuss how these applications can be extended and improved for better utilization of the process repositories by (1) deploying a larger set of semantic models; and (2) integrating complementing applications.

Keywords: Business process model standardization, Business process repositories, Natural language processing.

1 Introduction

Business process repositories are considered an important resource of organizational knowledge. These repositories facilitate visibility into the business of organizations, and therefore have a central role in enterprise analysis, strategy, and Information Technology (IT) efforts [4]. Therefore, in recent years, researchers have become increasingly interested in developing methods and tools for promoting the utilization of process repositories, and the topic has been discussed intensively both in academia and in industry [17]. This work is aimed at suggesting methods for enabling the utilization of such process repositories for business process management applications.

Our work presents a content-based utilization framework that relies on the standardization of the content layer of business process repositories, as a basis for enabling several applications that leverage the usage of these knowledge reservoirs.

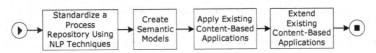

Fig. 1. A high-level framework for utilizing standardized process repositories for content-based applications

P. Herrero et al. (Eds.): OTM 2012 Workshops, LNCS 7567, pp. 173–182, 2012.

We propose a four-step meta process to utilize process repositories, as illustrated in Fig. 1 (using "Yet Another Workflow Language" (YAWL) [14]). First, we apply previously suggested methods for creating an operationally meaningful decomposition of a process repository. We use state-of-the-art Natural Language Processing (NLP) techniques to automatically decompose the content layer (text) of the repositories into its structured linguistic components (objects and actions and their qualifiers). As part of this decomposition, each business activity is encoded automatically as a *descriptor*, using the Process Descriptor Catalog ("PDC") notation [10]. The collection of all descriptors formulates a *descriptor space*, and distances between every two space coordinates are calculated in terms of business process conduct proximity. Second, by analyzing the generated decomposition, we create seven action and object models, that represent operational aspects of the process repository, as suggested in [8,7]. Third, we present applications from previous works that use action and object models for solving problems related to the utilization of the process repository in the following domains: (1) design of new process models; (2) validation of changes in the repository; (3) search of process segments in the repository, (4) similarity measurement between process models; and (5) construction of process data ontologies, as a basis for further understanding the logic of process models. As a fourth step, we discuss how these applications can be extended and improved for better utilization of the process repositories by (1) deploying a larger set of semantic models; and (2) integrating complementing applications.

The suggested framework is demonstrated using a process repository that consists 31 real-life processes and 183 related activities from the high-tech industry.

The rest of the paper is organized as follows: we present related work in Section 2, positioning our work with respect to previous research. In Section 3 we present an activity decomposition model that is gathered from previous works, and is used in this work as the foundation for creating action and object taxonomies. We then present applications from previous works that currently rely on some parts of the standardized repository, and discuss how they can be extended in Section 4. We conclude in Section 5.

2   Related Work

Research on standardization and analysis of the content layer of business process models mainly focuses on the analysis of linguistic components - actions and objects that describe business activities. Most existing languages for business process modeling and implementation are activity-centric, representing processes as a set of activities connected by control-flow elements indicating the order of activity execution [16]. In recent years, an alternative approach has been proposed, which is based on objects (or artifacts/entities/documents) as a central component for business process modeling and implementation. This relatively new approach focuses on the central objects along with their life-cycles. Such object-centric approaches include artifact-centric modeling [12,2], data-driven modeling [11] and proclets [13].

Although most works in the above domain are either object or activity centric, only a few works combine the two approaches in order to exploit an extended knowledge scope of the business process. The work in [5] presents an algorithm that generates an information-centric process model from an activity-centric model. The works in [10,8,7] present the concept of business process descriptor that decomposes process names into objects, actions and qualifiers, and suggest several taxonomies to express the operational knowledge encapsulated in business process repositories. In this work we take this model forward by: (a) testing it on real-life processes from the high-tech domain; (b) showing how the suggested taxonomies can assist in common usages of business process management.

3   The Activity Decomposition Model

This section describes a formal model of business process decomposition and analysis, gathered from previous works. We first introduce the descriptor model (Section 3.1). Then, based on the descriptor model, we introduce seven taxonomies of objects and actions (Section 3.2). To illustrate the taxonomies we make use of the high-tech repository (see Chapter 1).

3.1   The Descriptor Model

In the Process Descriptor Catalog model ("PDC") [10] each activity is composed of one action, one object that the action acts upon, and possibly one or more action and object qualifiers, as illustrated in Fig. 2. Qualifiers provide an additional description to actions and objects. State-of the art Natural Language Processing (NLP) systems, e.g., the "Stanford Parser,"[1] can be used to automatically decompose process and activity names into *process/activity descriptors*. For example, the activity "Develop requested functionality" generates an activity descriptor containing the action "develop," without an action qualifier, the object "functionality" and the object qualifier "requested."

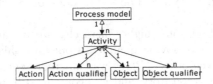

Fig. 2. The activity decomposition model

---

[1] http://nlp.stanford.edu:8080/parser/index.jsp

3.2   Action and Object Based Taxonomies

The descriptor model has two basic elements, namely objects and actions, and it serves as a basis for several state of the art taxonomies, as follows: (1) in [9] it was enhanced to create the *action hierarchy model*, the *object hierarchy model*, and the *action sequence model*, and the *object lifecycle model*; and (2) in [7] it was enhanced to create the *action scope model*, the *object grouping model*, and the *action influence model*.

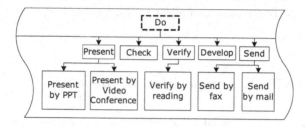

Fig. 3. Segment of an action hierarchy model from the high-tech repository

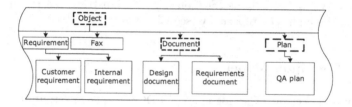

Fig. 4. Segment of an object hierarchy model from the high-tech repository

The Action and Object Hierarchy Models. The action and object hierarchy models organize a set of activity descriptors according to the hierarchical relationships among business actions and objects, respectively. This hierarchical dimension of actions and objects is determined by their qualifiers (see illustrations in Fig. 3 and Fig. 4). For example, consider the complete action "Send by fax." It is a subclass (a more specific form) of "Send" in the action hierarchy model, since the qualifier "By fax" limits the action of "Send" to reduced action range.

It is worth noting that some higher-hierarchy objects and actions are generated automatically by removing qualifiers from lower-hierarchy objects and actions. For example, the object "Plan" was not represented without qualifiers in the high-tech process repository, and was completed from the more detailed object: "QA plan" by removing its object qualifier ("QA") (see Fig. 4).

The Action Sequence Model. The action sequence taxonomy model organizes a set of activity descriptors according to the relationships among business

Fig. 5. Segment of an action sequence model from the high-tech repository

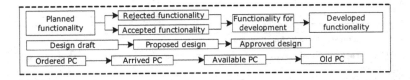

Fig. 6. Segment of an object lifecycle model from the high-tech repository

actions and objects in terms of execution order. In this model, each object holds a graph of ordered actions that are applied to that object. A segment of the action sequence model of a high-tech repository is presented in Fig. 5. For example, the object "Student" is related to the following action sequence: "Interview" followed by "Accept," "Sign," and finally "Update."

The Object Lifecycle Model. The object lifecycle taxonomy model organizes a set of activity descriptors according to the relationships among business actions and objects in terms of execution order. For example, the object "Functionality" is part of the following object lifecycle: "Planned functionality"–> "Rejected/Accepted functionality"–>"functionality for development"–> "Developed functionality."

The Action Scope Model. The action scope model represents the relationship between an action within a process name (a "primary action") and the actions in its corresponding process model. The fact that a process repository consists of pre-defined process models is being used for learning about the scope of actions in the following way. Each primary action in the repository is related with a set of directional graphs of actions that represent the order of actions within this primary action's segments. Since such a primary action can be part of more than one primary names, and since the same complete action may be represented more than once in the same process model segment - each edge in the action scope model is labeled with its weight, calculated by the number of its repetitions in the related process model segments. Graph splits are also represented in the action scope model.

Consider the following two processes from the high-tech repository: "Develop customer requirement" and "Develop a new idea." These processes are illustrated in Fig 7a. Using these two process models, it is possible to generate an action scope model for the action "Develop" (Fig 7b). According to this example, there are two optional action paths compatible to the "Develop" action starting by

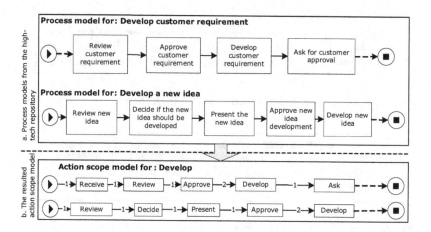

Fig. 7. A segment of the action sequence model for the action "Develop"

either "Receive" or "Review." Since "Develop" follows "Approve" twice in this model, the respective edge weight is set to 2.

The Object Grouping Model. The object grouping model represents the relationship between a primary object and the objects in its corresponding model segments. Since such a primary object can be part of more than one primary process segment, and since the same object may be represented more than once in the same process model segment - each object in the object grouping model is labeled with its weight calculated by the number of its repetitions in the related process model segments.

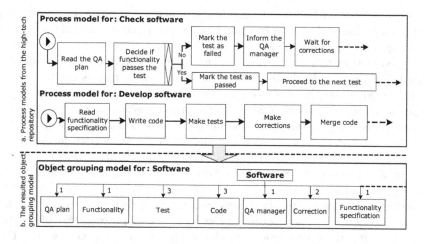

Fig. 8. A segment of the object grouping model for "Software"

To illustrate, consider two processes from the high-tech repository: "Check software" and "Develop software." These processes are represented by corresponding graph segments as illustrated in Fig 8a. Using these two process models, it is possible to generate an object grouping model for the object "Software," as illustrated in Fig 8b.

The Action Influence Model. An action influence model represents the relationship between a primary action and the flow of states (object qualifiers) of the primary object in model segments that correspond to the primary action. Each edge in the action influence model is labeled with its weight representing the number of its repetitions in the related process model segments.

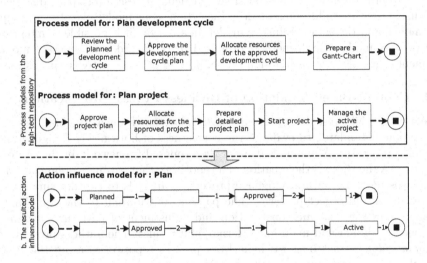

Fig. 9. A segment of the action influence model for the action "Plan"

To illustrate, consider the two process models named: "Plan development cycle" and "Plan project." They both deal with *plan,* but focus on different objects (see illustration in Fig. 9a). By following changes to the qualifiers of the primary object in these process models we end up with the action influence model for "Plan" as illustrated in Fig. 9b.

4   Applications

In Section 2 we showed how the content layer of business process repositories can be standardized using the activity decomposition model. In this section we show how such standardized process repositories can be utilized for several applications in the domain of business process management. The presented applications are based on previous works that applied semantic analysis of standardized business process repositories, using natural language processing techniques.

4.1   Machine-Assisted Design of Business Process Models

The work in [8] suggests a generic method for designing new business process models related to any functional domain. The suggested method guides business analysts that opt to design a new business model, by suggesting process steps (activities) that are relevant to the newly created process model. The business logic for such suggestions is extracted from the following four models: the action and object hierarchy model, the action sequence model and the object lifecycle model. Each activity is encoded automatically as a *descriptor*, using the "PDC" notation. The collection of all descriptors formulates a *descriptor space*, and distances between every two space coordinates are calculated in terms of business process conduct proximity.

To elaborate this work, it is possible to calculate descriptor space distances also using the three additional models: the action scope model, the object grouping model, and the action influence model. In addition, it is possible to integrate the process model search method proposed in [7] in order to generate model segment suggestions at each design phase, instead of single activity suggestions.

4.2   Content-Based Validation of Business Process Modifications

The work in [6] presents a content-based validation framework that uses organizational standards to evaluate the correctness of both newly designed and modified processes. A unique feature of the proposed framework, in the context of process validation, is the creation of a repository that captures organizational standards by using natural language processing analysis to capture simultaneously action and object patterns. The paper's contribution to the compliance domain is in the *dynamic* construction and adjustment of patterns - avoiding the need to design and maintain external, static rules. The authors propose to *automatically* extract business logic from process repositories using the PDC model, and the taxonomy models of action sequence, object lifecycle, and object and action hierarchies that support the validation process. The proposed method includes three steps for content-based validation: (1) deficiency identification (using existing descriptors as a benchmark reference), (2) validation score calculation, and (3) generation of a ranked list of possible corrections.

Similarly to the former method, we suggest elaborating this work, by referring also to the three additional models: the action scope model, the object grouping model, and the action influence model. In addition, we suggest to integrate the method proposed in [15] for measuring the similarity between process models using semantic analysis. This method may assist in ranking the generated correction suggestions, by comparing the suggestions to the original user intention (the change he made to the process repository).

4.3   Searching Business Process Repositories Using Operational Similarity

The search framework proposed in [7] receives natural language queries and returns a ranked list of related process models. The business logic is extracted from process repositories through the analysis of the following three taxonomies: the action scope model, the object grouping model, and the action influence model (see Section 3). The proposed method *dynamically* segments a process repository according to the ad-hoc request as expressed in the user's search phrase.

We propose elaborating the segmentation process by referring also to execution flows as expressed by the action sequence model and the object lifecycle model. In addition, an integration of the query-by-example approach proposed in [1] may extend the returned result range and may produce better search results.

4.4 Measuring Similarity between Process Models

The work in [15] proposes a method for measuring the similarity between process models using semantic analysis. Similarity in this paper is based on textual proximity of process components.

We suggest elaborating this similarity method proposed in [15] by referring also to operational similarity, as expressed in the activity decomposition model. Distances in this case can be calculated in terms of separating in the seven taxonomies.

4.5 An Automatic Construction of Process Data Ontologies

Some works focus on automatic construction of process data ontologies, as a basis for further understanding the logic of process models. Several works have been suggested, each focuses on extracting different aspects of the business conduct as encoded in the process repository. The work in [1] proposes a query-by-example approach that relies on ontological description of business processes, activities, and their relationships, which can be automatically built from the workflow models themselves. The work in [3] automatically extracts the semantics from searched conceptual models, without requiring manual meta-data annotation, while basing its method on a model-independent framework.

We suggest extending the above methods by targeting the automatic extraction and usage of the operational layer (the "how-to") and the business rules encapsulated in the process repository. These can be explored using the taxonomies presented in Section 3.

5   Conclusions

We presented a framework to standardize the content layer of business process models as a basis for utilizing them for business process management purposes. The proposed framework provides a starting point that can already be applied in real-life scenarios, yet several research issues remain open. We mention two such extensions here. First, extending the list of relevant applications that can utilize the standardized model. Second, adding a case study and experiments to measure the efficiency of the proposed improvements to the listed applications.

References

1. Belhajjame, K., Brambilla, M.: Ontology-Based Description and Discovery of Business Processes. In: Halpin, T., Krogstie, J., Nurcan, S., Proper, E., Schmidt, R., Soffer, P., Ukor, R. (eds.) Enterprise, Business-Process and Information Systems Modeling. LNBIP, vol. 29, pp. 85–98. Springer, Heidelberg (2009)
2. Bhattacharya, K., Gerede, C.E., Hull, R., Liu, R., Su, J.: Towards Formal Analysis of Artifact-Centric Business Process Models. In: Alonso, G., Dadam, P., Rosemann, M. (eds.) BPM 2007. LNCS, vol. 4714, pp. 288–304. Springer, Heidelberg (2007)
3. Bozzon, A., Brambilla, M., Fraternali, P.: Searching Repositories of Web Application Models. In: Benatallah, B., Casati, F., Kappel, G., Rossi, G. (eds.) ICWE 2010. LNCS, vol. 6189, pp. 1–15. Springer, Heidelberg (2010)
4. Krumbholz, M., Maiden, N.: The implementation of enterprise resource planning packages in different organisational and national cultures. Information Systems 26(3), 185–204 (2001)
5. Kumaran, S., Liu, R., Wu, F.Y.: On the Duality of Information-Centric and Activity-Centric Models of Business Processes. In: Bellahsène, Z., Léonard, M. (eds.) CAiSE 2008. LNCS, vol. 5074, pp. 32–47. Springer, Heidelberg (2008)
6. Lincoln, M., Gal, A.: Content-Based Validation of Business Process Modifications. In: Jeusfeld, M., Delcambre, L., Ling, T.-W. (eds.) ER 2011. LNCS, vol. 6998, pp. 495–503. Springer, Heidelberg (2011)
7. Lincoln, M., Gal, A.: Searching Business Process Repositories Using Operational Similarity. In: Meersman, R., Dillon, T., Herrero, P., Kumar, A., Reichert, M., Qing, L., Ooi, B.-C., Damiani, E., Schmidt, D.C., White, J., Hauswirth, M., Hitzler, P., Mohania, M. (eds.) OTM 2011, Part I. LNCS, vol. 7044, pp. 2–19. Springer, Heidelberg (2011)
8. Lincoln, M., Golani, M., Gal, A.: Machine-Assisted Design of Business Process Models Using Descriptor Space Analysis. In: Hull, R., Mendling, J., Tai, S. (eds.) BPM 2010. LNCS, vol. 6336, pp. 128–144. Springer, Heidelberg (2010)
9. Lincoln, M., Golani, M., Gal, A.: Machine-assisted design of business process models using descriptor space analysis. Technical Report IE/IS-2010-01, Technion (March 2010), http://ie.technion.ac.il/tech_reports/ 1267736757_MachineAssisted_Design_of_Business_Processes.pdf
10. Lincoln, M., Karni, R., Wasser, A.: A Framework for Ontological Standardization of Business Process Content. In: International Conference on Enterprise Information Systems, pp. 257–263 (2007)
11. Müller, D., Reichert, M., Herbst, J.: Data-Driven Modeling and Coordination of Large Process Structures. In: Meersman, R., Tari, Z. (eds.) OTM 2007, Part I. LNCS, vol. 4803, pp. 131–149. Springer, Heidelberg (2007)
12. Nigam, A., Caswell, N.S.: Business artifacts: An approach to operational specification. IBM Systems Journal 42(3), 428–445 (2003)
13. Van der Aalst, W.M.P., Barthelmess, P., Eliis, C.A., Wainer, J.: Proclets: A framework for lightweight interacting workflow processes. International Journal of Cooperative Information Systems 10(4), 443–482 (2001)
14. van der Aalst, W.M.P., Ter Hofstede, A.H.M.: YAWL: yet another workflow language. Information Systems 30(4), 245–275 (2005)
15. van Dongen, B.F., Dijkman, R., Mendling, J.: Measuring Similarity between Business Process Models. In: Bellahsène, Z., Léonard, M. (eds.) CAiSE 2008. LNCS, vol. 5074, pp. 450–464. Springer, Heidelberg (2008)
16. Wahler, K., Küster, J.M.: Predicting Coupling of Object-Centric Business Process Implementations. In: Dumas, M., Reichert, M., Shan, M.-C. (eds.) BPM 2008. LNCS, vol. 5240, pp. 148–163. Springer, Heidelberg (2008)
17. Yan, Z., Dijkman, R., Grefen, P.: Business Process Model Repositories-Framework and Survey. Technical report. Beta Working Papers

Post-via: After Visit Tourist Services Enabled by Semantics

Ricardo Colomo-Palacios[1], Alejandro Rodríguez-González[2],
Antonio Cabanas-Abascal[1], and Joaquín Fernández-González[3]

[1] Computer Science Department, Universidad Carlos III de Madrid
Av. Universidad 30, Leganés, 28911, Madrid, Spain
{ricardo.colomo,antonio.cabanas}@uc3m.es
[2] Bioinformatics at Centre for Plant Biotechnology and Genomics UPM-INIA,
Polytechnic University of Madrid
Campus de Montegancedo, 28660 Boadilla del Monte, Madrid, Spain
alejandro@alejandrorg.com
[3] EgeoIT
Av. Brasil 17, 28020 Madrid, Spain
joaquin.fernandez@egeoit.com

Abstract. The Internet has disrupted traditional tourism services. Thus, knowing tourists' travel experience becomes a privileged tool to enable new business strategies based on the feedback provided by the tourists themselves. Post-Via captures and effectively manages tourists' feedback and, based on semantic technologies, integrates opinions and services to enhance tourists' loyalty. In a nutshell, Post-Via tries to unite on one platform the necessary components to perform traditional Customer Relationship Management functions and opinion mining techniques to provide services of direct marketing using web semantic components and recommender systems.

Keywords: Semantic Technologies, Tourism, After Visit Services, Ontology.

1 Introduction

Tourism encompasses all kind of heterogeneous activities related to tourists' needs satisfaction, and borrows from equally uneven multiple activities [1]. In this kaleidoscopic scenario digital networks are transforming tourism in depth, as long as the importance of the Internet for travel and tourism industry has dramatically increased over the past few years [2]. ICT praxis in tourism industry is heavily affecting how its products/services marketing is planned and managed and generating strong and permanent changes in its distribution systems [3]. This ICTs impact is becoming increasingly stronger and unanimously considered as an substantive breakthrough for this sector competitiveness[4].

The tourism sector is composed of heterogeneous agents whose boundaries between competition and cooperation have evolved (and blurred) with the use of the Internet, resulting in a massive re-organization of the markets and the industry as a

P. Herrero et al. (Eds.): OTM 2012 Workshops, LNCS 7567, pp. 183–193, 2012.

whole[1]. One of the main actors in tourism business are tourism organizations. Focusing on those players, ICT contribution has also changed radically their efficiency and effectiveness, changing the way their businesses are conducted in the marketplace, as well as how they interact with consumers[5]. This timely ICT contribution can of course boost staff morale, managerial effectiveness, productivity and profitability for these players [6], but only if they are able to quickly respond to the changing demands of customers and suppliers, and to new opportunities and environmental needs [7].

This paper presents Post-Via, an ICT platform devoted to support after visit tourist services offered by local tourism organizations by delivering relevant after visit raw data and assorted analytic tools. The remainder of the paper is organized as follows: Section 2 surveys the relevant literature about semantic technologies and their use in tourism environments. Section 3 describes Post-Via project. Section 4 brings the main project conclusions and depicts future works.

2   Literature Review

Semantic technologies ever-increasing presence in the ICT domain has been driven by the works of Tim Berners-Lee [8]. Semantic technologies lay on a set of technologies among which the Ontology is the main one. Ontologies define common, shareable and reusable views of a domain, and they give meaning to information structures that are exchanged by information systems [9]. The use of semantic support in ICT-based solutions allows the introduction of "intelligence" in software based systems, making it possible to introduce computer based reasoning and so enabling process automatization [10] and the performance of sophisticated tasks [11]. Several authors have highlighted the importance of semantic technologies in organizations. Ding [12] stated that the semantic web is fast moving in a multidisciplinary way and Breslin et al. [13] confirmed that industry is adopting semantic technology applications. In sum, Semantic-based technologies have been steadily increasing their relevance in recent years in both the research and business worlds [14].

As a result of this, semantic technologies and tourism have work together in the past. For instance, [15] proposed a semantically enriched recommendation platform for tourists on route, later expanded to Destination Management Organizations [16]. [17] presented a semantic technology based platform to support cultural tourism. [18] used ontologies combined with Bayesian networks to provide recommendation in the context of the city of Tainan (Taiwan). Recommendation is the field of study chosen by [19] to design and present a tool based on semantics and fuzzy logic. And more recently, in [20], authors present a Web-based system that provides personalized recommendations of touristic activities properly classified and labeled according to a specific ontology, which guides the reasoning process. Finally, [21] provide personalized recommendations of cultural and leisure activities when the tourist has already arrived at the destination partially based on semantic technologies.

However, these works are not focused on dealing with tourists once the trip is over. It's the main aim of Post-Via.

3   Post-via: Architecture and Implementation

Post-Via 2.0 platform is based on the conviction that information and communications technologies (ICT) can be heavily applied to the tourist domain with the aim of significantly improving quality of those services offered by tourism providers to final users.

This section presents the semantic architecture proposed for Post-Via project. Firstly, the main architecture of the whole system is showed describing briefly the workflow and the use of the semantic infrastructure. And secondly, a detailed description of the semantic component is provided. Finally, an example of the use of the semantic model is presented showing a couple of examples of the SPARQL queries which will be launch against the model.

3.1   Main Architecture

The main architecture of the entire Post-Via platform is depicted in Figure 1. As can be seen Post-Via is made up of several components which are interconnected using the Model-View-Controller pattern design.

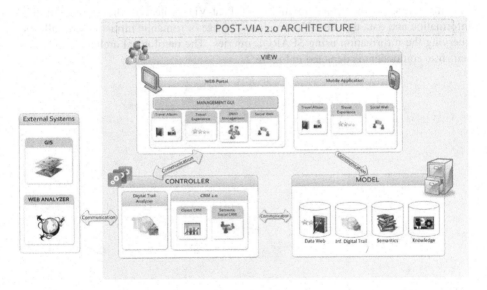

Fig. 1. Post-Via Architecture

In this paper, the semantic component is explained in detail, paying attention to the main entities which make up this component, and the relations among them. The behavior of the platform depends on user needs. However, most of the interactions of the platform will make use of the semantic model. This is because Post-Via has been designed as a semantic platform (a platform with an internal behavior based on semantic technologies). This means that most of the useful information of Post-Via, provided by the user is stored using the semantic model.

Each query or data entry in Post-Via makes use of the semantic platform and the relational database. When a user introduces data in the platform, this information is divided into several items depending on the entities which affect the data introduced. Once the information has been divided, an internal ID is assigned to each of the parts of the data. The main information is stored in the semantic model using this ID as part of the URI of the different instances which will be created (for example, a user with ID 45 will generate at URI like http://postviahost.com/postvia.owl#USER45). At the same time, this ID is stored in the instances with the "id" data property value. Also, in the relational database, the additional information about the data introduced is stored. The reason behind this is to avoid a possible overload of the semantic model.

The semantic model needs concrete information to handle SPARQL queries. This information is referred to the relations existing between the different entities. However, some extra information such as, for example, the comments or opinions provided by the user is not stored in the semantic model. Post-Via only stores a reference which allows us to know if a given comment has been introduced.

3.2   Semantic Model

The main aim of the semantic model of Post-Via project is the storage of the information and data that Post-Via handles. The use of semantic infrastructures allows querying the information using SPARQL queries. The ontological architecture of the semantic component is depicted in Figure 2.

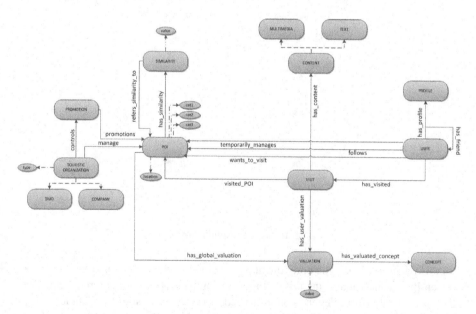

Fig. 2. Conceptual Semantic Model

In what follows the conceptual semantic models of Post-Via platform are explained:

- **User:** This entity represents tourist. Each tourist registered in the platform will be identified by an instance in the ontological model.
- **Profile:** Each user can have several (1-n) profiles. The profile class represents each possible profile existing in the platform. A profile defines the set of preferences for a tourist. Profile allows making recommendations between users based on their profiles. For instance, given a profile which reflects that the user likes some kind of restaurants, through the use of the platform it is possible to make recommendations to other users with similar preferences.
- **Visit:** This entity represents the visit that a concrete user has made on a concrete time and place. When a user visits a given POI (Point of Interest), a new instance of visit is created to store all the information related to the visit.
- **Valuation:** This entity represents the valuation of a visit. It can make reference to a concrete visit made by the user, or to the global valuation of a POI (calculated based on the valuation of the users). The instances of this entity present an attribute (value) to establish the weight of the valuation.
- **Concept:** This entity represents the concept that the user has valuated. It is also used by the global valuation. The concept can make reference to several things such as accommodation, cleanliness, food, etc.
- **POI:** It represents a concrete point of interest.
- **Similarity:** This entity represents the similarity which exists between several POIs. The instances of this entity present an attribute (value) to establish the similarity level.
- **Content:** This entity makes reference to the content which can be associated to a concrete visit (multimedia: pictures, videos, audio, etc...) or text (mainly comments).
- **Touristic Organization:** This entity is used to make reference to the organization which is in charge of the management of a given POI. It is mainly divided in two sub elements: private companies or DMO (Destination Management Organization).
- **Promotion:** This entity represents the promotions offered by the POIs. These promotions are managed by touristic organizations.

The different relations, which have been included in the semantic model of Post-Via, are presented in Table 1.

Table 1. Relations of the semantic model

Relation	Domain	Range	Inverse Relation
has_profile	User	Profile	is_profile_of
has_friend	User	User	is_friend_of
has_visited	User	Visit	was_done_by
has_user_valuation	Visit	Valuation	makes_reference_to
has_global_valuation	POI	Valuation	is_global_valuation_of
has_valuated_concept	Valuation	Concept	is_valuated_in

Table 1. (*Continued*)

visited_POI	Visit	POI	was_visited_in
has_similarity	POI	Similarity	refers_similarity_to
promotes	Promotion	POI	is_promoted_by
manages	Touristic Organization	POI	is_managed_by
controls	Touristic Organization	Promotion	is_controlled_by
follows	User	POI	is_followed_by
has_content	Visit	Content	is_content_of
has_multimedia_content	Visit	Multimedia	is_multimedia_content_of
has_text_content	Visit	Text	is_text_content_of
temporarily_manages	User	POI	is_temporarily_managed_by
wants_to_visit	User	POI	will_be_visited_by

The explanation of each relation is as follows:

- o **has_profile:** This relation is used to establish a relation between a concrete user and one or more profiles. As explained before, the idea is to provide the system with the ability of querying the model in order to know possible associations or relations between users based on their similarities using their profiles. It is a non-functional relation because one user can present several profiles.

- o **has_friend:** This relation is used to model a friendship link between two users. This relation allows knowing which users are friends. The aim of this relation is to create recommendation profiles based on several parameters such as friendship. For the sake of simplification, authors decided to use a new relation instead of using existing approaches such as Friend of a Friend (FOAF). It is a non-functional relation because one user can have several friends.

- o **has_visited:** This relation is used to model a relationship between a user and his or her visits. It is a non-functional relation because one user can made several visits.

- o **has_user_valuation:** This relation is used to perform a valuation on a concrete visit. It models a relation between a concrete visit and a concrete instance of valuation type. At the same time, the valuation will be related with a concept as explained in the relation *has_valuated_concept*. It is a non-functional relation because each visit has several valuations which cover the different concepts that can be evaluated.

- o **has_global_valuation:** This relation is used to model a relation between a concrete POI and a valuation instance. Thus, it's possible to have a global valuation about a concrete POI based on the individual valuations of the users. It is a non-functional relation because a POI can have several valuation instances.

- o **has_valuated_concept:** This relation is used to know which concept has been evaluated on a concrete "valuation" instance. Each POI has several items to valuate (e.g. in a hotel a given user can evaluate the quality of the service, comfort, cleanliness, etc. meanwhile, for instance, a restaurant the quality of the food can be assessed). Thus, it is necessary to establish the concept which has been valuated. It is a functional relation because a valuation can make reference only to a concrete concept. This is because the valuation contains a numerical value.

o **visited_POI:** This relation is used to establish, on a concrete visit, which POI has been visited. Given that the relations between POIs and visits are unary, this relation is functional.

o **has_similarity:** This relation is used to set the similarity between two POIs. Thus, it is possible to know if two POIs are similar and how similar they are (based on the similarity level). With this information it is possible to make recommendations to the users. It is a non-functional relation because a POI can be similar to several.

o **promotions:** This relation is used to establish the relation between a concrete promotion, created or managed by a touristic organization, and the POI affected by this promotion. It is a non-functional relation because a promotion can affect several POIs.

o **manages:** This relation is used to establish a relation between a touristic organization and a POI. It is a non-functional relation because a touristic organization can manage several POIs.

o **controls:** This relation is used to establish a relation between a touristic organization and a promotion. It is a non-functional relation because a touristic organization can control several promotions.

o **has_content:** This relation is used to establish a relation between a visit and a content. It is a non-functional relation because a visit can have several contents.

o **has_multimedia_content:** This relation is used to establish a relation between a visit and a multimedia content. It is a non-functional relation because a visit can have several multimedia contents. This relation is sub property of *has_content* and hence it is not depicted in the diagram.

o **has_text_content:** This relation is used to establish a relation between a visit and a text content. It is a non-functional relation because a visit can have several text contents. This relation is sub property of *has_content* and for hence it is not depicted in the diagram.

o **temporarily_manages:** This relation is used to establish a relation between a user and a POI. With this relation we can know which POIs were created and are currently managed by a user. When a user adds a POI in Post-Via, the user is the manager of the POI until a Touristic Organization takes the control of it.

o **wants_to_visit:** This relation is used to establish a relation between a user and a POI. It is a non-functional relation because a user has the intention of visit several POIs.

Table 2 presents data properties of the semantic model. Special attention should be paid to "id" property. This property contains the ID, which represents a concrete instance in the semantic model. With the ID of the instance it is possible to query the relational database in order to obtain more information if needed.

Table 2. Data properties of the semantic model

Property	Domain	Range
type	Touristic Organization	Literal
value	Valuation Similarity	int
location	POI	Literal
id	Thing	Literal
description	Similarity	Literal
cat1	POI	Literal
cat2	POI	Literal
cat3	POI	Literal

To conclude with the description of the model, Figure 3 provides a representation of the semantic model painted with OntoGraf plugin of Protégé tool.

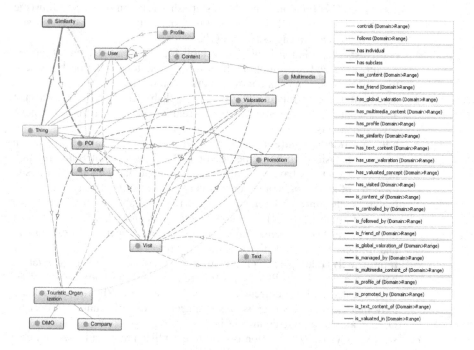

Fig. 3. OntoGraf representation of the semantic model

3.3   Accessing the Model

The access to the semantic model can be performed using several ways. Depending on the operation needed (store or retrieve), a concrete solution is adopted. Thus, in order to store information in the semantic model, authors have chosen Jena API as main framework to load the ontology model and store the data. The access to semantic model and relational database is handled by a middleware that manages the dealing and storage of information in both persistence mechanisms, using Jena API to access semantic model.

On the other hand, in query issues, two main options are available for semantic frameworks. The first one consists on the use of Jena API. The main problem of this option is that it is slower and more difficult to implement because it requires knowing which exact classes and instances are you going to need. The second option, which is the one implemented in Post-Via, is the use of SPARQL. Once Post-Via requires information about the model, a middle interface is executed. This interface receives the information required and is in charge of generating the appropriate SPARQL query to access the semantic model. Most of the queries are fixed and, for hence, the associated SPARQL query is static. In those cases where the query is dynamic, the interface generates the SPARQL associated to the query asked by the interface. However, it is important to remark that the interface of Post-Via platform has been developed in such a way that it is not possible to process any type of query. For this reason, the numbers of queries that can be done against the semantic model are limited. The following snippets depict a small example about a typical query which can be made against the semantic model:

```
PREFIX rdf: <http://www.w3.org/1999/02/22-rdf-syntax-ns#>
PREFIX owl: <http://www.w3.org/2002/07/owl#>
PREFIX pv: <http://127.0.0.1/postvia.owl#>
SELECT *
WHERE {
?u pv:has_visited ?v .
?v pv:visited_POI ?p .
}
```

Snippet 1. SPARQL Query to get users and visits

In Snippet 1 the SPARQL query which obtains all the visits made by all the users of the platform is showed. It returns the instance which represents the visit and the instance which represents the user.

```
PREFIX rdf: <http://www.w3.org/1999/02/22-rdf-syntax-ns#>
PREFIX owl: <http://www.w3.org/2002/07/owl#>
PREFIX pv: <http://127.0.0.1/postvia.owl#>
SELECT ?v ?p
WHERE {
?u pv:has_visited ?v .
?v pv:visited_POI ?p .
FILTER regex(str(?u), "US001")
}
```

Snippet 2. SPARQL Query to get POIs of visits of a concrete user

Snippet 2 shows the SPARQL query which obtains all the visits (and the POI associated to each visit) of a concrete user (US001).

4   Conclusions and Future Work

In new scenarios in which the internet has deeply changed tourism services provision patterns, tourism organizations behaviour is changing to wisely adapt to these new circumstances. Post-Via framework provides a new platform built to help tourism organizations to attract tourists to places they already have visited before. Based on a set of cutting edge technologies (geographical information systems, recommender systems, customer relationship management, social networks, mobility and semantic technologies), Post-Via represents a novel approach to achieve tourism loyalty by means of allowing the user to have a platform that assists him once his trip has finished.

Future research will be focused on the development of DL axioms or rules which allows the execution of inference engines over the semantic model to infer useful knowledge based on the descriptions of the domain. Future works also will be centered on the testing and discussion of the platform along with its comparison to other systems similar in terms of technology, aims and functionalities.

Acknowledgement. This work is supported by the Spanish Ministry of Industry, Tourism, and Commerce under the project *"Diseño, desarrollo y prototipado de una plataforma TIC de servicios post-viaje a los turistas"* (IPT-2011-0973-410000).

References

[1] Aldebert, B., Dang, R.J., Longhi, C.: Innovation in the tourism industry: The case of Tourism@. Tourism Management 32(5), 1204–1213 (2011)
[2] Garín-Muñoz, T., Pérez-Amaral, T.: Internet usage for travel and tourism: the case of Spain. Tourism Economics 17(5), 1071–1085 (2011)
[3] Berné Manero, C., García-González, M., García-Uceda, M.E., Múgica Grijalba, J.M.: Modelización de los cambios en el sistema de distribución del sector turístico debidos a la incorporación de las tecnologías. Cuadernos de Economía y Dirección de la Empresa (in press, 2012)
[4] Ip, C., Leung, R., Law, R.: Progress and development of information and communication technologies in hospitality. International Journal of Contemporary Hospitality Management 23(4), 533–551 (2011)
[5] Buhalis, D., Law, R.: Progress in information technology and tourism management: 20 years on and 10 years after the Internet—The state of eTourism research. Tourism Management 29(4), 609–623 (2008)
[6] Buhalis, D.: Strategic use of information technologies in the tourism industry. Tourism Management 19(5), 409–421 (1998)
[7] Cooper, C.: Knowledge management and tourism. Annals of Tourism Research 33(1), 47–64 (2006)

[8] Berners-Lee, T., Hendler, J., Lassila, O.: The semantic web. Scientific American 284(5), 34–43 (2001)
[9] Brewster, C., O'Hara, K.: Knowledge representation with ontologies: Present challenges—Future possibilities. International Journal of Human-Computer Studies 65(7), 563–568 (2007)
[10] Álvarez Sabucedo, L.M., Anido Rifón, L.E., Corradini, F., Polzonetti, A., Re, B.: Knowledge-based platform for eGovernment agents: A Web-based solution using semantic technologies. Expert Systems with Applications 37(5), 3647–3656 (2010)
[11] Durgin, J.K., Sherif, J.S.: The semantic web: a catalyst for future e-business. Kybernetes 37(1), 49–65 (2008)
[12] Ding, Y.: Semantic Web: Who is who in the field—a bibliometric analysis. Journal of Information Science 36(3), 335–356 (2010)
[13] Breslin, J.G., O'Sullivan, D., Passant, A., Vasiliu, L.: Semantic Web computing in industry. Computers in Industry 61(8), 729–741 (2010)
[14] Janev, V., Vraneš, S.: Applicability assessment of Semantic Web technologies. Information Processing & Management 47(4), 507–517 (2011)
[15] García-Crespo, A., Chamizo, J., Rivera, I., Mencke, M., Colomo-Palacios, R., Gómez-Berbís, J.M.: SPETA: Social pervasive e-Tourism advisor. Telematics and Informatics 26(3), 306–315 (2009)
[16] García-Crespo, Á., Colomo-Palacios, R., Gómez-Berbís, J.M., Chamizo, J., Rivera, I.: Intelligent Decision-Support Systems for e-Tourism. International Journal of Decision Support System Technology 2(1), 36–48 (2010)
[17] Bordoni, L.: Technologies to support cultural tourism for Latin Latium. Journal of Hospitality and Tourism Technology 2(2), 96–104 (2011)
[18] Huang, Y., Bian, L.: A Bayesian network and analytic hierarchy process based personalized recommendations for tourist attractions over the Internet. Expert Systems with Applications 36(1), 933–943 (2009)
[19] García-Crespo, Á., López-Cuadrado, J.L., Colomo-Palacios, R., González-Carrasco, I., Ruiz-Mezcua, B.: Sem-Fit: A semantic based expert system to provide recommendations in the tourism domain. Expert Systems with Applications 38(10), 13310–13319 (2011)
[20] Moreno, A., Valls, A., Isern, D., Marin, L., Borràs, J.: SigTur/E-Destination: Ontology-based personalized recommendation of Tourism and Leisure Activities. Engineering Applications of Artificial Intelligence (in press, 2012)
[21] Batet, M., Moreno, A., Sánchez, D., Isern, D., Valls, A.: Turist@: Agent-based personalised recommendation of tourist activities. Expert Systems with Applications 39(8), 7319–7329 (2012)

Ontology-Based Support for Security Requirements Specification Process

Olawande Daramola[1,2], Guttorm Sindre[2], and Thomas Moser[3]

[1] Department of Computer and Information Sciences
Covenant University, Ota, Nigeria
Olawande.daramola@covenantuniversity.edu.ng
[2] Department of Computer and Information Science
Norwegian University of Science and Technology (NTNU), Norway
{wande,guttors}@idi.ntnu.no
[3] Christian Doppler Laboratory for Software Engineering
Integration for Flexible Automation Systems
Vienna University of Technology, Austria
thomas.moser@tuwien.ac.at

Abstract. The security requirements specification (SRS) is an integral aspect of the development of secured information systems and entails the formal documentation of the security needs of a system in a correct and consistent way. However, in many cases there is lack of sufficiently experienced security experts or security requirements (SR) engineer within an organization, which limits the quality of SR that are specified. This paper presents an approach that leverages ontologies and requirements boilerplates in order to alleviate the effect of lack of highly experienced personnel for SRS. It also offers a credible starting point for the SRS process. A preliminary evaluation of the tool prototype – *ReqSec tool* - was used to demonstrate the approach and to confirm its usability to support the SRS process. The tool helps to reduce the amount of effort required, stimulate discovery of latent security threats, and enables the specification of good quality SR.

Keywords: security requirements, ontology, requirement boilerplates, information extraction, security threats.

1 Introduction

The increasing opportunities for systems integration, remote access, and sharing of resources across heterogeneous platforms by diverse software agents have made security requirements engineering (SRE) a major aspect of software system development in recent times. The Security requirements specification (SRS) process, which entails the formal documentation of identified security needs of a system, is an integral aspect of SRE [1]. However, there is a lack of sufficiently experienced security experts or security requirements engineers in many organizations, which limits the quality of SRS. SR becomes too vague or too specific in many cases due to the absence of

P. Herrero et al. (Eds.): OTM 2012 Workshops, LNCS 7567, pp. 194–206, 2012.
© Springer-Verlag Berlin Heidelberg 2012

experienced SR personnel [2, 3]. This scenario implies the need for a tool-based framework that is capable of supporting the SRS process. The framework will: 1) assist the requirements engineer (REng) in the identification of security threats, which is usually a manual procedure that depends largely on the expertise of human personnel; 2) stimulate the adoption of appropriate defence strategies to deal with the identified security threats; 3) enable the formulation of SR in a consistent way, eliminating ambiguity, and ensuring correctness of SR; and 4) reduce the effort needed for SRS by allowing the reuse of previously specified SR in subsequent instances. The aim is to assist the REng in the process of SRS so that the quality of SRS can be enhanced and effort reduced.

To achieve these objectives, we have integrated the use of ontologies and requirements boilerplates within a semantic framework-based tool to aid the REng personnel. The use of ontologies provides the necessary background knowledge, and domain knowledge that is required to identify security threats, and recommend appropriate countermeasures, while the requirements boilerplates provide a reusable template for writing SR in a consistent way in order to eliminate ambiguity. The uniqueness of our approach stems from the provision of a more elaborate procedure for supporting the SRS process relative to existing approaches because our approach: 1) enables identification of security threats; 2) provides recommendation of defence actions as countermeasure to identified security threats; and 3) enables pattern-based reuse of boilerplates when writing SR. The evaluation experiment that we conducted, reveal that our approach is usable to support SRS.

The rest of this paper is as follows. Section 2 gives an overview of background and related work, while Section 3 presents a detailed overview of our approach. Section 4 discusses the evaluation, results, and threats to validity. The paper is concluded in Section 5 with a discussion of further work.

2   Background and Related Work

In this section, we present an overview of ontology support for security requirements engineering (SRE), boilerplates for security requirements. Additionally, we discuss the related work.

2.1   Ontology Support for Security Requirements Engineering (SRE)

There is a lack of systematic processes for attaining software security [1], hence SRE attempts to add security considerations into software requirements engineering. SRE aims to integrate the security needs of a system particularly from the attacker's perspective into the software development process as early as possible. According to [3], SR objectives can be categorized as authentication, authorization, integrity, intrusion detection, non-repudiation, confidentiality, and auditing. Some well-known SRE approaches include Comprehensive, Lightweight Application Security Process (CLASP) [4], System Quality Requirements Engineering (SQUARE) [5], Common Criteria [6], Secure Tropos [7], and Misuse Case [8].

Ontologies as the semantic representation of the conceptualization of a domain have an important role to play in SRE. Research efforts on security ontologies such as [9, 10, 11] attest to this. In [12] the use of ontology was suggested as the solution to the problem of vaguely defined vocabularies among security practitioners.

According to [13], specific applications of ontologies to SRE include security taxonomies, general security Ontologies, specific security ontologies, security ontologies for Semantic Web, security ontologies for risk analysis, and ontologies for security requirements.

Generally, a good ontology will facilitate more effective reporting of incidents, sharing of information, and interoperable security collaborations among different organizations. Our proposed framework uses ontology to ensure the standardization of vocabulary in SRS, threat identification, and the recommendation of appropriate countermeasure to identified threats.

2.2 Boilerplates for Security Requirements

The notion of requirements boilerplates (RB) which stems originally from the work of [14], and subsequently applied in [15] enables the writing of requirements in a consistent manner. A requirement boilerplate is a pre-defined structural template for writing requirement statements. It imposes a uniform structure on the way requirements are written, by affording a level of expressivity akin to using of natural language, yet minimising ambiguity in requirement statements. The fixed parts of requirement boilerplate are reused when writing requirements, while the REng can fill in the parameter parts manually.

An example of a boilerplate taken from the webpage[1] is:

"*BP2*: **The <system> shall be able to <action> <entity>**"

Here, *BP2* is the label of this particular boilerplate. The terms in < > brackets are parameters where something must be filled in when the boilerplate is instantiated to a concrete requirement. The words that are outside brackets are the fixed syntax elements (FSE) that will be kept as-is when the boilerplate is instantiated. An example of an instantiation of this particular boilerplate, would be *"The payroll system shall be able to display login details of all its users"*. In this case *<action>* has been replaced by "display login details" and *<entity>* by "all its users". In some cases, several boilerplates may be combined to make precise and testable requirements, e.g. combining *BP2* with *BP37* **...at least <percentage> of the time** will yield the requirement *"The payroll system shall be able to display login details of all users at least 100% of the time"*.

Thus, the use of boilerplate will ensure that a unified structure and style of writing is used for requirements that pertain to specific classes of system function, capability, goals, or constraints. The FSE in each boilerplate will remain the same for all requirements that used a certain boilerplate. For instance, all who used BP2 + BP37 to specify that the system should be able to do something with some specific frequency,

---

[1] http://www.requirementsboilerplates.org

will now use phrases "shall be able to", "at least", "times per", rather than various other phrases that could have more or less the same meaning, e.g., "have the ability to", "be capable of", "a minimum of", "more than", "shots per", etc.

Firesmith in [16] identified four different types of defence against security threats, which can be used to assign specific security threats to the types of defence actions to counter them. These are:

(i) Prevention of malicious harm, security incident, security threats and security risks.

(ii) Detection of malicious attack, security incidents, security threats, and security risks.

(iii) Reaction to detected malicious attack.

(iv) Adaptation of system to avoid or minimize the negative consequences of the malicious harm, security incidents, security threats and security risks. This could also be in terms of recovery of system from attacks.

For each of the defence types, Firesmith also gave specific examples.

The examples in [16], could be the basis for some generic SR boilerplates, e.g.

SecBP1: **The** <*system*> **should [prevent | detect] at least** <*percentage*> **of** <*harm | incident | threat | risk*>

SecBP2: **Upon detection of** <*harm | incident | threat | risk*> **the system shall** <*action*>

SecBP11: **...of attacks with maximum duration** <*time unit*>

SecBP12: **...made by attackers with profile** <*attacker profile*>

SecBP21: **...at least** <*percentage*> **of the time**

Here, *SecBP11*, *SecBP12*, and *SecBP21* are parts that could be optionally concatenated with *SecBP1* or *SecBP2* respectively.

To use boilerplates for SRS in practical terms will entail the formulation of requirement boilerplates for the different aspects of security such as authentication, authorization, integrity, intrusion detection, non-repudiation, confidentiality, and auditing. Therefore, more boilerplates could be formulated, both as core parts and as attachments, but since boilerplates for security will vary for different domains, we cannot go into more detail here. However, experienced personnel must create the boilerplates prior to SRS as an upfront investment, while it should be updated periodically as new types of requirements emerge. By so doing, the boilerplate repository becomes an organisational asset for SRS that can be useful when there is paucity of experienced security REng personnel.

2.3 Related Work

We shall classify tool support for SRE into two broad categories – front-end tools and back-end tools. Front-end tools and approaches are those that facilitate the elicitation, modelling, and analysis of security threats in order to derive SR, while the back-end tools are those that help with the specification and validation of SR, and their integration with other requirements. Notable examples of front-end tools include: SecTro [17], - a CASE tool that supports automated modelling and analysis of security requirements based on Secure Tropos approach. The ST-Tool [18] supports the Secure

Tropos methodology. Its main goals are to support the translation of Secure Tropos models into formal specifications, and serve as a front-end tool for formal analysis of Secure Tropos models. The jMUCMNav (Java Use Case Map Navigator, [19]) editor is a modelling tool for Misuse Case Maps (MUCMs) in designing secure architectures for business processes. jUCMNav simply focuses on modelling for use case maps (UCM) and supports all UCM notations. Other front-end SRE tool that are worth mentioning are: SeaMonster [20, 21], and Surakasha security workbench [22].

Currently, there are more front-end tools than back-end tools for SRE. The SQUARE tool [5] is a back-end managerial tool that is designed to increase the quality of SRE process for the adopters of the SQUARE methodology. It support core SRE aspects such as definitions, searching, and addition of new terms, identification of security goals, assets and privacy goals, performing risk assessment, identifying threats, prioritizing requirements, traceability, and exporting of requirements to other requirements management tool. Similarly, the prototype tool - *ReqSec tool* – that we have developed is an eclipse-based back-end tool that supports SRS, and enables the integration of SR with other types of requirements. The unique feature of the ReqSec tool compared to other SRE back-end tools stems from its capability to facilitate automatic analysis of natural language requirements in order to assist the REng during SRS. It represents a first attempt to use semantic-based procedures for supporting both security threat identification and SRS. In the wider requirements engineering context, approaches such as [23] – ambiguity detection-, [24, 25] – requirement quality assessment-, are also based on natural language (NL) text analysis but did not use ontologies. The DODT [26] tool does not have a focus for SRE, but it bears similarity with our approach, because it combines the use of ontologies and boilerplates to enable semi-automatic transformation of NL requirements into boilerplate requirements. However, it can only ensure the correctness of requirements based on the underlying domain ontology, and the writing of boilerplate requirements. Our approach does more, in that it entails the discovery of latent security threats contained in NL descriptions, and the recommendation of probable defence actions that aids the formulation of semi-formal boilerplate SR. Hence, the novelty of our approach is the provision of a backend tool for SRE that will minimize effort needed for SRS, and offer a credible starting point for SRS, particularly in cases where there is paucity of experienced personnel.

3   Approach Overview

A high-level schematic overview of our approach is presented in Fig. 1. The process starts with input of description of the security threat scenario, which should be represented as a textual Misuse Case (TMUC) [8]. This is followed by identification of type of attack and required defence action through semantic text analysis of the TMUC, thereafter suggestion of boilerplates to be used to the REng, and finally specification of SR by the REng.

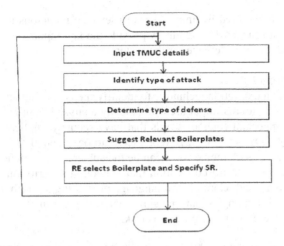

Fig. 1. Activity Workflow of the tool-supported SR Specification Process

3.1   Database Tampering - Example

In order to demonstrate how our tool-supported framework can be applied, we hereby consider the example of a security threat description of database tampering scenario. The detail of the scenario is presented in Table 1 using a TMUC template.

Table 1. TMUC for Database Tampering Case

Code: QC1	
Misuse Case Title	Tamper with database by web query manipulation
Name of System	Web Query System
Summary	A crook manipulates the web query, submitted from a search form, to update or delete information, or to reveal confidential information;
Basic Path	The crook provides some values on a product search form and submits. The system displays the product(s) matching the query. The crook alters the submitted URL, introducing a query error, and resubmits. The query fails and the system displays the database error message to the crook, revealing more about the database structure. The crook alters the query further, for instance adding a nested query to reveal secret data or update or delete data, and submits. The system executes the altered query, changing the database or revealing content that should have been secret.
Alternative Path	The crook does not alter the URL in the address window, but introduces errors or nested queries directly into form input fields.

Input TMC Details

The TMUC template [8] has two core aspects namely the basic path, and the alternative path. The basic path describes the security threat scenario that could be used by an attacker to cause harm to a system, while the alternative path specifies the other options that may be explored by an attacker or user with malicious intent. These two aspects together with the TMUC summary provide the key inputs used to identify the type of attack, and required defence for the system.

Identify Type of Attack

We used information extraction technique to identify the type of attack described by a TMUC template. The textual input are semantically analysed in order to identify and extract the most important (theme) words that have security implications. The basic threat ontology (BTO) (see Fig. 2), WordNet ontology, and the domain ontology (DO) are used to do this. A theme word can be the subject of a sentence (noun), or an action word (verbs) or a word collocation that connote a security threat to a system when it has been analysed. Core natural language processing algorithms for tokenization, parts-of-speech tagging, syntax parsing, morphological analysis, and ontology-based inferencing were used to achieve this task.

Determine the Type of Defence Using the Basic Threat Ontology (BTO)

The BTO contains a mapping of different kinds of security threats to specific defence actions based on information that was gathered from the literature and a number of existing security ontologies. The BTO is a major investment and a core knowledge infrastructure of the framework. The defence actions are the ones proposed by Firesmith in [16]. We reused all the essential aspects of the threat description in Security Ontology [11] as foundation for developing the BTO, which included some additional concepts. The BTO has a total of 98 classes, 46 restrictions and 9 object properties. The key object properties include *hasDefense* – which associates a threat with a specific defensive action, *hasThreat* – which associate a threat with an asset, *isThreatenedBy* – inverse of hasThreat, *isThreatTo*, *isSameAs*, - which describes equivalent concepts. Each security threat in the BTO was mapped to one or more defence actions (viz. detect, prevent, adapt, react, recover) using the *hasDefense* object property. Figure 2, presents a view of the BTO illustrating how specific types of attacks have been mapped to corresponding defence actions. The knowledge contained in the BTO is used for automatic recommendation of appropriate defence actions when a particular type of attack has been identified from the TMUC input details. The Pellet OWL Descriptive Logics (DL) reasoner was used as the ontology reasoning engine for the BTO.

Suggestion of Relevant Boilerplates

The information extraction process generates a set of recommendations comprising a pair of defence-action and attack-type. Fig. 3 shows the recommended pairs for the Database Tampering example. The recommended pairs are extracted directly from the BTO after the semantic analysis of the TMUC. Ontology reasoning and other semantic capability were facilitated using Stanford NLP toolkit[2], Word Net java API, and the Jena semantic framework[3]. Per-time, the REng will have to select a specific <defence-action, attack-type> pair from the list of recommendations, and appropriate

---

[2] http://nlp.stanford.edu/software/lex-parser.shtml
[3] http://jena.sourceforge.net/

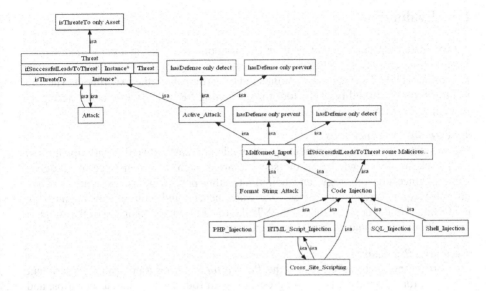

Fig. 2. A view of the description of Malformed Input threat in the BTO using OntoViz

boilerplate, prefix and suffix, from the boilerplate repository to formulate a security requirement automatically. However, the tool is able to learn by keeping track of the combinations of <defence-action, attack-type> pairs and boilerplate patterns that tend to go together based on user's preferences. Subsequently, once a <defence-action, attack-type> pair is selected, the tool automatically displays a list of fully formulated boilerplate SR for the user to select from. This way, the fixed syntax elements (FSE) of the selected boilerplate are reused, while the selected <defence-action, attack-type> substitutes the <action> placeholder in the selected boilerplate. The REng can then fill in the remaining part of the boilerplate requirements that require specific data to complete the formulation of the SR (see Fig. 3).

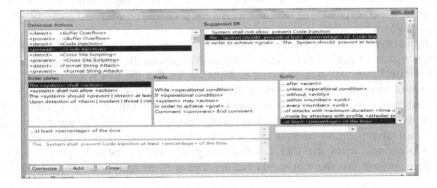

Fig. 3. A snapshot of suggestions for database tampering from the tool

4   Evaluation

We conducted a preliminary evaluation of our approach by using a controlled experiment with seven subjects. The subjects were Master degree students of software engineering of NTNU, Norway, who volunteered to participate in the experiment. The aim was to assess the usability of the tool for supporting SRS. The participants were paid for taking part in the experiment.

Background of Participants
The response to a pre-experiment questionnaire revealed that the participants had good background knowledge in the specific areas such as system security, requirements engineering, ontology, and boilerplates that pertain to the experiment. They have all taken two relevant courses – software security and requirements engineering and testing – in the department – IDI / NTNU. In addition, the majority of the subjects also claim to have some industrial work experience.

Evaluation Procedure
The participants were asked to use the *Reqsec tool*[3] during a controlled experiment that lasted for 1.5 hours. They were presented with four security threat scenarios, and asked to formulate SR for each case by using the tool. All the participants performed the same task at any given time during the experiment. The participants were given a five minutes tutorial on the use of the tool[4] before they commenced the experiment. They were required to assess the tool along six dimensions - *perceived usefulness (PU), perceived ease of use (PEOU), intention to use (ITU), reuse (reu), accuracy (acc), and serendipity (sere)* - through a post-experiment questionnaire. The mean score out of a maximum of 5.0 for each of the six dimensions are shown in Table 1.

4.1   Results

The analysis of the results from the post-experiment questionnaire revealed that the tool had its highest mean rating in the aspects of *perceived ease of use (PU)*, and *serendipity (sere)* – the users acknowledged that the tool offered suggestions that they had not thought about originally. The tool also had good rating in other aspects such as *reuse, accuracy,* and *intention to use*. All the participants stated emphatically that they would use the tool.

In the free comments feedback section of the questionnaire, the participants revealed a positive general perception of the tool as potentially viable to support SRS, and admitted their willingness to use it. Most agreed that the tool is easy to use, and capable of assisting a REng. A few of them were particularly impressed that the tool enabled them to write security requirements that they did not think about initially until when they saw the suggestions from the tool. They all agreed that although the tool offers useful support for SRS, it cannot be solely relied upon. This is because there were occasions when the tool failed to suggest certain expected options. Some of them advised that the tool would perform better if the quality of the underlining

---

[3] https://www.idi.ntnu.no/~wande
[4] https://www.idi.ntnu.no/~wande/Guide_for_Reqsec_Tool.htm

ontology is improved. They also mentioned a number of areas that should to be improved in the tool. This includes the fact that 1) the tool's interface did not scale well on the MacOs systems compared to Windows; and 2) the need to be able to save the requirements that pertain to a TMUC all at once in the repository and not one at a time. We agree with the observations of the participants and would seek to revise the subsequent version of the tool based on the observations by participants.

Generally, the result of the evaluation demonstrates the potential of the tool to first, simplify, and significantly aid the REng during the SRS process, particularly when the REng is not highly experienced. Second, facilitate a reduction in the effort expended on SRS, particularly as the process progresses. Third, ensure that correct terms are used when formulating SR, and in a consistent way without ambiguity. However, our inspection of the specified security requirements revealed consistency in the use of language and pattern of expression in formulated SR that pertain to same security threat scenario by different individuals, which is mainly due to the use of boilerplates and ontologies.

Table 2. Mean score rating for Tool Assessment

Metric	Mean	Std
PU	3	0.433013
PEOU	3.714286	0.698638
ITU	3.357143	0.481039
Reu	3.214286	0.393398
Acc	3.285714	0.95119
Sere	4	0.816497

4.2   Lessons Learned

Our experience from the evaluation emphasised the need for high quality underlying ontologies – BTO, DO - and the boilerplate repository. Hence, an upfront and crucial investment is to ensure that good quality BTO, DO and a rich boilerplate repository are available at the onset of the tool. In order to cater to this, the tool comes pre-loaded with the BTO and the boilerplate repository as basic artefacts, while a DO can be imported into the tool. Also, provision was made to ensure the evolution of the BTO, DO, and boilerplate repository with time. To do this, we have made it possible to continually revise the ontologies BTO, DO, and boilerplate repository from within the tool's environment. The tool includes an ontology management module that allows the addition of new concepts, properties, and axioms to an existing ontology, while the boilerplate management module allows the boilerplate repository to be updated. Thus, the tool can be customised, and adapted to cater for future emerging requirements.

4.3   Evaluation Threats

Ordinarily, an industrial case study would give a different perspective to the evaluation of the tool and the quality of tool support. However, the subjects used for the experiment are sufficiently knowledgeable in the relevant areas such as requirements engineering, system security, ontologies, and requirements boilerplates having taken taught courses in these areas. This makes them suitable as reasonable substitutes for real experts in a preliminary evaluation. Also, the evaluation was performed with only seven users, but although the statistical significance is reduced, the results are indicative of the acceptance of the approach evaluated. Moreover, our objective is to assess the potential usability of the tool to support SRS. Evidence in literature suggests that a minimum of 5 subjects are sufficient to get a valid opinion on the usability of a tool [27].

Another perspective to the evaluation could be to evaluate the tool alongside other tools or to compare its performance with humans, either of, which could also lead to a different result compared to what we have reported. However, comparative evaluation with other tools is not attractive as at now because, hardly could we find any other tool that have the same focus, and is set out to do exactly a similar thing as we envisioned. The option to compare the tool capacity with human is a possibility for the future, after this preliminary evaluation.

5   Conclusion

In this paper, we have presented the notion of ontology-support for security requirements specification. Our approach employs a tool-based framework that uses a combination of ontologies and boilerplates to aid a requirements engineer in the process of security threat identification and eventual formulation of quality SR. It provides the attendant benefits of reducing the effort need for the SRS process, and offers a good starting point in cases when sufficiently experienced REng may not be available. The preliminary evaluation of the approach confirms that it is viable and usable for supporting SRS. In future work, we will conduct a more elaborate evaluation by using industrial case studies to further validate the approach. Also, we shall seek means to further improve the performance of the tool, and extend the concepts to the aspect of safety.

Acknowledgment. The Norwegian Research Council through the ReqSec project, Norway, has supported this work while the first author of this paper was a Research Scientist at NTNU, Norway. This work has been supported by the Christian Doppler Forschungsgesellschaft and the BMWFJ, Austria.

References

1. Rushby, J.: Security Requirements Specifications: How and What? Symposium on Requirements Engineering for Information Security (SREIS), Indianapolis (2001)
2. Firesmith, D.: Specifying Reusable Security Requirements. Journal of Object Technology 3(1), 61–75 (2004)
3. Chandrabrose, A.: Alagarsami: Security Requirements Engineering – A Strategic Approach. International Journal of Computer Applications 13(3), 25–32 (2011)

4. Viega, J.: The CLASP Application Security Process. Training Manual, vol. 1(1). Secure Software Inc. (2005)
5. Mead, N., Stehney, T.: Security quality requirements engineering (SQUARE) methodology. In: Proceedings of International Conference on Software Engineering for Secure Systems (SESS 2005), pp. 1–5 (2005)
6. Common Criteria Implementation Board. Common Criteria for Information Technology Security Evaluation, Part 2: Security Functional Requirements (1999)
7. Mouratidis, H., Giorgini, P.: Secure Tropos: A security-oriented extension of the Tropos methodology. International Journal of Software Engineering and Knowledge Engineering 17(2), 285–309 (2004)
8. Sindre, G., Opdahl, A.: Eliciting Security Requirements with Misuse Cases. Requirements Engineering 10(1), 34–44 (2005)
9. Fenz, S., Ekelhart, A.: Formalizing information security knowledge. In: 4th International Symposium on Information, Computer, and Communications Security (ASIACCS 2009), pp. 183–194 (2009)
10. Kim, A., Luo, J., Kang, M.: Security Ontology for Annotating Resources. In: 4th International Conference on Ontologies, Databases, and Applications of Semantics, ODBASE 2005 (2005)
11. Herzog, A., Shahmehri, N., Duma, C.: An Ontology of Information Security. International Journal of Information Security 1(4), 1–23 (2007)
12. Donner, M.: Toward a Security Ontology. IEEE Security and Privacy (2003)
13. Souag, A., Salinesi, C., Wattiau, I.: Ontologies for Security Requirements: A Literature Survey and Classification. In: WISSE 2012 in Conjunction with 24th International Conference on Advanced Information Systems Engineering (CAiSE 2012), pp. 8 pages (June 2012)
14. Hull, E., Jackson, K., Dick, J.: Requirements Engineering. Springer (2004)
15. Daramola, O., Stålhane, T., Sindre, G., Omoronyia, I.: Enabling Hazard Identification from Requirements and Reuse-Oriented HAZOP Analysis. In: Proceeding of 4th International Workshop on Managing Requirements Knowledge, pp. 3–11. IEEE Press (2011)
16. Firesmith, D.: A Taxonomy of Security-Related Requirements. In: Proceedings of the International Workshop on High Assurance Systems (RHAS 2005), Paris, France (2005)
17. Pavlidis, M., Islam, S., Mouratidis, H.: A CASE Tool to Support Automated Modelling and Analysis of Security Requirements, Based on Secure Tropos. In: Nurcan, S. (ed.) CAiSE Forum 2011. LNBIP, vol. 107, pp. 95–109. Springer, Heidelberg (2012)
18. Giorgini, P., Massacci, F., Mylopoulos, J., Siena, A., Zannone, N.: ST-Tool: A CASE Tool for Modeling and Analyzing Trust Requirements. In: Herrmann, P., Issarny, V., Shiu, S.C.K. (eds.) iTrust 2005. LNCS, vol. 3477, pp. 415–419. Springer, Heidelberg (2005)
19. Bizhanzadeh, Y., Karpati, P.: jMUCMNav: an Editor for Misuse Case Maps. In: First Int. Workshop on Alignment of Business Process and Security Modelling (ABPSM 2011), Riga, Latvia (2011)
20. Tøndel, I.A., Jensen, J., Røstad, L.: Combining misuse cases with attack trees and security activity models. In: Proc. ARES 2010, pp. 438–445 (2010)
21. http://sourceforge.net/apps/mediawiki/seamonster/
22. Maurya, S., Jangam, E., Talukder, M., Pais, A.R.S.: A security designers' work-bench. In: Proc. Hack. in 2009, pp. 59–66 (2009)
23. Gleich, B., Creighton, O., Kof, L.: Ambiguity Detection: Towards a Tool Explaining Ambiguity Sources. In: Wieringa, R., Persson, A. (eds.) REFSQ 2010. LNCS, vol. 6182, pp. 218–232. Springer, Heidelberg (2010)

24. Wilson, W., Rosenberg, L., Hyatt, L.: Automated Analysis of Requirement Specifications. In: Proceedings of the International Conference on Software Engineering (ICSE 1997), pp. 161–171 (1997)
25. Fabrini, F., Fussani, M., Gnesi, S., Lami, G.: An Automatic Quality Evaluation for Natural Language Requirements. In: Proceeding of the Seventh International Workshop on Requirements Engineering Foundation for Software REFSQ 2001, Interlaken, Switzerland, pp. 150–164 (2001)
26. Farfeleder, S., Moser, T., Krall, A., Stålhane, T., Zojer, H., Panis, C.: DODT: Increasing Requirements Formalism using Domain Ontologies for Improved Embedded Systems Development. In: Proceedings of 14th IEEE Symposium on Design and Diagnostics of Electronic Circuits and Systems (DDECS 2011), pp. 1–4 (2011)
27. Nielsen, J., Landauer, T.: A mathematical model of the finding of usability problems. In: Proceedings of ACM INTERCHI 1993 Conference, pp. 206–213 (1993)

Formalization of Semantic Annotation for Systems Interoperability in a PLM Environment

Yongxin Liao[1,2], Mario Lezoche[1,2], Eduardo Loures[1,5],
Hervé Panetto[1,2], and Nacer Boudjlida[3,4]

[1] Université de Lorraine, CRAN, UMR 7039, Boulevard des Aiguillettes B.P.70239,
54506 Vandoeuvre-lès-Nancy, France
[2] CNRS, CRAN, UMR 7039, France
[3] Université de Lorraine, LORIA, UMR 7503, Boulevard des Aiguillettes B.P. 70239,
54506 Vandoeuvre-lès-Nancy, France
[4] CNRS, INRIA, LORIA, UMR 7503, France
[5] Industrial and Systems Engineering, Pontifical Catholic University of Parana,
Imaculada Conceicao 1155, Curitiba, Brazil
{Yongxin.Liao,Mario.Lezoche,Herve.Panetto}@univ-lorraine.fr,
eduardo.loures@pucpr.br, Nacer.Boudjlida@loria.fr

Abstract. Nowadays, the need for systems collaboration across enterprises and through different domains has become more and more ubiquitous. Due to the lack of standardized models or architecture, as well as semantic mismatching and inconsistencies, research works on information and model exchange, transformation, discovery and reuse are carried out in recent years. One of the main challenges in these researches is to overcome the semantic gap between enterprise applications along any product lifecycle, involving many distributed and heterogeneous enterprise applications. We propose, in this paper, an approach for semantically annotating different knowledge views (business process models, business rules, conceptual models, and etc.) in the Product Lifecycle Management (PLM) environment. These formal semantic annotations will make explicit the tacit knowledge generally engraved in application models and act as bridges to support all actors along the product lifecycle. A case study based on a specific manufacturing process will be presented for demonstrating how our semantic annotations can be applied in a Business to Manufacturing (B2M) interoperability context.

Keywords: Ontology, Semantic Annotation, Systems Interoperability, Business Process, PLM.

1 Introduction

The opening of enterprise information systems towards integrated access has been the main motivation for the interest around systems interoperability. In order to achieve the main objective of the enterprise, the business domain and the manufacturing domain need to exchange information and to synchronise their knowledge concerning the related product. Over the last ten years complex engineered products have

P. Herrero et al. (Eds.): OTM 2012 Workshops, LNCS 7567, pp. 207–218, 2012.
© Springer-Verlag Berlin Heidelberg 2012

discovered the benefits of PLM solutions and are adopting efficient PLM software in increasing numbers [1]. Contemporary PLM systems typically use workflow technology to provide support for process management. From many common business processes in the manufacturing industry in areas such as accounting, engineering design, product release, process planning, and production control, emerges the problem on versioning policies [2]. PLM represents an all-encompassing vision for managing all data relating to the design, production, support and ultimate disposal of manufactured goods. PLM can be thought of as both a repository for all information that affects a product, and a communication medium between product stakeholders: principally marketing, engineering, manufacturing and field service. The PLM system is the first place where all product information from marketing and design comes together, and where it leaves in a form suitable for production and support. In the same philosophy the product centric vision developed by [3] theorizes an omnipresence of the product related knowledge in the product itself.

Panetto et al. [4] postulate that an ontological model of a product may be considered as a facilitator for interoperating all applications software that share information during the physical product lifecycle. Their approach concerns the formalization of all technical data and concepts contributing to the definition of a Product Ontology, named ONTO-PDM, embedded into the product itself and making it interoperable with applications, thus minimizing loss of semantics. The ONTO-PDM acts as a common core model for enterprise applications interoperability in manufacturing process environment. Chen et al. [5] proposes an ontology-based framework for sharing and integrating product lifecycle knowledge. The authors present a mechanism that integrates ontology-based product lifecycle knowledge distributed among different cooperative enterprises allowing all knowledge actors to share product lifecycle knowledge. Wang et al. [2] stress out those current methods of process modelling which lack adequate specification of terminology used in supply chain process models. In a complete supply chain process, this leads to inconsistency and semantic conflicts between the interchanging of various process models. They propose combining BPMN ontology with SCOR ontology, deriving the so-called scorBPMN ontology, which specifies the semantics in supply chain processes.

The enterprise models are mainly related to some views and artefacts such as processes, behaviours, activities, data, resources, material and information flows, infrastructure and architecture. These models must contain the necessary and sufficient semantics in order to be intelligible and then enabling the global Enterprise Interoperability [6]. Semantic Annotations are generally used in heterogeneous domains and help to bridge the different knowledge representations [7]. There are several methods for modelling semantic annotations that vary in their referenced ontology (languages, tools and design), models and corresponding applications, as presented in our previous paper [8]. For example, the semantic business process model defines in details the business process flows, modelling the information, resource policy, business rules and other element encompassed in a workflow [9]. In [10], the author presents a complete overview on business process semantic annotations and divides the existing proposals into two groups: (i) adding semantics to specify the dynamic behaviour exhibited by a business process; (ii) adding semantics to specify the meaning of the entities of a process. In our approach, a semantic annotation is formally represented by the so-called semantic annotation structure model (SASM). The additional knowledge provided by the SASM makes bridges between different models to support the different actors in PLM environment.

This paper is organized as follows. Section 2 presents an updated version of the formal definition of semantic annotation, SASM and semantic annotation framework. In section 3, a real case study is presented in order to demonstrate the applicability of our framework. Section 4 concludes the paper and presents the future research.

2   Formalization of Semantic Annotation

2.1   Formal Definition of Semantic Annotation

A semantic annotation can be considered as a formal model which describes the relationship between the original information source and an ontology [9]. We proposed a formal definition: semantic annotation SA is a tuple $(\mathcal{M}, R)$ that is composed by two parts: the structural part, a set of mappings $\mathcal{M}$, between a set of elements of knowledge $\mathcal{E}$ and a powerset of ontology $\mathcal{P}(O_l)$; and the representational part, a set of meta-model references R [8].

$$SA = \{\mathcal{M}(\mathcal{E}, \mathcal{P}(O_l)), R\}$$

Where:

$\mathcal{E} = \{e_1, e_2, ..., e_n\}$, $\mathcal{E}$ is composed by a set of element e_i from different knowledge views, which represents the knowledge that needs to be annotated.

$O = \{o_1, o_2, ..., o_r\}$, O is composed by a set of ontology o_k, which represents the specific knowledge in a formal way. An *Ontology* $o_k \in O$ is a 4-tuple $(C_k, is\_a, RN_k, \sigma_k)$, where C_k is a set of *concepts*, is_a is a partial order relation on C_k, RN_k is a set of relation names, and $\sigma_k: RN_k \rightarrow (C^+)$ is a function which defines each relation name with its arity [11].

$\mathcal{P}(O_l) = \{p_1, p_2, ..., p_m\}$, $\mathcal{P}(O_l)$ is composed by a set of powerset of ontologies p_j, which brings meaning to annotated element of knowledge.

$p_j = \{\prod_{k=0}^{z} o_k \,|\, o_k \in \prod_{l=1}^{s} O_l\}$, p_j is composed by different concepts that referenced from one or more ontologies.

$\mathcal{M} = \{m_x\langle e_i, p_j\rangle \,|\, e_i \in \mathcal{E} \times p_j \in \mathcal{P}(O_l)\}$, $\mathcal{M}$ is composed by a set of mapping m_x, which describes the semantic relationship between e_i and p_j.

- $m_\sim(e_i, p_j)$: Equivalence relationship, which states that e_i is semantically equivalent to p_j;
- $m_\supset(e_i, p_j)$: Subsumes relationship, which states that e_i subsumes the semantics of p_j;
- $m_\subset(e_i, p_j)$: Subsumed by relationship, which states that e_i is subsumed by the semantics of p_j;

- $m_\cap (e_i, p_j)$: Intersection relationship, which states that e_i intersects with the semantics of p_j

$R = \{r_1, r_2, ..., r_t\}$, R is composed by a set of meta-model representation r_y, which represents the meta-model specification for the element of knowledge.

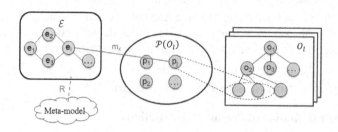

Fig. 1. Formal Definition of Semantic Annotation

The constituent parts of a formal semantic annotation are illustrated in Figure 1. On the left side, it indicates that an element of knowledge e_i in $\mathcal{E}$ is annotated with the powerset of ontology p_j in $\mathcal{P}(O_l)$ with their semantic relationship m_x. On the right side, it shows that the powerset p_j is composed by one or more concepts from one or more ontology O_l. The relationship R describes the referenced meta-model that expresses the annotated knowledge in the language represented.

2.2   Semantic Annotation Structure Model (SASM)

One of the well-known studies in semantic annotation area is proposed by SAWSDL Working Group[1]. They developed SAWSDL (Semantic Annotation for Web Services Definition Language) [12], which provides two kinds of extension attributes as follow: (i) modelReference, which is used for identifying the reference from a WSDL (Web Services Definition Language) or a XML Schema component to a semantic concept; (ii) liftingSchemaMapping and loweringSchemaMapping, which are used for describing the mappings between semantic data and WSDL type definitions in XML [13]. This approach cannot be easily used in a PLM environment when the business processes are represented with the help of formal or semiformal notations. In spite of some constraints that SAWSDL imposes [12], as well the need to represent with more details the procedural knowledge, we focus our study on discovering an appropriate SASM for our annotation.

In general, the common components of a SASM are elements of knowledge, powerstes of ontology, the semantic relations that relate them and a reference to the language meta-model. The meta-model of SASM is described in Figure 2. One element of knowledge has zero or more semantic annotations. One semantic annotation is composed by one powerset of ontology and defined by one annotation type. An element of knowledge corresponds to one or more elements of meta-model.

---

[1] SAWSDL Working Group.
http://www.w3.org/2002/ws/sawsdl/#Introduction

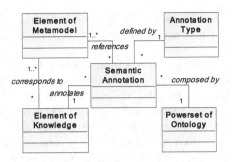

Fig. 2. Semantic Annotation Structure Meta-model

2.3   Semantic Annotation Framework

In a PLM environment, enterprises are using different kinds of engineering systems to manage their products. Applications in these engineering systems create many corresponding knowledge views for their product information flows. But because of the different specifications, the information among products is represented in many styles. When collaborative actors in or between enterprises need to cooperate, the tacit knowledge that hides behind these knowledge views must be made explicit. Figure 3 illustrates our semantic annotation framework in a PLM environment. There are four main modules: different knowledge views (KVs), knowledge cloud (KC), set of Meta-models (MM) and the formal semantic annotation (SA).

System of interest is represented into many different KVs along the product lifecycle. For example, business process models graphically depict their internal business procedures [14], conceptual models express the concepts and their mutual relationships

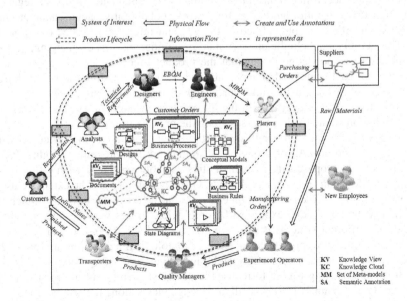

Fig. 3. Semantic Annotation Framework in PLM environment

[15], state machine diagrams represent the dynamic behaviour of an entity based on its response to events [16], Computer-Aided Design (CAD) models create a prototype of a product [17], and so on.

KC, in this context, is considered as a formal shared definition of concepts and relationships used for describing a domain of knowledge. In the same philosophy of Big Data [18], the ontology concepts that are combined in this KC are integrated from different sources and different levels. KC is composed by several interrelated ontologies and some common relevant domain concepts. They are structured as a loosely connected graph in three different abstract levels: general product ontology, top level, is the common share understanding of product definition and evolution; domain product ontology, middle level, capture the main structure concepts of product; instance product ontology, base level, instantiated the product information in the domain ontology. The links between them are done through similar concepts, for the moment this mapping is done manually. There are many approaches that are focused on representing the product knowledge: ONTO-PDM [4], Edinburgh enterprise ontology [19], PRONTO [20], OntoSTEP [21] and etc.

The set of MM refers to knowledge representation, which is used to explain the semantics of the different elements of knowledge. This set includes, among many others, UML 2.0 meta-model for specifying, constructing, and documenting the artefacts of systems [22], BPMN 2.0 meta-model for business process modelling [14], PNML meta-model (Petri Net Markup Language) for developing an XML-based interchange format Petri nets [23].

The formal semantic annotation $SA = \left\{ \mathcal{M}\left(\mathcal{E}, \mathcal{P}(O_l)\right), R \right\}$ is presented in section 2.1 and 2.2. It makes explicit the hidden semantics embedded in all KVs with their meta-model specifications. The annotations are created and used by all participants (analysts, designers, engineers, planners, operators, quality managers, transporters, new employees, etc.) according to the corresponding confidential and privacy strategies.

Through this semantic annotation framework, collaborative actors annotate their own KVs with the concepts defined in the KC and refer them to the corresponding MM. This activity can help the process of co-designing, sharing, exchanging, versioning and aligning knowledge throughout the product lifecycle: (i) All the associated knowledge for each annotated element can be located via this framework; (ii) Different knowledge views can be underhanded by their meta-model specifications; (iii) Tacit knowledge that is engraved in the different knowledge views can be made explicit. It will contribute to all processes along the product lifecycle.

Some approaches are similar to our method, but there are some differences that have to be pointed out. An ontology-based framework for integrating product lifecycle knowledge is proposed in [5], which stresses more on the reorganisation of the internal knowledge to fit the external needs. Our method, through the extensive use of semantic annotations, focuses more on carrying out the different views and much less on changing the knowledge expressed by ontologies. In this way the interoperability between the different systems is preserved using the local expressed and formalized knowledge. Li, C. et al present a standardised ontological annotation approach [24], OntoCAD, which is used to support multiple engineering viewpoints in CAD Systems. It is an interesting way to formalise the design step and it mostly focuses on the CAD part. Our domain of interest is all knowledge views along the product lifecycle.

3   Case Study

In order to explain how this semantic annotation proposition can be applied, in this section, we focus on the semantic annotation of the manufacturing processes in a product lifecycle. This case study is based on the cooperative production between two production sites: AIPL (Atelier Inter-Établissements de Productique Lorrain, France) and DIMeG (Dipartimento di Innovazione Meccanica e Gestionale, Italy).

Product models are designed at DIMeG with ProEngineer CAD system, which generates product technical and geometrical information into an EBOM (Engineering Bill of Material). However, the EBOM information represents the product structure from the designer point of view, which may not include every data needed by ERP (Enterprise Resource Planning) system and MES (Manufacturing Execution System) to support production [25]. For this reason, when AIPL received EBOM from DIMeG, they need to create a BOP (Bill of Process) according to EBOM. As can be seen from Figure 4, the manufacturing processes are planned as follow:

- Bar cutting process, cut 3 meter aluminium bar into 1 meter.
- Base turning process, chip a bar into the several design bases.
- Disc cutting process, cut galvanized plate and magnetic plate and into discs.
- Part sticking process, stick galvanized or magnetic discs with different bases.
- Product assembling process, use parts to assemble products.

After combining BOP with EBOM (also with other associated information, such as machine capability, stocks, company schedules and etc.), MBOM (Manufacturing Bill of Material) is generated.

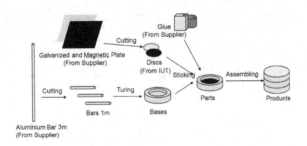

Fig. 4. Manufacturing Processes of AIPL Products

Sage X3 ERP system and Flexnet MES are used in AIPL. This site is in charge of purchasing row materials, outsourcing components and manufacturing products.

- In the purchasing part, based on the stock states and resources, ERP will generate a set of purchasing orders. The row materials (aluminium bar 3m, galvanized plate, magnetic plate and glue) will be purchased from different suppliers.

- In the outsourcing part, because the lack of disc cutting equipment, AIPL can't perform the disc cutting process. Galvanized plate and magnetic plate need to be delivered to IUT (Institute Universitaire de Technologie Nancy-Brabois).
- In the manufacturing part, the ERP system sends work order suggestions to the MES, which proposes the production schedules, and the MES performs the production and updates the stocks information for the ERP system.

At the end, all the qualified products are packaged in boxes and dispatched from AIPL to DIMeG, which will be delivered to the customers. The business process models in Figure 5 represent the product lifecycle of the AIPL products.

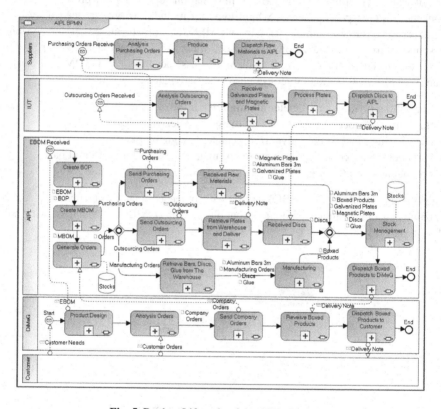

Fig. 5. Product Lifecycle of the AIPL Products

Because of the page limit, we will only present the part of the semantic annotations in this section that will be related to the sticking process of parts and assembling process of Prod5. Figure 6 illustrates these two processes:

- On the left side of the figure, it shows that glue A (AN 302-50) is used to stick galvanized disc with base (P11 and P60), glue B (HR-496) is used to stick magnetic disc with base (P10 and P88).
- On the right side of the figure, it shows that product Prod5 is composed by one P10, one P11, one P88 and one P60.

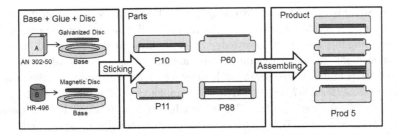

Fig. 6. Sticking and Assembling Processes of Prod 5

There is some tactic knowledge hidden in the experienced operator's and in the process designer's mind, for example:

- Under the conditioning temperature of around 20°C, the full cure time of glue A is 6 hours, and glue B is 24 hours. The sticking parts will be not stable if they are assembled before the full cure time. In this case, the stock of parts will became available only if they achieve the full cure time.
- In order to improve the production rate, Prod 5 can be assembled in different ways, which is dependent on the stock level of four parts. There exist three possible configurations named g1, g2 and g3: (i) g1 is the minimum stocks of p60 and p88; (ii) g2 is the minimum stocks of p11 and p88; (iii) g3 is the minimum stocks of p10 and p11. The associated business rule is:

  − If (g1 >= g2) and (g1 >= g3) then perform start assembly with P60,88;
  − If (g2 >= g3) and (g2 > g1) then perform start assembly with P88,11;
  − If (g3 > g2) and (g3 > g1) then perform start assembly with P11,10.

Figure 7 illustrates the semantic annotation example for above processes. In this figure, there are: three types of knowledge view: business process model (Petri net and BPMN 2.0 instances), business rule and conceptual model; five powerset instances: P001, P002, P003, P004 and P005; two ontologies: Onto-PDM [4] (top and middle level) and AIPL-Ontology (base level); seven semantic annotations.

In BPMN 2.0 instances, "Sticking" is annotated as $AIPL\_Manufacture\_001 = \{m_{\backsim}\langle Sticking, P001\rangle, "SubProcess, BPMN\,2.0"\}$, in which, P001 is labelled by the ontology concept "$Sticking:ProductSegmentType$". "Assemble Prod5" is annotated as $AIPL\_Manufacture\_002 = \{m_{\backsim}\langle Assemble\,Prod5, P002\rangle, "SubProcess, BPMN\,2.0"\}$, in which, P002 contains the ontology concept "$Prod5\_Assembly:ProductSegmentType$". "P10" is annotated as $AIPL\_Manufacture\_003 = \{m_{\exists}\langle P10, P003\rangle, "Date\,Object, BPMN2.0"\}$, in which, P003 is composed by two ontology concepts from different ontologies: "$P10:ProductDefinitionType$" and "$P10:ProductModelInCatalog$".

In Petri net, "Prod5 assemble states" is annotated as $Petri\_net\_001 = \{m_{\backsim}\langle Prod5\,assemble\,states, P002\rangle, "PNML"\}$. Through the connection between "Prod5 assemble states" and "Assemble Prod5", Petri net can help us to fully explain the state changes and rules during the whole Prod5 assemble process.

In business rules, "Sticking Rule" is annotated as $Business\_Rule\_001 = \{m_{\backsim}\langle Sticking\,Rule, P001\rangle, "Natural\,Language"\}$. We can easily find the connection between "Sticking" process and "Sticking Rule". This business rule is in the form of natural language, which lets emerge the tactic knowledge in "Sticking" process. New operators using this associated knowledge in the sticking process can avoid mistakes.

In conceptual model, "Operation" is annotated as $Conceptual\_Model\_001 = \{m_\cap \langle Operation, P004\rangle, "Class, UML\ 2.0"\}$, in which, P004 is labelled by the ontology concept "*ProductSegmentType*". "Article" is annotated as $Conceptual\_Model\_002 = \{m_\cap \langle Article, P005\rangle, "Class, UML\ 2.0"\}$, in which, P005 is labelled by the ontology concept "*ProductDefinitionType*". The semantic annotation helps in typing and clustering different parts of all product related processes to let simply reuse them into other contexts.

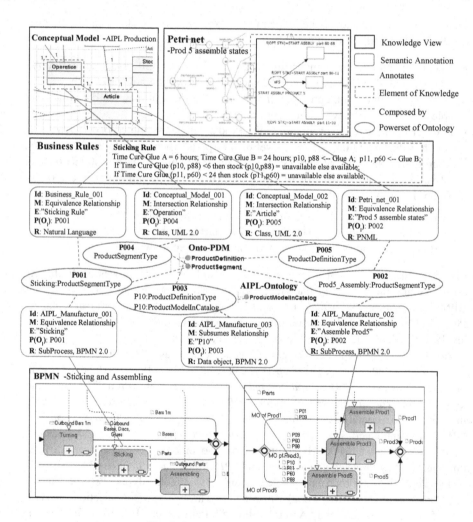

Fig. 7. Semantic Annotation Examples

This example shows the possible use of semantic annotation to create formal connection between different knowledge representations: behavioural knowledge (BPMN diagram, Petri net, business rule) and structural knowledge (conceptual model).

4 Conclusions

This paper provides a semantic annotation approach, which focused on the interoperability problem, to overcome the semantic gap between enterprise applications along the product lifecycle. We first introduced the system interoperability issues in PLM environment. Then we illustrated an updated semantic annotation definition and structure model. We proposed a semantic annotation framework that can help collaborative actors to overcome the semantic gaps. Finally, a case study based on AIPL and DIMeG product lifecycle is presented for demonstrating how our semantic annotations can be applied in a Business to Manufacturing interoperability context.

Future research will be focused on the following aspects: deeply analyse the interoperability requirements among the enterprise applications during the product lifecycle; use semantic annotation to help the evaluation of semantic gap between collaborative systems; explore the way to make heterogeneous enterprise systems and application interoperate, to help enterprises that use different process model notations to exchange process models and to operate on them; investigate the confidential and privacy strategies of the knowledge sharing in and between enterprises.

References

1. Marchetta, M.G., Mayer, F., Forradellas, R.Q.: A reference framework following a proactive-product approach for Product Lifecycle Management. Computers in Industry 62, 672–683 (2011)
2. Wang, X., Li, N., Cai, H., Xu, B.: An Ontological Approach for Semantic Annotation of Supply Chain Process Models. In: Meersman, R., Dillon, T.S., Herrero, P. (eds.) OTM 2010. LNCS, vol. 6426, pp. 540–554. Springer, Heidelberg (2010)
3. Morel, G., Panetto, H., Zaremba, M., Mayer, F.: Manufacturing Enterprise Control and Management System Engineering: Paradigms and Open Issues. IFAC Annual Reviews in Control 27(2), 199–209 (2003)
4. Panetto, H., Dassisti, M., Tursi, A.: ONTO-PDM: Product-driven ONTOlogy for Product Data Management interoperability within manufacturing process environment. Advanced Engineering Informatics 26(2) (April 2012)
5. Chen, Y., Chen, Y., Chu, H.: Development of a mechanism for ontology-based product lifecycle knowledge integration. Expert Systems with Applications: An International Journal 36(2), 2759–2779 (2009)
6. Yahia, E., Lezoche, M., Aubry, A., Panetto, H.: Semantics enactment for interoperability assessment in Enterprise Information Systems. Annual Reviews in Control 36(1) (April 2012)
7. Boudjlida, N., Panetto, H.: Enterprise Semantic Modelling for Interoperability. In: Proceedings of the 12th IEEE International Conference on Emerging Technologies and Factory Automation, ETFA 2007, Patras, Greece, pp. 25–28 (2007)

8. Liao, Y., Lezoche, M., Panetto, H., Boudjlida, N.: Semantic Annotation Model Definition for Systems Interoperability. In: Meersman, R., Dillon, T., Herrero, P. (eds.) OTM-WS 2011. LNCS, vol. 7046, pp. 61–70. Springer, Heidelberg (2011)
9. Lin, Y.: Semantic Annotation for Process Models: Facilitating Process Knowledge Management via Semantic Interoperability. PhD thesis, Norwegian University of Science and Technology, Trondheim, Norway (2008)
10. Di Francescomarino, C.: Semantic Annotation of Business Process Models. PhD thesis. International Doctorate School in Information and Communication Technologies. University of Trento, Trento, Italy (2011)
11. Stumme, G., Maedche, A.: Ontology Merging for Federated Ontologies on the Semantic Web. In: Proceedings of the International Workshop for Foundations of Models for Information Integration (2001)
12. Kopecký, J., Vitvar, T., Bournez, C., Farrell, J.: SAWSDL: Semantic Annotations for WSDL and XML Schema. IEEE Internet Computing 11(6), 60–67 (2007)
13. Verma, K., Sheth, A.: Using SAWSDL for Semantic Service Interoperability. Tutorial at Semantic Technology Conference, San Jose, CA, USA (2007)
14. Business Process Model and Notation (BPMN) Version 2.0. In: OMG Standard, http://www.omg.org/spec/BPMN/2.0/
15. Winkler, M., Staníček, Z.: Conceptual modelling using the HIT method. Practical tutorial. Masaryk university Faculty of Informatics (2011)
16. Ambler, S.W.: The Elements of UML 2. Cambridge University Press, New York (2005)
17. Patel, M., Ball, A., Ding, L.: Curation and Preservation of CAD Engineering Models in Product Lifecycle Management. In: Proceedings of the 14th International Conference on Virtual Systems and Multimedia, Limassol, Cyprus, pp. 59–66 (2008)
18. Jacobs, A.: The pathologies of big data. Communications of the ACM 52(8) (August 2009)
19. Uschold, M., King, M., Moralee, S., Zorgios, Y.: The Enterprise Ontology. The Knowledge Engineering Review 13, 31–89 (1998)
20. Vegetti, M., Leone, H., Henning, G.: PRONTO: An ontology for comprehensive and consistent representation of product information. Engineering Applications of Artificial Intelligence, 1305–1327 (2011)
21. Krima, S., Barbau, R., Fiorentini, R., Sudarsan, R., Foufou, S., Sriram, R.D.: OntoSTEP: OWL-DL Ontology for STEP. In: Proceedings of 6th International Conference on Product Lifecycle Management, Bath (2009)
22. Unified Modeling Language (UML) Version 2.0. In: OMG Standard, http://www.omg.org/spec/UML/2.0/
23. Hillah, L.M., Kindler, E., Kordon, F., Petrucci, L., Trèves, N.: Petri Net Newsletter. In: 10th International workshop on Practical Use of Colored Petri Nets and the CPN Tools, pp. 9–28 (2009)
24. Li, C., McMahon, C., Newnes, L.: Progress with OntoCAD: A Standardised Ontological Annotation Approach to CAD Systems. In: International Conference on Product Lifecycle Management (PLM 2011), Eindhoven, Netherlands (2011)
25. Tursi, A.: Ontology-Based Approach for Product-Driven Interoperability of Enterprise Production Systems. Comentorship PhD Thesis. University Henri Poincaré (France) and Politecnico di Bari, Italy (2009)

Meta4eS 2012 PC Co-chairs Message

The future eSociety - renamed OnTheMoveSociety in the context of OTM 2012 - is a society created by extensive use of digital technologies at all levels of interaction between its members. It is a society that evolves based on knowledge and that empowers individuals to be active participants of the worlds economy by creating virtual communities that benefit from social inclusion, access to information, enhanced interaction and freedom of expression, among others.

In this context, the role of the World Wide Web in the way people and organizations exchange information and interact in the social cyberspace is crucial. Large amounts of structured data are being published and shared on the Web and a growing number of services and applications emerge from it. The applications must be designed in such a way to help people use their knowledge at best and generate new knowledge in return, while keeping intact their privacy and confidentiality. A current popular initiative adopted by a growing number of actors from transversal domains (e.g. governments, city municipalities, etc.) encourage publishing structured data (e.g. RDF) on the Web of Data. Managing such data in order to produce services and applications for end-user consumption is presently a huge challenge. Finally, the barrier between end-users and information and communication technologies should be lowered by techniques stemming from the fields of multilingual information, information visualization, privacy and trust, rich multimedia retrieval, etc.

To discuss, demonstrate and share best practices, ideas and results, the 1st International IFIP Workshop on Methods, Evaluation, Tools and Applications for the Creation and Consumption of Structured Data for the e-Society (Meta4eS 2012), an event supported by IFIP TC 12 WG 12.7 and the Open Semantic Cloud for Brussels project, brings together researchers, professionals and experts interested to present original research results in this area.

We are happy to announce that, for its first edition, the workshop raised interest and good participation in the research community. After a rigorous review process, with each submission was refereed by at least three members of the workshop Program Committee, we accepted 6 full papers and 9 poster and demo abstracts covering topics such as ontology engineering, multilingual terminology, multimedia annotation, security and privacy, knowledge creation and sharing, social semantics, and usability, and applied to the fields of linked cities, e-Democracy, energy efficiency and personal data management.

We thank the Program Committee members for their time and effort in ensuring the quality during the review process, as well as all the authors and the workshop attendees for the original ideas, the inspiring discussions and for making Meta4eS possible. Also, we thank the OTM 2012 Organizing Committee members for their continuous support. We are confident that Meta4eS will push forward the research boundaries towards the future eSociety.

July 2012

Ioana Ciuciu
Anna Fensel

P. Herrero et al. (Eds.): OTM 2012 Workshops, LNCS 7567, p. 219, 2012.

A Methodological Framework for Ontology and Multilingual Termontological Database Co-evolution[*]

Christophe Debruyne[1], Cristian Vasquez[1],
Koen Kerremans[2], and Andrés Domínguez Burgos[2]

[1] Semantics Technology and Applications Research Lab (STARLab),
Vrije Universiteit Brussel
{chrdebru,cvasquez}@vub.ac.be
[2] Centre for Special Language Studies and Communication, Erasmushogeschool Brussel
{Koen.Kerremans,Andres.Dominquez.Burgos}@ehb.be

Abstract. Ontologies and Multilingual Termontology Bases (MTB) are two knowledge artifacts with different characteristics and different purposes. Ontologies are used to formally capture a shared view of the world to solve particular interoperability and reasoning tasks. MTBs are general, contain fewer types of relations and their purposes are to relate several term labels within and across different languages to categories. For regions in which the multilingual aspect is vital, not only does one need an ontology for interoperability, the concepts in that ontology need to be comprehensible for everyone whose native tongue is one of the principal languages of that region. Multilinguality provides also a powerful mechanism to perform ontology mapping, content annotation, multilingual querying, etc. We intend to meet these challenges by linking both methods for constructing ontologies and MTBs, creating a virtuous cycle. In this paper, we present our method and tool for ontology and MTB co-evolution.

Keywords: Ontology Engineering, Multilingual Termontology Bases, Ontology Evolution.

1   Introduction

A computer-based, shared, agreed formal conceptualization is known as an ontology. Ontologies constitute the key resources for realizing a Semantic Web. The problem is not so much what ontologies are, but how they come to be. Methods are needed to support communities in reaching the meaning agreements necessary for semantic interoperability between two or more autonomously developed information systems for a particular goal. In previous work [5], we introduced a formalism for hybrid ontology engineering. In hybrid ontologies, concepts are both described in terms of natural language and formal descriptions. To this end, the ontologies are complemented with a glossary, containing the natural language descriptions. Just like the ontology, this glossary is in function of the community's semantic interoperability requirement. The natural language descriptions are used to drive the formal descriptions of these concepts.

---

[*] This work was partially funded by the Brussels Institute for Research and Innovation through the Open Semantic Cloud for Brussels Project.

P. Herrero et al. (Eds.): OTM 2012 Workshops, LNCS 7567, pp. 220–230, 2012.

In general, ontologies are used to capture a shared view of the world in a formalism to solve particular interoperability and reasoning tasks. Multilingual termontology bases (MTBs) are terminology bases in which ontological information is made explicit. They contain fewer types of relations and their purposes are to relate several term labels within and across different languages to categories. MTBs are used in a way that surpasses their 'traditional' role as terminological dictionaries for human users (e.g. by translators who often need to verify the right verb or adjective to combine with a given noun a set of candidate words with similar meanings). Given one or several predefined functions, MTBs need to represent (in natural language) those items of knowledge that are considered relevant for supporting specific tasks (e.g. domain modeling), applications (e.g. information extraction tools) or users (e.g. domain experts). These new needs have defined new methods in terminology analysis, new types of information to be included in MTBs as well as new ways of visualizing or representing this information. See for instance: [17,1,3,2,4].

The special linguistic resource in hybrid ontologies was not meant for capturing appropriate linguistic (syntactic, morphological, semantic and pragmatic) information of the natural language descriptions as well as to cope with multiple languages. In hybrid ontologies, we assume one community to agree on one common language. The linguistic resource is rather meant for facilitating meaning agreements on the formal description of concepts. MTBs do take into account this information. In line with the mission statement of the Ontology-Lexica Community Group[1], we bring hybrid ontologies and MTBs together in this paper. This enables – amongst others – capturing how elements in the (hybrid) ontology are realized in multiple languages, enable multilingual querying of the annotated datasets and provide additional documentation and information while consulting the (hybrid) ontology. We furthermore show how the methods for developing hybrid ontologies and MTBs are furthermore driven by each other. In the architecture that we will present, both methods are connected by means of SPARQL services.

2   Related Work

In ontology engineering, it is important that the community members first agree on the meaning of the concepts to be represented before formally describing them. Such agreements among community members can be reached on the basis of discussions in natural language, which will eventually lead to the creation of natural language definitions of concepts to which all members have contributed and agree. Quite a few surveys on the state of the art in ontology engineering methods exist [8,15,16]. However, we noted that for ontology development (for the Semantic Web), relatively few methods take into account a special linguistic resource for natural language definitions: DOGMA [10] and GOSPL [5,6], HCOME [12] and UPON [7]. Other methods do mention the idea of drawing inspiration from existing linguistic resources, but do not treat these resources as an integral part of the method. In the case of HCOME, it should be noted that users were seemingly not able to update this resource.

---

[1] http://www.w3.org/community/ontolex/

3   Method

In this section, we explain the ontology engineering and multilingual termontological database methods adopted in this paper and present how both methods can co-evolve. We will explain how these two representations with distinct degrees of precision (the first serving a specific purpose and thus containing only the relations needed for this purpose, the latter a general description with general relations). The two are thus complementary and - as we will explain - can benefit from each other's construction process. As we will adopt a method for hybrid ontology engineering, we will use the words hybrid ontology and ontology interchangeably.

3.1   Ontology Engineering Method

In hybrid ontologies, communities are promoted to first-class citizens, part and parcel of the formalism, such that the interactions within the evolving community leads to a series of change-operations applied to the ontology. The evolution of the interactions thus has a direct impact on the evolution of the ontology. The natural language aspect is vital, as the closer the link between human communication and the resulting system and/or business communication, the more likely such systems will work as intended by their various stakeholders. Concepts are described both informally by means of natural language descriptions stored in a *glossary* and formally by means of binary fact-types coming from a community and grounded in natural language called *lexons* [13], e.g., <*Cultural Domain Community, Event, starting on, end of, Date*>. A fact type is the collection of objects linked by the predicate. A fact is an element of the population of the fact type, e.g. "Event A" starting on "2012-05-22". A series of social processes have been defined which allows the ontology to evolve with the community and the community's agreements. Table 1 contains some of the social processes defined in GOSPL. A lexon is more "understandable" by people without training than, for instance, ontology languages such as OWL. The goal of the DOGMA framework is not to invent another ontology language, but rather to present a formalism for developing ontologies from which "implementations" in other formalisms can be distilled.

Table 1. Social processes in GOSPL

Social process: Request to ...		
Remove gloss from lexon or term	Add lexon	Add constraint
Change gloss of lexon or term	Remove lexon	Change role hierarchy
Add gloss to lexon or term	Remove constraint	Remove synonym
Change supertype of term	Add synonym	

Fig. 1 summarizes the different processes in GOSPL. Starting from co-evolving communities and requirements, the informal descriptions of key terms have to be gathered before formally describing those concepts. Constraints and application commitments to these formal descriptions can be expressed in commitment languages, such as Ω-RIDL [18]. During the processes from creating the glossary to committing to the ontology, the communities can make agreements on gloss-equivalences (an agreement that two descriptions refer to the same concept) and synonyms (an agreement that two terms refer to the same concept). The ontology, and the data described with those commitments can then be re-internalized by the community for another iteration. This allows communities to gradually build up the domain that needs to be captured by the ontology. Knowledge proposed by the *goal-driven* community typically comes from their existing autonomously developed and maintained information systems. In that sense, (hybrid) ontologies are rarely built from scratch. By capturing the social processes leading to ontology evolution, we do not only store the changes in the ontology, but also register the thought processes of communities that have lead to those changes.

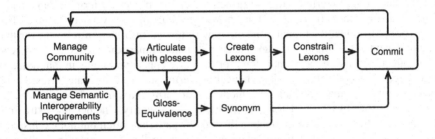

Fig. 1. The GOSPL method

3.2   Termontology Mining Method

In [11] a method called termontography was described for developing multilingual termontological databases, i.e. terminological resources which make explicit both terminological/linguistic and ontological/conceptual information. Termontological databases are in this respect similar to terminological knowledge bases, as defined by [14]. Unlike TKBs, termontological databases following the termontographic approach rely on a predefined categorization structure, which is used to identify and classify terminology in different natural languages. The categorization structure corresponds to an ontological structure listing the important categories and their relationships that are derived from a user requirements analysis. These relationships are not strictly confined to the typical hierarchical relationships (i.e. partitive and generic relationships) found in thesauri or taxonomies but can also encompass generic relationships expressing like causality, location and function. In the termontographic approach, the categorization level interconnects with a linguistic level, providing a wide range of information about the use of any term in natural language to express the meaning to which it is associated at the category level. The category level can be used by terminographers to classify multilingual terminology. It supports the processes of terminology analysis and management. The linguistic level provides additional information for analysis and production of human language.

This detailed information has always been relevant for human purposes. Translators, for instance, often need to verify the right verb or adjective to combine with a given noun within a set of candidate words with similar meaning. The framework can also be useful within the realm of natural language processing to overcome the gap between natural language and ontologies. Take for instance the term "opera".

Even within one short text, opera can refer to either the building or the music genre. When we read that an opera is performed, we know it is about a piece of that music. When we read an opera is "re-furbished", we know the word denotes something different as compared to when we say that it is "being visited". Very often the correct meaning can be derived from looking at the correlation between the ambiguous term and some context words. For instance 'opera' and 'visit' vs. 'opera' and 'perform'. Still, in other cases, determining the real meaning of opera could above all depend on the syntactic paradigm used, as in "he was at the opera" (we cannot say the verb "be" and its possible meaning is determining our judgment here).

Fig. 2 shows how the TermontoPlatform supports the extraction and modeling of an MTB according to termintological principles. In this process, a terminologist and a human domain expert first define the knowledge domain they want to tackle. They then proceed to select document collections with textual information relevant for that domain. Using automatic means -term extraction- and human knowledge they proceed to compile a list of seed terms that stand for the basic conceptual items in that domain. They agree on a taxonomic model where these terms stand for the categories. Using expert knowledge and yet again the modules for term extraction, they identify the relationships they want to identify in the texts. They verify whether the extraction modules have the right rules to identify the kind of patterns - often but not exclusively verbal phrases - expressing those relationships. To do that they examine primarily documents where the seed terms are particularly relevant. They can modify and add new linguistic patterns to detect these relationships. Once this is done, they run the mining modules on the domain documents. The extracted terms and possible relationships are then verified, modified if needed, and exported. New data can be imported from other databases by adapting a filter module that converts other sources into data types of the MTB.

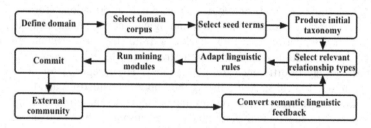

Fig. 2. A general view of the MTB process: ontological and other updates from the external community are taken over to perform a new mining and modeling cycle. The Termonto Platform supports humans through different steps. The mining modules in the middle of the process use the incoming rules, predefined seed terms and statistic criteria to extract possible terminological and ontological-relevant information that terminologists validate for internal and external consumption.

The MTB distinguishes a semantic level from a linguistic level. Labels attached to categories are not per se "terms" in the linguistic way: they are only tags that help identify categories more easily as the unique identifiers at semantic levels. A category label in the MLB model can exist for one or more languages. The same label can be visualized in different languages but only once for a given category in one specific language. The categories themselves can be connected to one or more terms within a context.

The term "opera" within a specific context has a meaning and is attached to the category with the English label "opera as piece". In other contexts that term is attached to two other different categories. In Fig. 3 you can see how two terms, opera and opera house, are attached to the category opera_house. These are synonyms. The stars represent preferred synonym. At the linguistic level, each term within a context can be attached to one or more lexical relations, which can be seen as links to other co-occurring terms. These other terms can help in the analysis of texts to detect which context and hence which concept is meant.

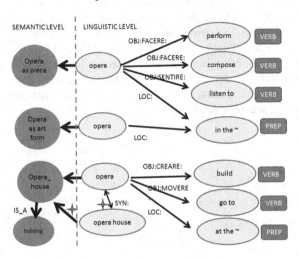

Fig. 3. A fragment of the linguistic data of a MTB: here, terms associated with categories such as opera as art piece, as art form or opera house. Special lexical relations linking to collocate words to these terms can help in disambiguation processes. They can also be used to identify possible raw data for identifying semantic relations.

3.3   Ontology and MTB Co-evolution

Fig. 4 depicts the co-evolution of the ontology and the MTB. Communities can use the MTB as a starting point to build up or adapt the ontology to–their needs by re-internalizing the ontology and start interacting. The social processes (for reaching agreements) result in several ontology evolution operators during externalization. Externalization here means the process of a community formally "writing" down their thoughts in artifacts that describe the universe of discourse. The social processes and changes in the ontology can be queries to refine or steer the crawling processes of the MTB. The interactions on terms are available through an API, table or as RDF. The crawler can be steered by analyzing the number of activity of terms in the ontology within a time window. The link between the ontology and the MTB is captured in externalization and is used to provide links from the implemented ontology to the MTB.

In the previous Section, we described some of the data types present in the MTB. The structure between the Categories and Terms allow us to query the MTB based on the term labels in the ontology's facts. This can be used to retrieve glosses from the category definitions and information about the fact's term labels from the MTB term entries. Category relations that connect two categories in the MTB even serve as inspiration to add facts to the ontology; i.e. a linguistic knowledge "graph" on the side. The next section will go into more detail on how this is precisely implemented and how the MTB is queried.

As can be seen from Fig. 2 and Fig. 4, the TermontoPlatform can also import data from other knowledge systems. As Fig. 2 shows, a module is used to determine how the import process takes place. That means the module needs to know what data types are relevant and to what data types or rules they can be mapped. "Terms" as used in GOSPL are not necessarily reliable to determine linguistic terms. They need to be verified by a terminologist before they can overwrite or serve as a synonym. Still, they can be used to improve the term detection in the text miner modules. The lexons can be mapped to correct and expand the semantic level of the MTB. New lexons that represent a semantic relationship between two objects or instances can be used in the module for semantic relation detection (Fig. 2) in order to identify new linguistic patterns in the domain documents that can be selected to add yet new rules for further automatic detection of semantic relations.

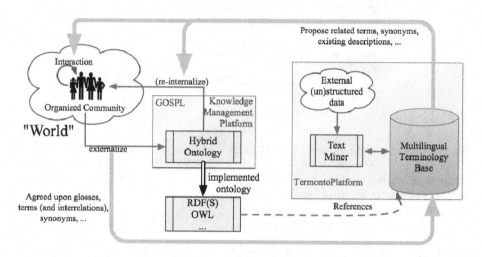

Fig. 4. Co-evolution of the ontology and the MTB. The MTB is used as a source of inspiration in the community interactions that will result in ontology evolution operators. The hybrid ontology can - at any time - be transformed into other formalisms referring to the MTB for documentation and additional context.

4   Tool

The GOSPL [6] prototype is the tool we have adopted for hybrid ontology engineering. The core of GOSPL is a series of services for hybrid ontology engineering to which multiple (types of) clients can connect. Services include: community management, ontology retrieval, starting and resolving discussions involving requests, etc. Discussions involve around requests to evolve the ontology. The interface depicted in Fig. 5 is a screenshot of one such client.

The MTB's schema was lifted to an ontology using the GOSPL platform. This ontology was then used to publish the MTB as RDF triples on the Web. There are currently 20430 triples available. The SPARQL endpoint is then used to link the knowledge management platform with the MTB. Fig. 6 contains an RDF description of the English term opera.

The community working on the ontology using GOSPL with an integrated multilingual termontology base can - at each time - ask for an implementation of the hybrid ontology in OWL. The translation of a fact-oriented formalism into another formalism has already been presented, for instance in [9]. The generation of the OWL implementation of the ontology now incorporates links with the MTB as well as additional annotation for documenting purposes next to the labels and glosses of the hybrid ontology.

The benefits of this approach on the information service level are twofold. First, it gives pointers to the MTB for multilingual understanding of some of the facts and concepts in the ontology. Secondly, it enables querying the information not only via the ontology, but also via the concepts and terms of the MTB, allowing for querying using synonyms (within one language and across languages). The community has been externalizing their perception of reality through modeling processes driven by glosses, of which a subset is provided by the MTB. Thanks to this link between the

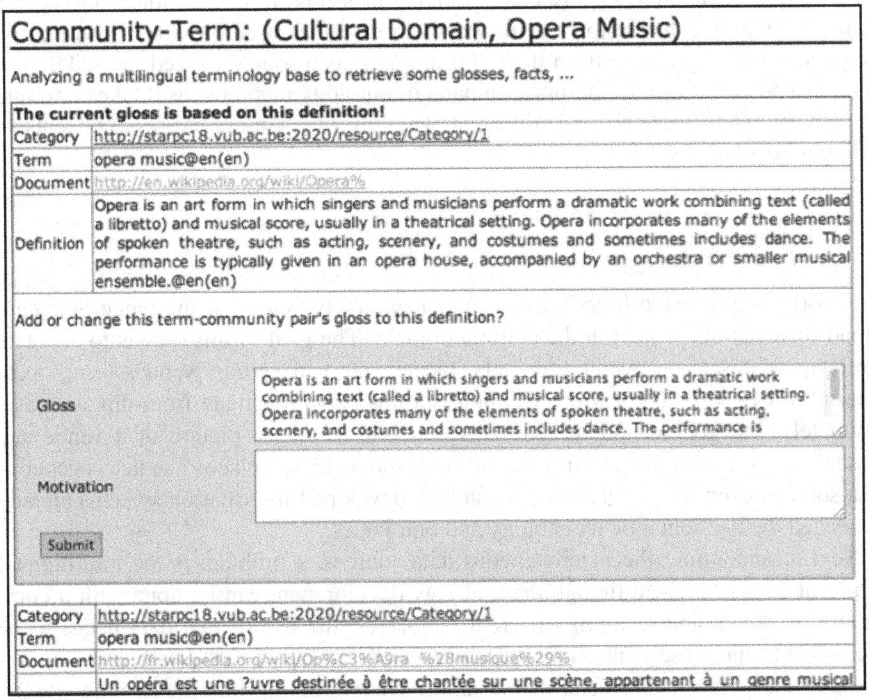

Fig. 5. The GOSPL [6] prototype linked with the MTB. Users can ask for a list of definitions that they can adopt as a gloss. Note that the user is shown on which definition the current gloss is based on (if the gloss came from a definition from the MTB). Also note that a user can alter the definition, but a link with the original definition is kept.

Property	Value
is ont:Category_with_Term of	<http://localhost:2020/resource/Category/169>
is ont:Collocation_of_Term of	<http://localhost:2020/resource/Collocation/15>
is ont:Collocation_of_Term of	<http://localhost:2020/resource/Collocation/16>
is ont:Collocation_of_Term of	<http://localhost:2020/resource/Collocation/17>
is ont:Collocation_of_Term of	<http://localhost:2020/resource/Collocation/18>
is ont:Linguistic_Context_of_Term of	<http://localhost:2020/resource/LinguisticContext/51>
ont:Term_with_Gender	none
ont:Term_with_Gramatical_Number	singular
ont:Term_with_Syntactical_Pattern	noun
ont:Term_with_Term_Label	opera (en)
rdfs:label	opera (en)
rdf:type	ont:Term

Fig. 6. Triples of a term in the MTB. Namespaces have been omitted

purpose driven ontology and more general MTB, the community will potentially understand this query. The benefits of this approach on the methodological level are threefold. First, it helps users discover new facts and textual description from the MTB, facilitating ontology development. Different communities and their corresponding ontologies evolve towards each other by agreeing on the relations (e.g., equality) of their concepts. Secondly, the discussions provide points of interest for the MTB development by - for instance - looking at terms in the ontology that are the source of an active discussion but for which no gloss has been provided. And thirdly, the glosses not originating from the MTB are used as a source to feed the MTB. The MTB is a powerful tool for automating parts of ontology mapping, as it takes also into account language variation, i.e. different ways in which users express concepts in different languages.

5   Case

The work we presented here is the result of one of the cases in the Open Semantic Cloud for Brussels project in the cultural domain. The goal of this case is to annotate a relevant datasets on events (concerts, theater, etc.) in various venues (e.g., opera houses) in Brussels. The various examples in this paper originate from this use case. Ultimately, the goal would be that a user is able to take a picture of a venue and present the user with, for instance, the current shows taking place. The heterogeneous data sources from the different autonomously developed information systems already motivated the use semantic technology and ontologies.

Next to annotating the heterogeneous data sources, a problem is the multilingual nature of Brussels. Even though the ontology development can be done with a community of stakeholders having different languages, the use of that data needs to be accessible to most users, not only to build services on top of that data but also to understand the concept and facts in the ontology. By linking ontologies with MTBs, queries expressed in different languages about the same concepts can be formulated. Currently, the MTB is being developed while the community in the cultural domain is working on the ontology. One of the results is facilitating the mapping of concepts when multiple ontologies have linkages to the same MTB.

6   Conclusions

In this paper, we presented a methodological framework for ontology and multilingual termontological database co-evolution. Ontologies stem from the community's need to exchange information for a particular purpose and are the result of a series of meaning agreements. In hybrid ontology engineering, those agreements are driven by the natural language descriptions formulated by the community. Multilingual termontological databases are general-purpose multilingual thesauri with general semantic relations (e.g., subsumption, part-whole, etc.), storing variances in meaning across languages. The hybrid ontology engineering processes can use the MTB as a useful source for natural language descriptions and general relations between concepts, and the MTB construction processes can benefit from the hybrid ontology engineering activities to pinpoint the communities topics of interest, e.g., to steer the mining process or adapt the seed terms.

To this end, we have published the MTB as RDF on the Web to facilitate the integration with the GOSPL knowledge management platform. Information on the interactions between the communities is provided via an API or as RDF. Those interactions are annotated by means of SIOC. These descriptions are then used to mine the points of interest of the community by for instance pointing to the terms and lexons that more strongly engaged people in interacting with one another than other terms or lexons.

References

1. Aussenac-Gilles, N., Condamines, A., Szulman, S.: Prise en compte de l'application dans la constitution de produits terminologiques. Actes des 2e Assisses Nationales du GDR I3 (2002)
2. Cabré, M.T.: El principio de poliedricidad: la articulación de lo discursivo, lo cognitivo y lo lingüístico en Terminología (I). IBÉRICA 16, 9–36 (2008)
3. Collet, T.: What's a term? An attempt to define the term within the theoretical framework of text linguistics. Linguistica Antverpiensia 3, 99–111 (2004)
4. Faber, P. (ed.): A Cognitive Linguistics View of Terminology and Specialized Language. Mouton De Gruyter (2012)
5. Debruyne, C., Meersman, R.: Semantic Interoperation of Information Systems by Evolving Ontologies through Formalized Social Processes. In: Eder, J., Bielikova, M., Tjoa, A.M. (eds.) ADBIS 2011. LNCS, vol. 6909, pp. 444–459. Springer, Heidelberg (2011)
6. Debruyne, C., Reul, Q., Meersman, R.: GOSPL: Grounding ontologies with social processes and natural language. In: Latifi, S. (ed.) ITNG, pp. 1255–1256. IEEE Computer Society (2010)
7. De Nicola, A., Missikoff, M., Navigli, R.: A software engineering approach to ontology building. Information Systems 34, 258–275 (2009)
8. Gomez-Perez, A., Fernandez-Lopez, M., Corcho, O.: Ontological Engineering with examples from the areas of Knowledge Management. In: e-Commerce and the Semantic Web. Springer-Verlag New York, Inc., Secaucus (2003) ISBN: 1852335513
9. Hodrob, R., Jarrar, M.: Mapping ORM into OWL 2. In: Alnsour, A., Aljawarneh, S. (eds.) ISWSA, p. 9. ACM (2010)

10. Jarrar, M., Meersman, R.: Ontology Engineering - the DOGMA Approach. In: Dillon, T.S., Chang, E., Meersman, R., Sycara, K. (eds.) Advances in Web Semantics I. LNCS, vol. 4891, pp. 7–34. Springer, Heidelberg (2008)
11. Kerremans, K., Desmeytere, I., Temmerman, R., Wille, P.: Application-oriented terminography in financial forensics. Terminology 11(1), 83–106 (2005)
12. Kotis, K., Vouros, A.: Human-centered ontology engineering: The hcome methodology. Knowledge Information Systems 10(1), 109–131 (2006)
13. Meersman, R.: The use of lexicons and other computer-linguistic tools in semantics, design and cooperation of database systems. In: CODAS, pp. 1–14 (1999)
14. Meyer, I., Skuce, D., Bowker, L., Eck, K.: Towards a new generation of terminological resources: an experiment in building a terminological knowledge base. Presented at the, Nantes, France (1992)
15. Simperl, E.P.B., Tempich, C.: Ontology Engineering: A Reality Check. In: Meersman, R., Tari, Z. (eds.) OTM 2006. LNCS, vol. 4275, pp. 836–854. Springer, Heidelberg (2006)
16. Siorpaes, K., Simperl, E.: Human intelligence in the process of semantic content creation. World Wide Web 13(1-2), 33–59 (2010)
17. Temmerman, R.: Towards New Ways of Terminology Description: The Sociocognitive-Approach. John Benjamins Publishing Company, Amsterdam (2000)
18. Verheyden, P., De Bo, J., Meersman, R.: Semantically Unlocking Database Content Through Ontology-Based Mediation. In: Bussler, C.J., Tannen, V., Fundulaki, I. (eds.) SWDB 2004. LNCS, vol. 3372, pp. 109–126. Springer, Heidelberg (2005)

F-SAMS: Reliably Identifying Attributes and Their Identity Providers in a Federation

David W. Chadwick and Mark Hibbert

School of Computing
University of Kent
{d.w.chadwick,m.j.m.hibbert}@kent.ac.uk

Abstract. We describe the Federation Semantic Attribute Mapping System (F-SAMS), a web services based system that automatically collects, in a trustworthy manner, the semantic mappings of Identity Provider (IdP) assigned attributes into a federation agreed set of standard attributes. The collected knowledge may be used by federation service providers (SPs) to support the dynamic management of IdPs and their assigned attributes.

Keywords: semantic access control, federation interoperability, identity management.

1 Introduction

A federation is defined as "A collection of domains that have established trust and it typically includes a number of organizations that have established trust for shared access to a set of resources" [1]. Although the members of the federation share their resources with other members, they remain in complete control of them and often govern the authorization and access control to their resources through the use of policies about a user's attributes. These members are known as service providers (SPs). The federation members who authenticate and identify the users are known as identity providers (IdPs), those who simply provide attributes about the users, attribute authorities (AAs).

One crucial consideration when establishing a federation is reaching a common understanding of an accepted vocabulary for such things as the user roles and attributes (and their associated privileges) which need to be understood throughout the entire federation. Traditionally, the problem of federation interoperability is addressed by all members of the federation agreeing upon a standard set of attributes that will be assigned to all users by the IdPs/AAs and will be used in access control decisions by the SPs. This is the approach adopted by the UK Access Management Federation (UKAMF) [2], which passes eduPerson attributes [3] between federation members. However, this approach is not scalable and can be difficult to maintain by IdPs and AAs when they have large numbers of users, and/or are members of multiple federations, as the new federation agreed attributes may need to be assigned (or mapped) to each of their users. It also poses difficulties for SPs, since they need to be

P. Herrero et al. (Eds.): OTM 2012 Workshops, LNCS 7567, pp. 231–241, 2012.

sure that each IdP/AA is a trusted member of the appropriate federation and is entitled to assign the federation attributes that it does. The UKAMF partially addresses this problem by regularly distributing metadata between its members, which lists details about the current members of the federation. But it does not yet fully address the trust issues. But by not supporting the federation agreed set of standard attributes, the situation is worse, since SPs will not be able to interpret the semantics of attributes originating from IdPs and AAs outside their domain. However the current federation solution does not mirror the existing physical world.

Consider a university which gets applications for its degree courses from students from every country of the world. Each student presents his/her original paper qualification certificates which are issued by different educational organizations the world over. These have different grading schemes, different pass marks, and different levels of attainment, in short, different attributes issued by different authorities. But the admissions officer needs to know how each of these qualifications maps into the local ones that he is familiar with, in order to know if the student is sufficiently qualified to enroll on the degree course. In the UK, some help is at hand from UK Naric (http://www.naric.org.uk), which provides a directory of foreign educational institutions, the qualifications they offer, and a best guestimate mapping of these into their equivalent UK counterpart. But the mapping is advisory only and each UK admissions officer has to make his own decisions about the trustworthiness and mapping of the foreign qualification attribute. Germany has a more advanced system, in that Uni-Assist (http://www.uni-assist.de) acts as a trusted third party and provides validated mappings of foreign qualifications into their German equivalent. In order to validate the authenticity of the paper certificate, the student has to have it stamped by the German embassy in its country of issuance.

Our Federation Semantic Attribute Mapping System (F-SAMS) system is designed to more closely mirror, and improve upon, the physical world by:

i)   allowing IdPs and AAs to send their locally assigned roles and attributes to SPs, rather than having to send a set of standard federation agreed attributes

ii) automating the collection of IdP and AA issued roles and attributes as well as their semantic mappings into a set of federation agreed attributes (the knowledgebase), and

iii) using a novel trust model, builds a trust base that allows SPs to automatically validate unknown IdPs and AAs and their attributes.

The remainder of this paper is structured as follows; section 2 describes the F-SAMS model; section 3 describes the attribute mappings; section 4 explains the crawler which collects the attribute mappings into a knowledge base; section 5 introduces the knowledgebase queries; section 6 discusses related work, whilst section 7 concludes and discusses future directions of F-SAMS research and development.

2   The F-SAMS Model

In a F-SAMS federated environment, users can access resources from SPs without any prior interactions taking place between the SP and the user's IdP/AA. Fig. 1 depicts a typical access control request by a user's agent. When the SP receives the request, it first discovers the user's IdP/AA and then redirects the user's agent to there, along with an authentication and attribute request. As the IdP/AA has no existing relationship with the SP, it does not want to release the user's personal information (attributes) until it knows that the SP is a trusted member of the federation. The IdP/AA queries F-SAMS with the SP's X.509 public key certificate (PKC). F-SAMS looks up the SP in its trust base and returns the result to the IdP/AA. If the SP is a trusted federation member, the IdP/AA can continue with authenticating the user. The IdP/AA returns a signed attribute response to the SP, via the user's agent. When the SP receives the response, it must first validate the IdP/AA and its attributes before granting access to the user. The SP queries F-SAMS i) to determine if the IdP/AA is in the trust base, and ii) to discover the semantics of the IdP/AA's attributes. If the IdP/AA is a trusted federation member, F-SAMS returns a set of mapped federation attributes, which the SP can use to make an access control decision.

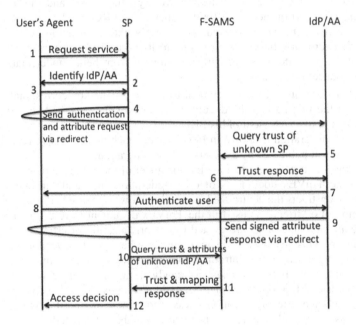

Fig. 1. F-SAMS access control process

The F-SAMS model revolves around the trust and vocabulary expression (TruVEx) document that is published by each IdP/AA member or candidate member of a federation. Each document contains three parts:

- the X.509 PKC of the (candidate) member. This can be a self-signed certificate, or one issued by a CA. The only restriction is that it must contain the uniformResourceIdentifier component of the subject alternative name (SAN) extension and hold the URI of the web location storing the detached signature of the member's TruVEx document. The candidate member determines this URI at the time his PKC is issued, even though the location will initially be empty.

- an attribute mapping part, expressing in RDF the relationships between the attributes in the (candidate) member's local vocabulary and those in the federation vocabulary. Each of the member's vocabularies are aligned with those of the other members using the federation vocabulary as the common ontology that binds them all together. By aligning the vocabularies with the federation ontology, relationships will automatically be inferred between the attributes of the separate organizational vocabularies without any of them possessing prior knowledge of the other vocabularies. The federation vocabulary is published by the federation root of trust (FRoT), the FRoT being the organization that initially establishes the federation and invites other candidate members to join. As the federation evolves, the FRoT may dynamically expand the federation vocabulary to include other attributes that are of interest to the federation's members, and members may update their TruVEx documents accordingly. This allows finer grained access controls to be introduced.

- a friends part, which contains for each friend (i.e. candidate member that this member (the introducer) asserts to be trustworthy): their PKC and the hash of the attribute mapping part of their TruVEx document. The PKC enables the TruVEx document of the friend to be discovered, as the SAN extension points to the TruVEx detached signature and the signature points to the TruVEx document. By including the hash of the attribute mapping part, this stops it from being undetectably altered after the introducer has validated it.

Each member signs his TruVEx document using the private key corresponding to the public key in the first part of the document, and stores the detached signature at the URI contained in the SAN field of his PKC.

An example federation is shown in Fig. 2. where each named square represents the TruVEx document published by a member of the federation.

A web crawler starts from the TruVEx document of the FRoT, and crawls the web picking up the TruVEx documents of other federation and candidate members and from these it constructs the centralized federation knowledgebase and trust base.

The notion of a "friend" is used in the TruVEx document to refer to an organization whose attribute mappings are trusted by the organization asserting the friendship (the introducer). This "friendship" is not required to be mutual; instead it merely indicates that one organization (the introducer) trusts, or has confidence in, another organization's semantic attribute mappings. All candidate members are given a trust score based on this friendship. As more members add a candidate member to their friends' parts, then the candidate organization's trust score increases until it is sufficient to reach the trust threshold required to become a member of the federation. The new member is then assigned a level of trust by F-SAMS, but this trust level decreases, the further the member is away from the FRoT. A member's trust level is used in computing the trust score of new federation candidates that this member introduces (as a friend). A fuller description of the trust model and trust scoring mechanism is outside the scope of this document.

A TruVEx document is signed for two reasons: the first is to prove the integrity of the document's content, and the second is to verify the assertions made about friends that the introducer trusts. This is similar to a signed X.509 PKC where the signer asserts that the public key mentioned in the certificate belongs to the named subject of the certificate. In the F-SAMS case, the introducer is asserting that he has confidence that his friend's attributes do map into the federation agreed ones as specified in the friend's TruVEx document.

Members can update and re-sign their TruVEx documents as often as they want, with the following provisos:

— each time the document is signed its detached signature must be stored at the signature URI contained in the SAN field of the signer's PKC (otherwise no-one will be able to verify the document's integrity)

— if a member changes his asymmetric key pair or PKC or attribute mapping part he must notify the introducers who have his details stored in the friends' parts of their TruVEx documents (see Fig.2).

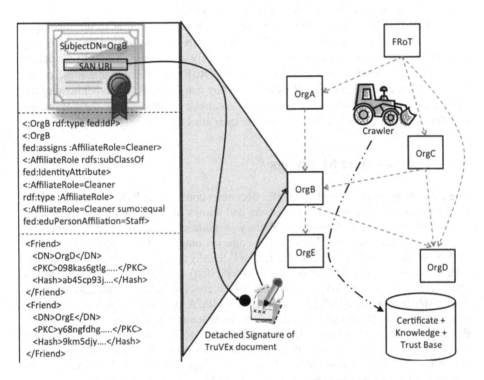

Fig. 2. A TruVEx document from an example F-SAMS federation

A member can update his friends list as often as he wishes without notifying anyone. However, when a member updates the attribute mapping part of its TruVEx document, this alters the hash value so that it no longer matches those published by the introducers of this document. For the document to remain trusted and for F-SAMS to process it, each introducer must re-validate and re-publish the new hash of the attribute mapping part. To assist with the automation of updating the attribute mapping part, members should maintain a separate list of introducers (LOI) that will contain the email addresses of their introducers. The LOI can then be used to inform the introducers when the attribute mappings are updated. The introducers can either confirm the mappings are valid and update their friend's entry accordingly, or if the mappings are no longer valid, the friend's entry can be removed as this member is no longer trusted by the introducer. If the introducer does nothing, it is equivalent to the latter.

The member's X.509 PKC is used for verification of the distinguished name (DN) and public key of the member. Note that a member may assert its own DN, by issuing a self-signed certificate, but its friends will validate this when they add the member to their friends' lists. The PKC is used by the crawler to confirm the subject's DN with the one constructed from the friend assertions made by already trusted introducers in their TruVEx documents. The PKC is also used to confirm that the TruVEx document was signed by the correct entity. Thus F-SAMS does not rely on, nor require, any CA infrastructure. The validated member's PKC is stored in the certificate base by the crawler, for subsequent use by other federation members.

The FRoT's TruVEx document contains additional information to the members' TruVEx documents. It contains the SP members part and the federation vocabulary part. The SP members part contains a list of (possibly self-signed) X.509 PKCs of SPs that are trusted members of the federation. The FRoT has validated that these public keys do belong to the named SP members. They can be used for authenticating the SPs in message exchanges. The federation vocabulary part contains the vocabulary that the members of the federation will base their attribute mappings on.

3   The Attribute Mappings

The attribute mapping part of a TruVEx document conveys via RDF statements which attributes the IdP/AA assigns to its users and shows how they relate to the federation's attributes. The federation vocabulary is made up of a subset of concepts and object properties from the SUMO upper common ontology [4], supplemented by F-SAMS, as shown in Fig. 3 and Table 1. The F-SAMS upper common ontology in Fig. 3 shows how the SUMO (sumo) and F-SAMS (fed) concepts and object properties connect. We have extended the SUMO Attribute concept to include IdentityAttribute, with a subclass of EmailAddress. This allows IdPs/AAs to define their own identity attributes (as subclasses) and map them into the federation vocabulary. The Organization concept from SUMO has been extended to include the three types of organization that F-SAMS will encounter: IdP, AA, and SP. IdPs/AAs will classify themselves as one or both of these, whilst the FRoT will classify the SPs. Fig. 3 also shows the object properties (defined in Table. 1) used in F-SAMS.

Table 1. The relationships used by F-SAMS

Relationship	Object property	Definition of object property
Superior role/attribute	sumo:subAttribute	The object of the triple is a subordinate attribute of the subject of the triple
Equivalent or better	sumo:equal	The subject of the triple is at least equivalent to the object of the triple
Property of	sumo:property	The object of the triple is an attribute of the subject (any entity) of the triple
Assigns	fed:assigns	The object of the triple is an identity attribute assigned by the subject of the triple

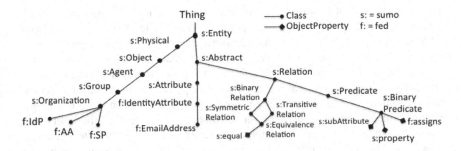

Fig. 3. The F-SAMS upper common ontology

This upper common ontology is then extended by the FRoT to include the federation's application specific objects and attributes. All concepts in the F-SAMS ontology are related using the rdfs:subClassOf property. Individuals are connected to their concept via the rdf:type property. All attributes are represented as type/value pairs (e.g. Role=Professor), and are instances of their attribute type concept. These attributes may be hierarchically related to each other (i.e. superior or subordinate) and the SUMO property subAttribute is used to define the subordinate attribute relationship. When an IdP/AA asserts that one of its attributes is equivalent to a federation attribute, the SUMO equal relationship is used. When an IdP/AA wishes to map one of its identity attributes to a non-equivalent federation attribute, the IdP/AA attribute must be superior to the federation attribute.

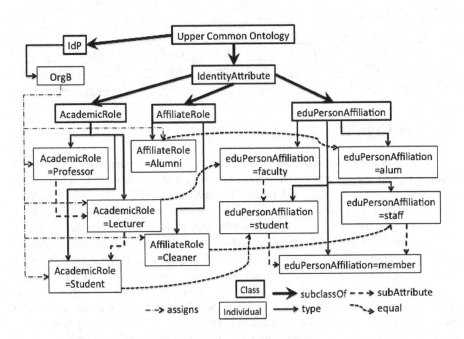

Fig. 4. Example attribute mappings

A pictorial example of (a subset of) a federation vocabulary that might be used by an academic federation is shown on the right hand side of Fig. 4. This is taken from the eduPerson schema [3]. The left hand side shows the mappings that might be made by the OrgB IdP, which issues two types of attribute: academic roles (in a hierarchy) and two unrelated affiliate roles. OrgB is linked to its attribute values using the assigns property. Some of these can be mapped into equivalent federation eduPerson Affiliation attribute values. Other relationships can be inferred from these mappings. For example, the AcademicRole=Lecturer attribute is equivalent to the eduPerson Affiliation=faculty attribute. As AcademicRole=Lecturer is a subAttribute of AcademicRole=Professor, it can be inferred that AcademicRole=Professor is also equivalent to eduPersonAffiliation=faculty. Similarly, eduPersonAffiliation=member is a subAttribute of eduPersonAffiliation=student, and the latter is a subAttribute of eduPersonAffiliation=faculty, therefore both AcadmicRole=Lecturer and Academic Role=Professor will inherit the privileges of eduPersonAffiliation=faculty, eduPerson Affiliation=student and eduPersonAffiliation=member. Fig. 2 shows part of Table 2 represented as RDF in OrgB's TruVex document.

Table 2. Example triples from Fig.4

Subject	Predicate	Object
AcademicRole	subClassOf	IdentityAttribute
eduPersonAffiliation	subClassOf	IdentityAttribute
AcademicRole=Professor	type	AcademicRole
OrgB	assigns	AcademicRole=Professor
AcademicRole=Professor	subAttribute	AcademicRole=Lecturer
AffiliateRole=Cleaner	type	AffiliateRole
eduPersonAffiliation=staff	type	eduPersonAffiliation
eduPersonAffiliation=staff	subAttribute	eduPersonAffiliation=member
AffiliateRole=Cleaner	equal	eduPersonAffiliation=staff

4   The Crawler

The crawler is the element of F-SAMS that discovers the vocabularies, verifies the documents, and builds the knowledgebase, trust base and certificate base. The crawler runs periodically to maintain and update the information. The crawler is initialized with the PKC of the FRoT and the URI of the FRoT's TruVex document. The crawler begins by retrieving the FRoT's TruVex document, which it verifies with the PKC, before dissecting it to extract the various parts. The FRoT's federation vocabulary part contains the federation ontology, which F-SAMS uses as the foundation for the knowledgebase. The SP members part is used to create the list of SP PKCs in the F-SAMs certificate store. Only these SPs will be entitled to use the web service to validate IdPs/AAs and their attributes. The FRoT's friends' information is used to create the crawler's initial list of friends (LOF). As the FRoT is fully trusted, its friends are trusted to join the federation as IdPs/AAs, and their certificates are added to the F-SAMs certificate store. However, their trust levels are set to a reduced level.

The crawler then works through the LOF to read, verify and analyze their trusted TruVEx documents. As it does so, it dynamically updates the knowledgebase from their attribute mapping parts, and its LOF and internal certificate store from their friend's parts. The crawler then proceeds to compute the trust scores of the friends of the friends of the FRoT, using the entries in its LOF. The more friends a candidate member has, the higher its trust score. If a candidate does not have a trust score which passes the required membership threshold, its details (PKC and hash) are still added to the LOF, but the TruVEx document is not read in or processed until its trust score satisfies the membership threshold. Once this occurs, the crawler computes a reduced trust level for this new member, adds its PKC to the F-SAMS certificate store, reads in its TruVEx document, validates it, then includes its friends in its LOF and its attribute mapping part in the F-SAMS knowledge base. The crawler continues this process until either no more entries are added to its LOF, or no more trusted candidates remain unprocessed. Once the crawl is complete, any candidates with a trust score under the threshold are kept in the LOF, but are not included in the trust base, so that SP's only have access to a completely trusted set of IdPs/AAs and their attribute mappings. Periodically, at a frequency determined by the FRoT, the crawler starts to crawl the federation again, starting with the TruVEx document of the FRoT. If a previously trusted member become untrusted, then its details are removed from the F-SAMS certificate, knowledge and trust bases.

5   F-SAMS Queries

To query F-SAMS, the SP establishes a TLS session with the F-SAMS web service, and sends a request containing the PKC and the (unknown to the SP) attribute(s) of the issuing IdP/AA. F-SAMS initially attempts to retrieve the trust score for the IdP/AA from its trust base, and if it is found, will proceed to map the IdP/AA's attribute(s) into federation attributes. The response to the SP contains one of the following:

- a response code of -2 if the IdP/AA is not trusted;
- the trust score of the IdP/AA (which will always be above the membership threshold), followed by one of the following for each IdP/AA attribute:
  - o   a response code of 1 and the mapped federation attribute, or
  - o   a response code of 0 and the dominant federation attribute, meaning that the attribute is known to F-SAMS but is not equivalent to or superior to any federation attribute. The dominant federation attribute represents the closest match. The SP can then unilaterally decide to either grant the unknown attribute equivalent or downgraded privileges compared to the dominant federation attribute, or simply ignore it.
  - o   a response code of -1 when the attribute is unknown to F-SAMS.

As the knowledgebase is built by aligning only vocabularies that are fully trusted, i.e. from IdPs and AAs that have a trust score of at least the threshold, the relationships returned by F-SAMS can be completely trusted even though the trust is transitive and not direct. This is because each SP has complete trust in the FRoT, and through chains of trust from the FRoT to every IdP/AA member in the federation, trust remains strong regardless of how far that latter is away from the FRoT, since more introducer chains are needed the further an IdP/AA is away from the FRoT.

An IdP or AA may query F-SAMS to determine whether an SP is a trusted member of the federation. An IdP/AA establishes a TLS connection with F-SAMS and sends the SP's PKC. F-SAMS checks the certificate base and returns a binary response of true if the SP is a federation member, and false if not.

6   Related Work

Our work is related to the work presented in [5], OBIS, which enables semantic interoperability within federations. More specifically, the knowledgebase that we present is a relationship lookup service similar to OBIS. However, OBIS is grounded in natural language, whereas F-SAMS is based on the standardized RDF and OWL languages [6, 7]. In addition to the relationship lookup service, we present a federation infrastructure for building the knowledge base and a trust model for dynamically expanding the IdP/AA membership.

The Semantic Access Control (SAC) Model [8] was specifically designed to enforce ABAC policies in heterogeneous and distributed environments. It maps policies to resources dynamically based on the semantics of policies and resources. F-SAMS allows the SP to keep their existing policies, mapping instead the user's attributes into their local SP equivalents.

The Semantic Access Control Enabler (SACE) [9] was developed to enforce RBAC when accessing heterogeneous databases. This approach allows each organization to define their resources as concepts (classes) and then use schema mapping techniques to resolve the semantic interoperability. Thus, the SP's resources in the request can be mapped to concepts representing a resource in the ontology by a trusted third party mediator which makes the access control decisions on behalf of the SP. So the permissions are associated to classes in the ontology rather than to the actual resources. In comparison, F-SAMS leaves the access control decisions in the hands of the SP and maps the requester's roles/attributes into SP understood ones, rather than mapping the requested resources. F-SAMS therefore has wider applicability.

[10, 11] both suggest the use of RDF ontologies to create and manage policies, whereas, [12] extends this presenting the ROWLBAC model, which discusses the use of OWL to represent policies in RBAC. They argue that the use of established access control techniques (such as XACML) requires all roles to be established at initialization time and it is therefore advantageous to use OWL to generate policies. F-SAMS similarly does not require all roles to be known at initialization time, but enables the dynamic mapping of roles/attributes rather than the dynamic generation of policies.

7   Conclusions and Future Work

We have presented F-SAMS, a web services based system for use in federations to enhance interoperability, using semantic mappings to understand attributes from unknown IdPs and AAs. Its trust model allows for the automatic sharing of vocabularies between members, and using levels of trust, ensures that SPs can have complete trust in the mappings without even knowing the IdP/AA or its vocabulary. Combining a trust base and a knowledge base allows SPs to not only verify attribute assertions from an unknown IdP or AA, but also interpret the unknown request attributes. This provides flexibility within the federation, as IdP/AAs do not have to update their attributes to accommodate the federation attributes. Instead, they can map their attributes into the federation's, where they can be securely collected and stored centrally for SPs to query whenever unknown attributes are encountered. It also means that the SPs and IdP/AAs do not have to engage in any prior trust relationships.

Future work will include the design and building of a vocabulary creator that will allows members to create, edit and sign their TruVEx documents using a GUI. The F-SAMS infrastructure will be extended to allow SPs to dynamically introduce new SPs to a federation, and to include Levels of Assurance in IdPs.

References

1. Federation definition, http://msdn.microsoft.com/en-us/library/ms730908.aspx
2. UK Access Management Federation, http://www.ukfederation.org.uk
3. EduPerson Schema, http://middleware.internet2.edu/eduperson/
4. Niles, I., Pease, A.: Towards a Standard Upper Ontology. In: Welty, C., Smith, B. (eds.) Proc. of the 2nd Int. Conf. on Formal Ontology in Information Systems (FOIS 2001), Ogunquit, Maine, October 17-19 (2001)
5. Ciuciu, I., Zhao, G., Chadwick, D.W., Reul, Q., Meersman, R., Vasquez, C., Hibbert, M., Winfield, S., Kirkham, T.: Ontology-based Interoperation for Securely Shared Services. In: Proc. IEEE Int. Conf. on New Technologies, Mobility and Security (NTMS 2011), Paris, France (2011)
6. RDF Concepts – W3C Recommendation (February 10, 2004) http://www.w3.org/TR/rdf-concepts/
7. OWL – W3C Recommendation (October 27, 2009), http://www.w3.org/TR/owl2-primer/
8. Yagüe, M.I., Gallardo, M.-d.-M., Maña, A.: Semantic Access Control Model: A Formal Specification. In: de Capitani di Vimercati, S., Syverson, P.F., Gollmann, D. (eds.) ESORICS 2005. LNCS, vol. 3679, pp. 24–43. Springer, Heidelberg (2005)
9. Mitra, C.C.P.P., Liu, P.: Semantic Access Control for Information Interoperation. In: Proceedings of the 11th ACM Symposium on Access Control Models and Technologies, pp. 237–246 (2006)
10. Uszok, A., Bradshaw, J., Johnson, M., Jeffers, R., Tate, A., Dalton, J., Aitken, S.: KAoS Policy Management for Semantic Web Services. IEEE Intelligent Systems 19(4), 32–41 (2004)
11. Kagal, L., Berners-Lee, T., Connolly, D., Weitzner, D.: Using semantic web technologies for policy management on the web. In: Cohn, A. (ed.) Proceedings of the 21st National Conference on Artificial Intelligence, vol. 2, Boston, Massachusetts, July 16-20. Aaai Conference on Artificial Intelligence, pp. 1337–1344. AAAI Press (2006)
12. Finin, T., Joshi, A., Kagal, L., Niu, J., Sandhu, R., Winsborough, W.H., Thuraisingham, B.: ROWLBAC - Representing Role Based Access Control in OWL. In: Proceedings of the 13th Symposium on Access Control Models and Technologies, pp. 73–82. ACM Press (June 2008)

Assessing the User Satisfaction with an Ontology Engineering Tool Based on Social Processes

Ioana Ciuciu and Christophe Debruyne

Semantics Technology and Applications Research Laboratory
Vrije Universiteit Brussel, Belgium
{iciuciu,chrdebru}@vub.ac.be

Abstract. This study discusses one of the three measures defined within the usability testing, namely the user satisfaction, when evaluating an ontology engineering tool based on social processes. The motivation of our focus lays in the fact that being driven by communities through social interactions, the ontology engineering process depends on what the user does, sees and feels when using the system. The evaluation criteria proposed here are therefore developed by looking at the people involved, the processes and their outcomes, mostly taking into account the user experience, in an approach that goes beyond usability. The paper identifies the problems the users encounter when using the system, both at a technical level and psychometric level. A set of recommendations is proposed in order to overcome these problems and to improve the user experience with the system.

Keywords: usability engineering, user satisfaction, hybrid ontology engineering, social processes, community, human-computer interaction, socio-technical systems theory.

1   Introduction

The present study is part of the community evaluation task of the Open Semantic Cloud for Brussels (OSCB[1]) project. OSCB aims at providing a cloud of structured data for the city of Brussels and a platform for publishing and consuming it. Communities work collaboratively on the platform to unlock their data which in turn can be used by other parties to create services for users around the data. The OSCB platform is intended to enable communities of users to represent their knowledge using natural language. The knowledge is further captured in an ontology which is used to annotate data and resources on the web. The ontology is grounded in natural language. The ontology creation is a community effort and is supported by the OSCB knowledge-engineering platform. Note that the multilingual aspect is taken into account in the platform for the particular case of Brussels (i.e. data available in English, French and Dutch).

---

[1] http://www.oscb.be/

P. Herrero et al. (Eds.): OTM 2012 Workshops, LNCS 7567, pp. 242–251, 2012.

As already mentioned, the aim of this study is to evaluate the ontology-engineering platform of OSCB from the usability engineering point of view. However, our aim is to go beyond usability and to analyze the user experience with the system from a socio-technical perspective: what the user does, sees, and feels when using the platform. The user feedback will be constructively used in order to improve the next iteration of the platform.

This paper reports on the user satisfaction with the OSCB ontology-engineering platform. Based on that, we identify the main (usability) problems and draw valuable conclusions and recommendations for improvement.

The rest of the paper is organized as follows: Section 2 constitutes the paper background. The usability (socio-technical) test design is described in Section 3. Section 4 reports on the results and presents some recommendations for improvement. Section 5 is the related work of the paper. Section 6 concludes and presents the future work of this research.

2   Background

2.1   The Post-study System Usability Questionnaire (PSSUQ)

Satisfaction was measured using the standardized Post-Study System Usability Questionnaire (PSSUQ [1,2]) developed by IBM. PSSUQ originally consisted of 19 questions, each question being a statement about the usability of the system. Participants need to answer each statement using a Likert scale of 7 points, where 1 indicates that the user "strongly agrees" with the statement whilst 7 indicates that the user "strongly disagrees" with it. PSSUQ is based on a comprehensive psychometric analysis, providing scales for three sub-factors, namely: (1) system usefulness; (2) information quality; and (3) interface quality. The short (and most recent) version of PSSUQ, illustrated in Table 1, was used, in order to save study time.

Table 1. PSSUQ – short version [3]

Item	Item Text
Q1	Overall, I am satisfied with how easy it is to use this system.
Q2	It was simple to use this system.
Q3	I was able to complete the tasks and scenarios quickly using this system.
Q4	I felt comfortable using this system.
Q5	It was easy to learn to use this system.
Q6	I believe I could become productive quickly using this system.
Q7	The system gave error messages that clearly told me how to fix problems.
Q8	Whenever I made a mistake using the system, I could recover easily and quickly.
Q9	The information (such as on-line help, on-screen messages and other documentation) provided with this system was clear.

Table 1. (*continued*)

Item	Item Text
Q10	It was easy to find the information I needed.
Q11	The information was effective in helping me complete the tasks and scenarios.
Q12	The organization of information on the system screens was clear.
Q13	The interface of this system was pleasant.
Q14	I liked using the interface of this system.
Q15	This system has all the functions and capabilities I expect it to have.
Q16	Overall, I am satisfied with this system.
SysUse = Average Items 1 through 6 *IntQual* = Average Items 13 through 15 *InfoQual* = Average Items 7 through 12 *Overall* = Average Items 1 though 16	
*Table note*s: *SysUse* = *system usefulness; InfoQual* = *information quality; IntQual = interface quality; Scores can range from 1 (strongly agree) to 7 (strongly disagree), with lower scores better than the higher scores.*	

In this study, we use PSSUQ in order to measure the user satisfaction when dealing with an ontology-engineering tool based on social processes, which is described in the following section. The reason for choosing PSSUQ for this study is mainly the rich information it provides, with little effort from the user, and the extensive IBM documentation and experience for the statistics it can provide. Besides the 16 items in the test, the test participants can make comments and elaborate on their answers. Based on these comments, we will draw conclusions and try to provide recommendations for improving the human-system interaction.

2.2   Grounding Ontologies with Social Processes (GOSPL)

GOSPL [6] is a method and its supporting tool[2] for collaborative hybrid ontology engineering. It supports communities of stakeholder in collaboratively achieving an approximation of the domain to support their semantic interoperability requirements. Hybrid ontologies are ontologies where concepts are both described informally in natural language by means of glosses for high level reasoning between the community members and formally suitable for machine reasoning and data annotation. Concepts are formally described by means of lexons [8], expressing plausible binary relations that hold within a community and expressed in natural language. An example of a lexon is ⟨Cultural Domain, Concert, is a, subsumes, Event⟩, which states that – in the Cultural Domain community- the concept referred to with term "Concerts" plays the role of "is a" on the concept with term "Event" and the concept with term "Event" plays the role of "subsumes" on the concept with term "Concert". A lexon should – ideally – result in two coherent sentences when read in both directions, but assuring this quality is the responsibility of the community. The community that wishes to interoperate formulates semantic interoperability requirements and the social processes

---

[2] For access to a running instance of GOSPL, please contact the authors.

within that community leading to closer approximations of their domain are driven by those glosses. Meaning agreements across communities reside at two levels, the glossary and the formal descriptions. This allows agreements within the formal and informal part of the hybrid ontology to evolve asynchronically. Ideally, if two communities agree that two descriptions refer to the same concept, the labels associated with those descriptions should be considered equal as well; this is called the glossary consistency principle [6]. All social processes are stored on the platform, adding an additional layer of traceability; not only information is kept about changes in the ontology, the whole discussion leading to this decision is also stored for future reference.

Some of the social processes in the GOSPL methodology include a request to: remove gloss from lexon or term, change gloss of lexon or term, add gloss to lexon or term, change super-type of term, remove gloss-equivalence, add lexon, remove lexon, remove constraint, add synonym, add constraint, change role hierarchy, remove synonym, and add gloss-equivalence. Users are thus able to propose adding, removing, and (sometimes, depending on the subject) change parts of the hybrid ontology. Terms are labels referring to concepts and lexons are binary relations between those terms. Users can create a hierarchy of terms and roles and also describe terms and lexons with a gloss. Synonyms are agreements that two terms refer to the same concept, and gloss-equivalences are agreements that two descriptions refer to the same concept.

Fig. 1. summarizes the different processes in GOSPL [6]. Starting from co-evolving communities and requirements, the informal descriptions of key terms have to be gathered before formally describing those concepts. Communities define the semantic interoperability requirements, out of which a set of key terms is identified. Those terms need to be informally described before the formal description can be added. In order for a lexon to be entered, at least one of the terms needs to be articulated. The terms and roles in lexons can be constrained and the community can then commit to the hybrid ontology by annotating an individual application symbols with a constrained subset of the lexons. At the same time, communities can interact to agree on the equivalence of glosses and the synonymy of terms. Committing to the ontology allows for the data to be explored by other agents via that ontology. Commitments also enable the community to re-interpret the ontology with its extension (i.e. the instances in each annotated system). This will trigger new social processes that lead to a better approximation of the domain, as the community is able to explore the increasingly annotated data, e.g., by formulating queries. We will not go into detail about the commitments, but a description of one such language can be found in [9].

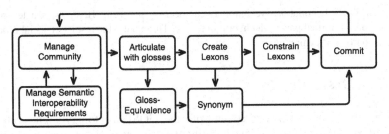

Fig. 1. The GOSPL methodology

Fig. 2 shows a screenshot of the lexons and constraints in the Event Community, which aims to provide a high level, light weight descriptions of events at a particular location and happening at a certain time. This description will be used by more specialized community to "subclass" the concept of Event. Those facts and constraints are the results of discussions between the community members. The screenshot also shows that users have access to the glossary and they can obtain an OWL implementation of the ontology. Indeed, the aim of GOSPL is not to come up with yet another ontology language, but rather use a formalism closer to natural language for ontology engineering out of which other formalisms can be distilled for immediate deployment with other Semantic Web technologies.

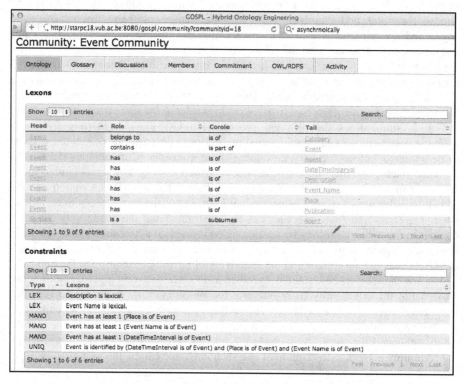

Fig. 2. The GOSPL collaborative ontology-engineering platform. Here, we see lexons and constraints on the formal part of the hybrid ontology. These were the results of social processes within that particular community

3   Test Design

The user satisfaction when interacting with the GOSPL ontology-engineering tool was assessed within a wider usability testing experiment undertaken with a group of master student volunteers of a course on ontology engineering. The goal of the test is to evaluate the usability of GOSPL in two dimensions: *formative* and *summative*, from the user satisfaction point of view. The formative usability testing aims at identifying the usability problems of the tool. The summative UT consists of a series of measurements (e.g. effectiveness, efficiency, satisfaction) which are performed in order to compare the usability results against a set of predefined objectives.

The objective of the experiment is to create a prototype ontology capturing the (shared) concepts and relations of two applications involving cultural events (e.g. concerts, exhibitions). One information system (IS) is developed by the experiment participants and one application whose database schema and data is provided to them. Both applications are portals. The objectives identified in the test are thus: (1) the ontology creation and (2) the annotation (of the IS and the existing database) with the ontology, together with their subsequent subtasks:

— Propose discussion (the social processes defined in Section 3.1)
— Discuss (vote);
— Conclude (accept/reject discussion);
— Create a community;
— Manage a community (add/delete members and roles);
— Use the ontology to annotate existing information systems.

The satisfaction test was undertaken by a group of fifteen volunteers, divided in four subgroups of three to four people. The volunteers were recruited from university students with the distribution of gender, age, education and occupation very close in the four groups. The participants are also grouped by the community in which they get involved based on their application: the 'Date and Time' community, the 'Ticket' community, the 'Venue' community, etc.

The overall usability testing was carried out both implicitly by analyzing the data logs and the user-system interactions and explicitly, by collecting the user feedback via several questionnaires. The outcome of the experiment highlights three aspects of the evaluation: 1) effectiveness; 2) efficiency and 3) satisfaction [3]. Following the recommendations in [10] we have developed the evaluation criteria looking at the people involved, the processes and their outcomes.

The purpose of this study is to assess the user satisfaction with the system. The results are reported in the following section.

4   User Satisfaction. Results and Recommendations

4.1   Summative User Satisfaction

The results delivered by the PSSUQ questionnaire are as follows: the overall (average) user satisfaction shows a value of 3.4, the system usefulness 3.1, information quality 3.9 and interface quality 3.4 (see Table 2). There were four groups of volunteers involved in the study, denoted as: A, B, C and D. The group the most satisfied overall is group C, the group the most satisfied with the system is the same group C, the group the most satisfied with the information quality is group B and the group the most satisfied with the interface quality is group A. The overall satisfaction ranking over the four groups is therefore: group C (most satisfied), group B, group D and group A (least satisfied).

Table 2. Summative user satisfaction

Metric	A	B	C	D	Average
SysUse	3.4	3	**2.8**	3.1	3.1
InfoQual	4.1	**3.8**	3.9	3.9	3.9
IntQual	**3.1**	3.6	3.3	3.6	3.4
Overall	3.6	3.4	**3.3**	3.5	3.4

We have compared these results with the system logs indicating the number of user-system interactions per group, in order to justify the differences on the satisfaction levels per group. The logs show that the average number of interactions per group corresponds to the overall satisfaction per group: 1) group A - 94 interactions; 2) group B - 270 interactions; 3) group C - 350 interactions; and 4) group D - 176 interactions. These results are also correlated with the quality of work of each group, reflected also by the final project grade. It is curious, however, to observe that the group which has used the interface the least often (group A) is the most satisfied with the interface quality. Overall, they are the least satisfied with the system.

4.2 Formative User Satisfaction

The problems identified by the users in the comments section of each item are illustrated in Table 3.

Table 3. Formative user satisfaction

Usability Problem	Nature	No of reports
1. The (error) messages displayed by the system were often not clear to the user. There was in general no on-line help or documentation available	InfoQual	6
2. There is no "undo" or "edit" option available	InfoQual IntQual	5
3. No (top menu) link to the current community in the discussion page	IntQual InfoQual	5
4. It took a while to understand how the system works	SysUse	3
5. Sometimes, listing items in the dynamic tables didn't go well when after returning to a page it displayed the first item again	IntQual	2
6. There was no "delete" option for the communities who "died" during the process	InfoQual IntQual	1
7. The user name is not clear (just email addresses appear)	IntQual	1
8. Sometimes, more clicking necessary that one would expect (e.g. when browsing through several discussions)	SysUse	1

The problem they faced most often was linked to the absence of intelligible (error) messages and on-line help/documentation. Other often cited problems are related to the lack of "edit" and "undo" options; also, the users mention the need for a better organization and links regarding the (current and visited) communities. Other problems include clarification of the user names, the "back" button or the missing request to add gloss in the list box.

4.3   Recommendations for Improvement

Taking the satisfaction results obtained from PSSUQ and the user comments, we drive the following conclusions: out of the three sub-factors identified by PSSUQ, the *system usefulness* measure performed best (3.1); the *information quality* of the system is the sub-factor that needs most improvement (3.9). This also corresponds to the (InfoQuality-related) problems the most cited by the users: usability problems 1, 2 and 3 in Table 3. Therefore, summative and formative usability testing deliver similar results when it comes to user satisfaction in this study. An improvement regarding problem 1 is to introduce more *information support* for the user in the form of intelligible error messages or documentation. The students recommend an option to activate/disable these messages.

Regarding the *"delete"* and *"edit"* options, the students were explained that we were reluctant for allowing editing of posts/comments (e.g. to prevent abuse). Most of them would be content with a feature that allows a post to be edited within a number of seconds.

Regarding the problems related to *communities*, the users mention that there is no link to the current community in the discussion page. Such a link exists, but the users didn't notice it. Even though it was styled as a link with the website's style sheet, the users seemed to have overlooked it. There was also a wish from the users to delete communities, in particular the communities that became obsolete (or – as the users put it – "dead") as the different communities evolved. Even though they understood that even those communities might once again become active, they would be happy to be able to "filter" the dead communities from the list and toggle that filter.

Other identified improvements are as follows: the *organization of the information* could be improved (e.g. show more entries by default – the default number of items shown in a table is 10 and users wish to augment this number for caret browsing, more clearly show in which community you are at a certain moment, the visited communities, etc.); *notifications* from the system could be useful and/or a list of changes after the last visit; showing the *user name*, not just email addresses; more *visibility* with respect to the *visited communities* would be very handy (more forum-like).

5   Related Work

Usability is defined by the ISO-9241 standard [11] as the *effectiveness, efficiency* and *satisfaction* with which specified users can achieve specified goals in particular environments. Usability is a key factor in making the (computer) systems easy to learn and to use. Usability testing has been extensively studied and applied by Lewis [3] at IBM Software Group. The results of the usability testing improve the design of a system by evaluating the organization, presentation and interactivity of the system interface.

The subject of this study is the *user satisfaction*, evaluated while using an ontology-engineering system. A standard instrument to assess the user satisfaction is the *Post-Study System Usability Questionnaire* (PSSUQ). PSSUQ was developed for scenario-based usability evaluation at IBM [1]. The environment used was enterprise-wide and networked office application suites. A follow up study by IBM [2] was performed in the domain of speech recognition [5] using data from five years of usability studies. The follow up produced similar psychometric properties as the original survey. Fruhling [4] validates these results of the PSSUQ instrument and assesses its adaptability to other domains, such as telemedicine.

Socio-Technical Systems Theory (STST) has been widely applied in the domain of information systems implementation [12]. Even though older than 50 years, STST witnesses a revival in the information age. Eason [13] stresses that the important aspect about STST is that it provides the means of understanding the way in which people at work collaborate and use technical artifacts to achieve their tasks. It has been argued that STST determined the movement towards a user-centered approach [14].

Nowadays, we witness the tendency to combine the socio-technical concepts and usability engineering in the design of information systems [15]. In [10], the author questions: *"Is usability enough?"*, arguing that the existing usability measures are not capturing all that is of interest in order to design more innovative systems. According to that study, the user experience exists at three levels: the process, the outcome and the affect. More precisely, one needs to analyze what the user does, what the user attains and what the user feels. Not all of these aspects have a direct and clear way of being measured. Taking into account the emotional and affective factors would help to understand the human-system dynamics more efficiently.

6   Conclusion and Future Work

We conclude the paper by reminding that the aim of the study was to assess the user satisfaction with the GOSPL ontology-engineering tool, which is part of a larger, multi-lingual knowledge-engineering platform. The standard PSSUQ IBM questionnaire was used as instrument for the evaluation of the tool with 15 master students in Open Information Systems. The results show that the system performs best regarding the system usefulness sub-factor (3.1 on a scale from 1 to 7 were 1 is the best result and 7 is the worst result) and that it needs some improvements regarding the way the information and interface are structured and presented to the user for interaction.

The study not only takes into account the classic usability testing measures, but also brings together the usability measures and the socio-technical systems theory principles in a user-centric approach.

A reiteration of the test with an improved version of the interface, after taking into account the recommendations from this paper is work in progress. Future work includes testing the user satisfaction (and the usability in general) from a socio-technical systems theory point of view with users from various domains, different than students, preferably within one the OSCB project use cases.

Acknowledgments. This study is supported by the INNOViris Open Semantic Cloud for Brussels (OSCB) project, financed by the Brussels Capital Region.

References

1. Lewis, J.R.: IBM Computer Usability Satisfaction Questionnaires: Psychometric Evaluation and Instructions for Use. Technical Report 54.786 (1993)
2. Lewis, J.R.: Psychometric Evaluation of the PSSUQ Using Data from Five Years of Usability Studies. J. of Human-Computer Interaction 14(3), 463–488 (2002)
3. Lewis, J.R.: Usability testing. In: Handbook of Human Factors and Ergonomics, 4th edn., pp. 1267–1312. John Wiley, New York (2012)
4. Fruhling, A., Lee, S.: Assessing the Reliability, Validity and Adaptability of PSSUQ. In: Americas Conference on Information Systems, Omaha, USA (2005)
5. Lewis, J.R.: Psychometric Evaluation of the PSSUQ Using Data from Five Years of Usability Studies. J. of Human-Computer Interaction 14(3), 463–488 (2002)
6. Debruyne, C., Meersman, R.: GOSPL: A Method and Tool for Fact-Oriented Hybrid Ontology Engineering. In: Morzy, T., Haerder, T., Wrembel, R. (eds.) ADBIS 2012. LNCS, vol. 7503, pp. 153–166. Springer, Heidelberg (2012)
7. Debruyne, C., Meersman, R.: Semantic Interoperation of Information Systems by Evolving Ontologies through Formalized Social Processes. In: Eder, J., Bielikova, M., Tjoa, A.M. (eds.) ADBIS 2011. LNCS, vol. 6909, pp. 444–459. Springer, Heidelberg (2011)
8. Meersman, R.: The use of lexicons and other computer-linguistic tools in semantics, design and cooperation of database systems. In: CODAS 1999, pp. 1–14. Springer (1999)
9. Verheyden, P., De Bo, J., Meersman, R.: Semantically Unlocking Database Content Through Ontology-Based Mediation. In: Bussler, C.J., Tannen, V., Fundulaki, I. (eds.) SWDB 2004. LNCS, vol. 3372, pp. 109–126. Springer, Heidelberg (2005)
10. Dillon, A.: Beyond usability: process, outcome and affect in human-computer interactions. Canadian Journal of Library and Information Science 26(4), 57–69 (2001)
11. ISO. ISO 9241-11:1998: Ergonomic requirements for office work with visual display terminals (VDTs) – Part 11: Guidance on usability. Source (1998), http://www.iso.org/iso/catalogue_detail.htm?csnumber=16883
12. Eason, K.: Information Technology and Organizational Change. Taylor and Francis, London (1988)
13. Eason, K.: Sociotechnical systems theory in the 21st Century: another half-filled glass?, Sense in Social Science: A collection of essays in honour of Dr. Lisl Klein, Desmond Graves, Broughton, pp. 123–134 (2008)
14. Baecker, R., Grudin, J., Buxton, W., Greenberg, S.: Readings in Human-Computer Interaction. In: Toward the Year 2000. Morgan-Kaufman, New York (1995)
15. Dillon, A.: Group dynamics meet cognition: combining socio-technical concepts and usability engineering in the design of information systems. In: The New Socio Tech: Graffitti on the Long Wall, pp. 119–126. Springer, London (2000)

Ontology Supported Policy Modeling
in Opinion Mining Process[*]

Mus'ab Husaini[1], Andrea Ko[3], Dilek Tapucu[1,2], and Yücel Saygın[1]

[1] Faculty of Engineering and Natural Sciences, Sabancı University, Istanbul, Turkey
[2] Dept. of Computer Engineering, Izmir Institute of Technology, Izmir, Turkey
[3] CUB, Hungary
{musabhusaini,dilektapucu,ysaygin}@sabanciuniv.edu,
andrea.ko@uni-corvinus.hu

Abstract. In e-Society the spreading services offered by Social Web has changed the way of communication and cooperation among citizens, policy-makers, governance bodies and civil society actors. One of the main goals of policymakers is to motivate citizens for participation in policy-making processes. UbiPOL ((Ubiquitous Participation Platform for Policy-making, ICT-2009.7.3(ICT for Governance and Policy Modelling), 2009-2011) aimed to develop a ubiquitous solution, which emphasizes citizens' participation in policy-making processes (PMPs) regardless of their current location and time. Ontology-based opinion mining component of Ubipol system has a crucial role in citizens' commitment, because it empowers them to contribute in policy making. This paper presents the ontology-based semi-automatic approach and tool for sentiment analysis in Ubipol system, which include lexicon extraction from a large corpus of documents. Aspect-based opinion summarization of user reviews and its combination with domain ontology development are discussed as well.

1   Introduction

Ubiquitous Participation Platform for Policy-making (UbiPOL) project aimed to provide a ubiquitous participation platform that allows citizens to participate in the policy making process during their everyday life through providing relevant policies and others opinions that a affect their life wherever they are located. The specific objectives of UbiPOL are to [6]:

- develop an executable policy making process model that is related with geography through,
- geocode policy issues,
- attached policy issues to existing site objects (point of interests, POIs) and
- track the policy making process which is formed by citizen's opinions according to citizen's location and input opinions

[*] This work was developed in the context of UBIPOL (Ubiquitous Participation Platform for Policy Making) project funded by European Commission, FP7.

P. Herrero et al. (Eds.): OTM 2012 Workshops, LNCS 7567, pp. 252–261, 2012.
© Springer-Verlag Berlin Heidelberg 2012

It provides context-aware knowledge provision with regard to policy-making. Citizens using UbiPOL will be able to identify any relevant policies and other citizen's opinions whenever they want and wherever they are, in accordance with and fitting in with their as-usual life pattern. With the platform, citizens are expected to become more widely aware of any relevant policies and PMPs for involvement during their as-usual life; thus, there will be improved citizens' engagement and empowerment. Also, the platform provides policy-tracking functionality via a workflow engine and opinion tag concept to improve the transparency of policy-making processes. Ubipol system enables policy-makers to collect citizen opinions more efficiently as the opinions are gathered as soon as they are created in the middle of the citizens' usual life. UbiPOL provides security and an identity management facility to ensure that only authorised citizens have access to the relevant policies. UbiPOL services are provided through a scalable platform ensuring that a large number of citizens can make use of the system at the same time (for example, for e- Voting applications) via its well-proven automatic load balancing mechanisms. The privacy-ensuring opinion mining engine prevents the unwanted revealing of citizen identities and the mining engine stops any unrelated commercial advertisements from being included in the opinion base, to minimise misuse of the system.

Ontologies have a crucial role in Ubipol system, they help to structure the policy related context, provide conceptualization for policy domain and used in the opinion mining process. In order to create an ontology that is useful for sentiment analysis, we have to cover a large set of opinion documents from a certain domain. In this process, a person (domain expert) defines all the domain concepts (aspects) and corresponding features from the corpus, which is extended and updated continuously through the opinion processing. Aspect is a key term in our opinion mining solution; it describes certain characteristics of a domain, like environmental issue in policy issues domain. In this paper, we present an ontology based opinion mining engine to enrich policy modeling process (Figure 1). This engine analyzes a domain- specific opinion corpus, meanwhile it is assisting the user with the updating of a domain ontology and then determines the polarity of opinion on the various domain aspects.

In this engine, the context of a word a effects its meaning, specially whether it has a positive or negative or even neutral orientation. Before processing the text to determine its sentiment orientation, the policy domain aspect has to be identified (namely which policy category is represented by the concept). This identification is supported by the policy modelling ontology in Ubipol system, which describes the most important policy - related classes (aspects) and structure. To identify those policy issues, which require special attention is a key goal of policy maker. Ontology-based opinion mining highlights the most important issues, their aspects; polarity (positive, neutral or negative attitude of writers) and life cycle for the decision makers and citizens, through the continuous analyses of opinions and comments. During this process, several research questions emerge. How the set of aspects domain specific features of opinions (aspects) can be obtained? How they are linguistically expressed? How they are related

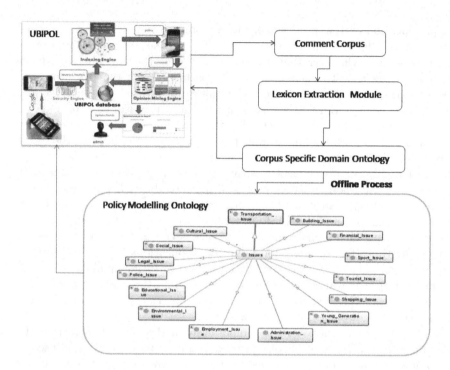

Fig. 1. UBIPOL Architecture and Our Approachthe Ontology-based Opinion Mining Solution

to each other? According to the questions above, the main research questions discussed in our paper are the following: How can we identify and monitor those policy issues, which require special attention or immediate action using citizens' opinions? What kind of algorithms can be applied to extract aspects (decisive characteristics of domain specific opinions) in a reusable manner? How can we structure these characteristics to gain semantic layer (ontologies) which can be integrated with the policy making process?

To answer these questions, we propose an ontology based opinion mining solution. Our main contribution is the ontology based opinion mining process and tool, more precisely the combination of Eagerly Greedy Set Cover algorithm (discussed in detail in section 4) with domain ontology development and maintenance. We aim to identify the smallest set of documents in a given corpus which provide appropriate information needed to develop domain ontology.

2   Related Work

This section gives a literature overview about the main areas; feature extraction and review summarization related to our research challenges. Using feature extraction for sentiment analysis has been studied extensively. In this area, Hu [5] introduced a technique that uses association rules and the most frequent nouns in a given set of reviews. Based on these rules, a set of features can be synthesized for the domain. In another work [8] a similar concept is used to find frequent noun phrases from the review dataset and then extract the product's parts and properties based on point-wise mutual information scores between these phrases and meronymy descriptors related to the product are found. These technique only focus on the overall features and not the keywords associated with them. In wider domains, this approach will yield large feature sets which are not necessarily useful for aggregation and summarization. In this work, we assume that the real set of features is limited and that various keywords are used to represent these features in opinion documents. The method proposed in [4] takes into account the relationship between a term and its related opinion information. Blair-Goldensohn et al. [1] have also reported a sentiment summarizer with aspect information for local service reviews. In [3] and [7], the authors suggested using a clustering algorithm for aspect identification.

A supervised method which combines frequency, syntax tokens, and domain knowledge to find the product features has been used in [12] to extract product features. The induction of domain knowledge aims to improve the quality of extraction. Gupta and Lehal [2] propose a keyword extraction method to support topic detection and document summarization.

3   Problem Definition and Theoretical Background of Our Research

The main objective of our research is to discover the smallest set of documents in a given corpus to provide appropriate information needed to develop a domain ontology. Before proceed with an explanation of our approach, it will be helpful to outline assumptions, define the problem, and disambiguate the terms commonly used in this paper.

To simplify our problem, we will assume that the corpora are domain-specific, i.e., all opinion documents in a given corpus are concerned with only one domain. An ontology, in turn, contains relationships among the domain, its *aspects*, and their respective *keywords*.

Definition 1 (Ontology). An ontology is a triple of the form, O = (D;A;K), where D is the corpus domain, A is the collection of aspects in domain D, and K is the collection of all keywords in domain D.

Definition 2 (Aspect). An aspect instance is the tuple, A = (a;KA), where a is a noun that denotes a certain characteristic of the domain that can be subject to opinion and KA is the collection of keywords used to represent aspect A. Aspects are also termed to domain features.

Definition 3 (Keyword). A keyword k , is a noun that can be used to represents a given aspect, A, in an opinion document.

An opinion document can then regarded as a set of words containing both keywords and non-keywords. Definitions mentioned above, we can also formalize the definitions of corpora and opinion documents.

Definition 4 (Corpus). A corpus is a tuple of the form, C = (D;R), where D is the corpus domain and R is the collection of opinion documents in the corpus.

Definition 5 (Opinion Document). An opinion document (or simply document) instance, R, is a set of m words such that,

$$R = \{w_1, w_2, w_3, ..., w_m \mid m > 0\}$$

Having defined the problem, we now turn to outlining our approach which consists of approximating keywords and using a clustering technique to find the subset of the corpus that minimizes the number of documents required and maximizes the amount of information available to create an ontology.

Our contribution is to provide a user-friendly and minimal-effort environment for producing gold-standard domain aspect lexica and better understanding of the issues and problems. Our approach is primarily intended for use by sentiment analysis researchers to study aspect lexicon generation and sentiment analysis techniques, and to a certain extent, practitioners. It can also be used by domain experts to study aspect lexicon generation.

4   Ubipol Approach for Opinion Mining

In sentiment analysis, the context of a word affects its meaning, specifically whether it has a positive or negative or even neutral orientation. Before processing for orientation, the concept that the word represents has to be known, which can be defined with a concept ontology. In order to create a robust ontology that is useful for sentiment analysis, we have to cover a large set of opinion documents. In this process, a person (domain expert) possessing domain knowledge defines all the domain concepts (aspects) and corresponding features from the corpus, which becomes increasingly expensive as the size of the corpus increases.

Our tool is designed as a self-contained web application that can be deployed to any Java-based web server. This system provides an interactive interface for users to import a domain corpus into the application in a variety of formats including text and XML. This corpus is then analyzed to obtain the most informative corpus documents from which the user extracts domain aspects and related keywords to create the aspect lexicon. The user also has the option to upload a pre-generated lexicon instead of manually extracting it. The lexicon, manually extracted or user-provided, is then used by the sentiment analysis engine to process the corpus. Finally, results are displayed to the user for further analysis. Fig.2 and Fig.3 illustrates this workflow with the help of screenshots. This system is publicly accessible online by visiting http://ferrari.sabanciuniv.edu/sare, and a demo video explaining how to use the system can be downloaded from the same address. The major components of the system are described below.

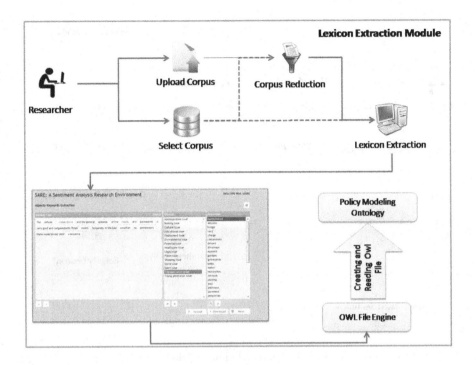

Fig. 2. Lexicon Extraction Module

4.1   Corpus Reduction

This module deals with the problem of aspect lexicon extraction by corpus summarization and user annotation. We approximate aspect keywords with corpus nouns and apply Eagerly Greedy Set Cover algorithm (a variation of the *Greedy Set Cover* algorithm, that we developed) called *Eagerly Greedy Set Cover* algorithm to find the minimum set of documents that cover all nouns in the corpus.

Eagerly Greedy, is given as follows: We maintain a candidate set cover initialized to an empty set, and iterate through the document collection R sequentially. For each document encountered, we consider the set of all nouns in the document and attempt to sequentially consume its elements into the candidate cover sets, i.e., members of the candidate set cover. Each time a candidate cover set consumes (presumes covered) an element, it increments its own utility score by one and removes the element from the new set. If the candidate cover set is a subset of the new set, then the candidate cover set is itself entirely consumed and replaced by the superset (with utility score being set to the sum of existing utility plus the size of the new set). This process continues until either all of the elements in the new set are consumed or we run out of candidate cover sets to process. In the latter case, a new candidate cover set is formed from the contents of the uncovered nouns with the utility score being initialized to its size. It should be noted that while the composition of sets may be changed changed

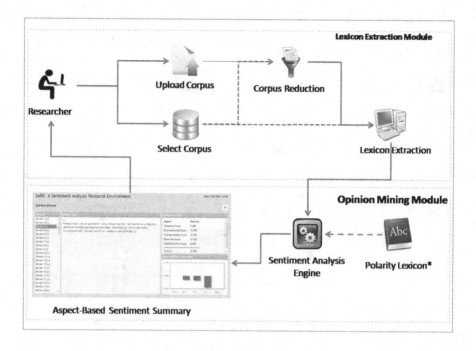

Fig. 3. Opinion Mining Module

by the end of each iteration, each candidate cover set maintains its identity such that the original set can be recovered as needed.

In order to evaluate the extent of data reduction obtained by the *Eagerly Greedy Algorithm*, we need to compare it with the best and the worst approximations of set cover problems. In this case, the worst case approximation is the random selection approach; that is to say, randomly choosing sets from the collection until all the elements in the universe are covered. The best approximation, as referenced previously, is the classical greedy algorithm.

Since our overall goal is to reduce the amount of data presented to the domain expert, we observe the performance of these three algorithms as a function of the amount of data reduction achieved.

Results. The amount of data reduction achieved by each of the algorithms is given in Table 1. We also experimented with several values of $\hat{\tau}$ to observe the value that provides us with the best reduction while incurring the least amount of loss in utility. As shown by the plot of $\hat{\tau}$ against $\Delta(EG_{\hat{\tau}})$. Thus, we can achieve very high utility coverage with a smaller part of the corpus by allowing for some outlier documents to be ignored. The comparison of algorithms shows that while the reduction achieved by the greedy algorithm is slightly higher than our algorithm (a difference of 2.81%), we can leverage the pruning capabilities of our algorithm to dramatically widen the gap in the opposite direction by

Table 1. Algorithm Comparison

Algorithm [α]	Data Reduction [$\Delta(\alpha)$]
Random	0%
Greedy	68.2%
Eagerly Greedy ($\hat{\tau} = 0\%$)	65.39%
Eagerly Greedy ($\hat{\tau} = 8\%$)	96.72%

introducing a small tolerance to error – the error tolerance of 8% that we have chosen for this corpus gives our algorithm an edge of 28.52% over the greedy algorithm.

4.2 Lexicon Extraction

We were also interested in employing a domain expert to discover features from the corpus. Since we do not have a standard ontology for our corpus domain, we had to evaluate the result qualitatively rather than empirically.

Setup. We developed a user interface to facilitate identification of features from provided examples. In this application, the user is sequentially provided with examples from the reduced set for annotation. To help the user easily spot keywords from the larger text, we also highlight all the nouns in a given document. An illustration of a hotel review as displayed in the application is given in Fig. 2. Based on the review that the user is shown, they can then add aspects and related keywords to their respective lists as shown in the same figure.

Our opinion corpora were drawn from a set of *TripAdvisor*[1] hotel reviews as published in [11]. This dataset consists of 235,793 reviews on various hotels that were aggregated over a one month period. For each experiment, we sampled a consistent but random subset of these reviews as will be detailed under each experiment. The experiments were performed using a Java implementation, and document nouns were extracted using the Stanford POS tagger presented in [9].

Results. The application detailed above was used to create an ontology for the any domain from the generated in the earlier steps. From this experiment, we determined that the domain has several aspects, and also obtained several keywords in each of these aspects. A breakdown of domain aspects and number of corresponding features has been provided in Table 2.

4.3 Opinion Mining Module

The objective of this module is to use ontology based approach for representing corpus-specific knowledge and to present aspect-based score value to summarize results in a scorecard structure. Our contribution is to provide a domain-independent approach in a user-friendly fashion. Thus, firstly corpus-based

---

[1] Online hotel booking and reviews site [10].

Table 2. Keyword Breakdown By Aspect for the Hotel Domain

Aspect	Number of Keywords
Business service	34
Check in/front desk	31
Cleanliness	42
Location	105
Rooms	138
Service	147
Value	23
Total	520

aspects and aspect-related keyword sets are extracted as described in Sec. 4.2 to create a corpus- specific ontology. Then a polarity ontology is created from SentiWordNet [www.sentiwordnet.com]. Finally, polarity-placement algorithm is used to calculate score values for each aspect. The idea of the algorithm is to get initial polarity value from the polar- ity ontology for any opinion word in a given comment and to transfer polarity value from polarity keywords to aspect- related keywords by using the Stanford NLP API. The reason for using the Stanford NLP API is to generate dependency tree graphs for a given sentence. After polarities are transferred on a correct token, aspect-based score value is calculated for each comment. A detailed aspect-based sentiment summary is displayed as illustrated in Fig. 3.

5   Conclusion and Future Work

This paper presented an ontology-based semi-automatic approach and tool for sentiment analysis in Ubipol system. The problem of lexicon extraction from a large corpus of documents was discussed with a focus on the aspect-based opinion summarization of user reviews. The main components of our solution are the lexicon extraction module, feature extraction module, which are detailed in section four.

The main challenge was to identify the smallest set of documents for a given corpus that provide appropriate information for domain ontology development. Eagerly Greedy Set Cover algorithm was suggested as a solution, because of its advantageous characteristics. In section four we showed that it provides better results in data reduction than the other approaches, like random and Greedy algorithms. Another advantage of our opinion mining process is that it supports domain ontology maintenance through the continuous processing of citizens' opinions. Policy modelling ontology can be utilized as an aspect/keyword set and fine-tuned in the steps of opinion mining. In spite of the fact, that we offer a user-friendly environment the main target group of the solution include sentiment analyses researchers, practitioners and domain experts. In wider context opinion mining component of Ubipol system supports policy makers to monitor citizens' opinions and they get immediate feedback if special attention or action is needed in a certain policy area.

Future work involves comparison the accuracy and the computational efficiency of our aspect extraction method with other approaches. In addition, larger scale quantitative evaluation of our opinion mining method will be conducted.

References

1. Blair-goldensohn, S., Neylon, T., Hannan, K., Reis, G.A., Mcdonald, R., Reynar, J.: Building a sentiment summarizer for local service reviews. In: NLP in the Information Explosion Era (2008)
2. Gupta, V., Lehal, G.: A survey of text mining techniques and applications. Journal of Emerging Technologies in Web Intelligence 1(1) (2009)
3. Hadano, M., Shimada, K., Endo, T.: Aspect identification of sentiment sentences using a clustering algorithm. Procedia - Social and Behavioral Sciences 27(0), 22–31 (2011), http://www.sciencedirect.com/science/article/pii/S1877042811024062; Computational Linguistics and Related Fields
4. Hana, J., Dongwook, S., Joongmin, C.: Ferom: Feature extraction and refinement for opinion mining. ETRI Journal 33(5), 720–730 (2011)
5. Hu, M., 0001, B.L.: Mining opinion features in customer reviews. In: McGuinness, D.L., Ferguson, G. (eds.) AAAI, pp. 755–760. AAAI Press/The MIT Press (2004), http://dblp.uni-trier.de/db/conf/aaai/aaai2004.html#HuL04
6. Irani, Z., Lee, H., Weerakkody, V., Kamal, M.M., Topham, S.: Ubiquitous participation platform for policy makings (ubipol): A research note. IJEGR 6(1), 78–106 (2010)
7. Ly, D.K., Sugiyama, K., Lin, Z., Kan, M.Y.: Product review summarization based on facet identification and sentence clustering. CoRR abs/1110.1428 (2011), http://dblp.uni-trier.de/db/journals/corr/corr1110.html#abs-1110-1428
8. Popescu, A.M., Etzioni, O.: Extracting product features and opinions from reviews. In: Proceedings of the Conference on Human Language Technology and Empirical Methods in Natural Language Processing, pp. 339–346. Association for Computational Linguistics (2005)
9. Toutanova, K., Klein, D., Manning, C.D., Singer, Y.: Feature-rich part-of-speech tagging with a cyclic dependency network. In: Proceedings of the 2003 Conference of the North American Chapter of the Association for Computational Linguistics on Human Language Technology, NAACL 2003, pp. 173–180 (June 1, 2003)
10. The TripAdvisor website (TripAdvisor LLC) (2011), http://www.tripadvisor.com
11. Wang, H., Lu, Y., Zhai, C.: Latent aspect rating analysis on review text data: A rating regression approach. In: Proceedings of the 16th ACM SIGKDD International Conference on Knowledge Discovery and Data Mining, pp. 783–792 (2010), http://portal.acm.org/citation.cfm?id=1835903
12. Zhang, S., Jia, W., Xia, Y., Meng, Y., Yu, H.: Product features extraction and categorization in chinese reviews. In: ICCGI 2011, The Sixth International Multi-Conference on Computing in the Global Information Technology, pp. 38–42 (2011)

Asking the Right Question:
How to Transform Multilingual Unstructured Data
to Query Semantic Databases

Andrés Domínguez Burgos, Koen Kerremans, and Rita Temmerman

Centre for Special Language Studies and Communication
Department of Applied Linguistics
Erasmus University College Brussels
Pleinlaan 5, B-1050 Brussels, Belgium
{andres.dominguez.burgos,koen.kerremans,rita.temmerman}@ehb.be

Abstract. Ontology engineers have long tried to develop mechanisms to automatically transform natural language statements into queries knowledge-systems can deal with. This has been an enormous challenge as natural languages are highly ambiguous and contexts for disambiguating are seldom identifiable through simple linguistic patterns. To circumvent these difficulties, developers of knowledge bases have often opted for the use of a restricted vocabulary and syntax. Normal users, nevertheless, prefer to express themselves in their language. Special languages or schemas tend to reflect one language – the developer's – and make extensibility more difficult. Also multilingual access can be more difficult to handle in that way. In this article we present strategies for transforming queries of natural languages into language-neutral representations that can be more easily transformed into semantic queries. We describe a tool that combines a multilingual database and natural processing modules with a semantic database in order to transform queries in Dutch, French and English into queries from which ambiguity at syntactic and semantic levels have been reduced. We focus on certain aspects of natural language such as negation and collocation preferences to deal with semantics.

Keywords: collocation, natural language queries, negation, structured data, ontology, unstructured data.

1   Introduction

The Semantic Web was conceived with the vision of making the access to knowledge more accessible through the use of semantic information. This semantics was conceived mainly as semantic markers that people or automatic processes add to structured and unstructured data. Humans, though, prefer to use natural language. If they want to search these semantic web repositories, they need to 1) try different keywords or 2) interact by using some query language. The first approach – semantic marking by humans - is time-consuming and ultimately frustrating for users. If users restrict themselves to key words, they cannot resort to constraints that help making the search

P. Herrero et al. (Eds.): OTM 2012 Workshops, LNCS 7567, pp. 262–271, 2012.
© Springer-Verlag Berlin Heidelberg 2012

more precise. Using a query language is not an option for most users – it implies learning non-trivial syntax, getting to know a certain vocabulary and having an idea about the structure of the data model behind the data collection the user wants to search. The need to facilitate semantic search has a long tradition. Seminal work can be traced back to the first efforts to create interfaces to access conventional databases in the late sixties. Enhancing search through the use of semantics has been one of the key research areas in the Web in the last few years [1]. In section 2, we present the state of the art. Section 3 discusses general issues regarding ambiguity in natural language queries. Section 4 shows an overview of the natural language components of LinSigna, a tool that converts natural language queries from different languages into a normalized form, a semantic representation, used for querying. Section 5 discusses initial results. Section 6 reports on work ahead and section 7 has the conclusions.

2   State of the Art

The transformation of natural language into some formal representation has a long tradition in different fields: from machine translation and Q&A systems to semantic search. [2] presented an overview of problems found when trying to close the breach between natural language and databases and discussed some of the initial work.

Querix was a natural language interface to the Sematic Web [3]. The system does not try to solve human-language ambiguities but asks questions to the user for further clarifications. Ginseng was another tool that presented itself as a semantic engine with a full natural language interface. In reality, the system used an entry form that shaped – or restricted – the kind of queries that can be asked. Keywords are "suggested" from the vocabulary loaded from the chosen ontologies [4].

Form-based interfaces that guide users can be well suited for domain-specific purposes but they are difficult to extent. As Damjanovic points out, the development of natural language interfaces (NLI) has not been very widespread because of the high development and customization costs associated with them. SemSearch and AquaLog [5] were some other attempts. The former did not deal with natural language processing. A google-like query interface allowed users to specify the subject and three basic operators: ":" for specifying and the boolean operators "and" and "or". It matched keys to the labels of concepts and semantic relationships. Finally, it used query templates to transform user queries into formal queries. AquaLog used Word-Net and shallow parsing. One of the problems was that it required syntactically correct sentences. AutoSparql [6] was another attempt to enable queries in natural language and converting them into SPARQL. QuestIO was a tool that interacted with ontologies using unconstrained language-based queries [7]. It aimed at minimal customization and robustness. [8] describes an approach for dynamically extending the vocabulary that supports a controlled natural language.

Summing it up, the main advantages for a natural language component are: a) external users do not need to learn a query language or have an understanding of the data model, b) users only need to use an input field and c) some user errors' are usually dealt with natural language interface for data bases (NLIDBs) – at least to some extent. The main disadvantages are as follows: a) a system for natural language processing can only cover a subset of possible human inputs – those it has been trained to cover; humans tend to under-estimate human language productivity and complexity and b) it is difficult for the system to give an appropriate feedback when an input was not understood. We believe a NLIDB interface offers other major advantages if rightly conceived: it can help in keeping data models and general semantic mechanisms apart from human language issues and it becomes easier to add other human languages to the interface. In this article, we present some mechanisms we have developed to allow more user-friendly queries.

3   Some Issues in Interpreting Natural Language for Queries

Our general aim was to develop a system that could interpret short but non-trivial queries in different languages without naïve users having to learn some restricted language and use this interpretation to produce semantic queries. We believe the idea should be to make users go beyond isolated key word queries without having them to formulate queries in full-blown sentences, for which many do not have the time.

There has been a discussion on how users modify across time their own strategies for search [9, 10]. These strategies are the product of trial and error with the systems available in document search, in QA systems or in systems that try to take a hybrid attempt. Organizations working on search technology keep adjusting their strategies to cope with users' queries. Users and engines have been adapting their strategies over the years responding to societal and technological evolution. We think a more robust interface will enable users to ask more complex queries.

The current situation can be described as follows: many users do not want to deal or do not even know how to deal with formalisms for logic operators. Still, they express those operators routinely in their own natural language. Users are less inclined to type in long sentences reflecting some formal language syntax. Still, they can intuitively formulate queries in natural language that enables us to produce a unified representation of a complex query. This formal representation can be language-independent and can be more easily translated into a SPARQL query or another database query language.

The system we have developed reads short queries in Dutch, English or French and transforms them into a formal language Common Semantics (CS) that can be easily parsed to produce semantic queries. First, the system does a shallow parsing of the sentences. After that, the system identifies the natural language elements that may stand for logic operators. It then identifies scope and precedence of the operators. After that, it detects the possible candidates for entities, concepts and relationships. Once this process is concluded, the system tries to solve some conceptual disambiguation when it has encountered several candidates for concepts or relationships. We understand for a concept a unit of meaning that can be located in a hierarchy with other objects and which contains specific properties.

3.1   Conceptual Ambiguity

Conceptual ambiguity is a well-known phenomenon, which has not yet been entirely solved. Natural language terms are highly ambiguous. Even in domain specific utterances, a given term can often be employed to refer to different concepts.

3.2   Syntactic Ambiguity and Scope

Negation

Negation in natural language can be applied to alter the meaning of nouns, verbs, adjectives, whole nominal or verbal phrases. Negation can also have different scopes. Although the mechanisms for expressing negations have been extensively studied, few work has been carried out on the automatic detection of negation semantics. [11] works on strategies for detecting negation by identifying the focal term through a learning algorithm. The following example is a Dutch query in which a user expresses that (s)he wants to see a movie, provided that it is not an action movie or a movie for children:

>> *Film, Actiefilm noch kinderfilm*

In English, this Dutch query can be literally translated as follows: "Movie, neither action nor children's movie". The pattern "neither...nor ..." points at another scope than "... noch ...". The following English and Dutch queries express the search for any concert, except for world music concerts:

>> *Concert anything but world music*
>> *Concert geen wereldmuziek*

To be able to analyse these patterns, we developed a simple rule-based module called ScopeIdentifier (see section 4). Our system is designed to capture negations and resolve their scope for each language. The negation can be transformed into a negation of a concept, of a table or other collection of semantic items.

Modifiers

A typical problem in natural language processing is to ascertain the real scope of prepositions and other items with the role of modifiers. This happens very often in the case of prepositions linking two nouns or noun phrases. In the query "I want to go to the movies on Saturday", the pattern 'on Saturday' primarily refers to the predicate. In the query "Movies on science", the pattern "on science" is likely to determine and restrict the scope of movies. Different languages have different strategies to solve this and this issue again needs to be solved in the parsing mechanisms for each separate language.

All in all, different languages develop different strategies for shortening queries. Our initial observations with native speakers adapting the queries for tests has been that French speakers tend to skip certain prepositions, more so than articles. English and Dutch speakers tend to eliminate prepositions less often but virtually all articles. Linguistic rules for finding the syntactic relationship between the parts – mostly groups of nouns and how they depend on each other, where the modifier is and where the modified – obviously depend from language to language.

4   Tool Design

LinSigna is a tool that transforms natural language queries into a formal language – a common and unambiguous representation which we call CS, Common Semantics. This representation can be later used to generate semantic queries.

LinSigna uses a basic set of natural language processing modules to generate a shallow parsing of the input, identify the possible concepts and relationships, disambiguate concepts and solve the scope of logical operators based on rules. Once this is carried out, a template matrix generates the possible statements in the formal language. After that, a normalized interpretation of the input is produced.

LinSigna uses two sets of linguistic data resources: 1) a resource containing basic dictionaries and inflection forms, part-of-speech disambiguation rules and syntactic rules for the general linguistic analysis (including shallow parsing) and 2) a linguistic-semantic resource that is used for tagging the linguistic elements with conceptual items and for the process of sense disambiguation. The second resource is most relevant for this work and will be further discussed in section 4.1. In section 4.2, we will list the software components that produce the analysis and describe the general analysis of a human language query.

4.1   Linguistic-Semantic Model

The linguistic-semantic model comprises both linguistic and semantic layers. The most important items in the semantic layer are the concepts. Concepts are interlinked by means of semantic relations. They can be visualized by means of concept labels in several natural languages. These concept labels should not be confused with linguistic terms. They can be seen as base material to build up an ontology. A given concept can be connected to one or more term groups in any natural language. A term group is a set of terms that for a given context are connected to a given concept. A term X can be present in one or more term groups, which means it is connected to different concepts. The term "film" (see picture 1), for instance, can be connected to the concept of film as artistic product – a movie - or as the photographic film.

A term in a given term group can appear in collocations, i.e. linguistic patterns in which terms frequently tend to appear together. A collocation record is a lexical relation (LER) between the focal term (film) and a collocate like "shoot". An LER is similar to the lexical functions (LFs) in the Text-Meaning Theory [12]. The main difference between the LERs and the LFs is that the former can have more than one value. LERs with more than one value assign a probability for each value. For instance, given a LER x, it can have a value v1 with a probability 0.9 and a value v2 with a probability 0.1. That means that the lexical relationship is expressed 90% of the time in a given corpus with a value v1 (for instance, *watch a movie* as opposed to *see a movie*). The LERs can be used to try to determine whether an ambiguous term found in unstructured data should be better linked ton one or the other term group – depending on the values present for the LERs in those term groups in the linguistic database. Different LERs for a given focal term may signal different meanings of the term. LER values are thus context terms that can be used for disambiguation and that have been classified in our database. We will discuss this further in 4.3.

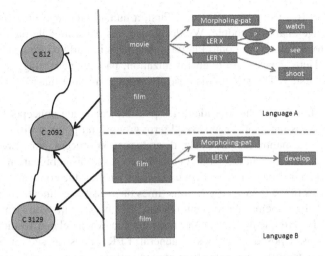

Fig. 1. The linguistic semantic model connects the linguistic layer containing possible terms in different languages (right side) with a concept in the semantic layer (left side)

4.2   Software Modules and Process

LinSigna contains the following modules: the Sentence Analyzer, the TermConcept-Mapper, the SenseSelector, the ConnectorFinder, the ScopeIdentifier and finally the StatementGenerator. Later on we plan to build a module to convert the normalized, disambiguated output into database queries.

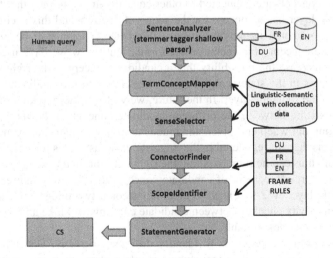

Fig. 2. LinSigna's main components

The process is illustrated in figure 2. First, a human language input *I* goes into a natural language analysis module. We developed this basic module ourselves as part of a suite of tools called Termonto Platform that helps in building up lexical and onto-logical data. Here, *I* passes through tokenization, part-of-speech tagging, stemming and shallow parsing. The system also tries to recover missing diacritics for Dutch or French.

Once this stage ends, the tool identifies possible candidate concepts for the input terms. Some terms may appear in several term groups and point at different concepts in the linguistic semantic resource. The disambiguation process takes two steps: syn-tactically-based disambiguation and context-based sense disambiguation. The Sense-Selector checks for each of the concept candidates whether the collocate values match with other terms in the input query *I*. Sometimes the possible collocation values give a hint. If *I* is "what cinema shows Untouchables?", the system will identify that the term "show" is a frequent LER of the term cinema when related to the concept of movie theatre as opposed to movies in general. LER values (as seen in Fig 1) were previously obtained by processing large amounts of documents from a general and a domain specific corpora. Collocates were automatically classified by part of speech and frequency and assigned a LER label by semi-automatic means – some values tend to perform the same semantic relation but need to be verified. Some LERs have a limited set of possible values – like prepositions or verbs denoting realization. A term can have different or the same values when linked to two different concepts. Only when the values for one sense and the other are different or their likelihood for one sense is much greater than for the other can they be used for sense disambiguation. Found collocations through LERs increase the assignment of a term to a concept.

The SenseSelector proceeds to see for terms with more than one candidate concept whether those concepts are connected to other concepts linked to the other terms in *I*. If the semantic layer has a concept for the action of <show> and this is connected to the concept of <cinema as movie theater>, this latter concept will be given more weight than the concept of <cinema as art form>. Until now we have used a rather trivial way to increase the possibility that a candidate concept is the right one based on other concepts in the statement: we give a preference to the candidate with more connections in the semantic layer. In the future, we will consider the kind of semantic relationship existing between the different candidate concepts. Likewise, the tool is simply checking out whether a given ambiguous term in a human statement is present with other terms that are registered in the linguistic layer as values for one or the other term group and thus can help in assigning the right concept. In a next stage, we would like to consider reinforcement of candidate concepts that are only indirectly linked in the semantic layer. We will need to take into account two things here: how much time this connectivity checkup between candidate concepts will take and what seman-tic relation types are most reliable.

The ConnectorFinder proceeds to identify different operators. Depending on the natural language, these operators may appear at different positions in a sentence. The system is, for the moment, ruled-based. We believe this suffices with the kind of short queries normal users are bound to choose. In English, a user may negate with neither X nor Y. In Dutch, this pattern corresponds with the pattern 'X noch Y'. The ConnectorFinder maps words in the input to the best logical operator. For the moment, the analysis is restricted to deal with basic patterns for basic operators as well as interrogative function words that help to identify possible tables in a database. The ScopeIdentifier tries to identify the scope of the operators (what is negated) by using predefined frames and reorders the sense if necessary. The StatementGenerator reorders the identified components according to frames.

5   Initial Results

We have decided to elaborate our own queries. The main reason for this is that we wanted to use a specific domain where multilingualism plays a very important role: Brussels and its cultural events. We also decided to elaborate queries that are natural for normal users: statements that go beyond lists of keywords but that are often shortened versions of standard sentences, i.e. statements that show already a succinct but clear structure. We derived inspiration from the data set of [13] but adapted it according to the previous criteria. Initially we have 80 queries for English and the same amount for Dutch and French. The Dutch and French queries are semantically equivalent to the English original, even if they are adapted to language traditions of shortening messages. It can be argued that the adaptations, especially the idiomatic changes, inevitably lead to differences in focus and intention, but we believe users in these three languages would basically use such statements to look for the same piece of information. Three examples (in English, French and CS) are shown in table 1.

Table 1. Examples of queries and their Common Semantic expression

English	French	CS
Rock concerts in Brussels during weekend	Concerts rock à Bruxelles pendant le weekend	concert#rock where location#Brussels, when#Monday-Sunday
Family movie after 8pm	Comédie familiale après 8pm	movie#family where time#>=20
Theatre in Ixelles in French	Théâtre à Ixelles en Français	theatre#any where location#Ixelles, language#French

So far we have managed to produce rules for interpreting basic negations, conjunctions, different forms of time and duration and location. The system manages to produce as output similar statements in a formal language (CS) whether the original input was in English, Dutch or French.

6   Work Ahead

Our next step is to implement a converter to SPARQL. Once that is done we will be able to test the system's response on a large scale to test queries in Dutch, English and French against real data. The translation of those queries into CS statements should produce basically comparable results for a large amount of cases. As mentioned in Section 3, one of the problems of natural language interfaces is how to send back in an appropriate manner a feedback when the query has not been understood or other problems occurred. Several strategies will need to be worked out for different cases: a) when the error is a product of the human language input – either because the query was not properly formulated or the system is not robust enough to analyze it, b) when there is a limitation in the expressiveness of CS and c) when the database was properly accessed but no result was found. The system currently deals with one do-main – cultural events - and possible common – ambiguous – general language that can appear in queries related to it, but we believe the way it is conceived   allows for expansion to other domains. We think it offers more power than one that deals with isolated key words only or one that forces users to write full formal sentences and special languages.

7   Conclusion

In this article, we presented the LinSigna tool combining a multilingual database and natural processing modules with a semantic database in order to transform natural language queries into semantic queries from which ambiguity at syntactic and seman-tic levels have been reduced. The tool we have described so far and the strategies behind it can enable semantic search for naïve users using different natural languages. They won't have to restrict themselves to a form of pseudo English or fill in cumber-some forms but state a query in their own language.

Acknowledgments. This research has been partially financed with funds from the Brussels Region in the framework of the Open Semantic Cloud for Brussels project in the Innoviris program.

References

1. Damjanovic, V., Kurz, T., Westenthaler, R., Behrendt, W., Gruber, A., Schaffert, S.: Semantic Enhancement: The Key to Massive and Heterogeneous Data Pools. In: Proceed-ings of IEEE-ERK, Portoroz (2011)
2. Chandra, Y.: Natural language interfaces to databases (2006)
3. Kaufmann, E., Bernstein, A., Zumstein, R.: Querix: A Natural Language Interface to Query Ontologies Based on Clarification Dialogs. In: Cruz, I., Decker, S., Allemang, D., Preist, C., Schwabe, D., Mika, P., Uschold, M., Aroyo, L.M. (eds.) ISWC 2006. LNCS, vol. 4273, pp. 980–981. Springer, Heidelberg (2006)

4. Bernstein, A., Kaufmann, E., Kaiser, C., Kiefer, C.: Ginseng: A guided input natural language search engine for querying ontologies. In: Jena User Conference, pp. 144–157 (2006)
5. Lopez, V., Pasin, M., Motta, E.: AquaLog: An Ontology-Portable Question Answering System for the Semantic Web. In: Gómez-Pérez, A., Euzenat, J. (eds.) ESWC 2005. LNCS, vol. 3532, pp. 546–562. Springer, Heidelberg (2005)
6. Lehmann, J., Bühmann, L.: AutoSPARQL: Let Users Query Your Knowledge Base. In: Antoniou, G., Grobelnik, M., Simperl, E., Parsia, B., Plexousakis, D., De Leenheer, P., Pan, J. (eds.) ESWC 2011, Part I. LNCS, vol. 6643, pp. 63–79. Springer, Heidelberg (2011)
7. Damljanovic, D., Tablan, V., Bontcheva, K.: A text-based query interface to owl ontologies. In: 6th Language Resources and Evaluation Conference (LREC), Marrakech, Morocco (2008)
8. Damljanovic, D., Agatonovic, M., Cunningham, H.: Natural language interfaces to ontologies: Combining syntactic analysis and ontology-based lookup through the user interaction. The Semantic Web: Research and Applications, 106–120 (2010)
9. Muramatsu, J., Pratt, W.: Transparent Queries: investigation users' mental models of search engines. In: Proceedings of the 24th Annual International ACM SIGIR Conference on Research and Development in Information Retrieval, pp. 217–224 (2001)
10. Huang, J., Efthimiadis, E.N.: Analyzing and evaluating query reformulation strategies in web search logs. In: Proceedings of the 18th ACM Conference on Information and Knowledge Management, pp. 77–86 (2009)
11. Blanco, E., Moldovan, D.: Semantic representation of negation using focus detection. In: Proceedings of 49th Annual Meeting of the Association for Computational Linguistics, pp. 19–24 (2011)
12. Mel'čuk, I.: Lexical functions: a tool for the description of lexical relations in a lexicon. Lexical Functions in Lexicography and Natural Language Processing 31, 37–102 (1996)
13. Quarteroni, S., Guerrisi, V., La Torre, P.: Evaluating Multi-focus Natural Language Queries over Data Services. In: Proceedings of LREC 2012, Istanbul, pp. 2547–2552 (2012)

Semantic Policy-Based Data Management for Energy Efficient Smart Buildings

Vikash Kumar, Anna Fensel, Goran Lazendic, and Ulrich Lehner

The Telecommunications Research Center Vienna (FTW),
Donau-City-Straße 1, A-1220 Vienna, Austria
{kumar,fensel,lazendic,lehner}@ftw.at

Abstract. We describe how the semantics can be applied to the smart buildings, with the goal of making them more energy efficient. Having designed and implemented a semantically enabled smart building system, we discuss and evaluate the typical data management challenges connected with the implementation, extension and (re-)use of such system when employing them in the real buildings. The results demonstrate a clear benefit from semantic technologies for integration, efficient rule application and data processing and reuse purposes, as well as for alignment with external data such as tariffs, weather data, statistical data, data from other similar smart home systems. We outline the typical data management operations needed in the real life smart building system deployment, and discuss their implementation aspects.

1 Introduction

Energy efficiency is a topic of acute and growing importance, as achieving 20% savings of energy consumption by 2020 through energy efficiency is one of the key measures to keep CO2 emissions under control[1]. By 2050, EU's goal is to cut greenhouse gas emissions by 80–95% and two thirds of the energy in the EU should come from renewable sources[2]. Also widely known are regulations of EU-wide introduction of smart meters - to be implemented within the next few years - it is estimated that the *"world will have 250 million smart meters by 2015, representing a $3.9 billion market"*[3]. The related markets of energy efficiency, building automation, smart homes are accordingly rapidly growing, particularly, close to exponential in the renewable energies sector[4]. All these factors lead to the appearance of vast amounts of data, followed by the need to efficiently manage it, and enable services addressing the drastically changing energy efficiency data economy.

---

[1] EU climate and energy "20-20-20" package, URL: http://ec.europa.eu/clima/policies/brief/eu/package_en.htm
[2] "Energy Roadmap 2050", European Union 2012, URL: http://ec.europa.eu/energy/publications/doc/2012_energy_roadmap_2050_en.pdf.
[3] Pike Research, URL: http://seekingalpha.com/article/170629-250m-smart-meters-3-9b-market-by-2015-pike-research-says
[4] "Clean Energy Trends 2012", March 2012, URL: http://www.cleanedge.com/reports/clean-energy-trends-2012

P. Herrero et al. (Eds.): OTM 2012 Workshops, LNCS 7567, pp. 272–281, 2012.
© Springer-Verlag Berlin Heidelberg 2012

On the technical side, as the integration of the Internet and physical reality is increasing, analytical and sensor-based systems and services tend to rely on knowledge representations with shared, well-known structures (ontologies) for improved interoperability. This data can serve as a basis for various added value services. Currently this data is often collected, processed and analyzed manually and individually by the companies, whereas automation, optimization and sharing would not only be possible but also generating an enormous value chain in such a large and important market as energy efficiency.

In this work, we present a use case for energy efficiency, supported by a semantic system combining particularly home automation techniques, smart metering and sensor data, deployed in two real buildings (a school and a factory) allowing advanced monitoring and control of energy consumption. We describe the developed system and the deployment set up, as well as the available data. Apart from contribution to establishment of the best practice techniques in implementation of such systems, we identify and study in detail the required automation processes for data, semantics and rules usage, and draw evaluation conclusions on the applicability and success of large-scale data reuse practices.

This paper is structured as follows. In Section 2, we describe the problem statement and motivation for the paper and approach. In Section 3, we discuss our energy management hardware and software design, detailing in particular the use of semantic technologies and data management. In Section 4, we present the evaluation set up and results. Section 5 discusses the related work. Finally, Section 6 concludes and summarizes our paper.

2   Problem Statement and Motivation

As the vision of Internet of Things[5] moves towards mainstream reality, several new challenges needs to be addressed for a better adaptation and interconnectivity of such systems. A common understanding of data emanating from all such systems to enable them to talk, interact and respond to events in each others' environments are essential to achieve this goal. Increased data volumes would also require smart planning of system architectures that are scalable to accommodate such data as well as perform efficient processing to derive meaningful information from them.

A typical case in point is the proliferation of commercial smart home and building systems [3][4][5][6][9] where the common goal is to use latest technologies for improving the quality of living and, in most cases, also to enable energy savings. Even with the success of these systems in standalone buildings, their shortcomings in the broader vision of smart cities cannot be ignored where there is an increasing need for reduction in efforts for their setup and standardization of underlying technologies right from data representation to intra as well as inter building communications. Besides this, expansions in such installations are themselves constantly vulnerable to changes like appliance manufacturers, types of energy used in different buildings, etc. notwithstanding the changes required in the user interfaces [10].

In this paper, we argue that providing a semantic layering on top of a data prosuming ecosystem consisting of sensors and receivers provides manifold added value and

---

[5] Internet of Things: http://en.wikipedia.org/wiki/Internet_of_Things

benefits such as: (a) enabling easy exchange and integration of data among interconnected smart building systems, (b) providing "intelligence" to the system by way of reasoning almost with little or no overhead costs, (c) minimizing adaptation costs for installations in new environments, and (d) ease of scalability in terms of addition of new and existing setups in the ecosystem.

We validate our claims in the setup of a building automation system containing sensors to gather data and actuators and central controllers to control various devices. Superimposing a semantic layer on top of it enabled the introduction of policy-based intelligence to the system and heterogeneous useful apps and services for the users. The whole setup was installed at a school in Kirchdorf, Austria, and then later replicated on a factory floor in Chernogolovka, Russia. The results demonstrated a very high efficiency in the amount of time required to replicate the data layer and adapt the policies between the setups despite the core components of the system being vastly different.

3   System Description

While the general architecture of our implemented smart energy efficient building deployment is shown in Figure 1, in the following subsections we describe the hardware, semantic software and user interface parts of our system.

3.1   Hardware – Physical Layer Settings

The installation was carried out on two separate locations and different types of buildings. The installation in Kirchdorf in Austria consists of sensors, meters for measuring consumption of electrical energy in three classrooms, plugs for measuring electrical consumption of individual appliances, and a power management service (PMS), for monitoring and controlling the state of all computers installed in these three rooms. The installation at factory in Chernogolovka in Russia includes only sensor devices for measuring room temperatures and temperatures of incoming and outgoing airflow of heating system in factory. In the complete version of our system, the following set up has been applied:

Sensors. Sensor devices for measuring temperature, humidity and light were battery powered autonomous systems pushing their data over wireless LAN internet connection to a cloud service exposing collected data via REST interface.

Meters. Power consumption meters were installed in the housing of already existing distribution cabinets at school. Collected data was exposed over a serial interface on metering device and transferred to persistent storage through a wireless bridge to be finally exposed via REST interface for external use.

Smart Plugs. Smart plugs from Plugwise[6] were used to measure the consumption of individual devices at school in Kirchdorf, consisting of one beverage machine, one coffee machine and a wall socket where pupils in school connect their laptops. The data of smart plugs is exposed over Web Service interface for external use.

---

[6] Plugwise: http://www.plugwise.com

Power Management Service (PMS). The PMS is a service for monitoring the state of computers installed in the three classrooms as well as for shutting down and restarting them remotely.

Hardware Setup Overview. The whole trial setup consists of sensors, meters, plugs and PMS where all delivered data is accessed either by REST or Web Service interface processed by connector software where it is prepared for semantic storage in an OWLIM semantic repository.

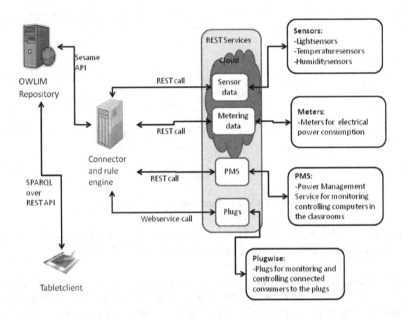

Fig. 1. SESAME-S School Setup at Kirchdorf, Austria

3.2 Data and Software Layer – Semantics

An OWLIM-Lite [7] based semantic repository is central to the data layer of our smart building architecture. OWLIM is a Sesame SAIL (Storage and Inference Layer) where Sesame[7] itself is a framework for analyzing and querying RDF data stored in a triple store [1]. This serves as the triple store for all the data received from various sensors and also provides RDFS-optimized reasoning capabilities necessary for our use cases. Rules in the native PIE format are supported but have limited expressive capabilities.

The connector software itself reads data from school via REST and Web Services on the one side and prepares and stores that data in OWLIM repository by using native Java Sesame 2.0 API on the other side. Besides this functionality and due to limitations of OWLIM for implementing custom rules, the connector software is doing custom reasoning over data in OWLIM store via SPARQL Construct queries

---

[7] SESAME: http://www.openrdf.org/

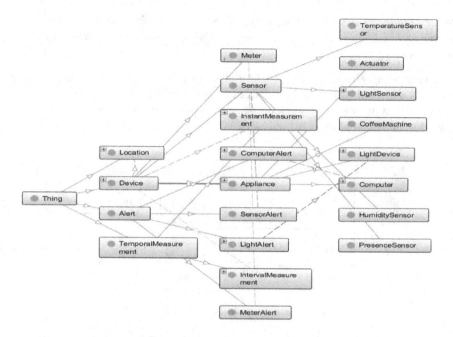

Fig. 2. Core of SmartBuilding Ontology

implementing rules for our use cases. Client side devices like tablets and phones query the repository utilizing REST interface offered by OWLIM store.

SmartBuilding Ontology. The ontology defining our data structure is described below, and its class hierarchy is shown in Figure 2. Disjoint classes represent various aspects of a smart building environment: Devices, Locations, Time bound measurements (Temporal Measurement) and Alerts.

Several datatype properties are used to describe device features like control type (manual or automatic), function (heating, cooking, etc.), power source (battery, electricity, self generating, etc.), state (ON/OFF/Idle), specifications, manufacturer, name, etc. Instances of the subclass "InstantMeasurement" shows instantaneous readings of devices in the "Device" class by datatype property "hasMeasurement" at the instant represented by another datatype property "atInstant". "IntervalMeasurement", another subclass of TemporalMeasurement is similar to "InstantMeasurement" with the only difference being the time for measurements being represented by two data properties (instead of one), "intervalStarts" representing the start of measurement interval and "intervalEnds" representing end of the measurement interval.

Data properties "atInstant" and "hasAlertState" describe the time as well as the state of the alerts in "Alert" class respectively. "hasAlertMessage" describes the message accompanying a particular alert instance. Object properties like "alertFromSensor", "alertFromComputer", etc. connect the SensorAlert (& ComputerAlert respectively) as domain to the Sensor (or Computer) generating that alert as range. The "locatedAt" object property connects the "Device" class as domain with "Location" class as range. "locationHas" is the inverse of the "locatedAt" property. The "hasInstantMeasurement" object property has "Device" class as domain and "InstantMeasurement" class as range. The "hasIntervalMeasurement" class similarly connects "Device" and "IntervalMeasurement" classes respectively.

The Policy Based Approach towards Intelligent Decision Making. A policy based approach towards providing personalized and flexible services to users lies at the core of our design that enables easy adaptation of the framework to different environments. With the data arriving from heterogeneous sources structured and updated in the central repository almost in real time, we utilize the feature to create complex rules and policies to administer this setup. Several services and end user interfaces were created in which rule based modeling of user side constraints were utilized in the monitoring and administration of the system. In the first phase of implementation, most of our tasks involved monitoring of the system and only one use case takes care of administrative jobs.

The OWLIM uses TRREE (Triple Reasoning and Rule Entailment Engine) which is a forward-chaining R-Entailment [2] for providing in-memory reasoning and query evaluation functionalities. Existing rule-sets can be extended with custom rules expressed in the native Pie format. However, several limitations in this format (like not supporting mathematical operators) greatly restrict the potential advantages one could harness with custom rules.

We therefore resorted to using SPARQL[8] Construct queries as a workaround for this handicap. The end user services in our setup do a constant querying of the status of changes in repository at regular intervals. These intervals are flexible and in all our installations, fixed at 15 minutes. Each time an application sends a query to the repository, a set of SPARQL Construct queries are executed by the connector software. Each of these Construct queries contains the logic and constraints relating to the user/system policies. If the constraints are matched with existing environmental conditions represented in the repository, new triples pertaining to respective alerts are generated and added to the triple store. In our setup, all these triples are added to the class "Alert", connecting them to the device and time at which they were generated along with a message. The Application queries the "Alert" class each time to check if a new alert was generated in the system since the last check.

3.3 End User Interfaces and Client Side Data Acquisition

The end user interfaces were developed on top of the Android platform and consisted of a tablet and a smartphone interface allowing comparisons in the usage scenarios. The features include real time feedback on power consumption visualized as line chart, real time data on appliance level (ON/OFF/Idle), historical comparison of past consumption, remote shutdown mechanism for computers and a notification system that reminds the user of unused computers (Figure 3). We used an ACER ICONIA Tab A501 with a 10.1" WXGA display in our evaluations.

The mobile phone application version has a user interface design consistent to the tablet application, but is adapted to the special constraints of the device's smaller

---

[8] SPARQL: http://www.w3.org/TR/rdf-sparql-query/

Fig. 3. Dashboard of the Tablet Software

form factor (like splitting the features into different screens). Because the phone version is not supposed to run all the time, we enhanced the notification system with the standard Android notifications. This behavior is same as receiving a text message reminding users of any idle computers.

4   Evaluation of Data Management

The evaluations of the installation and its services were carried out on our setup at a school in Kirchdorf, Austria. The parts of evaluations showing the flexibility of the system to adapt and scale to a new setup are explained in this paper.

4.1   Evaluation Setup

As described in Section 3, the school setup consists of 3 rooms attached with light, humidity and heat sensors as well as smart meters receiving consumption data from various devices. The semantic data management and services described in Section 3 were tested for their ability to adapt themselves to a new smart building setup. The total volume of data collected from this installation over several months is amounting to ca. 3 million triples. We also observed the effort needed to formally induct the data from a new setup classified according to our existing, generic in its nature, ontology.

4.2   Results

While the initial creation of the connector software linking various data sources to central repository took a typical amount of required man hours, once it is implemented, linking additional sources in general was very easy. Below we describe the adaptability of this framework on the basis of various criteria as tested in real installations:

Adding New Buildings to the System. Dramatically reducing the efforts required in adding new buildings to this framework according to us is the most outstanding achievement of this work. Most of the existing energy monitoring systems use Excel sheets for maintaining their data in a structured format and integrating such data back into new systems or extending it for changes in existing systems is very cumbersome [10]. On the other hand, to induct a new building installation to the framework of our SESAME system, the raw data coming from various sources in this building along with respective timestamp and source information need to be provided to our data layer preferably via a REST/Web service interface.

Since our *SmartBuilding* ontology is very generic in nature, any new location names, devices and corresponding alert types can be readily added to extend the ontology as well as in the Connector software. Such a modification to include data from Russian factory setup in our main repository took not more than half a day by a single person. We also argue that for the adaptation of ontology, a semantic expert is not necessarily needed as including a new setup requires only an extension of the ontology and not the redefining or modification of underlying logic.

Adding New Devices. Addition of a new device to the system can be done in the following steps: (a) installation of the device (b) inserting an instance of it in the appropriate class (Appliance/Meter/Sensor) of the ontology and connect it to other entities as needed (c) provide a REST/Web Service interface of the data coming from this device. For step (c), if there is no way to monitor individual consumption (e.g. toaster, fans, etc.) then it can also be connected via a Plugwise smart plug for which we have installed interfaces to the system. Most of the smart meters and sensors in the market already provide a standard REST/Web service access to their data and thus our system doesn't require any specific non standard access to data making it very easy to add a new device to the system.

In our setup, we tested this with the addition of sensor data in a factory setup in Chernogolovka in Russia where three combined sensor sets are involved for measuring inside room temperature, incoming airflow temperature, outgoing airflow temperature and one Boolean value indicating whether the heater is turned on or off. As the setup here uses the same hardware sensor devices as the setup in school at Kirchdorf/Austria no adaptation of connector software was needed, except for REST access interface.

Aligning Old and New Data. The process of aligning new data to the system besides hardware installation requires adaption of connector software in relation to new REST/Web Service interface offered by the new device added to the system. This means introducing new interface classes in Java to represent the new data structure.

Another aspect in aligning new data refers to end user interface and presentation of new data to the user. The principle in our system uses SPARQL Construct queries for custom rules and resulting triples representing alerts generated by our rules. The system requires only an addition of new SPARQL query for retrieving new alerts based on new use case and change of labeling to conform to this use case and to be meaningful for the user. As the presentation layer is totally decoupled from underlying data layer, custom individual user interfaces for every use case are possible and require no deep understanding of the whole system.

Adapting the Policies. Since the policies for our school setup was created mostly for monitoring the system based on daily routine of school, we could adapt most of these generic looking policies for the Russian factory setup as well. An example was sending out alerts if light was left on after school hours (for the school setup) or after factory working hours (for the factory setup).

Although the effort needed for adapting the policies manually was around half a day for each policy, significant knowledge of semantic web technologies was required to achieve this. We therefore decided to work on an automatic policy adaptation tool that would take care of such policy adaptation tasks automatically reducing the dependence on core semantic expertise [8].

Since all our application services use structured data from the repository and include intelligent reasoning over them, we argue that just by simplifying the data acquisition from a new setup to our framework makes this framework highly scalable along with the value addition of using semantic intelligence.

5   Related Work

Home automation has been defined in [6] as "The introduction of technology within the home to enhance the quality of life of its occupants, through the provision of different services such as telehealth, multimedia entertainment and energy conservation." There has been extensive work in making home automation systems by using different technologies and utilizing innovative techniques [3][4][5]. The aim of authors in [3] is to achieve a more efficient remote control and monitoring of networked enabled devices in a house. They investigate the use of ZigBee towards creating a flexible automation system. The system has however not been tested with real installations and hence the scalability cannot be ascertained. Another example of such an implementation using knowledge representation techniques for smart university application is shown in [6]. This approach is based on semantic web service middleware enriched with capabilities like dynamic composition adapted specifically for university buildings and similar educational facilities. Such a system is therefore far from generic to be implemented across the board in all kinds of buildings. After an initial study into such systems, we believe that our approach provides a unique mix of the qualities (mentioned in earlier sections) that can be practically used in mainstream smart building systems.

6   Conclusions

We have presented a semantically enabled real life smart buildings deployment, and have described and analyzed the data processing techniques. We have shown the feasibility of such deployment in use, and the benefits the semantic technologies are bringing to such development. While many data operations are shown to be made very efficiently, it would be of interest to see the aspects of even larger scale deployments of that character, e.g. as a part of a smart city. The main contributions of this work are as follows:

-    Real life use case with real data and users, its design, implementation, deployment, as an innovative development for the semantic web community;
-    Illustrated clearly the cases of added value of the semantic technologies in the real-life settings;

- Analyzed the typical data management implementations for this smart building use case, and showed their implementation feasibility with the current state of art.

The collected and semantically represented data has a large potential for being combined, extended and reused for numerous scenarios and parties, such as grid operators seeking the balance on their smart grids, utilities, looking after optimal energy trading prices - based on real, and not synthetic user profiles, and municipalities, looking for more information about the citizens. Mechanisms to adequately access and commercialize such data within services (in particular, complying with the rigid security and privacy requirements typical for smart home use cases) are certainly among the next most relevant research questions.

Acknowledgments. This work is supported by the FFG COIN funding line, within the SESAME-S project (http://sesame-s.ftw.at). FTW is supported by the Austrian government and the City of Vienna within the competence center program COMET. The authors thank the SESAME-S project team for valuable contributions.

References

1. Rusher, J.: Semantic Web Advanced Development for Europe (SWAD-Europe). Workshop on Semantic Web Storage and Retrieval - Position Papers
2. ter Horst, H.J.: Combining RDF and Part of OWL with Rules: Semantics, Decidability, Complexity. In: Gil, Y., Motta, E., Benjamins, V.R., Musen, M.A. (eds.) ISWC 2005. LNCS, vol. 3729, pp. 668–684. Springer, Heidelberg (2005)
3. Gill, K., Yang, S.-H., Yao, F., Lu, X.: A zigbee-based home automation system. IEEE Transactions on Consumer Electronics 55(2), 422–430 (2009)
4. Byun, J., Park, S.: Development of a self-adapting intelligent system for building energy saving and context-aware smart services. IEEE Transactions on Consumer Electronics (2011)
5. Bromley, K., Perry, M., Webb, G.: Trends in Smart Home Systems, Connectivity and Services (2003), http://www.nextwave.org.uk
6. Stavropoulos, T.G., Tsioliaridou, A., Koutitas, G., Vrakas, D., Vlahavas, I.: System Architecture for a Smart University Building. In: Diamantaras, K., Duch, W., Iliadis, L.S. (eds.) ICANN 2010, Part III. LNCS, vol. 6354, pp. 477–482. Springer, Heidelberg (2010)
7. Kiryakov, A., Ognyanov, D., Manov, D.: OWLIM – a Pragmatic Semantic Repository for OWL. In: Proc. of International Workshop on Scalable Semantic Web Knowledge Base Systems (SSWS 2005), WISE 2005, New York City, USA, November 20 (2005)
8. Kumar, V.: A Semantic Policy Sharing and Adaptation Infrastructure for Pervasive Communities. In: Proc. of ACM World Wide Web (WWW-PhD Symposium) 2012, Lyon, France, pp. 155–160 (2012)
9. Tomic, S., Fensel, A., Schwanzer, M., Kojic-Veljovic, M., Stefanovic, M.: Semantics for Energy Efficiency in Smart Home Environments. In: Sugumaran, V., Gulla, J.A. (eds.) Applied Semantic Technologies: Using Semantics in Intelligent Information Processing. Taylor and Francis (2011)
10. Capehart, B. L., Middelkoop, T.: Handbook of Web Based Energy Information and Control Systems, 565 pages. Fairmont Press (July 26, 2011)

Towards Using OWL Integrity Constraints
in Ontology Engineering*

Trung-Kien Tran and Christophe Debruyne

STARLab, Department of Computer Science, Vrije Universiteit Brussel
{truntran,chrdebru}@vub.ac.be

Abstract. In the GOPSL ontology engineering methodology, integrity constraints are used to guide communities in constraining their domain knowledge. This paper presents our investigation on OWL integrity constraints and its usage in ontology engineering.

Keywords: Ontology, Integrity Constraint, Ontology Engineering.

1 Introduction

The information contained in legacy systems can be exposed as RDF by annotating the system's symbols with concepts and relations in ontologies. Those mappings, however, sometimes disregard relational constraints [4]. In addition, annotated data also should meet some intended hypothesis in the ontologies. Therefore checking constraints against the annotated data-sources is important. This problem can be addressed by using OWL axioms as *integrity constraints* [5,9]. For example, the following constraint is common in cultural application domain: *every Event must has a Location where it takes place*. It can be expressed in OWL axiom (1).

$$Event \sqsubseteq \exists hasLocation.Location \tag{1}$$

Suppose that in our dataset *beerFestival* is annotated as an instance of *Event*. In database setting, constraint (1) is violated. However, in OWL semantics, constraint (1) is not violated as it can be satisfied by unknown instances. The mismatch between Open World Assumption (OWA) in OWL and Closed World Assumption (CWA) in relational database needs to be addressed in order to use OWL axioms as integrity constraints. In this paper, we present a survey of prominent approaches, analyze the advantages and disadvantages, and an ongoing prototype validator.

2 OWL Integrity Constraints

In relational databases, *Integrity constraints* are used to validate the integrity of data. This idea is brought to knowledge representation and reasoning to enforce the legal state of a knowledge base [7,8]. We discuss some proposals here.

---

* This work was partially funded by the Brussels Institute for Research and Innovation through the Open Semantic Cloud for Brussels Project.

P. Herrero et al. (Eds.): OTM 2012 Workshops, LNCS 7567, pp. 282–285, 2012.

Definition 1 (Integrity constraints by consistency [3]). *A knowledge base $\mathcal{K}$ satisfies an integrity constraint IC iff $\mathcal{K} \cup IC$ is satisfiable.*

Example 1. Let IC_1 contains only axiom (1), $\mathcal{K}_1$ consists of the following axioms.

$$MusicEvent(jazzNight), MusicEvent \sqsubseteq Event \qquad (2)$$

Obviously $\mathcal{K}_1 \cup IC_1$ is satisfiable, then $\mathcal{K}_1$ satisfies IC_1 by Definition 1. However, it does not fit our purpose: we want to have explicit location for $jazzNight$.

Definition 2 (Integrity constraints by entailment [7]). *A knowledge base $\mathcal{K}$ satisfies an integrity constraint IC iff $\mathcal{K} \models IC$.*

Example 2. Let IC_2 contains only axiom (1), $\mathcal{K}_2$ consists of (2) and (3).

$$hasLocation(jazzNight, grandPalace), Location(grandPalace) \qquad (3)$$

Follow our intuition, $\mathcal{K}_2$ should satisfies IC_2. However, there is a model model $\mathcal{I}_1$ of $\mathcal{K}_2$ but $\mathcal{I}_1 \not\models IC_2$. By Definition 2, $\mathcal{K}_2$ does not satisfies IC_2.

$$\mathcal{I}_1 = \{MusicEvent(jazzNight), hasLocation(jazzNight, grandPalace)$$
$$Location(grandPalace), Event(jazzNight), Event(beerFestival)\}$$

The above example suggests that entailment in Definition 2 should be restricted to *minimal models* of $\mathcal{K}$. This idea has been nicely captured in [5], where *outer skolemization* [6] is applied to deal with existential quantifiers.

Definition 3 (Integrity constraints by minimal models and skolemization [5]). *Let $\pi(\mathcal{K})$ and $\pi(IC)$ are first-order formulae that express $\mathcal{K}$ and IC respectively, and $\mathsf{sk}(\mathcal{K})$ is obtained from $\pi(\mathcal{K})$ by skolemization. $\mathcal{K}$ satisfies integrity constraint IC iff $\mathcal{I} \models \pi(IC)$ (simply written as $\mathcal{I} \models IC$) for every minimal (Herbrand) model $\mathcal{I}$ of $\mathsf{sk}(\mathcal{K})$.*

Reconsidering Example 1, the only minimal model of $\mathcal{K}_1$ is $\mathcal{I}_0 = \{Event(jazzNight), MusicEvent(jazzNight)\}$. By Definition 3, $\mathcal{K}_1$ does not satisfy IC_1 because $\mathcal{I}_0 \not\models IC_1$. In Example 2, the only minimal model of $\mathcal{K}_2$ is $\mathcal{I}_2 = \mathcal{I}_1 \setminus \{Event(beerFestival)\}$. $\mathcal{I}_2 \models IC_2$, then $\mathcal{K}_2$ satisfies IC_2. This matches our intuition, however *skolemization* could lead to unexpected consequences.

Example 3. Let $\mathcal{K}_3$ consists of axiom (2) and (4), IC_3 contains only the axiom (5).

$$Event \sqsubseteq \exists hasLocation.Location \qquad (4)$$
$$MusicEvent \sqsubseteq \exists hasLocation.Location \qquad (5)$$

We have $\mathcal{I}_3$ is the minimal Herbrand model of $\mathcal{K}_3$, where $unknownLocation$ is generated by skolemization of axiom (4).

$$\mathcal{I}_3 = MusicEvent(jazzNight), hasLocation(jazzNight, unkownLocation)$$
$$Event(jazzNight), Location(unknownLocation)$$

Since $\mathcal{I}_3 \models IC_3$, $\mathcal{K}_3$ satisfies the IC_3 although $jazzNight$ has an unknown location.

To overcome this unexpected consequence, one can use a special concept O to bind the existential variables to known individuals. In addition, every known individual should be the instance of O. An alternative for the semantics of OWL integrity constraints has been proposed in [9]. Given a knowledge base $\mathcal{K}$ and a set of its models $\mathcal{U} = \{\mathcal{I}_1, \ldots, \mathcal{I}_n\}$, a concept name A, role name R and individual a are interpreted under *IC-interpretation* $\mathcal{I}_\mathcal{U}$ as follows:

$$A^{\mathcal{I}_\mathcal{U}} = \{d^{\mathcal{I}} \mid d \in N_I \text{ such that } d^{\mathcal{J}} \in A^{\mathcal{J}}, \text{for all } \mathcal{J} \in \mathcal{U}\}$$
$$R^{\mathcal{I}_\mathcal{U}} = \{(c^{\mathcal{I}}, d^{\mathcal{I}}) \mid c, d \in N_I \text{ such that } (c^{\mathcal{J}}, d^{\mathcal{J}}) \in R^{\mathcal{J}}, \text{for all } \mathcal{J} \in \mathcal{U}\}$$
$$a^{\mathcal{I}_\mathcal{U}} = a^{\mathcal{I}}$$

In addition to the new semantics, this approach utilizes the notion of *Weak Unique Name Assumption* (WUNA), that is: in the model of $\mathcal{K}$, *equalities* are derived as less as possible. The resulting model is called the *minimal equality model*. The integrity constraint satisfaction is then defined in Definition 4.

Definition 4 (Integrity constraints by WUNA and *IC-interpretation* [9]). *A knowledge base $\mathcal{K}$ satisfies integrity constraint IC iff for every axiom $\alpha \in IC$ and for all model $\mathcal{I} \in \mathcal{U}$, $\mathcal{I}_\mathcal{U} \models \alpha$; where $\mathcal{U}$ is a set of minimal equality models of $\mathcal{K}$ and $\mathcal{I}_\mathcal{U}$ is an IC-interpretation.*

Reconsidering previous examples, it is easy to check that Definition 4 matches our intuition. We agree with the proposed semantics of integrity constraints. However, we claim that UNA is more suitable. The reason is that *equality* can be seen as a special role and should be interpreted likes other roles in the integrity constraints. UNA, therefore, correctly captures semantics of *equality* under IC-interpretations.

3   Using OWL Integrity Constraints in Ontology Engineering

We will briefly describe the ontology-engineering method adopted within this project; GOSPL [1]. It is a hybrid approach as a special linguistic artifact is used to describe terms by means of natural language definitions for human reasoning on one side, and formal descriptions based on the other. For the formal part, the world is described by means of binary fact-types, which are generalizations of facts observed in the world. For instance, the observed fact "Christophe attends U2 360 tour" is refined into "the person with name "Christophe" attends the concert with concert title "U2 360" and then generalized into the following binary fact-types: (i) Person with / of Name, (ii) Concert with / of Concert Title, and (iii) Person attends / attended by Concert. Fact-types hold within a particular community, and the community is used as a means to disambiguate the labels inside those facts.

Commitments in GOSPL are a selection of lexon that are constrained to describe the intended usage of these facts. Commitments also contain information on how one individual application commits to the ontology[1]. The constraints are based on ORM [2].

The adoption of GOSPL within OSCB is motivated by the fact that the fact-types are grounded in natural language and that everything is described in terms of fact-types (no separate notions of concepts and properties), leveraging the modeling activities for domain experts.

---

[1] For more information on this part, we refer the reader to [1].

4   Implementation and Conclusion

We have implemented a prototype validator that can check three types of constraint: *mandatory constraint, uniqueness constraint*, and *key constraint* [2]. Table 1 shows the SPARQL queries (without prefixes) to check the validity of those integrity constraints and get the counter examples. To get complete answers, we use HermiT[2] reasoner to perform *forward reasoning* before running those SPARQL queries.

Table 1. SPARQL queries for integrity constraints

Constraint type / OWL integrity constraint	SPARQL query
Mandatory constraint / $C \sqsubseteq \exists R.D$	`SELECT ?x WHERE {?x rdf:type C. OPTIONAL {?x R ?y. ?y rdf:type D. } FILTER (!BOUND(?y))}`
Uniqueness constraint / $C \sqsubseteq\, \leq 1R.D$	`SELECT ?x WHERE {?x rdf:type C; R ?y1; R ?y2. ?y1 rdf:type D. ?y2 rdf:type D. FILTER (?y1 !=?y2)}`
Key constraint / $haskey(C, R)$	`SELECT ?x1 ?x2 WHERE {?x1 rdf:type C; R ?y. ?x2 rdf:type C; R ?y. FILTER (?x1!=?x2)}`

Our prototype validator is under development. Although we have not performed experiments on well-known benchmarks, our validator is tested with some toy ontologies. We plan to support more constraint types (cfr. ORM [2]), do further experiments, and fully integrate it to our ontology engineering platform.

References

1. Debruyne, C., Meersman, R.: Semantic Interoperation of Information Systems by Evolving Ontologies through Formalized Social Processes. In: Eder, J., Bielikova, M., Tjoa, A.M. (eds.) ADBIS 2011. LNCS, vol. 6909, pp. 444–459. Springer, Heidelberg (2011)
2. Halpin, T.: Information Modeling and Relational Databases. Morgan Kaufmann, San Francisco (2008)
3. Kowalski, R.A.: Logic for data description. In: Logic and Data Bases, pp. 77–103 (1977)
4. Lausen, G., Meier, M., Schmidt, M.: Sparqling constraints for rdf. In: EDBT, pp. 499–509 (2008)
5. Motik, B., Horrocks, I., Sattler, U.: Bridging the gap between owl and relational databases. J. Web Sem. 7(2), 74–89 (2009)
6. Nonnengart, A., Weidenbach, C.: Computing small clause normal forms. In: Handbook of Automated Reasoning, pp. 335–367 (2001)
7. Reiter, R.: Towards a logical reconstruction of relational database theory. In: On Conceptual Modelling (Intervale), pp. 191–233 (1982)
8. Reiter, R.: On integrity constraints. In: TARK, pp. 97–111. Morgan Kaufmann (1988)
9. Tao, J., Sirin, E., Bao, J., McGuinness, D.L.: Integrity constraints in owl. In: AAAI. AAAI Press (2010)

---

[2] http://www.hermit-reasoner.com

Table4OLD: A Tool of Managing Rules of Open Linked Data of Culture Event and Public Transport in Brussels

Yan Tang Demey

Semantic Technology and Application Research Laboratory (STARLab),
Department of Computer Science,
Vrije Universiteit Brussel, Pleinlaan 2 B-1050 Brussels, Belgium
yan.tang@vub.ac.be

Abstract. This paper records a brief description of an online tool and web service called Table4OLD (decision table for Open Linked Data, culturebrussels.appspot.com), with which we manage decision rules defined on top of domain ontologies. These decision rules are presented in the form of (semantic) decision tables. In the demonstration, we use a use case in the field of culture event and public transport in Brussels. We intend to show how easy a semantic decision table can be used as a user interface for non-technical people. In the meanwhile, it also gives enough technical transparency and modification possibilities to technicians and amateurs.

Keywords: ontology, Semantic Decision Table, Open Data, Linked Data, Open Linked Data, Knowledge Management.

1 Introduction

In the Open Semantic Cloud for Brussels (OSCB) project (www.oscb.be), a use case has been designed for detecting public transport means for a culture event. There are two domain ontologies – a culture event ontology developed with Agenda (www.agenda.be) and a public transport ontology developed with STIB/MIVB (www.mivb.be). We want to use semantic decision tables (SDT, [1]) to model decision rules for managing user preferences.

An SDT is a decision table enriched with formal domain semantics. It contains a tabular presentation, a set of binary fact types, constraints, dependency rules and operators over those fact types. In some cases, the fact types and constraints are the result of annotating a decision table.

Table 1 shows an example. It contain the semantics defined in the domain ontologies (see L1~4), table structural information (see L 5 and 11 etc.), and the value types of the decision items (see L 8~10). We include a meta-rule for this decision table, which is "IF the value of [PT Available] is [Y], THEN the value of [Show PT info.] should be [*]". This rule is modeled in Semantic Decision Rule Language (SDRule-L, [2]).

The meta-rule in an SDT can be used to check the consistency in the rules of a decision table. In this paper, we will not focus on this issue. We would rather focus on

P. Herrero et al. (Eds.): OTM 2012 Workshops, LNCS 7567, pp. 286–289, 2012.

Table 1. An SDT of deciding whether or not to recommend a cultural event based on the price, language and availability of the public transport (PT)

Condition	1	2	3	4	5	6	7	8	9	10	11	12
Price	<=5						>5					
Language	EN		FR		NL		EN		FR		NL	
PT Available	Y	N	Y	N	Y	N	Y	N	Y	N	Y	N
Action												
Recommend	*	*					*				*	
Show PT info.	*		*		*		*		*		*	

	Binary fact types		
1	$\langle \gamma_1, Event, with, of, Price \rangle$	8	$\langle \gamma_3, Price, has\ value\ type\ of, is\ value\ type\ of, Float \rangle$
2	$\langle \gamma_1, Event, with, of, Language \rangle$	9	$\langle \gamma_3, Language, has\ value\ type\ of, is\ value\ type\ of, String \rangle$
3	$\langle \bar{a}_1, Event, with, of, Address \rangle$	10	$\langle \bar{a}_3, PTAvailable, has\ value\ type\ of, is\ value\ type\ of, Boolean \rangle$
4	$\langle \bar{a}_2, Bus, connects, is\ connected\ by, Address \rangle$	11	$\langle \bar{a}_3, Recommend, is\ a, is, ActionStub \rangle$
5	$\langle \bar{a}_3, Price, is\ a, is, ConditionStub \rangle$		...

Meta-rules in SDRule-L [2]

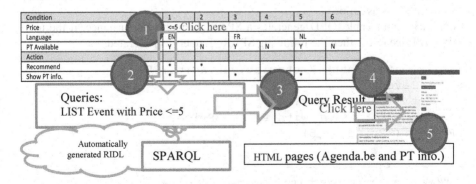

the management issues of an SDT by considering it as a user interface for non-technical people. In the meanwhile, we also want our tool to give enough technical transparency and modification possibilities.

2 Design and Result

The functional design of Table4OLD is illustrated in **Fig. 1**.

Fig. 1. Functional design of Table4OLD (5 steps)

Before allowing non-technical users to use Table4OLD, we, as knowledge engineers, have selected a few concepts from the domain ontologies and group them into two groups: *conditional* and *decisional*. A conditional concept often points to a web service that consumes data. A decisional concept often points to a web service that produces data.

Each SDT has a context, which is identified as a problem field. This context can as well be modelled as a concept in the domain ontologies. For instance, in the culture event ontology[1], the concept *Event* can be considered as a context. The concepts *Price* and *Language* are the two concepts considered conditional.

In this ontology, *Price* is linked to *Event* via an object property *Event_with_Price*, the domain of which is *Event* and the range of which is *Price*. The inverse property of *Event_with_Price* is *Price_of_Event*. Similarly, *Language* is linked to *Event* via an object property *Event_with_Language*, the inverse property of which is *Language_of_Event*.

The concept *PT Available* is defined in an application ontology[2]. It is linked to *Event* using *Event_with_PTAvailable* and *PTAvailable_of_Event*. It uses the object property *DetectPTAvailable_for_PTAvailable* to be further connected with *Detect PT Available*, which is a subtype of *Web Service*. The type of the value of *PT Available* is Boolean.

A user can build an SDT in Table4OLD by simply selecting conditional and decisional concepts. In the step of designing decision rules, he can make some meaningful combinations of those concepts. If a conditional concept has a value range, then Table4OLD will propose to use ranges. If the concept has disparate countable members, then it will propose the user with the choices. If the value of the concept is a Boolean value, then it will use "Y" and "N" automatically.

After the table has been created, he can use Table4OLD to check whether the decision rules are properly built by validating it against the domain ontologies and the semantics in any other shared models, such as the meta-rules defined in SDRule-L.

When the user clicks on a condition, for instance, "Price <= 5" in Table 1, Table4OLD will look at the open linked data from Agenda.be and provide a list of culture events that cost less than or equal to 5 euro. When he clicks on a column, e.g., column 1 in Table 1, a list of events that meet the conditions of "Price <= 5", "Language – EN", "PT Available – Y" is illustrated. What happened in Table4OLD in this scenario is as follows.

For each click, Table4OLD generates a SPARQL query. For instance, if the user clicks on "Price <=5", then the following SPARQL query is generated.

```
@prefix Onto: <http://starlab.vub.ac.be:8080/>
select ?event {
    ?event a Onto: Event.
    ?event Onto: Event_with_Price ?Price.
    Filter (?Price <= 5).
}
```

---

[1] http://www.starlab.vub.ac.be/website/files/agenda2012-07-13.owl

[2] http://www.starlab.vub.ac.be/website/files/publictransportapplicationV0.1.owl

As the result, the list of web pages will be shown to the user. If a link is clicked by the user, then he will be forwarded to the right web page at www.agenda.be.

Another possible scenario of using the SDT in Table 1 is as follows. A user can ask for the recommendations for future cultural events. For instance, if he specifies the time slot, e.g. within a week, then he will get a list of events with recommendations as illustrated in Table 2.

Table 2. A result of recommendation using Table 1

Event	Fired Rules	Action
Bruxelles Les Bains	1, 3, 5	**Recommended**, Metro 2, 6, Bus 51
Foire du Midi	1, 3, 5	**Recommended**, Metro 2, 6, Bus 3, 4, 51
Sinon la Famille ça va ?	9	Metro 1, 5, Bus 51
...	...	...

In Table4OLD, the results shown in Table 2 are decorated with other information from these events, such as images, logos and short descriptions. A hyper link to each event is a necessary.

3 Discussion and Conclusion

We have designed and implemented Table4OLD for culture events and public transports in Brussels. We use semantic decision tables (SDTs) to consume open linked data on the Web.

The SDTs in this paper are manageable and executable, meaning that all the decision items (conditions and actions) are linked to web services.

Table4OLD uses multiple domain ontologies. In the future, we need to study how non-technical end users can provide their "new" concepts to the conceptual models without making an extra effort.

References

[1] Tang, Y.: Semantic Decision Tables - A New, Promising and Practical Way of Organizing Your Business Semantics with Existing Decision Making Tools. LAP LAMBERT Academic Publishing AG & Co. KG, Saarbrücken (2010) ISBN 978-3-8383-3791-3
[2] Tang, Y., Meersman, R.: SDRule Markup Language: Towards Modeling and Interchanging Ontological Commitments for Semantic Decision Making. In: Chapter V (Section I) in Handbook of Research on Emerging Rule-Based Languages and Technologies: Open Solutions and Approaches. IGI Publishing, USA (2009) ISBN: 1-60566-402-2

Fact-Based Web Service Ontologies

Peter Bollen

Department of Organization & Strategy
School of Business and Economics
Maastricht University

1   Introduction

The service-oriented architecture paradigm has gained attention in the past years, because it promised to lay the foundation for agility, in the sense that it would enable companies to deliver new and more flexible business processes to improve customer satisfaction [1, 2, 3]. In the *service-oriented architecture* (SOA) paradigm, a *service requesting organization* (SRO) basically outsources one or more organizational activities or even complete business processes to one or more *service delivering organizations* (SDOs). The way this is done in a traditional way, is that the SRO 'outsources' a given business service to a 'third-party' SDO for a relative long period of time (3 months, a year). In an agile environment, the reconfigurable resources might face a life-span of a few days or even a few hours, in principle reconfiguration of business services can take place on a run-time time-scale, in the sense that for each new transaction a possibly different SDO must be configured into the value chain. The application of the service-oriented paradigm, therefore, allows the dynamic composition of business functionality by using the world-wide web [3, 4].

The problem with current approaches is that they cannot handle the semantic and ontological complexities caused by flexible participants having flexible cooperation processes.

In most business organizations the function that is responsible for information and knowledge management will have some kind of repository, schema or knowledge map that (ideally) defines the information objects (business repository or business ontology) and the semantic relationships between these business concepts (conceptual schema or a data description language (DDL) of some sort). At best (large) companies have a business glossary in which business concepts are defined precisely. When it comes to processes we must conclude that at best descriptions of procedural knowledge might be documented in some type of data flow diagram (DFD) or other process description logic (e.g. BPMN [5]). In most practical situations, however, the process logic is embedded in software code, and an explicit semantic description is lacking.

We will extend the current modeling capabilities of the fact-based approach with modeling constructs for the modeling of business services in the context of the service-oriented paradigm by extending the concepts definitions and derivation/ exchange rule modeling constructs [6] to cater for 'business services' that can be provided by either the SRO itself or by one or more (external) SDO(s).

P. Herrero et al. (Eds.): OTM 2012 Workshops, LNCS 7567, pp. 290–293, 2012.
© Springer-Verlag Berlin Heidelberg 2012

2   Business Ontology I: Concept Definitions

We will now take this set of 'explicit' verbalizations and abstract them into a set of concept definitions and fact type readings in a fact type diagram. This list of structured concept definitions (see table 1), should facilitate the comprehension of knowledge domain sentences and comprise the business domain ontology [7].

Table 1. List of concept definitions for SDO

Concept	Definition
Carrier	A third party logistics organization that ships packages for an [order] from a [SRO] to a client of the [SRO]
Carrier name	A name from the *carrier name* name class that can be used to identify a [carrier] among the set of [carriers]s that exist in the world.
Local delivery type	A label to refer to a specific type of service provided by a specific [carrier]
Carrier delivery type	A [local delivery type] that is offered by a [carrier]
Period length in days	A period or slice in time having a duration
Natural number	A name from the *natural number* name class that can be used to identify a [period length in days] among the set of [period length in days].
Money amount	A specific quantity of money
Dollars	A name from the *dollar* name class that can be used to identify a [money amount] among the set of [money amount]s.
Promotional price	A price that is charged per kg for a delivery service during a number of [week]s in a promotional period
Standard price	A price that is charged in a [week] for which no [promotional price] is charged
Maximum dimension	The maximum [size] for length * the maximum [size] for width * the maximum [size] for height of an [order] for which a given [delivery type] is still valid

3   Business Ontology II: Fact Types and Fact Type Readings

The domain sentences from the former sections can be abstracted and will lead to fact types and associated fact type readings. In figure 1 an example is given of the fact types and fact readings that have been abstracted from these example domain sentences for the example communication UoD for the SRO.

4   Business Rules I

The fact type diagram can be used as a starting point for a further explicitation and encoding of business rules in terms of constraints on the allowed populations of the fact type diagram as for example is given in figure 1.

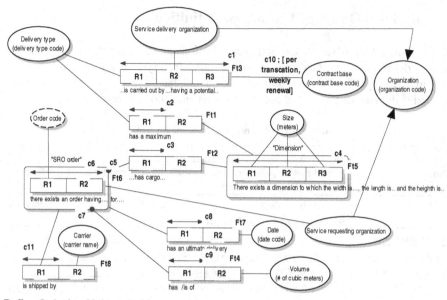

Define Order has Volume (cubic meters)
As Order has cargo Dimension **and** There exist a dimension for which the width is $Size_1$ and the length is $Size_2$ and the heighth is $Size_3$ **and** Volume= $Size_1 * Size_2 * Size_3$

Fig. 1. Complete conceptual schema for SRO (in combination with table 1) using ORM (I) notational conventions

5   Business Rules II: Exchange- and Event Rules

Adding the semantic definition of a (business) process to the list of concept definitions, is a pragmatic extension of the current definition of the list of definitions, which normally contains definitions for concepts in the ontology. From a theoretically point of view, however, if we consider a process base [8] as part of our UoD, then a semantic definition of a process type, should per definition be contained in the list of concept definitions.

Process: Calculate Volume	A process that has a a result: a rough indicator of the cubic [volume] of a package which is determined by multiplying its width, heighth and lenghth. **<Create(s) instance(s) of Ft4>**
Process: Add order	A transaction in which the [order] and the [dimension] and [delivery date] of the [order] are added to the information system.**<Create(s) instance(s) of Ft2 and Ft7>**
Process: Determine carrier for order	This process leads to the selection of a specific [SDO] for the shipment of an [order] under the best possible conditions for [delivery time] and [shipment price]**<Create(s) instance(s) of Ft8>**

6   Conclusions

In this article we have given additional modeling concepts in fact-based modeling (FBM) to cater for the explicit modeling of a application domain's ontology. The new modeling constructs allow us to capture the definitions of the fact-generating business processes. The practical relevance of the list of concept definitions is in the 'networked' society and business-world in which a traditional conceptual schema has to be 'upgraded' to cater for communication of the definition of business processes with potential external agents, e.g. customers, suppliers, web-service brokers, whose identity is not yet known to us at design time.

In line with semantic web developments, the conceptual schema needs a communication part that contains 'definition' instances to be shared with the potential agents in order for them to be able to communicate effectively and efficiently with a ('web-based') business application in which the 'traditional' allowed communication patterns and their state (transition) constraints will not be violated. This will significantly increase the perceived quality and ease-of-use of such a (web-based) application, since it has established a semantic bridge with the potential external users, allowing them to communicate in a direct way with the business application, by preventing semantic ambiguities from occurring in the first place.

References

1. Yusef, Y., Sarhadi, M., Gunasekaran, A.: Agile manufacturing: The drivers, concepts and attributes. International Journal of Production Economics 62(1-2), 33–43 (1999)
2. Demirkan, S., et al.: Service-oriented technology and management: Perspectives on research and practice for the coming decade. Electronic Commerce Research and Applications 7, 356–376 (2008)
3. Choy, L., et al.: Leveraging the supply chain flexibility of third party logistics – Hybrid knowledge-based system approach. Expert Systems with Applications 35, 1998–2016 (2008)
4. Grefen, P., et al.: Dynamic business network process management in instant virtual enterprises. Computers in Industry 60, 86–103 (2009)
5. OMG, Business process modelling notation (BPMN) specification, OMG (2007)
6. Bollen, P.: Fact-based modeling in the data-, process- and event perspectives. In: OTM 2007, ORM 2007. Springer, Vilamoura (2007)
7. Bollen, P.: Extending the ORM conceptual schema design procedure with the capturing of the domain ontology. In: EMMSAD 2007. Tapir Academic Press, Trondheim (2007)
8. Nijssen, G.: An axiom and architecture for information systems. In: Information Systems Concepts: An In-Depth Analysis (1989)

Combining Image Similarity Metrics
for Semantic Image Annotation

Bart Jansen[1,2,*], Tran Duc Toan[1,2], and Frederik Temmermans[1,2]

[1] Vrije Universiteit Brussel, Dept. of Electronics and Informatics, Pleinlaan 2, 1050
Brussels, Belgium
bjansen@etro.vub.ac.be
http://www.etro.vub.ac.be
[2] Interdisciplinary Institute for Broadband Technology (IBBT), Dept. of Future
Media and Imaging (FMI), Ghent, Belgium
http://www.ibbt.be

Abstract. This paper describes automated image annotation as an image retrieval problem, in which the distance metric used to express similarity among images is learnt from available distance metrics on several image descriptors. Rather than describing the problem as an optimization problem, we study it as a regression problem. On a limited dataset of images of buildings taken in the city center of Brussels, we illustrate the superior performance of the combined distance metrics over any of the considered individual distance metrics in automated image annotation.

Keywords: automated image annotation, distance metric learning.

1 Introduction

The domain of automated semantic image annotation studies how to automatically assign one or more semantic labels to images in a given database. Typically, these labels originate from a predefined ontology which is specific to the application. Automated image annotation (AIA) [8] is based on the retrieval of images similar to the given image from a database of already annotated images. As such, it relies on the assumption that *similarity* in the image domain relates to *similarity* in the semantic domain (see for instance [3] for a discussion on *the semantic gap*). Therefore, progress in the domain of AIA largely depends on advancements obtained in content based image retrieval (CBIR). In CBIR, the main challenges are to define image descriptors that are relevant for identifying similarity among images and to define methods to combine various descriptors. Image descriptors are typically based on interest point detectors (SIFT, SURF, ...) or on color, shape or texture (of objects present in) the images.

Although various methods exist for combining multiple descriptors, a common approach is to use machine learning techniques to train a classifier for each of the classes. One of the disadvantages of the classifier based approach is that a

---

* Bart Jansen is currently funded by Innoviris.

P. Herrero et al. (Eds.): OTM 2012 Workshops, LNCS 7567, pp. 294–297, 2012.

separate and independent classifier is most of the time trained for each class. Consequently, the importance and complexity of a second classification system for aggregating the votes of the individual classifiers grows with an increasing number of classes [8]. Such approaches are typically evaluated in CBIR tasks but far less often in AIA tasks.

2   Algorithms

Several methods exist for learning a distance metric based on a weighted combination of several distance metrics in a supervised learning scheme. We adopt the notation of [6] and adapt it to the specific case of CBIR and AIA.

Suppose there is a set of n single labeled images $\{(x_1, y_1), (x_2, y_2), ..., (x_n, y_n)\}$ where $x_i \in X$ and $y_i \in \{1, 2, ..., c\}$ and c is the number of unique classes. Each image x_i is represented by a vector $[x_i^1 ... x_i^m]$ where $x_i^l \in X_l, l = 1...m$ are different descriptors computed from the image x_i. Thus, $x_i \in X = X_1 \times ... \times X_m$. On each of the X_l spaces a distance metric D_l is defined. If D is defined as $D(x_i, x_j) = [D_1(x_i^1, x_j^1), ..., D_m(x_i^m, x_j^m)]^T$, then

$$D_A^2(x_i, x_j) = D(x_i, x_j)^T A \, D(x_i, x_j) \tag{1}$$

can be defined. In order to ensure that D_A is a valid pseudometric, A should be positive semi-definite, so $A = W^T W$.

Now, define S_S to be the set of all image pairs annotated with the same class and S_D to be the set of all image pairs with a different class. $S_S = \{(x_i, x_j) \mid y_i = y_j\}$ and $S_D = \{(x_i, x_j) \mid y_i \neq y_j\}$, then the metric learning problem in a supervised setting consists of an optimization problem:

$$\min_A F_A(S_S, S_D, D_A^2) \tag{2}$$

Depending on the definition of F, the within class distances are minimized, the between class distances are maximized, or combination of both, often resulting in complex optimization problems [7,2].

If we assume that A is a diagonal matrix, then the distance $D_A(x_i, x_j)$ reduces to a simple weighted sum of the distances $D_l(x_i, x_j)$ and the problem is reduced to the learning of the weights a_{ll}. By specifying that $D_A(x_i, x_j)$ should be 0 for all $(x_i, x_j) \in S_S$ and that $D_A(x_i, x_j)$ should be 1 for all $(x_i, x_j) \in S_D$, the weights can be learnt in a supervised binary classification problem. In this paper weights are learnt using linear regression and by back-propagation learning using a single layer neural network (NN).

3   Results

The proposed method is evaluated in a task of automated annotation of images of buildings in the city of Brussels. The database contains pictures of 28 different buildings in the city center of Brussels. Four images per class were selected for training (112 in total) and 1 image per class was used as an independent test set. This dataset is similar - but still smaller - than the ZuBuD dataset [1], often used in content based image retrieval tasks. A difference with ZuBuD is the rather big difference in views of the same buildings and the big differences in viewing distance.

On each image, the following MPEG-7 descriptors [4] were computed: Color Layout Descriptor (CLD), Color Structure Descriptor (CSD), Edge Histogram Descriptor (EHD), Homogenous Texture Descriptor (HTD) and Scalable Color Descriptor (SCD). Additionally, we complemented these image descriptors with SURF [1]. On each of the six interest point descriptors, we used an appropriate distance metric as specified in [4] and [5].

Results of this experiment are summarized in Table 1, in which the accuraies of several weighted distance metric combinations are listed. Rows 1 to 6 show the accuracies of the isolated use of each individual distance metric. Although all descriptors result in recognition rates far above random (which is only 1/28), there is as expected a clear performance difference between SURF and the MPEG-7 descriptors in this object recognition task. However, SURF in itself is not resulting in perfect recognition. This confirms our assumption that this dataset has more variety in viewing angles etc. compared to the ZuBuD dataset, on which SURF results in 100% correct recognition. Rows 7 and 8 list the results for the case in which a weighted combination of the different distance metrics are learned using linear regression (row 7) and NN (row 8), resulting in accuracies of 82.14% and 85.74% respectively, resulting in an increase of 4% to 7% when only using SURF. In both cases, a much higher weight was learned for SURF compared to the other descriptors, confirming the importance of SURF in object recognition tasks.

However, SURF is not a good descriptor for object class recognition tasks, where the kind of object rather than the exact object needs to be recognized. Therefore, it was investigated whether a combined metric can be learned only

Table 1. Experimental results

Nr	CLD	CSD	EHD	HTD	SCD	SURF	Accuracy
1	1	0	0	0	0	0	42.86
2	0	1	0	0	0	0	53.57
3	0	0	1	0	0	0	42.86
4	0	0	0	1	0	0	35.71
5	0	0	0	0	1	0	35.71
6	0	0	0	0	0	1	78.57
7	0.17	0.35	0.15	0	0	0.28	82.14
8	0.13	0.37	0.07	0.05	0.07	0.26	85.74
9	0.15	0.45	0.14	-0.01	0.04	0	71.42
10	0.21	0.40	0.20	0	0.03	0	75.00

---

[1] http://www.vision.ee.ethz.ch/showroom/zubud/

based on the MPEG-7 descriptors. Results are listed in rows 9 and 10 for linear regression and NN and show that although the combined metrics clearly outperform the individual metrics, performance is still slightly lower than only using SURF, i.e. 71.42% and 75.00% using all MPEG-7 descriptors against 78.57% for SURF only.

Given the low number of training images per class, the limited number of classes and the limited evaluation of the proposed methods, comparison results need to be interpreted with care. However, the initial experiments show the validity of the approach, which needs to be confirmed by further and more elaborate experiments.

4   Conclusion

This paper explored the learning of a combined distance metric on several image descriptors to improve annotation accuracy on a database of images of buildings in the city of Brussels. The problem was described as a supervised learning problem based on a dataset of annotated images. Results showed that both using linear regression and neural networks superior performance could be obtained compared to using any of the individual distance metrics.

References

1. Bay, H., Tuytelaars, T., Van Gool, L.: SURF: Speeded Up Robust Features. In: Leonardis, A., Bischof, H., Pinz, A. (eds.) ECCV 2006. Part I. LNCS, vol. 3951, pp. 404–417. Springer, Heidelberg (2006)
2. Globerson, A., Roweis, S.: Metric learning by collapsing classes. In: Weiss, Y., Schölkopf, B., Platt, J. (eds.) Advances in Neural Information Processing Systems 18, pp. 451–458. MIT Press, Cambridge (2006)
3. J.S. Hare, P.A.S. Sinclair, P.H. Lewis, K. Martinez, P.G.B. Enser, and J. S. Christine. Bridging the Semantic Gap in Multimedia Information Retrieval: Top-Down and Bottom-Up Approaches. In 3rd European Semantic Web Conference (ESWC 2006). LNCS, vol. 4011. Springer (2006)
4. Sikora, T.: The MPEG-7 visual standard for content description-an overview. IEEE Transactions on Circuits and Systems for Video Technology 11(6), 696–702 (2001)
5. Temmermans, F., Jansen, B., Deklerck, R., Schelkens, P., Cornelis, J.: The Mobile Museum Guide: Artwork Recognition with Eigenpaintings and SURF (2011)
6. Woznica, A., Kalousis, A., Hilario, M.: Learning to combine distances for complex representations. In: ICML 2007: Proceedings of the 24th International Conference on Machine Learning, Corvalis, Oregon, pp. 1031–1038. ACM (2007)
7. Xing, E., Ng, A., Jordan, M., Russell, S.: Distance Metric Learning with Application to Clustering with Side-Information. In: Advances in Neural Information Processing Systems. MIT Press, Cambridge (2003)
8. Zhang, D., Monirul Islam, M., Lu, G.: A review on automatic image annotation techniques. Pattern Recognition 45(1), 346–362 (2012)

Ranking and Clustering Techniques to Support an Efficient E-Democracy

Marlene Goncalves[1], Maria-Esther Vidal[1], Francisco Castro[2], Luis Vidal[1,2], and Maribel Acosta[1,3]

[1] Universidad Simón Bolívar, Venezuela
[2] Universidad Central de Venezuela, Venezuela
[3] Institute AIFB, Karlsruhe Institute of Technology, Germany
{mgoncalves,mvidal,macosta}@ldc.usb.ve, maribel.acosta@kit.edu

Abstract. We focus on ranking and data mining techniques to empower e-Democracy and allow the opinion of ordinary people to be considered in the design of electoral campaigns. We illustrate the quality of our approach on Venezuelan historical electoral data; ranking results are compared to ground truths produced by an independent study. Our evaluation suggests that the proposed techniques are able to identify up to 85% of the golden results by just analyzing 35% of the whole data.

Keywords: E-Democracy, Skyline, Top-k, Clustering.

1 Introduction

Digital and Information technologies as well as Semantic Web standards and tools, facilitate the publication of governmental data and the development of applications that can impact on the citizens' quality of life. For example, e-Government initiatives as the ones supported by the *Data.gov*[1] and *GovTrack*[2] projects make available more than 450,000 datasets to empower normal people participation in governmental processes. This democratization of the information facilitates citizens' daily activities and also provides the basis to discover properties and relationships that could not be identified years before. Nevertheless, because these open datasets can be extremely large, applications need to be designed not just to meet soundness and completeness of the solutions, but to provide few relevant solutions quickly. We propose the construction of a multi-dimensional dynamic model that is able to explore large volumes of data very quickly with no limitations on data patterns or sources of information. Particularly, we apply this approach to identify electoral citizens' patterns in voting historical data. The identified patterns are used to discover electoral regions where a given electoral option has the potential of switching intended votes into actual votes. These selected regions will be the basis for the design of effective electoral campaigns. Ranking [1,2] and data clusterings [4] techniques

---

[1] http://www.data.gov/
[2] http://www.govtrack.us/

P. Herrero et al. (Eds.): OTM 2012 Workshops, LNCS 7567, pp. 298–301, 2012.
© Springer-Verlag Berlin Heidelberg 2012

are combined into a two-fold solution to the problem of identifying these best regions. We demonstrate the benefits of the approach and show the following key issues: *i*) effectiveness of the approach on discovering the regions where an electoral option has good chances to win whenever the electoral champaign is intensified, and *ii*) efficiency by showing that the approach is able to identify up to 85% golden regions by just ranking 35% of the electoral data. The paper is composed of three additional sections. Section 2 defines our approach, and Section 3 reports the experimental results. Finally, we give our conclusions and future work in Section 4.

2 A Ranking and Clustering Approach

Our approach is comprised of two components: *i*) *Clustering* and *ii*) *Ranking*. The former offers different clustering algorithms, i.e., X-Means [4], to group multidimensional data according to the dataset attributes; voting centers with similar electoral patterns are placed together in the same cluster. Clusters' centroids correspond to a vector of the mean values of the electoral properties of the centers grouped in the cluster. The *Ranking* component implements techniques to identify the top-k electoral regions that best meet an electoral condition among the non-dominated regions. Non-dominated or *skyline* regions [1] are areas with at least one electoral value in the centroid that is better than the same electoral parameter of the centroids of the other areas. These areas have also at least one parameter in the centroid whose value than worse than the value of this parameter in centroids of the other non-dominated areas. Furthermore, a region is top-k if it is among the k regions with the smallest distance to the electoral condition; the ranking algorithm proposed by Goncalves et al. [3] is implemented.

3 Empirical Evaluation

The goal of our study is to analyze the efficiency and effectiveness of our approach in determining the parishes where one electoral option has the higher potential electoral value and at getting new votes. We compare the results obtained by our techniques to the results proposed by an independent study where the Venezuelan parishes were ranked according to the chances that an electoral option has to win in an electoral event. Analysis of past voting histories of two electoral events comprised our study. We analyzed an electoral dataset *ED* collected from the National Electoral Counsel[3]. This is comprised of 3,757 electoral centers distributed in 976 parishes which are grouped in 268 municipalities; 24 states comprise the municipalities. *ED* registered the electoral outcome of an event where citizens voted in a referendum to decide if an electoral option *A* was going to be included in the next national electoral event. Each electoral center of *ED* is characterized by: *i*) total number of registered voters (TNRV), *ii*) referendum election outcome (PEO), *iii*) number of votes in favor of option *A* (CFV),

---

[3] http://www.cne.gov.ve/web/index.php

iv) number of spoilt votes (NSV), and *v*) number of abstention (NA). Additionally, *ED* was enriched with two derived attributes which were computed in terms of historical data: *i*) number of potential intended voters (NPIV), *ii*) number of potential new voters (NPNV). We report on coverage measures of the percentage of parishes that are produced by our approach and that are present in the golden parishes (GP). A value of 100% indicates that all the top-k parishes produced by our technique are considered among the top-k in GP, while a value of 0%, suggests that none of these top-k parishes are in GP top-k parishes. Additionally, we measure performance as the percentage of electoral centers that were ranked to produce the top-k parishes. Evaluation steps are as follows:

Clustering of Electoral Centers: Two configurations of the X-Means algorithm implemented by WEKA[4], were used to cluster the electoral centers. [5]

Clustering 1: between 2 and 24 clusters were produced; the upper bound corresponds to the number of states in Venezuela. This configuration gives the algorithm the freedom to group the country according to their electoral characteristics and not in terms of an arbitrary lower bound.
Clustering 2: between 12 and 24 clusters were produced; the upper bound corresponds to the number of states and the lower bound is half of this number.

Computation of the Top-k Parishes: clusters were ranked according to the cluster centroid. Since centroids are multidimensional, a set of non-dominated parishes or skyline was computed. Additionally, to determine the top-k parishes among the skyline, the election condition was defined as those with NPIV at least of 50% and NPNV less or equal than 0. The Euclidean distance metric was used to calculate the distance between the centroids of the clusters in the skyline and the electoral condition; parishes in the top-k electoral regions were ranked in terms of the number of electoral centers.

Table 1. Clusters produced by two different configurations of the X-Means clustering algorithm; NC: Number of Generated Clusters; Min: Minimal Number of Electoral Centers per Clusters, Max: Maximal Number of Electoral Centers per Clusters; NCMRC: Number of Clusters that Meet Electoral Condition; PTEC: Percentage of electoral centers in NCMRC out of the Total Electoral Centers.

Strategy	# NC	(Min;Max)	NCMRC	PTEC
Clustering 1	4	(221;1,378)	3	94%
Clustering 2	20	(4;1,478)	4	12%

Table 1 describes the clusters produced by each cluster configuration. We can observe that *Clustering 1* is able to group a greater number of centers in fewer clusters, and it only generates a group of clusters where more than 75%

---

[4] http://www.cs.waikato.ac.nz/ml/weka/
[5] Information about location of the center was not considered.

of clusters meet the electoral condition, i.e., three out of four clusters belong to the skyline; also, the clusters that belong to the skyline group 94% of the total of electoral centers. Furthermore, Tables(a) and (b) report on the coverage of our proposed techniques; we can observe that grouping electoral centers into a small number of clusters may better approximate the current golden ranking; *Method 1* of *Clustering 1* is enough to identify up to 85% of the relevant parishes in the ground truths. Finally, Table(c) shows the percentage of centers that were considered in the ranking process; *Method 1* of *Clustering 1* is able to reach a coverage of 85% by just analyzing 35% of the centers.

Table 2. (a) and (b) Coverage of the top-k parishes with respect to the top-k in the ground truths. *Method i* indicates that top-i clusters are identified during the ranking process; (c) Percentage of the Total Electoral Centers considered by *Method i*.

(a) Clustering 1

top-k	Method		
	1	2	3
top-7	**85%**	**85%**	71%
top-30	46%	60%	56%
top-50	53%	58%	64%
top-100	**54%**	**64%**	63%

(b) Clustering 2

Top-k	Method		
	1	2	3
top-5	28%	14%	28%
top-30	13%	2%	2%
top-50	22%	22%	2%
top-100	24%	19%	19%

(c) Performance

Strategy	Method		
	1	2	3
Clustering 1	**35%**	57%	94%
Clustering 2	5%	10%	12%

4   Conclusions and Future Work

We describe a two-fold approach that relies on clustering and ranking techniques to identify electoral regions where a given option has the potential to win. Because these techniques consider the behavior of voters in different types of electoral events, they attempt to achieve campaigns that reflect the voting patterns of their participants. Empirically we probed that these techniques are able to predict up to 85% of the golden results identified by an independent study, while only 35% of the data is considered in the ranking. In the future, we plan to extend the study with other type of data, i.e., opinion polls.

References

1. Börzsönyi, S., Kossmann, D., Stocker, K.: The skyline operator. In: Proceedings of the 17th International Conference on Data Engineering, pp. 421–430. IEEE Computer Society, Washington, DC (2001)
2. Carey, M.J., Kossmann, D.: On saying "Enough already!" in SQL. SIGMOD Rec. 26(2), 219–230 (1997)
3. Goncalves, M., Vidal, M.-E.: Reaching the Top of the Skyline: An Efficient Indexed Algorithm for Top-k Skyline Queries. In: Bhowmick, S.S., Küng, J., Wagner, R. (eds.) DEXA 2009. LNCS, vol. 5690, pp. 471–485. Springer, Heidelberg (2009)
4. Pelleg, D., Moore, A.W.: X-means: Extending k-means with efficient estimation of the number of clusters. In: ICML, pp. 727–734 (2000)

Demo Paper: A Tool for Hybrid Ontology Engineering

Christophe Debruyne

Semantics Technology and Applications Research Lab, Vrije Universiteit Brussel
chrdebru@vub.ac.be

Abstract. We demonstrate a collaborative knowledge management platform in which communities representing autonomously developed information systems build ontologies to achieve semantic interoperability between those systems. The tool is called GOSPL, which stands for Grounding Ontologies with Social Processes and natural Language, and supports the method bearing the same name. Ontologies in GOSPL are hybrid, meaning that concepts are both described informally in natural language and formally. Agreements on these two levels are made simultaneously and the social interaction between and across communities drive the ontology evolution process.

Keywords: Hybrid Ontology Engineering.

1 Introduction

GOSPL was first mentioned in [2], in which a initial prototype was described for developing *hybrid ontologies*. Hybrid ontologies are ontologies in which concepts are both described informally by means of natural language descriptions called *glosses* and formally by means of *lexons* [4], and all operations on the hybrid ontology are parameterized with the community owning that ontology.

Lexons are binary-fact types of the form $\langle \gamma, h, r, c, t \rangle$ where - in some context referred to by $\gamma \in \Gamma$ - term h plays the role of r on term t and t the role of c on h. In hybrid ontology engineering, the context-identifiers refer to communities and help to disambiguate the concepts the terms in the lexons refer to. An example of a lexon is given below.

Example 1. $\langle \overbrace{Cultural\ Domain}^{\gamma}, \overbrace{Concert}^{h}, \overbrace{is\ a}^{r}, \overbrace{subsumes}^{c}, \overbrace{Cultural\ Event}^{t} \rangle$

Concepts are described informally by means of two functions: g_1 mapping community-term pairs to a gloss and g_2 mapping lexons to a gloss. Both functions show an explicit grounding with the community. Below is an example of a gloss for a community-term pair.

Example 2. $g_1(Cultural\ Domain, Concert) = $ *"A concert is a live performance (typically of music) before an audience."*

P. Herrero et al. (Eds.): OTM 2012 Workshops, LNCS 7567, pp. 302–305, 2012.

Glosses are used to circumscribe concepts linguistically and (mostly) declaratively by agreement within (human) communities. The lexons describe concepts formally (and unambiguously) for use in computer-based information systems. Glosses facilitate the communities in aligning their thoughts before describing the concepts formally, and also facilitate agreements across communities. In this demonstration, we present the method and tool for hybrid ontology engineering.

2   The Method

To support hybrid ontology engineering, the fact-oriented method for ontology engineering called DOGMA [3] was extended to define a framework for hybrid ontologies [1]: (i) the context-identifiers were limited to refer to communities, (ii) a special linguistic resource called *Glossary* containing natural language descriptions employed by these communities was introduced and (iii) a series of social processes for evolving the ontologies were defined. An example of a social process is the discussion to introduce a constraint on a role of a lexon, e.g., EACH Cultural Event has AT MOST ONE Date.

We built a method around this framework. Communities define the semantic interoperability requirements, out of which a set of key terms is identified. Those terms need to be informally described before the formal description (in terms of lexons) can be added. In order for a lexon to be entered, at least one of the terms needs to be articulated. The terms and roles in lexons can be constrained and the community can then commit to the hybrid ontology by annotating an individual application's symbols with a constrained subset of the lexons. At the same time, communities can interact to agree on the equivalence of glosses and the synonymy of terms. Indeed, we make a distinction between the agreement of descriptions referring to the same concept and terms in lexons referring to the same concept.

Commitments of individual applications to the hybrid ontology are described by means of Ω-RIDL [5]. Commitments in Ω-RIDL annotate the application's symbols (e.g. fields in a table of a relational database) with a selection of lexons. A commitment can also contain lexons and constraints specific to an application. Including application-specific knowledge in a commitment is for instance useful to annotate foreign keys; they are not part of the domain, but necessary to join related information when interoperating.

3   The Tool

The core of GOSPL is a series of services for hybrid ontology engineering on which multiple (types of) clients can connect to. Services include: community management, ontology retrieval, starting and resolving discussions involving requests, etc. Discussions involve around requests to evolve the ontology. Fig. 1 depicts a screenshot of the GOSPL prototype, and shows some lexons and constraints currently residing in the "Venue Community", which aimed to describe the venues in which cultural events take place.

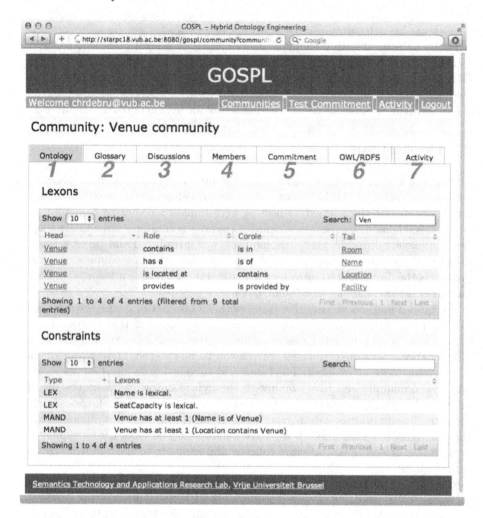

Fig. 1. GOSPL prototype

The tabs in this figure direct the user to: (1) The lexons and constraints currently agreed upon by the community. (2) The natural language descriptions for terms and lexon currently agreed upon by the community. This page also displays information such as the current gloss-equivalences. (3) The social processes as discussions to evolve the hybrid ontology and the semantic interoperability requirements. (4) Community management. (5) The list of commitments. Such commitments can exist without the platform knowing about its existence. However, the system can only query or test constraints proposed by the community on data of applications of which it the commitment is recorded. (6) The OWL implementation of the hybrid ontology. (7) Activity log of this particular community.

The tool supports the community's discussions on how the ontology should evolve in order to meet their goals defined by the semantic interoperability requirements. Important in GOSPL is that the result of community interaction evolves the hybrid ontology, i.e., the outcome of a discussion is translated into ontology evolution operators.

Acknowledgements. This work was partially funded by the Brussels Institute for Research and Innovation through the Open Semantic Cloud for Brussels Project.

References

1. Debruyne, C., Meersman, R.: Semantic Interoperation of Information Systems by Evolving Ontologies through Formalized Social Processes. In: Eder, J., Bielikova, M., Tjoa, A.M. (eds.) ADBIS 2011. LNCS, vol. 6909, pp. 444–459. Springer, Heidelberg (2011)
2. Debruyne, C., Reul, Q., Meersman, R.: GOSPL: Grounding ontologies with social processes and natural language. In: Latifi, S. (ed.) ITNG, pp. 1255–1256. IEEE Computer Society (2010)
3. Jarrar, M., Meersman, R.: Ontology Engineering - the Dogma Approach. In: Dillon, T.S., Chang, E., Meersman, R., Sycara, K. (eds.) Advances in Web Semantics I. LNCS, vol. 4891, pp. 7–34. Springer, Heidelberg (2008)
4. Meersman, R.: The use of lexicons and other computer-linguistic tools in semantics, design and cooperation of database systems. In: Zhang, Y., Rusinkiewicz, M., Kambayashi, Y. (eds.) The Proceedings of the Second Int. Symposium on Cooperative Database Systems for Advanced Applications (CODAS 1999), pp. 1–14. Springer (1999)
5. Verheyden, P., De Bo, J., Meersman, R.: Semantically Unlocking Database Content Through Ontology-Based Mediation. In: Bussler, C.J., Tannen, V., Fundulaki, I. (eds.) SWDB 2004. LNCS, vol. 3372, pp. 109–126. Springer, Heidelberg (2005)

Get Knowledge from the Knowledge

Steny Solitude

Perfect Memory S.A, Compiègne - France

Abstract. The Information Society is on its way and not only by or through the Broadcast Industry! Publishing rich media means moving from a data management system controlled by humans to a collaborative production process where machines manage migration, exchange and archiving. So it is necessary to manage the data, applications for data representation and especially the knowledge base that provides the link between the data and its meaning. Worldwide, there are standardized languages (W3C) which provide a scientific basis for this important technological move!

Semantic technologies are made to ensure the enhancement of data's, manage the sustainability of the link between the data and information (a meta/data), allowing the exchange of rich models between systems!

Keywords: AV Semantic middleware, media information representation, ontology, temporal objects, linked open data, 360° publishing.

Media deserves an information management (the meaning of the data) which must be independent of any application.

A clouded knowledge exploitation requires following tools:

1   A Semantic Wrapper

The USE (Unique Semantic Entity) contains all the data and relations necessary for the operation and interpretation of the information it encapsulates. The USE is an autonomous set of semantic knowledge and it contains the resources, and the ontology to make understand the resources. The USE is the basis package, providing information instead of data, thanks to the concepts always provided with the resources.

The USE structures:

- A physical layer (support for transport of essences (or carrier stream)
- A logical layer (representing the physical layer, the segmentation,…)
- A knowledge base (ontology MediaMap+ Core)

It can be distinguished:

- A header that includes, among others, an unique ID, and a set of pointers associated with metadata files included in the file and structured by the

P. Herrero et al. (Eds.): OTM 2012 Workshops, LNCS 7567, pp. 306–311, 2012.

MediaMap+ Core ontology. It also contains elements for communications and queries management.

- The structural metadata's include everything that is around "content object", "digital resources", "temporal object", "graphical object", "textual object" ...
- Administrative metadata's repeat everything about the "corporate body" as defined in the ontology
- Descriptive metadata's include everything that defines "editorial object", "annotation", "subject", "shot" ...
- Resources specify the production entity (corporate body, physical person, production management, ...). They also identify interfaces (APIs) that can form pages and view.
- References contain everything about ontology, the knowledge base installed, the linked open data (external links).
- The processes describe the production line with the material and human resources, tasks and objectives.

By each treatment of a USE, the ID will be changed to match the new version and preserve the uniqueness of the ID.

2   The Open Semantic Bus

The OSB is the of exchange system between USE and Local Operation Centre (LOC).

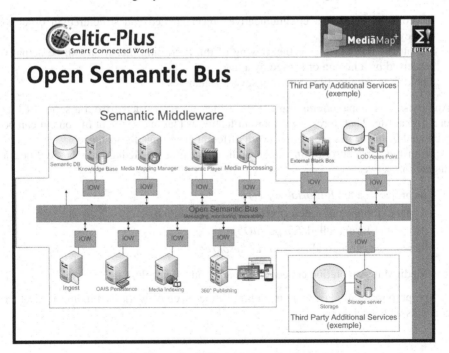

Fig. 1. Shows the OSB architecture implemented

This architecture allows:

- To integrate stakeholder type in the web production line
- To provide and enrich metadata
- To connected all the systems devices and make them interoperable
- To identify in detail the process and the involvement of different actors
- To preserve the link between metadata and the associated ontology
- To take into account the roles and skills
- To provide a specific view according to the roles and responsibilities of different actors

The OSB is based on a distributed network architecture. The spatial and temporal interoperability is provided by the Interoperability Window (IOW). Each Interoperability window uses an identified Profile (cf Profile part), and handles simply the mission to transform semantic knowledge into proprietary data, eventually execute proprietary processes and do the inverse transformation.

3   The Audiovisual Production Ontology

The Audiovisual Production Ontology is a conceptual model which can represent various audiovisual production projects in terms of tasks hierarchy, outputs, contributors, roles and rights. It enables to build custom-tailored access and view to the project information for each member of the project.

An audio visual object is all together:

- An editorial project: a communicative object created and structured in order to convey a message.
- a content : the viewing or the playing of this recording, i.e. what can be actually perceived by a human or sensed by a machine
- a recording : digital files stored in several databases.

Audiovisual is a spatio/temporal content which is reconstructed from a series of bits in a digital file. Therefore, one important feature is that one segment of content can be recreated from various recording – with different encodings for instance.

From this first description of the audiovisual object, MediaMap+ has defined a distinction between:

- its project (called *EditorialObject)*
- its prescription and/or description (called *Annotation*)
- its playing form (called *TemporalObject*)
- its recording form (called *MaterialResource*)

The MediaMap Annotation concept is generic and extensible.

The purpose is to enrich the modeling of the piece of work by binding it to other concepts with 4 relations:

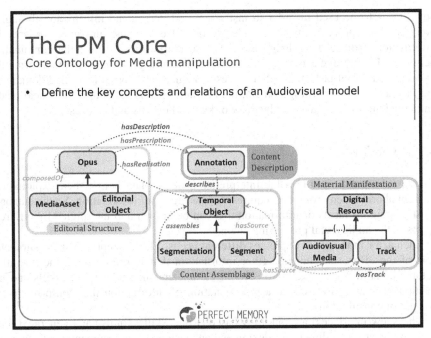

Fig. 2. Depicts the main relations between these concepts

- prescriptive annotations which reflects the editorial intentions (relation *hasPrescription* with *Annotation* as range).
- descriptive annotations which reflect the editorial choices made during production (relation *hasDescription* with *Annotation* as range).
- its potential realizations (*hasRealization*) with *TemporalObject* as range).
- a portion of video material which has either been the result of an original creation or a selection of existing content (relation *hasSource* with *MaterialObject* as range).

The *Audiovisual Annotation Ontology* is a conceptual model which provides high-level descriptors for audiovisual content. These descriptors are based on the audiovisual scripting vocabulary used by professionals in documents like the screenplay, the synopsis or the shooting script.

The annotations can be indexed by a human being or extracted by automatic analysis.

An Annotation is an element which either prescribes or describes one particular aspect of an editorial object (*hasPrescription, hasDescription* relations) and related to a specific content object (describes relation).

4   The Profile

By choosing a set of representation formats with a choice of parameters, it is possible to get the capacity to represent information for a class of application. The aim of an ontology is to be used in order to instantiate and understand information through a process. Any process must be able to mobilize existing universal or specific information, from a Knowledge Base. We so define the Profile : the combination between a Knowledge Base and an Ontology, structuring and limiting the information of the execution of tasks through a process. For instance, for an identified domain, as the Physical media handling domain, the Profile to use is the couple "Physical media handling ontology" – "Knowledge base of known Formats and Codecs".

5 The View

Digital information involves the interpretation of the data before their exploitation. The collaborative environment requires the sharing of all information. So the database must contain all facets of information that can be known and interpreted by different actors in the audiovisual processing chain.

Each actor in the chain expresses different needs. The concept of VIEW automates part of the effort to adapt and filter information that is presented to the operating actor. The adjustment takes into account parameters such as the role, skills and the manipulated entity to produce a representation of information that conforms to the context of consultation.

The View(interfaces) are ontology based (Role, Skills, Entity) and generated for a creator (scripting), a director (indexing and enhancement), a documentalist (inference: automatic enrichment), ... they offer:

- an easy segmentation in chapter, scene, shots, shot value for video and audio
- a synchronized tagging for metadata's (text, pictures and other temporal objects!)
- the enhancement and enrichment during a collaborative process through semantic inferences
- a structured collaborative enrichment through semantic tags and their linking to open semantic databases (via Linked Open Data),
- consolidated information available on the content whether centralized or distributed
- 360° publishing with a real rights management system

6 The Semantic Player

It is a tool that goes beyond the simple storage and interconnection of data repositories to provide a representation of information that is independent of any application or database. It is a tool for production/exploitation of multimedia data (video, audio, image, text) which allows the establishment of a non-sequential supply chain.

The player uses a semantic middleware that includes an ontology and a knowledge base, inference rules are implemented to provide intuitive navigation, and a semantic database.

Spatio/temporal semantic objects offer:

- synchronized visualization of metadata's (text, pictures and other temporal objects!)
- consolidated information available on the content whether centralized or distributed for explicit exploration of a set of properties (minimum FRBR, and much more with personalized profiles)
- the interpretation of the consultation contexts that present the right visualization facets to the user

In addition it allows users, who wish to become a source of data, to guarantee accessibility to their knowledge.

The properties of the USE, the distributed architecture of the network exchange (OSB), the Ontology, the Profile and the View:

- provide a highly collaborative production chain
- ensure interoperability over time (sustainability) and space (interoperability between heterogeneous systems)
- cover the dynamic aspects of interchanges
- present to users relevant information based on their roles and skills.

The objectives of this middleware, in addition to the assisted capture of rich and structured information, were the simplification of exploration, visualization and exploitation of the data all along its life cycle.

remix: A Semantic Mashup Application

Magali Seguran, Aline Senart, and David Trastour

SAP Research, SAP Labs France
805 Avenue du Dr. Maurice Donat
06254 Mougin, France
firstname.lastname@sap.com

Abstract. With today's public data sets containing billions of data items, more and more companies are looking to integrate external data with their traditional enterprise data to improve business intelligence analysis. These distributed data sources however exhibit heterogeneous data formats and terminologies and may require helping the user merging data coming from heterogeneous sources.

remix is a Business Intelligence (BI) solution that offers business users a productive environment to easily create highly formatted reports they would ultimately like to see. Via rich visual context-aware interactions, users can quickly combine shared data sets and reuse report parts. This enhanced collaboration combined with the provision of a multi-source semantic layer give users the power to make more effective and informed decisions on virtually any relevant data source or BI resource wherever they are.

Keywords: semantic mashup, semantic web, schema matching, semantic enrichment.

1 Introduction

Whether freely available in the case of "open data", or commercially available in data aggregators or marketplaces, data on the web is growing at fast pace in several domains: government, financial, science, biology. This structured knowledge available in the future e-society will make it feasible for companies to mine huge amount of public data and integrate it in their next-generation enterprise information management systems. Analyzing this new type of data within the context of existing enterprise data should bring them new or more accurate business insights and allow better recognition of sales and market opportunities (*1*).

Unfortunately, current BI applications and solutions cannot easily consume structured data available on the web. These new distributed sources raise tremendous challenges. They have inherently different file formats, access protocols or query languages. They possess their own data model with different ways of representing and storing the data. Data across these sources may be noisy (e.g. duplicate or inconsistent), uncertain or be semantically similar yet different (*2*). Integration and provision of a unified view for these heterogeneous and complex data structures therefore require powerful tools to map and organize the data.

P. Herrero et al. (Eds.): OTM 2012 Workshops, LNCS 7567, pp. 312–315, 2012.

2   Proposition

While there are a number of high-quality tools in the BI domain (*3,4*), it is very difficult for end users to consume structured data from the web today. By leveraging technology from the linked data community, we propose an innovative self-service BI tool that bridges this gap and allows non-technical business users to easily augment enterprise content with external content. *remix* combines, recommends and presents information from any structured data source from the enterprise and web world. In particular, it offers the following key features:

- **Self-service BI for external data**. *remix* enables mashups of enterprise data and external data. *remix* adds business context to the data and builds semantic links into a unified and consolidated view.
- **Query-free**. Business users do not write queries but simply graphically build what they have in their mind. It's a direct and intuitive way to build reports without requiring the user to understand IT concepts.
- **Guided interaction**. *remix* provides contextualized recommendations to the business users to increase quality when possible, suggest new insights and save them valuable report design time. *remix* helps the business user to find relevant data sources, formulas, visualization, and assists in the data reconciliation process.
- **Collaboration and sharing**. Business users are able to share their data sets and report parts allowing other users to quickly build new reports.

3   Research Challenges

The two key challenges that we encountered in developing *remix* are the provision of the multi-source semantic layer and the recommendation system.

- **Multi-source semantic layer**. In order to interlink data from different sources, we leverage vocabularies and metadata that are readily available on the web. We map cell values with instances, and column headers with types from popular data sets from the Linked Open Data Cloud (e.g. dbpedia). Once raw data has been enriched, schema matching can be performed. Specific algorithms on rich types from vector algebra and statistics have been developed and results show that the use of our multi-source semantic layer greatly improves the matching process (*5*). For example, schemas can be discovered if column headers are not defined and can be improved when they are not named or typed correctly.
- **Recommendation system**. In order to facilitate the reuse of BI artifacts (reports, dashboards, etc.), and easily adapt existing reports to new data, we developed a recommendation system. Based on user profile, historical usage and content similarity (on visualization, query or data elements), the system aggregates data and make recommendations to users at all stages of the data mashup process. The real greatest impediment is to evaluate our results. Until we have a sufficiently large amount of users and BI artifacts in the *remix* repository, the system cannot return interesting advices. To overcome this bootstrapping issue, we focus our efforts on

users' habits and preferences that are well-known and we plan to exploit user traces from other SAP products in the future.

4   Demo and User Benefits

Our demo is based on a use case taken from the healthcare domain. We will run a scenario illustrating how Doctor H., a physician with a speciality of infectious diseases at the Nice Hospital (France) is able to perform easily and quickly data mashup on his medical reports with external data. In the demo, we will show that Doctor H. will discover the source of local suspicious infection with the help of *remix*. Merging different sources of data (external pollution report, hospital medical reports) will lead him to the conclusion that most of his patients suffer from water pollution.

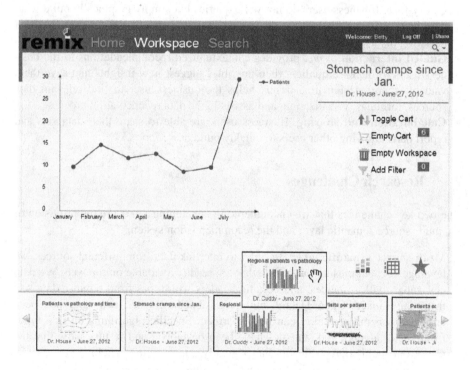

Fig. 1. *remix* tool, "your report on my data"

At the beginning of the scenario, Doctor H. builds his report following *remix*'s suggestions and becomes aware of a trend in his patients' visits. He decides to share his report with Doctor C. (his boss) who has access to more data at a regional level. Figure 1 shows how Doctor C. applies her data on Doctor H.'s report, confirming that there is an increasingly large amount of stomach cramps in the last month in the region. Remix suggests automatically how to merge the two reports and pre-selects the columns to match. After some investigation using *remix* (in particular, searching for relevant reports), the physicians perform a second merge between the patients's addresses and a report on the pollution of the river. *remix* shows a clear correlation between the location of patients and the pollution, enabling Doctor H. and Doctor C. to raise a healthcare alert.

This scenario shows that *remix* assists the users in all steps of the process: identification of relevant data sources, recommendation of reusable reports, suggestion in data processing and data alignment. This helps users to produce higher quality business analysis in a shorter time frame, therefore increasing efficiency of their work.

5   Conclusion

We propose to present *remix*, a new self-service BI tool that combines, recommends and presents information from any structured data source from the enterprise and web world. The tool is designed to help business analysts use existing knowledge and generate new knowledge in return. In future work, we plan to improve the recommendation engine and to evaluate mash up on big data.

References

1. LaValle, S., Lesser, E., Shockley, R., Hopkins, M.S., Kruschwitz, N.: Big Data, Analytics and the Path from Insights to Value. MIT Sloan Management Review (2011)
2. Kavitha, C., Sadasivam, Shenoy, N.: Ontology Based Semantic Integration of Heterogeneous Databases. European Journal of Scientific Research 64(1), 115–122 (2011)
3. QlikTech. QlikView: Business Discovery for Everyone, http://www.qlikview.com/ (accessed 2012)
4. Tableau Software, http://www.tableausoftware.com/ (accessed 2012)
5. Assaf, A., Louw, E., Senart, A., Follenfant, C., Troncy, R., Trastour, D.: Improving Schema Matching with Linked Data. In: First International Workshop on Open Data, Nantes, France (2012)
6. Peukert, E., Eberius, J.: Rahm Erhard. A Self-Configuring Schema Matching System. In: 28th IEEE International Conference on Data Engineering (2012)

ORM 2012 PC Co-chairs Message

Following successful workshops in Cyprus (2005), France (2006), Portugal (2007), Mexico (2008), Portugal (2009), and Greece (2010 and 2011), this is the eighth fact-oriented modeling workshop run in conjunction with the OTM conferences. Fact-oriented modeling is a conceptual approach for modeling and querying the semantics of business domains in terms of the underlying facts of interest, where all facts and rules may be verbalized in language readily understandable by users in those domains.

Unlike Entity-Relationship (ER) modeling and UML class diagrams, fact-oriented modeling treats all facts as relationships (unary, binary, ternary etc.). How facts are grouped into structures (e.g. attribute-based entity types, classes, relation schemes, XML schemas) is considered a design level, implementation issue irrelevant to capturing the essential business semantics. Avoiding attributes in the base model enhances semantic stability, simplifies populatability, and facilitates natural verbalization, thus offering more productive communication with all stakeholders. For information modeling, fact-oriented graphical notations are typically far more expressive than other notations. Fact-oriented modeling includes procedures for mapping to attribute-based structures, so may also be used to front-end those other approaches.

Though less well known than ER and object-oriented approaches, fact-oriented modeling has been used successfully in industry for over 30 years, and is taught in universities around the world. The fact-oriented modeling approach comprises a family of closely related dialects, including Object-Role Modeling (ORM), Cognition enhanced Natural language Information Analysis Method (CogNIAM) and Fully-Communication Oriented Information Modeling (FCO-IM). Though adopting a different graphical notation, the Object-oriented Systems Model (OSM) is a close relative, with its attribute-free philosophy. The Semantics of Business Vocabulary and Business Rules (SBVR) proposal adopted by the Object Management Group in 2007 is a recent addition to the family of fact-oriented approaches.

Software tools supporting the fact-oriented approach include the ORM tools NORMA (Natural ORM Architect), ActiveFacts, InfoModeler and ORM-Lite, the CogNIAM tool Doctool, and the FCO-IM tool CaseTalk. The Collibra ontology tool suite and DogmaStudio are fact-based tools for specifying ontologies. Richmond is another ORM tool under development. General information about fact-orientation may be found at www.ORMFoundation.org.

This year we had submissions for the workshop contributed by authors from Australia, Belgium, Canada, Germany, Italy, Malaysia, Norway, The Netherlands, and the USA. After an extensive review process by a distinguished international program committee, with each paper receiving at least four reviews, we accepted the 10 papers that appear in these proceedings. Congratulations to the successful authors! We gratefully acknowledge the generous contribution of time and effort by the program committee, and the OTM organizing committee,

P. Herrero et al. (Eds.): OTM 2012 Workshops, LNCS 7567, pp. 316–317, 2012.
© Springer-Verlag Berlin Heidelberg 2012

especially Robert Meersman and Tharam Dillon (OTM General Co-chairs), Pilar Herrero (OTM General Co-chair and OTM Workshops General Chair), and Jan Demey (Logistics Team).

July 2012   Terry Halpin
                                                                          Herman Balsters

Applying Some Fact Oriented Modelling Principles to Business Process Modelling

Peter Spyns

Vlaamse overheid – Departement Economie, Wetenschap en Innovatie
Koning Albert II-laan 35, bus 10, B-1030 Brussel, Belgium
Peter.Spyns@ewi.vlaanderen.be

Abstract. In the context of a business process modelling task within a government department, an adapted version of the first two steps of fact oriented modelling has been proposed as an alternative strategy in the initial stage of business processes knowledge elicitation activities. As expertise and knowledge on organisational processes and procedures are in many cases implicit and embodied by support staff – rather than by highly skilled knowledge workers – it is extremely important to adopt an more accessible method to facilitate the elicitation and validation steps. This paper presents how a small scale experiment has been set up, its results and lessons learnt. Even if a thorough evaluation was out of scope, the experiment sufficiently demonstrated the strength of the analysis by natural language as included in the fact oriented modelling methodology.

1   Context and Motivation

One of the targets of the Flemish government, in particular in times of budgetary restrictions, is to have its administration function more efficiently, cut costs and become a leaner organisation. At the Flemish department of Economy, Science and Innovation (EWI) it was decided to analyse and re-engineer the most important business processes and lay out a roadmap from the "as is" situation to the "to be" ideal. An external consultant was contracted to facilitate and support this effort. A task group of civil servants received a first business process modelling assignment. It was striking to see that a majority had started to identify mainly activities and some choice points (or gateways), but without any connecting logic (see section 4.1). Hardly any connection between the process states was established. Also during subsequent discussion it became clear that many civil servants were much more at ease *talking* about the process flow (with the consultant as a Socratic knowledge elicitator) rather than drawing gateways and adding the connecting logic to it (see Fig. 2).

As fact oriented modelling distinguishes itself from other data modelling methodologies by its emphasis on the use of natural language as part of the methodology, it seemed natural to try to re-use and apply principles of fact oriented modelling [4:p. 64 f.f. section 3.3] to business processes or workflow modelling. After all, Natural-language Information Analysis Method (NIAM) [15] (by *Nijssen*) was the basis of fact oriented modelling: statements of domain experts are subsumed into sentence patterns (comparable with templates) to create an information model. The fact that the second

P. Herrero et al. (Eds.): OTM 2012 Workshops, LNCS 7567, pp. 318–327, 2012.

edition of the Object Role Modeling (ORM) reference work [4] includes a chapter on "process and state modelling" confirms our intuition that fact oriented modelling is not exclusively disjoint from process modelling. A limited literature review (see section 2) revealed that this topic, even if not entirely innovative anymore (cf. e.g. [10]), still leaves room for further thoughts and discussion. In addition, a case study emerged [11] that reported about a positive experience in this respect.

Hence, the major topic of this paper is to present an alternative to the initial stage in the workflow or process modelling method proposed by the external consultant. The alternative consists of a combination of analysis through natural language, typical of fact oriented modelling methodologies, and some knowledge breakdown steps, as included in the DOGMA modelling methodology [14]. Even if based on earlier acquired scientific insights, the experiment presented here does not make scientific claims, but rather is a report on how process modelling on the work floor by lay persons can be improved. The text is structured as follows. After having discussed some related work (section 2), we present the method and material (section 3) and explain in section 4 how the process modelling exercise has been set up. Results and experiences of the experiment are amply discussed in section 5. The paper ends with some ideas for future work (section 6) as well as with a concluding section (7).

2   Related Work

Seen our context (governmental organisation, no scientific ambitions, report on practical experience), we focused on the combination of business process modelling with fact oriented modelling. To our – albeit probably limited – knowledge, only a few authors mention this combination. Even if the ORM2 handbook [4: chapter 15 pp. 773 - 833] includes a chapter on business process modelling, *Halpin and Morgan* rather provide an introduction to workflow modelling (and popular graphical notations) in general. The structure of a process, represented by several ORM2 meta-models of process constructs is their main focus [4: p.780, 7].

Bollen models processes by starting from a data model that is the result of fact oriented modelling steps (the inside-out approach) [2]. His basic idea is that the relevant static domain description is represented by the data model so that the knowledge engineers have to additionally model the dynamic aspects, and map these into Business Process Modelling Notation (BPMN) constructs [1]. In his view this can to a very large extent be done by including derivation rules – see [1] for an overview on the matter – in the data model. The process flow is considered as a set of (approved) transitions from one stage of the knowledge grammar to another. He has created an ORM meta-model for palette 1 BPMN constructs using the fact oriented modelling methodology [3]. As far as we know, he has not (yet ?) applied his model to real-life business process modelling cases.

Less directly related, but nevertheless still relevant for our purposes, work concerns the story telling based (or narratological) ontology modelling technique by *Zhao* [16] integrated in the DOGMA approach [14]. A story seems to be a natural "vehicle" to describe a workflow in an almost casual way. Reducing stories into episodes, which are further to be segmented into elementary sentences, is a crucial step to distil lexons (i.e. the DOGMA denomination defined by *Meersman* for a more formal – but still linguistic form of – plausible binary fact types about a universe of discourse [5,12]). A subsequent step is to semantically ground the constituents of a lexon [13].

Another not so remotely related modelling standard is SBVR (Semantics of Business Vocabulary and Business Rules) [9] by the OMG Group (Object Management Group). Although the immediate aim of the EWI business process modelling exercise was not to define precise semantics or to create an ontology, it will in the long run be advantageous if the business process vocabulary is grounded by precise semantics.

3   Material and Method

Just as in any important knowledge engineering project, some preparatory actions were executed before the experiment at hand started. The preparation stage mainly concerned defining the scope of the overall project, the identification (and prioritisation) of major processes in the EWI department, and the selection of a method and tools. We will not elaborate on these aspects as most of them do not present any general (scientific) interest.

The EWI department subsequently set up an internal enterprise architecture project team. The team members hold different functions, have various backgrounds[1] and different levels of initial expertise with knowledge modelling and enterprise architecture. An external consultant, PriceWaterhouseCoopers Belgium (PWC), was contracted to facilitate and support the modelling exercises. One can reasonably expect the PWC team members to be professional experts in business process engineering. In order to familiarise the EWI project team involved in the process (re-)engineering effort, the consultant gave an introductory course on workflow and enterprise architecture modelling. Eventually the EWI project team members were supposed to model and (re-) engineer themselves the EWI business processes and enterprise architecture. After the introductory course, three subgroups of the project team each had to model an important process within the department as an exercise.

In this paper, we discuss the process of handling incoming requests for information.[2] At the end of a modelling session, the external consultant should have gathered enough information to draw a process model. The external consultant used MS Visio as complementary tool (with a specific

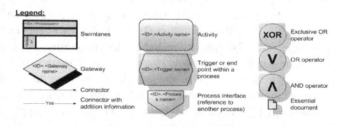

Fig. 1. Some BP modelling constructs

---

[1] Such as economy, library science, chemistry, bio-engineer, public administration.

[2] We have selected this particular process for this paper as it is quite universal.

cil) to draw the workflows (see Fig. 1 for the constructs used[3]). For subsequent modelling steps, the consultant developed some specific Excel forms to capture additional textual information, e.g., to describe information objects and applications used.

The experiment took place during two sessions: a so-called naive process modelling session (see section 4.1) and a fact oriented session (section 4.2). The former consisted of the steps and activities following the methods of the consultant as foreseen in his contract with EWI. The author, who is part of the EWI project team, participated in both sessions. At the same time, he observed his colleagues and the consultants. Afterwards, he analysed their results and interactions in order to formulate an alternative method. During the latter, the author applied this alternative method to another major administrative (and formally constraint) process as well: providing a reply by the minister to a question by a member of the Flemish Parliament. Nevertheless, for the easy of reading of this paper and due to space restrictions, the "request for information" process is elaborated in the following sections.

4   Two Ways of Modelling Business Processes

4.1   "Naive" Business Process Engineering

The (few) EWI civil servants quite familiar with (or interested in) formal information modelling and/or MS Visio managed to structure their conceptualisation of the process resulting in a nicely drawn flow. Fig. 2 however displays a model prepared by a less "knowledge engineering savvy" group. What immediately strikes the eye is the (almost complete) absence of connecting edges, logical operators, swim lanes and end point. One can summarise safely that these civil servants were well able to distinguish the main activities, decision points and certain activity sequences (although represented implicitly by the position of the activity boxes), but did not master the (graphical) modelling language and principles well enough.[4] This initial model has been discussed and enriched in subsequent discussions by the entire EWI project team. The consultant facilitated the discussions by reconciling various points of view, noting down the intermediate conclusions and using post-its to lay out the process flow on the wall.

With this material the consultant subsequently created an "as-is" workflow model (after a final validation by the project team). The consultant was, as expected, at some points unfamiliar with the terminology used by the civil servants. Some semantic assumptions, being important for a correct "as-is" flow, remained implicit and led the consultant on the wrong track. Some misunderstandings were clarified during the first

---

[3] This stencil has been made by the consultant without any further explanation. The number of BP modelling constructs is very limited and basic – e.g., no timing or event primitives – maybe to reduce the learning curve for the EWI team members. Its idiosyncratic notation seems to be only remotely inspired by BPMN.

[4] Some actually stated that they did not have enough time (or interest ?) to invest into using Microsoft Visio and the modelling stencil prepared by the consultant – see Fig. 1. Another explanation could be that they didn't master MS Visio enough.

group discussion; others were only detected during the final validation phase. And as with any group discussion, group dynamics sometimes may lead to adopting the position expressed by the loudest voice, which is not necessarily the most correct voice. In short, the primary means to convey domain or process information during these modelling sessions was natural language (spoken and written), which echoes findings of another recent real life fact oriented modelling case study [8: p. 751]. Hence, improving the knowledge elicitation steps implies applying and improving techniques focusing on the use of natural language.

Fig. 2. Initial model for the EWI business process "finding information"

4.2   Fact Oriented Inspired Business Process Engineering

The idea, as explained in [14,16], is to firstly compose a story (from scratch by an individual, as a summary of existing documents or as a result from an initial group discussion) – see Fig. 3. Available documents describing official procedures already contain important parts of such a story, or even the entire story in "disguise".

Depending on the complexity of the domain, the skills of the domain expert with fact oriented analysis through natural language, the volume of available text, (s)he can immediately produce elementary sentences (see Table 2) starting from the story itself or proceed via an intermediate stage first. In the latter case, one first decomposes a story into several episodes (see Table 1).

External persons send requests for information to the EWI info email address from where the EWI communication manager routes the question to the most appropriate head of division, who in turn forwards the question to his most appropriate collaborator. Or the head of division returns the question, possibly on behalf of his/her collaborator, as not relevant/related to his/her division – maybe suggesting another, more appropriate division or civil servant.

The collaborator who accepted the question composes an answer after having browsed through his/her (physical) sources of information and/or having consulted other (external) parties responsible for a part of the answer. If the collaborator is not the most appropriate person (s)he explains why not.

The head of division might perform some quality control on the proposed answer and sends the final answer to the EWI contact-point who archives the answers and eventually provides the requester with the answer.

Fig. 3. A simplified "information request" story

Table 1. Episodes of the "information request" story – cf. Fig. 3

E.1	A request for information is received.
E.1.1	The communication manager receives a request for information.
E.1.2	(s)he passes the question on to the most appropriate head of division.
E.1.3	The head of division forwards the question to his most appropriate collaborator.
E.2	The head of division returns the question, possibly on behalf of his/her collaborator, as not relevant/related to his/her division – maybe suggesting another division or civil servant.
E.3	The collaborator processes the request.
E.3.1	The collaborator rejects the question and explains why.
E.3.2	The collaborator accepts the question.
E.3.3	(s)he browses through his/her (physical) sources of information and/or consults other (external) parties responsible for a part of the answer.
E.3.4	The collaborator composes an answer and sends it to his/her head of division.
E.4	The head of unit processes the answer.
E.4.1	The head of unit reviews the answer.
E.4.2	(s)he forwards the answer to the contact point or ask his/her collaborator to improve the answer.
E.5	The communication manager archives the answer.
E.6	The communication manager sends the answer to the requesting party

An episode can be loosely considered as a "part of the story plot" or an intermediary level (E1, E2, …, E6) of granularity that groups some related activities (e.g., E.3.1, … E3.4). Creating episodes is a first way of decomposing a story into smaller units that are usually chronologically and hierarchically ordered. Some similarities with drawing activity hierarchies (cf. [4: p.779]) hold. As Zhao proposes [16], simple techniques (segmentation and highlighting) can be applied and specific forms can be used to document the various modelling rounds [14,16].

A domain expert can subsequently transform the sentences of the episodes into elementary sentences (see Table 2) that are defined as sentences that cannot be reduced into smaller ones without a loss in "vital" information [4: p.63] – e.g., no subordinated sentences. Many of the "rules" described in the step 1 of the ORM conceptual schema design procedure (CSDP) [4: p. 63-81] can be applied to reduce sentences of a story or of an episode into elementary sentences. It is expected that natural language processing tools (parser) can largely automate this procedure. As noted by Proper et al. [10], and quite common knowledge in the field of linguistics, activities are mostly expressed by a particular class of verbs (not surprisingly called *action verbs*). When creating elementary sentences, care should be taken to include a meaningful *actor* and *item* of the activity as they represent relevant business information objects and roles. A tripartite template "*actor – activity – item*" was used.

Table 2. Some sample elementary sentences derived from Fig. 3

Actor (subject)	Activity (verb)	Item (object)
Person	Mails	Request
Communication manager	Receives	Request
Communication manager	Forwards	Request
Communication manager	Forwards to	Head of division
Head of division	Forwards to	Collaborator
Head of division	Quality checks	Proposed answer
Head of division	Forwards	Request
Collaborator	Assesses	Request
Collaborator	Accepts	Request
Collaborator	Consults	Sources
Collaborator	Forwards	(sub)request
Collaborator	Refuses	Request
Collaborator	Composes	Answer
Communication manager	Archives	Final answer

A first draft of a graphical BP model can be drawn on the basis of the set of elementary sentences or triples (= a row of Table 2) as a result of the following transformation. The *actor* slot of a triple contains the basic label for a BP swim lane, the *activity* slot includes information on the BP activity boxes while many relevant information objects can be found in the *item* slot.

Various (real life) examples are used to check whether or not Table 2 contains all the elementary sentences needed (no unused triples and no missing triples). Example cases are "navigated" through the activity boxes while checking the corresponding triple. At the same occasion, the activity boxes are (graphically) arranged in a sequential manner. One can mark (or count) the triples "passed through" to detect unused triples that might be superfluous. Missing triples (= missing activities in the flow) are detected when the example case cannot "reach" an end situation. Also artificial (counter-)examples can be introduced to have the domain experts additionally (in)validate the model. These two activities more or less resemble the CSDP step 2 of drawing the fact types and applying a population check.

5   Discussion and Lessons Learnt

Similar techniques as used in NIAM/ORM to reduce a complex sentence into elementary fact types are easily applied to business process modelling – e.g., to avoid the introduction of complex activities (e.g., "compose and send letter" becomes "compose letter" followed by "send letter") in the model. By applying the *"actor – acts on – item"* template the domain experts are much more inclined to include all the relevant information on objects and actors in the analysis right away. Otherwise, there is a tendency to overlook these objects and roles in the heat of discussions or reflections on the process flow. Breaking down complex sentences into elementary ones makes domain experts express their thoughts more clearly and concisely (i.e. drop irrelevant details). However, not all relevant information can be captured in this way, in particular, the gateways or connectors and their related logic.

Evidently, performing the analysis by natural language constitutes a working technique much easier for a domain expert or informant, having no prior formal modelling experience, to learn than a graphical notation, even if the latter has been simplified. As a consequence, domain experts feel much more at ease to participate actively in the analysis, which, in addition, results in a richer description than when using from the start a graphical notation. Once a set of elementary sentences is available, it is also easier for domain experts to validate the elementary sentences (or triples) and "supervise" their transformation by a knowledge engineer into a graphical BP model.

Currently, only a very simple (and idiosyncratic) BP modelling notation was used (cf. Fig. 1). Subsequent steps similar to ORM CSDP steps are probably useful to add sophistication to this basic model – e.g. to define state conditions (including timers). In particular, if the business processes modelling exercise does not remain limited to the "happy flow" – as often is the case[5] – expressing conditions correctly and clearly becomes more important in a flow with (many) ramifications. In addition, a preliminary phase of vocabulary uniformisation by the individual experts should happen. And one could also use n-ary sentences - e.g., an actor forwards something to someone else. Currently, inspired by the DOGMA tradition of fact based modelling [6], only binary elementary sentences have been used.

The following remark might seem obvious, but it must be stressed that appropriate domain experts are to be included in the modelling project team (there is a substantial difference between people simply willing to participate and actual domain experts). Also, all relevant (and only the relevant) documentation (e.g., regulations or existing descriptions) has to be available in its most recent form. Translated in methodological terms, this corresponds to what is usually called "preparing and scoping"

---

[5] Evidently the happy flow exhibits less complexity, requires less time to model and less knowledge of all the intrinsics of an organisation's procedures and working habits, and hence, less effort. In addition, employees are not always eager to reveal their procedural short-cuts (sometimes "illicit").

(e.g., [14:p.19]) and constitutes an integral part of any serious knowledge engineering project. Even though the consultant did include scoping in his proposal for a modelling methodology, in practice it turned out that not all relevant (human) sources of expertise and knowledge for the process under scrutiny had been gathered from the start on.

6   Future Work

Currently, mainly impressionistic and subjective feedback has been gathered from the participants in the modelling experiment (loose talks, intuitive comparison of graphic BP models etc.). Hence, before exploring new research avenues on combining process modelling and fact oriented modelling (e.g., adapting the other CDSP steps, verbalising the graphical process model, formalising the various steps, developing guidelines to make the method more widely applicable, …), the benefit of the method presented here should be validated more solidly. This involves more modellers, more and different processes and a number of evaluation criteria (e.g., perceived simplicity and experienced time gain for the lay modellers/experts, efficiency gain for the professional (external) knowledge engineers, improved quality and completeness of the knowledge elicitation results, overall cost reduction, etc.). An often used method consists of inviting subjects to fill out questionnaires and attribute scores (using a Likert scale). Further statistical analysis of the scores should determine whether or not this alternative method constitutes an effective improvement over the working method proposed by the consultant. Nevertheless, the results of the experiment seem promising enough to make the organisation of a solid evaluation worthwhile. Involving more modellers and more processes to be modelled will also prove beneficial for formalising the process described in this paper and for transforming the business process modelling craftsmanship of individuals in a methodology applicable by others and teachable to others.

7   Conclusion

Combining fact oriented modelling and story telling principles, as an alternative method to initial business process or workflow modelling knowledge elicitation steps, seems to improve, for the limited EWI experiment, the overall quality and completeness of the model as well as the level of commitment of individual project team members having various backgrounds and functions. Non formally oriented modellers/experts felt more comfortable in the way of providing information to professional knowledge engineers. Nevertheless, "hard" and objective evidence to substantiate this claim is currently not yet available, although the experiment reported on seemingly provided promising results.

Acknowledgements. We'd like to thank our colleagues of the EWI enterprise architecture team, the PWC consultant team, who all have been – without actually being aware of it – the trigger of this paper and our object of behavioural observation, as well as the anonymous reviewers for their useful comments.

References

1. Bollen, P.: BPMN as a Communication Language for the Process- and Event-Oriented Perspectives in Fact-Oriented Conceptual Models. In: Meersman, R., Herrero, P., Dillon, T. (eds.) OTM 2009 Workshops. LNCS, vol. 5872, pp. 639–648. Springer, Heidelberg (2009)
2. Bollen, P.: A Fact-Based Meta Model for Standardization Documents. In: Meersman, R., Dillon, T., Herrero, P. (eds.) OTM 2010. LNCS, vol. 6428, pp. 464–473. Springer, Heidelberg (2010)
3. Bollen, P.: BPMN, a meta-model for the happy path, Maastricht University METEOR Technical Report 10/003 (2010)
4. Halpin, T., Morgan, T.: Information Modeling and Relational Databases, 2nd edn. Morgan Kaufmann, San Francisco (2008)
5. Meersman, R.: An essay on the role and evolution of (data)base semantics. In: Meersman, R., Mark, L. (eds.) Database Application Semantics, Proceedings of the Sixth IFIP TC-2 Working Conference on Data Semantics (DS-6), IFIP Conference Proceedings, vol. 74, pp. 1–7. Chapman and Hall (1996)
6. Meersman, R.: Ontologies and Databases: More than a Fleeting Resemblance. In: d'Atri, A., Missikoff, M. (eds) OES/SEO 2001 Rome Workshop. Luiss Publications (2001)
7. Morgan, T.: Business Process Modeling and ORM. In: Meersman, R., Tari, Z. (eds.) OTM-WS 2007, Part I. LNCS, vol. 4805, pp. 581–590. Springer, Heidelberg (2007)
8. Nijssen, M., Lemmens, I., Mak, R.: Fact-Orientation Applied to Develop a Flexible Employment Benefits System. In: Meersman, R., Herrero, P., Dillon, T. (eds.) OTM 2009 Workshops. LNCS, vol. 5872, pp. 745–756. Springer, Heidelberg (2009)
9. Object Management Group, Semantics of Business Vocabulary and Business Rules (SBVR) v1.0, http://www.omg.org/spec/SBVR
10. Proper, H.A(E.), Hoppenbrouwers, S.J.B.A., van der Weide, T.P.: A Fact-Oriented Approach to Activity Modeling. In: Meersman, R., Tari, Z. (eds.) OTM-WS 2005. LNCS, vol. 3762, pp. 666–675. Springer, Heidelberg (2005)
11. Rozendaal, J.: Industrial Experience with Fact Based Modeling at a Large Bank. In: Meersman, R., Tari, Z. (eds.) OTM-WS 2007, Part I. LNCS, vol. 4805, pp. 678–687. Springer, Heidelberg (2007)
12. Spyns, P., Meersman, R., Jarrar, M.: Data modelling versus Ontology engineering. SIGMOD Record Special Issue 31(4), 12–17 (2002)
13. Spyns, P.: Adapting the Object Role Modelling Method for Ontology Modelling. In: Hacid, M.-S., Murray, N.V., Raś, Z.W., Tsumoto, S. (eds.) ISMIS 2005. LNCS (LNAI), vol. 3488, pp. 276–284. Springer, Heidelberg (2005)
14. Spyns, P., Tang, Y., Meersman, R.: An ontology engineering methodology for DOGMA. Journal of Applied Ontology 1-2(3), 13–39 (2008)
15. Verheyen, G., van Bekkum, P.: NIAM, aN Information Analysis Method. In: Olle, T., Sol, H., Verrijn-Stuart, A. (eds.) IFIP Conference on Comparative Review of Information Systems Methodologies, Noord-Holland (1982)
16. Zhao, G., Gao, Y., Meersman, R.: An ontology-based approach to business modelling. In: Proceedings of the International Conference of Knowledge Engineering and Decision Support (ICKEDS 2004), pp. 213–221 (2004)

The Interplay of Mandatory Role and Set-Comparison Constraints

Peter Bollen

Department of Organization and Strategy
School of Business and Economics
Maastricht University
P.O. Box 616
6200 MD Maastricht, The Netherlands
p.bollen@maastrichtuniversity.nl

Abstract. In this paper we will focus on the interplay of mandatory role and set-comparison (equality-, subset- and exclusion-) constraints in fact based modeling. We will present an algorithm that can be used to derive mandatory role constraints in combination with non-implied set-comparison constraints as a result of the acceptance or rejection of real-life user examples by the domain expert.

Keywords: Mandatory role constraint, set-comparison constraint, implied constraint, CSDP.

1   Introduction

Fact-based modeling (FBM) is a conceptual modeling approach that is rooted in the field of conceptual modeling for database systems [11]. The features of FBM have inspired the development of a standard language for business rules (SBVR) in which the fact type construct and many other essential FBM modeling constructs have been incorporated [6]. FBM's *conceptual schema design procedure* (CSDP) [9, 13] can be considered one of the earliest business rule derivation technologies [12]. Some examples of contemporary incarnations of FBM are ORM [9], CogNiam [15] and FCO-IM [2].

In this paper we will investigate those steps in the CSDP that derive mandatory role and set-comparison constraints. We will present a mandatory role constraint derivation algorithm in tandem with the algorithm for deriving set-comparison constraints (as presented in [7: p. 332-333]). By combining the derivation procedure for these two constraint types we can avoid duplication in the process of business rule extraction by simultaneously deriving instances of both constraint types. Therefore, the main objective of this paper is to derive an algorithm that can be used to derive all mandatory role and set-comparison constraints in one procedure. This paper will lean heavily on the results that were presented in [7].

The paper is structured as follows. In section 2 we will define the mandatory role and set-comparison constraints. In section 3 we will investigate in what ways

P. Herrero et al. (Eds.): OTM 2012 Workshops, LNCS 7567, pp. 328–337, 2012.

mandatory role and set-comparison constraints can be derived in a CSDP. In section 4 we will present an integrated algorithm for deriving mandatory role and set-comparison constraints. In section 5 we will consider the integration of conceptual schemas. Finally in section 6 conclusions will be given.

2   Definition of Mandatory Role and Set-Comparison Constraints

In the FBM defining literature a mandatory role is defined as follows: 'A role is mandatory if and only if, for all states of the database, the role must be played by every member of the population of its object type; otherwise the role is optional' [9: p. 162]. When it comes to defining mandatory role *constraints* in a conceptual schema, ORM-(2) allows to leave out explicit mandatory role constraints if a (primitive) object type plays only one role [9: p.164, 14: p.115]. In order to explicitly show that object types can 'exist', without having to play at least one fact role, ORM has defined the concept of *independent object type* as 'a primitive object type whose fact roles (if any) are collectively optional' [9: p. 291]. In Fully Communication Oriented Information Modeling (FCO-IM), independent object types can be modeled using existence postulating fact types [1]. In CogNiam (and some of its predecessors) [10, 13] independent object types are implied whenever all roles of the fact types in which they are involved have the status *optional*.

Set comparison constraints are population constraints that restrict the way in which the population of (a) role (combinations) relates to the population of another role (combination) [9: p. 224]. The three set comparison constraint type are the *subset, equality* and *exclusion* constraints. For an in-depth coverage of these constraint types we refer to [9: p.224-228].

3   The Derivation of Mandatory Role and Set-Comparison Constraints

In some knowledge domains the business rules might be provided in such a way that mandatory roles and set-comparison constraints can be easily added to a fact type diagram (e.g. the outside-in approach). If we for example consider the following fact types: *Person lives at Address* and *Person owns Car* and the following documented business rule: *For every Person an Address must be recorded*, we can see that this business rule maps straightforward to a mandatory role constraint defined on the *Person* role of the *Person lives at Address* fact type. In some exploratory knowledge domains, the constraints that govern the domain can only be detected by rigorously applying a conceptual schema design procedure in which the FBM analyst will meticulously present permutations of domain examples to the domain expert in order to derive instances of domain constraints. It is for these domains specifically that we need an integrated mandatory role and set-comparison constraint derivation algorithm.

In the ORM conceptual schema design procedure the mandatory role constraints are derived in step 5 and the set-comparison constraints are derived in step 6 [7, 9]. Some of the set-comparison constraints that will be derived in step 6 especially the subset and equality constraints, therefore will be 'implied' [8: p.6.8-6.26].

In the CogNIAM fact-based dialect [15] (and its predecessors NIAM2007 [10] and Kenniskunde [13]) the mandatory role constraints are derived after the set-comparison constraints. In this application sequence of constraint derivation sub-procedures, some mandatory role constraints can potentially be implied (by a configuration of set-comparison constraints).

3.1   Recap of the Procedure for Deriving Set-Comparison Constraints

In [7: p.332-333] we have given a fully specified derivation procedure in which in an analyst-user dialogue, exclusively based on the acceptance or rejection of 'real-life' domain examples or 'data use-cases' all set-comparison constraints that exists in an application domain can be detected. This algorithm is presented here as a decision-table in which for a given combination of allowed existence or non-allowed existence of each of the example extensions (at most) one set-comparison constraint will be derived (see table 1).

Table 1. Decision logic from the set-comparison constraint derivation algorithm [7, p.334][1]

	1	2	3	4
EXT1 pop(Ft1)= {a1} pop(Ft2)= empty	Allowed	Not Allowed	Not Allowed	Allowed
EXT2 pop(Ft1)= {a1} pop(Ft2)= {a1}	Allowed	Allowed	Allowed	Not Allowed
EXT3 pop(Ft1)= {a1} pop(Ft2)= {a1, a2}	Not Allowed	Allowed	Not Allowed	Not Allowed
Constraint type	Subset1 (FT2->FT1)	Subset2 (FT1->FT2)	equality	exclusion

The scope of the set-comparison algorithm in [7] is one pair of role(s) (combinations) in which in principle the same object type(s) (or nested object type(s) or a combination of (an) object type(s) and (a) nested object type(s)) are involved. It should be noted that the set-comparison constraint configuration that is derived by executing this algorithm for all possible pairs of role(s) combinations of a given object type (or nested object type(s) or a combination of (an) object type(s) and (a) nested object type(s)) is complete, and therefore contains all implied set-comparison constraints. In the example in figure 1 set comparison constraint *C3* is implied by the combination of subset constraints *C1* and *C2*. The application of the algorithm will always lead to the 'complete'[2] configuration of set comparison constraints as exemplified by the information model in figure 1(A).

---

[1] We note that for the other 4 (2^3-4) possible outcomes of the algorithm no set-comparison constraints will be derived.

[2] Complete means that all implied set-comparison constraints are derived.

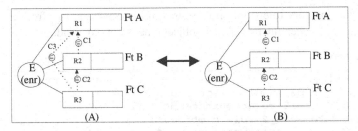

Fig. 1. Equivalent subset constraint configurations (example 1)

4   An Integrated Algorithm to Derive Mandatory Role and Set- Comparison Constraints

We will now take the set-comparison constraint derivation algorithm in [7] as a starting point for an integrated algorithm (see algorithm A on next page) in which we can 'derive' the mandatory role constraints by analyzing the subset and equality constraint configurations that are centered around a given object type. It is further assumed that the 'independence' status [9: p.219] of this object type is known. The integrated algorithm will contain the set-comparison derivation algorithm from [7]. The outcome of the first step in the algorithm will contain all set-comparison constraints between pairs of role(s) (combinations), and will therefore lead to a constraint configuration as is shown in figure 1(A) which is tabled in table 2(A).

Table 2. Tabular format set- comparison constraints

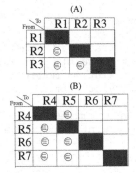

(A)

From \ To	R1	R2	R3
R1			
R2	⊆		
R3	⊆	⊆	

(B)

From \ To	R4	R5	R6	R7
R4		⊆		
R5	⊆			
R6	⊆	⊆		
R7	⊆	⊆		

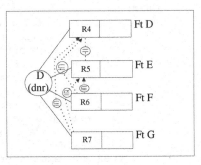

Fig. 2. Example subset constraint configuration (example 2)

Figure 2 will be replaced by the subset constraint entries: *from R2 to R1* and *from R1 to R2* in table 2(B). The next step in the algorithm is an inspection of the set-comparison constraint tables as exemplified in table 2. For each column in which all

Cells contain a subset constraint, a mandatory role will be defined on the column role In table 2(B) we have given the tabular format for the set-comparison constraints in example 2 (see figure 2). It should be noted that an *equality* constraint in the schema will be replaced by two *subset* constraints each opposite to the diagonal from the table. For example the equality constraint between roles R1 and R2 of the example in

('...*A* has a mandatory role *r* only if there is a subset constraint to *r* from each of *A*'s roles' [9: p. 226]) when the role playing object type is not independent.

Algorithm A

```
BEGIN Algorithm derive set-comparison and mandatory role
     (fact type model,object type).
     WHILE still rolecombinations left
     DO Take next_2_role_combination
      Algorithm SETCOMPARISON_on_2_rolecombinations(see [7])
     ENDWHILE³
     create a tabular format by
     1. copying subset constraints 1-on-1 into the table
     2. copying exclusion constraints into exactly one
     of the applicable table cells.
     3. copying an equality constraint as 2 subset
   constraints, mirrored across the diagonal of the table
     4. remove all copied set-comparison constraints from the
information model
          take the first column from the table
          WHILE still columns left
          DO    Take next column. Check all entries in the column
          IF (all column entries = subset constraint AND object
                  type IS NOT independent)
          THEN mandatory role defined for the role on the
          column. Remove subset constraints from column
          ENDIF
          ENDWHILE
          WHILE still constraint entries in table
          DO check next constraint
               IF constraint=subset
               THEN check for mirrored constraint
                      IF mirrored constraint exist
                      THEN add equality constraint in model
                       Remove both subset constraints fr table
                      ELSE add subset constraint in model
                       Remove sub-set constraint from table
                      ENDIF
               ELSE add exclusion constraint to model
                      Remove exclusion constraint from table
               ENDIF
          ENDWHILE
   Remove implied constraints⁴
   END
```

³ We will refer to the bold italic segment of the algorithm as procedure SETCOMPOBJ(object type).
⁴ In [8, section 6] an overview is given of a number of implied constraints for set-comparison and mandatory role constraint configurations. The algorithm can remove the implied constraints in for example the following cases: [(A is subset of C) AND (C is subset of B) → (A is subset of B)]; [(C is subset of A) AND (B is subset of C) → (B is subset of A)]; [(A is disjunct with B) AND (A = C) → (C is disjunct with B)].

After we have removed the content of the cells for the mandatory role columns we can map the remaining constraints back to the conceptual schema in which case the mirrored sub-set constraint pairs will be transformed back to equality constraints. The outcome of this algorithm applied on examples 1 and 2 will lead to the conceptual schemas as given in figure 3.

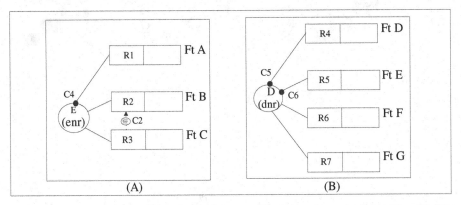

Fig. 3. Final mandatory role and set-comparison configurations for examples 1 (A) and 2 (B)

4.1 An Example of the Application of the Set-Comparison and Mandatory Role Derivation Algorithm

In example 3 (see figure 4) we need to investigate the mandatory role and set-comparison constraint configuration centered around the *TaxPayer* object type. The example in figure 4 contains the set-comparison constraints that have been derived using the set-comparison algorithm from [7].

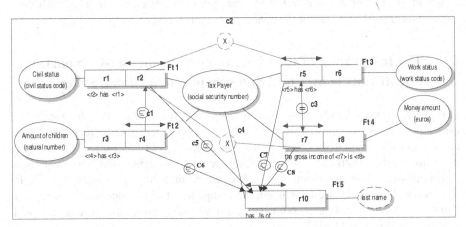

Fig. 4. Example 3 (based upon the example in [7])

Table 3. Transformation of tables in set-comparison and mandatory role algorithm

(A)

From \ To	R2	R4	R5	R7	R9
R2	■		⊗	⊗	⊆
R4	⊆	■			⊆
R5			■	⊆	⊆
R7			⊆	■	⊆
R9					■

(B)

From \ To	R2	R4	R5	R7	R9
R2	■		⊗	⊗	
R4	⊆	■			
R5			■	⊆	
R7			⊆	■	
R9					■

(C)

From \ To	R2	R4	R5	R7	R9
R2	■			⊗	
R4	⊆	■			
R5			■	=	
R7				■	
R9					■

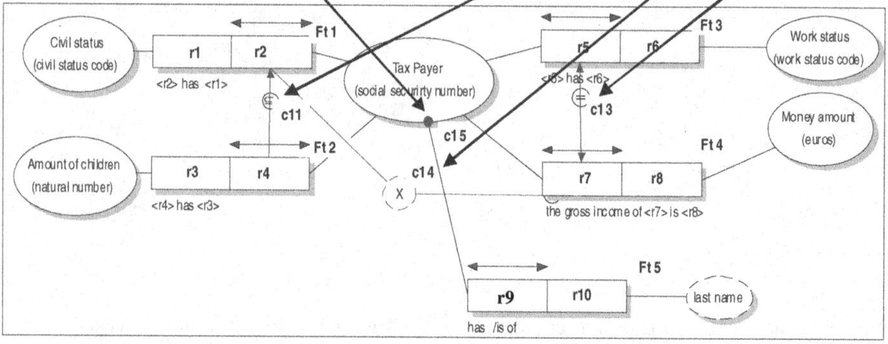

Fig. 5. In-between results and result of applying the algorithm derive set-comparison and mandatory role constraints

The constraint configuration in table 3(A) points at the existence of mandatory role constraint *c15* in figure 5. After removing the subset constraints in the mandatory role column (table 3(B)) and the collapse of 'opposite' subset constraints from table 3(B) into an equality constraint in table 3(C), and the removal of the implied exclusion constraint (from role *R2* to role *R5*) we can map the table entries in table 3(C) onto constraints *c11*, *c13* and *c14* of the conceptual schema, respectively.

5 The Integration of the Mandatory Role and Set-Comparison Constraints from Local Sub-schemas to a Global Schema

In [5: p.135] it was already shown that by integrating two conceptual schemas, (some of) the mandatory role constraints in the local conceptual schema(s) cannot directly be copied into the integrated schema that captures the global 'semantics' of the local mandatory role constraint. We therefore, propose to apply the set-comparison constraint derivation algorithm in [7] first when analyzing the 'local' UoD's. in figures 6 (A) and 6 (B) we have given the completed (local) conceptual schemas for UoD1 and UoD2. In figures 6(C) and 6(D) we have given the proto-conceptual schemas for UoD1 and UoD2.

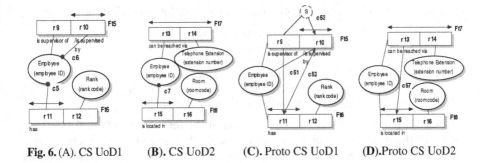

Fig. 6. (A). CS UoD1   (B). CS UoD2   (C). Proto CS UoD1   (D).Proto CS UoD2

In UoD1 we have fact types and constraints that represent the following (local) domain semantics:

> *Each employee has exactly one rank.*
> *Each employee has exactly one supervisor*
> *Each supervisor is an employee.*

In UoD2 we have the following (local) domain semantics[5]:

> *Each employee is located in exactly one room*
> *An employee can be reached via zero, one or more telephone extensions.*

If we now want to integrate the completed conceptual sub-schemas for UoD1(figure 6(A)) and UoD2 (figure 6(B))we can merge the fact types and uniqueness constraints into one integrated conceptual schema. However, we can not merge the mandatory role constraints, because in the integrated (global) UoD the mandatory participation in some roles does no longer hold. It is because we have to consider the 'global characteristics' that emerge when we add 'individual views'. These characteristics can lead to new and/or adapted constraints that have to be added to/adapted in the model of the 'global view' [4: p. 338].

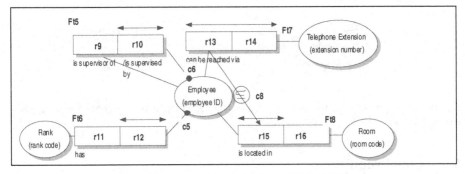

Fig. 7. Conceptual schema integrated UoD (IUoD)

---

[5] Note that in UoD2 only a subset of the 'global' employee population is relevant: those employees that are located in a room. This explains the existence of mandatory role constraint *c7* in figure 6(B).

We have summarized the semantics of the integrated domain (IUoD) as follows[6]:

Each employee has exactly one rank.
Each employee has exactly one supervisor
Each supervisor is an employee.
An employee can be located in a room.
An employee that is located in a room can be reached via
zero, one or more telephone extensions

If we carefully analyze the conceptual schema of the integrated UoD in figure 7 we notice that the result of the integration of the local schemas into a global schema with global semantics has had the following implications in terms of the mandatory role and set-comparison constraints: mandatory role constraint *c7* in the local schema has been replaced by subset constraint *c8* in the global schema (see figure 7). In this case it is recommended to apply the set-comparison derivation algorithm in [7] for the creation of the local proto conceptual schemas. In an integration step of two (or more) proto conceptual schemas the same algorithm can be applied on those new role combinations that have emerged from the federation of the local proto conceptual schemas into the new 'global' proto-conceptual schema (procedure beta in figure 8). The latter schema can now serve as input for procedure gamma (in figure 8), i.e. the application of the 2nd part of the set-comparison and mandatory role derivation algorithm (A) to map the set-comparison constraints to mandatory role and remaining (non-implied) set comparison constraints (see figure 8).

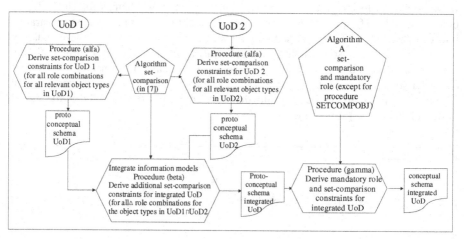

Fig. 8. The application of the mandatory role and set comparison algorithm for integrating (conceptual) sub-schemas

6   Conclusion

In this article we have shown that the algorithm for the 'example-based' derivation of set-comparison constraints can be used as a starting point for an integrated algorithm

---

[6] Note that in the integrated UoD not all employees have to be located in a room.

that will generate the mandatory role and the non-implied set-comparison constraints. We have also shown that for the integration of multiple 'local' conceptual schemas, the logic of the algorithm allows us to integrate those sub-schemas with a minimum of integration effort. By expressing the mandatory role constraints in the local (proto) schema as (combinations of) set comparison constraints the process of data federation can focus on the derivation of set-comparison constraints for the 'new' role combinations that govern the integrated UoD.

References

1. Bakema, G.P., Zwart, J.P., van der Lek, H.: Fully communication oriented NIAM. In: Nijssen, G., Sharp, J. (eds.) NIAM-ISDM 1994 Conference (1994)
2. Bakema, G.P., Zwart, J.P., van der Lek, H.: Fully communication oriented information modeling (2002), http://www.fco-im.nl/pdfFiles/FCO-IM%20book.pdf
3. Balsters, H., Halpin, T.: Modeling Data Federations in ORM. In: Meersman, R., Tari, Z. (eds.) OTM-WS 2007, Part I. LNCS, vol. 4805, pp. 657–666. Springer, Heidelberg (2007)
4. Batini, C., Lenzerini, M., Navathe, S.: A comparative analysis of methodologies for database schema integration. ACM Computing Surveys 18(4), 323–336 (1986)
5. Bollen, P.: A formal transformation from object-role models to UML class diagrams. In: Halpin, T., Siau, K., Krogstie, J. (eds.) Seventh CAiSE/IFIP-WG8.1 International Workshop on Evaluation of Modeling Methods in Systems Analysis and Design (EMMSAD 2002), pp. 132–143 (2002)
6. Bollen, P.: SBVR: A Fact-Oriented OMG Standard. In: Meersman, R., Tari, Z., Herrero, P. (eds.) OTM-WS 2008. LNCS, vol. 5333, pp. 718–727. Springer, Heidelberg (2008)
7. Bollen, P.: A Derivation Procedure for Set-Comparison Constraints in Fact-Based Modeling. In: Meersman, R., Dillon, T., Herrero, P. (eds.) OTM-WS 2011. LNCS, vol. 7046, pp. 329–338. Springer, Heidelberg (2011)
8. Halpin, T.: A logical analysis of information systems: static aspects of the data-oriented perspective. Ph.D thesis. Department of Computer Science. University of Queensland (1989)
9. Halpin, T., Morgan, T.: Information Modeling and Relational Databases; from conceptual analysis to logical design, 2nd edn. Morgan-Kaufman, San-Francisco (2008)
10. Lemmens, I.M.C., Nijssen, M., Nijssen, S.: A NIAM2007 Conceptual Analysis of the ISO and OMG MOF Four Layer Metadata Architectures. In: Meersman, R., Tari, Z. (eds.) OTM-WS 2007, Part I. LNCS, vol. 4805, pp. 613–623. Springer, Heidelberg (2007)
11. Nijssen, G.: On the gross architecture for the next generation database management systems. In: Information Processing. IFIP (1977)
12. Nijssen, G.: Mini cookbook to prepare a conceptual schema or conceptualization procedure in fourteen major steps, University of Queensland, Australia (1982), http://www.sjirnijssen.eu/documents.aspx
13. Nijssen, G.: Kenniskunde 1A. PNA publishing, Heerlen (2001)(in Dutch)
14. Nijssen, G., Halpin, T.: Conceptual schema and relational database design: a fact oriented approach. Prentice-Hall (1989)
15. Nijssen, G., Le Cat, A.: Kennis gebaseerd werken: de manier om kennis produktief te maken. PNA publishing, Heerlen (2009) (in Dutch)

CCL: A Lightweight ORM Embedding in Clean

Bas Lijnse[1,2], Patrick van Bommel[1], and Rinus Plasmeijer[1]

[1] Institute for Computing and Information Sciences (ICIS),
Radboud University Nijmegen, The Netherlands
[2] Faculty of Military Sciences,
Netherlands Defense Academy, Den Helder, The Netherlands
{b.lijnse,pvb,rinus}@cs.ru.nl

Abstract. Agile software development advocates a rapid iterative process where working systems are delivered at each iteration. For information systems, this drive to produce something working soon, makes it tempting to skip conceptual domain modeling. The long term benefits of developing an explicit conceptual model are traded for the short term benefit of reduced overhead. A possible way to reconcile conceptual modeling with a code-centric agile process is by embedding it in a programming language. We investigate this approach with CCL, a compact textual notation for embedding Object-Role Models in the functional language Clean. CCL enables specification of Clean types as derivatives of conceptual types. Together with its compact notation, this means that defining data types with CCL as intermediary requires no more programming effort than defining data types directly. Moreover, because embedded ORM is still ORM, mappings to other ORM representations remain possible at any time.

1 Introduction

The foundation of a successful information system is a solid understanding of the domain it represents. A way of capturing such understanding on a conceptual level is through the use of Object-Role Models (ORM [4]). They allow modelers to express the conceptual relationships in a domain without committing to the level of detail that implementation data structures require. A common approach to ORM is to make models with dedicated tools as analysis and design activity, and use them to bootstrap development of information systems by generating relational schemas and template code. An implicit assumption of this approach is that the development process has a requirements analysis or design phase prior to a construction or programming phase. With the increasing popularity of Agile development [2] this assumption does no longer always hold. Agile development advocates an iterative process with short cycles in which working systems are delivered at each iteration and stakeholders are actively involved in the development. In such a process, with a focus on delivering working systems in a short amount of time, it is tempting to skip conceptual modeling, because the overhead of using dedicated modeling tools while already programming an information system may outweigh the short-term benefits. Unfortunately this

P. Herrero et al. (Eds.): OTM 2012 Workshops, LNCS 7567, pp. 338–347, 2012.

means that the long-term benefit of an explicit conceptual model that can be used in communication with stakeholders is also lost.

A possible way to reconcile conceptual modeling with a code-centric Agile development process is by embedding ORM in a programming language. At first glance, this appears to be a compromise. For ORM modelers, it means that conceptual models have to be specified textually instead of graphically in order to let it be embeddable in the structured text of a programming language. For programmers this means that they cannot define data types directly, but that they need to specify a conceptual model of the domain first. Yet, we expect that embedding ORM in a programming language can have several benefits: First, conceptual relations between different data structures used in the code of an information system are often implicit. By making them explicit, data types can be specified more compactly as derivatives of shared conceptual types, giving programmers an immediate short-term benefit. It also gives compilers additional opportunities to check code and detect programming mistakes.

Second, because models are integrated in the source code of information systems there is a direct link between the model and the working information system. This means there cannot be discrepancies between the ORM models and the behavior of the information system caused by misinterpretation of the models during implementation. Moreover, embedded ORM models are still ORM models. This makes it possible to maintain bidirectional mappings to representations used by other ORM notations and tools.

In this paper we investigate the embedded ORM approach with CCL (Concepts in CLean), a compact notation for embedding ORM models in the pure functional programming language Clean [10]. Clean is a statically typed language where data types play an important role. Not only are they used to detect programming errors, but they are also for type-driven generic programming, a technique in which data types are used to parameterize algorithms. Contemporary Clean frameworks like iTasks [6] aim to improve agility by enabling large parts of information systems to be generated from abstract patterns that depend on types. This makes specification of data types a key element of agile Clean programming.

The main contributions of this paper are:

- We provide a new compact textual notation of a core subset of ORM.
- We demonstrate how this notation is used to embed ORM in a programming language.
- We extend the Clean language with the possibility to specify conceptual types underlying multiple data types.

The remainder of this paper is organized as follows: We start with an example of CCL in Section 2. We then continue with an explanation of the notation of ORM constructs for defining conceptual models in CCL in Section 3 and for defining derivative data types in Section 4. We reflect on the benefits as well as the scope and limitations of our work in Section 5 and put it the context of related work in Section 6. In Section 7, we end with concluding remarks and an outlook on future work.

2   A CCL Example

Before going into technical details of the CCL notation, we present a simple, yet nontrivial example. We model a personal audio catalogue of digital audio files like for example a collection of ripped CD's or an iTunes library. The central concept is an album, which can be a music album or an audiobook. Additionally songs, artists and authors of audiobooks are modeled.

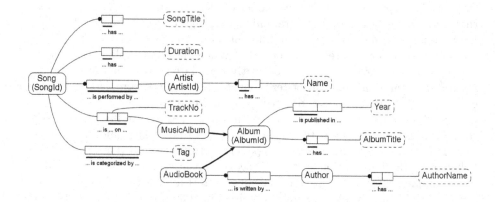

Fig. 1. ORM diagram of a personal audio collection

Figure 1 shows the ORM2 diagram of such an audio collection which is defined by the CCL code in Figure 2. This definition consists of three parts. A series of object type definitions consisting of entity type definitions and value type definitions, a series of fact type definitions and a series of fact container type definitions that define Clean data types in terms of the conceptual definitions. In the next section we explain this definition in more detail.

3   Defining Conceptual Models with CCL

Conceptual models are defined as structured text in CCL source modules, text files with .ccl as extension. Each CCL module starts with a module header defining its module name.

concept module AudioCollection

By giving each module a name we make it compatible with the module system of Clean such that we can refer to its content from within other modules.

The module header is followed by a series of declarations. These can be *object type* declarations, *fact type* or declarations, that define the model, or *fact container type* declarations that link the conceptual level to concrete first-order data structures. In Table 1 an overview of the CCL declarations is listed together with examples and their corresponding ORM diagrams.

Table 1. CCL Language Constructs

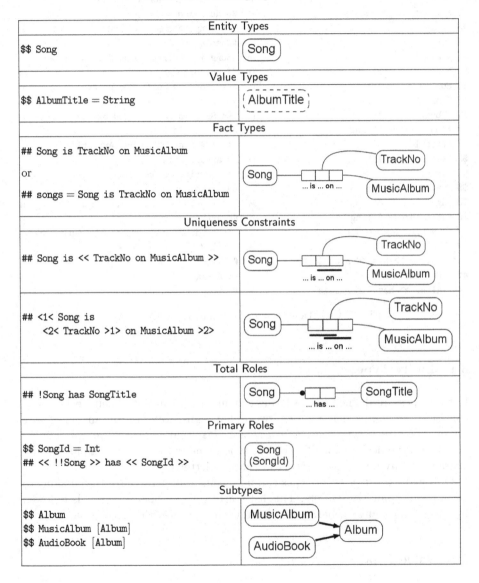

Entity Types	
$$ Song	Song
Value Types	
$$ AlbumTitle = String	AlbumTitle
Fact Types	
## Song is TrackNo on MusicAlbum or ## songs = Song is TrackNo on MusicAlbum	Song ... is ... on ... TrackNo MusicAlbum
Uniqueness Constraints	
## Song is << TrackNo on MusicAlbum >>	Song ... is ... on ... TrackNo MusicAlbum
## <1< Song is <2< TrackNo >1> on MusicAlbum >2>	Song ... is ... on ... TrackNo MusicAlbum
Total Roles	
## !Song has SongTitle	Song ... has ... SongTitle
Primary Roles	
$$ SongId = Int ## << !!Song >> has << SongId >>	Song (SongId)
Subtypes	
$$ Album $$ MusicAlbum [Album] $$ AudioBook [Album]	MusicAlbum AudioBook Album

342   B. Lijnse, P. van Bommel, and R. Plasmeijer

```
//Module header                          1   ## album_year =                        27
concept module AudioCollection           2     << Album >> is published in Year     28
// Entity types                          3   ## song_id =                           29
$$ Album                                 4     << !!Song >> has << SongId >>         30
$$ AudioBook [Album]                     5   ## title =                             31
$$ Author                                6     << !Song >> has SongTitle            32
$$ MusicAlbum [Album]                    7   ## duration =                          33
$$ Artist                                8     << Song >> has Duration              34
$$ Song                                  9   ## songs =                             35
// Value types                          10     Song is << TrackNo on MusicAlbum >>  36
$$ Name        = String                 11   ## performed_by =                      37
$$ SongId      = Int                    12     << !Song is performed by Artist >>   38
$$ SongTitle   = String                 13   ## tags =                              39
$$ AlbumId     = Int                    14     << Song is categorized by Tag >>     40
$$ AlbumTitle  = String                 15   ## artist_id =                         41
$$ ArtistId    = Int                    16     << !!Artist >> has << ArtistId >>    42
$$ Year        = Int                    17   ## artist_name =                       43
$$ Duration    = Time                   18     << !Artist >> has Name               44
$$ TrackNo     = Int                    19   ## author_name =                       45
$$ Tag         = String                 20     << !Author >> has AuthorName         46
$$ AuthorName  = String                 21   ## author =                            47
// Fact type definitions                22     << !AudioBook is written by Author >> 48
## album_id =                           23   // Fact container types                49
  << !!Album >> has << AlbumId >>        24   #: Album    = Album {..}               50
## album_title =                        25   #: Artist   = Artist {..}              51
  << !Album >> has AlbumTitle           26   #: Song     = Song {..}                52
```

Fig. 2. CCL Definition of Personal Audio Collection

3.1 Entity Types

Entity types are defined by declaring a name for a concept. Their declarations consist of an *object type marker*, two dollar signs, followed by an *object type name*. The object type marker is a symbol (**$$**) that indicates we are defining an object type declaration. The object type name must consist of alphanumeric characters only and must start with a capital letter.

Optionally a list of super types can be specified after the object type name to declare subtyping constraints. This list starts with an open bracket, is followed by entity type names separated by commas and ends with a closing bracket.

3.2 Value Types

Value types are defined by assigning a name to a first-order Clean type. They are declared the same way as object types, but with the addition of an equals sign, followed by the name of a first-order Clean type. Specification of super types is not allowed for value types.

3.3   Fact Types

Fact type declarations are defined by a *fact type marker* (##) followed by a sentence consisting of capitalized words and all lowercase words. The captilized words are interpreted as names of object types.

It is allowed to reference object types that are not explicitly declared by an object type declaration. Undefined references are interpreted as implicit entity type declarations. It is recommended to explicitly declare entity types, but by allowing implicit use it is possible to construct a model by supplying fact types only. The CCL compiler can detect implicit references and issue warnings.

Optionally one can assign names to fact types by adding a *fact type name* followed by an equals sign between the fact type marker and the sentence. Assigning a name to a fact type makes it possible to reference the fact type in the declaration of *fact container types*.

3.4   Uniqueness Constraints

Uniqueness constraints are expressed by annotations in fact type declarations. Unique sets of roles can be marked by enclosing parts of the sentence with double angle brackets (<< >>). When multiple uniqueness constraints within the same fact type overlap making their definition becomes ambiguous. This can be resolved by labeling the constraints with a unique number. This number is placed between the angle brackets. Non-adjacent uniqueness can be specified by using the same label on multiple annotations.

3.5   Mandatory and Primary Roles

Mandatory role constraints are specified by prefixing object type references in a fact type declaration with an exclamation mark (!).

To indicate that a mandatory role is not only mandatory, but that the associated value type(s) may be used as reference for an entity type, we use an annotation to mark a role as the *primary* role. Because it is essentially a stronger version of a mandatory constraint, we use a double exclamation mark as annotation (!!).

This annotation does not necessarily have to be used together with uniqueness constraints, but if it is used in a binary fact type between an entity type and a value type with two unique roles, the value type is depicted with the shorthand notation for standard names in the derived diagram. Each entity type can have only one primary role annotation.

4   Defining Clean Types with CCL

To manipulate facts in Clean programs, we need to represent them in compound data structures. Because Clean is a strong statically typed language that uses Burstall-style algebraic data types to type compound structures, we need to define (Clean) types of such data structures representing facts. To achieve this, CCL offers notation to define Clean types in terms of CCL fact types, which are automatically expanded. This way, the specification of CCL fact types reduces the specification effort of Clean types, because a single fact type can contribute to the definition of multiple Clean types if it relates to multiple entity types. Even for the simple model in Section 2 the CCL definition is more concise than the expanded Clean data types derived from it.

4.1 Fact Container Types

To define Clean types that can contain composite structures of facts, CCL offers so called *fact container types*. Their notation is similar to the notation for *record types* in Clean. For example:

```
#: SongSummary = Song {song_id,title,songs}
```

Which expands to the following Clean record type:

```
:: SongSummary =
  { song_id :: SongId
  , title :: SongTitle
  , songs :: [(TrackNo,AlbumId)] }
```

A fact container type definition starts with a *container type marker* (#:), followed by a type name and and equals sign. The righthand side of the equals sign consists of a *focus entity* and a selection of facts that get mapped to field names. The focus entity is the name of a conceptual entity type, that we collect facts about. It is implicit in all the facts that the type contains. The selection of facts is a comma separated list of named facts in which the focus entity has a role. Each fact maps to a field in the expanded record type. The types of the fields (in Clean denoted with the double colon) do not have to be specified because they can be inferred from the conceptual model. For value types this is simply their Clean type. For entity types, the type of the fact type with a primary role annotation is used. This inference makes the type specifications more concise.

4.2 Complete Container Types

To make the definition of data types even more concise, a shorthand notation is available for defining fact container types that contain *all* facts about an entity. To define a type that expands to include all named facts a focus entity has role in, one can use the following notation:

```
#: Album = Album {..}
```

4.3 Explicit Field Type Specifications

If more control over the data types of fields in fact container types is desired, selected facts may be annotated with type information. To not just reference related entities, but to include facts about them one could for example specify:

#: SongSummary = Song {song_id,title,songs :: (TrackNo,Album)}

The name of a fact in the selection is annotated by a double colon followed by a comma separated list of Clean types enclosed in parenthesis for all roles except the role of the focus entity. For binary facts the parenthesis may be omitted because only one role remains.

5   Discussion

5.1   Conceptual Modeling

CCL is a lightweight embedding of ORM that provides notation for a core set of ORM constructs only. The reason for this is partially intentional and partially practical. Covering all ORM constraints fully would make the CCL language more complex while the additional value is uncertain. Because we are embedding ORM in a general purpose programming language, we don't need to be complete. Many constraints can also be expressed alternatively in Clean and addition would only duplicate existing functionality. The supported ORM subset adds the structural conceptual level that could not be expressed explicitly in Clean. Exploration of the effects of additional constraints remains a topic for future research.

Although unnecessary for the generation of Clean code, the CCL notation uses complete sentences to define fact types. For constraints however, it uses annotations instead of a more verbose verbal form. This approach aims to provide a notation that is concise but still contains all information necessary for verbalization. The notation is therefore not as close to natural language as for example SBVR, but still starts from stating facts about a universe of discourse.

5.2   Effects on Agility

The use of CCL as intermediate step in the definition of collections of data types, may improve agility of a Clean programmer in two ways. First, it reduces the amount of code that has to be written, because CCL makes the definition of types more compact. Secondly, it automatically keeps the data types that represent entities that share fact types consistent. This makes it easier to incrementally extend the system under development, because changes that involve multiple conceptual entities can be made in one place.

A possible negative effect may be that too much of a domain is modeled. If in CCL more types are defined than are used in the current iteration of an information system, time is spent on something that does not contribute to the working system. Luckily this can easily be detected by the compiler.

5.3   Implementation

To be able to test and investigate the use of CCL in information systems developed with Clean, we have implemented a basic compiler. This is a proof-of-concept compiler that serves as a preprocessor to the Clean compiler. The primary purpose of our compiler is to compile CCL to Clean. Although CCL's syntax is designed to avoid conflict with Clean's syntax such that CCL can be mixed with Clean in the same module, we currently only support separate CCL modules that can transparently be compiled to Clean using the Clean IDE's preprocessing support.

The secondary purpose is to generate representations of the conceptual models for communication with domain experts. Currently we support the generation of ORM2 diagrams, but one could also think of verbalizations, or a combination of both in hyperlinked documents. Because, CCL does not allow the specification of diagram layout, we use the popular open-source Grapviz tool, to visualize CCL. The CCL compiler generates a graph structure in the DOT language which is rendered by Graphviz. All diagrams shown in Section 2 and Section 3 have been generated from CCL in this way.

Both the CCL notation, and the CCL compiler have many opportunities for improvement. Obvious additional targets are the generation of relational schema's for storage, and access functions for conversion between flat relational structures and CCL fact container types. Another area in which the CCL compiler could be improved, is interoperability with formats from tools such as Norma, or languages as CQL or SBVR.

6   Related Work

It is obvious that CCL as presented in this paper is not intended to replace any of the current ORM notations and tools, but rather to introduce ORM in a new context where explicit conceptual models have added value. Therefore it may be less obvious where to position CCL in the ORM literature. Unlike most concrete ORM notations, like the earlier NIAM [9], FCO-IM [1] or more recent ORM2 [4], CCL is a textual language with a formal concrete syntax, instead of a graphical language. In its textual approach it is closer to SBVR vocabularies [3] or CQL [5], but less natural language oriented. CCL is a pure data definition language. Where languages as RIDL [8] and LISA-D [11], as well as CQL incorporate the querying and manipulation of information, CCL defines only the conceptual structure. Manipulation of data is already provided by the host language Clean. In its aim to accommodate an agile process and use of a text oriented approach, CCL has some overlap with CQL. However, because CCL is an embedded language it has a different focus. CCL's syntax emphasizes concise notation, to align with the host language, whereas CQL chooses a linguistic approach for better alignment with domain experts. CCL is less expressive as CQL, because it is just a lightweight embedding, not a standalone language. With regard to information system development in Clean, CCL can be related to earlier work on automated mapping between relational tables and Clean data types [7]. That approach relied on the encoding of conceptual relations in Clean types because no explicit ORM model could be expressed. CCL could be used to improve this mapping.

7   Conclusions

In this paper we have presented CCL, a lightweight embedding of ORM in the functional programming language Clean. We have shown that it is possible to define conceptual models from within a programming language without additional overhead. Because derivation of data types from conceptual types enables a more concise specification of collections of data types that model a domain, the additional effort of specifying the conceptual types pays off immediately. Moreover, because a tightly integrated conceptual model is developed from within the programming language, ORM diagrams or verbalizations can be extracted from an information system's source code at any time.

References

1. Bakema, G., Zwart, J., van der Lek, H.: Fully Communication Oriented Information Modelling. FCO-IM Consultancy (2002)
2. Fowler, M., Highsmith, J.: The agile manifesto. Software Development 9, 28–35 (2001)
3. O.M. Group. The semantics of business vocabulary and business rules (2009), http://www.omg.org/spec/SBVR/1.0/
4. Halpin, T.: ORM 2. In: Meersman, R., Tari, Z., Herrero, P. (eds.) OTM-WS 2005. LNCS, vol. 3762, pp. 676–687. Springer, Heidelberg (2005)
5. Heath, C.: The Constellation Query Language. In: Meersman, R., Herrero, P., Dillon, T. (eds.) OTM 2009 Workshops. LNCS, vol. 5872, pp. 682–691. Springer, Heidelberg (2009)
6. Jansen, J.M., Plasmeijer, R., Koopman, P., Achten, P.: Embedding a web-based workflow management system in a functional language. In: Brabrand, C., Moreau, P.-E. (eds.) Proceedings 10th Workshop on Language Descriptions, Tools and Applications, LDTA 2010, Paphos, Cyprus, March 27-28, pp. 79–93 (2010)
7. Lijnse, B., Plasmeijer, R.: Between Types and Tables - Using Generic Programming for Automated Mapping Between Data Types and Relational Databases. In: Scholz, S.-B., Chitil, O. (eds.) IFL 2008. LNCS, vol. 5836, pp. 272–290. Springer, Heidelberg (2011)
8. Meersman, R.: The RIDL conceptual langue. Technical report, International Centre for Information Analysis Services, Control Data Belgium Inc. (1982)
9. Nijssen, G.M., Halpin, T.A.: Conceptual schema and relational database design: A fact oriented approach. Prentice-Hall, New York (1989)
10. Plasmeijer, R., van Eekelen, M.: Clean language report, version 2.1 (2002), http://clean.cs.ru.nl
11. ter Hofstede, A., Proper, H., van der Weide, T.: Formal definition of a conceptual language for the description and manipulation of information models. Information Systems 18(7), 489–523 (1993)

Formalization of ORM Revisited

Terry Halpin

INTI International University, Malaysia and LogicBlox, Australia
`terry.halpin@logicblox.com`

Abstract. Fact-oriented modeling approaches such as Object-Role Modeling (ORM) and Natural Language Information Analysis Method (NIAM) enable conceptual information models to be expressed using graphical diagrams that may be assigned formal semantics by mapping them onto sets of logical formulae. Various formalizations for such mappings exist. This paper extends such previous work by providing a new approach to formalizing second generation ORM (ORM 2). We show that the metalevel association between semantic value type and data type must be a mapping relationship rather than a subtyping relationship, and we axiomatize a special representation relationship to support this mapping at the instance level. Our new formalization includes coverage of preferred reference schemes and additional constraints introduced in ORM 2. Other issues examined briefly include the use of finite model theory, sorted logic, and practical choices for implementing certain kinds of logical formulae as constraints or derivation rules.

1 Introduction

For conceptual data modeling, fact-oriented approaches such as Object-Role Modeling (ORM) [11,15] and Natural Language Information Analysis Method (NIAM) [23] differ from Entity Relationship Modeling (ER) [3] and class modeling in the Unified Modeling Language (UML) [22] by uniformly modeling facts as unary or longer relationships that are instances of fact types (e.g. Person smokes, Person was born on Date) instead of modeling only some facts as relationships and others as instances of attributes (e.g. Person.isSmoker, Person.birthdate). This attribute-free approach enables all facts, constraints, and derivation rules to be verbalized naturally in sentences easily understood and validated by nontechnical business users using concrete examples, and promotes semantic stability, since one never needs to remodel existing structures in order to add facts about attributes [9]. ORM's graphical notation for data modeling is also far more expressive than that of industrial ER diagrams or UML class diagrams [15].

To ensure that fact-oriented models and queries are unambiguous and executable, it is essential to formalize them in terms of underlying logics. The first formalization of a fact-oriented approach appeared in 1989 in our doctoral thesis [5], which provided an algorithm to map an extended version of NIAM to predicate logic in which deduction trees (semantic tableaux augmented by natural deduction) were used to test whether a conceptual schema is strongly satisfiable (consistent when populated) and

P. Herrero et al. (Eds.): OTM 2012 Workshops, LNCS 7567, pp. 348–357, 2012.
© Springer-Verlag Berlin Heidelberg 2012

whether one schema implies or is equivalent to another, using conservative extensions to define predicates unique to the other schema prior to the evaluation.

In the 1990s, other formalizations of fact-oriented modeling were produced (e.g. [4, 17]), and we extended NIAM further to become ORM. In 2005 we introduced second generation ORM (ORM 2) [6], which modified the graphical notation to remove all English-specific symbols, and added features (e.g. role value constraints, semiderived fact types, asserted subtypes, and deontic constraints). Recently, various researchers have proposed ways to transform many ORM 2 constructs into description logics (e.g. [18]), noting that some features such as acyclic ring constraints have no such mapping. In 2011, ORM 2 support for ring constraints was modified and extended to cater for local reflexivity, transitivity, and strong intransitivity [14]. From now on, we use "ORM" to mean the current version of ORM 2.

The rest of this paper focuses on formalization issues for ORM, and is structured as follows. Section 2 discusses the top level partition of types, including a new treatment for relating semantic values to data values. Section 3 illustrates how fact types, fact instances, and constraints and reference schemes are formalized, including an example relating to ORM's adoption of finite model theory. Section 4 briefly discusses asserted, derived and semiderived fact types and subtypes, and practical choices for implementing certain kinds of logical propositions as constraints or derivation rules. Section 5 concludes by summarizing the main contributions, identifying areas for future research, and listing the references cited.

2   Entities, Semantic Values, and Data Values

Our original formalization [5] treated named value types (e.g. CountryCode) as subtypes of conceptual datatypes (e.g. String), as shown in the metamodel fragment Figure 1(a). Our new formalization treats semantic values as ontologically distinct from data values, replacing the subtyping relationship by a mapping relationship as in Figure 1(b).

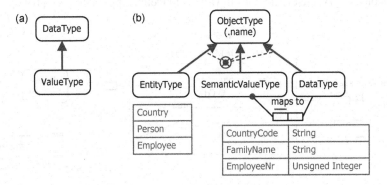

Fig. 1. Value types and data types in (a) original formalization, and (b) new formalization

In ORM, an object is the same as an individual in logic, and is either an entity, a semantic value or a data value. Figure 1(b) includes fact tables with sample populations of the meta-object types and the meta-fact type SemanticValueType maps to DataType. A complete treatment of this mapping includes discussion of finer aspects about data types, such as facets (e.g. assigning country codes a fixed length of 2 characters), but such aspects are ignored in this paper.

Our main reason for distinguishing between semantic values and data values is to ensure a formalization that is consistent with the *Principle of Indiscernibility of Identicals* (*PII:* identical objects have exactly the same properties). Using Φ as variable ranging over predicates, this may be formalized in second-order logic as follows: $\forall x,y$ $[x = y \rightarrow \forall \Phi\ (\Phi x \equiv \Phi y)]$. In first-order logic this corresponds to the Substitutivity of Identicals (SI) inference rule.

For example, consider the following objects: the country code 'CH', and the IATA airline code 'CH'. Are these objects identical? If we adopt the subtyping semantics in in Figure 1(a), they are identical, since each is just the character string 'CH'. The country code 'CH' was chosen for Switzerland because the Latin name for Switzerland is '*Confederatio Helvetica*', so sentence (1) below expresses a true proposition. The IATA airline code 'CH' is used for Bemidji airlines (a small airline company based in Bemidji, Minnesota), but the choice of this airline code has nothing to do with Latin. Hence, sentence (2) below expresses a false proposition.

(1) The country code 'CH' is based on a term in Latin.
(2) The IATA airline code 'CH' is based on a term in Latin.

Since the property of being based on a Latin term holds for the country code 'CH' but not the IATA airline code 'CH', it follows from PII that the country code 'CH' is *not* identical to the IATA airline code 'CH'. Hence the subtyping pictured by the Euler diagram in Figure 2 is *incorrect* (the string 'CH' cannot be both a country code and an IATA airline code). Though the codes are not identical, their mapped data values may be equated. Any logical attempt to deny our distinction between semantic values and data values must move the semantics of the type names into the associated predicates (e.g. CountryCode is a country code based on a term in Language), but this option is clearly inferior as it hinders reuse and leads to unnatural verbalization. For some related discussion on entity/value distinctions in various modeling approaches see [10].

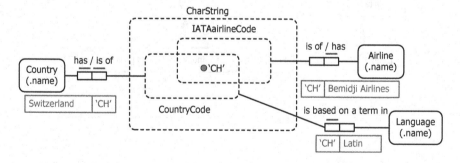

Fig. 2. A diagram that wrongly treats a semantic value as identical to a data value

Fig. 3. Graphic notation for partitioning objects into entities, semantic values and data values

At the business domain level, the type partitioning in Figure 1(b) is displayed graphically by using different line styles for the named, soft rectangles that denote the object types. Entity types use solid lines, semantic values types used dashed lines, and data types use dotted lines, as shown in Figure 3. The graphical display of data types is being added to ORM at the time of writing. ORM satisfies finite model theory [20], so for each state of the model the *population* of each of its types is finite. Although the usual axioms for data types allow infinite sets (e.g. each integer has a successor), ORM models use data values only to represent semantic values, and data types are implicitly independent. In any state, the semantic value population is finite, and hence so is the data value population in use. As in datalog [1], syntactic restrictions are placed on derivation rules and queries in ORM to ensure that use of data type operations (e.g. numeric addition or string concatenation) do not generate infinite sets.

Every ORM model implicitly includes the unary type predicates *Entity*, *Semantic-Value*, and *DataValue* to convey the kind of object type. Hence the schema fragment shown in Figure 3 may be formalized as follows. In our logical notation, type predicates are written in prefix notation without parentheses. For example, "Country *x*" abbreviates Country(*x*) and is read "x is a country".

$\forall x$ (Country $x \rightarrow$ Entity x)
$\forall x$ (CountryCode $x \rightarrow$ SemanticValue x)
$\forall x$ (String $x \rightarrow$ DataValue x)

A model comprises a schema plus a population. Figure 4(a) shows an example of the simplest kind of populated ORM model: a semantic value type populated with one instance. The enclosing single quotes on the value instance indicate that the code is represented by a character string value, as shown explicitly in Figure 4(b). For explanation purposes, the *typed constant* "CountryCode 'US'" is used here for the country code in the representation relationship, to distinguish it from the character string 'US'. In typical ORM diagrams, the representation relationship is suppressed, and semantic values are normally displayed in context without their type name, as in Figure 4(a).

The identity relationship "=" is defined between objects of any type. This may be formalized by using *Object* for a universal type predicate, and adding the axiom$\forall x,y$ [$x = y \rightarrow$ (Object x & Object y)]. The usual axioms for identity (e.g. Reflexive, Symmetric, Transitive, and SI) apply. We reserve the predicate symbol $\approx$ for the *representation relationship* that provides an injective (mandatory 1:1 into) mapping from semantic values of a given type to data values, so "$x \approx y$" is read "x is represented by y".

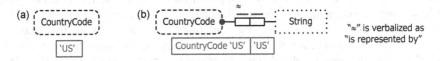

"$\approx$" is verbalized as "is represented by"

Fig. 4. A simple ORM model displayed in (a) compact form, and (b) expanded form

The representation relationship $\approx$ is axiomatized as follows, to allow its reuse between many different kinds of semantic values and data values. Since $\approx$ is predefined and is the same for all semantic value types, this formally allows us to treat semantic values simply as typed constants (e.g. "CountryCode 'CH'" may be unabbreviated to the definite description "**the** CountryCode **that** is represented by **the** String 'CH'"). Axioms A2 and A3 capture the mandatory role and uniqueness constraints for $\approx$ using the numeric quantifiers "$\exists^1$" (there is exactly one) and "$\exists^{0..1}$" (there is at most one). These may be unabbreviated to expressions using simple quantifiers and the identity relation thus: $\exists^{0..1}x \; \Phi x =_{df} \forall x,y \; [(\Phi x \; \& \; \Phi y) \rightarrow x = y]; \; \exists^1 x \; \Phi x =_{df.}.\exists x \; [\Phi x \; \& \; \forall y \; (\Phi y \rightarrow y = x)].$

A1 $\forall x,y \; [x \approx y \rightarrow (\text{SemanticValue } x \; \& \; \text{DataValue } y)]$
A2 $\forall x \; (\text{SemanticValue } x \rightarrow \exists^1 y \; x \approx y)$
A3 $\forall y,T \; \exists^{0..1}x \; (Tx \; \& \; x \approx y)$ 2nd-order axiom, where T is a type variable

For any given ORM model, the axiom A3 may be implemented in first-order logic by replacing the quantification over types by a conjunction over the finite set of domain type predicates (e.g. each string 'US' represents at most one countrycode and at most one pronoun etc.). The model in Figure 4(b) may now be formalized as follows. Here 'US' is an individual constant denoting itself (the character string 'US').

$\forall x \; (\text{CountryCode } x \rightarrow \text{SemanticValue } x) \; \& \; \forall x \; (\text{String } x \rightarrow \text{DataValue } x)$
$\forall x,y \; [(\text{CountryCode } x \; \& \; x \approx y) \rightarrow \text{String } y]$
$\exists x \; (\text{CountryCode } x \; \& \; x \approx \text{'US'})$

If we expand the model as shown in Figure 5, the additional part of the model may be formalized as follows. Although CountryCode and Pronoun are mutually exclusive types, their data types are compatible, so one may perform lexical comparisons between their instances by comparing the data values that represent those instances.

$\forall x \; (\text{Pronoun } x \rightarrow \text{SemanticValue } x)$
$\forall x,y \; [(\text{Pronoun } x \; \& \; x \approx y) \rightarrow \text{String } y] \; \& \; \exists x \; (\text{Pronoun } x \; \& \; x \approx \text{'US'})$

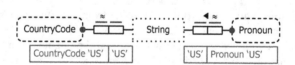

Fig. 5. A populated ORM model with two semantic value types based on the data type String

ORM includes Formal ORM Language (FORML), a textual language for verbalizing ORM models in semi-natural language that is intelligible to nontechnical users [12]. Its latest version, FORML 2, is designed for both input and output [16]. To facilitate compact expression in this language, mapping from entities to semantic values, and from semantic values to data values is often implicitly performed. For example, given the refmode declaration Gender(.code), the condition "Gender 'M'" is implicitly expanded to "Gender **that** has GenderCode **that** $\approx$ 'M'". Moreover, a user comparison between semantic values (e.g. CountryCode = Pronoun) is interpreted as a comparison between their data value representations, as this is the likely intent. In practice, such mappings can be implemented efficiently (e.g. using tagged types and autoboxing/unboxing).

3   Facts, Fact Types, Constraints and Reference Schemes

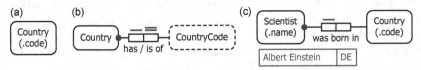

Fig. 6. A refmode in (a) compact and (b) expanded form, and (c) a populated fact type

Figures 6(a) and 6(b) display an entity type with a reference mode, in compact and expanded forms. The short predicate reading "has" is convenient for compact display, but for formalization this is auto-expanded to the predicate name "hasCountryCode". In principle, one could instead use "has" as the full predicate name, but this would often require long disjunctive type declarations for predicates, e.g. $\forall x,y$ (x has $y \rightarrow$ [(Country x & CountryCode y) $\vee$ (Scientist x & ScientistName y) $\vee$ ...]). If necessary, short predicate readings are auto-expanded to fact type readings to ensure they are distinct. For example, the inverse predicate reading "is of" expands to "CountryCodeIsOfCountry" An ORM fact type corresponds to a set of one or more typed predicates. Binary predicates with no front or trailing text are placed in infix position. In general, ORM supports mixfix predicates of any arity. This schema may be formalized thus:

$$\forall x \text{ (Country } x \rightarrow \text{ Entity } x) \ \& \ \forall x \text{ (CountryCode } x \rightarrow \text{ SemanticValue } x)$$
$$\forall x,y \ [x \text{ hasCountryCode } y \rightarrow (\text{Country } x \ \& \ \text{CountryCode } y)]$$
$$\forall x \text{ (Country } x \rightarrow \exists^1 y \ x \text{ hasCountryCode } y)$$
$$\forall y \text{ (CountryCode } y \rightarrow \exists^{0..1} x \ x \text{ hasCountryCode } y)$$
$$\forall x,y \text{ (} x \text{ CountryCodeIsOfCountry } y \equiv y \text{ hasCountryCode } x \text{)}$$
$$\forall x \text{ (} x \text{ isIdentified } \rightarrow \text{ Entity } x)$$
$$\forall x,y \ [x \text{ hasCountryCode } y \rightarrow x \text{ isIdentified}]$$

The notion of *preferred reference* (indicated by the double uniqueness bar) is formalized by reserving the postfix predicate isIdentified for "is identified by a preferred reference scheme", allowing its use for any entity by the penultimate declaration above, and then indicating a fact type (as in the last formula above), or a conjunction or disjunction of fact types, used to provide the identification.

Figure 6(c) displays a binary fact type and sample fact. The entity type Scientist and its refmode may be formalized in a similar way to Country. The below formalization of the fact type Scientist was born in Country using the predicate name "was born in" assumes this short predicate reading is not used for another predicate in the schema (e.g. in fact types such as Horse was born in Country or "Person was born in City"). If this assumption does not hold, expand the predicate name with object type names as needed. Such expansions have no impact on ORM diagrams (which use predicate readings not predicate names) and can often be avoided by renaming (e.g. rename Horse was born in Country to Horse was foaled in Country). For discussion of an alternative approach allowing reuse of predicates with disjunctive type arguments see [8].

$$\forall x,y \ [x \text{ was born in } y \rightarrow (\text{Scientist } x \ \& \ \text{Country } y)]$$
$$\forall x \text{ (Scientist } x \rightarrow \exists^1 y \ x \text{ was born in } y)$$

In ORM, an object type is said to be a top-level object type if it is not a subtype of any domain object type (excluding Entity, SemanticValue, DataValue, and Object if included). In ORM, top-level entity types are implicitly mutually exclusive, so if Scientist and Country in Figure 6(c) are top-level, the following constraint applies implicitly: $\forall x$ (Scientist x → ~Country x). Similarly, top-level semantic value types are implicitly mutually exclusive, so if ScientistName and CountryCode are top-level, the following constraint applies implicitly: $\forall x$ (ScientistName x → ~CountryCode x).

Given the schema formulae, *fact populations* may be formalized as existential assertions. We allow individual variables to start with any letter and include more letters or digits, permitting suggestive individual variable names. For example, using "*s*" for scientist, "*sn*" for scientist name, "*c*" for country, and "*cc*" for country code, the fact depicted in Figure 6(c) may be formalized thus: $\exists s,sn,c,cc$ (s hasScientistName sn & $sn \approx$ 'Albert Einstein' & c hasCountryCode cc & $cc \approx$ 'DE' & s wasBornIn c).

Most ORM constraints may now be formalized using formulae that are basically equivalent to those used in our doctoral thesis [5], but supplemented where needed by preferred reference declarations. For example, the preferred external uniqueness constraint in Figure 7(a) may be formalized thus:

$$\forall c,sc \; \exists^{0..1}s \; (s \text{ isInCountry } c \; \& \; s \text{ hasStateCode } sc)$$
$$\forall s,c,sc \; [(s \text{ isInCountry } c \; \& \; s \text{ hasStateCode } sc) \rightarrow s \text{ isIdentified}]$$

ORM allows reference schemes of arbitrary complexity, which may include entity-to-entity relationships. As a trivial example, the schema for President in Figure 7(b), which identifies a president by the country of which he/she is president, may be formalized using techniques already discussed. As a recent extension to ORM 2, Figure 7(c) shows a disjunctive reference scheme in which a chief officer is identified by the company to which he/she bears exactly one of two relationships, e.g. "the CEO of Megasoft" or "the CTO of Megasoft". The reference scheme may be formalized thus:

$$\forall x,y \; [x \text{ is chief executive officer of } y \rightarrow (\text{ChiefOfficer } x \; \& \; \text{Company } y)]$$
$$\forall x,y \; [x \text{ is chief technical officer of } y \rightarrow (\text{ChiefOfficer } x \; \& \; \text{Company } y)]$$
$$\forall x \; [\text{ChiefOfficer } x \rightarrow \exists^1 y \; (x \text{ is chief executive officer of } y$$
$$\vee \; x \text{ is chief technical officer of } y)]$$
$$\forall x,y \; [x \text{ is chief executive officer of } y \rightarrow {\sim}\exists z(x \text{ is chief technical officer of } z)]$$
$$\forall y \; (\text{Company } y \rightarrow \exists^{0..1}x \; x \text{ is chief executive officer of } y)$$
$$\forall y \; (\text{Company } y \rightarrow \exists^{0..1}x \; x \text{ is chief technical officer of } y)$$
$$\forall x,y \; [(x \text{ is chief executive officer of } y \vee x \text{ is chief technical officer of } y)$$
$$\rightarrow x \text{ isIdentified}]$$

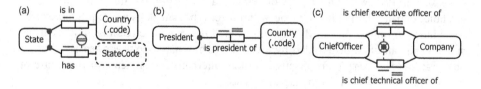

Fig. 7. Some different kinds of preferred reference schemes

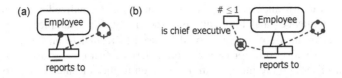

Fig. 8. (a) An incorrect ORM schema fragment, and (b) a correct ORM schema fragment

The ORM schema in Figure 8(a) includes an acyclic ring fact type. Formalization of all ring constraints in ORM is discussed in detail in [14], so is omitted here, other than noting that recursive constraints such as acyclicity and strong intransitivity are assigned fixed point semantics. The combination of mandatory role, uniqueness, and acyclicity constraints in Figure 8(a) says that each employee has exactly one employee to which he/she reports, and the reporting relation is acyclic. This is allowed in classical logic, where the Employee domain may be infinite. However, this constraint pattern is illegal in ORM because all its domain predicates (including the Employee type predicate) must be *finite*. The schema in Figure 8(b) fixes the problem by using an exclusive-or constraint to ensure that each employee is either a chief executive or reports to a manager but not both. A chief executive may now reside at the top of the reporting hierarchy without reporting to any employee.

The *role cardinality constraint* "# ≤ 1" ensures that there is at most one employee who is chief executive, i.e. $\exists^{0..1} x$ x is chief executive. This is one of the new kinds of constraint introduced in ORM 2, along with deontic constraints, value-comparison constraints and others. By interpreting a state of the business model as a possible world, the constraints discussed so far may be treated as alethic, implicitly prepending the alethic necessity operator □ of modal logic to the usual constraint formula, e.g. □ $\forall x$ (Scientist $x \rightarrow \exists^1 y$ x was born in y). *Deontic* constraints are obligations rather than necessities, and are formalized by prepending the deontic "it is obligatory that" operator O to the usual constraint formula. For example, $O\forall x$ (Driver $x \rightarrow x$ is licensed to drive). For further discussion of deontic constraints, see [7]. There is no space here to formalize all the constraint varieties in ORM 2, but the constraint formalization patterns not discussed here are typically straightforward or are discussed elsewhere.

The formalizations provided here use unsorted logic, but may trivially be re-expressed using *sorted logic*, where the individual variables range over specific object types. For example, $\forall x$(Country $x \rightarrow$ Entity x) may be reformulated as $\forall x$:Country Entity x. Sorted logic formulae correspond more closely to FORML verbalizations, which use subscripted variables to distinguish variables of the same type (e.g. x:Person and y:Person may be rewritten as Person$_1$ and Person$_2$).

4   Derivation Options

ORM 2 fact types and object subtypes may be asserted, derived, or semiderived [15]. A semiderived type may have asserted instances and derived instances. Derivation rules for derived fact types and derived subtypes may be complete (iff-rules) or incomplete (if-rules). Complete derivation rules are formalized as universally quantified equivalences, e.g. $\forall x,y[x$ is father of $y \equiv (x$ is a parent of y & x is male)]. Incomplete derivation rules and semiderived rules are formalized as universally quantified implications, e.g. $\forall x,y[x$ is a grandparent of $y \leftarrow \exists z(x$ is a parent of z & z is a parent of $y)]$.

In ORM, equality and subset constraints are also formalized using universally quantified equivalences and implications respectively. For example, the conditional $\forall x[x$ is cancer prone $\leftarrow x$ smokes) could be used to formalize an ORM subset constraint or the derivation rule for an incomplete derived fact type or a semiderived fact type. Which of these three interpretations is given to the formula is an important implementation choice. For example, if we use a subset constraint then we cannot add the fact that Pat smokes without explicitly adding the fact that Pat is cancer prone. However, with a derived or semiderived fact type we can add the fact that Pat smokes, and leave it to the system to infer that Pat is cancer prone. In ORM, this implementation choice is reflected by explicitly classifying the declaration as a constraint or derivation rule, and this choice is depicted graphically in different ways on ORM diagrams. When mapping from ORM to Datalog^{LB}, we map constraints to "right-arrow rules" using the forward implication operator "->", and we map derivation rules to "left-arrow rules" using the converse implication operator "<-", since this is how Datalog^{LB} distinguishes syntactically between these choices [13].

There is no space here to give a full account of derivation in ORM, but we note in passing that the description logics and the Web Ontology Language (OWL) [24] currently have no way to choose to implement conditionals as integrity constraints [19], though some proposals have been made to extend OWL in this direction [21].

5   Conclusion

This paper extended previous work on formalization of ORM by replacing the former metalevel subtyping association between semantic value type and data type by a mapping relationship, axiomatizing a special representation relationship to support this mapping at the instance level, formalizing preferred reference schemes and various constraint and rule patterns, and briefly discussing the use of finite model theory, sorted logic, and choices for implementing certain kinds of logical formulae as constraints or derivation rules. Current and future research efforts in this regard are focused on providing a more rigorous and complete formalization and implementation of ORM derivation and query facilities, including negation, bag functions, and extended support for dynamic constraints and rules [2].

Acknowledgement. This paper's treatment of semantic values has benefited from discussion with colleagues, especially Matt Curland, Andy Carver and Lex Spoon.

References

1. Abiteboul, S., Hull, R., Vianu, V.: Foundations of Databases. Addison-Wesley, Reading (1995)
2. Balsters, H., Halpin, T.: Formal Semantics of Dynamic Rules in ORM. In: Meersman, R., Tari, Z., Herrero, P. (eds.) OTM-WS 2008. LNCS, vol. 5333, pp. 699–708. Springer, Heidelberg (2008)
3. Chen, P.P.: The entity-relationship model—towards a unified view of data. ACM Transactions on Database Systems 1(1), 9–36 (1976), http://csc.lsu.edu/news/erd.pdf
4. De Troyer, O.: On Data Schema Transformations. PhD Thesis, Tilburg University (1993) ISBN 90-9005913-X

5. Halpin, T.: A Logical Analysis of Information Systems: static aspects of the data-oriented perspective. Doctoral dissertation, University of Queensland (1989), http://www.orm.net/Halpin_PhDthesis.pdf
6. Halpin, T.: ORM 2. In: Meersman, R., Tari, Z., Herrero, P. (eds.) OTM-WS 2005. LNCS, vol. 3762, pp. 676–687. Springer, Heidelberg (2005)
7. Halpin, T.: Modality of Business Rules. In: Siau, K. (ed.) Research Issues in Systems Analysis and Design, Databases and Software Development, pp. 206–226. IGI Publishing, Hershey (2007)
8. Halpin, T.: Predicate Reference and Navigation in ORM. In: Meersman, R., Herrero, P., Dillon, T. (eds.) OTM 2009 Workshops. LNCS, vol. 5872, pp. 723–734. Springer, Heidelberg (2009)
9. Halpin, T.: Object-Role Modeling: Principles and Benefits. International Journal of Information Systems Modeling and Design 1(1), 32–54 (2010)
10. Halpin, T.: Structural Aspects of Data Modeling Languages. In: Halpin, T., Nurcan, S., Krogstie, J., Soffer, P., Proper, E., Schmidt, R., Bider, I. (eds.) BPMDS 2011 and EMMSAD 2011. LNBIP, vol. 81, pp. 428–442. Springer, Heidelberg (2011)
11. Halpin, T.: Fact-Orientation and Conceptual Logic. In: Proc. 15th International EDOC Conference, pp. 14–19. IEEE Computer Society, Helsinki (2011)
12. Halpin, T., Curland, M.: Automated Verbalization for ORM 2. In: Meersman, R., Tari, Z., Herrero, P. (eds.) OTM 2006 Workshops. LNCS, vol. 4278, pp. 1181–1190. Springer, Heidelberg (2006)
13. Halpin, T., Curland, M., Stirewalt, K., Viswanath, N., McGill, M., Beck, S.: Mapping ORM to Datalog: An Overview. In: Meersman, R., Dillon, T., Herrero, P. (eds.) OTM 2010. LNCS, vol. 6428, pp. 504–513. Springer, Heidelberg (2010)
14. Halpin, T., Curland, M.: Enriched Support for Ring Constraints. In: Meersman, R., Dillon, T., Herrero, P. (eds.) OTM-WS 2011. LNCS, vol. 7046, pp. 309–318. Springer, Heidelberg (2011)
15. Halpin, T., Morgan, T.: Information Modeling and Relational Databases, 2nd edn. Morgan Kaufmann, San Francisco (2008)
16. Halpin, T., Wijbenga, J.P.: FORML 2. In: Bider, I., Halpin, T., Krogstie, J., Nurcan, S., Proper, E., Schmidt, R., Ukor, R. (eds.) BPMDS 2010 and EMMSAD 2010. LNBIP, vol. 50, pp. 247–260. Springer, Heidelberg (2010)
17. ter Hofstede, A., Proper, H., van der Weide, T.: Formal definition of a conceptual language for the description and manipulation of information models. Information Systems 18(7), 489–523 (1993)
18. Keet, C.: Prospects for and issues with mapping the Object-Role Modeling language into DLRifd. In: 20th Int. Workshop on Description Logics (DL 2007). CEUR-WS, vol. 250, pp. 331–338 (2007)
19. Krötzsch, M., Simancik, F., Horrocks, I.: A Description Logic Primer, eprint arXiv:1201.4089 (2012), http://arxiv.org/abs/1201.4089
20. Libkin, L.: The Finite Model Theory Toolbox of a Database Theoretician. In: PODS 2009 (2009) ACM 978-1-60558-553-6/09/06
21. Motik, B., Horrocks, I., Sattler, U.: Bridging the Gap Between OWL and Relational Databases. J. of Web Semantics 7(2), 74–89 (2009)
22. Object Management Group: Unified Modeling Language Specification, version 2.4.1 (2011), http://www.omg.org/spec/UML/2.4.1/
23. Wintraecken, J.: The NIAM Information Analysis Method: Theory and Practice. Kluwer, Deventer (1990)
24. W3C: OWL 2 Web Ontology Language: Direc Semantics (2009), http://www.w3.org/TR/owl2-direct-semantics/

ORM Logic-Based English (OLE) and the ORM ReDesigner Tool: Fact-Based Reengineering and Migration of Relational Databases

Herman Balsters

University of Groningen
Faculty of Economics and Business
P.O. Box 800 9700 AV Groningen,
The Netherlands
h.balsters@rug.nl

Abstract. The problem of database reengineering stems from (legacy) databases that are hard to understand (incorrect-, incomplete- or missing semantics) or that perform inefficiently. Reengineering is often cumbersome due to lack of semantics of the original database, and often the data migration target is also unclear. This paper addresses those two problems. We shall show how fact-based modeling, in particular ORM and its representation in (sugared) Sorted Logic, can help in reengineering (relational) databases. We reconstruct the semantics of the source database by offering a set of natural-language sentences capturing conceptual structure and constraints of the source. These sentences are written in a structured natural language format, coined as OLE: *ORM Logic-based English*. OLE is then used to define the mappings from the original source to a reengineered and restructured target database. We shall also discuss the ORMReDesigner: a semi-automatic tool, based on OLE and NORMA, available as a research prototype, used for reengineering and migrating relational databases.

Keywords: Reengineering, data migration, fact-based modeling, structured English, derivation rules.

0   Introduction

Object-Role Modeling (ORM) is a fact-oriented approach for modeling information in terms of the underlying facts, where facts and rules may be verbalized in a language easily understandable by non-technical domain experts. In contrast to Entity-Relationship (ER) modeling [8] and Unified Modeling Language (UML) class diagrams [27], ORM models are attribute-free, treating all facts as relationships (unary, binary, ternary etc.). ORM does, however, include procedures (e.g. the RMap [18]) for mapping to attribute-based structures, such as those of ER or UML. For a basic introduction to ORM see [17], for a thorough treatment see [18]. We will use the term Fact-based modelling (FBM [14]) as the general name of several fact-based conceptual data modelling dialects, such as ORM, Natural language Information

P. Herrero et al. (Eds.): OTM 2012 Workshops, LNCS 7567, pp. 358–367, 2012.

Analysis Method (NIAM) [17], and Fully-Communication Oriented Information Modeling (FCO-IM) [1].

Database reengineering of a source database, and subsequent data migration to some target database, is an important activity in both academia and current database practice [2,3,4,5,12,21,22,24,25,28,29]. Reengineering is often cumbersome due to lack of semantics of the original database, and often the data migration target is also unclear. In practice, it may be the case that the target schema is fixed, in which case there is similarity with the data exchange problem [13]. In our case, however, we deal with the situation where we are free in choosing a suitable target schema.

Reengineering involves the reconstruction of the semantics of some source database. Subsequent data migration involves mapping a source database schema to a target database schema. We shall show how Fact-based modeling, in particular ORM and its representation in (sugared) Sorted Logic [7], can help in reengineering (relational) databases. We reconstruct the semantics of each table from the source database by offering a set of natural-language sentences capturing the intended semantics of that table, as well as its conceptual structure and constraints. These sentences are written in a structured natural language format, coined as OLE: *ORM Logic-based English*. OLE closely follows the representation of ORM models in terms of Sorted Logic as offered in [15]. OLE is used to specify elementary facts and constraints in ORM. The OLE-syntax is consistent with a subset of Common Logic Controlled English (CLCE, [11]). CLCE has been adopted by the OMG [26], and is accepted as an ISO standard [23]. A related specification language used to describe the contents (facts and rules) of ORM models is CQL [20]. Texts in CQL can be seen as an alternative for ORM diagrams to model the Universe of Discourse (UoD). FORML2 [19], a highly expressive natural-language based specification language for derivation rules in ORM, but FORML2 (unlike OLE) is not directly based on logic.

OLE expressions are used as input for the NORMA tool [9,10], to generate associated ORM models. OLE will be used to read and write derivation rules for derived fact types. Since the derivation rules are written in a structured natural language format, they can be easily validated by non-technical domain experts. Since NORMA does not support view definitions in SQL, we will use OLE, and the so-called CoRef-version of ORM [18], to eventually obtain fully-defined view-version DDL. Our method for reengineering and migrating is supported by a semi-automatic tool [28] called ORMReDesigner. In section 1, we describe the migration problem using a simple case, and offer an introduction to the OLE language. Section 2 shows how to apply OLE to reengineer the semantics of a source database. Section 3 shows how OLE offers derivation rules that eventually lead to a view-version DDL of the target database. Section 4 offers some notes on OLE and the ORMReDesigner tool. Finally, in Section 5, we offer some conclusions. This paper uses basic ORM notations, cf. [16,18].

1   Structured English for Reengineering

The main reasons for reengineering an existing database system usually deal with that system being incorrect, incomplete, or inefficient. Reengineering, or restructuring, such a system entails that the redesigner has to construct a model of the existing system, as well as construct a model of the improved database. Designers want to specify facts and rules to describe their business context, and how that context relates to the database that has to be redesigned. For that purpose, they don't want to use SQL, e.g., since SQL -for this purpose- will be too technical, too implementation directed, and too difficult to validate directly. What they would like, is a language that is easy to read and write by both designers and domain experts: hence, the facts and rules should be able to be validated by a non-technical domain expert. At the same time, the language has to be expressive enough to capture typical business rules and constraints, and also be precise enough to eventually translate to a technical platform.

We will reconstruct the semantics of each database table from a given source database by offering a corresponding natural language sentence capturing the intended meaning of the table heading. The first offering of this sentence can be in informal semantics/syntax. This soft-semantics sentence is then rewritten to a structured format, coined as **OLE**: *ORM Logic-based English*. This format is mandatory and fixed for the user. OLE is a sugared form of Sorted Logic, and is easy to read and write by non-technical domain experts. OLE expressions are expressed as elementary facts. Objects are categorized as entities and values, and entities are offered reference modes. All elementary facts in OLE may be added with the following relevant constraints: uniqueness, mandatory constraints , external uniqueness, and subtyping. Entities may also be identified by using compound reference schemes.

Let's start by offering an example of a very simple database in need of redesign. Consider the following source table

STUDENT(nr, project, mentor, projectDescription)

where this table has the key (nr, project). The semantics of this table could be offered by: *"Student is identified by number and has mentor for the project described by projectDescription"*. Note that this semantics is offered as an informal English sentence, hence providing a soft semantics definition of the table meaning. Also note that this table is a candidate for reengineering, because the semantics definition reveals that we are dealing with a composite fact type. In general, we could say that a table is in *acceptable format*, when the table is normalized (no redundancy), and has a correct and complete semantics (including all relevant constraints and derivation rules). Our example table is therefore not acceptable, because it contains a non-key dependency *project → projectDescription*, telling us that the STUDENT table is not normalized.

The following section introduces the OLE language and ORMReDesigner method, and shows how to apply this method to our example source table STUDENT in order to transform it into an acceptable database.

2   OLE and ORM ReDesigner Method

In order to reengineer our example table, we (i.e, the redesigner) try to discover (together with the domain expert) all of the elementary facts within our soft-semantics description of the source table. In our case, we find the following fact types

- Student has Mentor for Project
- Project is described by ProjectDescription

The elementary fact types are the basic building blocks for our target model (avoiding eventual redundancy in the resulting databases).

Subsequently, for each elementary fact, we list all entities and values, along with reference modes and associated basic types. In our case we find

- Student **is Entity (and is referred to by** nr **(of type** integer**))**
- Mentor **is Entity (and is referred to by** name **(of type** varchar(25)**)))**
- Project **is Entity (and is referred to by** code **(of type** char(4)**)))**
- Description **is Value (with Datatype** varchar(20)**))**

The third step involves listing all uniqueness constraints for each elementary fact

- **for each** Student **and** Project, **there is at most one** Mentor, **such that** Student has Mentor for Project
- **for each** Project, **there is exactly one** Description, **such that** Project has Description

Note that all of the expressions listed above are examples of valid OLE-expressions (where bold-case syntax indicates a reserved word). Also note that any **such that**-part always binds to the **there is**-part that is nearest to it; in that way no ambiguity can arise from its reading. In Sorted Logic the last two OLE-expressions would read as

- ∀x:Student ∀y:Project ∃$^{0..1}$z:Mentor Student has Mentor for Project
- ∀x:Project ∃^{1}y:Description Project has Description

Our ORM ReDesigner tool will assist in offering suggestions for the second and third steps listed above. Inputting the fact types, entities, values, and constraints into the *NORMA tool* will yield the following proper ORM model (intended to replace the schema of the original STUDENT base table)

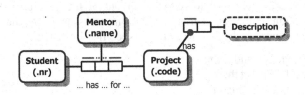

Fig. 1. Target Model M1

Our aim is to eventually construct a set of views in SQL that serve as a (virtual) target database: the original source database STUDENT is used to populate this set of views (which we shall call the Target View). In order to do so, we will perform a *binary breakdown* of the Target model M1 by taking the *co-referenced* version of model M1. In CoRef-ORM, only binary fact types with functional uniqueness constraints have to be considered, along with subtyping relations and all constraints. The CoRef-version of model M1 results in the following model M2

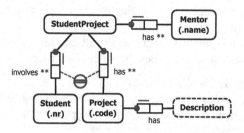

Fig. 2. Target Model M2

Model M2 is the direct conceptual counterpart of a relational view used as the starting point for an eventual implementation of our target view. M2 has the following advantages over model M1

- it is the model format that is *as close as possible* to the desired view-table format
- it is, however, still possible to reason *completely on the conceptual level* about M2 (semantics are given by fully validated elementary fact statements), this in contrast to the corresponding relational view DB-Target (table headings do **not** offer the underlying fact types!)
- it offers fully re-engineered, re-structured and validated semantics of the original source database

For all of the above-mentioned reasons, we use this binary model M2 as the basis for offering the derivation rules that will eventually calculate the population of our Target View. These derivation rules (fully defined in OLE) offer what we call the *binary build-up* of the restructured database (our Target View). We note that very basic CoRef-versions of ORM models can also be *generated* by the NORMA tool (the modeler will, however, often have to redo the layout of the generated model). In deriving the population of the target model M2 from an assumed population of the source model M1, we employ the following rules (specified in OLE):

(1) **for each** Student, Project, **and** Mentor,
if Student has Mentor for Project **then**
there is some StudentProject , **such that**
StudentProject involves Student **and**
StudentProject involves Project **and**
StudentProject has Mentor

(2) **for each** StudentProject, Student, Project, **and** Mentor,
if StudentProject involves Student **and**
StudentProject has Project **and**
StudentProject has Mentor **then**
Student has Mentor for Project

Rule (1) tells us that entity type StudentProject is *at least* populated by taking instances from fact type Student has Mentor for Project from Model M1. Rule (2) tells us that entity type StudentProject is *at most* populated by instances taken from fact type Student has Mentor for Project from Model M1. We can now prove the following properties, written in OLE (proof is based on previous rules (1, 2) and the uniqueness constraints taken from M1):

(i) **for each** Student **and** Project,
there is at most one StudentProject, **such that**
StudentProject involves Student **and**
StudentProject has Project

(ii) **for each** StudentProject,
there is exactly one Student, **such that**
StudentProject involves Student

(iii) **for each** StudentProject,
there is exactly one Project, **such that**
StudentProject has Project

We shall refrain from offering the actual proofs (that would be out of the scope of this paper), but these could be offered by coding OLE-expressions (1, 2) as well as the OLE-expressions (i, ii, iii) as formulas in first-order logic, and then provide the proofs by using, e.g., natural deduction trees [15] .

Properties (i), (ii), and (iii) now allow us to introduce the following (derived) *compound reference scheme* for StudentProject written in OLE:

StudentProject **is Entity (and is referred to by** Student **and** Project, **where**
StudentProject involves Student **and** StudentProject has Project)

Rules (1, 2) are sufficient for target model M2 to have all of the desired properties of the CoRef-version of model M1. Equipped with this knowledge, we shall proceed, in the subsequent section, by defining derivation rules for the target view.

3   Derivation Rules for the Target View

In this section, we aim to define a virtual target database (Target View) with the following schema where all of the attributes and all of the constraint properties (PK, FK) are derived.

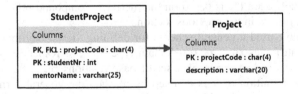

Fig. 3. Target View

We note that this target view has model M2 as its (full) conceptual counterpa

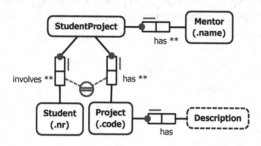

where all of the (binary and functional) fact types and all of the constraint properties (uniqueness constraints, mandatories) are derived (cf. previous section).

We now offer a list of derivation rules -specified in OLE- that takes the source base relation STUDENT(nr,mentor,project,projectDescription) as the input schema, and offers definitions of the derived attributes in the target view:

(1) **for each** Nr, Name, **and** Code,
  there is some StudentProject, **such that**
    the studentNr **of** StudentProject **is that** Nr **and**
    the mentorName **of** StudentProject **is that** Name **and**
    the projectCode **of** StudentProject **is that** Code
iff
there is some STUDENT, **such that**
  STUDENT.nr = Nr **and**
  STUDENT.project = Code **and**
  STUDENT.mentor = Nam

(2) **for each** Nr, Name, String **and** Code,
  there is some Project, **such that**
    the projectCode **of** Project **is that** Code **and**
    the Description **of** Project **is that** Name
iff
there is some STUDENT, **such that**
  STUDENT.nr = Nr **and**
  STUDENT.project = Code **and**
  STUDENT.mentor = Name **and**
  STUDENT.projectDescription = **that** String

We note that definition (1) is based on the (derived) compound reference scheme for StudentProject, proved in the previous section.

Here, we have used a general scheme for defining views. Say that we have some view V, with attributes $x_1, .., x_n$, (of domain type $X_1, .., X_n$ respectively), and that the view is to be defined in terms of a set of base relations $B_1, .., B_m$. If the predicate describing the definition of V is denoted by Ψ, then the general formula (in Sorted Logic) stating that V is defined in terms of Ψ can be stated as

$$\forall x_1{:}X_1, .., \forall x_n{:}X_n \ [\exists v{:}V \ v(x_1, .., x_n) \Leftrightarrow \exists b_1{:}B_1, .., \exists b_m{:}B_m \ \Psi(b1, .., bm, x_1, .., x_n)]$$

Note that our OLE-specifications (1,2) offered directly above, refer to the base relation STUDENT. The general idea is that we take the original base relations of the (to be reengineered) source database, which subsequently offer the input population for the derivation rules of a target view. In this manner we migrate the data from the source database to a target view. Once this process has been completed, we can change the status of the target view into that of the actual target database. OLE-definitions offer an alternative for SQL-syntax; an OLE-text easy to read and write – and, hence, validated- by non-technical domain experts.

The ORMReDesigner tool assists in writing OLE-specifications like (1, 2) listed above; in this case the tool will generate the following specifications

Define the target table StudentProject
with column names StudentNr, projectCode, mentorName **as:**
rows consisting of STUDENT.nr, STUDENT.project, STUDENT.mentor
for each STUDENT

Define the target table Project
with column names projectCode, description **as:**
rows consisting of STUDENT.project, STUDENT.projectDescription
for each STUDENT

and subsequently the tool generates the following view definitions in SQL

```
CREATE VIEW `Project` (`projectCode`, `descriptionName`)
AS SELECT `STUDENT`.`Project`, `STUDENT`.`ProjectDescription`
FROM `STUDENT`;

CREATE VIEW `StudentProject` (`studentNr`, `projectCode`, `mentorName`)
AS SELECT `STUDENT`.`nr`, `STUDENT`.`Project`, `STUDENT`.`Mentor`
FROM `STUDENT`;
```

4 Some Notes on OLE and the ORMReDesigner

OLE has been offered a full BNF language specification [6], which was implemented in the ORMReDesigner [28]. In [6] we have made a comparison between OLE, ORM, and first-order predicate logic (in particular Sorted Logic), and we demonstrated that

- OLE contains at least the expressive power of Sorted Logic
- OLE can handle most of ORM's fact type constructions and constraints

Space limitations, however, do not allow for more details on the above-mentioned aspects of OLE. In this paper, we have taken only a simple base relation as a case study; we have, however, successfully applied OLE and the ORMReDesigner to larger case studies (e.g. migrating patient medical records from two different hospitals to a common EPD (Electronic Patient Dossier) database). Both OLE and the ORMReDesigner proved in practice to be reasonably simple to use, both by the non-technical domain expert (involved in the validation of the OLE-specifications) and professional designer (using the tool to migrate databases).

5   Conclusions

The problem of database reengineering stems from (legacy) databases that are hard to understand (incorrect and/or incomplete semantics) or that perform inefficiently. Database reengineering is often cumbersome due to lack of semantics of the original database, and often the data migration target is also unclear. We have shown how fact-based modeling, in particular ORM and its representation in (sugared) Sorted Logic, can help in reengineering (relational) databases. We reconstruct the semantics of the source database by offering a set of natural-language sentences capturing the conceptual structure and constraints of the source. These sentences are written in a structured natural language format, coined as OLE: *ORM Logic-based English*. OLE is used to define the mappings from the original source to a reengineered target database. We have also discussed the ORM ReDesigner: a semi-automatic tool, based on OLE and NORMA, available as a research prototype, used for reengineering and migrating relational databases.

References

1. Bakema, G., Zwart, J., van der Lek, H.: Fully Communication Oriented Information Modelling. Ten Hagen Stam (2000)
2. Balsters, H., de Brock, E.O.: Integration of Integrity Constraints in Federated Schemata Based on Tight Constraining. In: Meersman, R. (ed.) OTM 2004. LNCS, vol. 3290, pp. 748–767. Springer, Heidelberg (2004)
3. Balsters, H., Halpin, T.: Modeling data federations in ORM. In: Meersman, R., Tari, Z. (eds.) OTM-WS 2007, Part I. LNCS, vol. 4805, pp. 657–666. Springer, Heidelberg (2007)
4. Balsters, H., Huitema, G.B.: Semantics of Outsourced and Interoperable Information Systems. In: Morel, M. (ed.) Interoperability for Enterprize Software and Applications. Springer, Berlin (2007)
5. Balsters, H., Haarsma, B.: An ORM-Driven Implementation Framework for Database Federations. In: Meersman, R., Herrero, P., Dillon, T. (eds.) OTM 2009 Workshops. LNCS, vol. 5872, pp. 659–670. Springer, Heidelberg (2009)
6. Balsters, H.: ORM Logic-based English (OLE) and the ORM ReDesigner tool: Fact-based Re-engineering and Migration of Relational Databases, Technical Report, Faculty of Economics and Business (May 2012)
7. Chang, C.C., Keisler, H.J.: Model Theory. Studies in Logic and the Foundations of Mathematics, vol. 73. North Holland Publishing Company (1977)
8. Chen, P.P.: The entity-relationship model—towards a unified view of data. ACM Transactions on Database Systems 1(1), 9–36 (1976)
9. Curland, M., Halpin, T.: Model Driven Development with NORMA. In: Proc. 40th Int. Conf. on System Sciences (HICSS-40). IEEE Computer Society (January 2007)

10. Curland, M., Halpin, T.: The Norma Tool for Orm 2. In: Pernici, B. (ed.) Advanced Information Systems Engineering. LNCS, vol. 6051. Springer, Heidelberg (2010)
11. Common Logic, http://www.Common-Logic.org
12. Drumm, C., Schmitt, M., Do, H.H., Rahm, E.: Quickmig: Automatic schema matching for data migration projects (2007)
13. Embley, D.W., Xu, L., Ding, Y.: Automatic direct and indirect schema mapping: experiences and lessons learned. SIGMOD Record 33(4), 14–19 (2004)
14. FBM working group: Fact-based modeling exchange schema. Version 20111021c (2011), http://www.factbasedmodeling.org/
15. Halpin, T.: A Logical Analysis of Information Systems: static aspects of the data-oriented perspective. Doctoral dissertation, University of Queensland (1989), http://www.orm.net/Halpin_PhDthesis.pdf
16. Halpin, T.: ORM 2. In: Meersman, R., Tari, Z., Herrero, P. (eds.) OTM-WS 2005. LNCS, vol. 3762, pp. 676–687. Springer, Heidelberg (2005)
17. Halpin, T.: ORM/NIAM Object-Role Modeling. In: Bernus, P., Mertins, K., Schmidt, G. (eds.) Handbook on Information Systems Architectures, 2nd edn., pp. 81–103. Springer, Heidelberg (2006)
18. Halpin, T., Morgan, T.: Information Modeling and Relational Databases, 2nd edn. Morgan Kaufmann, San Francisco (2008)
19. Halpin, T., Wijbenga, J.P.: FORML 2. In: Bider, I., Halpin, T., Krogstie, J., Nurcan, S., Proper, E., Schmidt, R., Ukor, R. (eds.) BPMDS 2010 and EMMSAD 2010. LNBIP, vol. 50, pp. 247–260. Springer, Heidelberg (2010)
20. Heath, C.: The constellation query language. In: OTM 2009: ORM Workshop, OTM 2009, pp. 1–10 (2009)
21. Henrard, J., Roland, D., Cleve, A., Hainaut, J.-L.: An Industrial Experience Report on Legacy Data-Intensive System Migration. In: IEEE International Conference on Software Maintenance, pp. 473–476 (2007)
22. Hull, R.: Managing Semantic Heterogeneity in Databases. In: ACM PODS 1997. ACM Press (1997)
23. ISO, http://standards.iso.org/ittf/licence.html
24. Lenzerini, M.: Data integration: a theoretical perspective. In: ACM PODS 2002. ACM Press (2002)
25. Lin, C.Y.: Migrating to relational systems: Problems, methods, and strategies. Contemporary Management Research 4(4), 369–380 (2008)
26. OMG/FUML, http://www.omg.org/spec/FUML
27. OMG/UML: OMG Unified Modeling Language (OMG UML), Superstructure, Version 2.3 (May 2010)
28. Pastoor, J.J.: Database-migratie en -normalisatie in ORM Logic-based English (in Dutch), Bachelor's thesis, University of Groningen (2012)
29. Sluis, T.C.: The ORM Infusion Migration Method, Master's Thesis, University of Groningen (2011)
30. Wu, L., Sahraoui, H., Valtchev, P.: Coping with legacy system migration complexity. In: 10th IEEE International Conference on Engineering of Complex Computer Systems, ICECCS 2005, pp. 600–609 (2005)

ORM2: Formalisation and Encoding in OWL2

Enrico Franconi[1], Alessandro Mosca[1], and Dmitry Solomakhin[2]

Free University of Bozen-Bolzano, Italy
lastname@inf.unibz.it,
Dmitry.Solomakhin@stud-inf.unibz.it

Abstract. This paper introduces ORM2^{plus} – a new linear syntax and complete semantics expressed in first order logic of ORM2 – which can be shown correctly embedding the original proposal. A provably correct encoding of the core fragment ORM2^{zero} in the $\mathcal{ALCQI}$ description logic (a fragment of OWL2 with qualified cardinality restrictions and inverse roles) is presented. Complexity of reasoning on ORM2 conceptual schemas, and the EXPTIME-membership of reasoning on ORM2^{zero}, are also shown. On the basis of these results, a systematic critique of alternative approaches to the formalisation of ORM2 in (description) logics published so far is provided. A prototype has been implemented providing a backend for the automated support of implicit constraints deduction, schema consistency checks, and user-defined constraints entailment, for ORM2^{zero} conceptual schemas along with its translation into $\mathcal{ALCQI}$ knowledge bases.

1 Introduction

The NIAM language, ancestor ORM, has been equipped with a first order logic (FOL) semantics in 1989 [1]. Since then, despite the remarkable evolution in terms of expressivity that ORM2 has experienced, much less attention has been paid to its formal foundations. This paper can be considered as an attempt to fill this gap. In particular, the issue of providing a logic formalism, equipped with sound and complete reasoning services, that captures the expressiveness of ORM2 is addressed, and a 'practical' fragment of ORM2 is introduced. The first contribution of the paper is thus the introduction of a completely new linear syntax and FOL semantics for a generalisation of ORM2, called ORM2^{plus}, allowing for the specification of join paths over an arbitrary number of relations. The syntax can be used to express the full set of ORM2 graphical symbols introduced in [2]. The new semantics has been proved to be equivalent with the original FOL semantics of NIAM, up to the differences in the expressivity of the two languages. The second contribution of the paper is driven by a practical objective: We identified a 'core' fragment of ORM2, called ORM2^{zero}, that can be translated in a sound a complete way into the EXPTIME-complete description logic (DL) $\mathcal{ALCQI}$ [3]. Finally, we implemented a first prototype, built on top of available DL reasoners which provides an automated support for **schema consistency** checks, **implicit constraints deduction**, and user-defined **constraints entailment**. The rest of the paper is organised as follows: Section 2

P. Herrero et al. (Eds.): OTM 2012 Workshops, LNCS 7567, pp. 368–378, 2012.

introduces syntax and semantics of ORM2^{plus}. ORM2^{zero} is presented in Section 3 together with its encoding in $\mathcal{ALCQI}$. A critique of alternative approaches to the formalisation of ORM2 in (description) logics published so far is provided in Section 4. Section 5 gives an overview of the implemented prototype. See [4] for a complete account of the work behind this paper, including full proofs.

2   ORM2 from a Formal Perspective

The modelling activity in ORM2 is supported by several tools that provide user friendly graphical interfaces to build complex conceptual schemas in real world application domains. Among these, the Natural Object-Role Modelling Architect (NORMA) tool is a plug-in to MS Visual Studio providing the most complete support for the ORM2 notation. This tool performs syntactic check on the graphical notation, returns warnings for not-admitted combinations of basic elements and constraints, and drives the modelling activity according to the ORM2 *Conceptual Schema Design Procedure* [2]. Nonetheless, the ability to avoid the definition of syntactically correct schemas that resolve to be semantically inconsistent is currently left to expertise and skill of the modeller itself. It is known that, due to design mistakes, a syntactically correct schema may (i) not admit any instantiation without the violation of some constraints, or (ii) admit only a partial instantiation. *Schema consistency, consistency of an object type*, and the fact that some constraints is already present in a schema as *implicit consequences*, are typical properties of a schema that, once checked, significantly improve its quality. The automated verification of these properties depends on the possibility to perform reasoning on the schema by means of a logic representation of it. With this goal in mind, this section presents the ORM2^{plus} language. For each construct φ in the syntax, its corresponding semantics expressed in FOL is introduced in tables 1 and 2. The signature $\mathcal{S}$ of the linear syntax is made of the following symbols: (i) A set $\mathcal{E}$ of *entity types*; (ii) a set $\mathcal{V}$ of *value types* (a set of *object types* $\mathcal{O} = \mathcal{E} \cup \mathcal{V}$); (iii) a set $\mathcal{R}$ of *relations*; (iv) a set $\mathcal{A}$ of *roles*; (v) a set $\mathcal{D}$ of *domains*, and a set Λ of pairwise disjoint sets of values. Then, a binary relation $\varrho \subseteq \mathcal{R} \times \mathcal{A}$ linking role to relation symbols is also in $\mathcal{S}$: $R.a$ is the atomic elements of the syntax (given a relation symbol R, $\varrho_R = \{R.a | R.a \in \varrho\}$ is the set of *localised roles* w.r.t R, and $|\varrho_R| = arity(R)$). Finally, for each relation symbol R, a bijection $\tau_R \colon \varrho_R \to [1..|\varrho_R|]$, mapping role components and argument positions in a relation, is defined.

Given the signature $\mathcal{S}$, an ORM2^{plus} *conceptual schema* Σ over $\mathcal{S}$ includes a finite combination of the constructs in tables 1 and 2. The list of constraints graphically introduced in [2] can now be linearised using a specialisation of the new syntax, where: (1) TYPE is for role **typing**; (2) FREQ for **frequency occurrence**; (3) MAND for **mandatory participation**; (4) R-SET$_\text{H}$ for the family of **set-comparison** constraints; (5) O-SET$_\text{H}$ for the family of **subtyping** constraints; (6) O-CARD and R-CARD for **object** and **role cardinality**; and (7) OBJ for **objectification**; (8) RING for **ring** constraints; and (9) V-VAL for **object value** constraints. Below, an example on how the introduced syntax can be used to encode a fragment of the schema in fig. 1.

Table 1. Linear Syntax (■) and FOL Semantics (□) table

■ TYPE $\subseteq \wp \times (\mathcal{E} \cup \mathcal{V})$

□ If TYPE$(R.a, O) \in \Sigma$ then $\forall x_1 \ldots x_{\tau(R.a)} \ldots x_n . R(x_1, \ldots, x_{\tau(R.a)}, \ldots, x_n) \to O(x_{\tau(R.a)})$

■ FREQ $\subseteq \wp(\varrho) \times (\wp(\varrho) \times \wp(\varrho)) \times (\mathbb{N} \times (\mathbb{N} \cup \{\infty\}))$

□ If FREQ$(\{R^1.a_{11}, \ldots, R^1.a_{1n}, \ldots, R^k.a_{k1}, \ldots, R^k.a_{km}\}, \bowtie_{\mathbf{R}}, (\min, \max)) \in \Sigma$ then

$$\exists \bar{y}[\exists \bar{x}^1 \ldots \bar{x}^k (\bigwedge_{j=1}^k R^j(\bar{x}^j) \wedge \bigwedge_{i1=1}^n (x^1_{\tau(R^1.a_{111})} = y_{1i1}) \wedge \ldots \wedge \bigwedge_{ik=1}^m (x^1_{\tau(R^1.a_{11k})} = y_{1ik}) \wedge \bigwedge_{\bowtie_{\mathbf{R}}} (x^{r^+}_{\tau(R^{r^+}.a_r + \mathbf{v}_r)} = x^{r^-}_{\tau(R^{r^-}.a_r - \mathbf{w}_r)})] \to$$

$$\exists^{\geq \min; \leq \max} \bar{y}[\exists \bar{x}^1 \ldots \bar{x}^k (\bigwedge_{j=1}^k R^j(\bar{x}^j) \wedge \bigwedge_{i1=1}^n (x^1_{\tau(R^1.a_{111})} = y_{1i1}) \wedge \ldots \wedge \bigwedge_{ik=1}^m (x^1_{\tau(R^1.a_{11k})} = y_{1ik}) \wedge (\bigwedge_{\bowtie_{\mathbf{R}}} x^{r^+}_{\tau(R^{r^+}.a_r + \mathbf{v}_r)} = x^{r^-}_{\tau(R^{r^-}.a_r - \mathbf{w}_r)}))]]$$

where:

(1) $\bowtie_{\mathbf{R}} = \{\ldots, \langle R^i.a_{iv} = R^j.a_{jw}\rangle, \ldots\}$, with $i \neq j$ and $1 \leq i, j \leq k$, is the finite set of join (role) pairs (given k relations $\mathbf{R}$, $|\bowtie_{\mathbf{R}}| = k - 1$)

(2) $R^i.a_{ix} \in \varrho_{R^i}$ for any $R^i \in \mathcal{R}$, and

(3) the equalities in $\bigwedge_{\bowtie_{\mathbf{R}}}$ are specified according to $\bowtie_{\mathbf{R}}$

(e.g. given $\bar{x}^1, \bar{x}^2, \bar{x}^3$ s.t. $R^1(\bar{x}^1), R^2(\bar{x}^2), R^3(\bar{x}^3)$, if $\bowtie_{\mathbf{R}} = \{(R^1.a, R^2.b), (R^2.c, R^3.d)\}$ then $\bigwedge_{\bowtie_{\mathbf{R}}} =_{\text{def}} (x^1_{\tau(R^1.a)} = x^2_{\tau(R^2.b)}) \wedge (x^2_{\tau(R^2.c)} = x^3_{\tau(R^3.d)})$

■ MAND $\subseteq \wp(\varrho) \times (\mathcal{E} \cup \mathcal{V})$

□ If MAND$(\{R^1.a_{11}, \ldots, R^1.a_{1n}, \ldots, R^k.a_{k1}, \ldots, R^k.a_{km}\}, O) \in \Sigma$ then

$$\forall y[A](y) \to \bigvee_{i=1}^n \exists \bar{z}^i (R^1(\bar{z}^i) \wedge (z^i_{\tau(R^1.a_{1i})} = y)) \vee \ldots \vee \bigvee_{j=1}^m \exists \bar{z}^j . R^k(\bar{z}^j) \wedge (z^j_{\tau(R^k.a_{kj})} = y)]]$$

Table 1. (*continued*)

■ $\text{R-SET}_H \subseteq (\wp(\varrho) \times (\wp(\varrho) \times \wp(\varrho))) \times (\wp(\varrho) \times (\wp(\varrho) \times \wp(\varrho))) \times (\mu \colon \varrho \to \varrho)$ where $\mathsf{H} = \{\mathsf{Sub}, \mathsf{Exc}\}$

□ • If $\text{R-SET}_{\mathsf{Sub}}((\{R^1.a_{11}, \ldots, R^1.a_{1n}, \ldots, R^k.a_{k1}, \ldots, R^k.a_{km}\}, \bowtie_\mathbf{R}), (\{S^1.b_{11}, \ldots, S^1.b_{1v_{\mathfrak{s}}}, \ldots, S^q.b_{q1}, \ldots, S^q.b_{qw}\}, \bowtie_\mathbf{S}, \mu) \in \varSigma$ then

$$\forall \overline{y} [\forall \overline{x} \exists^k (\bigwedge_{j=1}^k \overline{x}^k (\bigwedge_{j=1}^q \overline{x}^j)) \wedge \bigwedge_{i1=1}^n (x^1_{\tau(R^1.a_{1i1n})} = y_{1ik}) \wedge \cdots \wedge \bigwedge_{ik=1}^m (x^{r^+}_{\tau(R^{r^+}.a_r + \mathbf{v}_r)} = x^{r^-}_{\tau(R^{r^-}.a_r - \mathbf{w}_r)})) \to$$

$$\exists \overline{z}^1 \ldots \overline{z}^q (\bigwedge_{i=1}^q S^i(\overline{z}^i) \wedge \bigwedge_{i1=1}^n (z^{f_\mu(1i1)}_{\tau(\mu(R^1.a_{1i1}))} = y_{1i1}) \wedge \cdots \wedge \bigwedge_{ik=1}^m (z^{f_\mu(1ik)}_{\tau(\mu(R^1.a_{1ik}))} = y_{1ik}) \wedge \bigwedge_{\bowtie_\mathbf{S}} (z^{s^+}_{\tau(S^{s^+}.b_s + \mathbf{v}_s)} = z^{s^-}_{\tau(S^{s^-}.b_s - \mathbf{w}_s)})]]$$

□ • If $\text{R-SET}_{\mathsf{Exc}}((\{R^1.a_{11}, \ldots, R^1.a_{1n}, \ldots, R^k.a_{k1}, \ldots, R^k.a_{km}\}, \bowtie_\mathbf{R}), (\{S^1.b_{11}, \ldots, S^1.b_{1v}, \ldots, S^q.b_{q1}, \ldots, S^q.b_{qw}\}, \bowtie_\mathbf{S}, \mu) \in \varSigma$ then

$$\forall \overline{y} [\forall \overline{x} \exists^k (\bigwedge_{j=1}^k \overline{x}^k (\bigwedge_{j=1}^q \overline{x}^j)) \wedge \bigwedge_{i1=1}^n (x^1_{\tau(R^1.a_{1i1})} = y_{1i1}) \wedge \cdots \wedge \bigwedge_{ik=1}^m (x^{r^+}_{\tau(R^{r^+}.a_r + \mathbf{v}_r)} = x^{r^-}_{\tau(R^{r^-}.a_r - \mathbf{w}_r)})) \to$$

$$\neg (\exists \overline{z}^1 \ldots \overline{z}^q (\bigwedge_{i=1}^q S^i(\overline{z}^i) \wedge \bigwedge_{i1=1}^n (z^{f_\mu(1i1)}_{\tau(\mu(R^1.a_{1i1}))} = y_{1i1}) \wedge \cdots \wedge \bigwedge_{ik=1}^m (z^{f_\mu(1ik)}_{\tau(\mu(R^1.a_{1ik}))} = y_{1ik}) \wedge \bigwedge_{\bowtie_\mathbf{S}} (z^{s^+}_{\tau(S^{s^+}.b_s + \mathbf{v}_s)} = z^{s^-}_{\tau(S^{s^-}.b_s - \mathbf{w}_s)})))]$$

where:

(1) given $\varrho^{\mathsf{C_A}} = \{R^1.a_{11}, \ldots, R^1.a_{1n}, \ldots, R^k.a_{k1}, \ldots, R^k.a_{km}\}$, and $\varrho^{\mathsf{C_B}} = \{S^1.b_{11}, \ldots, S^1.b_{1v}, \ldots, S^q.b_{q1}, \ldots, S^q.b_{qw}\}$, we have $\varrho^{\mathsf{C_A}} = \{R.a | \mu(R.a) \in \varrho^{\mathsf{C_B}}\}$, and μ is a partial bijection s.t. for any $\langle \varrho^{\mathsf{C_A}}, \varrho^{\mathsf{C_B}}, \mu \rangle \in \text{R-SET}_{\mathsf{H}}$

(2) $f_{\mu(xy)} = z$ iff $\mu(R^x.a_{xy}) \in \varrho^{S^z}$

ENTITYTYPES :{PhoneCall, MobileCall, PhonePoint, Cell, Landline, HomePoint}
VALUETYPES :{PhoneCall_Id, PhonePoint_♯}
  RELATIONS :{HasOriginFrom, HasDestinationTo, HasMOriginFrom, HasPhoneCall_Id,
              HasPhonePoint_♯}
    TYPE(HasOriginFrom.1, PhoneCall) MAND({HasOriginFrom.1}, PhoneCall)
                                     FREQ({HasOriginFrom.1}, {}, (1, 1))
    TYPE(HasOriginFrom.2, PhonePoint)
    TYPE(HasDestinationTo.1, PhoneCall) MAND({HasDestinationTo.1}, PhoneCall)
    TYPE(HasDestinationTo.2, PhonePoint)
    TYPE(HasMOriginFrom.1, MobileCall)
          TYPE(HasMOriginFrom.2, Cell)
    TYPE(HasPhoneCall_Id.1, PhoneCall)
  : MAND({HasPhoneCall_Id.1}, PhoneCall)
                                     FREQ({HasPhoneCall_Id.1}, {}, (1, 1))
    TYPE(HasPhoneCall_Id.2, PhoneCall_Id) FREQ({HasPhoneCall_Id.2}, {}, (1, 1))
    TYPE(HasPhonePoint_♯.1, PhonePoint) MAND({HasPhonePoint_♯.1}, PhonePoint)
                                     FREQ({HasPhonePoint_♯.1}, {}, (1, 1))
    TYPE(HasPhonePoint_♯.2, PhonePoint_♯) FREQ({HasPhonePoint_♯.2}, {}, (1, 1))
    O-SET$_{Tot}$({Landline, Cell}, PhonePoint)
    O-SET$_{Ex}$({Landline, Cell}, PhonePoint)
  O-SET$_{Ex}$({HomePoint, Landline}, PhonePoint)
R-SET$_{Sub}$({HasMOriginFrom.1, HasMOriginFrom.2}, {}), ({HasOriginFrom.1, HasOriginFrom.2}, {}),
    {(HasMOriginFrom.1, HasOriginFrom.1), (HasMOriginFrom.2, HasOriginFrom.2)}

ORM2^{plus} covers ORM2[1]; in particular, *external* and *internal* forms are represented by means of different specialisations of the same constructs; the FREQ construct can now be applied to arbitrary role sequences no matter about the arity of involved relations, and the same holds for the R-SET$_H$ constructs. Additional sequences of role pairs (see $\bowtie_R$, and $\bowtie_S$) are among the arguments of both FREQ and R-SET$_H$, and used to specify the roles where the joins must be computed. Uniqueness constraints are viewed as frequency occurrence constraints with a fixed range $(1, 1)$, and several other constraints can now be derived as shown in table 2. The 'strict' version of the subtyping relation, that is assumed as primitive in [2], is seen here as a derived constraint: Given a non-strict semantics for the subtyping relation, the strict one can be represented by a combination of partition, cardinality constraint, and the introduction of a a new fresh object type symbol ('equality' can also be expressed using a similar pattern, where the cardinality of the new introduced symbol is zero).

Note that the FOL semantics is based on a signature that perfectly matches the one of the linear syntax (n unary entity type predicates, m value type predicates, and l domain symbol predicates are introduced). Nonetheless, the following set of *background axioms* is needed in order to force the interpretation of the symbols in the FOL knowledge bases (KBs) to be correct w.r.t. the intended semantics of the corresponding ORM2 symbols:

$$\forall x. E_i(x) \to \neg(D_1(x) \lor \cdots \lor D_l(x)), \text{ for } 1 \le i \le n \tag{1}$$

$$\forall x. V_i(x) \to D_j(x), \text{ for } 1 \le i \le m, \text{ and some } j \tag{2}$$

$$\forall x. D_i(x) \leftrightarrow (x = d_1 \lor x = d_2 \lor \ldots), \text{ for all } d_i \in \Lambda_{D_i} \tag{3}$$

$$\forall x_1, \ldots, x_n, z_1, \ldots, z_n. \text{ID}(\bar{\mathbf{x}}) = \text{ID}(\bar{\mathbf{z}}) \leftrightarrow \bar{\mathbf{x}} = \bar{\mathbf{s}}, \text{ for } n = 1, \ldots, n_{max} \tag{4}$$

---

[1] We consider here the standard ORM2 as defined in the book [2]; it is not hard to characterise in FOL, e.g., the additional constraints introduced by [5].

Table 2. Linear Syntax (■) and FOL Semantics (□) table (contd)

■ O-SET$_H$ ⊆ ℘($\mathcal{E} \cup \mathcal{V}$) × $\mathcal{E} \cup \mathcal{V}$ where H = {Isa, Tot, Ex}

□ • If O-SET$_{Isa}$({$O_1, \ldots, O_n$}, O) ∈ Σ then $\forall y.O_i(y) \rightarrow O(y)$ for all $i = 1, \ldots, n$

  • If O-SET$_{Tot}$({$O_1, \ldots, O_n$}, O) ∈ Σ then

$$\begin{cases} \forall y.O_i(y) \rightarrow O(y) \\ \forall y.O(y) \rightarrow O_1(y) \vee \cdots \vee O_n(y), \text{ for all } i = 1, \ldots, n \end{cases}$$

  • If O-SET$_{Ex}$({$O_1, \ldots, O_n$}, O) ∈ Σ then

$$\begin{cases} \forall y.O_1(y) \rightarrow O(y) \wedge \neg O_2(y) \wedge \cdots \wedge \neg O_n(y) \\ \forall y.O_2(y) \rightarrow O(y) \wedge \neg O_3(y) \wedge \cdots \wedge \neg O_{n-1}(y) \\ \cdots \\ \forall y.O_{n-1}(y) \rightarrow O(y) \wedge \neg O_1(y) \\ \forall y.O_n(y) \rightarrow O(y) \end{cases}$$

■ O-CARD ⊆ ($\mathcal{E} \cup \mathcal{V}$) × (ℕ × (ℕ ∪ {∞}))

□ If O-CARD(O) = (min, max) ∈ Σ then $\exists^{\geq min} y.O(y) \wedge \exists^{\leq max} y.O(y)$

■ R-CARD ⊆ ℘(ϱ) × (ℕ × (ℕ ∪ {∞}))

□ If R-CARD($R.a$) = (min, max) ∈ Σ then

$$\exists^{\geq min} x_{\tau(R.a)}.R(x_1 \ldots x_{\tau(R.a)} \ldots x_n) \wedge \exists^{\leq max} x_{\tau(R.a)}.R(x_1 \ldots x_{\tau(R.a)} \ldots x_n)$$

■ OBJ ⊆ $\mathcal{R}$ × ($\mathcal{E} \cup \mathcal{V}$)

□ If OBJ(R, O) ∈ Σ then $\forall x.O(x) \leftrightarrow \exists \overline{y}.R(\overline{y}) \wedge \text{ID}^{|\varrho_R|}(\overline{y}) = x$

■ RING$_J$ ⊆ ℘($\varrho \times \varrho$) where J = {Irr, Asym, Trans, Intr, Antisym, Acyclic, Sym, Ref, ...}

□ E.g. If RING$_{Irr}$($R.a, R.b$) ∈ Σ then $\forall x_{\tau(R.a)}, x_{\tau(R.b)}.R(x_{\tau(R.a)}, x_{\tau(R.b)}) \rightarrow \neg R(x_{\tau(R.b)}, x_{\tau(R.a)})$

■ V-VAL: $\mathcal{V} \rightarrow$ ℘(Λ_D) for some $\Lambda_D \in \Lambda$ (where $\Lambda_{(\cdot)}$ associates an extension to each domain symbol)

□ If V-VAL(V) = {$d_1, \ldots, d_n$} ∈ Σ then $\forall x.V(x) \rightarrow (x = d_1) \vee \cdots \vee (x = d_n)$

Table 3. Derived constraints

Uniqueness:	FREQ({$R^1.a_{11}, \ldots, R^1.a_{1n}, \ldots, R^k.a_{k1}, \ldots, R^k.a_{km}$}, ⋈$_\mathbf{R}$, ⟨1, 1⟩)
Role value:	TYPE($R.a, V^*$) where V^* is a new fresh value type symbol
	V-VAL(V^*) ⊆ {$v_1^D, \ldots, v_n^D$}
Equality:	R-SET$_{Sub}$(({$R^1.a_{11}, \ldots, R^1.a_{1n}, \ldots, R^k.a_{k1}, \ldots, R^k.a_{km}$}, ⋈$_\mathbf{R}$),
	({$S^1.b_{11}, \ldots, S^1.b_{1v}, \ldots, S^q.b_{q1}, \ldots, S^q.b_{qw}$}, ⋈$_\mathbf{S}$), μ)
	R-SET$_{Sub}$(({$S^1.b_{11}, \ldots, S^1.b_{1v}, \ldots, S^q.b_{q1}, \ldots, S^q.b_{qw}$}, ⋈$_\mathbf{S}$)
	({$R^1.a_{11}, \ldots, R^1.a_{1n}, \ldots, R^k.a_{k1}, \ldots, R^k.a_{km}$}, ⋈$_\mathbf{R}$), μ^-)
Exclusive-Or:	MAND({$R^1.a_{11}, \ldots, R^1.a_{1n}, \ldots, R^k.a_{k1}, \ldots, R^k.a_{km}$}, O)
	R-SET$_{Exc}$(({$R^1.a_{11}, \ldots, R^1.a_{1n}$}), ({$R^2.a_{21}, \ldots, R^2.a_{2n}$}), μ_1)
	R-SET$_{Exc}$(({$R^1.a_{11}, \ldots, R^1.a_{1n}$}), ({$R^3.a_{31}, \ldots, R^3.a_{3n}$}), μ_2), $\cdots$,
	R-SET$_{Exc}$(({$R^{k-1}.a_{k-11}, \ldots, R^{k-1}.a_{k-1n}$}), ({$R^k.a_{k1}, \ldots, R^k.a_{kn}$}), μ_k)
Partition:	O-SET$_{Tot}$({$O_1, \ldots, O_n$}, O)
	O-SET$_{Ex}$({$O_1, \ldots, O_n$}, O)
Strict Subtyping:	O-SET$_{Tot}$({O_1, O^*}, O)
	O-SET$_{Ex}$({O_1, O^*}, O)
	O-CARD(O^*) = (1, inf) where O^* is a new fresh object type symbol

where, axiom (1) forces the interpretation of each entity type to be disjoint from the interpretation of the domain symbols; axiom (2) says that objects in the interpretation of a value type must be also in the interpretation of a specific domain symbol; axiom (3) forces the interpretation of a domain symbols to be among the set of values predefined by $\Lambda_{(.)}$, while axiom (4) captures the injective nature of each ID function and the fact that tuples of different length will never agree on the same identifier (where $n_{max} = \max\{|\varrho_R| \| R \in \mathcal{R}\}$). A FO interpretation is a **model** for an ORM2^{plus} schema if it satisfies the background axioms and the corresponding FOL KB built as described in tables 1 and 2. We can prove that, when the schema is restricted to a NIAM schema, the models of the corresponding ORM2^{plus} schema are the same as the FO models of the NIAM schema as specified in [1].

3   Encoding in $\mathcal{ALCQI}$

With the main aim of relying on available tools to reason in an effective way on ORM2 schemas, we present here the encoding in the logic $\mathcal{ALCQI}$ for which tableaux-based reasoning algorithms with a tractable computational complexity have been developed [3]. $\mathcal{ALCQI}$ corresponds to the basic DL $\mathcal{ALC}$ equipped with *qualified cardinality restrictions* and *inverse roles*, and it is a fragment of OWL2. The difficulty implied by the absence of n-ary relations has been overcome by means of *reification*: For each relation R with arity $n \geq 2$, a new atomic concept A_R and n functional roles $\tau(R.a_1), \dots, \tau(R.a_n)$ one for each component of R are introduced. Due to the tree-model property of $\mathcal{ALCQI}$, the reification process provides a sound and complete translation w.r.t. concept satisfiability, such that each instance of the new introduced concept is a representative of one and only one tuple of R. Given as such, the tree-model property guarantees the *correctness* of the $\mathcal{ALCQI}$ encoding w.r.t. the reasoning services over ORM2. Besides reification, we can prove that the expressiveness of $\mathcal{ALCQI}$ does not allow to fully capture ORM2: $\mathcal{ALCQI}$ does not admit neither arbitrary set-comparison assertions on relations, nor external uniqueness or uniqueness involving more than one role, nor arbitrary frequency occurrence constraints. The analysis of these restrictions thus led to identification of the fragment ORM2^{zero} that is maximal with respect to the expressiveness of $\mathcal{ALCQI}$, and still expressive enough to capture the most frequent usage patterns of the modelling community in ORM2 [2]. Let ORM2$^{zero} =$ {TYPE, FREQ$^-$, MAND, R-SET$^-$, O-SET$_{Isa}$, O-SET$_{Tot}$, O-SET$_{Ex}$, OBJ}   be   the fragment of ORM2 where: (i) FREQ$^-$ can only be applied to single roles, and (ii) R-SET$^-$ applies either to relations of the same arity or to two single roles. The encoding of the semantics of ORM2^{zero} shown in table 3 is based on the $\mathcal{S}^{\mathcal{ALCQI}}$ signature made of: (i) A set $E_1, E_2, \dots, E_n$ of concepts for *entity types*; (ii) a set $V_1, V_2, \dots, V_m$ of concepts for *value types*; (iii) a set $A_{R_1}, A_{R_2}, \dots, A_{R_k}$ of concepts for objectified n-ary *relations*; (iv) a set $D_1, D_2, \dots, D_l$ of concepts for *domain symbols*; (v) $1, 2, \dots, n_{max} + 1$ roles.

The correctness of the introduced encoding is guaranteed by the following theorem (whose complete proof is available online at [4]):

Theorem 1. *Let Σ^{zero} be an ORM2^{zero} conceptual schema and $\Sigma^{\mathcal{ALCQI}}$ the $\mathcal{ALCQI}$ KB constructed as described above. Then an object type O is consistent in Σ^{zero} if and only if the corresponding concept O is satisfiable w.r.t. $\Sigma^{\mathcal{ALCQI}}$.*

As a matter of fact, all the reasoning tasks for a conceptual schema can be reduced to object type consistency. Let us conclude this section with some observation about the complexity of reasoning on ORM2 conceptual schemas. Undecidability of the ORM2 object type consistency problem can be proved by showing that arbitrary combinations of subset constraints between n-ary relations and uniqueness constraints over single roles are allowed [6] (*a fortiori*, ORM2^{plus} is also undecidable). As for ORM2^{zero}, one can conclude that object type consistency is ExpTime-complete: The upper bound is established by reducing the ORM2^{zero} problem to concept satisfiability w.r.t. $\mathcal{ALCQI}$ KBs (which is known to be ExpTime-hard) [7], the lower bound by reducing concept satisfiability w.r.t. $\mathcal{ALC}$ KBs (which is known to be ExpTime-complete) to object consistency w.r.t. ORM2^{zero} schemas [8]. Therefore, we obtain the following result:

Theorem 2. *Reasoning over ORM2^{zero} schemas is ExpTime-complete.*

Table 4. $\mathcal{ALCQI}$ encoding

Background domain axioms:	$E_i \sqsubseteq \neg(D_1 \sqcup \cdots \sqcup D_l)$ for $i \in \{1, \ldots, n\}$
	$V_i \sqsubseteq D_j$ for $i \in \{1, \ldots, m\}$, and some j with $1 \le j \le l$
	$D_i \sqsubseteq \sqcap_{j=i+1}^{l} \neg D_j$ for $i \in \{1, \ldots, l\}$
	$\top \sqsubseteq A_{T_1} \sqcup \cdots \sqcup A_{T_{n_{max}}}$
	$\top \sqsubseteq (\le 1i.\top)$ for $i \in \{1, \ldots, n_{max}\}$
	$\forall i.\bot \sqsubseteq \forall i+1.\bot$ for $i \in \{1, \ldots, n_{max}\}$
	$A_{T_n} \equiv \exists 1.A_{T_1} \sqcap \cdots \sqcap \exists n.A_{T_1} \sqcap \forall n+1.\bot$ for $n \in \{2, \ldots, n_{max}\}$
	$A_R \sqsubseteq A_{T_n}$ for each atomic relation R of arity n
	$A \sqsubseteq A_{T_1}$ for each atomic concept A
TYPE$(R.a, O)$	$\exists \tau(R.a)^-.A_R \sqsubseteq O$
FREQ$^-(R.a, \langle min, max \rangle)$	$\exists \tau(R.a)^-.A_R \sqsubseteq \; \ge \min \tau(R.a)^-.A_R \sqcap \le \max \tau(R.a)^-.A_R$
MAND$(\{R^1.a_1, \ldots, R^1.a_n,$	$O \sqsubseteq \exists \tau(R^1.a_1)^-.A_{R^1} \sqcup \cdots \sqcup \exists \tau(R^1.a_n)^-.A_{R^1} \sqcup \cdots \sqcup$
$\ldots, R^k.a_1, \ldots, R^k.a_m\}, O)$	$\exists \tau(R^k.a_1)^-.A_{R^k} \sqcup \cdots \sqcup \exists \tau(R^k.a_m)^-.A_{R^k}$
$^{(A)}$ R-SET$^-_{\mathsf{Sub}}(A, B)$	$A_R \sqsubseteq A_S$ $^{(A)} A = \{R.a_1, \ldots, R.a_n\}, B = \{S.b_1, \ldots, S.b_n\}$
$^{(A)}$ R-SET$^-_{\mathsf{Exc}}(A, B)$	$A_R \sqsubseteq A_{T_n} \sqcap \neg A_S$
$^{(B)}$ R-SET$^-_{\mathsf{Sub}}(A, B)$	$\exists \tau(R.a_i)^-.A_R \sqsubseteq \exists \tau(S.b_j)^-.A_S$ $^{(B)} A = \{R.a_i\}, B = \{S.b_j\}$
$^{(B)}$ R-SET$^-_{\mathsf{Exc}}(A, B)$	$\exists \tau(R.a_i)^-.A_R \sqsubseteq A_{T_n} \sqcap \neg \exists \tau(S.b_j).A_S$
O-SET$_{\mathsf{Isa}}(\{O_1, \ldots, O_n\}, O)$	$O_1 \sqcup \cdots \sqcup O_n \sqsubseteq O$
O-SET$_{\mathsf{Tot}}(\{O_1, \ldots, O_n\}, O)$	$O \sqsubseteq O_1 \sqcup \cdots \sqcup O_n$
O-SET$_{\mathsf{Ex}}(\{O_1, \ldots, O_n\}, O)$	$O_1 \sqcup \cdots \sqcup O_n \sqsubseteq O$ and $O_i \sqsubseteq \sqcap_{j=i+1}^{n} \neg O_j$ for each $i = 1, \ldots, n$
OBJ(R, O)	$O \equiv A_R$

4   Related Works

In the last few years, several papers addressed the issue of encoding ORM2 conceptual schema into DL KBs [9,10,11,12]. Among those proposals, [9] goes through the encoding with a formal perspective. [9] introduces an encoding of a fragment of ORM2 into the logic $\mathcal{DLR}_{ifd}$, an extension of $\mathcal{DLR}$ with *identification assertions* on concepts, and *functional dependencies* assertions on relations [6]. Except for the presence of uniqueness constraints spanning over arbitrary sequence of n roles of the same relation, and external uniqueness over 2 roles, that are represented in the paper by means of suitable identification assertions, ORM2^{zero} and the fragment identified in [9] agree on the same expressive power. Unfortunately, the proposal is somehow sloppy, and it is wrong w.r.t. the semantics specified in [1] (e.g., the semantics of 'objectification' and frequency occurrence constraints is wrong).

As regards to [10], already [9] claimed its limits. It should be also noticed that [11,12] suffer from the same formal inconsistencies and limitations of [10]. In particular, [10] is sloppy with respect to the underlying DL formalism: distinct extensions of the adopted logic (e.g. $\mathcal{DLR}$ plus $\mathcal{DLR}$-*Lite*) and distinct DL languages (e.g. $\mathcal{DLR}$, plus $\mathcal{DLR}$-*Lite*, plus $\mathcal{SROIQ}$, plus 'role composition' operator) are mixed together. No semantics nor complexity results are is provided for these combinations.

In [13], a list of nine 'unsatisfiability constraint patterns' is introduced with the aim of supporting the automatic detection of unsatisfiable schema elements. The patterns discussed in the paper represent a subset of all the possible sources of inconsistency that can occur in a conceptual schema, and it is therefore severely *incomplete*.

Similar to [13], a paper focused on the encoding of ORM2 in OWL has been recently published [14]. The paper introduces a set of informal 'rules' devoted to the mapping of a subset of the ORM2 constructs into OWL. Unfortunately, the paper is wrong in several respects: (i) the OWL EquivalentTO, instead of the SubClassOf, is erroneously introduced; (ii) optionality of uniqueness constraints is lost. In general, the paper covers a fragment that is smaller than ORM2^{zero}, and the proposed mapping mostly remains formally unjustified.

Finally, in [15] the *converse* (incomplete) encoding of OWL-DL into ORM2 is presented. In the paper, the authors claim that 'universal restrictions' of the form $A \sqsubseteq \forall R.B$ cannot be translated in ORM2 in a way that preserves the semantics of the original constructs. But, this is not the case: A viable translation into ER has been introduced in [8], where covering (i.e. total subtyping) and disjointness (i.e. exclusive subtyping) between relationships are used, and a second one into UML can be found in [7], making use of reification of roles. Both translations can be straightforwardly rephrased into ORM2.

A detailed account of all the problems in the related work can be found in [4].

5 Automated Reasoning Support Tool

With the main goal of providing automated reasoning services facilitating the conceptual modelling activity, a prototype of ORM2^{zero} modelling support tool has been implemented for NORMA. The prototype takes an ORM2 schema produced by NORMA as input, and encodes it into the linear syntax using an XSLT script. By relying on existing OWL2 reasoners (e.g. HermiT, FaCT++), the tool provides the following functionality:

- **Implicit constraints deduction.** Derived implicit ORM2^{zero} constraints, including inconsistent object types and fact types, are displayed in distinct pop-up windows. The computation is complete, but only cognitively relevant constraints are visualised, e.g. redundant transitive links are not visualised.
- **Translation into OWL2 ontology.** In order to facilitate web-data exchange and to make conceptual schemas readily accessible to automated processes, the prototype features a translator from ORM2^{zero} schema into OWL2 ontology, which can then be saved in various formats.

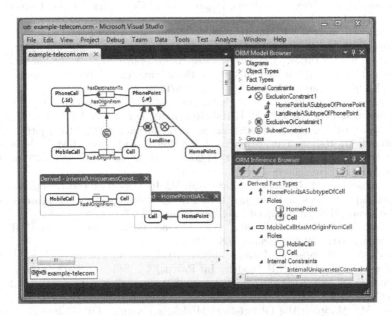

Fig. 1. Graphical interface of the prototype

Let us now illustrate the essential functionality of the prototype using the example introduced on fig. 1. Among the key constraints, the schema involves the uniqueness constraint imposed on the origin of a phone call as well as the hierarchical constraints describing the nature of possible phone points. Therefore, with a single click we can obtain the following relevant deductions for the given conceptual schema: FREQ({hasMOriginFrom.1}, {}, (1,1)) and O-SET$_{\text{Isa}}$({HomePoint}, Cell), i.e. it is true that any home point is also a cell point, and each mobile call may have an origin from at most one cell point. In order to understand why this is true, consider the following. The class of home points is a sub class of all the phone points, and it is disjoint from the class of landline points. Since any phone point is either a cell point or a landline point, then any home point should necessarily be a cell point. The hasMOriginFrom binary relation is included in the hasOriginFrom binary relation. Since each call participates exactly once as first argument to the hasOriginFrom, if we take a generic sub class of calls, such as the class of mobile calls, and a sub relationship of the hasOriginFrom relation, such

as hasMOriginFrom, then we can conclude that necessarily each mobile call participates at most once as first argument to the hasMOriginFrom relation. The full list of
the inferred constraints is displayed in the ORM2 *Inference Browser* window while
selected deductions are illustrated by relevant fragments of the inferred schema in
pop-up windows over the initial schema.

References

1. Halpin, T.: A Logical Analysis of Information Systems: Static Aspects of the Data-
   oriented Perspective. PhD thesis, Department of Computer Science, University of
   Queensland (1989)
2. Halpin, T., Morgan, T.: Information Modeling and Relational Databases: From
   Conceptual Analysis to Logical Design, 2nd edn. Morgan Kaufmann (2001)
3. Baader, F., Calvanese, D., McGuinness, D.L., Nardi, D., Patel-Schneider, P.F.
   (eds.): The description logic handbook: theory, implementation, and applications.
   Cambridge University Press, New York (2003)
4. Franconi, E., Mosca, A.: The formalisation of ORM2 and its encoding in OWL2.
   Technical Report KRDB12-2, KRDB Research Centre, Free University of Bozen-
   Bolzano (2012), http://www.inf.unibz.it/krdb/pub/TR/KRDB12-2.pdf
5. Curland, M., Halpin, T.A., Stirewalt, K.: A Role Calculus for ORM. In: Meersman,
   R., Herrero, P., Dillon, T. (eds.) OTM 2009 Workshops. LNCS, vol. 5872, pp. 692–
   703. Springer, Heidelberg (2009)
6. Calvanese, D., De Giacomo, G., Lenzerini, M.: Identification constraints and functional dependencies in description logics. In: Proceedings of the 17th International
   Joint Conference on Artificial Intelligence, pp. 155–160 (2001)
7. Berardi, D., Cali, A., Calvanese, D., Giacomo, G.D.: Reasoning on UML class
   diagrams. Artificial Intelligence 168 (2003)
8. Artale, A., Calvanese, D., Kontchakov, R., Ryzhikov, V., Zakharyaschev, M.: Reasoning over Extended ER Models. In: Parent, C., Schewe, K.-D., Storey, V.C.,
   Thalheim, B. (eds.) ER 2007. LNCS, vol. 4801, pp. 277–292. Springer, Heidelberg
   (2007)
9. Keet, M.: Mapping the Object-Role Modeling language ORM2 into description
   logic language $\mathcal{DLR}_{ifd}$. Technical Report KRDB07-2, KRDB Research Centre,
   Faculty of Computer Science, Free University of Bozen-Bolzano (2007)
10. Jarrar, M.: Towards Automated Reasoning on ORM Schemes. Mapping ORM into
    the $\mathcal{DLR}_{ifd}$ Description Logic. In: Parent, C., Schewe, K.-D., Storey, V.C., Thal-
    heim, B. (eds.) ER 2007. LNCS, vol. 4801, pp. 181–197. Springer, Heidelberg (2007)
11. Jarrar, M.: Mapping ORM into the $\mathcal{SHOIN}$/OWL description logic. In: Proc. of
    the International Workshop on Object-Role Modeling (ORM 2007), pp. 729–741.
    Springer (2007)
12. Hodrob, R., Jarrar, M.: ORM to OWL2 DL mapping. In: International Conference
    on Intelligent Semantic Web: Applications and Services. ACM (2010)
13. Jarrar, M., Heymans, S.: Unsatisfiability reasoning in orm conceptual schemes. In:
    Proc. of the IFIP-2.6 International Conference on Semantics of a Networked World,
    pp. 517–534. Springer (2006)
14. Wagih, H.M., ElZanfaly, D.S., Kouta, M.M.: Mapping Object Role Modeling 2
    schemes to OWL2 ontologies. In: Proc. of the 3rd IEEE International Conference on
    Computer Research and Development (ICCRD), pp. 126–132. IEEE Press (2011)
15. Bach, D.B., Meersman, R., Spyns, P., Trog, D.: Mapping OWL-DL into OR-
    M/RIDL. In: Proceedings of the 2007 OTM Confederated International Confer-
    ence, OTM 2007, pp. 742–751 (2007)

Fact-Based Specification of a Data Modeling Kernel of the UML Superstructure

Joost Doesburg[1] and Herman Balsters[1]

University of Groningen, The Netherlands

Abstract. Data schemas are an important part of the software design process. The Unified Modeling Language (UML) is the lingua franca in current software engineering practice, and UML class diagrams are used for data modeling within software-engineering projects. Fact-based modeling (FBM) has many advantages over UML, for data modeling. Database engineers that have specified their data schemas in FBM, are often faced with difficulties in communicating these schemas to software engineers using UML. We wish to tackle this communication problem by eventually offering a translation from the FBM-specifications to UML class diagrams. Such a translation requires a formal meta-model description of both FBM and a data-modeling kernel of UML. This paper describes an FBM-based specification of a data-modeling kernel of the UML Superstructure. This kernel will be fact-based, with the added advantage of enabling validation of this FBM-specification.

Keywords: meta-model, fact-based modeling, UML, ORM.

1 Introduction

Fact-based modeling (FBM) is a methodology for modeling the universe of discourse (UoD) of an information system. The main purpose of fact-based modeling is to capture the semantics of the UoD, and to validate results with a domain expert. Unlike object-oriented modeling, FBM treats all facts as relationships. FBM facilitates natural verbalization and thus productive communication (and validation) between stakeholders. FBM is also used as the general name of several fact-based conceptual data modeling dialects, such as Object Role Modeling (ORM), the Natural language Information Analysis Method (NIAM) [6], and Fully-Communication Oriented Information Modeling (FCO-IM) [1]. This paper uses basic ORM2 notations [8], as supported by the NORMA tool [3].

The goals of the Unified Modeling Language (UML) include to provide modelers with a ready-to-use, expressive, and visual modeling language to develop and exchange meaningful methods; support specifications that are independent of particular programming languages and develop processes; and to support higher-level development concepts [14]. In order to support modeling both the static, structural aspects of software and its behavior, UML has multiple diagram types

---

The authors thank Serge Valera for his contributions.

P. Herrero et al. (Eds.): OTM 2012 Workshops, LNCS 7567, pp. 379–388, 2012.

that support different software aspects [13]. UML is most often used to design object-oriented software, but it is also used to generate conceptual schemas for databases [7,15]. Some authors have compared UML and ORM with respect to data modeling (e.g. [7,11]). This will be treated in some more detail in Sect. 5 of this paper. In this paper, UML version 2.3 is used.

Drawbacks of UML in data modeling have been extensively described in [7,10]. We can safely say that UML was never intended as a conceptual data modeling language. UML does not, for example, have a facility for directly specifying keys in class models, and also it has no facility for directly specifying a large class of constraints specific to roles inside a particular fact type (e.g. most set-comparison constraints, frequency constraints, and ring constraints). UML is used in more than 90 percent of the Fortune 500 companies [14, p. XI]). UML is the lingua franca for modeling in the software development process.

The expressibility of the data-oriented aspects of UML is less than that of FBM [11]. Database engineers that have specified their data schemas in FBM, however, are often faced with difficulties in communicating their FBM-schemas to software engineers using UML. We wish to tackle this communication problem by eventually offering a translation from the FBM-specifications to UML class diagrams. An algorithm for such a translation was created in [4], and is discussed shortly in Sect. 5. There have been other attempts to translate ORM-models to UML-models [2,10]. The algorithm in [10] was only informal, while both algorithms in [2,10] were not implemented. In both cases, the translation was not based on (formal, published) meta-model descriptions of the two languages.

A translation algorithm requires a formal meta-model description of both FBM and a data-modeling kernel of UML. This paper has as its main focus to realize an FBM-based specification of a data-modeling kernel of the UML Superstructure. Since this kernel will be fact-based, we have as an added advantage that this FBM-specification can be validated. It also demonstrates FBM's data-modeling differences with and advantages over UML. As far as we know, our work offers the first fact-oriented specification of a data-modeling kernel of the UML Superstructure.

We note that as a basis for our algorithm, we take that all of the ORM models offered as input to our algorithm are in so-called co-referenced format (CoRef-format). That means that only binary fact types with functional uniqueness constraints have to be considered, along with subtyping arrows and a basic set of constraints. All ORM models can be translated to such a format, as can be found in [10]. Since CoRef-FBM is taken as a starting point, the algorithm can be relatively simple [4]. We note that some advantages of ORM are lost when transforming to Co-Ref form, such as easy, natural verbalization of fact types. We also note that using CoRef-format for our ORM input models will result in a UML-specification that is very close to a relational view of that input model.

The rest of this paper is structured as follows. Section 2 provides a description of our particular choice for a data modeling kernel of the UML Superstructure, based on ORM's Conceptual Schema Design Procedure (CSDP) [10]. Section 3 describes the meta-models of our data-modeling kernel pertaining to pure data structures, while Sect. 4 provides descriptions (on the meta-level) of the constraint section of the data-modeling kernel. Section 5 offers an overview of the translation algorithm, and offers an example of a translation output. Section 6 summarizes the main contributions, and notes some further research options.

2   The Data Modeling Kernel

As mentioned in the introduction, UML was designed to model the structure and behavior of object-oriented software. For conceptual modeling, not all supported constructs are needed. To determine which UML constructs are required for the data modeling kernel, the Conceptual Schema Design Procedure (CSDP) from [10, pp. 62–63] is used. The CSDP is a structured method to create a conceptual data schema, and is not confined to FBM. The data modeling kernel of UML should contain those constructs that are required by the CSDP.

The first steps of the CSDP are concerned with transforming information examples into elementary facts. UML is object-oriented, so instead of entity-, value-, and fact types; classes, attributes, and associations will be used. These are the basic constructs in UML. Note that these do not directly correspond to the FBM constructs. Some way of defining data types is also necessary, as well as some method of defining derivations.

In the fourth step of the CSDP, uniqueness constraints are added. Some of these constraints can be captured by using UML multiplicity, but this does not cater for all situations. A different approach is presented in Sect. 4.

CSDP step 5 concerns mandatory constraints. While most of the semantics are captured in UML multiplicity, it cannot cater for all situations. Some mandatory constrains will necessarily be captured by comments.

In the next step, value-, set comparison- and subtyping constraints are added. UML enumerations can be used for some value constraints, but UML does not provide graphical support for other value constraints. Subtyping is supported, as well as subtyping constraints. Set comparison constraints can only be captured in specific situations, and are not treated in this paper due to space limitations.

In the last step of the CSDP, other constraints are added, and final checks are performed. We will capture this latter category of constraints by comments.

In the following sections, a formal meta-model for UML for data modeling is defined. The UML superstructure [13] has been followed as closely as possible. Where the text from [13] was unclear or open to interpretation, we have made our own choice for a semantics. These choices will be explicitly mentioned below.

3   Basic Constructs

In this section, the constructs that capture facts from the UoD are introduced.

UML is object-oriented, so facts are captured in classes, attributes and associations. In the UML superstructure [13], every construct is a subtype of 'element'. While this construct never explicitly occurs in UML diagrams, it provides a reference scheme for all subtypes, and provides the capability to attach comments to any such element. All elements have a Universally Unique IDentifier (UUID) for machine identification. This is depicted in the FBM-model pertaining to the UML-concept of 'element', as on the left-hand side of Fig. 1.

We deviate from the superstructure in the following manner. Firstly, all abstract subtypes of element were removed, since on a conceptual level, only those constructs that can be instantiated are actually necessary. In the superstructure, an association is also a type. Since we conceive of associations and types as being largely different, we refrain from treating associations as types. Additionally, a comment is an element in the superstructure; since a comment does not have a structural role (it is only a piece of text), we refrain from considering a comment as a subtype of element.

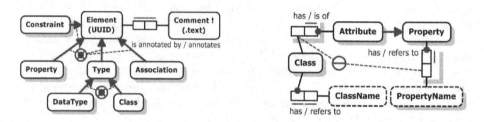

Fig. 1. *Left:* Everything is an element in UML. *Right:* UML class

Classes are the most important data structure for conceptual modeling in UML. A class can participate in associations with other classes, and have any number of attributes. Attribute names are unique within a class. For purposes of user-defined identification, a class also has a unique name. This is depicted in the FBM-model on the right-hand side of Fig. 1.

For conceptual modeling in UML, the methods of a class are not relevant, so these too are not included in the data modeling kernel. Grouping classes into packages is a logical activity, instead of conceptual, so this concept is not included either.[1] The same goes for defining classes as leaf- or abstract classes.

The 'property' construct from the superstructure can have either of two roles in a class diagram. The first role is that of an attribute of a class, and the other is the role of being the end of an association. While the two concepts (i.e. attributes and association ends) share some characteristics (e.g. they both have a multiplicity), their purpose in a class diagram is substantially different. Therefore, in the data modeling kernel, attributes and association ends are defined separately. Each property has a name and multiplicity, and references a type. Properties can be derived, as depicted in the left-hand side of Fig. 2. Note that the 'property' construct as used in UML is different than the one used in mathematics: in UML it is only the supertype of both an association end, and an attribute.

---

[1] In the UML superstructure, a class name is unique within a package. Since packages are out of scope for this paper, they are considered unique.

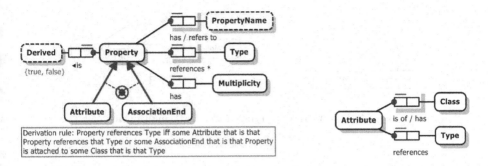

Fig. 2. *Left:* UML property. *Right:* UML attribute

Every attribute is of exactly one class and references one type, as displayed on the right-hand side of Fig. 2. The type of an attribute is generally a data type, but could also be a class.

Figure 3 shows the other function of a property, as an association end. In this setting, the association end gets an aggregation kind, and is attached to a class. An association has two member association ends, can have a (not necessarily unique) name, and can be derived.

In the superstructure, associations of any arity greater than one are allowed. Because CoRef-FBM is taken as a starting point in this paper, we limit ourselves to exactly two association ends per association. The superstructure also allows for the aggregation kind 'shared', but the semantics of this concept are rather vague[2], so we have not included this concept in the data modeling kernel.

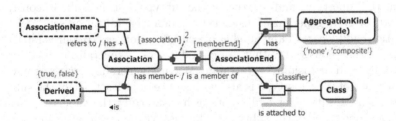

Fig. 3. UML association and association end

UML has a number of primitive data types built in (integer, string, boolean, null and unlimited natural), and provides support for defining new data types. The exact definition of these primitive data types is outside the scope of this paper. As the left of Fig. 4 shows, a data type can also be an enumeration, which we treat in Sect. 4.

---

[2] "Precise semantics of shared aggregation varies by application area and modeler." [13, p. 38].

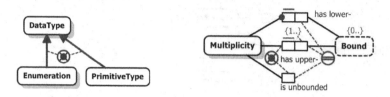

Fig. 4. *Left:* UML data type. *Right:* UML multiplicity

4   Constraints

Now that the information-holding constructs have been defined, constraints on that information are investigated.

UML does not use uniqueness and mandatory constraints, but a concept called 'multiplicity'. Multiplicity defines how many instances of a certain property are allowed for a class or association. As the right side of Fig. 4 shows, every multiplicity has a lower bound, and also either has an upper bound, or is unbounded. We always have that lower bound ≤ upper bound; an upper bound, if defined, is at least 1.

The superstructure allows for expressions as bounds, but requires that they always evaluate to some integer. This option for expressions has been left out of our model.

The UML construct for subtyping is called a 'generalization', and is depicted in the FBM-model in Fig. 5. A generalization is diagrammatically displayed as a subtyping arrow on a class diagram. Generalizations can only be defined for types, i.e. classes and data types. Every generalization has one type that functions as the supertype, and one that is the subtype. It is possible to constrain a set of two or more generalizations by the use of a 'generalization set', and a generalization can be part of any number of generalization sets. In our version of the kernel, the only constraints that are considered on a generalization set are the 'is covering' and 'is disjoint' constraints. When a generalization set is covering, each instance of the supertype is also an instance of at least one of the subtypes. When a generalization set is disjoint, each instance of the supertype is an instance of at most one of the subtypes. The case where a generalization set is not covering, or not disjoint, is interpreted as the absence of that constraint. Every generalization set has a unique name. In the superstructure, a generalization set constrains zero or more generalizations. As the covering and disjoint constraints are meaningless when the generalization set has less than two generalizations, the two or more constraint was added.

UML provides for a way to define a list of possible (discrete) values: an enumeration. An enumeration has one unique name, and a list of one or more enumeration literals. The names of enumeration literals within an enumeration are unique, as displayed in Fig. 6. As an enumeration is a type, it can be used as the data type for attributes, effectively limiting the values of that attribute to the literals within the enumeration.

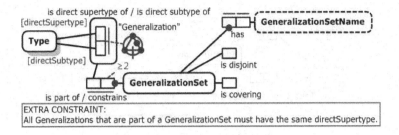

Fig. 5. UML subtyping

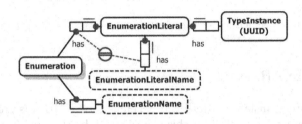

Fig. 6. UML enumeration

The UML superstructure does not support a user-defined reference scheme for objects. While a UUID is sufficient when a computer needs to keep track of objects, it is not suited for human communication. Additionally, the superstructure does not provide a way to define that a combination of properties is unique. In [7], Halpin uses the notations {P} and {Un} to denote primary and secondary identification, respectively. While this is a step up from no value-based identification at all, this is not formally defined in UML yet; also, this approach does not allow for association ends to be used in an identification. Here, an identification mechanism based on [12] is used: UML is extended with an 'identification' construct, as depicted at the top of Fig. 7. This identification construct is added to UML, using the official UML extension method: a profile that defines a stereotype [13]. The UML syntax definition is listed at the bottom of Fig. 7, but keep in mind that the semantics are defined at the top.

The identification construct is analogous to the uniqueness constraint as defined in the FBM exchange schema [5]. Every identification has a unique name, and provides either a primary or secondary identification for a class. An identification is built up from one or more properties (i.e. attributes or association ends). The combination of these properties is unique. Every class in a data schema has one way in which it is preferably identified: through one of its superclasses, or by an identification. Classes can have any number of direct secondary identifications.

For an example of the identification construct in practice, we refer to Sect. 5.

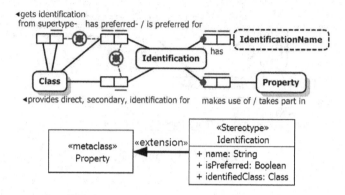

Fig. 7. *Top:* FBM specification of the identification construct. *Bottom:* UML profile for the identification stereotype.

5   Algorithm Results

An algorithm to translate CoRef-FBM schemas into UML was created in [4]. Space limitations do not allow for this algorithm to be thoroughly treated here, but the main decision steps will be presented, along with an example transformation.

Since CoRef-FBM has been taken as a starting point, the algorithm can be relatively simple. Only binary fact types with functional uniqueness constraints have to be considered, along with subtyping arrows and a basic set of constraints.

The algorithm consists of three main steps. First, it is decided which object types translate to a class. Special attention is given to (binary) fact types containing two uniqueness constraints. The second step decides what to do with the fact types, and translates each fact type to an association or an attribute. In the third step, constraints are translated, and identification stereotypes are created.

In the upper part of Fig. 8, an example schema is presented. It features many common modeling constructs: subtyping arrows, internal and external uniqueness constraints, and two value constraints.

In the first step, the algorithm will decide that Person, Teacher and Student will be translated to a class, because they are involved in a subtyping fact type. Booking and CourseEnrollment are also translated to classes, as they have functional roles that do not provide their reference modes. Lastly, SexCode is translated to an enumeration, as it has a list of possible values.

In the second step, all fact types are considered. A fact type, where both object types have been mapped to a class, is translated to an association, while a fact type where only one object type is mapped to a class will be translated to an attribute. The results can be found at the bottom of Fig. 8.[3]

In the last step of the algorithm, all constraints that have not been translated to UML multiplicities are translated. All external uniqueness constraints

---

[3] The little black triangle on the association designates the reading direction. It does not have any semantics.

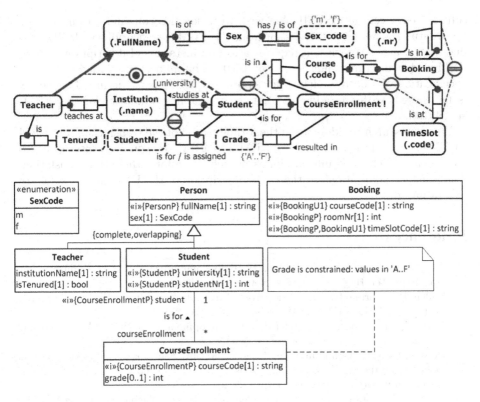

Fig. 8. *Top:* example FBM schema. *Bottom:* the translated UML class diagram

are translated to an identification stereotype. To save space, the name of the stereotype is shortened to «i», the name of the identification includes the name of the identified class, and the name includes a modifier P or U*n*. In the class Booking, the timeSlotCode attribute takes part in two identifications.

The value constraint on the value type Sex_code is translated to the enumeration SexCode. The kernel does not define an equivalent to the value constraint on Grade, so it is translated to a comment.

Note that all fact type readings for attributes are lost, as well as the reverse readings for associations. Because the superstructure does not support many common constraints on data [9], the formality of these constraints is also lost. Note that the resulting UML class diagram is object oriented, so this translation does not help to provide UML with any real fact orientation.

6   Conclusions

Fact-based modeling (FBM) has many advantages over UML, for conceptual modeling. Database engineers that have specified their data schemas in FBM, however, are often faced with difficulties in communicating these schemas to software engineers using UML. We wish to tackle this communication problem by eventually offering a translation from the FBM-specifications to UML class diagrams. Such a translation requires a formal meta-model description of both FBM and a data-modeling kernel of UML. This paper offers an FBM-based specification of a data-modeling kernel of the UML Superstructure. This kernel is fact-based, with the added advantage of enabling validation of this FBM-specification.

Future research could focus on the formalization of the translation from FBM to UML, and the translation from UML to FBM. It would be interesting to investigate which extra information is needed to perform the latter translation. The required adaptations to the FBM description of the UML meta-model are also of interest.

References

1. Bakema, G., Zwart, J., van der Lek, H.: Fully communication oriented information modelling. Ten Hagen Stam, The Netherlands (2002)
2. Bollen, P.: A formal transformation from object role models to UML class diagrams. In: Proc. of EMMSAD 2002 Workshop, vol. 2 (2002)
3. Curland, M., Halpin, T.: Model driven development with NORMA. In: System Sciences, HICSS 2007, p. 286a. IEEE (2007)
4. Doesburg, J.L.H.: Communicating Conceptual Data Schemas in ESA Space System Projects: Producing UML class diagrams from FBM conceptual schemas. Master's thesis, University of Groningen (April 2012)
5. FBM working group: Fact-based modelling exchange schema. Version 20111021c (2011), http://www.factbasedmodelling.org/
6. Halpin, T.: Object-role modeling (ORM/NIAM). In: Handbook on Architectures of Information Systems, pp. 81–102 (1998)
7. Halpin, T.: UML Data Models From An ORM Perspective: Parts 1–10. Journal of Conceptual Modelling, 1–10 (1998), http://orm.net/uml_orm.html
8. Halpin, T.: ORM 2. In: Meersman, R., Tari, Z. (eds.) OTM-WS 2005. LNCS, vol. 3762, pp. 676–687. Springer, Heidelberg (2005), http://dx.doi.org/10.1007/11575863_87
9. Halpin, T., Bloesch, A.: Data modeling in UML and ORM: a comparison. Journal of Database Management 10(4), 4–13 (1999)
10. Halpin, T.A., Morgan, T.: Information modeling and relational databases, 2nd edn. Morgan Kaufmann (2008)
11. Keet, C.: A formal comparison of conceptual data modeling languages. In: 13th International Workshop on Exploring Modeling Methods in Systems Analysis and Design (EMMSAD 2008), Montpellier, France, pp. 16–17. Citeseer (2008)
12. Keet, C.: Enhancing identification mechanisms in uml class diagrams with meaningful keys (2011)
13. OMG: OMG Unified Modeling Language (OMG UML), Superstructure. Version 2.3 (May 2010)
14. Pender, T., McSheffrey, E., Varveris, L.: UML bible. Wiley (2003)
15. Simsion, G.: Data Modeling: Theory and Practice. Technics Publications LLC (2007)

Exploring the Benefits of Collaboration between Business Process Models and Fact Based Modeling - ORM

Necito dela Cruz, Connie Holker, and Miguel Tello

Boston Scientific, Clinical IS, St. Paul, MN, USA
{Necito.DelaCruz,Connie.Holker,Miguel.Tello}@bsci.com

Abstract. Companies are continually striving to reduce issues leading to failed projects and the costs associated with them. The use and collaboration of business process mapping and ORM data modeling can help improve the success rate of a project. This project incorporated lean business practice deliverables such as business process maps along with ORM data models. The output from the two sessions revealed a gap in knowledge around business rules which led to the creation of decision tables. The knowledge gained from the three components (process maps, ORM models and business rules) had numerous benefits including cross-validation of models, increased user involvement, definition of user acceptance tests, and ease in eliciting requirements. The collaboration of business process and data modeling drives accuracy and efficiency in requirements and can reduce or eliminate many of the issues identified as causes of failed projects.

Keywords: Lean Business Process, ORM, Supply Chain, Clinical Device Tracking, Business Requirements Elicitation, User Involvment.

1 Introduction

Many statistics have been presented during numerous professional development courses that indicate the importance of clear, complete, testable requirements and the correlation between poor requirements and project failure. A recent 2010-2011 industry survey identified issues around requirements elicitation and management. The study was conducted by Geneca LLC [1] and asked 600 Business and IT practitioners to answer questions around why teams struggle to meet the business expectations for their projects. According to the study, significant contributing factors to an individual's view on whether their project would be a success include:

Re-work expectations: 80% of the respondents of the Geneca study indicated that they expected to spend at least half of their time completing re-work tasks. The need for re-work can often be linked back to a poor understanding of business needs and lack of requirements documentation.

Quality business involvement: Often the business feels that creation of requirements is an IT task and doesn't understand the criticality of providing comprehensive, detailed

P. Herrero et al. (Eds.): OTM 2012 Workshops, LNCS 7567, pp. 389–398, 2012.
© Springer-Verlag Berlin Heidelberg 2012

requirements that clearly define the business need and capture the business' expectations. Without thoughtful participation from the business, the chance of the system meeting business needs and expectations is nominal. The lack of collaboration between IT and the business is often exposed during user acceptance testing when it is found that the acceptance tests have little or no correlation to system requirements.

Synchronicity between members of the business: Often software requirements are defined at the start of the project and the system is designed based on those defined requirements. However, business needs often change and by the time the system is deployed, the initial requirements may no longer be valid. Another issue is the lack of agreement among the members of the business team as to what the requirements really are. It is critical that the business users stay engaged throughout the lifecycle of the project and that they communicate any suspected issues as soon as they are known in an effort to minimize confusion and disappointment at the end of the project.

Clarity around business objectives: Not understanding the underlying business objectives behind the creation of new software can derail a project. This is troubling given that only 55% of the survey respondents felt they understood the business objectives both conceptually and in the details.

Consistent definitions: Less than 20% of survey respondents described requirements as the articulation of a business need, revealing a belief that requirements are system specific rather than expressing a particular business objective. This lack of understanding that a requirement is a representation of the business need feeds and exacerbates all of the issues listed above. It also provides a glimpse into a larger consistent language problem that infiltrates many projects.

All of these issues can be tied back to the requirements definition and management process. Project members need a way to minimize these issues so they can feel confident that their projects will be a success. Eliciting accurate, relevant and complete business requirements at the start of the project can minimize the risks of scope creep, re-work and communication issues that result in over budget, overdue, and poor quality projects that do not meet customer expectations.

2   The Project

This white paper focuses on a project initiated to create a new system that tracks clinical devices once the device leaves the distribution center, allowing internal visibility and reconciliation of clinically labeled investigational devices. The system records transactional information of all movements during the lifecycle of a clinical device such as shipment, receipt, usage and return of the device. In addition, the system provides methods to control the movement of devices based on pre-determined inventory levels and shelf-life dates. The system is known as the Clinical Device Tracking System (CDTS).

For this illustration, we'll be discussing the movement of a serialized device. A serialized device is part of a batch. Multiple batches of the same product may be manufactured; all of these products have the same UPN (universal part number).

3   Project Framework

3.1   Lean Business Process Tools

The project started out with an IS initiative constraint to implement Lean Business Process (LBP) tools in an effort to start with a solid understanding of the business process we were trying to automate. Tools from each of the DMAIC (Define, Measure, Analyze, Implement, Control) phases were selected.

Current state process maps, one of the LBP deliverables, were created by the Business Analyst, utilizing existing documented procedures and work instructions and collaborating with the Business Lead. Swim lanes were included for each functional area involved in the process as well as lanes for data and tools. This provided a quick, clear method of identifying high level or major data components captured in each process and the tools used to create or obtain that data. The information provided on the cross-functional maps could be used by Enterprise Architects to complete their enterprise analysis.

The current state process maps were reviewed by the business during a two day Kaizen Event during which the maps were used to drive a SWOT analysis where the **S**trengths, **W**eaknesses, **O**pportunities and **T**hreats of the current process were identified and then correlated to specific process boxes within the overall process maps.

The next step involved walking through the current state maps end-to-end and identifying changes to create the future state. Each weakness and opportunity identified as part of the SWOT analysis was addressed in the appropriate map. The end result was an expected future state process map (see condensed version in Figure 2).

3.2   ORM Conceptual Data Models

After reviewing the project assessment, the Data/Information Architect recommended holding an ORM session to harvest the detailed data requirements for the device tracking project. The argued benefit was an increased understanding by the business of the system definitions and the relationships between objects. It would provide a common language for the project team to use for the duration of the project. "Object-Role Modeling (ORM) simplifies the analysis and design process by using natural language, intuitive diagrams, and examples, and by examining the information in terms of simple, elementary facts. By expressing the model in terms of natural concepts, such as objects and roles, this fact-oriented method provides a truly conceptual approach to modeling [2]."

Two initial sessions were held via conference call followed by a four day on-site session. Each session was facilitated by the Data/Information Architect and attended by the Business Analyst and Business Users. The previously constructed future state maps were used as the framework during the fact-based modeling sessions. This framework provided a number of benefits including:

Semantics: the sessions provided an opportunity to engage in quality dialogue with the business users, creating a common language understood by all team members and confirming that the object relationship interpretations of IT were correct.

Structure: the maps provided a structure to the fact based modeling discussions. Because scope was previously defined and outlined, the group could focus its time and attention on the data details of the process.

Efficiency: fourteen individual sub process maps were initially created; however the underlying data elements were consistent and the modeling sessions identified commonalities between the process maps.

Validation: stepping through each process map to gather the data components revealed both the validity of the previously created maps and the inaccuracies. Based on discussions held during these sessions, the maps were modified to reflect the exposed discrepancies.

Gap Identification: based on the discussions held during the process mapping sessions and the conceptual data modeling sessions, a gap in knowledge was identified around business rules. This gap led to the creation of decision tables.

3.3   Decision Tables (Business Rules)

While the knowledge gained during the process mapping and data modeling sessions was extensive, further analysis revealed a gap in requirement details. The collaboration of the two analysis techniques uncovered areas where detailed business rules needed to be documented in order to fully understand system functionality. It was understood that the ORM models would need to change once the business rules were established.

The system has two primary functionalities: 1) records each movement transaction that occurs for a device throughout its lifecycle and 2) displays current inventory levels at each inventory location. Examples that illustrate the knowledge gaps that were uncovered within each of these two core functional components are presented below.

Example 1: Device Movement

Devices can be shipped to four types of inventory locations: Distribution Center (DC), Clinical Site, Field Clinical Engineer (FCE), and Stocking Location. Inventory location was a concept adopted by generalizing the four individual location types listed above into one ORM object type because they are executing the same device movement process. However, each inventory location type has a distinct and unique id and is used as an alternate reference scheme (see Figure 1).

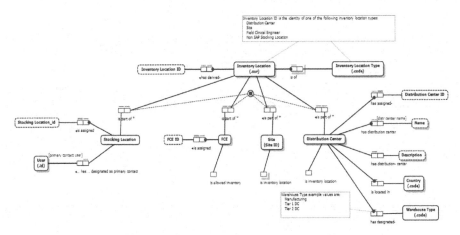

Fig. 1. Inventory Location ORM Model

Process mapping identified nine unique sub process maps involved in the tracking of device movements (Figure 2). The boxes circled in Figure 2 represent four types of device movements modeled during the ORM sessions: DC to DC movement (2.1), transfer (2.6), shipment (2.2, 2.8), and return (2.4). A fifth movement type, in transit, occurs whenever one of the other movement types occurs.

The ORM sessions revealed data commonalities between four of the five movement types, as seen in Figure 3. The DC to DC movement is a unique type of movement that is not consistent with the others (Figure 4).

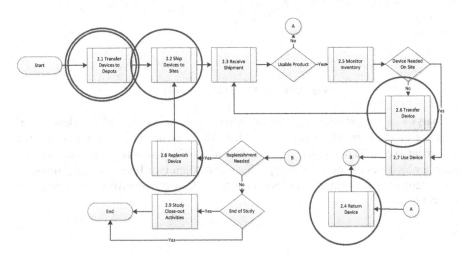

Fig. 2. High Level Tracking Device Process Map

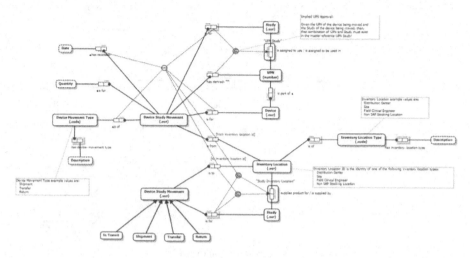

Fig. 3. Device Movement – Shipment, Transfer, Return, In Transit

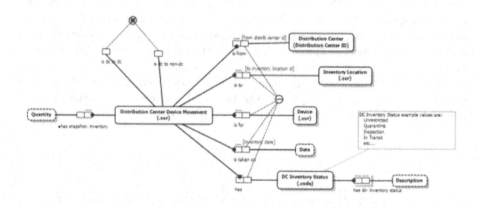

Fig. 4. Device Movement - DC to DC

Analysis of the process maps and data models revealed a need for clear representation of the correlation between each of the four inventory locations and the movement types. Table 1 displays the decision table that was created to visually present which device movement type occurs between two Inventory Locations. In transit movements occur in conjunction with each of the identified movements in the grid below.

Table 1. Device Movement Matrix

Ship From	Ship To			
	SAP DC	**Clinical Site**	**FCE**	**non-SAP Stocking Location**
SAP DC	InventorySnapshot	Shipment	Shipment	Shipment
Clinical Site	Return	N/A	N/A	Return
FCE	Return	Transfer	Transfer	Return
non-SAP Stocking Location	Return	Transfer	Transfer	Transfer

Transfer	initiated within CDTS
Shipment	initiated within SAP
N/A	not allowed
InventorySnapshot	snapshot from SAP, update to inventory levels
Return	return to DC or Stocking Location

The above matrix helped align IT and the business with a common language and an understanding of the terminology. This matrix was referenced frequently during the requirements sessions to remind the project team of the definitions of each of the movement types.

Example 2: Inventory Management. During the ORM sessions, several device status categories were identified throughout the business process. After the ORM sessions, it was evident that simplification of the numerous statuses was required; however, business rules needed to be solidified before simplification could occur. The Business Analyst created decision tables around the device statuses that could occur during a device's lifecycle which led to the creation of the Inventory Category and its subcomponents Physical Inventory and Disposition Inventory.

The following process flow illustrates the workflow involved in inventory management that was identified as a result of solidifying business rules and identifying valid inventory categories.

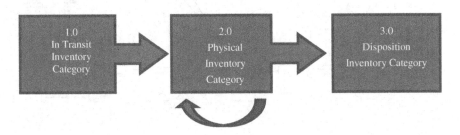

Fig. 5. Inventory Management Workflow

1.0 In Transit (Figure 5)

Upon shipment of a device to the Ship To location, the inventory category is set to In Transit. Once received at the Ship To inventory location, it is assigned to a Physical Inventory category.

2.0 Physical Inventory Category (Figure 5)

The Physical Inventory Category is composed of statuses that indicate that a device is in the physical custody of the inventory location. This is a temporary status during the lifecycle of a device. A device may be assigned to more than one physical inventory category before it is assigned a disposition inventory category.

3.0 Disposition Inventory Category (Figure 5)

The Disposition Inventory Category tells the story of the end of the device. Each device must be assigned a Disposition Category to complete the device lifecycle.

The above workflow revealed the need for additional business rules that documented which inventory categories a device could move to based on its current category. Table 2 displays one example of a complex decision table that was created as a result of the analysis.

Table 2. Allowable Transactions for Physical Inventory

Decrement Inventory	Increment Inventory												
	Physical Inventory Category								Disposition Inventory Category				
	Available	On-hold	Damaged	Expired	Opened/Used	Explanted	Pending Return	Return Received[3]	Lost in Transit	Discarded	Used[1]	Returned	Transferred[2]	Destroyed
Available	NA	√	√	√	NA	NA	√	NA	NA	√	√	NA	√	NA
On-hold	√	NA	√	√	NA	NA	√	NA	NA	NA	NA	NA	NA	NA
Damaged	√	NA	NA	NA	NA	NA	√	NA	NA	NA	NA	NA	NA	NA
Expired	√	NA	√	NA	NA	NA	√	NA	NA	√	√	NA	NA	NA
Opened/Used	NA	NA	NA	NA	NA	NA	√	NA	NA	√	NA	NA	NA	NA
Explanted	NA	NA	NA	NA	NA	NA	√	NA	NA	√	NA	NA	NA	NA
Pending Return	NA	NA	NA	NA	NA	NA	NA	NA	NA	NA	NA	√	NA	NA
Return Received[3]	NA	NA	NA	NA	NA	NA	√	NA	NA	NA	NA	NA	NA	√

exception rules

[1] Usage is valid only when inventory location = Clinical Site.

[2] Transfer is valid only when inventory location = FCE or Stocking Location.

[3] Return Received is valid only when inventory location = Stocking Location or DC.

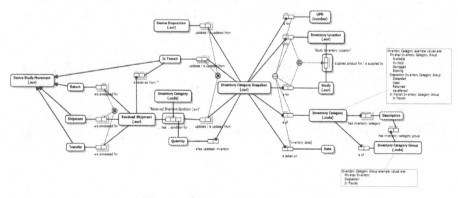

Fig. 6. Inventory Category Snapshot

The final step to the analysis was updating the ORM diagram based on the newly identified business rules. The multiple device status objects that were previously identified were condensed into the Inventory Category. The updated ORM diagram (Figure 6) reflects the fact types of counting inventory category.

The collaboration between process maps and data models revealed a gap in business rule definitions around the increment and decrement of inventory from one category to another. Although the ORM diagrams reflect a simple concept, the rules behind the diagrams are complex and require clear definition and documentation of those rules.

4   Benefits of Methodology

Beginning project discussions by documenting the process and following it with fact based modeling sessions with the business users has numerous benefits.

Multiple discussions, different perspectives: Prior to any formal requirements session, the business users were involved in numerous discussions regarding the project. These sessions forced the business users to thoroughly think and reflect on process, data and business rules and this reflection minimizes the potential for re-work. It allowed a platform for discussions among the user group that resulted in clarification of needs, scope and expectations. It built a solid foundation between members of IT and members of the business to help ensure that everyone was using the same language when discussing the project, which led to improved communication throughout the project and helped minimize misunderstandings between project members.

Stable database framework: The ORM sessions divulged 90% of the system's data components based on *business need* prior to any design or construction of the system. This framework was used to validate future requirements documentation to ensure that no data components were overlooked during requirements sessions.

Efficiency in business process/data gathering: The approach drove efficiencies in the business process maps by teasing out the inaccuracies in the maps through the data modeling discussions. It also drove efficiencies in the ORM sessions by providing an established framework to follow to ensure all processes were discussed. In addition, the process of defining and capturing business rules identified inefficiencies and inaccuracies within the data models which were then re-defined to accommodate the various business rules.

Driver for capturing business rules: A major benefit of the collaboration of methods is the clarity reached around the business rules of the system. This clarity is vital to the understanding and documentation of business requirements.

Framework for user acceptance tests: The process maps provide high level processes that need to be tested and can drive the test script creation process. In addition, conversations from the ORM sessions can be used to guide the testing of business rules.

Each of these benefits supports the requirements definition process. By following the above methodology, project members can feel confident that their projects will be a success. Business Analysts (in collaboration with actively involved business users) will be able to elicit accurate, relevant and complete business requirements and minimize the risks of scope creep, re-work and communication issues that result in over budget, overdue, and poor quality projects that don't meet customer expectations.

References

1. Geneca, LLC, http://www.genecaresearchreports.com/index.html
2. Halpin, T., Morgan, T.: Information Modeling and Relational Databases. Morgan Kaufmann, San Francisco (2008)

Enhanced Verbalization of ORM Models

Matthew Curland[1] and Terry Halpin[2]

[1] ORM Solutions, USA
[2] INTI International University, Malaysia and LogicBlox, Australia
mcurland@live.com, terry.halpin@logicblox.com

Abstract. Fact-oriented modeling approaches such as Object-Role Modeling (ORM) validate their models with domain experts by verbalizing the models in natural language, and by populating the relevant fact types with concrete examples. This paper extends previous work on verbalization of ORM models in a number of ways. Firstly, it considers some ways to better ensure that generated verbalizations are unambiguous, including occasional use of lengthier verbalizations that are tied more closely to the underlying logical form. Secondly, it provides improved verbalization patterns for common types of ORM constraints, such as uniqueness and mandatory role constraints. Thirdly, it provides an algorithm for verbalizing external uniqueness and frequency constraints over roles projected from join paths of arbitrary complexity. The paper also includes some discussion of how such verbalization enhancements were recently implemented in the Natural ORM Architect (NORMA) tool.

1 Introduction

When designing an information system, it is important to ensure that the data model accurately reflects the data requirements for the relevant business domain by validating the model with someone who understands the business domain, i.e. a domain expert. Since domain experts are often nontechnical, the data model should be communicated to them in language that is intelligible to them, without requiring mastery of a complex, technical syntax such as that of the Object Constraint Language (OCL) [17]. Fact-oriented modeling approaches are specifically designed to facilitate communication between modelers and domain experts by verbalizing the data model in natural sentences and populating the model's fact types with concrete examples of fact instances. A fact type corresponds to a set of typed predicates of arity one (e.g. Person smokes), two (e.g. Person was born on Date), or higher (e.g. Item contains Item in Quantity). This approach differs from Entity relationship (ER) modeling [3] and class diagramming within the Unified Modeling Language (UML) [19], which encode some facts in attributes (e.g. Person.isSmoker, Person.birthdate).

Fact-orientation's attribute-free nature promotes semantic stability (e.g. no remodeling is needed to talk about an attribute) and its graphical constraint notation for data modeling is much richer than that of industrial ER or UML. The family of fact-oriented modeling approaches include various dialects such as Object-Role Modeling (ORM), Natural-language Information Analysis Method (NIAM) [20],

P. Herrero et al. (Eds.): OTM 2012 Workshops, LNCS 7567, pp. 399–408, 2012.
© Springer-Verlag Berlin Heidelberg 2012

Fully-Communication Oriented Information Modeling (FCO-IM) [1] and the Predicator Set Model (PSM) [16]. This paper focuses on recent verbalization work within second generation ORM (ORM 2) [6]. Overviews of ORM may be found in [8, 9], and a detailed coverage in [14].

Our previous work on ORM verbalization and its automation is discussed in [13, 5, 10]. The rest of this paper discusses extensions to this work, and is structured as follows. Section 2 considers various ways to help ensure that generated verbalizations are unambiguous, noting some cases where lengthier verbalizations based more closely on logical formalization may be needed. Section 3 provides improved verbalization patterns for some common types of ORM constraints, such as uniqueness and mandatory role constraints. Section 4 provides an algorithm for verbalizing external uniqueness and frequency constraints over roles projected from join paths of arbitrary complexity, and discusses how such verbalization enhancements were implemented in the Natural ORM Architect (NORMA) tool.

2   Avoiding Ambiguity

In Figure 1(a), the binary fact types Person was born in Year and Person speaks Language are displayed with infix predicate readings. Readings are left-to-right unless reversed by an arrow-tip. The bar over the left-hand role of the birth predicate depicts a uniqueness constraint that we verbalize in ORM as "**Each** Person was born in **at most one** Year", and the dot on the line connected to the left-hand role of the speaks predicate depicts a mandatory role constraint that verbalizes as "**Each** Person speaks **some** Language". Using sorted logic with mixfix predicates, these constraints formalize respectively as $\forall p$:Person $\exists^{0..1}y$:Year p was born in y, and $\forall p$:Person $\exists l$:Language p speaks l.

We verbalize the universal quantifier $\forall$ as "**each**" rather than "**all**" or "**every**" because linguistically "**each**" is always a *distributive* quantifier, applying to individuals one at a time [1, p. 352]. In contrast, "**all**" and "**every**" may be used both collectively and distributively, which may lead to ambiguity. For example, "All baby whales weigh more than all baby humans" is true if "all" is interpreted distributively, but false if it is interpreted collectively (because there are many more humans). Another reason for avoiding "all" is that it requires pluralization (e.g. all persons). By default we verbalize the existential quantifier $\exists$ as "**some**", although we do plan to also support "**a**" or "**an**" as appropriate. Linguists regard the pattern "every-some" to be ambiguous [17]. For example, "Every person speaks some language" could mean either (a) For each person, that person speaks some language, or (b) There is some language such that every person speaks that language.

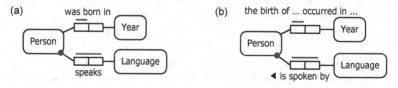

Fig. 1. Some predicate reading choices for ORM fact types

Because ORM supports mixfix predicates, allowing object terms to be placed at any position in a sentence, a predicate reading might include *front text* (before the first term) and/or *trailing text* (after the last term). The presence of front text often requires a different verbalization pattern to avoid ambiguity. For example, applying the simple pattern used earlier, the uniqueness constraint on the birth predicate in Figure 1(b) verbalizes thus "The birth of **each** Person occurred in **at most one** Year" which could be misunderstood by some users to mean that everybody was born in the same year. Hence we instead use the following verbalization: **For each** Person, the birth of **that** Person occurred in **at most one** Year. Our verbalization of a constraint on a role also depends on whether there is a predicate reading that starts at that role. For example, the mandatory role role constraint in Figure 1(b) verbalizes as "**For each** Person, **some** Language is spoken by **that** Person", rather than "**Some** Language is spoken by **each** Person" which linguistically untutored users might take to mean that there is some language that everyone speaks.

In previous work, we often used "**the same**" as a linguistic quantifier for verbalizing some leading existential quantifiers. For example, we verbalized the many-to-many nature of the spanning uniqueness constraint on the speaks predicate in Figure 1(a) thus: **It is possible that the same** Person speaks **more than one** Language **and that more than one** Person speaks **the same** Language. The problem with this is that "the same" can sometimes be misinterpreted as referring back to a previous instance. To avoid such misunderstanding, we now use the following verbalization if forward and converse predicate readings are available: **It is possible that some** Person speaks **more than one** Language **and that some** Language is spoken by **more than one** Person. If only a forward reading is available, we verbalize thus: **It is possible that some** Person speaks **more than one** Language **and that for some** Language **more than one** Person speaks **that** Language. In a few cases where "**the same**" is unambiguous, we still use it to provide a more natural verbalization.

To render natural rather than mathematical verbalizations, we verbalize correlations by using relative pronouns (e.g. "**who**", "**that**"), reflexive pronouns (e.g. "**itself**"), demonstratives (e.g. "**that**"), and typed variables, possibly subscripted (e.g. Person, Person$_1$), rather than resort to untyped variables (e.g. x, y) which are used in some controlled natural languages such as Common Logic Controlled English (CLCE) [20]. For further, related details on our Formal ORM Language (FORML) and its use as an input language as well as an output verbalization language, see [15].

Adverbs in predicate readings (e.g. "rarely" in Figure 2(a)) sometimes requires special care to clearly verbalize constraints, even though the meaning of fact instance verbalizations is clear (e.g. The Person named 'Ann Jones' rarely drives the Car that has CarRegNr 'ABC123'). For example, using our earlier pattern, the uniqueness constraint in Figure 2(a) verbalizes thus: **Each** Person rarely drives **at most one** Car.

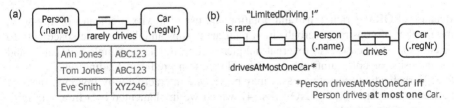

Fig. 2. Adverbs can raise further ambiguity issues with constraint verbalization

This ambiguous verbalization could mean either (a) For each person there is at most one car that he/she rarely drives, or (b) For each person, it is rare that he/she drives at most one car. There are competing linguistic and logical theories for dealing with adverbs that might shed some light on this issue [17, ch. 12], but these theories are complex, and their utilization would seem to require either substantial linguistic parsing machinery or the possession of sophisticated grammatical expertise by the user. We feel that the best way to resolve such ambiguities is to offer an expanded verbalization that more closely matches the underlying logical form of the ORM constraints. Every ORM constraint unambiguously maps to a logical form (e.g. see [4]), and in this example the uniqueness constraint requires interpretation (a), since uniqueness on a role means that entries in the fact column for that role are unique. This interpretation is clearly captured by the logical form of the uniqueness constraint: $\forall p$:Person $\exists^{0..1}c$:Car p rarely drives c, which directly maps to the expanded verbalization: **For each** Person, **there is at most one** Car **such that that** Person rarely drives **that** Car. Interpretation (b) is radically different since it predicates the rareness to the situation of a person driving at most one car, which may be modeled in ORM as in Figure 2(b) by objectifying a derived fact type. ORM formalizes objectification as situational nominalization rather than propositional nominalization [14].

While unambiguously rendering the required meaning, expanded logical form verbalizations are lengthy and awkward in comparison with our typical verbalizations (e.g. compare "**Each** Person was born in **at most one** Year" with "**For each** Person, **there is at most one** Year **such that that** Person was born in **that** Year"). Moreover, the cases where our simple verbalization patterns are ambiguous are rare in practice. As a pragmatic compromise, we generate the simple verbalization patterns by default, but plan to give users the option of seeing the logical form verbalizations whenever they wish (e.g. when the default verbalization provided seems unclear to them). For users who are poor at English grammar or logic, this facility would have the added benefit of improving their grammatical or logical expertise.

Verbalization of constraints and derivation rules may involve use of logical operators. To disambiguate the order in which logical operators are evaluated, we emulate bracketing by careful use of indentation rather than rely on artificial precedence rules (e.g. evaluate **and** before **or**) as is done in some other controlled natural languages. We also avoid well known ambiguous patterns (e.g. "all are not", which could mean either "none are" or "not all are"). Further examples of FORML in this regard may be found in [15].

3   Improved Verbalization Patterns

Because of ORM's rich constraint notation and use of mixfix predicates of any arity, the number of constraint verbalization patterns is substantial. We have space here to discuss only two cases: (a) external uniqueness constraints on simple join paths, and (b) inclusive-or constraints where each role starts a predicate reading with no front text. Verbalizations for other cases may be viewed interactively by invoking the verbalizer in a recent build of NORMA [4], which we implemented as a free plug-in to Microsoft Visual Studio.

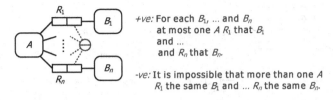

Fig. 3. New verbalization patterns for external uniqueness constraints

Figure 3 shows our new alethic constraint verbalization patterns for an *external uniqueness constraint* where the join object type A starts predicate readings with no front text for each of the n constrained predicates $R_1 .. R_n$. The object types $B_1 .. B_n$ may be entity or value types, and are not necessarily distinct. If two or more of the B_i are identical, their instances in the verbalization must be distinguished by subscripting. Previously, our verbalizations for such cases required declaration of a context clause to specify the relevant fact types, followed by another clause that referenced the constrained role combination within that context. Our new verbalizations are closer to the underlying logical form, and are easier for users to understand.

We provide positive verbalizations for all constraints, and negative verbalizations as well for some constraints. Positive verbalizations stress what must be satisfied while negative verbalizations indicate what cannot or must not be the case. Positive alethic constraint verbalizations may optionally be prepended by the modal necessity operator □ "**It is necessary that**". The *deontic* versions prepend the positive reading by the obligation operator O "**It is obligatory that**" and replace ~◊ "**impossible**" in the negative reading by F "**forbidden**". For further discussion of constraint modalities and the use of modal operators see [8]. Here are two examples:

+ve, alethic: **For each** Building **and** RoomNr,
                  at most one Room is in **that** Building **and** has **that** RoomNr.

-ve, deontic: **It is impossible that**
                  more than one Arrow is from **the same** Node₁ **and** is to **the same** Node₂.

The above patterns do not work if any predicate has *front text, or a predicate does not start at A*. For example, consider the fact types: "the location of Room is in Building; RoomNr is of Room". For such cases we use another pattern leading to the following verbalization for the positive alethic case: **For each** Building **and** RoomNr, **there is at most one** Room **such that** the location of **that** Room is in **that** Building **and that** RoomNr is of **that** Room.

For all cases, the constraint has the following logical forms. The initial formula in each case assumes there are predicates $R_1..R_n$ starting at an A role. For each fact type F_i where this is not the case, replace xR_iy_i by y_iS_ix where S is the preferred predicate starting at B_i and $1 \leq i \leq n$.

+ve alethic: $\Box\ \forall y_1{:}B_1..y_n{:}B_n\ \exists^{0..1}x{:}A(xR_1y_1\ \&\ ..\ xR_ny_n)$

+ve deontic: $O\ \forall y_1{:}B_1..y_n{:}B_n\ \exists^{0..1}x{:}A(xR_1y_1\ \&\ ..\ xR_ny_n)$

-ve alethic: $\sim\!\Diamond\ \exists y_1{:}B_1..y_n{:}B_n\ \exists^{2..}x{:}A(xR_1y_1\ \&\ ..\ xR_ny_n)$

-ve deontic: $F\ \exists y_1{:}B_1..y_n{:}B_n\ \exists^{2..}x{:}A(xR_1y_1\ \&\ ..\ xR_ny_n)$

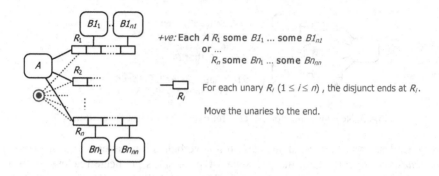

Fig. 4. A basic inclusive-or constraint verbalization pattern

Figure 4 shows the positive alethic verbalization pattern for an *inclusive-or constraint* where each constrained role starts a predicate reading with no front text. The object types are not necessarily distinct. Each predicate R_i may have ni roles ($ni \geq 0$) following the role played by A. So the predicates may all be of different arity (unary upwards). We verbalize all the non-unaries before all the unaries. The *deontic* version prepends "**it is obligatory that**" to the positive form. Here are two examples:

+ve, alethic: **Each** Partner became the husband of **some** Partner on **some** Date
                or became the wife of **some** Partner on **some** Date.

+ve, deontic: **It is obligatory that each** Vehicle was purchased from **some** AutoRetailer
                or is rented.

No negative verbalization is supplied for this constraint case, as it is awkward and adds no clarity. The logical form of the positive alethic constraint is shown below, where any disjuncts with unary predicates must appear only after all the disjuncts with non-unary predicates (if any). The deontic form simply replaces □ by O.

+ve alethic: $\Box \, \forall x{:}A \, (\, \exists x_1{:}B1_1..x_{n1}{:}B1_{n1} \, Rxx_1..x_{n1}$
$$\lor \dots$$
$$\lor \, \exists x_1{:}Bn_1..x_{nn}{:}Bn_{nn} \, Rxx_1..x_{nn} \,)$$

4   Implementing Verbalizations Involving One Join Path

In ORM, an external uniqueness or external frequency constraint applies to roles in more than one fact type, so a join path must be associated with that constraint to formally specify the relationship between the fact types. In most common cases, NORMA is able to automatically determine the join path for common patterns; more complex cases require user entry. For this discussion, we assume that an error-free join path has been implicitly or explicitly created for the verbalized multi-fact type constraints. For cases where the optimized verbalization patterns are not available due to complexity in the model structure or associated predicate readings, the verbalization engine relies on the join paths to generate verbalizations for the general logic-based forms.

We have previously discussed the use of *role paths* in NORMA to define fact type derivation rules [5]. This same underlying structure is also used to specify join paths for constraints. The primary difference is that fact type derivation rules project nodes from a role path onto roles of the derived fact type, while join paths project these same nodes onto *constraint roles*, meaning a use of role in the ordered list of roles restricted by the given constraint. In terms of predicate logic, the role path forms the body of a logic expression, while the projection targets (fact type roles for derivation and constraint roles for join paths) can be viewed as a list of variables in the head of the logic expression. Continuing with the logic parallels, each variable projected from the body (thus appearing in the head) is assumed to be *free* in the body, meaning that the value of the variable is known in the body and can be unambiguously referenced with a *that X* expression.

By default, the role path verbalization engine assumes that no variables are free in the path and existentially places [13] variables as needed. For example, given the Room/Building uniqueness example with the obvious role path (consisting of an and-split after Room), the path verbalization engine would produce *some Room is in some Building and has some RoomNr* for the simple reading, and *for some Room, the location of that Room is in some Building and that Room has some RoomNr* for the more complicated reading with front text.

Clearly, the path verbalizations with no free variables are of very little use, just as the body of an expression is of little use without a head. Forming full verbalizations, therefore, requires each type of role path use to tell the role path verbalizers which nodes are used in the head, thereby forming a meaningful verbalized statement. The general verbalization for a multi-fact type uniqueness constraint has gone through several stages:

1. The original form used a stated Context and no join path. This is not very readable and does not clearly state the relationship between the different fact types involved. The join information can be inferred for trivial cases, but this approach of simply listing the fact types is inadequate for non-trivial join paths.

   Context: Room is in Building;
   Room has RoomNr.
   In this context, each Building, RoomNr **combination occurs at most once.**

2. The first modification used a verbalized role path with no free variables to form the context. The main problem here is the ambiguity of the term *some* used to introduce variables in the verbalized path. The intent was to convey "any" in a universal sense (e.g. given *any* Room), but it can also be interpreted as applying to some (but not all) of the specified instances.

   Context: some Room is in **some** Building
   and has **some** RoomNr.
   In this context, each Building, RoomNr **combination occurs at most once.**

3. This form is improved by applying the universal quantifier to the projected variables before verbalizing the role path. Here, the items in the *for each* list correspond to the constraint roles, which are shown numbered on a diagram in NORMA when the constraint is selected. This form uses the *combination* suffix after the projection list so that we can use *that combination* without ambiguity in the later list. Note that this structure is used as the general form of a frequency constraint by modifying the quantifier (for example, replacing *occurs exactly once* with *occurs at most 2 times* verbalizes a frequency constraint over the same roles).

> **For each** RoomNr **and** Building **combination,**
> **if some** Room has **that** RoomNr
> **and** is in that Building
> **then that combination occurs exactly once in this context.**

It is also important that we can use the stronger *exactly once* phrase here instead of the earlier *at most once*. This is possible because the context is fully defined, so the quantifier applies only to states that are known to exist, implying *at least once*. This differs from the earlier forms, which did not have a complete logical context and could use only the weaker *at most once*.

4. While formally correct, the 3rd verbalization form lacks elegance because it still relies on the abstract notions of *combination* and *context* to express its meaning. The desired general verbalization brings us directly to the pure logical form discussed earlier by applying the at-most-one numeric quantifier to *Room* before verbalizing the role path—with both the universally and numerically quantified variables free in the path body.

> **For each** Building **and** RoomNr,
> **there is at most one** Room **such that**
> **that** Room is in **that** Building
> **and** has **that** RoomNr.

While the fourth form is clearly the most readable, it adds a non-trivial implementation challenge for the case of the fully generalized role path. The problem is that the projection list (used in the universal *for each* quantifier) is part of the model, as is the full role path, but the list of items to numerically quantify must be programmatically determined. It is common for the list of unique items to be the same as the remaining variables not under universal quantification, but this does not hold when additional conditions are applied to the role path. For example, we could add the many-to-many fact type Building has been certified by Inspector to the model and add this as a condition in the join path. We now want "**for each** Building **and** RoomNr, **there is at most one** Room **such that** that Room is in **that** Building **that** has been certified by **some** Inspector **and that** Room has **that** RoomNr." In this case the number of inspectors is irrelevant, so using "**at most one** Room **and** Inspector" as the numerically quantified list would be incorrect.

The algorithm used to determine the numerically quantified variable list takes advantage of the hierarchical nature of the role path structure, proceeding as follows:

1. Starting from the projected nodes, recursively step towards the top of the role path, record all passed nodes, and add all nodes that form a join to another fact type to the list of variables to be numerically quantified. This means that variables in n-ary fact types that are not directly joined to other fact types are not in the list.

2. If any node is passed—including those not added to the list—that is correlated with another node in the tree, then repeat the recursive algorithm beginning at each of the correlated nodes. Repeat until the top of the role path has been reached in all cases.

3. Provide a consistent order for the numerically quantified nodes determined by 1 and 2 by doing a depth-first walk from the top of the role path, ordering nodes in the order in which they are reached.

The point of this algorithm is to discover the nodes that must be unique, while not touching nodes (or the corresponding variables) from the conditional branches. The algorithm also covers cases where projected nodes are above or below each other in the path. For example, if our path starts at Building and steps over Room to RoomNr (instead of the default path that starts at Room and splits to Building and RoomNr), then this algorithm still identifies Room as the numerically quantified variable. This algorithm also correctly identifies variables for uniqueness constraints across longer role paths.

5   Conclusion

This paper extended our previous work on verbalization of ORM models, noting various techniques for avoiding ambiguity, including the use of expanded logic-based verbalizations to deal with problematic cases arising from the presence of adverbs in predicate readings. We also provided improved general verbalization patterns for some common kinds of ORM constraints, and discussed an algorithm for verbalizing external uniqueness and external frequency constraints over role combinations projected from join paths of arbitrary complexity.

We have implemented in NORMA all of the verbalization work described in this paper, as well as many other new verbalization patterns, with the sole exception of the expanded logic-based verbalization option, which we plan to soon support. Other research plans in this area include refining the verbalization of other constraints and derivation rules, fully implementing FORML as a language for inputting and querying ORM models, and providing verbalization in languages other than English.

Acknowledgement. Our verbalization research has benefited from reviewing linguistics publications suggested by our colleague Kurt Stirewalt, who also encouraged more use of logical forms.

References

1. Allen, J.: Natural Language Understanding, 2nd edn. Benjamin/Cummings (1994)
2. Bakema, G., Zwart, J., van der Lek, H.: Fully Communication Oriented Information Modelling. Ten Hagen Stam (2000)

3. Chen, P.P.: The entity-relationship model—towards a unified view of data. ACM Transactions on Database Systems 1(1), 9–36 (1976), http://csc.lsu.edu/news/erd.pdf
4. Curland, M., Halpin, T.: The NORMA Software Tool for ORM 2. In: Soffer, P., Proper, E. (eds.) CAiSE Forum 2010. LNBIP, vol. 72, pp. 190–204. Springer, Heidelberg (2011)
5. Curland, M., Halpin, T., Stirewalt, K.: A Role Calculus for ORM. In: Meersman, R., Herrero, P., Dillon, T. (eds.) OTM 2009 Workshops. LNCS, vol. 5872, pp. 692–703. Springer, Heidelberg (2009)
6. Halpin, T.: A Logical Analysis of Information Systems: static aspects of the data-oriented perspective. Doctoral dissertation, University of Queensland (1989), http://www.orm.net/Halpin_PhDthesis.pdf
7. Halpin, T.: Business Rule Verbalization. In: Doroshenko, A., Halpin, T., Liddle, S., Mayr, H. (eds.) Information Systems Technology and its Applications, Proc. ISTA-2004. Lec. Notes in Informatics, vol. P-48, pp. 39–52 (2004)
8. Halpin, T.: ORM 2. In: Meersman, R., Tari, Z., Herrero, P. (eds.) OTM-WS 2005. LNCS, vol. 3762, pp. 676–687. Springer, Heidelberg (2005)
9. Halpin, T.: Modality of Business Rules. In: Siau, K. (ed.) Research Issues in Systems Analysis and Design, Databases and Software Development, pp. 206–226. IGI Publishing, Hershey (2007)
10. Halpin, T.: Object-Role Modeling: Principles and Benefits. International Journal of Information Systems Modeling and Design 1(1), 32–54 (2010)
11. Halpin, T.: Fact-Orientation and Conceptual Logic. In: Proc. 15th International EDOC Conference, pp. 14–19. IEEE Computer Society, Helsinki (2011)
12. Halpin, T., Curland, M.: Automated Verbalization for ORM 2. In: Meersman, R., Tari, Z., Herrero, P. (eds.) OTM 2006 Workshops. LNCS, vol. 4278, pp. 1181–1190. Springer, Heidelberg (2006)
13. Halpin, T., Curland, M., Stirewalt, K., Viswanath, N., McGill, M., Beck, S.: Mapping ORM to Datalog: An Overview. In: Meersman, R., Dillon, T., Herrero, P. (eds.) OTM 2010. LNCS, vol. 6428, pp. 504–513. Springer, Heidelberg (2010)
14. Halpin, T., Curland, M.: Enriched Support for Ring Constraints. In: Meersman, R., Dillon, T., Herrero, P. (eds.) OTM-WS 2011. LNCS, vol. 7046, pp. 309–318. Springer, Heidelberg (2011)
15. Halpin, T., Harding, J.: Automated support for verbalization of conceptual schemas. In: Brinkkemper, S., Harmsen, F. (eds.) Proc. 4th Workshop on Next Generation CASE Tools, Univ. Twente Memoranda Informatica 93-32, pp. 151–161 (1993)
16. Halpin, T., Morgan, T.: Information Modeling and Relational Databases, 2nd edn. Morgan Kaufmann, San Francisco (2008)
17. Halpin, T., Wijbenga, J.P.: FORML 2. In: Bider, I., Halpin, T., Krogstie, J., Nurcan, S., Proper, E., Schmidt, R., Ukor, R. (eds.) BPMDS 2010 and EMMSAD 2010. LNBIP, vol. 50, pp. 247–260. Springer, Heidelberg (2010)
18. ter Hofstede, A., Proper, H., van der Weide, T.: Formal definition of a conceptual language for the description and manipulation of information models. Information Systems 18(7), 489–523 (1993)
19. Larson, R., Segal, G.: Knowledge of Meaning. MIT Press (1995)
20. Object Management Group: UML OCL 2.0 Specification (2005), http://www.omg.org/docs/ptc/05-06-06.pdf
21. Object Management Group: Unified Modeling Language Specification, version 2.4.1 (2011), http://www.omg.org/spec/UML/2.4.1/
22. Sowa, J.: Common Logic Controlled English (2004), http://www.jfsowa.com/clce/specs.htm
23. Wintraecken, J.: The NIAM Information Analysis Method: Theory and Practice. Kluwer, Deventer (1990)

A Validatable Legacy Database Migration Using ORM

Tjeerd H. Moes[1], Jan Pieter Wijbenga[1], Herman Balsters[2], and George B. Huitema[2]

[1] TNO
P.O. Box 1416 9701 BK Groningen,
The Netherlands
{tjeerd.moes,jpwijbenga}@tno.nl
[2] University of Groningen
Faculty of Economics and Business
P.O. Box 800 9700 AV Groningen,
The Netherlands
{h.balsters,g.b.huitema}@rug.nl

Abstract. This paper describes a method used in a real-life case of a legacy database migration. The difficulty of the case lies in the fact that the legacy application to be replaced has to remain fully available during the migration process while at the same time data from the old system is to be integrated within the new system. The target database schema was fixed beforehand, hence complicating and limiting our choices in constructing a possible target schema. The conceptual approach of the Object-Role Modeling (ORM) method helped us to better understand the semantics of the source and target system and enabled us to abstract from implementation choices in both the source and the target schemas. We discuss how our method could help in executing other legacy data migration projects.

Keywords: data migration, conceptual modeling, fact-oriented modeling, re-engineering, ORM, database schema mapping.

1 Introduction

Legacy IT systems form a growing problem for companies and other institutions. Their core business usually depends on legacy systems while at the same time knowledge of these systems may be fading or absent. Furthermore, as the organization changes, the legacy system may fall behind in terms of functionality, adaptability, reliability or user interface. Businesses must make an inconvenient tradeoff between the growing risk of using legacy systems and the often bigger risk of migration to newer systems. Considering the prevalence of legacy systems, one can conclude that many companies choose to stick with their legacy systems.

When, for whatever reason, a migration becomes inevitable it is critical that the migration process is well-manageable as well as well-managed. This is why legacy migration has received considerable attention in the literature, see [5], [12], [13] and [15].

P. Herrero et al. (Eds.): OTM 2012 Workshops, LNCS 7567, pp. 409–418, 2012.
© Springer-Verlag Berlin Heidelberg 2012

The problem of database re-engineering stems from (legacy) databases that are hard to understand or that perform badly. Database re-engineering involves the reconstruction of the (intended) semantics of some source database. Subsequent data migration involves mapping a source database schema to a target database schema. We shall show how Fact-based modeling, and in particular ORM, can help in re-engineering (relational) databases.

Fact-based modeling (FBM [6]) is a methodology for modeling the universe of discourse (UoD) of an information system. The main purpose of fact-based modeling is to capture the semantics of the UoD, and to validate results with a domain expert. Unlike Entity-Relationship (ER) modeling or object-oriented modeling, fact-based modeling treats all facts as relationships (unary, binary, ternary etc.). Fact-based modeling facilitates natural verbalization and thus enables productive communication (and, hence, validation) between stakeholders. FBM is also used as the general name of several fact-based conceptual data modeling dialects, such as Object Role Modeling (ORM [9]), Natural language Information Analysis Method (NIAM) [8], and Fully-Communication Oriented Information Modeling (FCO-IM) [1]. This paper uses basic ORM notations; the version of ORM discussed in this paper is ORM 2 [7], as supported by the NORMA tool [3], [4].

This paper provides a first case of applying a migration method using fact-oriented modeling for legacy databases after a method by [14] (explained in Section 3). Moreover our paper proposes a number of improvements to this method. It is structured as follows. Section 2 introduces the migration case. The developed migration method is shortly described in Section 3. Section 4 states the results and the experiences of applying this method. Finally, in Section 5 the conclusion is presented together with some guidelines for future research.

2   Case Description; Migration of a Legacy Online Survey Tool

A sales company, here referred to as SalesCo, uses an online survey tool to gather information on customer satisfaction. This monitoring tool, called KBM, produces on average 1000 survey invitations and processes 150 customer responses per week. The response data is used by SalesCo to manage the customer service and sales departments.

The tool KBM, developed in 2000, must be replaced by a newer and better survey tool LimeSurvey (LS). Continuing to operating the legacy KBM system imposes a big risk since the KBM system administrator is the only person who knows how to operate and maintain KBM. Moreover no system documentation exists at all.

Because of its importance to SalesCo and the frequent use by its customers, the service that KBM provides and the data it contains, must remain operational and accessible at all times. Therefore we have to find a migration method that will eventually result in a complete shutdown of KBM while SalesCo can continue to do online surveys and access the response data on the new LS system.

3   The Applied Migration Method; Re-engineering Steps

The migration method we apply in this paper is based on the experimental method by [14]. In this method the migration is performed on the conceptual level before the physical migration is started. We use elements of that method, add detail to the existing steps and add an extra step on the conceptual level that creates a conceptual model by following the conceptual schema design procedure CSDP [9].

In this section we will describe 5 steps that we conducted to better understand the source and target schema and design an initial mapping between the two. We call this the re-engineering phase of the migration. The steps of re-engineering the source and target schemas and creating the required mappings are as follows. Figure 2 visualizes the re-engineering phase and the created artifacts, illustrated by examples from the case. The prefix 'kbm_' stands for the source system; 'ls_' indicates the target system. A prefix of 'm_' indicates that the object type originates from the optimized model.

Step 1: Creating an Optimized and Correct Conceptual Model of Data to Be Migrated (Artifact A1). We select the subset that only contains data that has to be migrated from the source database. This model is created as if there is no target database to take into account and it abstracts from specific implementation choices of the source. Hence, this is the ideal target model and it is created using the CSDP [9] and input from the business analysis phase. The CSDP ensures that we capture the semantics in a complete and correct fashion. In this model we ignore parts of the source schema that are non-normalized.

Step 2: Creating an Unoptimized but Valid ORM Model of the Source Database (Artifact A2). The first purpose of this step is to help understand the semantics of the source schema and provide useful knowledge to extract the data correctly. This step uses an unoptimized ORM model (Artifact A2) that has correct ORM syntax. It is called unoptimized because it is not constructed using the CSDP, but using a simple reverse engineering procedure that has two substeps. First, we iteratively construct an ORM model where tables in the source schema are represented by object types that have binary relations with value types representing the table's columns. Secondly, we identify and add to the model all constraints that were left implicit in the original source database schema. These missing constraints may or may not be enforced in the application logic. Knowing these constraints simplifies data extraction. The second purpose of this step is that it indicates problems regarding data pollution and the presence of quirks in the schema. This provides valuable input for the process of cleaning the data and the source schema. For brevity reasons, we will not address the cleaning of data here.

We use an ORM-based questionnaire [14] to provide a systematic way to identify which tables and columns should be migrated from the source to the target database, as illustrated in Figure 1.

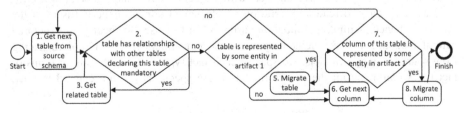

Fig. 1. ORM based questionnaire, after [14]

Artifact A1 (the ORM conceptual model of data to be migrated) serves as the first input for the procedure. It answers the question; which tables must be migrated? The second input for the procedure is the source database schema. It provides all available tables and columns.

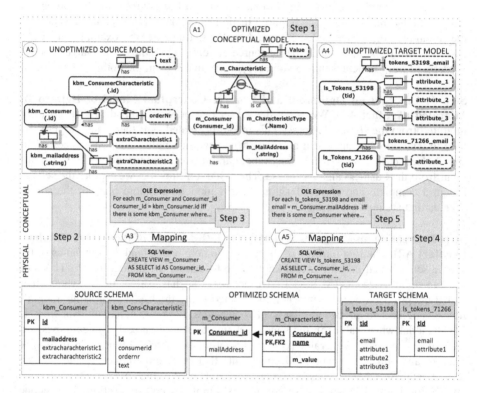

Fig. 2. The re-engineering and mapping phase of the migration method with process steps and artifacts

Step 3: Creating a Mapping between the Optimized Conceptual Model's Schema and the Unoptimized Source Schema (Artifact A3). The optimized and correct conceptual ORM model (A1) is mapped to the unoptimized ORM model (A2). This mapping uses sentences written in a structured format, coined as OLE: ORM Logic-based English [2] (not to be confused with Object Linking and Embedding). OLE aims at being easy to read and write by non-technical domain experts (users of the database), hence facilitating validation purposes. OLE is used to specify, in structured natural language format, elementary facts and constraints in ORM. For migrating from source to target models, we specify each fact type in a target table in terms of fact types coming from the source model. These specifications are entered in OLE into an experimental tool called the ORM ReDesigner that will automatically transform these OLE specifications of (derived) fact types into view definitions in SQL.

Step 4: Creating an Unoptimized ORM Model of the Target Database (Artifact A4). Similar to step 2, the resulting model provides valuable knowledge about the target schema for creating the mapping.

Step 5: Mapping between the Optimized Conceptual ORM Model's Schema and the Unoptimized ORM Target Schema (Artifact A5). OLE expressions map the optimized and correct conceptual ORM model (A1) to the unoptimized ORM target model (A4).This mapping facilitates insertion of the data into the target system.

After the re-engineering phase, the physical migration phase is started. A snapshot of the source schema is copied into a temporary migration database running on the target database server. A synchronization mechanism between source and temporary migration DBMS is implemented to propagate transactions between the two servers. The mapping A3 is implemented in the temporary migration database and the mapping A5 is implemented in the target database. A transaction propagation mechanism provides the final integration of data from the mapping A5 to into the target database.

4   Application of the Migration Method

KBM Database Details. The systems KBM and LS are running on different physical machines. Both systems use the same database management system (SQL Server 2008) for persistent data storage. The present system administrator explained that during the 12 years of operation KBM has received several ad-hoc database and application updates to meet new survey requirements.

All survey data, together with application data, is stored in the KBM database that contains 40 tables. An overview of the database schema shows some remarkable implementation choices: No primary key is defined for ten of the tables, 18 tables lack foreign key constraints that should be there or are improperly not referenced by a foreign key constraint in another table. Also, data relating to the same conceptual object type is spread over multiple tables.

Figure 3 below illustrates these findings. Tables 'optout' (short for 'optional out') and 'consumercharacteristic' do not have a primary key and both tables do not have any explicit relation to other tables. For the table 'consumercharacteristic' we can guess, based on the used naming convention, that the attribute 'consumerid' references the id in the table 'consumer' as a foreign key constraint. Probably, the mail addresses in 'optout' also relate to consumer, but we will come back to this later. The table 'providedanswer' stores response data of all surveys and does not contain a primary key or foreign key constraint either.

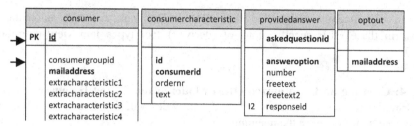

consumer		consumercharacteristic	providedanswer	optout
PK	id		askedquestionid	
	consumergroupid **mailaddress** extracharacteristic1 extracharacteristic2 extracharacteristic3 extracharacteristic4	**id** **consumerid** ordernr text	**answeroption** number freetext freetext2 I2 responseid	**mailaddress**

Fig. 3. Part of the ER model of the KBM database schema, (the arrows indicate a foreign key reference from another table not shown in this fragment, 'PK' indicates primary key)

The non-mandatory attributes 'extracharacteristic1' up to 'extracharacteristic4' are part of the 'consumer' table. But it appears that a consumer can have any number of characteristics since the 'consumercharacteristic' table also stores characteristics of consumers. So, these characteristics are stored over two tables, although there is no semantic difference.

LS Database Details. The target system LS is developed by the open source community of LimeSurvey.org. The LS database contains 24 base tables that store survey and application data. For each new survey two tables are added –called 'tokens_...' and 'survey_...' - to the database. These tables contain customer invitation data and survey response data. When we compare the database by the same implementation aspects as we did for KBM we get the following results: A primary key is defined for all 24 tables; There are no foreign key constraints in the schema and attributes relating to the same entity are properly located in the same table, as it seems for now.

survey_53198		tokens_53198		surveys	
PK	id	PK	tid	PK	sid
	submitdate lastpage **startlanguage**		firstname lastname email		**owner_id** admin **active**

Fig. 4. Part of the ER model of the LS database schema, only the first 7 attributes of each table are shown

Based on the table names we can guess that the last part (53198) of the 'survey_53198' and 'tokens_53198' table's names is a foreign key in the 'surveys' table.

This short analysis took the project team data model expert 1 day to make. Based on this analysis we conclude that many constraints on data of both databases are stored in application logic. We have to work with the system as is, and take the findings into account during the project execution.

4.1   Re-engineering Phase

Deriving semantics from the KBM database was difficult. No documentation was available and the system administrator could not provide detailed information about the meaning of tables and attributes either. So, understanding the semantics of the plain schema of the source database –containing 265 attributes in 40 tables- proved to be very hard. Looking at the source code of the application did not bring the team to a better understanding either. The application code contained many 'hacks' and was not systematically written using some particular design paradigm.

Analyzing the target LS system, the team found out that LS utilizes a completely different schema compared to that of KBM. Although LS was well-documented and the database schema was easier to understand than KBM's, it was hard to point out the relation between attributes in the target database schema and the attributes in the source schema. Apparently, the two databases were implemented very differently.

Re-engineering Step 1. To cope with different schema implementations, the team constructed an optimized and correct conceptual model that represents the information to be migrated in a fashion that is independent of implementation.

After 12 iterations and a final validation with the domain expert, the model contained fifteen entity types, eight value types and fifty roles. This model was Artifact A1 (see Figure 1); it contained the subset of all data required in the target system. Mapping this conceptual model to a relational schema (using the RMap procedure) provided 70 columns in 13 tables. This schema, together with semantic information from the ORM conceptual model, was validated by SalesCo and the project manager. Figure 5 shows a part of the first artifact.

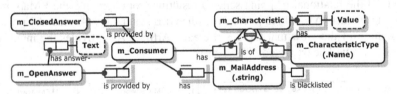

Fig. 5. Part of the optimized ORM conceptual model created as Artifact A1, the 'm_' prefix indicates that these entities refer to data to be migrated

This conceptual model provided abstraction from the implementation choices of the KBM schema and gives the correct semantics of the data. It allowed us to greatly simplify the information consumers' characteristics.

Re-engineering Step 2. During the database analyses we found out that many relations and constraints were implicit in the source schema. To solve this problem, the procedure was done iteratively and together with modeling the source schema in ORM. By closely examining the source schema and the source data, we were able to model all missing and implicit constraints in the source schema in an ORM model.

This ORM model now contains only the entities that must be migrated from the source and all constraints they are subject to. We name this second ORM model artifact A2. To illustrate this result, a part of artifact A2 is shown in Figure 7. This model shows the actual relations between e.g. 'kbm_ProvidedAnswer' and 'kbm_Consumer' that were implicit in the source schema. All constraints that were added are indicated with a model note.

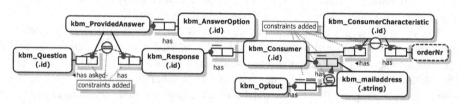

Fig. 6. Part of the ORM Reengineered source model created as artifact 2, the 'kbm_' prefix indicates that these entities refer to the source database

Re-Engineering Step 3. Creating the SQL statements for the first mapping proved to be a complex task. As shown in the previous examples (Figures 3-6), single entities in the target schema contain attributes from multiple tables in the source schema. We used OLE to describe the required mapping between the optimized conceptual model's schema and the unoptimized source schema. OLE is closer to natural language then SQL. Although validating the correctness of the OLE mapping statements is still not a trivial procedure, it proved to support the creation of, and communication about the mapping statements better then writing these directly in SQL statements. Hence it was more easy to validate the OLE with the source system expert.

We used the relational mapping schema resulting from applying the RMap procedure to the artifacts A1 and A2 to construct the OLE statements. Artifact A1 provided the definition of the view that OLE will create. Artifact A2 provides the input from which the data will be extracted.

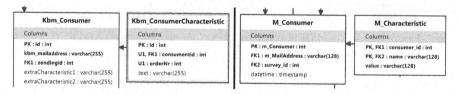

Fig. 7. Part of the ER schema produced from Artifact A2 (left) and Artifact A1 (right)

For each m_Characteristic and Value in m_Characteristic has Value,
(the Value of m_Characteristic is the text of kbm_ConsumerCharacteristic where there is some kbm_ConsumerCharacteristic and consumer_id = consumerid) or
(the Value of m_Characteristic is the extraCharacteristic1 of kbm_Consumer where there is some kbm_Consumer and consumer_id = id) or ...
(the same pattern holds for extraCharacteristic 2, 3 and 4).

OLE was translated manually into SQL code that is shown below:

```
CREATE VIEW m_Characteristic AS
SELECT kbm_CCh.consumerid AS consumer_id, kbm_CCh.text AS value, [..] FROM
kbm_ConsumerCharacteristic kbm_CCh, [..]
UNION SELECT kbm_C.id AS consumer_id, kbm_C.extraCharacteristic1 AS value FROM
kbm_Consumer kbm_C, [..].
```

Re-Engineering Step 4 and 5. Step 4 was similar to the re-engineering step 2. The target database also contained implicit constraints. The LS schema did not contain any foreign key constraints. In a test we confirmed that this a potential source of error. Step 5 was similar to step 3, but we found that the target schema contained less quirks than the source schema. The second mapping was still time-consuming, but less complex than the step 3 mapping process.

At the time of writing we are in the stage of the physical data migration. The mapping from the unoptimized source schema to the optimized schema has been implemented as a view. This implementation means that all updates, inserts and deletes on the source database are propagated to the target database server. The next step is to implement the mapping from the optimized schema to the target database schema and to propagate the transactions.

5   Conclusion

This paper described a legacy database migration method that employs ORM's conceptual approach. The ORM approach turned out to be a good implementation-independent way of expressing both domains in the same terms and to learn about the semantics of the model. And it allowed us to split up the mapping process into smaller steps. Despite the small size of our case, we directly experienced the need for a conceptual modeling approach, in order to abstract from the technical details of the source and target system. Future research will have to show that our method will work in different, more complex situations.

In this case, we experienced technical complexities such as a lack of primary keys, implicit constraints stored in the application, duplicate values in the source database, complex relations, conceptual objects represented in different numbers of tables in source and target and different implementation choices. We believe that whichever method may be chosen, these problems will always have to be addressed.

One could argue whether one mapping directly from source to target, instead of two would have been easier to maintain. Even so, the exercise of constructing the two slightly easier mappings may facilitate the construction of an eventual single mapping from source to target.

Problems of scalability are not addressed in this method. We realize that for databases with thousands of tables this method of re-engineering may introduce huge amounts of work and will be practically infeasible.

Future research will entail further validation of the applied method on migration projects that differ in any of the above aspects. Furthermore, creating the view statements that provide the mapping still involves some manual labor. This mapping process certainly will benefit from the further advancement of a natural language-like conceptual query language such as FORML [10], OLE and CQL [11].

References

1. Bakema, G., Zwart, J., van der Lek, H.: Fully Communication Oriented Information Modelling. Ten Hagen Stam (2000)
2. Balsters, H.: ORM Logic-based English (OLE) and the ORM ReDesigner tool: Fact-based Re-engineering and Migration of Relational Databases, Technical Report, Faculty of Economics and Business (May 2012)
3. Curland, M., Halpin, T.: Model Driven Development with NORMA. In: Proc. 40th Int. Conf. on System Sciences (HICSS-40). IEEE Computer Society (January 2007)
4. Curland, M., Halpin, T.: The norma tool for orm 2. In: Pernici, B. (ed.) Advanced Information Systems Engineering. LNCS, vol. 6051. Springer, Heidelberg (2010)
5. Drumm, C., Schmitt, M., Do, H.H., Rahm, E.: Quickmig: automatic schema matching for data migration projects (2007)
6. FBM working group: Fact-based modeling exchange schema. Version 20111021c (2011), http://www.factbasedmodeling.org/
7. Halpin, T.: ORM 2. In: Meersman, R., Tari, Z., Herrero, P. (eds.) OTM-WS 2005. LNCS, vol. 3762, pp. 676–687. Springer, Heidelberg (2005)
8. Halpin, T.: ORM/NIAM Object-Role Modeling. In: Bernus, P., Mertins, K., Schmidt, G. (eds.) Handbook on Information Systems Architectures, 2nd edn., pp. 81–103. Springer, Heidelberg (2006)
9. Halpin, T., Morgan, T.: Information Modeling and Relational Databases, 2nd edn. Morgan Kaufmann, San Francisco (2008)
10. Halpin, T., Wijbenga, J.P.: FORML 2. In: Bider, I., Halpin, T., Krogstie, J., Nurcan, S., Proper, E., Schmidt, R., Ukor, R. (eds.) BPMDS 2010 and EMMSAD 2010. LNBIP, vol. 50, pp. 247–260. Springer, Heidelberg (2010)
11. Heath, C.: The constellation query language. In: OTM 2009: ORM Workshop, OTM 2009, pp. 1–10 (2009)
12. Henrard, J., Roland, D., Cleve, A., Hainaut, J.-L.: An Industrial Experience Report on Legacy Data-Intensive System Migration. In: IEEE International Conference on Software Maintenance, pp. 473–476 (2007)
13. Lin, C.Y.: Migrating to relational systems: Problems, methods, and strategies. Contemporary Management Research 4(4), 369–380 (2008)
14. Sluis, T.C.: The ORM Infusion Migration Method, Master's Thesis, University of Groningen (2011)
15. Wu, L., Sahraoui, H., Valtchev, P.: Coping with legacy system migration complexity. In: 10th IEEE International Conference on Engineering of Complex Computer Systems, ICECCS 2005, pp. 600–609 (2005)

OnToContent 2012 PC Co-chairs Message

Semantics play an increasingly crucial role in large and complex networked information systems. Ontologies and semantic data all represent information sources valuable to end users and are fundamental resources that support a variety of applications in several domains, e.g., data integration, document management, information retrieval, web engineering, and so on. For this reason Onto-Content 2012 focuses on issues related to the creation and evaluation of content for ontologies and semantic data.

We have two tracks in the workshop. The first track focuses on ontology methodology and engineering. We are happy to have a first paper addressing the problem of negotiating ontology content in order to reach conceptual agreements. The other four papers address the application of ontologies for solving problems in specific domains, two of which propose ontologies that manage information related to information artifacts, and other two use ontologies in applications for supporting decisions in the digital libraries and risk management domains. This panel reflects an increasing acknowledgment of the usefulness of ontologies to solve problems in the field.

The second track acknowledges the increasing need for the automation and semi-automation of tasks that develop and evaluate ontology content, since manually developing and evaluating the content of ontologies is notoriously a time consuming task. The main topics investigated in the second part of this workshop are therefore related to the generation of content using semi-automated methods, by learning ontology modules from existing Web sources, by semi-automatic mapping ontologies and enriching their content, and by providing an end-to-end data and knowledge acquisition architecture with reference to a specific use case in the agrifood domain.

Finally, publishing public content under the form of high-quality governmental linked data will become an important driver for supporting applications implementing the vision of the Open Data initiative. An invited talk about strategies that can be undertaken to optimize the design of government linked data will be given by Aldo Gangemi (Head of Semantic Technology Lab, ISTC-CNR), who conducted outstanding research in fields such as pattern-based ontology design, semantic social networks, and collaborative modeling, with applications in several domains from Medicine to eGovernment.

The organization of this workshop is supported by the 7FP-INCO-295006 project SIERA: Integrating Sina Institute into the European Research Area. We are also grateful to all the reviewers, who carefully evaluated the submitted papers and provided authors with valuable comments to improve their work.

July 2012

Mustafa Jarrar
Amanda Hicks
Matteo Palmonari

P. Herrero et al. (Eds.): OTM 2012 Workshops, LNCS 7567, p. 419, 2012.
© Springer-Verlag Berlin Heidelberg 2012

Towards an Ontology of Document Acts: Introducing a Document Act Template for Healthcare

Mauricio B. Almeida[1], Laura Slaughter[2,3], and Mathias Brochhausen[4]

[1] Department of Information Theory and Management,
Federal University of Minas Gerais, Brazil
mba@eci.ufmg.br
[2] Department of Computer and Information Science, NTNU, Trondheim, Norway
[3] The Interventional Centre, Oslo University Hospital, Oslo, Norway
laura.slaughter@gmail.com
[4] Division of Biomedical Informatics, University of Arkansas for Medical Sciences,
Little Rock, AR, USA
MBrochhausen@uams.edu

Abstract. Background: In current information systems the pervasive role of documents and their ability of creating new entities are often overlooked. Regularly, documents are stored as mere files without analysis of their deontic powers. In order to make intelligent management of documents a real possibility, we propose an ontological representation of document acts. Objectives: This article summarizes first steps towards a sound ontological representation of documents in healthcare organizations by providing a template structure for documents acts. Methods: We rely on the theory of document acts to develop such a template for defining pragmatic aspects of documents and to provide examples of the application in healthcare procedures. Furthermore, we show how this research contributes for the development of an OWL representation of document acts. Results: We provide a template for document acts and show its usage in clinical guidelines. Conclusion: While the definition of pragmatic aspects contributes to a clearer representation of documents acts in the healthcare domain, further development needs to be carried out regarding representation of document acts in ontologies.

Keywords: ontologies, documents, document acts.

1   Introduction

Documents are valuable entities for different sorts of organizations, working as end-points of information flows. A wide variety of documents are used in a multitude of fields of human activity, which adds to the complexity of the task and makes systematic approaches necessary. Looking at examples from medical standards, e.g. HL 7, one can see the multiplicity of documents required to carry out an ordinary activity in healthcare organizations. In the case of blood donation looking at HL7 Version 3 we find documents primarily serving the function of recording data, for instance donor

P. Herrero et al. (Eds.): OTM 2012 Workshops, LNCS 7567, pp. 420–425, 2012.

questionnaires, lab results and donation event information [3]. Some documents, though, are bearers of additional properties. They give rise to new sorts of claims and obligations. For instance, in case of a blood donation order or a blood donation consent form [3].

We argue that information systems employed in healthcare organizations can take advantage of an appropriate characterization and formalization of documents, as well as both the actions they trigger and the states of affair they bring about. To achieve this aim, we present a template grounded on well-founded theories, which can be used as a guide for distinguishing types of documents in formal ontologies. In doing so, we rely on speech act[1] and document act theory [13] to explain the social consequences of documents. In addition, we adapt a framework for formalization [11] to determine the purpose of documents in a certain context. We look at a use case that stems from an ongoing project being conducted in healthcare organizations, dealing with medical guidelines to check generalizability. We explain how this research contributes to the development of an OWL representation of documents and document acts.

In this paper, we first describe theories to manage the complex phenomena arising from the usage of documents in everyday life focusing on healthcare organization environments. Then, we present a case study on which we develop a template for pragmatic characterization of documents present in medical institutions. We validate that step by proofing the applicability of the template for another aspect of healthcare. Finally, we discuss our findings and present the basis for the future development of an ontological representation of document acts in OWL.

2   Deontic Powers of Documents

The basis of document act theory is the recognition, which arose in 20th century philosophy of language, that we can use language to do other things beyond merely describing reality. This recognition led to the development of speech act theory [1, 10]. Austin states that some sentences, instead of describing something in the world, are enabling something to get done. They are performances of acts of certain kinds. These sentences are named performatives, by contrast with sentences in which something true or false is being stated, which are called constantives. Furthermore, speech acts theory establishes that, in any ordinary language, a speaker performs acts of three different kinds: locutionary acts, in which, more than merely uttering sounds, one is speaking the words with the meaning they really have; illocutionary acts, in which one is using the words in order to ask a question, give an order, make a promise, and so forth; and perlocutionary acts, used to convince someone to do something [1].

Important language features depend on the illocutionary acts being performed, rather than on the meaning of words and sentences [5]. Examples of ability of speech acts to bring about new entities are obligations and claims to which promises and orders give rise. The general speech acts theory was consolidated into a theoretical framework [9], in which the dimensions of utterance, meaning and action could be seen as being unified together.

Just as speech enables speech acts, documents can be more than just reports. They can spawn new entities in reality [13]. Searle [10] refers to the ability of documents to add something to reality as their *deontic power*. Smith [13] points out that according shifting from speech acts to document acts extents the purposes achievable by social action. Speech acts are events existing only in their execution and have a limited temporal and spatial reach, while document acts involve documents which endure through time. It is through documents that document acts do not underlie the temporal and spatial restrictions as speech acts.

3   Creating a Document Template

Within the healthcare segment, documents carry extensive economic, legal and medical entailments. Medical documents are complex instances employed for several purposes in healthcare processes and used to: to support patient care, to fulfill external obligations, to support administration, to support quality management, to support scientific research and to support clinical education.

Nevertheless, means to characterize documents regarding their *deontic power*s in medical organizations have not yet been implemented. In order to overcome this, we propose a template that is the result of an analysis of documents and document act in the process of using medical guidelines.

3.1   The Template

The first step in developing a template consists in selecting documents and characterize them according to three components based on Searle's theory of social action: the context, the content and the force [10]. The following paragraphs elucidates each of these components, according [11]:

Context concerns conditions of the world in which a document act is manifested. In order to characterize the context of a document, at a minimum the following questions should be considered: Who issues the document? Who receives the document? What is pertinent concerning the temporal and geographical aspects? Other contextual features that contribute to the success of the document act are gathered under the label contributory features.

Content consists of the proposition underlying the document act, that is, the common element that characterizes the effect of that document, independently of the form in which this element is presented.

Force aims to determine the commitments, that is, the organizational relationships established and the way in which the content is related to the institutions' environment. Searle and Vanderveken [11] give the following sub-components to specify the force of document acts:

- **Point** represents the purpose of a document act, namely, whether it is an assertive, a commissive, a directive, a declarative, or an expressive. An assertive point tells how the world is, for example, in predicting. A commissive point commits one to doing something, for example, promising. A directive point tries to get the receiver to do things, for example, ordering. A declarative point changes the world, for example, declaring. An expressive point expresses attitudes, for example, apologizing.

- **Degree** corresponds to the strength of a point, which is defined according to a taxonomy[11]. For example, assertives can be identified by the sequence of verbs: assert, claim, state, deny, argue, inform, suggest, to mention but a few. The verb "assert" produces an assertive stronger than the verb "suggest". Other sequences of verbs are organized in a similar fashion for commissives (e.g., commit, consent, etc.), directives (direct, recommend, etc.), declaratives (declare, endorse, etc.) and expressives (complain, protest, etc.).

- **Content conditions** are conditions required by the propositional content so a document act can be achieved. For example, invoicing can only refer to payments and not to salaries.

- **Preparatory conditions** are states of affairs that an entity must address for the success of the document act. For example, in placing an order the buyer presupposes that the supplier still sells those products.

Once presented the basic issues, we summarize the elements for the characterization into a template where some additional details and examples are added (Table 1):

Table 1. Template for the characterization of documents

Step	How to execute
Selecting document bearers of document-acts	Identify actions triggered by the document in its official usages Identify economic entities
Describing the context	Identify who issues and who receives the document Identify what are the related temporal and geographical aspects
Defining the content	Identify the underlying proposition of the document
Assigning the point	Identify the point according to the content defined. The point can be: an assertive, a commissive, a directive, a declarative, an expressive.
Assigning the degree	Identify the degree according to the point defined (ascending order): ▪ Assertives: assert > claim > state > assure > argue > inform > ... ▪ Commissives: commit > promise > threaten > refuse > offer ... ▪ Directives: direct > request > demand > advice > recommend ... ▪ Declaratives: declare > resign > appoint > approve > endorse > ... ▪ Expressives: apologize > thank > complain > protest > greet ...
Assessing content conditions	Identify premises that assure the point and degree feasibility.
Assessing preparatory conditions	Identify premises that assure the success of the point and degree.

3.2   Applying the Template

A template based on the aforementioned guidelines was applied to instances of documents pertaining to the scope of healthcare institutions. From the Evicare Project[1], a medical guideline was used to test the template. The results are depicted in Table 2. With these documents a receiver chooses to act (give a specific treatment) or not to act (does not act according to the original plan) after reading the contents stated as part of guideline recommendations. The force "degree" of these documents can be either "advice" or "recommendation".

---

[1] http://www.evicare.no/

Table 2. Template applied to a medical guideline

	Who issues	Guideline authoring panel
	Who receives	Physician
	Temporal aspect	Occasional, intermittent use during patient encounter
Context	Local aspect	In hospital, clinic or private practice within the area of application of the guideline authoring panel
	Contributory features	-Purpose: inform physicians of what a panel recommends they do based on evidence -Institutional system involved: healthcare -Possible actions: read, follow recommendations -Role of the agents: physician role
Content		x provides medical services in accordance with the guidelines to patient y
	Point	Directive
	Degree	Advice, Recommend
Force	Content conditions	The healthcare institution agrees that the guidelines are authoritative, up to date, and can be used by physicians that work
	Preparatory conditions	The physician can understand and carry out the recommendations in the guidelines.

4   Discussion and Future work

Above we demonstrated an application of Searle's work to create a comprehensive and consistent representation of document acts in the healthcare domain. However, the steps presented are merely preparatory to the final goal of providing an ontology of document acts in Web Ontology Language Version 2 (OWL 2) [8]. We argue that in order to achieve that goal, beyond the initial steps based on Searle's work, we really need to engage in in-depth ontological analysis of social action. Smith [14] argues that Searle's position, which restricts social ontology to elements reducible to physical entities, is lacking an analysis for the most central features of the social world: quasi-abstract entities that lie outside the world of physics, but are indeed fully part of the historical world [14].

Therefore, in creating the OWL representation of document acts we will base our efforts on Smith's proposal [14] to use Adolf Reinach's social ontology [9] as the foundation. This bases the existence of social entities on declarations which can be made portable and pertinent through time and space in documents. We hold that the key entities in a formal ontology of document acts based on Reinach are claims and obligations. Thus, the ontological status of these is a key issue that needs to be resolved.

The OWL implementation of our document act ontology which is still under development follows the OBO Foundry criteria [7][2].The ontology is based on Basic Formal Ontology (BFO) [2] and re-uses existing ontologies in the domain. Foremost, we imported classes from Information Artifact Ontology (IAO) [5], for instance *document* (http://purl.obolibrary.org/obo/IAO_0000310). With regard to the ontological status of claims and obligations, which are of crucial importance to document act

---

[2] For now the criterion of the ontology being publicly available is not fulfilled due to the fact that the size and stability of the OWL file is below initial release.

ontology, we agree with Smith [13] that both are instances of generically dependent continuants. However, the axiomatization of *document act* in OWL 2 based on these elements has proven to be the hard nut.

We expect to make continuing progress regarding the OWL implementation. Once this is achieved we aim for a complete coverage of the elements of the template, thus binding Searle's naturalist social ontology to a theory that allows for quasi-abstract entities.

An OWL implementation will allow not only capturing the subtleties of document act theory, but enable reasoning data annotated with terms from the template or the ontology. This will create the opportunity to reason over claims and obligations created and acted upon in healthcare, for instance in the case of checking the impact of clinical guidelines or ensuring the legality of blood specimens.

Acknowledgements. This work is partially supported by the Arkansas Biosciences Institute, the major research component of the Arkansas Tobacco Settlement Proceeds Act of 2000 and by award number 1UL1RR029884 from the National Center for Research Resources. The content is solely the responsibility of the authors and does not necessarily represent the official views of the National Center for Research Resources or the National Institutes of Health. Thanks are due to the Ontology Research Group team from the New York State University at Buffalo, US and to William R. Hogan, Division of Biomedical Informatics, UAMS, Little Rock, US.

References

1. Austin, J.L.: How to do things with words. Oxford University Press, Oxford (1962)
2. Basic Formal Ontology, http://www.ifomis.org/bfo (retrieved May 24, 2012)
3. HL7 Version 3 Standard: Blood, Tissue, Organ; Donation, Release 1, Committee Ballot 2 (January 2008), http://www.hl7.org (retrieved September 04, 2010)
4. Information Artifact Ontology, http://purl.obolibrary.org/obo/iao.owl (retrieved May 24, 2012)
5. Morris, M.: An Introduction to the Philosophy of Language. Cambridge Press, Cambridge (2005)
6. OBO Foundry Principles, http://obofoundry.org/crit.shtml (retrieved May 24, 2012)
7. OWL 2 Web Ontology Language. Overview, http://www.w3.org/TR/owl2-overview (retrieved May 24, 2012)
8. Reinach, A.: Sämtliche Werke. Textkritische Ausgabe in 2 Bänden, Smith, S.K. (ed.) Philosophia Verlag, München (1989)
9. Searle, J.: Expression and Meaning: Studies in the Theory of Speech Acts. Cambridge Press, Cambridge (1985)
10. Searle, J.: The Construction of Social Reality. Free Press, New York (1995)
11. Searle, J., Vanderveken, D.: Foundations of Illocutionary Logic. Cambridge Press, Cambridge (1985)
12. Smith, B.: An Essay on Material Necessity. In: Hanson, P., Hunter, B. (eds.) Return of the A Priori (Canadian Journal of Philosophy, Supplementary Volume 18), pp. 301–322 (1993)
13. Smith, B.: Document Acts, http://ontology.buffalo.edu/smith/articles/DocumentActs.pdf (retrieved July 02, 2010)

An Architecture for Data and Knowledge Acquisition for the Semantic Web: The AGROVOC Use Case

Maria Teresa Pazienza, Armando Stellato, Alexandra Gabriela Tudorache,
Andrea Turbati, and Flaminia Vagnoni

University of Rome Tor Vergata
Via del Politecnico 1, 00133 Rome, Italy
{pazienza,stellato,tudorache,turbati}@info.uniroma2.it,
f.vagnoni@gmail.com

Abstract. We are surrounded by ever growing volumes of unstructured and weakly-structured information, and for a human being, domain expert or not, it is nearly impossible to read, understand and categorize such information in a fair amount of time. Moreover, different user categories have different expectations: final users need easy-to-use tools and services for specific tasks, knowledge engineers require robust tools for knowledge acquisition, knowledge categorization and semantic resources development, while semantic applications developers demand for flexible frameworks for fast and easy, standardized development of complex applications. This work represents an experience report on the use of the CODA framework for rapid prototyping and deployment of knowledge acquisition systems for RDF. The system integrates independent NLP tools and custom libraries complying with UIMA standards. For our experiment a document set has been processed to populate the AGROVOC thesaurus with two new relationships.

1 Introduction

Nowadays we are surrounded by huge amounts of information: The World Wide Web, books, business documents, all creating a nearly infinite source of unstructured or weakly structured data. It is becoming mandatory to find novel ways to access, categorize and, most important, to extract meaningful knowledge from this virtual repository. Furthermore, to efficiently exploit such knowledge, it is necessary to structure it in a computer readable format. Processing, transforming and manipulating heterogeneous information is not an easy task and requires the integration of several dedicated tools. Frameworks for the integration, orchestration and harmonization of the different aspects related to content acquisition are thus an emerging need for industry-standard knowledge management systems.

In this work, we propose a knowledge elicitation scenario, where we report on the adoption of the CODA[1] framework [1] in a complete content production process,

---

[1] CODA – Computer Aided Ontology Development, http://art.uniroma2.it/coda

P. Herrero et al. (Eds.): OTM 2012 Workshops, LNCS 7567, pp. 426–433, 2012.
© Springer-Verlag Berlin Heidelberg 2012

ranging from content analytics, information extraction and triplification for Ontology development and enrichment.

The system aims to extract relations from unstructured web and textual documents to populate the AGROVOC[1] thesaurus with new relationships.

Currently the AGROVOC thesaurus contains more than 40 000 concepts in 21 languages and is widely populated with a few general semantic relations, such as: *broader term, narrower term, is used as, is part of.* Then, there are a series of more specific relations which have been only partially instantiated or even just defined, for future use. For a human expert, identifying such relations in free text content, with a good degree of confidence, requires not only specific skills but also a great amount of time. In the context of this experience, two different relations (and their inverses) will be extracted: *IsPestOf* and *IsInsecticideFor*. The *IsPestOf* relation is defined, but still not instantiated in AGROVOC, while *IsInsecticideFor* was not defined. The closest relation to *IsInsecticideFor* currently defined is *is_use_of* (e.g. "pesticide" <is use of> "ddt"), that relates one substance to its use as an insecticide, but not to its target pests.

This paper presents some notes on related work, the system architecture, the implementation choices and the experimental results. Moreover, conclusions will be drawn and future work will be discussed.

2 Related Work

In recent years, the research community showed a growing interest in the area of relation extraction and semantic role labeling, with different approaches being formulated as Machine Learning or Rule Based Systems [2]. While, machine learning systems have a better generalization power, they typically require extensive training and at least some seed data annotated by domain experts, rule based systems are better suited for specific tasks, but need a comprehensive support of domain experts. Considering that our application is domain related (Agriculture), and that we aim to perform high precision Relation Extraction for enriching AGROVOC (one of the biggest semantic resources on the Agriculture field), the second approach was selected. While maintaining an adequate recall, in the presented scenario, the precision was very important, to minimize the human experts' effort for validating the extracted triples.

Recently, several rule based information extraction systems were developed. Among them we cite: TextMarker [3], the AVATAR Information Extraction System [4] and, different systems for the medical [5] and biological (gene analysis) domains [6]. Furthermore, in the last decade, a number of ontology development related research directions emerged as: the automation of ontology development (KYOTO Project [7]), ontology and lexicon integration [8, 9], or ontology learning and population [1, 10]. In this context, open platforms and frameworks as GATE [11] and UIMA [12] were developed. Moreover, business oriented systems were designed as the ones for AGROVOC thesaurus enrichment including tasks as automatic term relationship cleaning and refinement [13] and vocabulary alignment [14].

---

[1] AGROVOC – FAO's Agricultural Thesaurus, www.fao.org/agrovoc/

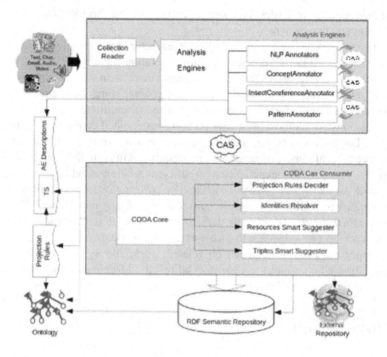

Fig. 1. System Architecture

While preexistent systems focus on general relations (broader and narrower term), the proposed system focuses on specific semantic relations extraction from free text, and concept alignment between different resources (e.g. *IsPestOf, IsInsecticideFor*).

3   Architecture

The architecture aims to optimize the Information Acquisition flow and to support the development of an easy and fast to integrate, modular system, complying with UIMA standards (see **Fig. 1**). The system is based on CODA framework and combines different NLP tools together with custom libraries and implements a complete NLP flow starting with collection reader, Information Extraction, more specifically relation extraction and ending with triplification and ontology enrichment/development.

In this context, the system implements different Analysis Engines, ranging from the reuse of available NLP annotators based on Stanford NLP Suite[1] and a few dedicated ones such as: *ConceptAnnotator*, *InsectCoreferenceAnnotator* and *PatternAnnotator*. Each annotator adds one ore more layers of semantic information having different roles in the workflow. NLP Annotators include: Segmenter, PosTagger, Lemmatizer, NamedEntityRecognizer, Parser and CoreferenceResolver

---

[1] Stanford Core NLP - http://nlp.stanford.edu/software/corenlp.shtml

Table 1. Triplification process

The sentence: "In the eastern US, the **gypsy moth**[c_30232] prefers **oaks**[c_6409], **poplar**[c_541], **apple**[c_6116]..." (Excerpt form testing file no 136).

Becomes the following **RDF triples:**
```
<rdf:Description rdf:about="http://aims.fao.org/aos/agrovoc#c_30232">
    <rdf:type rdf:resource="http://aims.fao.org/aos/agrovoc#Insect"/>
    <isPestOf xmlns="http://aims.fao.org/aos/agrovoc#"
            rdf:resource="http://aims.fao.org/aos/agrovoc#c_6409"/>
    <isPestOf xmlns="http://aims.fao.org/aos/agrovoc#"
            rdf:resource="http://aims.fao.org/aos/agrovoc#c_541"/>
    <isPestOf xmlns="http://aims.fao.org/aos/agrovoc#"
            rdf:resource="http://aims.fao.org/aos/agrovoc#c_6116"/>
</rdf:Description>
```

Where: c_XXXX stands for the AGROVOC concept ID

[15]. ConceptAnnotator's role is to annotate Insects and Plants found in text using existing resources as AGROVOC and NAL[1] thesauri. Concepts from other resources are aligned with AGROVOC concepts and concepts not present in AGROVOC are suggested as candidates for AGROVOC enrichment. InsectCoreferenceAnnotator is an ad-hoc coreference resolver that recognizes and tags different biological development forms of previously annotated insects as: eggs, larvae, pupae, and PatternAnnotator is an extensible annotator that recognizes different relations present in the analyzed text, each pattern being implemented as a different java class. The complete list of relations and correspondent patterns is presented in **Section 7**.

The role of building the Semantic Repository starting from the UIMA annotated data was delegated to CODA framework. For every annotated document, several RDF[2] triples are generated. Each triple represents a relation having one Subject and one Object. In the case of multiple subjects and/or objects, several triples will be generated one for each subject/object pair. Furthermore, the triples representing the inverse relations will be added (see **Table 1**).

4   Implementation

To start, a local domain knowledge base was constructed, by importing, merging and aligning the concepts of interest for the specific task. This newly created resource is based on AGROVOC and NAL thesauri. To include different forms of concepts and verbs a lemmatizer was used. Moreover, the lists of verbs expressing relations were expanded with their synonyms found in WordNet [16].

To extract *IsPestOf* and *IsInsecticideFor* relations eight different patterns were developed as summarized in **Table 2**. For each relation the aim was to use generalized

---

[1] NAL, National Agricultural Library's Agricultural Thesaurus, http://agclass.nal.usda.gov

[2] RDF, Resource Description Framework, http://www.w3.org/TR/rdf-primer

rules, to avoid overfitting. Furthermore, given the scope of this demo, we selected a small number of rules to speed up the annotation, development, experimental process and evaluation.

Table 2. Relation Extraction Pattern Summary

Relation	Pattern	Notes
IsPestOf	(insect)+ (MD)? be (pest|pests) (plant)+	This pattern recognizes if a previously annotated *insect(s) (be) pest of plant(s)*.
	(insect)+ (VB (including synonyms)) (plant)+	VB in {attack, damage, devastate, eat, feed on, feed upon, prefer, munch, enter, crawl, tunnel, infest, destroy} and synonyms.
IsInsecticid eFor	(pesticide)+ (MD)? be (pesticide(s)|insecticide(s)) (insect)+	One or more general pesticides (chemicals) are identified as insecticide(s) for specific insect(s).
	(pesticide)+ (MD)? be (used| (effective (including synonyms)) (against|on) (insect)+	[effective] ADJ and its synonyms.
	(pesticide)+ (VB (including synonyms)) (insect)+	VB in {repel, control, destroy, mitigate} and synonyms VB in {kill, defeat} without synonyms.
	(insect)+ (MD)? be (sensitive to|sprayed with) (pesticide)+	Identifies if insect(s) is/are sensitive to specific chemical.
General Patterns	Interrogative Pattern	Used to eliminate interrogative phrases that can introduce ambiguity
	Negation Pattern	Used to eliminate negative phrases that can introduce ambiguity

Where: MD – modal verb (can, may, could, should ecc.); VB – verb.

5   Corpus Description

The analyzed corpus has been collected as a selection of documents from a few publicly available websites (e.g. wikipedia.org, usda.gov, agric.wa.gov.au). This added different degrees of complexity to the analysis, due to the presence of not correctly formatted phrases (implicit subject or verb) or very long and complex ones, difficult to be understood even for human experts. For instance, in many cases the verb is missing as in: *"Moths of economic significance:* Gypsy moth *(Lymantria dispar), a pest of hardwood trees in North America."*.

Furthermore, often coreference analysis could not be applied as in several sentences the subject referred to the concept from the precedent section or in other cases was a specific instance of the concept present in the preceding sentence. *E.g. "The most serious pests are mealybugs that feed on citrus;* **other species** *damage sugarcane, (…)"*. It is difficult even for a human to understand that "other species" refers to other mealybugs not eating citrus.

The entire corpus contains 270 HTML files, of different lengths ranging from few sentences to several pages, each covering a specific arguments as insect pests (75%) or pesticides (25%), and was divided into training (170 files) and testing (100 files).

6   Experimental Setup and Evaluation Criteria

The aim of the experiments was to evaluate the relation extraction flow, including different annotators' contribution for two different relations: *IsPestOf* and *IsInsecticideFor*. In this context, different experiments were conducted, analyzing both HTML and well formatted txt files. Txt files were extracted from HTML pages and cleaned (tags, links and other specific HTML information was discarded).

Furthermore, as several sentences are difficult to be understood even by domain experts, both the existing resources and sentence complexity were considered for evaluation. Sentences in which a clear coreference relation was not found, or implied concepts and relations are present (subject or verb are missing), were not accounted (about 30%, mostly regarding insect pests). E.g. *"In late 2007, the moth eradication program involving (aerial spraying) of a product containing E. postvittana attractant sex pheromones as its active ingredient, among other substances not yet revealed to the public, over sixty square miles near the Pacific coast between Monterey and Santa Cruz was begun."*. In this case sex pheromones are not an insecticide but they can be used in an integrated pest control program.

To understand the contribution of each general annotator we designed four experiments over the baseline.

Baseline experiment includes ConceptAnnotator and PatternAnnotator without synonyms and InsectCoreferenceAnnotator. Furthermore, interrogative and negative sentences were not excluded and this is expected to introduce errors. Negative sentences are the sentences containing negation words as *not* and several negative adverbs and their synonyms such as: *never, uncommon, inconceivable, out of the question, unimaginable, unacceptable*. *Experiment1* consists on the baseline experiment to which was added the InsectCoreferenceAnnotator. *Experiment2* is the same as *Experiment1* from which interrogative and negative sentences were excluded. *Experiment3* adds synonyms to *Experiment2, while Experiment4* adds synonyms to *Experiment1*. In the context of AGROVOC enrichment, for each experiment the number of distinct extracted triples was analyzed. Results were evaluated using precision and recall as in Information Retrieval (see **Section 7**).

7   Results

The objective of preferring precision over recall was achieved as shown in **Table 3**. Each annotator has its own positive or negative contribution to the results. The best results were obtained within **Experiment4**, while **Experiment1** had a major contribution to results improvement.

Table 3. Experimental results

Relation	HTML Corpus								
	IsPestOf			*IsInsecticideFor*			*AllRelations*		
	Prec.	Rec.	F1	Prec.	Rec.	F1	Prec.	Rec.	F1
Baseline	*82.4*	*24.3*	*37.6*	*100.0*	*27.9*	*43.6*	*87.0*	*24.7*	*38.5*
Exp.1	87.2	34.5	49.4	100.0	30.2	46.4	90.0	33.3	48.6
Exp.2	87.2	28.6	43.0	100.0	25.6	40.7	90.0	27.8	42.5
Exp.3	83.3	25.2	38.7	100.0	25.6	40.7	87.2	25.3	39.2
Exp.4	**86.3**	**37.0**	**51.8**	**100.0**	**30.2**	**46.4**	**89.1**	**35.2**	**50.4**
Relation	Txt Corpus								
	IsPestOf			*IsInsecticideFor*			*AllRelations*		
	Prec.	Rec.	F1	Prec.	Rec.	F1	Prec.	Rec.	F1
Baseline	*75.0*	*14.5*	*24.3*	*100.0*	*20.9*	*34.6*	*81.8*	*16.2*	*27.0*
Exp.1	90.6	38.7	54.2	100.0	23.3	37.7	92.1	34.7	50.4
Exp.2	90.2	37.1	52.6	100.0	23.3	37.7	91.8	33.5	39.1
Exp.3	91.1	41.1	56.7	100.0	30.2	46.4	92.8	38.3	54.2
Exp.4	**91.4**	**42.7**	**58.2**	**100.0**	**30.2**	**46.4**	**93.0**	**39.5**	**55.5**

Furthermore, even if the hypothesis of eliminating Interrogative and Negative sentences (*Experiment2* and *Experiment3*) seemed promising in theory, the results showed that relevant information is lost.

Text files showed a higher precision as a result of well formatted corpus and *IsInsecticideFor* high precision was achieved being described by a simpler language.

8 Conclusions and Future Work

This paper presented a real life use case. The goal was to extract relations such as: *IsPestOf* and *IsInsecticideFor* from unstructured web documents for enriching FAO's AGROVOC thesaurus. This experience showed that it is possible to implement a fully functional Ontology Development workflow based on CODA architecture including different UIMA Annotators both for undertaking Information Extraction specific tasks and as wrappers to preexisting NLP tools. The developed system showed promising results in terms of thesaurus alignment, relation extraction and ontology population. The flexibility and modularity of the system permit both to expand the current analyzed relations and to change with little effort the application domain, by redefining the information sources and the extraction rules.

To contrast the effort needed for rule generation the system could be refined by learning new rules as in [17]. In this context, other relations as *[Plant X] benefits from [Substance Y]* or *[Substance X] is herbicide for [PestPlant Y]* could be analyzed and an ad-hoc coreference resolution system for insecticides could further improve results.

Moreover, to avoid creating domain related annotators the pattern matching algorithms could be rewritten in PEARL language [18] under CODA. And the syntactic analysis could be improved and internationalized by integrating different parsers as Chaos [19] that analyzes both English and Italian languages.

References

1. Fiorelli, M., Pazienza, M.T., Petruzza, S., Stellato, A., Turbati, A.: Computer-aided Ontology Development: an integrated environment. In: New Challenges for NLP Frameworks, Valletta, Malta, May 18 (2010)
2. Chang, C.-H., Kayed, M., Girgis, M.R., Shaalan, K.F.: A Survey of Web Information Extraction Systems. IEEE Transactions on KDE, 1411–1428 (October 2006)
3. Kluegl, P., Atzmueller, M., Puppe, F.: TextMarker: A Tool for Rule-Based Information Extraction. In: Unstructured Information Management Architecture (UIMA), 2nd UIMA@GSCL Workshop, 2009 Conference of the GSCL (2009)
4. Jayram, T.S., Krishnamurthy, R., Raghavan, S., Vaithyanathan, S., Zhu, H.: Avatar Information Extraction System. IEEE Data Eng. Bull., 40–48 (2006)
5. Regev, Y., et al.: Rule-based extraction of experimental evidence in the biomedical domain: the KDD Cup 2002 (task 1). SIGKDD 4(2), 90–92 (2002)
6. Mykowiecka, A., Marciniak, M., Kupsc, A.: Rule-based information extraction from patients' clinical data. Journal of Biomedical Informatics 42(5), 923–936 (2009)
7. Vossen, P., Soroa, A., Zapirain, B., Rigau, G.: Cross-lingual event-mining using wordnet as a shared knowledge interface. In: Proceedings of GWC 2012, Japan (January 2012)
8. Pazienza, M.T., Stellato, A.: Linguistic Enrichment of Ontologies: a methodological framework. In: OntoLex 2006, Genoa, Italy (2006)
9. Buitelaar, P., Cimiano, P., Haase, P., Sintek, M.: Towards Linguistically Grounded Ontologies. In: Aroyo, L., Traverso, P., Ciravegna, F., Cimiano, P., Heath, T., Hyvönen, E., Mizoguchi, R., Oren, E., Sabou, M., Simperl, E. (eds.) ESWC 2009. LNCS, vol. 5554, pp. 111–125. Springer, Heidelberg (2009)
10. Cimiano, P.: Ontology Learning and Population from Text Algorithms, Evaluation and Applications XXVIII. Springer (2006)
11. Cunningham, H.: GATE, a General Architecture for Text Engineering. Computers and the Humanities 36, 223–254 (2002)
12. Ferrucci, D., Lally, A.: Uima: an architectural approach to unstructured information processing in the corporate research environment. Nat. Lang. Eng. 10(3-4), 327–348 (2004)
13. Morshed, A., Keizer, J., Johannsen, G., Stellato, A., Baker, T.: From AGROVOC OWL Model towards AGROVOC SKOS Model. FAOAIMS (2010)
14. Morshed, A., Sini, M.: Creating and aligning controlled vocabularies. Report (2009)
15. Lee, H., et al.: Stanford's Multi-Pass Sieve Coreference Resolution System at the CoNLL-2011 Shared Task. In: CoNLL-2011 Shared Task (2011)
16. Miller, G.A.: WordNet: A Lexical Database for English. Communications of the ACM 38(11), 39–41 (1995)
17. Liu, B., Chiticariu, L., Chu, V., Jagadish, H.V., Reiss, F.: Automatic Rule Refinement for Information Extraction. PVLDB 3(1), 588–597 (2010)
18. Pazienza, M.T., Stellato, A., Turbati, A.: PEARL: ProjEction of Annotations Rule Language, a Language for Projecting (UIMA) Annotations over RDF Knowledge Bases. In: International Conference on Language Resources and Evaluation (LREC 2012), Istanbul, Turkey, May 21-27 (2012)
19. Basili, R., Zanzotto, F.M.: Parsing Engineering and Empirical Robustness. Journal of Natural Language Engineering 8 (June 2-3 2002)

Ontology Learning from Open Linked Data and Web Snippets

Ilaria Tiddi, Nesrine Ben Mustapha, Yves Vanrompay,
and Marie-Aude Aufaure

Ecole Centrale Paris, France
{ilaria.tiddi,nesrine.ben-mustapha,yves.vanrompay,
marie-aude.aufaure}@ecp.fr

Abstract. The Web of Open Linked Data (OLD) is a recommended best practice for exposing, sharing, and connecting pieces of data, information, and knowledge on the Semantic Web using URIs and RDF. Such data can be used as a training source for ontology learning from web textual contents in order to bridge the gap between structured data and the Web. In this paper, we propose a new method of ontology learning that consists in learning linguistic patterns related to OLD entities attributes from web snippets. Our insight is to use the Linked Data as a skeleton for ontology construction and for pattern learning from texts. The contribution resides on learning patterns for relations existing in the Web of Linked Data from Web content. These patterns are used to populate the ontology core schema with new entities and attributes values. The experiments of the proposal have shown promising results in precision.

1 Introduction

The Web of Linked Data contains solid structured data and aims to link them from different sources using equivalence statements based on an ontological representation. Efforts made by the Semantic Web community to connect data from diverse domains ensure their reliability and disambiguation. Moreover, the Web semantic evolution, by linking and structuring data, avoids the long manual ontology building process, and ontology learning techniques can take advantage from this. Such approaches aim at building ontologies from knowledge sources using a set of machine learning techniques and knowledge acquisition methods. Text-mining techniques for enriching ontologies with concepts and relationships starting from texts have been widely used in the knowledge engineering community. More recently, with the growth of the Web, it has become important to exploit its unstructured textual contents for knowledge acquisition.

In addition to this, a huge amount of information is available as a Web of structured data, in form of shared and open knowledge. Many efforts have been made so far in view of a global adoption of Linked Data[1]. Searching over aggregated data, semantic querying, and applications operating over global data

---

[1] http://linkeddata.org/

P. Herrero et al. (Eds.): OTM 2012 Workshops, LNCS 7567, pp. 434–443, 2012.

are just some of the main objectives for this new data sources format appearing in the Web[1]. Despite the Semantic Web Community's efforts to provide techniques for linking entities between knowledge sources, it is necessary to bridge the gap between structured data of the Semantic Web and web textual contents. Hence, ontology learning can tackle this issue by providing techniques able to structure a large amount of unstructured data without any human intervention.

In this paper, our first aim is to exploit these linked data as a starting point for ontology construction. The Linked Data is increasing in size and connections, and it can be useful to exploit the richness and scalability of this knowledge. Our insight is to use the **Linked Data as a skeleton for ontology construction and for pattern learning from texts**. The novelty is to focus on learning patterns for relations existing in the Web of Linked Data from Web snippets. These patterns are used to populate the ontology core schema with new entities and attributes values. In order to do this, we propose a hybrid approach based on linguistic and statistical techniques for **Pattern-based Entity Discovery from Web Snippets for ontology population**.

This paper is organized as follows. Section 2 presents related works. In Section 3 and 4, we present our approach followed by some experiments we conducted. In the final section, we discuss conclusions and future work.

2   Related Work

Linguistic patterns have been used in many fields namely in non-supervised information extraction and ontology learning. In linguistic approaches, lexico-syntactic patterns are manually defined by linguists and used for taxonomic relation discovery. Hearst pattern-based techniques have been successfully scaled up to the Web in order to identify certain types of relations such as hyponymy or meronymy[3]. *Lexico-syntactic patterns* are constructions that can indicate an interesting relation. Those satisfy the following needs: (i) they occur frequently, (ii) they (almost) always indicate the relation of interest and (iii) they can be recognized with little or no pre-encoded knowledge[4]. Some recent approaches have been proposed to automatically discover patterns. In [11], [5], [12], [7], authors focus on approaches using existing ontology to extract concepts linked by a relationship, and produce lexico-syntactic patterns. The interaction between natural language patterns and ontology relations for ontology population or entities extraction has been already explored.

However, with the increasing need for automatic pattern identification, research has focused on the use of *dependency grammars* for Named Entities Recognition and relation extraction (as an extension of it). *Dependency Trees* represent the syntactic relations between words by a list of tuples in the form *grammarRelation(regentWord, dependentWord)*. Each node is a word with its syntactic label, and each edge a grammatical relation between two words. Dependency patterns are the shortest path linking two words, the instance and its attribute value. This representation also includes the semantic information of a sentence, favoring the extraction relation linking two words[2]. Many efforts have been made using dependency parsing for semantic relations discovery or entity recognition. In [8], [9], [6], relations are extracted using dependency parsing. These approaches are mainly focused on specific grammatical relations, corresponding to the most common ones.

New trends focus on the use of Linked Data for data-mining and ontology matching [3],[13]. However, for the best of our knowledge, they have not been exploited yet for dependencies-based ontology learning. The main challenge of the present work is then to use structured data as training corpora, for dependency structures discovery from unstructured textual contents of the Web.

3   Pattern-Based Ontology Construction

We present our novel approach for ontology learning, using the Linked Data and Web snippets for pattern learning and entity discovery. Our structured approach consists in five main steps, which can be seen in Figure 1.

(1) **Linked Data Extraction.** Focusing on the DBPedia and the Schema.org datasets, which can be considered the backbone of the Linked Data, an existing concept (i.e. selected from the user) is retrieved with its attributes, the instances and their attributes values. Equivalence statements such as "same-as" are used to navigate the web of Linked Data, in order to discover new relations and update the attribute set.

(2) **Web Search.** Considering a couple *instance-attribute value*, the corpus constitution is led using web snippets provided by a search engine, instead of noisy Web pages.

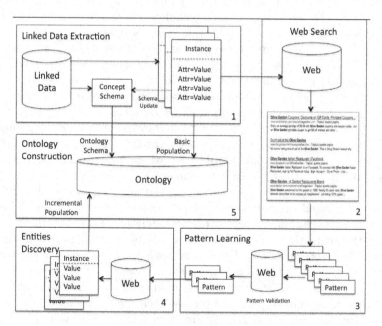

Fig. 1. General Architecture

(3) **Pattern Learning**. Snippets are parsed using Dependency Grammars and associated to a tree. The dependency trees are the key for the patterns collection and validatation. Patterns are discovered by extracting relations between entities.

(4) **Entity Discovery**. Validated dependency patterns are used to query the Web in order to discover new attribute values from new web snippets.

(5) **Ontology Population**. Extracted instances and their attribute values are used for the ontology enrichment.

In the next subsections, the different steps of the proposed approach will be detailed.

3.1 Linked Data Extraction

In order to construct the training corpus for patterns learning, the ontology schema with some related instances are extracted from the linked data knowledge. This step is composed of two tasks, as explained below.

The *Core Schema Extraction* aims to obtain a schema for a concept in the basic ontology provided, for instance, by the user. A set of attributes and some instances related to it alre also included in the schema. The concept and a basic set of attributes is extracted from the Schema.org ontology[2], which has been introduced by the main search engines in order to help web masters to semantically annotate their sites. This ontology provides standardized attributes for several domain concepts, avoiding redundancy or ambiguity in data structures. We then use the Schema.org structure as a starting point for the ontology schema construction.

The *Entities and Attributes values extraction* uses the DBPedia dataset[3] for instances and attributes values extraction. DBPedia is the backbone of the Open Linked Data. Thank's to its interlinking efforts, DBPedia is nowadays the intersection point among the huge Semantic Web Dataset and includes ontologies such as YAGO2, MusicBrainz, GeoNames, WordNet and many others. We exploit this interconnections for retrieving entities and attributes values of a same concept. As certain connections in the web of Linked Data may still be missing, we provide with a matching between Schema.org and DBPedia data, in order to avoid entities ambiguity.

The general schema of the ontology is a combination from the matchings between the *Schema.org* extracted schema and DBPedia instances.

3.2 Web Queries

This step consists in building a training corpus from the Web for the patterns learning. For example, considering a triple

<OliveGarden><parentCompany><DardenRestaurants>

web snippets containing the instance and its attribute value are extracted, by building a web query such as *"Olive Garden*Darden Restaurants"*. The term

---

[2] http://schema.rdfs.org/
[3] http://dbpedia.org/

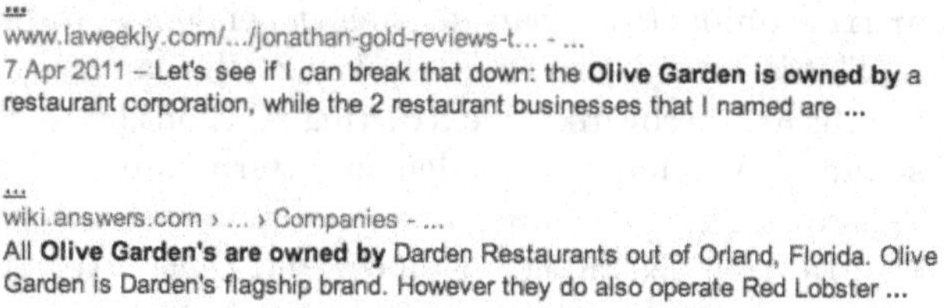

www.laweekly.com/.../jonathan-gold-reviews-t... - ...
7 Apr 2011 – Let's see if I can break that down: the **Olive Garden is owned by** a
restaurant corporation, while the 2 restaurant businesses that I named are ...

wiki.answers.com › ... › Companies - ...
All **Olive Garden's are owned by** Darden Restaurants out of Orland, Florida. Olive
Garden is Darden's flagship brand. However they do also operate Red Lobster ...

Fig. 2. Web Snippets examples

"snippet" we use here denotes a fragment of a Web page returned by remote
search engines (such as Google or Yahoo!) and summarizing the context of
searched pairs, as shown in Figure 2.

Our assomption, widely demonstrated by the literature, is that for each relation there exist in the natural language some universal grammatical patterns
for it. The hypothesis is that the use of Dependency Grammars for the patterns
design can be more efficient for the in information extraction task.

The set of resulting snippets composes the training corpus for the pattern
learning.

3.3   Pattern Learning

The objective of this step is to extract a set of candidate lexico-syntactic patterns
for a specific attribute. For instance, patterns for the attribute <parentCompany>
may be: "X_{NP}, *operates under* Y_{NP}", "*Owned by* Y_{NP}, X_{NP} ..." or "X_{NP},
part of Y_{NP}" For this purpose, Natural Language Processing techniques are
explored here. The step is composed by two phases: the extraction of a set of
candidate patterns from the training corpus, and their ranking by using their
frequencies.

The main objective of the *Dependency Analysis* phase is the acquisition of semantic relations expressed in natural language texts. Considering an input pair
(the instance and its attribute value) and a sentence from the Web corpus, the
structure of the latter is explored in order to retrieve the shortest *dependency path*
between the pair values, as shown in Algorithm 1. Therefore, sentences are analyzed through a dependency grammar parser[4]. Candidate patterns collected are
validated in the *Pattern Ranking* phase. In order to evaluate their accuracy, we
group patterns according to their dependencies. For instance, the pattern
$nsubjpass([start|find], X), agent([start|find], Y)$, refers to a dependency tree
including a passive nominal subject relation and an agent relation, linking the X
and the Y words with the verb is *start* or *find*. The selection of the best candidates
is based on the distributional analysis of patterns in the training corpus.

For validation purposes, we adapted the well known measure of *Term Fre-
quency/Inverse Document Frequency* ($tf * idf$) to our corpus and filter patterns
using their frequencies. The candidate pattern frequencies (i.e., how many times
the pattern is used in a single attribute), are multiplied with their inverse frequencies in each attribute (i.e., the general importance of such pattern among a

---

[4] http://nlp.stanford.edu/software/lex-parser.shtml

Algorithm 1. Pattern Extraction for an attribute

$corpus \leftarrow Entity1 + Entity2 : Sentence$
$patternsForAttribute \leftarrow emptySet()$
for $i = 0$ to $size(corpus)$ **do**
  $dependencyTree \leftarrow parseSentence(Sentence);$
  $head1 \leftarrow getHead(Entity1);$
  $head2 \leftarrow getHead(Entity2);$
  $pattern \leftarrow getPathBetweenNodes(head1, head2, dependencyTree);$
  if $pattern$ exists **then**
    $patternsForAttribute \leftarrow patternsForAttribute + pattern;$
  end if
end for

set of attributes) to obtain the candidate pattern importance. With this *Pattern Frequency/Inverse Document Frequency* ($pf * idf$) approach, most frequent patterns are discarded only if their frequency is too high in all the attributes set. The measure is computed as follows:

$$pf * idf(p, a, A) = pf(p, a) \times log\frac{|A|}{|\{a \in A : p \in a\}|} \tag{1}$$

where p is the candidate pattern, A the number of existing attributes and $|\{a \in A : p \in a\}|$ the number of attributes where the pattern p appears.

3.4 Entity Discovery

This process aims to extract new candidate entities from snippets provided by the search engine. Web queries are formulated using the validated patterns and a test set of entities, as follows: "CANDIDATE *is owned by*". Given the dependency tree of the resulting snippet, and the pattern, a matching between them is executed with the purpose of retrieving node entities. Considering a snippet sentence as "*Pizza Express is owned by One World Enterprises*", the resulting nodes will be X=Express and Y=Enterprises. A further step is necessary in order to retrieve the whole entity, in case it has children-dependencies (Child$_X$=Pizza and Child$_Y$=One,World). Figure 3 shows an example of the tree-matching phase.

3.5 Ontology Construction

The final phase concerns the ontology population with new discovered entities and attribute values. The input queries are made up with the validated patterns, and the ontology concept (i.e. "*Restaurant is owned by*"). While new entities (in our case, *Pizza Express*), corresponding to the X part of the pattern, are instance of the concept (*Restaurant*), attributes values are extracted with the Y part of the pattern (*One World Enterprises*).

This steps is shown in Figure 3.

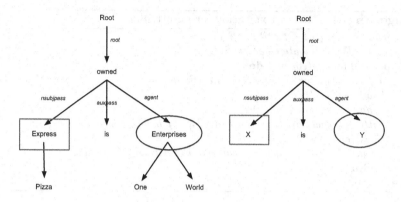

Fig. 3. Tree matching

4   Experimental Evaluation

In this section we give an overview of experiments aiming to evaluate our proposal. We are particularly interested in deriving quantitative insights about the accuracy of our pattern-based extraction approach.

Datasets and Corpora. The evaluation uses three datasets, partitioned into a training and a test corpus. Besides, we used the Schema.org ontology and DBPedia as structured knowledge bases, and the Web as unstructured textual corpus.

Pattern learning phase is carried on using the *Training corpus* built on these two types of sources. We used the Jena framework[5], and the SPARQL language for treating and querying data.

- From the **Schema.org ontology** we extract the basic structure for a given concept. It contains a fixed number of attributes we use for the core schema building of the ontology. We ran our experiment on the *restaurant* main concept.
- From the **DBPedia dataset** 40 instances and attributes values are selected, in order to build the web queries for the search engine.
- 20 snippets for each instance are extracted from the **Web** by using the Bing! Search API[6]. The resulting corpus contains almost 10000 snippets to parse.

A *Test corpus* has been built in order to apply the patterns extraction within the Entities Discovery step. Considering the main concept *Restaurant*, we focused our attention on 5 relations to build the test corpus: *location, founder, keyPerson, parentCompany, products*.

- 100 DBPedia new entities are extracted in order to reformulate new queries.
- 5 snippets for each entity are extracted from the Web and parsed for attribute values extraction.

---

[5] http://jena.apache.org/
[6] http://www.bing.com/toolbox/bingdeveloper/

Evaluation Criteria. Evaluation is based on two criteria.

Precision specifies whether attribute values are correctly extracted. It measures the percentage of correctly selected entities (attribute values) in relation to the total number of selected values.

$$Precision = \frac{correctly\_selected\_values}{total\_extracted\_values} \tag{2}$$

Recall shows how much of the existing knowledge is extracted. It is defined as follows:

$$Recall = \frac{correctly\_selected\_values}{total\_correct\_values} \tag{3}$$

We use DBPedia to judge the correctness of extracted values. If the DBPedia dataset contains the value and is related to the entity with the right attribute relation, it is considered correct. For instance, if the system retrieves $Y=Goldola$ *Holdings* and the entity $X=Pizza$ *Express* has an attribute *parentCompany* with Gondola Holdings as value, the discovered value is correct.

F-Measure is then calculated as:

$$F - Measure = \frac{2(Precision \times Recall)}{(Precision + Recall)} \tag{4}$$

Results. The $pf * idf$ ranking helps to filter on patterns according to their distribution. General common patterns, such as $nn[X, Y]$ (*"Darden Olive Garden"*) or $poss[Y, X]$ (*"Darden's Olive Garden"*), need to be discarded because of their low precision. On one side, it would be difficult to automatically decide to which attribute the extracted entities are related to (i.e. is *Darden* a person or an organization?). On the other, common patterns have a too large coverage on values retrieval and increase cases of syntactic ambiguity, particularly with complex noun phrases.

We evaluated the correctness of the extracted patterns for each attribute.

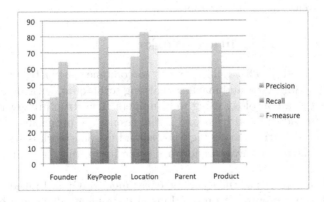

Fig. 4. Histogram for Precision, Recall, F-Measure

In general, better results are produced on attributes more frequent and widespread, as *location, founder* or *product*. Low scores are mainly due to the general evaluation of each attribute. In fact, by analyzing in detail each pattern result, an outstanding difference exists between patterns producing a high precision and recall scores, and the ones giving worse results. Hence, we show a summary table for the attribute *parentCompany*.

Summary table for ParentCompany				
Pattern	Freq.	P	R	F
$nsubjpass(owned, X), agent(owned, Y)$ Ex. "X is owned by Y"	47	95,7%	63.4%	76.3%
$partmod(X, owned), agent(owned, Y)$ Ex. "X, owned by Y"; "X, which is owned by Y"	19	84.2%	10.7%	19.1%
$appos(X, *), prep\_of(*, Y)$ * = (subsidiary|part) Ex. "X, subsidiary of Y"; "X, part of Y"	5	100%	13.1%	23.2%
$nsubj(operates, X), prep\_under(operates, Y)$ Ex. "X operates under Y"	3	66.6%	66.6%	66.6%

Promising results are obtained in precision. An higher precision is attempted by patterns containing a verbal node. The use of grammar relations reveals a good choice since we are able to retrieve sentences with different syntactic structures with a same pattern (such as *"Pizza Express, owned by One World Enterprises"*, "Pizza Express, which is owned by One World Enterprises"). However, some promising patterns have a too low frequency to be considered significant. Low recall is also due to external factors. First, results from web snippets can be non linguistically plain sentences: cut sentences, single linguistic phrases and other kind of noise can be returned from the search engines, and additional steps are necessary to avoid these phenomena. Second, short sentences of snippets may generate errors in parsing and affect precision and recall scores. Finally, using a bigger number of instances in the Entity Discovery phase is certainly necessary in order to increase recall in the approach.

5   Conclusion and Future Work

In summary, the idea behind this work is to combine unstructured and structured data using linguistic and machine learning techniques, with the purpose of the enrichment of an ontology using web snippets. The structure given from the Linked Data provide a good basis and initial results are promising. The dependency patterns we learn return a high precision, but some work is still necessary for improving them. We have put forward some future directions in which this might be done.

We intend to investigate the dynamic enrichment of Open Linked Data from unstructured web contents. The use of Linked Data knowledge could be promising also for entities classification or as test corpus, instead of web snippets. One further possibility is the treatment of snippets, or any other short textual content. Coreference resolution is also a step to explore for increasing parsing results. Unstructured information is often represented as multiple sentences referring to the same entity and linked by anaphoras or cataphoras. Then, coreference resolution would be a good way to increase accuracy of dependency patterns. On the other side, we are aware that we need to investigate for a bigger test corpus easier to parse and analyze, in order to avoid the affection of our pattenr learning.

References

1. Bizer, C., Heath, T., Berners-Lee, T.: Linked Data - The Story So Far. Int. J. Semantic Web Inf. Syst. 5(3), 1–22 (2009)
2. Marneffe, M.C., Manning, C.D.: The Stanford typed dependencies representation. In: Coling 2008: Proceedings of the workshop on Cross-Framework and Cross-Domain Parser Evaluation (CrossParser 2008), pp. 1–8. Association for Computational Linguistics, Stroudsburg (2008)
3. Sabou, M., Fernandez, M., Motta, E.: Evaluating Semantic Relations by Exploring Ontologies on the Semantic Web. In: Horacek, H., Métais, E., Muñoz, R., Wolska, M. (eds.) NLDB 2009. LNCS, vol. 5723, pp. 269–280. Springer, Heidelberg (2010)
4. Hearst, M.A.: Automatic Acquisition of Hyponyms. Technical Report. University of California at Berkeley, Berkeley, CA, USA (1992)
5. Ruiz-Casado, M., Alfonseca, E., Castells, P.: Automatising the learning of lexical patterns: an application to the enrichment of WordNet by extracting semantic relationships from Wikipedia. Data and Knowledge Engineering 61(3), 484–499 (2007)
6. Snow, R., Jurafsky, D., Ng, A.Y.: Learning syntactic patterns for automatic hypernym discovery. In: Proceedings of NIPS 17 (2005)
7. Alani, H.: Position paper: ontology construction from online ontologies. In: Proceedings of the 15th International Conference on World Wide Web (WWW 2006). ACM, New York (2006)
8. Ramakrishnan, C., Mendes, P.N., Wang, S., Sheth, A.P.: Unsupervised Discovery of Compound Entities for Relationship Extraction. In: Gangemi, A., Euzenat, J. (eds.) EKAW 2008. LNCS (LNAI), vol. 5268, pp. 146–155. Springer, Heidelberg (2008)
9. Zouaq, A., Gagnon, M., Ozell, B.: Semantic Analysis using Dependency-based Grammars and Upper-Level Ontologies. International Journal of Computational Linguistics and Applications 1(1-2), 85–101 (2010)
10. Kim, J., Kim, P., Chung, H.: Ontology construction using online ontologies based on selection, mapping and merging. IJWGS 7(2), 170–189 (2011)
11. Cimiano, P.: Ontology Learning and Population from Text: algorithm, evaluation and application. Springer (2006)
12. Maynard, D., Funk, A., Peters, W.: Using Lexico-Syntactic Ontology Design Patterns for ontology creation and population. In: WOP 2009 – ISWC Workshop on Ontology Patterns, Washington (2009)
13. D'Aquin, M., Kronberger, G., Suárez-Figueroa, M.: Combining Data Mining and Ontology Engineering to enrich Ontologies and Linked Data. In: Workshop: Knowledge Discovery and Data Mining Meets Linked Open Data - Know@LOD at Extended Semantic Web Conference, ESWC (2012)

An Ontology for the Identification
of the most Appropriate Risk Management Methodology

Silvia Ansaldi[1], Marina Monti[2], Patrizia Agnello[1], and Franca Giannini[2]

[1] INAIL - Centro Ricerche - Via Fontana Candida, 1 - 00040 Monte Porzio Catone (Roma)
{s.ansaldi,p.agnello}@inail.it
[2] CNR - IMATI , Via De Marini, 6 – 16149 Genova
{marina.monti,franca.giannini}@ge.imati.cnr.it

Abstract. Methods and technologies for risk management have been developed and consolidated over time in different sectors and to meet various needs. Recently, ISO organization published a set of documents for risk assessment. These guidelines are not specific to a particular sector, but can be undertaken by any public or private organization and can be applied to any type of risk. This paper presents a research work that aims to realize a knowledge-base for the development of a tool to support the identification of the most appropriate risk management methodology according to the specific characteristics of an organization.

Keywords: risk assessment, domain ontology, standard guidelines.

1 Introduction

Any working activity involves risks and organizations of any type and size have to be able to identify, analyze and evaluate risks at any time during their workflow; the overall process of identification, analysis and evaluation of risks is usually referred as risk assessment. Over the years, institutions and authorities, as well as large industrial groups, have developed many methods for identifying and managing potential sources of risk in order to prevent accidental scenarios and assess the impact they could have on people, the environment and plants' equipment.

Recently, ISO organization published a set of documents for a standard aimed at risk assessment, namely: ISO 31000, that outlines the principles and general guidelines on risk management, ISO 31010, that provides an overview of the techniques of risk assessment and ISO 73, corresponding to a vocabulary of terms for risk management domain. These guidelines are not specific to a particular sector, but can be undertaken by any public or private organization and may be applied throughout the life cycle of an organization and in all its business activities and can be applied to any type of risk, regardless of its nature and its possible consequences. This bench of documents provides the knowledge necessary to identify the most appropriate risk assessment technique for specific organizations and activities. However, accessing the right information and understanding which procedures are the most appropriate for the specific context and configurations might be not straightforward. It is even more

P. Herrero et al. (Eds.): OTM 2012 Workshops, LNCS 7567, pp. 444–453, 2012.

problematic for organizations of small size, where the access to the necessary resources is often difficult due to the unavailability of internal experts or time and cost constraints, and where often the definition and implementation of risk management procedure is delegated to external consultants; in this case tools supporting the comprehension of the proposed risk assessment methodology may greatly facilitate the validation and monitoring of the work entrusted to external specialists.

Formalize and exploit the knowledge available in this domain for the creation of tools that can help users to take decisions, considering all factors involved, may represent a progress of the utmost importance. This paper presents a research work aimed to develop a set of ontologies covering the risk management domain. In particular, the paper focuses on the knowledge formalized in two ontologies (OntologyGuide73 and OntologyRATIS - Risk Assessment Techniques Identification Support), used as knowledge-base for tools designed to facilitate the reading and understanding of the guidelines for risk assessment to support the choice of the most suitable for a given context among the available technologies.

The paper is structured as follows: section 2 introduces the domain knowledge, section 3 describes the methodology adopted for the identification and formalization of the domain knowledge in the ontology, section 4 concludes the paper.

2   The Domain Knowledge

Among the attempts to organize the domain knowledge for the risk assessment, Tixier et al. [1] present a review of the methodologies for risk analysis commonly adopted in the process industry, taking into account some general criteria for their classification. The presented 62 methods are described and classified according to four properties: deterministic, probabilistic, qualitative, quantitative. A particularly interesting aspect of this work is that the classifications of the methods are done on the basis of the type of input and output and according to application areas, such as: industrial, transportation of hazardous substances and human factors. A further attempt to classify risk assessment methods can be found in [2], where authors provide a survey that classifies and groups the main methodologies used for risk analysis and those published in scientific journals, applicable to various industrial sectors, such as process plant, process engineering, mechanical engineering, transport, chemistry and medicine. The classification adopted is very simple, the techniques are classified into three groups: qualitative, quantitative and mixed type. In the first group, the risk is considered as a quantity, which can be evaluated and expressed mathematically, even with the aid of recorded data relating to accidents. The paper compares the different methods of analysis and risk assessment based on the advantages and disadvantages, and it also provides interesting insights for future developments. In addition it provides a list of the scientific publications (404) of the last ten years regarding the analysis and assessment of risk, and for each indicates the techniques used, the type of data and the field of application considered.

As mentioned before, a set of standard ISO documents, recently published, aims at providing all the knowledge necessary to identify the most appropriate risk assessment technique for a specific organization and activity. The standard is divided into three different documents [3-5]:

- ISO 31000 (Risk Management - Principles and guidelines)
- ISO 31010 (Risk Management - Risk assessment techniques)
- ISO 73 (Risk Management - Vocabulary)

The document ISO 31000 [3] sets out the principles and general guidelines on risk management, providing a framework for the whole process, as shown schematically in Figure 1.

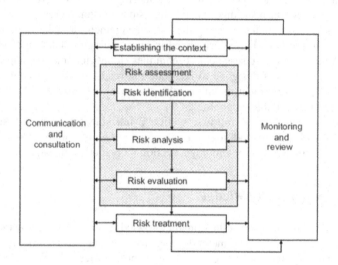

Fig. 1. Risk Management Process (Source: ISO 31000)

Overall, the process includes policies, procedures and organizational choices for managing risk across the entire organization at every level. In particular, it highlights the importance for those who must perform this process, to know: the context and the objectives, the extent and type of risks to be tolerated, how to treat risks considered not tolerable, how risk assessment is integrated in organizational processes, methods and techniques to be used for risk assessment, responsibilities for the process, the available resources, procedures for review and report.

The risk assessment process must provide the information necessary to decide: whether a specified activities has to be undertaken, how to maximize the opportunities, if certain risks should be treated, how to make a choice between different options that involve different risks, how to assign priority to different optional risk treatment, and what is the best strategy to take a risk to an acceptable level. The process includes risk identification, risk analysis and risk evaluation processes.

The risk identification is aimed at identifying situations that may prevent the achievement of objectives. The process includes the identification of causes, sources of risk and events that might have an impact on the objectives.

The risk analysis is mainly aimed to determine the consequences and the probability of the risks identified, taking into account the existing controls and their effectiveness. The combination of the consequences and the probability of occurrence determines the level of risk. There are several methods of risk analysis, and complex applications may require the combined use of different methods.

Risk evaluation consists of comparing the estimated level of risk with the risk criteria defined simultaneously with the definition of the context, to establish the importance of the level and type of risk. The process uses the understanding gained during the risk analysis to make decisions on possible future actions.

The document ISO 31010 [4] provides an overview of the most commonly used techniques for the identification, analysis and evaluation of risk; it classifies more than 30 different techniques into broad categories based on different points of view. The first classification provided is made on the basis of the applicability of the technique to the process of risk identification and /or risk analysis and/or risk evaluation. As shown in Table 1, for each step of the evaluation process the document specifies the applicability of the method at the different levels.

Table 1. Classification of risk assessment methods based on the applicability to risk identification, analysis and evaluation

Methods	Risk assessment process				
	Risk identification	Risk analysis			Risk evaluation
		Consequences	Probability	Risk level	
Brain-storming	Strongly applicable	Not applicable	Not applicable	Not applicable	Not applicable
HAZOP	Strongly applicable	Strongly applicable	Applicable	Applicable	Applicable
......					

The second classification groups the techniques into different macro-categories on the basis of the similarity of the methodological process, specifically: Look-up methods, Support methods, Scenario analysis, Evaluation of controls, Statistical methods, Functional analysis. In addition, for each technique some important characteristics are highlighted according to different points of view: the importance of some factors of influence on the method (resources and capabilities in terms of both budget and human resources, nature and degree of uncertainty, complexity) and whether or not the technique produces a quantitative result. The document illustrates the complexity of the risk assessment process and highlights factors to be considered in deciding the most appropriate strategy.

Finally, the document ISO 73 [5] provides an essential vocabulary to develop a common understanding on the concepts and terminology used in the management of risks across different organizations and different types of applications. The document underlines that when a term is used in the context of a standard it is of fundamental importance that its meaning is not misunderstood or badly used.

3   The Representation of the Domain Knowledge

The ISO documents described in the previous section are well structured and their reading is not particularly difficult. However, the variety of the concepts introduced and their relationships can make the consultation costly. In particular, the choice of the more appropriate risk assessment methodology has to take into account many factors, such as for example the organization and the tasks to consider, the available resources and skills, the objectives and the expected results. Thus, on the one hand, this type of knowledge navigation is demanding and might require very specific skills. On the other hand, risk assessment is one of the activities required by law for health and safety of workers in the workplace.

Ontology is a good means to specify and clarify the concepts employed in a specific domain [6]. In the field of risk management, in the MONITOR project [7], an ontology has been defined to formalize the knowledge necessary to identify the best technology for environmental risk management, in particular for monitoring methods and risk communication. Also in [8] authors propose a tool to support risk analysis based on a set of domain ontologies to support users in the retrieval of relevant information. While Gilmour et al. [9] developed an ontology focused on risk identification methods specific for the process industries.

The knowledge contained in the ISO documents presented in previous section can be exploited to:

- collect common vocabulary and concepts in the risk management domain
- formalise these basic concepts as an ontology in a computer readable format
- exploit this core ontology as a basis for the formalisation in domain ontologies of more complex and structured knowledge concerning specific aspects of the risk management process
- use the resulting ontologies as a knowledge base, for the creation of software tools that can support users in the decision process for the management of risks, allowing them to take into account all the factors involved and the dependency relationships among them.

The design and development of an ontology may follow different methodological approaches; in this research we adopted a top-down method [10], according to which, starting from the domain of interest and the objectives, ontology is developed in various steps up to reach the definition of all the classes, properties and relations:

- Determine the domain and purpose of the ontology,
- Consider the reuse and expansion of existing ontologies,
- Enumerate important terms of ontology and define the classes,
- Define the properties of classes and their relationships

Focusing on the ontology reuse, although we considered several ontologies defined in the course of research projects aimed at supporting the process of risk assessment we decided to develop a new ontology. There are two main reasons which have led to this choice: the requirement of a knowledge base fully compliant with the ISO 31000 document suite, and the objective to provide an ontology generally applicable to all areas where it is required to perform a risk assessment. In this perspective, to allow future reuse of the ontology, we adopted a layered approach which includes the definition of a core ontology that can be exploited by more specific domain ontologies. In Figure 2 the adopted ontology layered structure is depicted.

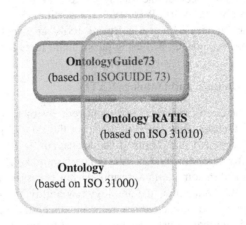

Fig. 2. Layered structure of the defined ontology

OntologyGuide73 is built starting from the content of the document ISO 73, which contains the reference vocabulary of the risk management domain and consequently provides the reference concepts. OntologyGuide73 can be considered the "core ontology" in the domain of risk management on the basis of which other more focused domain ontologies can be defined: for example, ontologies oriented to specific operations, such as maintenance, inspection and service activities, or to different contexts such as industrial environments or civilian complexes.

All the terms defined in the glossary ISO 73 were considered as reference elements (classes) possibly in relation to each other. Furthermore, from the definitions provided by the guide, other concepts have been extracted and modeled in the ontology, that do not have a formal definition in the document, but they have been recognized fundamental for the description of the characteristics of concepts that must be represented, such as the characteristics of the risk assessment technologies formalized in OntologyRATIS. As an example, the term Organization appears very often in the documents, in particular in ISO 73, although it is not explicitly defined; thus it was introduced as a class in the auxiliary OntologyGuide73.

OntologyRATIS, created starting from OntologyGuide73, contains the concepts extracted from the document ISO 31010 that have been identified to provide the technical knowledge necessary to choose the most appropriate risk assessment methodology with respect to the characteristics of a specific organization and of the activities to consider. The analyzed regulations do not provide real taxonomies of risk assessment methodologies, but various types of classification according to different factors that need to be taken into account. Examples of characteristics adopted for the classification are the applicability of the technique to a specific process of risk assessment (see Table 1) and the type of results produced, whether quantitative or qualitative. These categories are treated in the ontology by defining relations or properties of classes. As for the core ontology, also for ontologyRATIS it has been necessary to introduce concepts that do not have an explicit definition but are required for the completion of the knowledge base.

The ontologies have been defined using the tool Protégé[1], taking into account the guidance provided by the World Wide Web Consortium (W3C). In addition to make the ontology easily accessible to software tools an Application Programmable Interface (API) has been developed using the standard tools SPARQL[2] and Jena[3].

3.1   OntologyGuide73 and OntologyRATIS

At the top level the OntologyGuide73 has four root abstract classes, the first three are corresponding to the elements explicitly listed in the ISO 73 glossary: Terms_Risk, Terms_Risk Management and Terms_Risk_Management_Process, while the fourth class Auxiliary_Resources includes all the concepts not explicitly defined in the glossary and mentioned in some term description, but necessary for the specification of other main concepts. To facilitate the ontology readability, the suffix Terms_ has been added to the name of abstract classes referring the most general concepts. Since abstract classes do not have instances but are used to model common concepts, here their use permits to reflect the terminology structure adopted in the ISO 73 document. For instance, the abstract class Terms_Risk_Management has four sub-classes: Risk_Management_Framework, Risk_Management_Plan, Risk_Management and Risk_Management_Policy. The focus of this research is mainly on the abstract class Terms_Risk_Management_Process, that has, among other sub-classes, the abstract sub-class Terms_Risk_Assessment, that has in turn a sub-class named Risk_Assessment_Method containing all the classes corresponding to each risk assessment method included in ISO 31010. The properties and relationships that can better characterize the specific methods are identified and defined in the ontology. In Figure 3 a partial view of ontologyRATIS including the Risk_Assessment_Method class is depicted: rectangles are classes representing the domain concepts and the enclosed labels indicate the class names. Bold class labels indicate concepts of the OntologyGuide73 (Terms_Risk_Assessment, Risk_Assessment, Risk_Evaluation, Risk_Identification, Risks_Analysis, People). Classes with labels in italic (i.e. Terms_Risk_Assessment, Risk_Assessment, Risk_Assessment_Method) are abstract.

[1] http://protege.stanford.edu/
[2] www.w3.org/TR/rdf-sparql-query
[3] http://jena.apache.org/

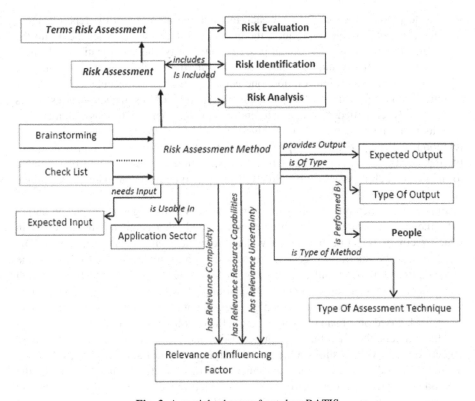

Fig. 3. A partial schema of ontologyRATIS

Unlabelled thick arrows represent the relationship "is-a". For example, Risk_Assessment "is-a" (specific type of) Terms_Risk_Assessment. The relationship "is-a" enables property inheritance among the classes involved, and through this relationship the ontology concepts are classified and organized in taxonomies. Moreover, relationships have a direction, and in this example may have multiple target. For the sake of comprehension, in the picture composite class names are strings with blank spaces. In addition to the taxonomies and the direct relationships, some restrictions have been introduced in order to design most of the concepts included in ISO documents, but explicitly defining only a small set of properties. For example, in ISO 73, Risk_Identification is defined as a "process of finding, recognizing and describing risk. It involves the identification of risk source, events, their causes and their potential consequences". In OntologyGuide73 this concept has been modeled as the restriction applied to Risk_Identification class: "providesOutput some (Risk or Risk_Source or Event)". Risk_Analysis has a similar restriction "providesOutput some (Level_Of_Risk or Consequences or Likelihood)", which models the concept "is a process... to determine the level of risk". These particular restrictions are also used to infer some concepts from the explicit definitions, for instance the classification of the risk assessment techniques. All the methods contained in ISO 31010 are designed as sub-classes of Risk_Assessment_Method class, and their instances are the specific techniques implemented for each method. On the basis of the type of output which a technique is able to produce, the ontology infers and classifies them into the most suitable type of risk assessment process. In this way, the classification in Table 1 has not been explicitly modeled but has been inferred by the reasoner. Among the advantages of such a design solution, one is that a new risk assessment technique can be introduced directly in the Risk_Assessment_Method, or in some sub-classes, but is automatically classified (through inference) into the appropriate class of methods, such as Risk_Identification, Risk_Analysis or Risk_Evaluation. On the contrary, the relation isOfType in Figure 3 explicitly indicates if a method is able to provide quantitative, semi-quantitative or qualitative results. In future, ontology will be extended to infer also such a classification directly from the type of output which a technique is able to produce .

Finally, each method is mainly described in terms of its target, the expected output data, the required input, the required expertise, and other characteristics, such as in which sector it is applicable, or on which life-cycle phase it can be adopted. The ontology can be queried by general questions, such as for example: "What are the methods used for risk identification? For risk analysis? For the evaluation?, Which methods provide quantitative output? Or qualitative?". Moreover the questions can be combined to make matters more complex, e.g.: "what kind of qualitative methods can be applied, based on a team of experts during the operating phase of a plant?".

This reflects the fact that OntologyRATIS has been modeled with the main objective to answer questions aimed at identifying the most suitable risk assessment methods, according to different requirements. In order to fulfill such objectives, the methodology proposed consists of a process which reduces the set of candidates by choosing from time to time some conditions depending on available resources. For example, starting from the expected results (output data), methods can be chosen by discriminating between input required and data available; or vice versa if some input data is available, only risk assessment methods compatible with those data are identified. The other characteristics may be conveniently used to reduce the list of candidates. Of course, each choice increases the complexity of the query, for example the question "Which methods can be used to identify explosive hazards in batch processes industry?" can be described in SPARQL language, as depicted in Figure 4, with the results achieved in the example.

---

select distinct ?a where { ?a rdf:type ?c. ?a XX:isUsableInSector ?sec.
?a XX:isApplicableToSituation ?sit. ?a G73:providesOutput ?out.
Filter ((?c= XX:Risk_Assessment_Method) && (?sec=XX:Batch_Process) &&
(?sit=XX:Industrial_installations) && (?out=XX:Explosive_Hazard)).} ORDER BY str(?a)

| XX: Air_Blust_Index_Method_DL334 |

|XX :Blust_Index_Method_DL334 |

| XX:Dow_Index_Method_DL334 |

| XX:General_Index_Method_DL334 |

Fig. 4. Example of SPARQL query and achieved results

4   Conclusions

The research presented in this article focuses on the definition of an ontology designed to support the implementation of ISO standards on identification, analysis and risk assessment to facilitate the choice of the risk management techniques most suited to the needs of a specific organization. Ontology formalization includes all concepts defined in the considered ISO documents and in addition those concepts that, although lacking a formal definition in the document, were considered necessary in the description and characterization of risk assessment methods. The design of the presented ontologies tries to minimize the explicit definitions of the identified concepts, exploiting the reasoning facilities offered by the ontology language, in order to infer implicit knowledge as much as possible. A preliminary evaluation of the usefulness of the ontology to meet the users 'requests have been carried out by domain experts.

To make the exploitation of the developed ontologies effective for users, a software tool with an adequate user interface is currently under development, that would facilitate the navigation in the knowledge base, taking into account all the factors involved in the choice of the risk assessment method. Moreover, the application will allow users to directly add instances of risk assessment methods or specify the knowledge required to define new classes of methods.

References

1. Tixier, J., Dusserre, G., Salvi, O., Gaston, D.: Review of 62 risk analysis methodologies of industrial plants. Journal of Loss Prevention in the Process Industries 15(7), 291–303 (2002)
2. Marhavilas, P.K., Koulouriotis, D., Gemeni, V.: Risk analysis and assessment methodologies in the work site: On a review, classification and comparative study of the scientific literature of the period 2000-2009. Journal of Loss Prevention in the Process Industries 24(5), 477–523 (2001)
3. ISO 31000 Risk Management-Principles and Guidelines, ISO/FDIS 31000:2009(E)
4. ISO 31010 Risk Management- Risk Assessment techniques, IEC/ISO 31010
5. ISO GUIDE 73 Risk Management-Vocabulary, ISO GUIDE 73: 2009(E/F)
6. Gruber, T.R.A.: Translation approach to portable ontology specification. Knowledge Acquisition 5, 199–220 (1993)
7. Kollarits, S., Wergles, N.: MONITOR – an ontological basis for risk management, http://www.monitor-cadses.org/documents/MONITOR_ BaseOntology_Report_1_0.pdf (accessed July 20, 2011)
8. Assali, A.A., Lenne, D., Debray, B.: Ontology Development for Industrial Risk Analysis, Information and Communication Technologies: From Theory to Applications. In: ICTTA 2008, pp. 1–5 (2008)
9. Gilmour, R.: An Ontology for Hazard Identification in Risk Management, Thesis, Department of Chemical Engineering (2004)
10. Noy, N.F., McGuinnes, D.L.: Ontology Development 101: A Guide to Creating Your First Ontology. Stanford Knowledge Systems Laboratory Technical Report KSL-01-05 and Stanford Medical Informatics Technical Report SMI-2001-0880 (2001)

SAM: A Tool for the Semi-Automatic Mapping and Enrichment of Ontologies

Vincenzo Maltese and Bayzid Ashik Hossain

DISI – University of Trento, Trento, Italy

Abstract. Ontologies are fundamental tools used with different purposes and with different modalities in different areas and communities. To guarantee the right level of quality, the most widely used ontologies are man-made. However, developing and maintaining them turns out to be extremely time-consuming. For this reason, there are approaches aiming at their automatic construction where ontologies are incrementally extended by extracting and integrating knowledge from existing sources. However, these approaches tend to reach an accuracy that, according to the application they need to serve, cannot be always considered satisfactory. Therefore, when a higher accuracy is necessary, manual or semi-automatic approaches are still preferable. In this paper we present a technique and a corresponding tool, that we called SAM (semi-automatic mapper), for the semi-automatic enrichment of an ontology through the mapping of an external source to the target ontology. As proved by our evaluation, the tool allows saving around 50% of the time required by purely manual approaches.

Keywords: Ontologies, mapping, semi-automatic enrichment.

1 Introduction

Ontologies are used in different communities, for different purposes and with different modalities [2]. Many definitions of *ontology* have been provided. Studer et al. [3], by extending the famous definition by Gruber [4], define it as *a formal, explicit specification of a shared conceptualization*. The notion of conceptualization refers to an abstract model of how people theorize (the relevant part of) the world in terms of basic cognitive units called *concepts*. Concepts represent the intention, i.e. the set of properties that distinguish the concept from others, and summarize the extension, i.e. the set of objects having such properties. Concepts basically denote classes of objects. For instance, the medicine domain can be theorized in terms of doctors, patients, body parts, diseases, their symptoms and treatments used to cure or prevent them. Explicit specification means that the abstract model is made explicit by providing names and definitions for the concepts. In other words, the name and the definition of the concept provide a specification of its meaning in relation with other concepts. The specification is said to be formal when it is written in a language with formal syntax and formal semantics, i.e. in a logic-based language such as Description Logic [5]. The conceptualization is shared in the sense that it captures knowledge which is common to a community of people and therefore represents concretely the level of agreement

P. Herrero et al. (Eds.): OTM 2012 Workshops, LNCS 7567, pp. 454–463, 2012.
© Springer-Verlag Berlin Heidelberg 2012

reached in that community. By providing a common formal terminology (i.e. a vocabulary of terms) and understanding of a given domain of interest, ontologies allow for automation (logical inference), support learning, reuse and favor interoperability across applications and people. When an ontology is populated with the instances of the classes, i.e. the individuals, it is called a *knowledge base*. In literature (see for instance [5]) the terms TBox and ABox are often used to denote what is known about the classes and about the individuals, respectively.

In order to guarantee the right level of quality, the most successful and widely used ontologies are man-made. We can mention for instance WordNet [6], Cyc [7], SUMO [8], Agrovoc[1] and UMLS[2]. The latter two are domain specific ontologies, in agriculture and medicine, respectively. However, maintaining them is extremely costly.

Attempts have been made to overcome this limitation by constructing ontologies automatically. One of the best examples in this direction is provided by YAGO [9], an ontology where the skeleton, constituted by WordNet, is progressively enriched with knowledge automatically extracted from Wikipedia[3]. This is done by mapping Wikipedia categories to WordNet synsets. Wikipedia categories can be seen as folders containing articles about individuals. For instance, the category *Italian scientists* contains an article about *Antonio Meucci*. WordNet synsets are groups of words which are synonyms, i.e. words with the same meaning, and corresponding definition. For instance, the synset containing the words *scientist* and *man of science* is defined as *a person with advanced knowledge of one or more sciences*. Basically, each category can be seen as a class of individuals that is mapped to a concept in the ontology; with the mapping, the ontology is enriched with knowledge coming from the *external source*. This mapping has a pretty high claimed accuracy of 90-95%.

As a matter of fact, computing the mapping between two ontologies is an essential step towards their integration [11]. Many projects have dealt with this problem. In the context of digital libraries this is a hot problem. We can mention for instance CARMEN[4], Renardus [13] and OCLC initiatives [14]. One possible approach is to exploit mappings from a reference scheme to search and navigate across a set of satellite vocabularies. For instance, Renardus and HILT [15] use the Dewey Decimal Classification (DDC). Some others prefer the Library of Congress Subject Headings (LCSH) [16, 17]. Both manual and semi-automatic solutions are proposed. Lauser et al. [18], with a focus on the agricultural domain, compare the two approaches and conclude that automatic procedures can be very effective but tend to fail when domain specific background knowledge is needed. Approaches to this problem have been proposed (see for instance [12]), but their accuracy still remains pretty low. It is therefore clear that automatic approaches typically require some form of manual validation [20], but limited work has been done in this direction and current interfaces to this purpose hardly scale with the size of the two ontologies [21, 22, 23]. A good survey of the state of the art in automatic tools for mapping computation can be found in [19], while the OAEI[5] initiative annually provides an evaluation of these tools.

---

[1] www.fao.org/agrovoc/
[2] http://www.nlm.nih.gov/research/umls/
[3] http://en.wikipedia.org/
[4] http://www.bibliothek.uni-regensburg.de/projects/carmen12
[5] http://oaei.ontologymatching.org/

For what said above, it is clear that when a very high accuracy is necessary purely manual or semi-automatic approaches, even if more time-consuming, are still preferable. Following this line, in this paper we present a technique for the semi-automatic mapping of generic categories to ontology concepts. As part of the proposed solution, we developed a tool - that we called SAM - that, as proved by our evaluation, allows saving around 50% of the time required by purely manual approaches.

The rest of this paper is organized as follows. Section 2 provides a motivating example showing the mapping process and typical problems that need to be faced. Section 3 describes the process of manual mapping. Section 4 presents the semi-automatic mapping approach and how the steps are supported by the SAM tool. Section 5 provides corresponding evaluation. Finally, Section 6 concludes the paper by summarizing the work done and outlining future work.

2   A Motivating Example

Consider the example in Fig. 1. It provides a small ontology where classes are represented with circles and individuals with squares; solid arrows represent relations between classes; dashed arrows represent relations between individuals or between an individual and corresponding class. Classes and relations between them constitute the TBox where the backbone is typically represented by *is-a* relations. Knowledge about the individuals forms the ABox where the relation between an individual and corresponding class is typically *instance-of*. Similarly to WordNet, each class can be associated a set of synonyms (here we do not provide definitions).

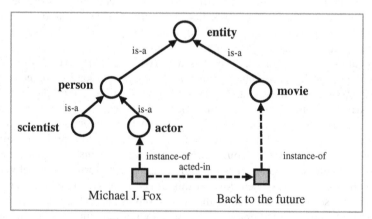

Fig. 1. A sample target ontology

Suppose that our task is to extend the ontology by importing knowledge from the external source depicted in Fig. 2. As it often happens, the source is only partially structured, in the sense that none of its elements is explicitly marked as class, individual or relation. This makes the process of extracting knowledge approximate due to errors that might be made in interpreting them.

Existing knowledge extraction techniques, for instance those at the basis of YAGO, rely on the identification of known terms in the phrases denoting category names, i.e. terms that already appear as labels of concepts in the ontology we want to extend. This is done by first identifying what in linguistics is known as the *head of the phrase* and by mapping it with a concept in the ontology. For instance, the head of *Italian scientists* is *scientist* (in its root form) which is in the ontology. This allows mapping them and enriching the ontology with the individuals extracted from the external source, thus importing *Antonio Meucci* as instance of *scientist*.

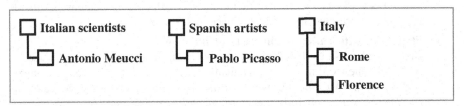

Fig. 2. A sample external source

However, especially if automated, during this process many mistakes may arise. The identification of the head, which in turn is typically based on part of speech (POS) tagging, is an approximated process with accuracy that varies according to the tool and the dataset used to train it. For instance, POS tagging reaches 97.24% accuracy on the Penn Treebank WSJ dataset [1]. However, mistakes are amplified when the POS is used to identify the head. Even if the head is correctly identified, there might be cases in which the head is not in the ontology and cases in which more than one sense for it is available. In the former case, YAGO enriches the ontology by linking the category directly to the root of the ontology. For instance, since *artist* (the head of *Spanish artists*) is not in the ontology, *artist* is directly linked to *entity* (while a better choice would be *person*). In the latter case, YAGO as main heuristic selects the sense with higher rank in WordNet. Notice that the head of a phrase is always a common noun. The categories in which it is not present (for instance in the category

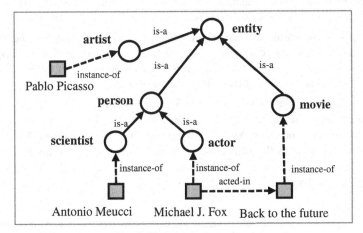

Fig. 3. The enriched ontology

Italy that is a proper noun) are simply ignored. The ontology that is obtained after the enrichment[6] is shown in Fig. 3.

3   Manual Mapping

The steps that we follow to manually map categories from an external source to the target ontology and consequently enrich it are as follows:

- **Step 1 - Filtering out proper nouns:** when the category represents a proper noun, it is marked as noise and filtered out. For example the category *Crittenden County* represents the name of a place in Arkansas, USA.

- **Step 2 - Identification of the head of the category:** when the category is a single word, it is clearly selected as head. When the category is constituted by more than one word the head is manually selected. For instance, for the category *Iraqi Sunni Muslims* the word *Muslim* is selected, while for the category *racehorses trained in Italy* the word *racehorse* is selected. In some cases a multiword has to be selected. For instance, for the category *amusement parks in New England* the multiword *amusement park* is selected.

- **Step 3 - Mapping the head to a concept:** a suitable concept corresponding to the head is searched in the target ontology. Possible candidates are evaluated and one of them is selected trying to understand the most suitable one. If a good one is found the process is completed.

- **Step 4 - Creation of a new concept:** if no suitable concept is found for the head of the category, an additional external vocabulary is used to determine a definition for it. A good definition should provide *genus et differentia*, i.e. it should provide information about the kind (the genus) and how it differs from the kind (the differentia). For example, *pathologist* can be defined as *a scientist who studies parasites and their biology and pathology* where scientist is the genus and the rest represents the differentia.

- **Step 5 - Identification of the parent:** similarly to Step 3, the genus in the definition is used to identify a suitable parent concept, if any, in the target ontology. For example, *scientist* is a suitable parent for *pathologist*.

- **Step 6 – Enriching the target ontology:** by using the mapping between the categories and the concepts in the ontology (either as direct mapping or through a parent) the ontology is enriched with new concepts and corresponding individuals extracted from the external source.

To evaluate the potential of this method, we took WordNet as target ontology and YAGO as external source. In fact, even if YAGO is already the result of a mapping between Wikipedia and WordNet, we found out that 15,480 Wikipedia categories were directly mapped to the root concept *entity* of WordNet. We applied the steps above to 2,000 of these categories randomly selected. The results are provided in Table 1 and show that:

---

[6] Notice that here we imported only the head and the entities while in YAGO also the categories themselves are imported.

Table 1. Results of the manual mapping

Categories analyzed	Proper Nouns	Concepts found	Concepts created
2000	358	1120	522

- 18% of the mapped categories are actually proper nouns
- 56% of the categories can be mapped to a more specific concept in WordNet
- 26% of the categories can be better mapped if a new concept is created and mapped to an existing parent concept in WordNet

4   Semi-Automatic Mapping

By applying the manual steps we can clearly achieve a very accurate mapping and enrichment, however at the price of a higher cost in terms of human resources and time needed. To overcome this limitation, we developed the SAM tool (implemented in Java) to assist the user (typically an ontology expert) and partially automate the necessary steps. The steps remain pretty much the same but the process is preceded by a preprocessing phase during which the system is trained in order to automatically recognize a category as proper noun or in alternative to identify its head. For each of the categories, the steps are as follows:

- **Step 1 - Filtering out proper nouns:** if the system recognizes the category as a proper noun no head is computed. The user is free to accept the suggestion or proceed to the next step.

- **Step 2 - Identification of the head of the category:** the system computes a head for the category. The user is free to accept the suggestion or provide an alternative one.

- **Step 3 - Mapping the head to a concept:** since the system keeps track of previous choices made by the user, if the head of the category corresponds to a word which has been already processed in the past then the system suggests previously assigned concepts. To help the user deciding, it shows them in a list with corresponding categories. For instance, in processing the category *Mexican Americans* and by automatically identifying *American* as head, it pops up the information that this head appeared in the previously processed category *Jamaican Americans in the Unites States Military* such that the same concept can be selected. If no similar cases are found or none of them is considered relevant by the user, the system looks up in the target ontology to identify the concepts corresponding to the head. They are given in a list as shown in Fig. 4. The user can pick one of them or, if none is found or none of them is considered correct, move to the next step.

- **Step 4 - Creation of a new concept:** the system queries an external vocabulary to identify useful information that the user can utilize to determine a suitable definition for the head.

- **Step 5 - Identification of the parent:** similarly to Step 3, the genus of the definition provided by the user is used to look into the target ontology for candidate concepts for the parent. The user is free to select one of the suggestions or reject them. If none of them is considered appropriate, the system asks for an alternative definition by coming back to step 4. A new concept is otherwise generated by the system and linked to the corresponding parent in the target ontology.

- **Step 6 – Enriching the target ontology:** At the end of the process, the entities associated to the category are automatically used to populate the ontology.

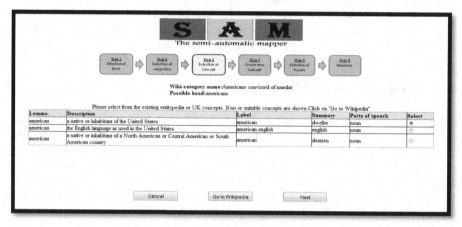

Fig. 4. A snapshot of the SAM interface

5   Evaluation

To evaluate SAM we used Entitypedia [10] as target ontology and the 15,480 categories of YAGO that were directly mapped to *entity* as external resource. Wikipedia was used as external vocabulary at Step 4. Developed at the University of Trento in Italy, Entitypedia is a knowledge base with a precise split between individuals (the ABox), classes, attributes and relations (the TBox) and their lexicalization as proper nouns and common nouns, respectively. Entitypedia is progressively extended by collecting knowledge from several sources, including WordNet.

With the pre-processing, the 15,480 categories of YAGO were POS tagged by using the Stanford NLP POS tagger [1]. After the tagging, a set of patterns were identified in order to automatically recognize the head. This was done by looking at common noun plural tags (/NNS). 8,998 categories were found to have exactly one such tag; 292 of them with more than one; 6,190 of them do not have any. In the first case the corresponding word was selected as head; in the second and third case 7 and 33 different patterns were identified respectively and for each of them a different choice was made also taking into account the mistakes made by the POS tagger. Patterns are also used to identify proper nouns. An example of pattern is:

{JJ}+ {NNP}* {NNPS}+

where {JJ}+ indicates one or more adjectives, {NNP}* zero or more proper nouns and {NNPS}+ one or more common nouns in plural form. An example of category matching this pattern is *Indian Zen Buddhists* with *Buddhist* its head. By evaluating a sample of 500 categories we found that this approach leads to an accuracy of 98.4% (only 8 mistakes).

The evaluation process comprises of 2 parts. During the first part, a trained user was given 200 YAGO categories randomly selected to be mapped manually. During the second part, the user was asked to use SAM to map 200 new YAGO categories different from the previous ones. By trained user we mean a user who was familiar with the manual mapping process as he was involved in the analysis phase described in Section 3 but not at all familiar with SAM. In other words, the user neither participated to the design nor to the implementation of the tool. The user was given precise evaluation guidelines including clear steps about the tasks to be done and was monitored during the whole experiment. Table 2 provides some examples of mapped categories. In the table, the head of each category is given in bold followed by either the concept found in the target ontology or the definition of the new concept otherwise.

Table 2. Examples of mapped categories

Category: Futurologists *Concept found*: - *Concept created*: futurologist (scientist and social scientist whose speciality is to attempt to systematically predict the future, whether that of human society in particular or of life on earth in general)
Category: Rare diseases *Concept found*: disease (an impairment of health or a condition of abnormal functioning) *Concept created*: -
Category: Landforms of Turkey *Concept found*: - *Concept created*: landform (is largely defined by its surface form and location in the landscape)
Category: Germans of Polish descent *Concept found*: german (a person of German nationality) Concept created: -
Category: Pharaohs of the Twenty-sixth dynasty of Egypt *Concept found*: pharaoh (the title of the ancient Egyptian kings) *Concept created*: -
Category: Roman Catholic dioceses in the Holy Roman Empire *Concept found*: diocese (the territorial jurisdiction of a bishop) *Concept created*: -
Category: Recipients of the Distinguished Service Cross (United States) *Concept found*: recipient (a person who receives something) *Concept created*: -
Category: Sexually transmitted diseases and infections *Concept found*: disease (an impairment of health or a condition of abnormal functioning) *Concept created*: -

With the evaluation, we took note of the number of proper nouns, concepts found and new concepts created as well as of the time taken. Figures for both the first and second part of the experiment are reported in Table 3.

Table 3. Manual and semi-automatic mapping compared

Mapping	Manual Mapping	Semi-automatic Mapping
Proper Nouns	11	12
Concepts found	122	111
Concepts created	67	77
Amount of Time (minutes)	169.22	89.98

As it can be noticed from the table, the distribution of the different cases is slightly different. For instance, during the semi-automatic mapping more concepts had to be created. As it can be noted from the description of the steps, these cases are those requiring more time. Nevertheless, with the help of the tool the user was able to complete the process in around half of the time.

6   Conclusions

In this paper we have shown that the process of manually enriching ontologies with knowledge coming from external sources can be significantly speed up, still guaranteeing a high level of accuracy, by using tools that interactively support the user during the mapping phase. In fact, our experiments show that by using the SAM tool it is possible to save around 50% of the time needed by purely manual approaches.

As future work we plan to conduct accurate usability studies on the user interface of SAM to identify critical parts that can be improved to facilitate or further speed up the process. The patterns used to identify proper nouns and the head of the categories will be tested against a broader set of categories to verify how the accuracy varies on unseen data and to eventually extend the number of patterns. SAM has been customized to work on YAGO (input) and Entitypedia (output), while a future extension may allow generalizing the input/output.

Acknowledgment. The research leading to these results has received funding from the CUbRIK Collaborative Project, partially funded by the European Commission's 7th Framework ICT Programme for Research and Technological Development under the Grant agreement no. 287704. We would like to thank Professor Fausto Giunchiglia for his constant guidance and Suresh Daggumati for the evaluation.

References

1. Toutanova, K., Klein, D., Manning, C., Singer, Y.: Feature-Rich Part-of-Speech Tagging with a Cyclic Dependency Network. In: HLT-NAACL, pp. 252–259 (2003)
2. Giunchiglia, F., Soergel, D., Maltese, V., Bertacco, A.: Mapping large-scale Knowledge Organization Systems. In: 2nd International Conference on the Semantic Web and Digital Libraries, ICSD (2009)

3. Studer, R., Benjamins, V.R., Fensel, D.: Knowledge engineering: principles and methods. Data and Knowledge Engineering 25, 161–197 (1998)
4. Gruber, T.R.: A translation approach to portable ontology specifications. Knowledge Aquisition 5(2), 199–220 (1993)
5. Baader, F., Calvanese, D., McGuinness, D., Nardi, D., Patel-Schneider, P.F.: The Description Logic Handbook: Theory, Implementation and Applications. Cambridge University Press (2002)
6. Fellbaum, C.: WordNet: An Electronic Lexical Database. MIT Press (1998)
7. Matuszek, C., Cabral, J., Witbrock, M., DeOliveira, J.: An introduction to the syntax and content of Cyc. In: AAAI Spring Symposium (2006)
8. Pease, A., Sutcliffe, G., Siegel, N., Trac, S.: Large theory reasoning with SUMO at CASC. AI Communications 23(2-3), 137–144 (2010)
9. Suchanek, F.M., Kasneci, G., Weikum, G.: YAGO: A Large Ontology from Wikipedia and WordNet. Journal of Web Semantics (2011)
10. Giunchiglia, F., Maltese, V., Dutta, B.: Domains and context: first steps towards managing diversity in knowledge. Journal of Web Semantics, Special Issue on Reasoning with Context in the Semantic Web (2012), doi: 10.1016/j.websem.2011.11.007
11. Noy, N.: Semantic Integration: A survey of ontology-based approaches. SIGMOD Record 33(4), 65–70 (2004)
12. Giunchiglia, F., Shvaiko, P., Yatskevich, M.: Discovering missing background knowledge in ontology matching. In: Proceedings of the 17th European Conference on Artificial Intelligence (ECAI), pp. 382–386 (2006)
13. Koch, T., Neuroth, H., Day, M.: Renardus: Cross-browsing European subject gateways via a common classification system (DDC). In: McIlwaine, I.C. (ed.) Subject Retrieval in a Networked Environment. Proceedings of the IFLA satellite meeting held in Dublin - IFLA Information Technology Section and OCLC, pp. 25–33 (2003)
14. Vizine-Goetz, D., Hickey, C., Houghton, A., Thompson, R.: Vocabulary Mapping for Terminology Services. Journal of Digital Information 4(4), Article No. 272 (2004)
15. Nicholson, D., Dawson, A., Shiri, A.: HILT: A pilot terminology mapping service with a DDC spine. Cataloging & Classification Quarterly 42(3/4), 187–200 (2006)
16. Whitehead, C.: Mapping LCSH into Thesauri: the AAT Model. In: Beyond the Book: Extending MARC for Subject Access, p. 81 (1990)
17. O'Neill, E., Chan, L.: FAST (Faceted Application for Subject Technology): A Simplified LCSH-based Vocabulary. In: World Library and Information Congress: 69th IFLA General Conference and Council, Berlin, August 1-9 (2003)
18. Lauser, B., Johannsen, G., Caracciolo, C., Keizer, J., van Hage, W.R., Mayr, P.: Comparing human and automatic thesaurus mapping approaches in the agricultural domain. In: Proc. Int'l Conf. on Dublin Core and Metadata Applications (2008)
19. Euzenat, J., Meilicke, C., Stuckenschmidt, H., Shvaiko, P., Trojahn, C.: Ontology Alignment Evaluation Initiative: Six Years of Experience. In: Spaccapietra, S. (ed.) Journal on Data Semantics XV. LNCS, vol. 6720, pp. 158–192. Springer, Heidelberg (2011)
20. Maltese, V., Giunchiglia, F., Autayeu, A.: Save up to 99% of your time in mapping validation. In: 9th International Conference on Ontologies, Data Bases, and Applications of Semantics, ODBASE (2010)
21. Robertson, G.G., Czerwinski, M.P., Churchill, J.E.: Visualization of mappings between schemas. In: SIGCHI Conference on Human Factors in Computing Systems (2005)
22. Halevy, A.: Why your data won't mix. ACM Queue 3(8), 50–58 (2005)
23. Falconer, S., Storey, M.: A Cognitive Support Framework for Ontology Mapping. In: Aberer, K., Choi, K.-S., Noy, N., Allemang, D., Lee, K.-I., Nixon, L.J.B., Golbeck, J., Mika, P., Maynard, D., Mizoguchi, R., Schreiber, G., Cudré-Mauroux, P. (eds.) ASWC 2007 and ISWC 2007. LNCS, vol. 4825, pp. 114–127. Springer, Heidelberg (2007)

Mining Digital Library Evaluation Patterns Using a Domain Ontology

Angelos Mitrelis[1], Leonidas Papachristopoulos[1], Michalis Sfakakis[1],
Giannis Tsakonas[1,2], and Christos Papatheodorou[1,3]

[1] Department of Archives and Library Science, Ionian University, Corfu, Greece
[2] Library, Neapolis University Pafos, Pafos, Cyprus
[3] Digital Curation Unit, IMIS, "Athena" Research Center, Athens, Greece
{111mirt,111papa,papatheodor,sfakakis,gtsak}@ionio.gr

Abstract. Scientific literature is vast and therefore the researchers need knowledge organization systems to index, semantically annotate and correlate their bibliographic sources. Additionally they need methods and tools to discover scientific trends and commonly acceptable practices or areas for further investigation. This paper proposes a clustering-based data mining process to identify research patterns in the digital libraries evaluation domain. The papers published in the proceedings of a well known international conference in the decade 2001-2010 were semantically annotated using the Digital Library Evaluation Ontology (DiLEO). The generated annotations were clustered to portray common evaluation practices. The findings highlight the expressive nature of DiLEO and underline the potential of clustering in the research activities profiling.

Keywords: research trends discovery, clustering, digital library evaluation.

1 Introduction

By nature a digital library (DL) is "a very complex and challenging proposition" [1] and therefore its evaluation on aspects of quality, effectiveness and excellence employs many researchers and concerns different domains. Each contributing field of DLs brings in evaluation its own background, terminology and implementation methods. Moreover, many studies can be conducted for the same DL differing at the goals and the used methods. Consequently this diversity indicates the need of decision making mechanisms, based on the existing knowledge, to assist the evaluation experiments planning in terms of its scope, aims, methods and instruments.

This paper exploits the Digital Library Evaluation Ontology (DiLEO) [2], to semantically annotate the literature of the European Conference on Digital Libraries (ECDL, Theory and Practice of Digital Libraries - TPDL since 2011) in the period of the 2001-2010 decade. Clustering techniques are then applied on the derived DiLEO instances in an effort to harvest usage patterns of the ontology in order to investigate how they are actually used so as to suggest evaluation practices to DL researchers. The present study is structured as follows: the next section gives a review of the

P. Herrero et al. (Eds.): OTM 2012 Workshops, LNCS 7567, pp. 464–473, 2012.
© Springer-Verlag Berlin Heidelberg 2012

major accomplishments in DL and evaluation conceptual modeling. Section 3 presents the research settings and describes DiLEO ontology. Section 4 gives an overview and discusses the derived results, while in the last section the conclusions are drawn.

2   Background

Through the use of reference models and ontologies, researchers describe the whole life cycle of a DL consisting of services and processes. For instance, Kovacs and Micsik [3] suggested a four-layered ontology consisting of content, services, interface and community which apply as the most important elements of a DL, while Gonçalves' et al. [4] ontology developed the relation among them and introduced the concept of quality as a constituent. The Digital Library Reference Model (DLRM) [5] consolidates a collective understanding of DLs by abstracting the central concepts of the domain. The model defines a set of classes and properties, some of which are related to the evaluation through the concept of Quality. Recently, Khoo and McDonald [6] proposed a model for the evaluation of DL, acknowledging the effect of organizational communication. DiLEO [2] has been developed aiming to conceptualize the DL evaluation domain by exploring its key entities, their attributes and their relationships.

Ontologies are used extensively for the description, analysis and evaluation of the scholarly communication activities. For instance, OntoQualis [7] focuses on the assessment of the quality of scientific conferences, while MESUR [8] provides a framework for the analysis of scholarly communication data, such as references and citations. Furthermore the developments in the nanopublications area [9] provide tools for the semantic integration of the knowledge recorded in the literature enabling its organization and correlation.

In parallel, bibliometric techniques have been used to analyze the evolution of DLs [10] and other related domains, such as information retrieval [11, 12]. Biryukov and Donk investigated the interests of computer science researchers analyzing data from DBLP [13], while Reitz and Hoffman explored the connections and the evolution of topics through time [14]. This paper combines the ontology-based topical analysis of the literature with data mining techniques to reveal the trends of the DL evaluation domain.

3   Research Setting

3.1   The Digital Library Evaluation Ontology

The methodological fundamentals of DiLEO rely on the analysis of various DL evaluation models and the structural composition of the identified characteristics under a unified logic, depicted by a set of constraints.

DiLEO is a two-tiered ontology (Figure 1). The upper, the strategic, layer consists of a set of classes related with the scope and aim of an evaluation while the lower level, the procedural, encompass classes dealing with practical issues. The strategic layer consists of the classes *Goals, Dimensions, Dimensions Type, Research Questions, Levels*, evaluation *Objects* and *Subjects*. Each evaluation initiative is stimulated by a *Goal*, which may be a *description* of a state, the *documentation* of several actions or the enhancement of a *design*. The class *Dimensions* refers to the scope of an evaluation, measuring its *effectiveness, performance, service quality, outcome assessment* and *technical excellence* while the phase in which an evaluation is conducted is characterized as *summative, formative* or *iterative*. The *Research Questions* are directly related with the methodological design of the research and the expected findings, while the class *Levels* are the aspects of a DL which are assessed and include *content, engineering, processing, interface* or *individual, institutional* and *social* levels. An *Object* in the evaluation process is either a product or an operation, and a *Subject* is a *human* or *machine agent* participating in the process.

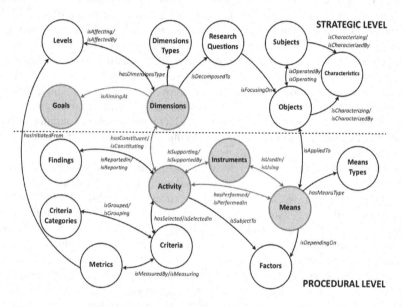

Fig. 1. The DiLEO classes and properties

The procedural layer includes classes that specify practical issues faced by every evaluation exertion. The *Activity* class includes the operations used to denature data to information after their collection by *recording* or *measuring*. Consequently, data are processed through *analyzing, comparing* and *interpreting* and finally are *reported* and *recommended*. The activities are affected by the *time, cost, infrastructure* and *personnel*, constituting the *Factors* class. A variety of *Means* are available, such as *logging studies, laboratory studies, expert studies, comparison techniques, field studies* and *survey studies*. DiLEO indicates the *Instruments* that are used, such as statistical analysis software, recording devices etc. Evaluators adopt or develop as reference points the *Objects* that can be valued while the *Criteria* are considered as controlling mechanisms of a measurement as well as a benchmarking process via standards and principles divided in certain *Criteria Categories*. The fulfillment of a criterion is a matter of measurement. *Metrics –user-originated, content-originated,* or *system-originated–* illustrate current conditions and indicate the gap between current and ideal states. Finally, the nature of *Findings* is determined by *Research Questions*, but is not specified and not predicted. DiLEO classes are co-related through a set of properties, while for each property particular constraints have been defined to support precise reasoning.

3.2 Semantic Annotation Process

The first step concerned the selection of the ECDL papers' that deal with evaluation. Two researchers worked independently judging the ECDL papers' relevance to evaluation by examining their title, abstract and author keywords (Figure 2). The absolute inter rater's agreement was estimated to be 78%. This result corresponds to a Cohen's Kappa measure – *"the proportion of agreement after chance agreement has been removed"* [15] – equal to κ=0.58, which indicates an acceptable level of agreement. For all the papers that a disagreement was identified a third researcher provided additional rankings. The selection process resulted to identify 119 out of 400 papers (29.5%) as those having evaluation interest.

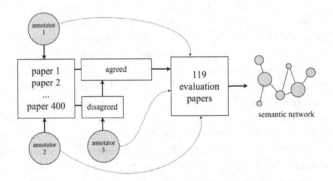

Fig. 2. Selection and annotation processes

The full text of the selected papers was semantically annotated manually by three experts with the goal to identify instances of the 21 subclasses of the DiLEO classes *Goals, Dimensions, Activities* and *Means* correlated with the properties *isAimingAt* (domain: *Dimensions*/range: *Goals*), *hasConstituent* (domain: *Dimensions*/range: *Activity*), *hasPerformed* (domain: *Activity*/range: *Means*). The annotators were familiar with both the instrument and the domain, agreeing beforehand on several thresholds, similarly to [16], and ensuring a common annotation method. To assess the correctness of annotation, random crosschecks were performed during that phase and any disagreements were resolved through discussion. The result of this process was the generation 1558 triples in the form of domain subclass – property – range subclass.

3.3 Clustering

In our experimentation we opted for K-Means, a well-known algorithm for partitioning M data points to K clusters. The 21 DiLEO subclasses, used as the vocabulary to annotate the documents, were considered as the features of the data points to be clustered.

Our dataset consists of 119 vectors of 21 features, representing the manually assigned annotations from the DiLEO vocabulary to the 119 ECDL papers related to DL evaluation. More specifically, the annotated documents are defined as vectors A_m = $(f_1, f_2, ..., f_n)$, where A_m, m= 1, ...,119 denotes an annotated document representation and f_n, n= 1, ..., 21 denotes a feature representing a DiLEO subclass.

The annotation vectors were partitioned to 11 clusters by applying the K-means algorithm. For the selection of the number of clusters K, the K-means was applied for the values of K between 1 and 25 recording the results of the objective (*cost* or *error*) function. Plotting the objective function results against the number of the clusters K the rate of decrease peaked at the values of K in between 9 and 13. Thereafter, we examined the clustering resulted by the K values equal to 11 and 12. The clustering resulted for a K value equal to 11 outperforms the other clustering, according to the evaluation procedure that follows. Moreover given that the K-means is highly dependent on the initialization of the centroids, it was run 200 times using different randomly initialized centroids. Then the clustering with the lowest cost was selected.

Two alternative formulations were tested for the annotation vectors A_m assigning different types of values to the features. In the first formulation, the values of the features were binary, therefore the feature f_i has the value one if the respective to f_i subclass was assigned to the document m, or zero otherwise. In the second formulation the value of the feature f_i was determined according to a variation of the *tf-idf* weighting scheme. To formulate this representation it should be remarked that every DiLEO subclass is annotated at most once to a document. Therefore, the *feature frequency* ff_i of the feature f_i in all vectors will be equal to one when the respective subclass was annotated to the respective document, or zero otherwise. In order to differentiate the values of the frequency of the same feature f_i in the different vectors and to correlate each value to the number of the annotations assigned to the document, the ff_i value is normalized by the number of the annotations to the respective document. Thereafter, given that the ff_i value corresponds to the *tf* part of the weighting scheme and its value is either 0 or 1, the feature f_i in the vector A_j is scored according to the following variation of the *tf-idf* schema:

$$nff_{i,j} = \frac{ff_{i,j}}{|A_j|}, \quad idf_i = \log\left(\frac{M}{1+df_i}\right), \quad tf-idf_{i,j} = nff_{i,j} \times idf_i$$

where, $nff_{i,j}$ is the normalized feature frequency of the feature f_i in the vector A_j, $|A_j|$ is the number of annotations to the document j, M is the number of documents, df_i is the document frequency of the feature f_i and idf_i expresses the inverse document frequency of the feature f_i.

To enable the discovery of patterns by characterizing each cluster with respect to the terms of DiLEO, we used the frequency increase measure (henceforth *FI*), which calculates the increase of the frequency of a feature f_i in the cluster k as compared to its document frequency df_i in the whole dataset. The frequency increase of the feature f_i in the cluster k, $FI_{i,k}$ is defined as the difference of the squares of the two frequency measures as specified by the formula:

$$FI_{i,k} = df_i^2 - ff_{i,k}^2$$

Intuitively, a representative feature for a cluster should be used to annotate a large number of documents in the cluster; hence its frequency in the cluster will be increased. In contrast, for a non representative feature the values of its *FI* measure will be low and probably negative. The definition of a representative feature for a cluster, is that $FI_{i,k}>\alpha$, where α is the required extent of frequency increase. If $\alpha>0$ then the frequency of a feature within a cluster is greater than the frequency of that feature in the initial dataset. If the *FI* value of a feature in a cluster becomes negative or lower than α then the feature will be filtered out from the representative features of that cluster, even if this feature has been assigned to several documents. The question that arises is to determine objectively the value of the threshold parameter α so that to define a set of features that characterizes a cluster.

In order to estimate the impact of the threshold parameter α, two indicators are defined: the *Coverage* and the *Dissimilarity Mean*. Hence, the selected value for the threshold α is the value that maximizes the combination of the *Coverage* and *Dissimilarity Mean* measures.

Coverage is defined as the proportion of the features participating in the clusters, for a particular *FI* value, to the total number of features used for annotation and is specified by the formula:

$$Coverage = \frac{\left| \bigcup_{k=1}^{K} \{f_i : FI_{i,k} \geq a\} \right|}{N}$$

Dissimilarity Mean expresses the average of the distinctiveness of the clusters and is defined in terms of the dissimilarity $d_{i,j}$ between all the possible pairs of the clusters. Specifically, the dissimilarity $d_{i,j}$ between the clusters i and j, the mean of dissimilarity $DMean_i$ of a cluster i and the *Dissimilarity Mean* are specified by the following formulas respectively:

$$d_{i,j} = 1 - \frac{\left| \{f_n : (FI_{n,i} \geq \alpha) \wedge (FI_{n,j} \geq \alpha)\} \right|}{\left| \{f_n : (FI_{n,i} \geq \alpha) \vee (FI_{n,j} \geq \alpha)\} \right|} \qquad DMean_i = \frac{1}{K-1}\sum_{j=1}^{K} d_{i,j} \ , \quad i \neq j$$

$$DissimilarityMean = \frac{1}{K}\sum_{k=1}^{K} DMean_k$$

F1-measure is the harmonic mean of the *Coverage* and the *Dissimilarity Mean* and expresses an acceptable balance between them. It is specified as follows:

$$F1-measure = 2 \times \frac{Coverage \ \times \ DissimilarityMean}{Coverage \ + \ DissimilarityMean}$$

The highest value of the *F1-measure* determines the desired value for the threshold parameter α.

Concluding, given the manually produced annotations based on the DiLEO ontology for the DL evaluation-related ECDL papers, the workflow for discovering patterns of evaluation practices consists of the following steps: (a) representation of the document annotations by two alternative vector models, the binary and the weighted *tf-idf*, (b) clustering of the vector representations of the annotations by applying the K-means algorithm, (c) assessment of the features of each cluster using the frequency increase metric, (d) selection of the threshold α that maximizes the *F1-measure* between the *Coverage* and the *Dissimilarity Mean* indicators, and (v) identification of the evaluation profiles based on the representative features of the clusters.

4   Findings and Discussion

In general the *tf-idf* weighted representation provides more precise results than the binary vector representation and this is evident by the K-Means objective function error for each representation; the error for the *tf-idf* representation is 0.03, while the error of the binary representation is 1.95. Moreover, for most of the threshold α values, both *Coverage* and *Dissimilarity Mean* indicate better performance and permit the selection of a higher value for α. As the value of α increases, the number of the representative features in the clusters decreases, while the clusters become more distinct, generating thus clear evaluation profiles.

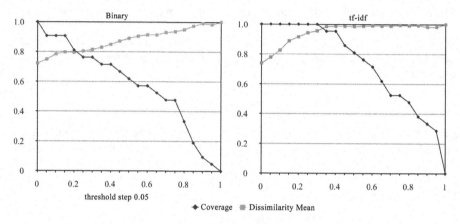

Fig. 3. *Coverage* and *Dissimilarity Mean* for the binary and *tf-idf* representations using different values for α

Figure 3 presents the curves of the *Coverage* and the *Dissimilarity Mean* with respect to the parameter α, as it varies in the range from 0 to 1 at a step of 0.05. The left part of the figure corresponds to the binary representation, while the right depicts the values of the *tf-idf* weighted representation. It is obvious that the *tf-idf* representation outperforms the binary representation for both indicators and permits a higher value for α to be selected.

In detail, the *Coverage* of the *tf-idf* representation remains equal to 1 meaning that all the features are present in the clustering, up to the point $\alpha=0.3$. The dissimilarity of the clusters increases quickly and its value is very close to its maximum at the same α value. Concerning the binary representation, the features are eliminated from the first step of α and the distinctiveness of the clusters reaches its maximum value near the highest α value. The outperformance of the *tf-idf* representation is also verified by the *F1-measure* values depicted in Figure 4.

The maximum score for the *F1-measure* is 0.98 when $\alpha=0.3$ for the *tf-idf* representation, while for the binary representation the *F1* maximizes at 0.85 when $\alpha=0.15$. Given these results we opted for the *tf-idf* representation and a *F1* value greater than or equal to 0.3 ($F1 \geq 0.3$). The features having FI values less than the threshold 0.3 will be excluded from the pattern description. The features resulted by this setting and describe each cluster are presented in Table 1.

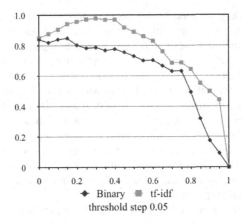

Fig. 4. F1-measure scores for the binary and *tf-idf* representations using different values for α

Table 1. The derived models of evaluation profiles and their frequencies

Cluster (Size)	Features for $FI \geq 0.3$
1 (7)	*interpret*: 0.97, *survey-studies*: 0.34, *analyze*:0.32
2 (19)	*description*: 0.69
3 (11)	*log_analysis_studies*: 0.94
4 (12)	*recommend*: 0.98, *effectiveness*: 0.35
5 (5)	*expert_studies*: 0.99, *documentation*: 0.87, *effectiveness*: 0.79, *comparison_studies*: 0.59, *comparison*: 0.42, *service_quality*: 0.34
6 (29)	*design*: 0.70, *technical_excellence*: 0.63
7 (7)	*service_quality*: 0.98, *record*: 0.31
8 (4)	*field_studies*: 0.99, *record*: 0.80, *analyze*:0.32
9 (15)	*documentation*: 0.74, *performance_measurement*: 0.63, *mesure*: 0.43, *laboratory_studies*: 0.41, *comparison*: 0.32
10 (4)	*outcome_assessment*: 0.99, *survey-studies*: 0.83, *analyze*: 0.32
11 (6)	*expert_studies*: 0.99, *technical_excellence*: 0.58, *laboratory_studie*: 0.54, *design*: 0.52, *record*: 0.50, *report*: 0.49, *description*: 0.39

All the clusters have at least one strong representative feature with FI value greater than 0.69. In particular, in three clusters the highest FI is close to 0.70, while the strongest feature of the other eight clusters has a FI value greater than 0.94.

Furthermore in ten clusters the FI value of the strongest feature is the highest from all the other FI values of the same feature in the other clusters. Hence, these features could be the starting points for formulating the evaluation pattern of the cluster they belong. One exception occurs for the feature *expert_studies*, which holds the same FI value in the clusters 5 and 11. However, clusters 5 and 11 have no other common feature, implying that even though the patterns start from the same feature, they follow different paths and express different evaluation practices.

Observing the lowest FI values in Table 1, it would be possible to filter more features from the clustering without affecting its structure. By increasing the value of α to 0.5, the features *analyze*, *measure* and *report* are filtered. The document frequency df_i of these three features is higher than 72%, meaning that these subclasses of the class *Activity* are widely adopted by the most papers. The removal of these features does not subtract any significant information, since it is known that almost every evaluation initiative includes these activities. The low impact of these features is implied by their *tf-idf* values, confirming, the outperformance of the *tf-idf* representation.

In general the evaluation profiles, presented in Table 1, are informative enough for investigating the DL evaluation trends in the last decade. Regarding the size of the clusters, it can be noted that the size of clusters 8 and 10 is small, each of them including four *tf-idf* weighted annotation vectors. However these clusters should not be merged with others, because the features with the highest *FI* value, *field_studies* and *outcome_assessment* respectively, correspond to subclasses not appeared in the patterns of the other clusters. Besides, these features hold the maximum *FI* value (0.99) of all the patterns in the other clusters, indicating their significance as starting points for formulating evaluation patterns.

The advantage of the presented method is that it reveals 'hidden' patterns not usually applied in the literature, such as the pattern of cluster 5, along with patterns representing frequently used evaluation practices, such as the pattern of clusters 8,9 and 10. For instance the pattern of cluster 9 implies that when a study aims to *document* the *performance* of a DL, then it consists of *measuring* activities, held –preferably– in a *laboratory setting*.

Some of the clusters are quite generic in the sense that the number of their representative features is quite small including a couple of features that usually refer to strategic level of the DiLEO schema, such as cluster 6 and cluster 2. This generic pattern corresponds to papers whose first priority is to present a new service or a system and for this purpose they provide evaluation results to describe the current state of that service or system. Cluster 3 consists also of a unique operational feature, the logging studies, indicating a significant trend in the literature.

The clustering process does not emerge any implications for modifying the ontology structure, in the sense that it does not reveal patterns that alter the structure of the ontology reasoning paths. Most of the patterns are identical to sequences of DiLEO triples (domain subclass –property– range subclass), such as the pattern of cluster 6, which is compatible to the DiLEO path *technical_excellence - isAimingAt- design*. This pattern is extended by the pattern of cluster 11, which emerges that when the goal is to improve the design of a DL, then the conduction of expert and laboratory studies contributes to the purpose of the technical excellence investigation; nevertheless the technical excellence investigation implies recording and reporting activities to be held. This pattern generates a set of DiLEO paths, indicatively *technical_excellence –hasConstituent– record* and *record –isPerformedIn– expert_studies*. Given these results, we consider that the application of clustering techniques on the instances of the DiLEO triples would discover complementary knowledge and therefore the future work will address this possibility.

5   Conclusions

Eleven groups of evaluation studies were generated after the semantic annotation of 119 papers and the application of the K-Means algorithm. These clusters, refined by statistical measures, such as the *FI*, provide meaningful patterns for the evaluation activities presented in ECDL among 2001-2010. We conclude that DiLEO provides the possibility to express meaningful annotations of the DL evaluation literature. Regarding the research questions of our work, we could confirm that the proposed approach can discover solid profiles of the evaluation research landscape, which reflect common practices and identify areas of interest.

References

1. Saracevic, T.: Introduction: the framework for digital library evaluation. In: Tsakonas, G., Papatheodorou, C. (eds.) Evaluation of Digital Libraries: an Insight to Useful Applications and Methods. Chandos Publishing, Oxford (2009)
2. Tsakonas, G., Papatheodorou, C.: An ontological representation of the digital library evaluation domain. JASIST 62(8), 1577–1593 (2011)
3. Kovács, L., Micsik, A.: An Ontology-Based Model of Digital Libraries. In: Fox, E.A., Neuhold, E.J., Premsmit, P., Wuwongse, V. (eds.) ICADL 2005. LNCS, vol. 3815, pp. 38–43. Springer, Heidelberg (2005)
4. Goncalves, M.A., Fox, E.A., Watson, L.T.: Towards a digital library theory: A formal digital library ontology. International Journal on Digital Libraries 8(2), 91–114 (2008)
5. Athanasopoulos, G., Candela, L., Castelli, D., et al.: The Digital Library Reference Model (2010)
6. Khoo, M., MacDonald, C.: An Organizational Model for Digital Library Evaluation. In: Gradmann, S., Borri, F., Meghini, C., Schuldt, H. (eds.) TPDL 2011. LNCS, vol. 6966, pp. 329–340. Springer, Heidelberg (2011)
7. Souto, M.A.M., Warpechowski, M., Oliveira, J.P.M.D.: An ontological approach for the quality assessment of Computer Science conferences. In: Advances in Conceptual Modeling: Foundations and Applications, pp. 202–212. Springer, Berlin (2007)
8. Rodriguez, M.A., Bollen, J., de Sompel, H.V.: A practical ontology for the large-scale modeling of scholarly artifacts and their usage. In: 7th ACM/IEEE-CS Joint Conference on Digital Libraries, pp. 278–287. ACM, New York (2007)
9. Groth, P., Gibson, A., Velterop, J.: The anatomy of a nanopublication. Information Services & Use 3, 51–56 (2010)
10. Bolelli, L., Ertekin, S., Zhou, D., Giles, C.L.: Finding topic trends in digital libraries. In: 9th Joint Conference on Digital libraries, pp. 69–72. ACM, New York (2009)
11. Rorissa, A., Yuan, X.: Visualizing and mapping the intellectual structure of information retrieval. Information Processing & Management 48, 12–135 (2011)
12. Smeaton, A.F., Keogh, G., Gurrin, C., Mcdonald, K., Sødring, T.: Content analysis of SIGIR conference papers. ACM SIGIR Forum 37, 49–53 (2002)
13. Biryukov, M., Dong, C.: Analysis of Computer Science communities based on DBLP. In: Lalmas, M., Jose, J., Rauber, A., Sebastiani, F., Frommholz, I. (eds.) ECDL 2010. LNCS, vol. 6273, pp. 228–235. Springer, Heidelberg (2010)
14. Reitz, F., Hoffmann, O.: An analysis of the evolving coverage of Computer Science subfields in the DBLP Digital Library. In: Lalmas, M., Jose, J., Rauber, A., Sebastiani, F., Frommholz, I. (eds.) ECDL 2010. LNCS, vol. 6273, pp. 216–227. Springer, Heidelberg (2010)
15. Cohen, J.: A coefficient of agreement for nominal scales. Educational and Psychological Measurement 20(1), 37–46 (1960)
16. Roberts, A., Gaizauskas, R., Hepple, M., et al.: The CLEF corpus: semantic annotation of clinical text. In: AMIA Annual Symposium Proceedings, pp. 625–629 (2007)

A Negotiation Approach to Support Conceptual Agreements for Ontology Content

Carla Pereira[1,3], Cristóvão Sousa[1,3], and António Lucas Soares[1,2]

[1] INESC Porto, Campus da FEUP, Rua Dr. Roberto Frias, 378, 4200-465 Porto, Portugal
[2] DEI, FEUP, University of Porto, Rua Dr. Roberto Frias, sn 4200-465 Porto, Portugal
[3] ESTGF-IPP, Apartado 205 4610 - 156, Felgueiras, Portugal
{csp,cpsousa,asoares}@inescporto.pt

Abstract. Conceptualisation processes are pervasive to most technical and professional activities, but are seldom addressed explicitly due to the lack of theoretical and practical methods and tools. However, it seems not to be a popular research topic in knowledge representation or its sub-areas such as ontology engineering. The approach described in this paper is a contribution to the development of methods and tools to collaborative conceptualisation processes. The particularly challenging problem of conceptual negotiation is here tackled through a combination of ColBlend method and an argumentation-based strategy, creating an innovative method to conceptual negotiation, *argile* method. This method was implemented in to the ConceptME platform as an advanced negotiation mechanism.

Keywords: conceptualisation process, argumentation-based strategy, collaborative networks.

1 Introduction

Collaborative knowledge representation is a research topic of utmost importance for the development of tools supporting collaborative human activities such as knowledge management or ontology content development. Nevertheless, it has not been researched as it would be expected. This is particularly evident in the lack of research literature about the early phases of ontology content development (or ontology specification), when the goal is to achieve a shared conceptualisation of a domain. Knowing more about collaborative conceptualisation processes and proposing new ways to support them is thus a challenging research. We have been researching these topics both by developing new "socio-semantic" methods and collaborative platforms to support the collective construction of conceptual representations. In this paper we will describe a method, based in argumentation techniques, aimed to support what we called "conceptual negotiation". Our context of use are "collaborative networks" involving independent actors (groups, organisations) that established trust, synergistic relationships and develop joint activities in technical domains.

P. Herrero et al. (Eds.): OTM 2012 Workshops, LNCS 7567, pp. 474–483, 2012.

2   Collaborative Conceptualisation and Conceptual Negotiation

An ontology can be viewed as "a specification of a conceptualisation" [10]. Furthermore, an ontology, as a knowledge representation artefact, is deemed to convey some shared conceptualisation of a domain, as perceived and understood by a social group. However, the terms "conceptual" or "conceptualisation" are seldom used in the discourse about the development of ontology content. The term "semantics" is rather preferred. "Conceptualisation" can be defined intuitively as "the relevant informal knowledge one can extract and generalize from experience, observation, or introspection" [18]. We can thus say that a conceptualisation is the result of a "conceptualisation process" (CP) that leads to the extraction and generalisation of relevant information from experience [18]. For an individual, the conceptualisation process of a given reality is a collection of ordered cognitive activities with information and knowledge that is internally or externally accessible to the individual as inputs and an internal or external conceptual representation as the output. Furthermore, a "collaborative conceptualisation process" (CCP) is a conceptualisation process that involves more than one individual producing an agreed conceptual representation. Besides individual CP activities, the collaborative CP involves social activities that include the negotiation of meaning and practical management activities for the collaborative process leading to a "semantic or conceptual agreement". By definition, an "agreement" means that two or more actors reached an understanding about something, approving and accepting it. But why are "conceptual agreements" needed? Simply because different groups, even participating in the same project, can conceptualise (and represent) the same reality in different ways. These differences are not expected to be dramatic, but even so important to hinder the achievement of a shared conceptualisation. Then, a CCP naturally includes understanding, arguing and compromising in order to achieve a conceptual agreement, in what can be called a conceptual negotiation process. Conceptual negotiation is thus a social interaction process leading to an agreement about the conceptual representation of a domain. A conceptual negotiation process establishes a "common ground" of understanding concerning the meaning of the represented conceptual structures and the associated terminology. In spite of considering an ontology as representing "semantic agreements", the research on ontology development didn't give much attention to the process of achieving such (conceptual) agreements. Only a few works acknowledge the importance of supporting the conceptualization phase [17]. Our research in socio-semantics addresses, between others [4], the support to CCP through collaborative conceptual models editing, discussion and negotiation (see figure 2, left). Part of this research resulted in the ColBlend method [1],[2], inspired in the Conceptual Blending Theory [3]. This method proposes a basic negotiation model based on conceptual spaces aimed at integrating ("blending") the conceptual structures contained in the input spaces [3]. In the next sections we present an approach to support conceptual negotiation based in argumentation techniques.

3   The *argile* Approach to Conceptual Negotiation

3.1   Overview of the ColBlend Method

The ColBlend method was designed to support a collaborative conceptualisation process, based on conceptual blending theory (CBT) [3]. In practical terms ColBlend aims to support the co-construction of conceptual representations (we can also call it *conceptual models*) which can serve as a specification for taxonomies, classifications or ontologies [1], [2]. In an overview, the process comprises a set of virtual spaces: a) the input spaces - where each party build models representing their conceptualisation of the domain; b) the blend space - containing the results from the analysis of the input spaces presented for discussion; moreover, it proposes new concepts from a global analysis of the current spaces content and c) the generic space - which contains the common domain model composed by the all parts of the proposals that were accepted by all and "published" to the this shared space. This method led to the development of the conceptME collaborative platform[1] [4], a "conceptual Modelling Environment" where groups of specialists can find tools and resources to collaboratively develop conceptual representations, organise them in libraries, share them with other colleagues and reuse them when needed. Currently, conceptME supports concept maps as representational notation.

3.2   The *argile* Method: High-Level Description

Starting from the ColBlend method, we present a new approach to conceptual negotiation that uses an argumentation-based strategy. Inspired in the Toulmin Model of argumentation [12], [13], the work described in [14], [15] and the argument mapping tutorials available in http://rationale.austhink.com/rationale2.0/tutorials/, a method organized in two level of conceptual negotiation is proposed (see figure 1). The first level refers to the creation, description and structural validation of conceptual structures (claims) in an individual level and their negotiation at group level. At the second level, a lightest conceptual negotiation iteration takes place, supporting the integration of the previously agreed conceptual structures (resulting form level 1) into the shared model. The goal is to define, collaboratively, the position of this new input in the global model. An initial proposal of the integrated conceptual model is created based on the blend execution (composition activity). The participant's role is to validate the proposal, if they agree the process is finished, else, they can present a different proposal for integration and a new light cycle of negotiation is started. These two negotiation levels rise from the fact that although all individuals involved in the process have accepted the simple conceptual structure (claim), it does not mean that the integrated model is compliant with all parties views, mainly due to the semantic changes that the integration can made in the global model. At the end, considering the conceptual structure integrated by running the completion and elaboration activities (blend execution) new conceptual structures can be

---

[1] http://www.conceptME.pt

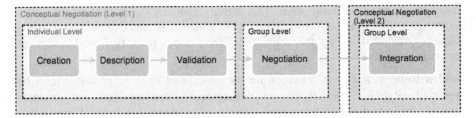

Fig. 1. The *argile* method activities

suggested to be included in the model. The execution of these activities triggers a new negotiation process.

3.3   The *argile* Method: Activities and Protocol Description

To the particular case of conceptual structures negotiation, the activities of the process are the following (see figure 1):

Conceptual Structure Creation: conceptual structure creation with the minimal degree of granularity (concept-relation-concept). During this activity, if a partner propose a conceptual structure whose concepts already exist in a another structure puts in discussion, the partner is alerted and their action is limited to the following speech-acts (defined according [12] and adjusted to conceptual negotiation (detailed description presented below)): counter-propose, defend, agree or refine.

Conceptual Structure Description: this activity include the introduction of information that support/justify the proposal. This is divided in 3 parameters:

(i) *Evidences* - are "meta-information" provided by the proponent. The "meta-information" can be the definition of the proposed concepts, a global definition of the conceptual structure proposed or documentation to support the proposal. (ii) *Social Value* - When a proposal is submitted, in an initial stage, their social value is directly dependent on proponent credibility. Social value is completed during the activity 4, considering the number of the speech-acts of type *Critique NOT*, *Defend* and *Agree* and the credibility of each participant. (iii) *User Credibility* - The user credibility is a value in the range 0 to 1. Initially, will assume a value according the reputation of the user on the group. This value will be updated according to the following parameters: i) degree of participation; ii) number of proposals made and; iii) their rate of acceptance. In practical terms the value is calculate as follows

$$(\alpha \cdot degreeOfParticipation + \beta \cdot noOfProposals + \delta \cdot acceptanceRate)$$
$$i) degreeOfParticipation = \sum UserSpeech-acts / \sum Speech-acts$$
$$ii) acceptanceRate = \sum UserProposals / \sum UserAcceptedProposals.$$

where α, β and δ are defined at the beginning of the process, corresponding to a weight between 0 and 1 and the parameters are calculated as follows:

Conceptual Structure Validation: This activity analyses the evidences to validate the presence of the terms constituents of the conceptual structure proposed in the evidences included during the activity 2. Here, some rules two used according argument mapping.

Golden Rule: at least one definition for the conceptual structure proposed must be presented. **Rabbit Rule:** based on the textual corpus-analysis and contexts identification, check the co-occurrence of the terms used in the conceptual structure.

Conceptual Structure Negotiation: Once validated, the proposal can be shared and the users can negotiate it. The users can act according the following speech-acts: *counter-propose, critique NOT, defend, agree* or *refine*. This activity occurs during a limited time period (time period agreed/defined by group members). At the end of this period, the conceptual structure value is calculated and the conceptual structure with highest value is suggested for integration into the global model. The conceptual structure value (is a value in the range 0 to 1) is calculated as follows (*n* is number of participants in the conceptual structure negotiation activity; A=1 if the participant *Depend* or *Agree* with the proposal; A=0 if the participant *Counter-Propose, Critique-Not* or *Refine* the proposal).

Conceptual Structure Integration in the Global (Shared) Conceptual Model: The fact of achieving consensus about the conceptual structure resulting from the first level of negotiation does not mean that the integration into the global model can be automatic (a collaborative activity is desirable). The integration proposal arises of the composition activity execution (blend execution). At this stage, the second level of the argile method initiates according to the description above (see 3.2).

$$[ProponentCredibility + \sum_{i=1}^{n} A * UserCredibility_i]/_n$$

4   The ConceptME Approach to Support Conceptual Negotiation

4.1   ConceptME Overview

The core of conceptME platform is on supporting collaborative modelling, allowing users to create and share conceptual models, focusing on graphical knowledge representations and terminological methods, accommodated into a service's library. The platform enhances negotiation and discussion capabilities by means of specific extensions, towards consensus reaching.

The platform is organised as follows (see figure 2, left): a) a set of functionalities to manage ongoing and previous collaborative modelling projects (generic project edition, definition and configuration of the enclosing collaborative spaces and related resources); b) a collaborative modelling environment, allowing users to build their models individually or editing them collaboratively (either on their own or through available templates), while discussing around concepts; c) a set of terminological services, based in terminological work methods and techniques, supported by a

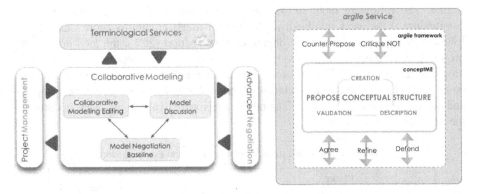

Fig. 2. ConceptME high-level architecture and method service protocol

domain specific textual corpus, allowing users to associate relevant resources to their projects, performing extraction operations to retrieve candidate terms that can be used in their conceptualisation process. At this level, conceptME provides means for corpus organisation and classification and real-time term contexts to detail existing representations; d) a model negotiation baseline enclosing a set of features (merging individual input structures, suggestion mechanism, cross-checking corpus-based validation, auto-complete and categorization, among others) to ensure simple negotiation mechanisms, towards a common shared model. This module provides the interface and environment conditions, allowing to connect other advanced negotiation mechanisms, such as, the argumentation-based conceptual negotiation approach described here.

4.2 Argumentation Service Support: An Illustration Scenario

To support the collaborative argumentation process, a negotiation service based on *argile* protocol was designed and implemented. Following the conceptME high-level architecture, the *argile* method was designed to implement a specific negotiation approach (argumentation based) on top of an existent negotiation baseline. As a service, *argile* main role is to account for decision support tasks taking place at negotiation process thresholds, providing mechanisms for individual proposals evaluation. Figure 2 (right), shows the main interactions (protocol) between the conceptME and the *argile* service. The proposed conceptual structures - developed individually - are published into a shared space within conceptME. At this common space, the claims (published conceptual structures) from each input space are available and the argumentation process starts over a claim on the list. Next, we describe a simple application scenario to illustrate the method. The example is based in a corpus about the domain of urban rehabilitation (http://www.h-know.eu/) used to support the development of the a collaborative platform project ontology. Thus, in the scope of urban rehabilitation, at a certain stage of conceptualisation process, the definition of a conceptual structure around the concept of "construction resource" was started. The following table shows the assumed status of the negotiation process comprising: i) the users involved; ii) the current user's credibility score - calculated following a weighted sum of the degree of participation (20%), the total amount of proposals and counter-proposals (30%) and the rate of proposals and counter-proposals acceptance (50%); iii) user's domain of expertise; iv) the actions performed so far and; v) the total accepted claims per user. Accepted claims comprises propose and counter-propose speech acts. The table values were dynamic and were updated as the negotiation process run.

Table 1. *Argile* Illustration Scenario - (**a**: initial assumed score)

User name	#User credibility value	#Performed actions (speech acts)		#Accepted claims
User1	0.50 + a	9	3 propose	4
			3 agree	
			3 counter-propose	
User2	0.56 + a	10	5 propose	4
			2 critique NOT	
			2 defend	
			1 agree	
User3	0.33 + a	15	3 propose	2
			1 counter-propose	
			3 agree	
			5 agree	
			1 defend	
			2 refine	

Going forward with the example, *user1* submitted the following conceptual structure to the common shared space as a new claim (claim #1): "*Construction agent is a type of construction resource*". On publishing, *argile* service has returned a golden rule warning exception, which means that no definition has been provided. Meanwhile, *user1* has decided to add a proper definition and resubmitted it for publication. *User2*, by his turn, has built the following structure (claim #2): "*Construction product is a type of construction resource*". The structure was validated, regarding the golden and rabbit rule and was appended to the claim list at the shared space. Afterwards, the discussion takes place around claim 1 and claim 2, from which two more claims arises: claim #3, counter proposing claim #2, stating that – "*Construction material is a type of construction resource*", and; claim #4, on defending claim #2 adding a warrant by specifying the original source documentation (ISO 12006-2 standard classes). The next table summarises the speech acts performed by each user and the conceptual structures to be integrated into the shared model (claim #1 and claim #3).

Table 2. Negotiation speech-acts - (Caption: * the proponent)

Claim thread	Claim ID	User1	User2	User3	Conceptual structure value	Selected claim
#1	#1	*	---	Agree	0,28	YES
#2	#2		*	Counter-propose		
#2	#3	Agree		*	0,28	YES
#2	#4	---	Defend	---	0,19	NO

5   Related Work

Researchers that study the collaborative creation of semantic artifacts have already pointed out the need for conceptual negotiation [5, 6, 7]. They state that many problems stem from the fact that various stakeholders with partially conflicting interests need to simultaneous collaborate on joint objectives. The incompatibilities are due the fact that these multidisciplinary teams have specific insight into certain sub-domains and use it to reach unrelated goals. [5] Presents an approach that models the members' commitments, interests and responsibilities using communicative workflow that allows for meaning negotiation. Ontology is used as a means of disambiguating communication. The meaning negotiation process used to attain consensus uses the DOGMA-MESS methodology [16]. [6] Also uses meaning negotiation in order to reach consensus via ontology integration. [7] Is similar to [5, 6] in that it deals with meaning negotiation; negotiation is based on the merging and alignment of local ontologies and; the resulting global ontology represents the shared agreement. The negotiation process is based on the extend DOGMA-MESS methodology resulting in an iterated four phase negotiation process. Unlike previous work however, [7] attempts to semi-automated the meaning negotiation process by providing an algorithm that tallies the changes that were made to the local ontologies and uses those values to make changes to the merged ontology. In essence this article presents a voting protocol, which according to [8], is not particularly flexible, efficient and effective. Although much work exists in the general area of agent based negotiation [9] to the best of our knowledge none deals with the specific problem of conceptual negotiation. The work that most closely resembles what we are attempting is described in [11]. It describes a general negotiation model and protocol based on speech-acts and argumentation in a knowledge intensive context (as opposed to the normal e-commerce setting such as supply chain management); the system does not use automated agent negotiation per se but provides support for designers to discuss issues based on CAD drawings; it deals with multi-issue negotiation, which is referred to as multiple interrelated negotiation and, as is required in any knowledge intensive negotiation process, the agent system promotes problem solving by generating alternatives. Our aim to provide a similar solution in the context of conceptual negotiation where the shared agreement is a conceptual model represented by concept maps.

6   Conclusions and Future Work

This paper brings into discussion the problems and requirements related to supporting collaborative conceptualisation processes, more specifically how to conduct the conceptual negotiation process. In this perspective, an innovative approach to conceptual negotiation, *argile* method, was presented. *Argile* method combines the principles of ColBlend method [2] with an argumentation-based strategy, and appears as the pilot proposal that deal with the specific problem of conceptual negotiation during the process of conceptual models construction. Together with other services (extraction services, templates, ontological guidance, and so on), this method was implemented in to the ConceptME platform as an advanced negotiation mechanism. Preliminary experiments were already run and the results showed that this approach improved the collaborative conceptualisation process in concepts elicitation and negotiation.

Future work will be focused on the running of experiments aimed at obtaining further feedback from specialists, in several domains, to improve and fine-tune the methods and tools developed so far. In what concerns to conceptual modelling this research is surely proposing a refreshing view on this subject.

Acknowledgements. This work is part-funded by the ERDF – European Regional Development Fund through the COMPETE Programme (operational programme for competitiveness) and by National Funds through the FCT – Fundação para a Ciência e a Tecnologia (Portuguese Foundation for Science and Technology) within project «PTDC/EIA-EIA/103779/2008 - CogniNET».

References

1. Pereira, C., Sousa, C., Lucas Soares, A.: A Socio-semantic Approach to Collaborative Domain Conceptualization. In: Meersman, R., Herrero, P., Dillon, T. (eds.) OTM 2009 Workshops. LNCS, vol. 5872, pp. 524–533. Springer, Heidelberg (2009)
2. Pereira, C., Sousa, C., Soares, A.L.: Supporting Conceptualisation Processes in Collaborative Networks: a Case Study on an R&D Project. International Journal of Computer Integrated Manufacturing, 1–21 (January 16, 2012)
3. Fauconnier, G., Turner, M.: Conceptual Integration Networks. Published in Cognitive Science 22(2), 133–187 (1998)
4. Sá, C., Pereira, C., Soares, A.: Supporting Collaborative Conceptualization Tasks through a Semantic Wiki Based Platform. In: Meersman, R., Dillon, T., Herrero, P. (eds.) OTM 2010. LNCS, vol. 6428, pp. 394–403. Springer, Heidelberg (2010)
5. Moor, A.D.: Ontology guided meaning negotiation in communities of practice. In: Mambrey, P., Grther, W. (eds.) Proc. of the Workshop on the Design for LargeScale Digital Communities at the 2nd Int. Conf. on Communities and Technologies (C&T 2005), Milan, Italy, pp. 21–28 (2005)
6. Oliveira, J., de Souza, J., de Paula, M.M., de Souza, J.M.: Meaning Negotiation for Consensus Formation in Ontology Integration. In: CSCWD, pp. 787–792. IEEE (2006)

7. Debruyne, C., Peeters, J., Arrassi, A.Z.: Semi-automated Consensus Finding for Meaning Negotiation. In: Meersman, R., Tari, Z., Herrero, P. (eds.) OTM-WS 2008. LNCS, vol. 5333, pp. 183–192. Springer, Heidelberg (2008)
8. Winoto, P., McCalla, G., Vassileva, J.: An extended alternating offers bargaining protocol for automated negotiation in multiagent systems. In: Eighteenth National Conference on Artificial Intelligence, pp. 969–970. AAAI, Menlo Park (2002)
9. Lopes, F., Wooldridge, M., Novais, A.Q.: Negotiation among autonomous computational agents: principles, analysis and challenges. Artif. Intell. Rev. 29(1), 1–44 (2008)
10. Gruber, T.: A Translation Approach to Portable Ontology Specifications. Knowledge Acquisition 5(2), 199–221 (1993)
11. Jin, Y., Geslin, M.: Argumentation-based negotiation for collaborative engineering design. Int. Journal of Collaborative Engineering 1(1/2), 125–151 (2009)
12. Toulmin, S.E.: The Uses of Argument. Cambridge University Press, Cambridge (1958)
13. Hitchcock, D., Verheij, B.: The Toulmin Model Today: Introduction to the Special Issue on Contemporary Work using Stephen Edelston Toulmin's Layout of Arguments. From the issue entitled "Special Issue: The Toulmin Model Today". Argumentation 19(3), 255–258 (2005)
14. Jin, Y., Geslin, M.: Argumentation-based negotiation for collaborative engineering design. International Journal of Collaborative Engineering 1(1/2), 125–151 (2009)
15. Rieke, R., Sillars, M., Peterson, T.: Argumentation and Critical Decision Making, 7th edn. Pearson (2008)
16. de Moor, A., Leenheer, P.D., Meersman, R.: Dogma-mess: A meaning evolution support system for interorganizational ontology engineering. In: Proc. of the ICCS 2006, Aalborg, Denmark, July 17-21 (2006)
17. Staab, S.: On understanding the collaborative construction of conceptualisations. In: International and Interdisciplinary Conference "Processing Text-Technological Resources" at the Center for Interdisciplinary Research, Bielefeld University, March 13-15 (2008)
18. Prévot, L., Huang, C., Calzolari, N., Gangemi, A., Lenci, A., Oltramari, A.: Ontology and the lexicon: a multidisciplinary perspective. In: Huang, C., et al. (eds.) Ontology and the Lexicon: A Natural Language Processing Perspective. Cambridge University Press

SeDeS 2012 PC Co-chairs Message

Decision support has gradually evolved in both the fields of theoretical decision support studies and practical assisting tools for decision makers since the 1960s. Ontology Engineering (OE) brings new synergy to decision support. On the one hand, it will change (and actually now is changing) the decision support landscape, as it will enable new breeds of decision models, decision support systems (DSS) to be developed. On the other hand, DSS can bring theories and applications that support OE, such as ontology integration, ontology matching and ontology integration.

The theme of the third international workshop on Semantics & Decision Support (SeDeS12) is to study how OE can bring extra advantages to DSS, especially with web technologies. SeDeS12 will have a special track from the 8th International IFIP Workshop on Semantic Web & Web Semantics (SWWS 2012), the theme of which is the study of Web Semantics.

After a thorough and extensive review process, this year we accepted 5 full papers and 2 posters for presentation at SeDeS12. Each of these submissions was rigorously peer reviewed by at least three experts. The papers were judged according to their originality, significance to theory and practice, readability, and relevance to workshop topics.

Papers selected for publication and presentation at the workshop were organized into a number of tracks, namely:

- Basic decision support theories and algorithms
- Decision support and Business applications
- Decision support for Ontology engineering

We would like to express our deepest appreciation to the Program Committee members and external reviewers for their generous contribution of time and effort in maintaining the quality during the review process. We would like to give special thanks to Dr. Peter Spyns for his valuable help. We would also like to thank the authors of the submitted papers and all the workshop attendees for their discussions and ideas and for turning the SeDeS12 workshop into a success. Lastly, we would like to thank the members of the OTM Organizing Committee, who played an important role in the smooth running of the workshop. We feel that the papers and discussions in the various tracks of SeDeS12 will further inspire research in the DSS and OE, especially in the areas of ontology development, semantic interoperability, decision support for human-computer interactions and semantic decision support systems in the fields of business management and Internet of Things.

July 2012

Yan Tang Demey
Jan Vanthienen

P. Herrero et al. (Eds.): OTM 2012 Workshops, LNCS 7567, p. 484, 2012.
© Springer-Verlag Berlin Heidelberg 2012

Nondeterministic Decision Rules
in Classification Process

Piotr Paszek and Barbara Marszał-Paszek

Institute of Computer Science, University of Silesia
Będzińska 39, 41-200 Sosnowiec, Poland
{paszek,bpaszek}@us.edu.pl

Abstract. In the paper, we discuss nondeterministic rules in decision tables, called the truncated nondeterministic rules. These rules have on the right hand side a few decisions. We show that the truncated nondeterministic rules can be used for improving the quality of classification.

We propose a greedy algorithm of polynomial time complexity to construct these rules. We use this type of rules, to build up rule-based classifiers. These classifiers, classification algorithms, are used not only nondeterministic rules but also minimal rules in the sense of rough sets. These rule-based classifiers were tested on the group of decision tables from the UCI Machine Learning Repository. The reported results of the experiment show that the proposed classifiers based on nondeterministic rules improve the classification quality but it requires tuning some of their parameters relative to analyzed data.

Keywords: classification, decision tables, nondeterministic decision rules, rough sets, rule based classifier.

1 Introduction

Over the years many methods based on rule induction and rule-based classification systems were developed [10,17]. Some of them are based on rough sets [2,6,14,15,18] and some of them are based on cluster analysis [7]. In this paper we show that exist possibility for improving the rule-based classification systems.

We discuss a method for rule inducing based on searching for strong rules for a union of a few relevant decision classes – nondeterministic decision rules. Because these rules are created by shortening the deterministic rules they are called truncated nondeterministic rules.

In the paper, the following classification problem is considered: for a given decision table T [11,12] and a new object v generate a value of the decision attribute on v using values of conditional attributes on v.

In [16] Skowron and Suraj shown that there exist information systems $S = (U, A)$ [11], where U is a finite set of objects and A is a finite set of attributes, such that the set U can't be described by deterministic rules. In [9] Moshkov shown that for any information system, the set can be described by nondeterministic

P. Herrero et al. (Eds.): OTM 2012 Workshops, LNCS 7567, pp. 485–494, 2012.
© Springer-Verlag Berlin Heidelberg 2012

(inhibitory) rules. Inhibitory rules [3] are a special case of nondeterministic rules. These results inspired us to use the nondeterministic rules in a classification process [8].

We present an application of (truncated) nondeterministic rules in construction of rule-based classifiers. We also include the results of experiments that shows that by combining the rule-based classifiers based on the minimal decision rules [11,15] with the nondeterministic rules that have sufficiently large support [1], it is possible to improve the classification quality and reduce the classification error.

The paper consists of six sections. In Section 2, we recall the notions of a decision table and deterministic and nondeterministic decision rules. In Sections 3 and 4 we present a greedy algorithm for nondeterministic decision rule construction and main steps in construction of classifiers enhanced by nondeterministic rules. In Section 5 the results of the experiments with real-life data from the UCI Machine Learning Repository [5] are discussed. Section 6 contains short conclusions.

2   Basic Notations

In 1982 Pawlak proposed the rough set theory as an innovative mathematical tool for describing knowledge, including the uncertain and inexact knowledge [11]. In this theory knowledge is based on possibility (capability) of classifying objects. The objects may be for instance real objects, statements, abstract concepts and processes.

Let $T = (U, A, d)$ be a *decision table*, where $U = \{u_1, \ldots, u_n\}$ is a finite nonempty set of *objects*, $A = \{a_1, \ldots, a_m\}$ is a finite nonempty set of *conditional attributes* (functions defined on U), and d is the *decision attribute* (function defined on U).

We assume that for each $u_i \in U$ and each $a_j \in A$ the value $a_j(u_i)$ belong to $V_{a_j}(T)$ and the value $d(u_i)$ belong to $V_d(T)$, where $V_d(T)$ denotes the set of values of the decision attribute d on objects from U.

2.1   Deterministic Decision Rules

In general, the *deterministic decision rule* in T has the following form:

$$(a_{j_1} \in V_1) \wedge \ldots \wedge (a_{j_k} \in V_k) \rightarrow (d = v),$$

where $a_{j_1}, \ldots, a_{j_k} \in A$, $V_j \subseteq V_{a_j}$, for $j \in \{1, \ldots, k\}$ and $v \in V_d(T)$. The predecessor of this rule is a conjunction of generalized descriptors and the successor of this rule is a descriptor.

In the rule-based classifiers, most commonly used are the rules in the form of Horn Clauses

$$(a_{j_1} = b_1) \wedge \ldots \wedge (a_{j_k} = b_k) \rightarrow (d = v)$$

where $k > 0$, $a_{j_1}, \ldots, a_{j_k} \in A$, $b_1, \ldots, b_k \in V_A(T)$, $v \in V_d(T)$ and numbers $j_1, \ldots, j_k$ are pairwise different. The predecessor of this rule (conditional part) is a conjunction of descriptors.

2.2   Nondeterministic Decision Rules

In this paper, we also consider nondeterministic decision rules. A *nondeterministic decision rule* in a given decision table T is of the form:

$$(a_{j_1} \in V_1) \wedge \ldots \wedge (a_{j_k} \in V_k) \to d = (c_1 \vee \ldots \vee c_s), \tag{1}$$

where $a_{j_1}, \ldots, a_{j_k} \in A$, $V_j \subseteq V_{a_j}$, for $j \in \{1, \ldots, k\}$, numbers $j_1, \ldots, j_k$ are pairwise different, and $\emptyset \neq \{c_1, \ldots, c_s\} \subseteq V_d(T)$.

Some notation about rules of the form (1) are introduced in [4].

Let us introduce some notation.

If r is the nondeterministic rule (1) then by $lh(r)$ we denote its left hand side, i.e., the formula $(a_{j_1} \in V_1) \wedge \ldots \wedge (a_{j_k} \in V_k)$, and by $rh(r)$ its right hand side, i.e., the formula $d = (c_1 \vee \ldots \vee c_s)$.

By $||lh(r)||_T$ (or $||lh(r)||$, for short) we denote all objects from U satisfying $lh(r)$ [12]. To measure the quality of such rules we use coefficients called the support and the confidence [1]. They are defined as follows. If r is a nondeterministic rule of the form (1) then the support of this rule in the decision system T is defined by

$$supp(r) = \frac{|\ ||lh(r)|| \cap ||rh(r)||\ |}{|U|},$$

and the confidence of r in T is defined by

$$conf(r) = \frac{|\ ||lh(r)|| \cap ||rh(r)||\ |}{|\ ||lh(r)||\ |}.$$

We also use a normalized support of r in T defined by

$$norm\_supp(r) = \frac{supp(r)}{\sqrt{|V(r)|}},$$

where $V(r) \subseteq V_d(T)$ is a decision values set from right hand side of the rule $(rh(r))$.

2.3   Truncated Nondeterministic Rules

Now we can define a parameterized set of truncated nondeterministic decision rules that are used in Section 4 for enhancing the quality of classification of rule-based classifiers. This type of nondeterministic rules appears as a result of shortening rules according to the principle MDL (Minimum Description Length) [13].

This parameterized set is defined as the set of all nondeterministic rules r (over attributes in T) such that:

1. On the left hand sides of such rules are only conditions of the form $a \in \{v\}$, where $v \in V_a$. We write $a = v$ instead of $a \in \{v\}$;
2. $conf(r) \geq \alpha$, where $\alpha \in [0.5, 1]$ is a threshold;

3. $|V(r)| \leq k < |V_d(T)|$, where k is a threshold used as an upper bound on the number of decision values on the right hand sides of rules – k is assumed to be small.

Hence, the *truncated nondeterministic decision rules* are of the form:

$$(a_{j_1} = b_1) \wedge \ldots \wedge (a_{j_k} = b_k) \rightarrow d = (c_1 \vee \ldots \vee c_s), \qquad (2)$$

where $a_{j_1}, \ldots, a_{j_k} \in A$, for $j \in \{1, \ldots, k\}$, $b_j \in V_{b_j}(T)$, numbers $j_1, \ldots, j_k$ are pairwise different, and $\emptyset \neq \{c_1, \ldots, c_s\} \subseteq V_d(T)$.

The algorithm presented in Section 3 is searching for truncated nondeterministic rules with sufficiently large support and relatively small (in comparison to the set of all possible decisions), sets of decisions defined by the right hand sides of such rules for the decision table T.

3   Algorithm for Nondeterministic Decision Rule Construction

Let us describe the algorithm with threshold $\alpha \in [0.5, 1]$ which constructs truncated nondeterministic decision rules for T. This algorithm is based on greedy strategy which is used to minimize the length of rules.

The algorithm consists of two main steps.

In the first step, the deterministic decision rules are constructed for a given decision table T. The different algorithms may be used to build up the set of deterministic rules. In Section 5 we present the influence of the choice of the deterministic rules that will be shorten in the second step of the algorithm on the classification quality.

In the second step, of the algorithm, the set of deterministic decision rules are shortened (truncated). *TruNDeR* (*Tru*ncated *N*ondeterministic *De*cision *R*ules) is the name of the algorithm implementing the second step. Algorithm 1 contains pseudo-code of algorithm *TruNDeR*.

Algorithm *TruNDeR*, for truncated nondeterministic rules construction, has polynomial computational complexity, which depends on number of deterministic rules, and number of objects and number of attributes in the decision table.

4   Classifiers

In this section, we present an application of nondeterministic rules for the classification process. We constructed two classifier *MDR* and *TNDR*.

The set of minimal rules, generated using *RSESlib* library (Rough Set Exploration System library) [2], and standard voting procedure to resolve conflicts between rules, were used to induce *MDR* classifier.

The set of truncated nondeterministic rules, generated by the *TruNDeR* algorithm and the set of minimal rules, generated using *RSESlib* library, are used to induce our second classifier (*TNDR*).

Algorithm 1. *TruNDeR* – greedy algorithm for truncated nondeterministic decision rule construction

Input: T – decision table, R_d – a set of deterministic decision rules of T, $\alpha \in [0.5, 1]$, k – upper bound on the number of decision values;
Output: $R_{nd}(\alpha)$ – a set of nondeterministic decision rules for T.

$R_{nd} \leftarrow \emptyset$;
for all $r \in R_d$ **do**
$\quad \{r : L \rightarrow (d = v); \ L = D_1 \wedge \ldots \wedge D_m; \ v \in V_d; \}$
$\quad STOP \leftarrow false$;
$\quad \lambda_L \leftarrow norm\_supp(L)$;
$\quad$**repeat**
$\quad\quad$**for all** condition attributes from r **do**
$\quad\quad\quad L^i = D_1 \wedge \ldots \wedge D_{i-1} \wedge D_{i+1} \wedge \ldots \wedge D_m$;
$\quad\quad\quad \{L^i$ is obtained by dropping i-th attribute from the left hand side of rule $r\}$
$\quad\quad\quad ||L^i||_T; \quad \theta = \{v \in V_d : \exists_{x \in U_{L^i}} d(x) = v\}$;
$\quad\quad\quad$Sorting in decreasing order θ;
$\quad\quad\quad \theta_i \subset \theta: conf(L^i \rightarrow (d = \theta_i)) = \frac{|||L^i|| \cap ||\theta_i|||}{|||L^i|||} \geq \alpha; \ \{\theta_i$ greedy selection$\}$
$\quad\quad\quad \lambda_{L^i} \leftarrow norm\_supp(L^i \rightarrow \theta_i)$;
$\quad\quad$**end for**
$\quad\quad \lambda_{max}^i \leftarrow argmax\{\lambda_{L^i}\}$;
$\quad\quad$**if** $\lambda_{max}^i \geq \lambda_L$ **then**
$\quad\quad\quad L \leftarrow L^i; \ \lambda_L \leftarrow \lambda_{max}^i; \ \{r_{nd} : L \rightarrow (d = \theta_i); \ \lambda_L\}$
$\quad\quad$**else**
$\quad\quad\quad STOP \leftarrow true$;
$\quad\quad$**end if**
$\quad$**until** STOP
$\quad$**if** $|\theta_i| \leq k$ **then**
$\quad\quad R_{nd} \leftarrow R_{nd} \cup \{r_{nd}\}$;
$\quad$**end if**
end for
return R_{nd};

Because we have two groups of rules in the classification process, in the *TNDR* classifier, we should negotiate between them.

For any new object the decision value set is generated as follows.

First, for any new object, all (truncated) nondeterministic rules matching the object are extracted. Next, from these matched rules, a rule with the largest normalized support is selected. In the case when several rules have the same support, the decision value set $V(r)$ of the nondeterministic rule r with the smallest set of decision value set ($|V(r)|$) is selected. If still several nondeterministic rules with the above property exist then first of them is selected.

Next, for this object, all minimal rules matching the object are extracted. We obtain a single decision value using standard voting procedure.

In this way, for any new object we obtain a decision value $v \in V_d(T)$ and a decision value set $V(r)$, where r is the rule selected from the set of nondeterministic rules.

The final decision for a given new object is obtained from the decision value v and decision value set $V(r)$ by the following strategy for resolving conflicts [8].

1. If for a given new object the standard voting based on minimal rules predicts the decision value v and $v \in V(r)$, (i.e., no conflict arises) then we take as the final decision the single decision v.
2. If for a given new object the standard voting based on minimal rules predicts the decision value v and $v \notin V(r)$ (i.e., conflict arises) then we take as the final decision value the single decision value v if support of the minimal (deterministic) rule is larger than the normalized support of nondeterministic decision rule r and selected for the given new object. In the opposite case, we take as the final decision a single decision value from the set $V(r)$, with the largest support in T among decisions from $V(r)$.
3. If for a new object, the standard voting based on minimal rules predicts the decision value v and this object does not match any nondeterministic rule then we assign the decision v as the final decision.
4. If a given new object does not match any of the minimal rules then we assign as the final decision the single decision from $V(r)$ with the largest support among decisions from $V(r)$, where r is the rule selected by voting on nondeterministic rules.
5. In the remaining cases, a given new object is not classified.

5   Experiments

We have performed the experiments on decision tables from the UCI Machine Learning Repository [5] using proposed *MDR* and *TNDR* classification algorithms.

The data sets selected for the experiments included the following: Balance Scale, Iris, Lymphography, Postoperative and Zoo.

Decision table *BalanceScale* was generated in 1976 to model psychological experimental results. *Iris* is the best known database to be found in the pattern recognition literature. *Lymphography* data is one of three domains provided by the University Medical Center, Institute of Oncology from Ljubljana. The classification task of decision table *Postoperative* is to determine when patients in a postoperative recovery area should be sent to the next one. Decision table *Zoo* is a simple database containing information about animals from the zoo.

The *MDR* classification algorithm is based on all minimal decision rules. The *TNDR* classification algorithm is based on all minimal decision rules and truncated nondeterministic rules.

On the input of the *TruNDeR* algorithm, which constructs truncated nondeterministic decision rules, we can use different sets of deterministic rules. Therefore, we can check how the choice of the deterministic decision rules in the *TruNDeR* algorithm influence the classification quality in the *TNDR* algorithm.

We used two types of deterministic rules. The first type of deterministic rules are minimal rules. In the Table 1, in the rows marked by (a) truncated rules are created from minimal rules.

The second type of deterministic rules are complete rules (rows from the decision table). In the Table 1, in the rows marked by (b) truncated rules are created from full rows from decision table.

Table 1. Accuracy of classifiers based on nondeterministic decision rules - cross-validation method

| Decision table | | Clas. | $MDR^{(1)}$ | Classification algorithm | | | | | | |
name	#dec.	factor		(3)	1.0	0.9	0.8	0.7	0.6	0.5
Balance	3	a×c	78.54	(a)	80.00	82.13	82.10	80.91	79.97	77.09
Scale		mrd	1.78		1.44	2.13	2.10	2.35	2.37	1.79
		a×c		(b)	79.46	**82.18**	82.16	80.96	79.84	77.10
		mrd			1.82	2.34	2.32	2.56	2.56	1.90
Iris	3	a×c	88.40	(a)	87.07	86.33	83.87	81.60	80.80	80.80
		mrd	7.07		7.07	11.67	10.53	9.07	9.87	11.47
		a×c		(b)	**88.73**	87.87	87.00	85.53	85.33	85.20
		mrd			7.40	10.53	9.67	9.53	9.33	10.53
Iris	3	a×c	94.13	(a)	94.13	93.20	92.40	88.53	87.87	86.33
(discret.)		mrd	4.80		4.80	5.47	12.40	11.20	10.53	10.33
		a×c		(b)	**94.20**	94.00	93.40	88.87	88.20	87.80
		mrd			4.87	4.67	10.73	11.53	10.87	9.13
Lympho-	8	a×c	37.36	(a)	37.36	37.36	37.36	37.36	37.36	37.36
graphy		mrd	4.26		4.26	4.26	4.26	4.26	4.26	4.26
		a×c		(b)	37.36	37.36	37.36	37.36	37.36	37.36
		mrd			4.26	4.26	4.26	4.26	4.26	4.26
Post-	3	a×c	65.44	(a)	65.67	65.67	65.67	67.67	68.78	**69.22**
Operative		mrd	3.44		3.44	3.44	3.44	5.44	3.22	2.56
		a×c		(b)	65.67	65.67	65.67	66.89	69.11	69.11
		mrd			3.44	3.44	3.44	4.67	2.44	2.44
Zoo	7	a×c	**93.37**	(a)	83.07	83.07	84.26	85.45	86.34	86.44
		mrd	5.25		3.07	4.06	2.87	2.67	3.17	3.27
		a×c		(b)	83.07	83.37	84.36	85.64	86.34	86.53
		mrd			3.07	3.76	2.77	2.48	3.17	3.37

[1] In the column marked by MDR the classification is defined by the classification algorithm based on deterministic rules. In the columns marked by $TNDR$ the classification is defined by the classification algorithm based on nondeterministic and deterministic rules.

[2] Confidence of nondeterministic rules generated by the algorithm is not smaller than the parameter α.

[3] In the rows marked by (a) nondeterministic rules are created from minimal rules. In the rows marked by (b) nondeterministic rules are created from rows from decision table (complete rules).

In evaluation of the accuracy of classification algorithms on a decision tables (i.e., the percentage of correctly classified objects) the 5–fold cross-validation method was used. For any considered data table, we used the classification algorithms for different values of parameter α. On testing sets the accuracy and the coverage factor were calculated. Also the maximal relative deviation (mrd) was calculated.

Table 1 contain the results of our experiments. The *TNDR* classifier was compared with *MDR* classifier.

For three decision tables – *Balance Scale, Iris, Iris (discretization)* – the classification quality measured by *accuracy × coverage* (marked in the table as the a×c) was better for the *TNDR* classification algorithm, when truncated rules are created from complete rules, than in the case of the *MDR* classification algorithm.

For the decision table *Post-Operative* the classification quality measured by *accuracy × coverage* was better for the *TNDR* classification algorithm, when truncated rules are created from minimal rules, than in the case of the *MDR* classification algorithm.

For one data set (*Lymphography*), the classification quality for both classifiers *TNDR* and *MDR* was equal.

For one data set (*Zoo*), using only deterministic rules in the classification process, the result was better than in case of the *TNDR* classification algorithm.

For obtaining those results it was necessary to optimize the threshold α for each data table. This means that the parameter α should be tuned for each data set.

6   Conclusions

The results of experiments with truncated nondeterministic rules are showing that these rules can improve the classification quality. We have demonstrated this by using classification algorithms based on minimal decision rules and truncated nondeterministic rules. The experiments have shown that proposed classifiers can improve classification accuracy, in our experiments the improvement was for the most decision tables.

The proposed *TNDR* (a) and *TNDR* (b) classifiers are comparable in case of the classification quality. For decision tables *Balance Scale, Iris, Iris (discretization)* and *Zoo* we got better result for the *TNDR* (b) classifier then for the *TNDR* (a) classifier. For Post-Operative data set we got better result for the *TNDR* (a) classifier then for the *TNDR* (b) classifier. For the data set *Lymphography*, the classification quality for both *TNDR* (a) and *TNDR* (a) classifiers is the same.

These results show that we can replace the minimal rules with the complete rules in the *TruNDeR* algorithm. This is important for this reason that the *TruNDeR* algorithm, for truncated nondeterministic rules generation, has polynomial computational complexity, which depends on number of objects and number of attributes.

At this moment the proposed *TNDR* classification algorithm uses nondeterministic rules (from the *TruNDeR*) and deterministic rules – minimal rules (from the *RSESlib*). The algorithm for constructing nondeterministic rules has polynomial computational complexity, and the algorithm for constructing minimal rules has exponential computational complexity. To decrease computational complexity of the *TNDR* algorithm, we plan to use others algorithms for constructing deterministic rules (e.g. based on subsets of minimal decision rules or decision trees).

In the future, we plan to compare the *TNDR* algorithm with other classifiers (e.g. decision trees, SVM).

References

1. Agrawal, R., Imielinski, T., Swami, A: Mining Association Rules Between Sets of Items in Large Databases. In: Buneman, P., Jajodia, S. (eds.) Proceedings of the 1993 ACM SIGMOD International Conference on Management of Data, pp. 207–216. ACM Press, New York (1993)
2. Bazan, J.G., Szczuka, M.S., Wojna, A., Wojnarski, M.: On the Evolution of Rough Set Exploration System. In: Tsumoto, S. et al (eds.) RSCTC 2004. LNCS, vol. 3066, pp. 592–601. Springer-Verlag, Heidelberg (2004)
3. Delimata, P., Moshkov, P., Skowron, A., Suraj, Z.: Inhibitory Rules in Data Analysis: A Rough Set Approach. Studies in Computational Intelligence, vol. 163, Springer. Heidelberg (2009)
4. Delimata, P. et al.: Comparison of Some Classification Algorithms Based on Deterministic and Nondeterministic Decision Rules. In: Peters, J.F. et al. (eds.) Transactions on Rough Sets XII. LNCS, vol. 6190, pp. 90–105, Springer, Heidelberg (2010)
5. Frank, A., Asuncion, A.: UCI Machine Learning Repository, University of California, Irvine (2010), http://archive.ics.uci.edu/ml/
6. Grzymala-Busse, J.W.: LERS - A Data Mining System. In: Maimon, O., Rokach, L. (eds.) The Data Mining and Knowledge Discovery Handbook, pp. 1347-1351, Springer, New York (2005)
7. Jach, T., Nowak-Brzezińska, A., Simiński, R., Xięski, T.: Towards a practical approach to discover internal dependencies in rule-based knowledge bases. RSKT 2011. LNCS, vol. 6954, pp. 232–237. Springer, Heidelberg (2011)
8. Marszał-Paszek, B., Paszek. P.: Minimal Templates and Knowledge Discovery. In: Kryszkiewicz, M. et al. (eds.) RSEISP 2007. LNCS, vol. 4585, pp. 411–416. Springer, Heidelberg (2007)
9. Moshkov, M., Skowron, A., Suraj, Z.: Maximal consistent extensions of information systems relative to their theories. Information Sciences 178 (12), 2600–2620 (2008)
10. Ryszard Michalski, http://www.mli.gmu.edu/michalski/
11. Pawlak, Z.: Rough Sets – Theoretical Aspects of Reasoning about Data. Kluwer Academic Publishers, Dordrecht (1991)
12. Pawlak, Z., Skowron, A.: Rudiments of Rough Sets. Information Sciences 177, 3–27 (2007); Rough Sets: Some Extensions. Information Sciences 177, 28–40 (2007); Rough Sets and Boolean Reasoning. Information Sciences 177, 41–73 (2007)
13. Rissanen, J.: Modeling by Shortest Data Description. Automatica 14, 465–471 (1978)

14. Rosetta, `http://www.lcb.uu.se/tools/rosetta/`
15. Rough Set Exploration System, `http://logic.mimuw.edu.pl/~rses`
16. Skowron, A., Suraj, Z.: Rough Sets and Concurrency. Bulletin of the Polish Academy of Sciences 41, pp. 237–254 (1993)
17. Triantaphyllou, E., Felici, G. (eds.): Data Mining and Knowledge Discovery Approaches Based on Rule Induction Techniques. Springer Science and Business Media, LLC, New York (2006)
18. Tsumoto, S.: Modelling Medical Diagnostic Rules Based on Rough Sets. RSCTC 1998. LNCS, vol. 1424, pp. 475–482, Springer-Verlag, Berlin (1998)

A Novel Context Ontology to Facilitate Interoperation of Semantic Services in Environments with Wearable Devices

Gregorio Rubio[1], Estefanía Serral[2], Pedro Castillejo[1], and José Fernán Martínez[1]

[1] DIATEL. Universidad Politécnica de Madrid
(grubio,pcastillejo,jfmartin)@diatel.upm.es
[2] PROS. Universidad Politécnica de Valencia
eserral@dsic.upv.es

Abstract. The LifeWear-Mobilized Lifestyle with Wearables (Lifewear) project attempts to create Ambient Intelligence (AmI) ecosystems by composing personalized services based on the user information, environmental conditions and reasoning outputs. Two of the most important benefits over traditional environments are 1) take advantage of wearable devices to get user information in a non-intrusive way and 2) integrate this information with other intelligent services and environmental sensors. This paper proposes a new ontology composed by the integration of users and services information, for semantically representing this information. Using an Enterprise Service Bus, this ontology is integrated in a semantic middleware to provide context-aware personalized and semantically annotated services, with discovery, composition and orchestration tasks. We show how these services support a real scenario proposed in the Lifewear project.

Keywords: Ontology, context, semantically annotated service.

1 Introduction

Wearable devices are becoming more advanced, accurate and capable of sensing. To take full advantage of them is necessary to combine their information with the obtained from the context and the own user. The amount and heterogeneity of the information that comes into play means that architectures and data models must be equipped with the features necessary to develop applications increasingly customized to the user and facilitate interoperation and information sharing.

The main concern has been to developed ontologies, middlewares and architectures to resolve problems related with ubiquitous computing, but, basically thinking in services provided to the web. With the advance of technology, new services based on the user information, environmental conditions and reasoning outputs are emerging in the context of Ambient Intelligence (AmI) ecosystems. Adding to these data a user profile a new ontology is developed including the entire information model. The integration of this ontology is simple: it is integrated as a new service in the Enterprise

P. Herrero et al. (Eds.): OTM 2012 Workshops, LNCS 7567, pp. 495–504, 2012.
© Springer-Verlag Berlin Heidelberg 2012

Service Bus (ESB). In this way, the ontology service can be used by other services or applications executing in the system.

The aim of this paper is to describe an ontology that allows integrating information about user context and semantic services. Using a test scenario, we show how this ontology considerably helps to provide context-aware personalized and semantically annotated services, with discovery, composition and orchestration tasks.

2   Related Work

To understand the scope of this paper in this section briefly present some of the research papers and projects related to sensor and context-aware of user ontologies and service-oriented middleware.

There are ontologies related to sensors used in different environments, like sensorML [1] or O&M Observation and Management [2-3] and even in [4] is presented a semantic sensor network ontology, like an approach to describe sensor assets and other ontologies summarized in [5]. Also, have been described ontology for context-aware environments in pervasive computing [6], modeling the context of a user. In [7] it is provided a means of acquiring, maintaining, and reasoning data about context, and different approach to service-oriented middleware to provide services based in sensor measures to other services and applications or built it [8]. Related to sensors, u-services like proposed in ITEA2 DiYSE project[1] [9], where a new middleware to provide u-services is presented.

This paper presents an integrated ontology, about users, with wearable devices, and services provided by a semantic middleware from the measurements provided by sensors, placed in a wearable device or context-aware, mixed with a dynamic user profile, all integrated in a very flexible architecture, in which the ontology is treated, like a service, being integrated trough an enterprise service bus.

3   Ontology Proposal

Different context models have been proposed until now to capture context in Pervasive Computing. Some of the most important examples are: object oriented models [10]; key-value models [11]; graphical models [12-14]; etc. However, several studies [6][15-16] state that the use of ontologies to model context is one of the best choices. They state that this model guarantees a high degree of semantic richness, exhibits prominent advantages for reasoning and reusing context, and facilitates the integration of different systems.

An ontology is a formal and semantic representation of a set of concepts and the relationships between those concepts within a domain. Some relevant examples of ontology-based approaches are SOUPA [17], COMANTO [18], and SOCAM [19]. A complete background of most of the ontologies proposed in Pervasive Computing can be found in [16]. None of the studied context ontologies cover adequately all the

---

[1] http://diyse.org:8080

context information identified in the previous subsection; however, the SOUPA ontology is of special interest for this work. SOUPA is a proposal for a Standard Ontology for Ubiquitous and Pervasive Applications that defines core concepts by adopting the following different consensus ontologies: FOAF, which captures personal information and social connections to other people; DAML-Time the Entry Sub-ontology of Time, which represent Time and facilitate the reasoning about the temporal orders of different events; OpenCyc Spatial Ontologies RCC, which allow space to be specified using geo-spatial coordinates or symbolic representation; Rei Policy Ontology, which specifies high-level rules for granting and revoking the access rights to and from different services.

For facilitating information sharing, we define a context ontology that adequately covers the context information needed for Lifewear systems by adopting as far as possible, suitable concepts of the SOUPA ontology. To build the context ontology of Lifewear, we follow a top-down approach, starting from the most coarse-grained concepts and dividing them up into finer-grained concepts. The coarse-grained concepts that we identify are: Environment, System, Person, Policy, Time, and Event. Dividing them into finer-grained concepts, we obtain the classes of the class diagram shown in Fig. 2.

To describe the environment where the user is, we reuse the OpenCyc Spatial and RCC ontologies that propose classes *SpatialThing* that is related to *LocationCoordinates* class. We have extended these ontologies with the *Location* class to describe the different areas that compose an environment by using a symbolic representation more intuitive for users (i.e., Kitchen, Corridor, etc.). Location has two subclasses; *indoor_location* and *outdor_location*; and can be related by the following relationships:

- *Subsumes:* indicates that a location contains other locations (e.g., the location First Floor subsumes the locations Kitchen, Hall and Living Room).
- *Adjacency:* indicates that two locations are physically together (e.g., the Parent Bedroom and the Children Bedroom are adjacent).
- *Mobility:* indicates that two locations are adjacent and there is a way for people to go from one location to the other (e.g., the Hall and the Living Room are adjacent and the Hall has a door to go to the Living Room).

In addition, we propose the term *EnvironmentProperty* to describe the properties (e.g., lighting intensity, presence detection, noise level, etc.) of a certain location.

To describe the system, we propose the terms *Service, ServiceCategory, Operation, Argument, and Process.* The central term is Service, which represents the services (e.g., Lighting, Multimedia Player, Alarm, etc.) that the system provides. Services can be classified into categories and are described by means of the following information:

- *Profile:* the public description of the service. It states the service *identification* (a unique identifier for the service), the service *functionality* (the service operation and their input and output arguments), the *security* profile (description of the security features under which the service will be provided) and *grounding* (protocol used between the service and application that use it).
- *Process:* the logic of the service. The *process* class is refined into *atomic and aggregated/complex processes. An atomic process* takes directly the information generated by sensors and, with the appropriated treatment provides the

functionality. In contrary, *aggregated process* providing new functionality that is not directly obtained from sensors by composing several atomic processes. The *aggregated process* can be built using a *sequence*, where the atomic process are executed in a sequential order; or *any_order*, where the order of the atomic process is irrelevant to the aggregated process.

- *Context*: the context conditions in which the service is provided. For instance, if the service is *static,* its functionality is always provided in the same location, or is *mobile*, like in the case of wearable devices where the location of the service can change.

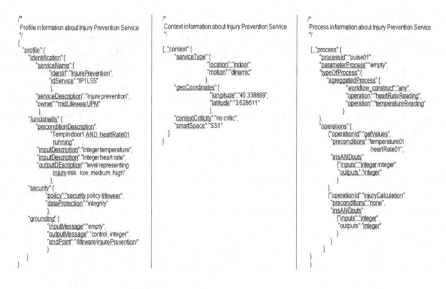

Fig. 1. Annotated service

To describe the users of the system, we reuse the FOAF SOUPA ontology, which propose the term *Person*. This term is described by a set of properties that include profile information (e.g., *name, gender, birth date*, etc.), contact information (e.g., *email, mailing address, phone numbers*, etc.), and *social* and *professional* relationships (e.g., people that a person knows, relatives, etc.). To properly describe the users, we add the *UserProperty* class, to represent the properties of users, such as user preferences (e.g., preferred music, preferred language, etc.), skills (abilities and disabilities that a person has and may affect to his/her interaction with the system, e.g., computer knowledge, deafness, diseases, etc.) and medical parameters (parameters that determine the user health). With regard to the location in which a person is, we define the *currentLocation* relationship, which relates each person to the location where it is in the current moment. Also, the user is related to the activity that is currently doing and his/her agenda, which describes the user appointments.

A *person* is also associated to *policies*. A policy represents a set of operations and/or services (which group a set of operations) that are permitted for a person. The policy also describes the context information that a person can see and/or modify.

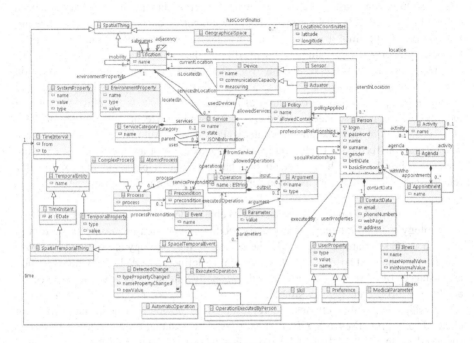

Fig. 2. Class diagram

To describe temporal aspects, we reuse the DAML-Time ontology and the Entry Sub-ontology of Time that SOUPA provides. These ontologies provide us with the term *TemporalEntity*, which is refined into *TimeInstant* and *TimeInterval*. The *TimeInstant* term is defined by using the *at* property that stores the value of time; while the *TimeInterval* term is defined by using the *from* and *to* properties that relate the time interval to the two corresponding time instants. In addition, these SOUPA ontologies provide useful temporal relationships to compare and order to different temporal entities, for instance: *after, before, sameTimeAs, startsLaterThan, startsSoonerThan, startsSameTimeAs, endsLaterThan, endsSoonerThan, endsSameTimeAs*. For avoiding overloading the model, we do not show these relationships in Figure 2. To these classes, we added the *TemporalProperty* class as another refinement of the TemporalEntity class. It represents temporal properties that are not identified as a time instant or a time interval, such as the day of the week, if it is holidays or working days, etc.

To describe the events that happen in the system, we reused the *Event* class proposed by the SOUPA ontology. In SOUPA, an event is a temporal and spacial thing. Thus, SOUPA provides the *SpatialTemporalThing* class, which is the intersection between *TemporalEntity* and *SpatialThing*. In addition, the *SpatialTemporalEvent* class is defined as the intersection of the Event and SpatialTemporalThing classes. The events in our systems can be a change detected by sensors, or can be an operation executed by a person or automated by the system. Thus, in order to better represent the events of our systems, we refine the SpatialTemporalEvent class in the DetectedChange class and the ExecutedOperation class. The DetectedChange represents a change that has been detected by the devices of the system (e.g., the temperature has increased, presence has been detected, the time goes by, etc.). This class is related with the environment or temporal property whose value has changed (e.g., the temperature of the kitchen). The ExecutedOperation class represents an event produced by the execution of an operation (e.g., switching on the light or playing a song). This class is related with the executed operation (e.g., the switch on operation of the lighting service or the play operation of the multimedia player service) and the arguments used for executing the operation. This class is refined in the OperationExecutedByPerson and AutomaticOperation classes. The OperationExecutedByPerson represents the execution of an operation by a person. This class is related with the person that has executed it by using the executedBy relationship. The AutomaticOperation represents the execution of an operation by the system.

To implement the ontology, we use the Web Ontology Language (OWL). OWL is an ontology markup language that greatly facilitates knowledge automated reasoning and is a W3C standard. Using OWL, the classes of the ontology are defined by OWL classes, and the context specific of the system is defined by OWL individuals, which are instances of these classes. In OWL, the properties of each class are represented by attributes whose data type is simple. These properties are *DatatypeProperties*. The relationships with other classes are represented by attributes whose data type is a class. These properties are *ObjectProperties*. For instance, a user named Bob is specified as an individual of the Person class whose *ID* datatypeProperty is *Bob*. Its preferred temperature is specified as an individual of the *Preference* class and added to the *userPreferences* objectProperty (which contains the list of user preferences) of the Bob individual.

4   Test Scenario

To demonstrate the use of the ontology, we designed a test scenario (Fig. 3). In this scenario, a user has a mobile phone with an android application that recommends him/her a sport routine and a diet according to his/her current condition. Regarding the user preferences, the app will prepare a specific daily training plan for losing weight and improving physical condition. The user can see these recommendations in an android device. The connectivity is by means of Bluetooth. Daily, the application should check the historical data of the user profile and adjust the weight loss plan, so the application could advice the client about its achievements and failures and encourage him to follow the plan of action.

At the end of each practice session, the user could view a list of recommendations that will be of interest to recover the biological deficiencies, mineral salts, liquid vitamins and diet-specific menu or could view a calorie intake recommendation.

Moreover, the application can analyze the experience of the user and decide whether the practice has been beneficial or detrimental to him/her. In this scenario, the ontology is the key to providing the integration of all needed information and make the services aware of user context.

An OWL context model based on the ontology presented in the previous section is created to manage and integrate all the needed information. In this model, the user information (such as age, tall, diet preferences, favorite sports, diseases, sex, food and environmental allergies) as well as the semantic information about the needed services (profile, context and process) is manually introduced by using Protègè [19].

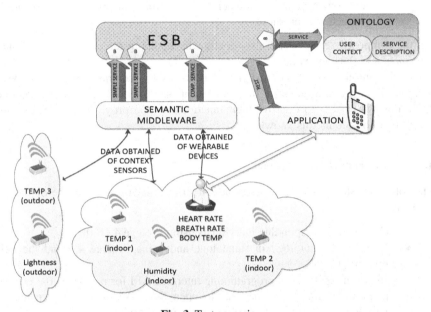

Fig. 3. Test scenario

When the user executes the application in the smartphone android, it uses the services semantically annotated provided by the semantic middleware to recollect data from all sensors and update the context model according to the sensed context.

The simple services provided by sensors are related with the dynamic measures such as heart rate, breathing rate, body temperature, location, indoor temperature in several places, indoor humidity, outdoor lightness or outdoor temperature.

In general, the service profile is static, while its context and process are dynamic. So, the service features can be known to create new composed services by using an orchestrator (dedicated mote). The composed services use and process the context information of the context model to provide the required application functionality.

Thus, the simple services semantically annotated in the context model, are used for the application for updating the sensed information in the context model. Processing this information, the following composed service is provided:

- Muscular Injury Prevention Service:
  a. Context information (provided by simple services) used: indoor temperature, body temperature, heart rate.
  b. Response: Injury levels, including low, medium and high, depending on the value of the context information parameters.

Using this composed service a new composed service can be also created:

- Alarm Muscular Injury Prevention Service: will be activated when the Injury level in the Response of Muscular injury prevention service is high (the gap between indoor temperature and body temperature is excessive, or indoor temperature, or skin temperature or heart rate has exceeded a threshold).

All the composed services are, also, continually updating the corresponding context information in the context model.

So, the ontology-based context model becomes the central point of the system integrating all the knowledge of the application (user context and required services) and allowing services to improve their functionality and provide composed services by taking into account this knowledge.

4.1   Test Scenario Deployment

The following steps have been performed in strict order to integrate the ontology in the ESB:

- Create the corresponding individuals using Protégé 4.1[20].
- Validate the ontology in standalone and using Protégé 4.1 and the Pellet reasoner [21].
- Build an Application programming interface API for managing the ontology at runtime: we used Jena [22] to open the OWL model and manage its individuals, TDB [23] for making the context model persistent and Pellet for providing reasoner. For developing this API we have applied the recommended best practices proposed in [24-25].
- Create a bundle to run the API in the ESB; in this way, services can easily access to the ontology and all the components are integrated.

5   Conclusions and Future Work

In this paper we have proposed an ontology that integrates all the information about user context and services running in a system and becomes a key point to improve the application features. The easiness of the ontology integration is also an important benefit of our proposal. As can be seen in the previous section, the ontology is integrated as a new service in the ESB. In this way, the ontology service can be used by other services that are running in the system.

Furthermore, we have developed a test scenario to demonstrate that the user, from him/her point of view, using only wearable devices, improve the experience of use of the application. What the user doesn't know is that this fact is possible because in the system exist the ontology showed in this paper.

Both the capabilities of the sensors as wearable devices constantly evolving, so, alike, ontology needs too constantly evolving to maintain the capability to represent the abstract content related whit sensors and users profile.

Keeping in mind that it will appear new manufacturers and new users with new profiles, the key point of future work will be to provide to the ontology capabilities of evolution and versioning [26]. To achieve this target it could be used methodologies like DOGMA-MESS [27-28], in a native way or adapting to the global system, like in DiYSE project, to gradually enrich the ontology.

It is also necessary to develop a powerful engine inference, providing the ontology to dynamically create new services based in the orchestration of the existing services.

Another future task is to test the global application in new scenarios, basically of ubiquitous computing, such us e-health, surveillance of young or elderly people, in a non-intrusive way.

In summary, the future work will be directed to adequate the ontology to let the creation of services each time closer to the user.

Acknowledgments. The work presented in this paper has been partially funded by the Spanish Ministry of Industry, Tourism and Trade in the framework of the European Research Project "LifeWear-Mobilized Lifestyle with Wearables" (TSI-020400-2010-100), which belongs to the ITEA 2 (Information Technology for European Advancement 2) program, and by the Spanish Ministry of Economy and Competitiveness in the AWARE Project (Ref. TEC2011-28397).

References

1. Botts, M., Robin, A.: OpenGis Sensor Model Lenguaje (SensorML) implementation Specification. OpenGIS Implementation Specification OGC 07-000. The Open Geospatial Consortium (2007)
2. Cox, S.: Observations and Measurements – Part 1– Observation Schema. OpenGIS Implementation Standard OGC 07-022r1 The Open Geospatial Consortium (2007)
3. Cox, S.: Observations and Measurements – Part 2– Sampling Features. OpenGIS Implementation Standard OGC 07-022r3 The Open Geospatial Consortium (2007)
4. The semantic sensor network ontology: a generic language to describe sensor assets. In: AGILE Workshop: Challenges in Geospatial Data Harmonization (2009)
5. Compton, M., Henson, C., Lefort, L., Neuhaus, H., Sheth, A.: A Survey of Semantic Specification of Sensors. In: Proc. Semantic Sensor Networks, pp. 17–32 (2009)
6. Chen, H., Finin, T., Joshi, A.: An ontology for context-aware pervasive computing environments. Special Issue on Ontologies for Distributed Systems, Knowledge Engineering Review 18(3), 197–207 (2004)
7. Chen, H., Finin, T., Joshi, A.: The SOUPA Ontology for Pervasive Computing. In: Ontologies for Agents: Theory and Experiences. Whitestein Series in Software Agent Technologies, pp. 233–258. Springer, Berlin (2005)
8. Gu, T., Pung, H.K., Zhang, D.Q.: A service-oriented middleware for building context-aware services. Journal of Network and Computer Applications 28(1), 1–18 (2005)

9. Tang, Y., Meerman, R.: DIY-CDR: An Ontology-based, Do-it-Yourself Components Discoverer and Recommender Theme Issue on Adaptation and Personalization for Ubiquitous Computing. Journal of Personal and Ubiquitous Computing (June 21, 2011) ISSN 1617-4909

10. Biegel, B., Cahill, V.: A framework for developing mobile, context-aware applications. In: 2nd IEEE Conference on Pervasive Computing and Communication (2004)

11. Dey, A.K.: Understanding and Using Context. Personal Ubiquitous Computing (2001)

12. Sheng, Q.Z., Benatallah, B.: ContextUML: a UML-based modelling language for model-driven development of context-aware web services. In: ICMB 2005, July 11-13, pp. 206–212. IEEE Computer Society, Washington, DC (2005)

13. Henricksen, K., Indulska, J.: Developing context-aware pervasive computing applications: Models and approach. Pervasive and Mobile Computing 2, 37–64 (2006)

14. Ayed, D., Delanote, D., Berbers, Y.: MDD Approach for the Development of Context-Aware Applications. In: Kokinov, B., Richardson, D.C., Roth-Berghofer, T.R., Vieu, L. (eds.) CONTEXT 2007. LNCS (LNAI), vol. 4635, pp. 15–28. Springer, Heidelberg (2007)

15. Baldauf, M., Dustdar, S., Rosenberg, F.: A Survey on Context-Aware Systems. International Journal of Ad Hoc and Ubiquitous Computing 2, 263–277 (2007)

16. Ye, J., Coyle, L., Dobson, S., Nixon, P.: A Unified Semantics Space Model. In: Hightower, J., Schiele, B., Strang, T. (eds.) LoCA 2007. LNCS, vol. 4718, pp. 103–120. Springer, Heidelberg (2007)

17. Chen, H., Perich, F., Finin, T., Joshi, A.: SOUPA: Standard Ontology for Ubiquitous and Pervasive Applications. In: The First Annual International Conference on Mobile and Ubiquitous Systems, August 22-26, pp. 258–267 (2005)

18. Roussaki, I., Strimpakou, M., Pils, C., Kalatzis, N., Anagnostou, M.: Hybrid context modeling: A location-based scheme using ontologies. In: Proceedings of the Fourth Annual IEEE International Conference on Pervasive Computing and Communications Workshops (PERCOMW 2006). IEEE Computer Society (2006)

19. Gu, T., Pung, H.K., Zhang, D.Q.: A service-oriented middleware for building context-aware services. Journal of Network and Computer Applications 28, 1–18 (2005)

20. The Protégé Ontology Editor and Knowledge Adcquisition, http://protege.stanford.edu

21. Pellet, OWL 2 Reasoner for Java, http://clarkparsia.com/pellet

22. Apache Jena, http://jena.apache.org

23. Apache Jena TDB, http://jena.apache.org/documentation/tdb/index.html

24. How To Design A Good API and Why it Matters. Google (2007)

25. Guy, M.: Report 2: API Good Practice Good practice for provision of and consuming APIs. Tech. rept. UKOLN (2009)

26. Khattak, A.M., Latif, K., Lee, S., Lee, Y.K.: Ontology Evolution: A Survey and Future Challenges. Communications in Computer and Information Science 62, 68–75 (2009)

27. de Moor, A., De Leenheer, P., Meersman, R.: DOGMA-MESS: A Meaning Evolution Support System for Interorganizational Ontology Engineering. In: Schärfe, H., Hitzler, P., Øhrstrøm, P. (eds.) ICCS 2006. LNCS (LNAI), vol. 4068, pp. 189–202. Springer, Heidelberg (2006)

28. De Leenheer, P., Debruyne, C.: DOGMA-MESS: A Tool for Fact-Oriented Collaborative Ontology Evolution. In: Meersman, R., Tari, Z., Herrero, P. (eds.) OTM-WS 2008. LNCS, vol. 5333, pp. 797–806. Springer, Heidelberg (2008)

Ontology Based Method for Supporting Business Process Modeling Decisions

Avi Wasser[1] and Maya Lincoln[2]

[1] University of Haifa, Israel
awasser@haifa.ac.il
[2] ProcessGene Ltd
maya.lincoln@processgene.com

Abstract. This work suggests a method for machine-assisted support of business process modeling decisions, based on business logic that is extracted from process repositories using a linguistic analysis of the relationships between constructs of process descriptors. The analysis enables the setup of a descriptor space, in which it is possible to analyze business rules and logic. The suggested method aims to assist process designers in modeling decision making, based on knowledge that is encapsulated within existing business process repositories. The method is demonstrated using a real-life process repository from the higher-education industry.

Keywords: Business process modeling decisions, Business process repositories, Semantic analysis, Process ontologies, Natural language processing.

1 Introduction

Our work presents a content-based utilization framework that standardizes the content layer of business process repositories, aiming to support the decision making of business analysts during their modeling work.

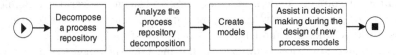

Fig. 1. A high-level framework for utilizing process repositories to support business process modeling decisions

We propose a four-step meta process to utilize process repositories for modeling decision support, as illustrated in Fig. 1 (using "Yet Another Workflow Language" (YAWL) [11]). First, we create an operationally meaningful decomposition of a process repository. We use state-of-the-art Natural Language Processing (NLP) techniques to automatically decompose the content layer (text) of the repositories into its structured linguistic components (objects and actions and their qualifiers). As part of this decomposition, each business activity is encoded automatically as a *descriptor*, using the Process Descriptor Catalog

P. Herrero et al. (Eds.): OTM 2012 Workshops, LNCS 7567, pp. 505–514, 2012.
© Springer-Verlag Berlin Heidelberg 2012

("PDC") notation [6] . As described in [4], the collection of all descriptors formulates a *descriptor space*, and distances between every two space coordinates are calculated in terms of business process conduct proximity. Second, we analyze the generated decomposition and third, we create action and object models, that represent operational aspects of the process repository. In total, seven such models are proposed in this work. As a fourth step, we use the above action and object models for creating a methodology aimed at assisting process analysts in decision making during the design of new processes. We instantiate the generic methodology for the following four decision support mechanisms: (1) generation of a next activity for the designed process model; (2) validation of changes made to an existing process repository; (3) search for process models using natural language queries. This mechanism can support decisions such as whether some parts of the modeled process already exist in the current repository; and (4) comparison between process models. The suggested method was demonstrated using a process repository that consists 24 real-life processes and 170 related activities from the higher-education industry.

The rest of the paper is organized as follows: we present related work in Section 2, positioning our work with respect to previous research. In Section 3 we present an activity decomposition model that is used as the foundation for creating action and object taxonomies. We then present the suggested method for decision support during process design in Section 4. We conclude in Section 5.

2   Related Work

Research on standardization and analysis of the content layer of business process models mainly focuses on the analysis of linguistic components - actions and objects that describe business activities. Most works in the above domain are either object or activity centric, only a few works combine the two approaches in order to exploit an extended knowledge scope of the business process. The works in [6,4,3] present the concept of business process descriptor that decomposes process names into objects, actions and qualifiers, and suggest several taxonomies to express the operational knowledge encapsulated in business process repositories. In this work we take this model forward by: (a) testing it on real-life processes from the higher-education domain; (b) showing how the suggested taxonomies can support business process modeling decisions.

Research on decision making during business process modeling mainly focuses on analyzing certain aspects of the rational encapsulated in the process model as a basis for reasoning and understanding the model. The work in [9] introduces a rationale-based architecture model that incorporates the design rationale, on which traceability techniques are applied for change impact analysis and root-cause analysis, thereby allowing software architects to better understand and reason about an architecture design. The work in [10] suggests a framework for supporting ontology based decision making, by modeling and visualizing ontological commitments using Semantic Decision Rule Language (SDRule-L). [1] proposes an approach to start from real known decision structures (like decision table hierarchies) and transform these into process models, in order to achieve tracability and maintainability during decision (re)design. The work in [8] focuses on context-aware decisions during process design, and the work in [7] presents an approach to process decision automation that incorporates data integration techniques, enabling significant improvements in decision quality. In this work we advance state of the art frameworks by extracting the *operational* logic encapsulated in process repositories using the process descriptor model and its derivative taxonomies.

3   The Activity Decomposition Model

This section describes a formal model of business process decomposition and analysis. We first introduce the descriptor model (Section 3.1), Then, based on the descriptor model, we introduce seven taxonomies of objects and actions (Section 3.2). To illustrate the taxonomies we make use of the higher education repository (see Chapter 1).

3.1   The Descriptor Model

In the Process Descriptor Catalog model ("PDC") [6] each activity is composed of one action, one object that the action acts upon, and possibly one or more action and object qualifiers, as illustrated in Fig. 2, using UML relationship symbols. Qualifiers provide an additional description to actions and objects. In particular, a qualifier of an object is roughly related to an object state. State-of the art Natural Language Processing (NLP) systems, *e.g.*, the "Stanford Parser,"[1] can be used to automatically decompose process and activity names into *process/activity descriptors*. For example, the activity "Manually update student information" generates an activity descriptor containing the action "update," the action qualifier "manually," the object "information" and the object qualifier "student."

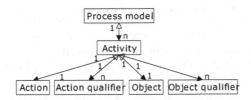

Fig. 2. The activity decomposition model

3.2   Action and Object Based Taxonomies

The descriptor model has two basic elements, namely objects and actions, and it serves as a basis for several state of the art taxonomies, as follows: (1) in [5] it

---

[1] http://nlp.stanford.edu:8080/parser/index.jsp

was enhanced to create the *action hierarchy model*, the *object hierarchy model*, and the *action sequence model*; and (2) in [3] it was enhanced to create the *object lifecycle model*, the *action scope model*, the *object grouping model*, and the *action influence model*.

The Action and Object Hierarchy Models. The action and object hierarchy models organize a set of activity descriptors according to the hierarchical relationships among business actions and objects, respectively. This hierarchical dimension of actions and objects is determined by their qualifiers: an addition of a qualifier to an action or an object makes them more specific, since the qualifier limits their meaning to a specific range.

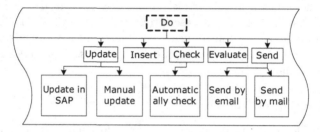

Fig. 3. Segment of an action hierarchy model

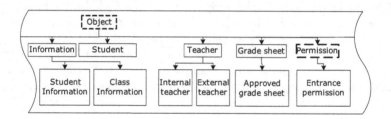

Fig. 4. Segment of an object hierarchy model

To illustrate the hierarchical dimension, a segment of the action hierarchy model of a higher education repository is presented in Fig. 3 and a segment of the object hierarchy model of a a higher education repository is presented in Fig. 4. In the action hierarchy model, for example, the action "Send by mail" is a subclass (a more specific form) of "Send," since the qualifier "by mail" limits the action of "Send" to reduced action range.

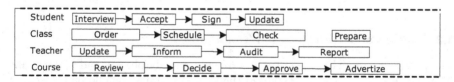

Fig. 5. Segment of an action sequence model

The Action Sequence Model. The action sequence taxonomy model organizes a set of activity descriptors according to the relationships among business actions and objects in terms of execution order. In this model, each object holds a graph of ordered actions that are applied to that object. A segment of the action sequence model of a higher education repository is presented in Fig. 5. For example, the object "Student" is related to the following action sequence: "Interview" followed by "Accept," "Sign," and finally "Update."

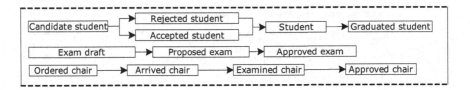

Fig. 6. Segment of an object lifecycle model

The Object Lifecycle Model. The object lifecycle taxonomy model organizes a set of activity descriptors according to the relationships among business actions and objects in terms of execution order. In this model, each object holds a graph of ordered objects that expresses the object's lifecycle, meaning - the possible ordering of the object's states. A segment of the object lifecycle model of a higher education repository is presented in Fig. 6. For example, the object "Student" is part of the following object lifecycle: "Candidate student"–> "Rejected/Accepted student"–>"Student"–> "Graduated student."

The Action Scope Model. The action scope model represents the relationship between an action within a process name (a "primary action") and the actions in its corresponding process model. The fact that a process repository consists of pre-defined process models is being used for learning about the scope of actions in the following way. Each primary action in the repository is related with a set of directional graphs of actions that represent the order of actions within this primary action's segments. Since such a primary action can be part of more than one primary names, and since the same complete action may be represented more than once in the same process model segment - each edge in the action scope model is labeled with its weight, calculated by the number of its repetitions in the related process model segments. Graph splits are also represented in the action scope model.

Consider the following two processes from the higher education repository: "Review student grades" and "Review teacher performance." These processes are represented in the higher education repository by corresponding graph segments as illustrated in Fig 7a. Using these two process models, it is possible to generate an action scope model for the action "Review" (Fig 7b). According to this example, there are two optional action paths compatible to the "Review" action starting by either "Receive" or "Review." Since "Decide" follows "Review" twice in this model, the respective edge weight is set to 2.

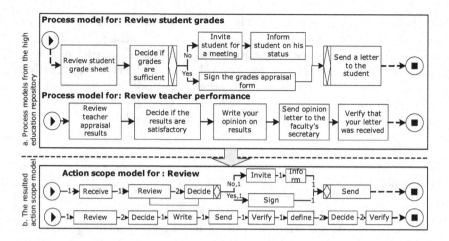

Fig. 7. A segment of the action sequence model for the action "Review"

The Object Grouping Model. The object grouping model represents the relationship between a primary object and the objects in its corresponding model segments. Since such a primary object can be part of more than one primary process segment, and since the same object may be represented more than once in the same process model segment - each object in the object grouping model is labeled with its weight calculated by the number of its repetitions in the related process model segments.

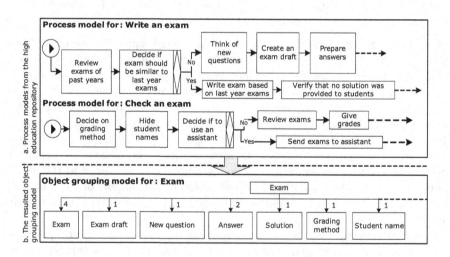

Fig. 8. A segment of the object grouping model for "Exam"

To illustrate, consider two processes from the higher education repository: "Write an exam" and "Check an exam." These processes are represented in the higher education repository by corresponding graph segments as illustrated in

Fig 8a. Using these two process models, it is possible to generate an object grouping model for the object "Exam," as illustrated in Fig 8b.

The Action Influence Model An action influence model represents the relationship between a primary action and the flow of states (object qualifiers) of the primary object in model segments that correspond to the primary action. Each edge in the action influence model is labeled with its weight representing the number of its repetitions in the related process model segments.

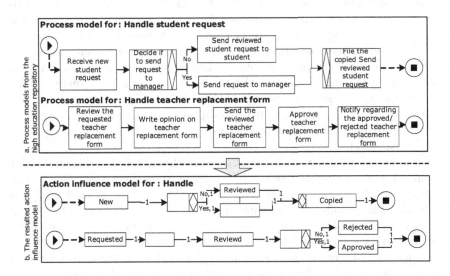

Fig. 9. A segment of the action influence model for the action "Handle"

To illustrate, consider the two process models named: "Handle student request" and "Handle teacher replacement form." They both deal with *handle*, but focus on different objects, "student request" and "teacher replacement form." These processes are illustrated in Fig. 9a. By following changes to the qualifiers of the primary object in these process models we end up with the action influence model for "Handle" as illustrated in Fig. 9b. In this example, the object state changes from "Reviewed" to "Copied" once in its corresponding process models and therefore the corresponding edge in the action influence model is labeled with weight of 1. In addition, empty rectangles represent no qualifiers.

4   Method for Supporting Business Process Modeling Decisions

In this section we present a framework for supporting business process modeling decisions based on the extraction of operational business logic as expressed in the descriptor model and its derivative taxonomies (Section 3).

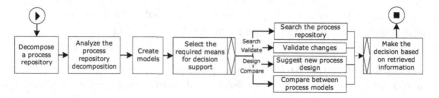

Fig. 10. A framework for supporting business process modeling decisions

We propose a six-step process to support business process modeling decisions, as illustrated in Fig. 10 (using "Yet Another Workflow Language" (YAWL) [11]). First, we create an operationally meaningful decomposition of a process repository. We use state-of-the-art Natural Language Processing (NLP) techniques to automatically decompose the content layer (text) of the repositories into its structured linguistic components (objects and actions and their qualifiers). As part of this decomposition, each business activity is encoded automatically as a *descriptor*, using the Process Descriptor Catalog ("PDC") notation.

Second, we analyze the generated decomposition and third, we create seven action and object models, that represent operational aspects of the process repository (Section 3.1).

As a fourth step, the process analyst decides which support is required for his current decision making. Decision support options include the following mechanisms: (1) generation of a next activity for the designed process model; (2) validation of changes made to an existing process repository; (3) search for process models using natural language queries. This mechanism can support decisions such as whether some parts of the modeled process already exist in the current repository; and (4) comparison between process models. In the fifth step we use the above action and object models for providing the required assistance. Although each mechanism is different they all share the following steps. They start with a user request phrased in natural language. Then, this input is decomposed into linguistic components. As a result of this phase both the user intention (input) and the methodology's underlying knowledge (the process repository) are represented in a common language. The next phase includes an analysis of the process repository and the user input aimed at fulfilling the specific goal. As a result, a set of solution suggestions is generated and then ranked according to the user's input, so that higher ranked suggestions are believed to be closer to the user needs. The specific methods for next activity generation, validation, search and comparison are detailed in Sections 4.1,4.2,4.3, and 4.4, correspondingly. Finally, at the sixth step the process analyst receives suggestions and supporting information and makes his decision accordingly.

4.1   Generation of the Next Activity for the Designed Process Model

This mechanism guides business analysts that opt to design a new business model, by suggesting process steps (activities) that are relevant to the newly created process model. For this purpose we use the framework suggested in [4], in which the business logic for such suggestions is extracted from the following four models: the action and object hierarchy model, the action sequence model and the object lifecycle model. Each activity is encoded automatically as a *descriptor*, using the "PDC" notation. The collection of all descriptors formulates a *descriptor space*, and distances between every two space coordinates are calculated in terms of business process conduct proximity. Each time the process analyst requests activity suggestions as part of the design process, the mechanism outputs a list of options, sorted according to the option's relevance to the modeled process and the current process repository.

4.2   Validation of Business Process Modifications

This mechanism assists process analysts in deciding whether modifications they made in the process repository are valid. To achieve this goal, we use the framework for content-based validation presented in [2], that uses organizational standards to evaluate the correctness of both newly designed and modified processes. This framework *automatically* extracts business logic from process repositories using the PDC model. Each process step is encoded automatically as a *descriptor* that represents objects, actions, and qualifiers. The collection of all process descriptors formulates taxonomy models of action sequence, object lifecycle, and object and action hierarchies that support the validation process.

The method includes three steps for content-based validation: (1) deficiency identification (using existing descriptors as a benchmark reference), (2) validation score calculation, and (3) generation of a ranked list of possible corrections.

4.3   Search for Process Models Using Natural Language Queries

The mechanism at this phase enables deciding whether a process model is already represented in the process repository. To do that, we use the search framework proposed in [3], which receives natural language queries and returns a ranked list of related process models. The business logic is extracted from process repositories through the analysis of the following three taxonomies: the action scope model, the object grouping model, and the action influence model (see Section 3). The proposed method *dynamically* segments a process repository according to the ad-hoc request as expressed in the user's search phrase.

4.4   Comparison between Process Models

This mechanism assists process analyst in deciding whether two or more process models are similar, and indicating which segments they share in common. To provide this capability, we use the work in [12] that proposes a method for measuring the similarity between process models using semantic analysis. Similarity in this work is based on textual proximity of process components. We elaborate this similarity method by referring also to operational similarity, as expressed in the activity decomposition model. Distances in this case can be calculated in terms of separating in the seven taxonomies.

5   Conclusions

We proposed a framework for machine-assisted support of business process modeling decisions, based on business logic that is extracted from process repositories using a linguistic analysis of the relationships between constructs of process descriptors.

The proposed framework provides a starting point that can already be applied in real-life scenarios, yet several research issues remain open. We mention two such extensions here. First, extending the list of supporting decision mechanism - to support additional decision use-cases. Second, adding a case study and experiments to measure the efficiency of the proposed framework.

References

1. De Roover, W., Vanthienen, J.: On the Relation between Decision Structures, Tables and Processes. In: Meersman, R., Dillon, T., Herrero, P. (eds.) OTM-WS 2011. LNCS, vol. 7046, pp. 591–598. Springer, Heidelberg (2011)
2. Lincoln, M., Gal, A.: Content-Based Validation of Business Process Modifications. In: Jeusfeld, M., Delcambre, L., Ling, T.-W. (eds.) ER 2011. LNCS, vol. 6998, pp. 495–503. Springer, Heidelberg (2011)
3. Lincoln, M., Gal, A.: Searching Business Process Repositories Using Operational Similarity. In: Meersman, R., Dillon, T., Herrero, P., Kumar, A., Reichert, M., Qing, L., Ooi, B.-C., Damiani, E., Schmidt, D.C., White, J., Hauswirth, M., Hitzler, P., Mohania, M. (eds.) OTM 2011, Part I. LNCS, vol. 7044, pp. 2–19. Springer, Heidelberg (2011)
4. Lincoln, M., Golani, M., Gal, A.: Machine-Assisted Design of Business Process Models Using Descriptor Space Analysis. In: Hull, R., Mendling, J., Tai, S. (eds.) BPM 2010. LNCS, vol. 6336, pp. 128–144. Springer, Heidelberg (2010)
5. Lincoln, M., Golani, M., Gal, A.: Machine-assisted design of business process models using descriptor space analysis. Technical Report IE/IS-2010-01, Technion (March 2010), http://ie.technion.ac.il/tech_reports/1267736757_Machine-Assisted_Design_of_Business_Processes.pdf
6. Lincoln, M., Karni, R., Wasser, A.: A Framework for Ontological Standardization of Business Process Content. In: International Conference on Enterprise Information Systems, pp. 257–263 (2007)
7. Niedermann, F., Maier, B., Radeschütz, S., Schwarz, H., Mitschang, B.: Automated Process Decision Making Based on Integrated Source Data. In: Abramowicz, W. (ed.) BIS 2011. LNBIP, vol. 87, pp. 160–171. Springer, Heidelberg (2011)
8. Ploesser, K., Recker, J., Rosemann, M.: Supporting Context-Aware Process Design: Learnings from a Design Science Study. In: Muehlen, M.Z., Su, J. (eds.) BPM 2010 Workshops. LNBIP, vol. 66, pp. 97–104. Springer, Heidelberg (2011)
9. Tang, A., Jin, Y., Han, J.: A rationale-based architecture model for design traceability and reasoning. Journal of Systems and Software 80(6), 918–934 (2007)
10. Tang, Y., Meersman, R.: Sdrule markup language: Towards modeling and interchanging ontological commitments for semantic decision making. In: Handbook of Research on Emerging Rule-Based Languages and Technologies: Open Solutions and Approaches. IGI Publishing, USA (2009)
11. van der Aalst, W.M.P., Ter Hofstede, A.H.M.: YAWL: yet another workflow language. Information Systems 30(4), 245–275 (2005)
12. van Dongen, B.F., Dijkman, R.M., Mendling, J.: Measuring Similarity between Business Process Models. In: Bellahsène, Z., Léonard, M. (eds.) CAiSE 2008. LNCS, vol. 5074, pp. 450–464. Springer, Heidelberg (2008)

Sensor Information Representation
for the Internet of Things

Jiehan Zhou[1], Teemu Leppänen[1], Meirong Liu[1], Erkki Harjula[1],
Timo Ojala[1], Mika Ylianttila[1], and Chen Yu[2]

[1] University of Oulu, Oulu, Finland
{firstname.lastname}@ee.oulu.fi
[2] Huazhong University of Science and Technology, Wuhan, China
yuchen@hust.edu.cn

Abstract. Internet of Things integrates wireless sensor networks into the
Internet, and paves the way to help people live seamlessly in both physical and
cyber worlds. In a synergizing Internet of Things application, various types of
sensors will communicate and exchange information for achieving user tasks
across heterogeneous wireless sensor networks. This application needs an information representation for uniformly developing and managing sensor data.
The information representation thus accelerates data integration and increases
Internet of Things application interoperability. In this paper, we present an
overview on existing technical solutions for representing sensor information.

Keywords: Internet of Things, sensor ontology, semantic Web, Web of Things.

1 Introduction

The Internet of Things (IoT) accelerates and facilitates the user to operate with information and communication technology through connecting wireless sensor networks.
These wireless sensor networks act much the way nerve endings do in the human body.
The sensors can be massively distributed in the living environment, and can be responsible for perceiving changes in the surroundings, while transmitting the data to the sink
node. Sensor networks can also be responsible for receiving and executing commands
from the central node. Wireless sensor networks can involve various application
domains such as home automation, logistics, factory systems, or medical domains. In a
synergizing application, wireless sensor networks commonly communicate and
exchange information across domains (Figure 1). Interoperability and efficient sensor
data transfer become crucial issues for realizing the Internet of Things.

Ontology methodology is often used to address application interoperability in
distributed systems. An ontology is a description of the contents or parts of a system,
and of how they relate. Design of ontologies serves to enable knowledge sharing and
re-use [1]. An ontology is also regarded as a data model that defines the primitive
concepts, relations, and rules comprising a topic of knowledge, in order to capture,
structure, or enlarge the explicit or tacit topic knowledge to be shared between people,
organizations, computers, or software systems [2]. From the viewpoint of a data

P. Herrero et al. (Eds.): OTM 2012 Workshops, LNCS 7567, pp. 515–524, 2012.
© Springer-Verlag Berlin Heidelberg 2012

model, an ontology is an hierarchical arrangement of metadata. As the Internet of Things has received widespread attention in the academia and industry, a number of researchers have studied and developed ontologies for specifying sensors. For example, the OntoSensor ontology [3] was intended as a generic knowledge base of sensors for query and inference. Avancha and Patel [4] designed the sensor node ontology for addressing wireless sensor network adaptivity. Neuhaus et al. [5] proposed a semantic sensor network ontology to describe sensors in terms of their capabilities and operations.

To accelerate and realize the vision of an Internet of Things, we proposed the Mammoth project,[1] funded by Tekes — the Finnish Funding Agency for Technology and Innovation. This project aims to facilitate information exchange and synergic performance between IoT things and people via global, massive-scale M2M (machine-to-machine) networks, and to provide M2M automatic metering, embedded web services, universal control of electricity or water utilities, etc. However, in the project initiation stage, we need a specification standard for describing sensors and data.

To meet the requirement for specification standards, this paper presents the requirement analysis of a synergizing IoT scenario, and overviews the state-of-the-art on information representation for the Internet of Things. The remainder of this paper is organized as follows: Section 2 briefly discusses the background of the Internet of Things, examines a typical synergizing IoT scenario, and analyzes requirements for representing sensor data. Section 3 reviews the state-of-art on information representation for the Internet of Things. Section 4 discusses the interesting research topic of semantic service composition, which is followed by conclusions.

2   Representing Sensor Information

2.1   Internet of Things (IoT)

As NIC defines the IoT concept,[2] *"IoT refers to the general idea of things, especially everyday objects, that are readable, recognizable, locatable, addressable, and/or controllable via the Internet — whether via RFID, wireless LAN, wide-area network, or other means."* This definition specifies key characteristics for IoT things: such things must be addressable, controllable, and use the Internet as the major means of interaction with other IoT things.

We describe the IoT concept in this paper from four perspectives: IoT things, IoT networks, IoT service systems, and IoT controls. IoT things refer to everyday objects, which are context aware, able to perceive, and able to extract information on their surroundings with the help of RFID (Radio-Frequency Identification) and sensor technology. People manipulate IoT things via IoT networks. For example, IoT sensors help monitor physical or environmental conditions, such as temperature, sound, vibration, pressure, humidity, or pollutants. These sensors cooperatively pass their data through the IoT network to an IoT things of server. The IoT network is a part of the Internet, and an extension of the Internet as an ubiquitous network. The IoT network

---

[1] http://www.mediateam.oulu.fi/projects/mammoth/?lang=en
[2] http://www.dni.gov/nic/PDF_GIF_confreports/disruptivetech/appendix_F.pdf

consists of smart everyday objects. These objects transmit data and exchange information with each other. Analogically, if the Internet is the artery for information exchange, then the Internet of Things is the capillary network for that information exchange, and its control system. The IoT network is ubiquitous, and has networking capabilities to support various classes of applications/services that require "any services, anytime, anywhere and any devices" operation. IoT networking capability should support human-to-human, human-to-object (e.g., device and/or machine), and object-to-object communications. IoT service systems refer to computer programs responsible for logics management, data processing, and storage for any purpose.

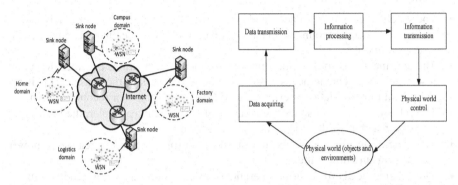

Fig. 1. Internet of Things with a synergizing application

Fig. 2. Information flow in an IoT application

Figure 2 illustrates information flow in an IoT application. To guarantee the information flow across heterogeneous sensor and network domains involves the questions of how to describe sensors as processing units, and how existing sensors can be composed to integrate. The next section will examine a synergizing scenario, and investigate the requirements for designing a sensor ontology.

2.2   A Synergizing Application and Requirement Examination

Take a synergizing application as an example of a smart-course schedule system.[3] Imagine everything as connected. Let us say a professor at the university is not feeling well, and calls in sick. The automatic system for the school sends an alert to all the students in the class, and cancels the class. Furthermore, this information is passed on to a system that adapts my agenda. It calculates the new time to my next class, which is two hours later, taking the transport timetable into account. The system could also re-set my alarm clock to wake me up later, and adjust the heating system and coffee machine.

In the above synergizing example, sensors are distributed across the university, the student dormitory, and the city travel system domains. The sensor involves different types of data, whether small and static, or big and dynamic. Fusion of data from multiple sensors leads to the extraction of knowledge that cannot be inferred from using individual sensors alone. There are still several impediments to data sensing in IoT. The network is limited by the lack of a well-developed common language for

---

[3] http://www.youtube.com/watch?v=kq8wcjQYW90

describing sensors, attributes, etc. This limits data fusion because different networks use different terminologies. The lack of integration and communication between these networks often isolates important data streams, or intensifies the existing problem of too much data and not enough knowledge. These systems need comprehensive sensor ontologies to establish a widely accepted terminology of sensors, properties, capabilities and services. It is necessary that the context terminology is commonly understood by all participating devices. Sensor ontology (i.e. representation scheme) is what facilitates the data fusion and increases interoperability, as well as providing contextual information essential for observations. An effective representation scheme must meet the following set of requirements:

- The scheme needs to be generic and extensible. Sensor nodes are extremely dense, and produce huge amounts of data. This data must be efficiently searched to answer user queries.
- The scheme needs to describe sensors' technical information, e.g. their temporal resolution. The scheme needs to describe how to access to the sensor. This is required not only for data retrieval, but also for sensor control or reconfiguration.
- The scheme needs to describe the location of a sensor, in particular, the location of the sensor with regard to the feature it is observing.
- The scheme needs to describe the physical sensor information regarding power source, consumption, batteries, etc.
- The scheme needs to describe operational information on process and results. A sensor may have a number of operations, with result information given in terms of inputs and conditions, accuracy, latency, resolution, effect, and the behavior description of the sensor.
- The scheme needs to be extensible, and to include larger macro instruments.

3   Information Representation for IoT Sensors

Many researchers have realized the problem of semantic integration of sensor data, and have tried to address the issue using semantic web technologies. This section presents a review on existing efforts or schemes for representing sensor data. Table 1 overviews the schemes developed for representing sensor data, with a brief description of each.

Table 1. Schemes for Representing Sensor Data

Name	Description
W3C SSN ontology (W3C)	Ten modules, consisting of 41 concepts and 39 object properties, built on four perspectives of sensor, observation, system, and property.
Ontology for adaptive sensor networks [4]	Networks involving the main concepts of processor CPU and memory, power supply, and radio or sensor modules.
Sensor network modeling frameworks [6]	Ontology describing the network topology and settings, sensor description, and data flow.

Table 1. (*continued*)

Ontology for sensor-rich information systems [7]	A UML-based representation for a vehicle/human detection ontology.
Sensor data ontology [8]	An initial class taxonomy which includes two main concepts: data and sensor.
Sensor data's pedigree ontology [9]	A refined pedigree ontology consisting of concepts regarding sensor, system, human, setting, software, InfoSource, report data, etc.
SensorML (Sensor Modeling Language)	A language that aims to describe the geometric, dynamic, and observational properties of dynamic sensors.
OntoSensor [3]	A system that includes definitions of concepts and properties adopted from SensorML, extensions to IEEE SUMO, references to ISO 19115, and constructs of the Web Ontology Language (OWL).
W3C Efficient XML Interchange (Efficient XML Interchange)	An IoT system that exploits the EXI format to mitigate the size and parsing complexity of the XML, while maintaining most of its capability.
DPWS (DPWS)	Defines a minimal set of implementation constraints to enable secure Web Service messaging, discovery, description, and eventing on resource-constrained IoT devices.
CESN ontology [10]	Core concepts are the physical sensor, Sensor; the *PhysicalProperty* that a *Sensor* can measure; and the measurement that a sensor has taken, *physicalPropertyMeasurement*.
CSIRO sensor ontology [5]	Organized around four core clusters of concepts: Feature, Sensor, Sensor Grounding, and Operation Model and Process.
WTN ontology [11]	Ontology based on OWL-S, and focused on the following aspects: services, manufacturer's view, bridging axioms, and syntactic description.

At the heart of semantic web technology is the concept of ontology. An ontology is defined as an explicit and formal specification of a conceptualization system [12]. There are four types of ontologies, namely top-level, domain, task, and application ontologies. At a broad level, Sheth et al. [13] classified ontologies according to the three types of semantics associated with sensor data – spatial, temporal, and thematic, in addition to ontological models representing the sensor domain. The many advantages of sensor ontology design include: a) classification of sensors according to functionality, output, or measurement method, b) location of sensors that can perform a particular measurement; collection of data spatially, temporally, or by accuracy, c) inference of domain knowledge from low-level data, and c) production of events when particular conditions are reached within a period. The efforts made to date concerning semantic sensor information representation are as follows.

The W3C Semantic Sensor Network Incubator group (the SSN-XG) [14] produced an SSN ontology to describe sensors, observations, and related concepts. SSN does not describe domain concepts, time, locations, etc. as these are intended to be included from other ontologies via OWL imports. The SSN ontology is organized into ten modules, consisting of 41 concepts and 39 object properties, directly inherited from 11 DUL (DOLCE-UltraLite) concepts and 14 DUL object properties. The SSN can describe sensors, the accuracy and capabilities of sensors, and observations or methods used for sensing. Also, concepts for operating and survival ranges are included. A structure for field deployments also describes deployment lifetime and sensing purpose of the deployed macro instruments. The SSN ontology is built on four main sensor perspectives: a sensor perspective (with a focus on what it senses, how it senses, and what is sensed), an observation perspective (with a focus on observation data and related metadata), a system perspective (with a focus on systems of sensors, deployments, platforms, and operating or survival conditions); and a feature and property perspective (focusing on what senses a particular property or what observations have been made about a property). The SSN ontology is currently used in a number of research projects, where its role is to describe sensors, sensing, the measurement capabilities of sensors, the observations that result from sensing, and the deployments in which sensors are used. The ontology is OWL-based, and covers large parts of the SensorML and O&M standards, omitting calibrations, process descriptions and data types.

Avancha et al. [4] described an ontology for adaptive sensor networks in which nodes react to available power and environmental factors, calibrate for accuracy, and determine suitable operating states. The sensor node ontology consists of the main concepts of processor CPU and memory, power supply, and radio or sensor modules. Five types of sensors are deployed in the sample network, namely vibration sensors, pressure-pad sensors, acoustic sensors, radioactive sensors, and sight optical sensors.

Jurdak et al. [6] defined an ontology that integrates high-level features to characterize sensor networks for customizing routing behavior. The ontology describes the network topology and settings, sensor description, and data flow. The two closely related topology features are location-awareness (i.e. whether or not the sensors are aware of their relative locations), and sensor deployment (i.e. the process by which the sensors are deployed). The network setting describes the communication media used, the transmission technology, operating environment, etc. The sensor description features routing protocols, memory size, battery lifetime, processor technology, etc. The data flow features data acquisition approaches such as time-driven, event driven, or demand-driven acquisition.

Enabling scalable sensor information access helps to define an ontology and its associated sensor information hierarchy in order to interpret raw data streams. Liu and Zhao [7] presented a UML representation for a vehicle/human detection ontology used for describing the data that can be provided by a sensor information system. Using this ontology, multiple end-users can simultaneously interact with a sensor-rich information system, and query the system for high-level events without dealing with raw signals.

To enable scalable and precise sensor information searches, Alamri et al. [8] defined an ontology that associates sensor information taxonomy for searching and interpreting raw data streams. The initial class taxonomy includes two main concepts: data and sensor. Data could be calibration, format, or parameter information. The sensors could be actuators and transducers. The experimental evaluation of this ontology is limited to validating the ontology's logical inconsistencies, and comparing the performance parameters of a search engine when utilizing the ontology as compared with traditional searching.

The pedigree or provenance of sensor data describes how the data was collected, and what it contributes to. It is extremely important to take data pedigree into consideration when performing level one fusion (i.e. attempts to combine data collected from multiple sensory sources into a single cohesive description). Matheus et al. [9] made efforts to develop an initial pedigree ontology for level-one sensor fusion, in which the highest level concept is "information object," represented by the InfoObject class. Associated with the InfoObject is its pedigree, which is represented by a class called InfoObjectMetaData. The refined pedigree ontology consists of concepts regarding sensor, system, human, setting, software, InfoSource, and report data etc. at the high level. The design and development of this pedigree ontology is based on a naval operation scenario examination.

The SensorML [15] aims to describe the geometric, dynamic and observational properties of dynamic sensors. This language goes beyond just describing individual sensors. Different sensor types can all be supported through the definition of atomic process models and process chains. Within SensorML, all processes and components are encoded as application schema of the Feature model in the Geographic Markup Language (GML) Version 3.1.1. This specification allows sensor providers to describe *in situ* what a sensor can observe, with what accuracy, etc. The language also introduces the notion of virtual sensors as a group of physical sensors that provide abstract sensor measurement.

The OntoSensor [3] was intended as a general knowledge base of sensors for query and inference. This system includes definitions of concepts and properties adopted in part from SensorML, and partly from extensions to IEEE SUMO, references to ISO 19115 and from constructs of the Web Ontology Language (OWL). OntoSensor adopts classes and associations from SensorML to create specific sensor profiles, and also extends IEEE Sumo concepts. In addition, the implementation of OntoSensor references the ISO 19115 constraints.

Considering means of reducing overhead, the W3C Efficient XML Interchange Working Group has developed an encoding system that allows efficient interchange of XML Information Set documents [16]. A major design decision in EXI is to use XML schema information for the encoding. Both endpoints must use the same schema files to generate the EXI grammar [17]. The IoT exploits the EXI format to mitigate the size and parsing complexity of the XML, while maintaining most of its capability for enhancing data with context information. EXI can reduce up to 90% of the original XML message size, thus carrying a rich set of information in very small packets. However, highly resource-constrained IoT devices are not capable of parsing and processing schema sets during runtime [18]. Hence the EXI grammar must be generated and integrated in the nodes at compile time, as described by Käbisch *et al.* [19].

The Devices Profile for Web Services (DPWS) is chosen as a suitable subset of web service protocols for machine-to-machine communication. DPWS defines a minimal set of implementation constraints to enable secure Web Service messaging, discovery, description, and eventing on resource-constrained IoT devices [20]. In addition, DPWS is fully aligned with Web Services technology, and includes numerous extension points, which allow for seamless integration of device-provided services in enterprise-wide application scenarios. In DPWS, service discovery can be done via multicast communication instead of querying a central service registry such as UDDI [17]. Research has also shown that DPWS can provide real-time capabilities [21].

To model IoT hardware used in the Coastal Environmental Sensor Networks (CESN), Matt et al. [22] developed the CESN sensor ontology to describe the relationships between sensors and their measurements. The CESN ontology [10] provides concepts about sensors and their deployments as seen by middleware responsible for database persistence. The core concepts in the CESN sensor ontology are the physical sensor devices themselves, *Sensor;* the *PhysicalProperty* that a *Sensor* can measure; and the measurement that a sensor has taken, or *PhysicalPropertyMeasurement*. The ontology is unconcerned with the sensor network's logical or physical topology, or with issues of intermediate aggregation within the sensor network. The ontology has a local knowledge base of facts describing particular CESN instrument deployments as instances of classes defined in the ontology. Moreover, the ontology has a collection of rule sets which represent the domain-specific knowledge and hypotheses of scientists. The main concepts found in the CESN sensor ontology are similar to the terminology described in SensorML.

A semantic sensor network would allow the network and its components to be organized, queried, and controlled thorough high-level specification. Neuhaus and Compton [5] developed the CSIRO sensor ontology for describing sensors and deployments. The CSIRO ontology is organized around four core clusters of concepts: those which describe the domain of sensing (feature), those describing the sensor (Sensor), those describing the physical components and location of the sensor (SensorGrounding), and those describing functions and processing (OperationModel and Process)—both processing on a sensor, and processing that can create a sensor from any number of data streams. CSIRO ontology does not serve to organize all concepts of sensing, but instead provides a language to describe sensors in terms of their capabilities and operations.

Undertaking research into simplifying the configuration and maintenance of wireless transducers (i.e. sensors and actuators) for wireless transducer networks (WTNs), Horan [11] summarized the requirements for transducer capability descriptions. Basically, the functionality of a device should be described in terms of its syntax and its semantics. The device and its description should be closely linked, the description should be machine-interpretable, and an *a priori* agreement on standards is insufficient. Further, Horan used the OWL-S as a basis for designing a framework for the exploitation of capability description focusing on the following aspects: services, manufacturer's views, bridging axioms, services provided by a class of devices, devices provided by themselves, and syntactic descriptions.

Other efforts have been made to describe the capabilities of sensor devices. Composite Capability/Preference Profiles (CC/PP) [23] are focused on describing the physical capabilities of a device such as its memory, CPU, etc. This standard is based on an extensible language, and it targets larger devices such as mobile phones and PDAs. TEDS [24] provides a similar description of transducers to SensorML, which provides a hardware description of the physical device, rather than of its functionality. A TEDS contains the information to identify, characterize, interface, and properly use the signal from an analogue sensor. The national marine electronics association standard 0183 [25] has become a standard protocol for interfacing navigational devices, for example Global Positioning System receivers. TinySchema [26], which is a schema for describing the attributes, commands, and events in TinyOS.

4   Conclusion and Discussion

The Internet of Things integrates wireless sensor networks with the Internet, and paves the way for people to live seamlessly in both the physical and cyber worlds. Those wireless sensor networks serve much like the nerve endings in the human body. The IoT requires information representation for uniformly developing and managing sensor data in wireless sensor networks. Thus it accelerates data integration and increases interoperability in sensor-intensive IoT applications. This paper discusses a generic Internet of Things structure, and examines requirements for designing information representation schemes for sensor nodes. The paper reviews the state of the art in sensor information representation for the Internet of Things. This work initiates the study of semantic information representation for the Mammoth project.

An interesting topic for future research concerns semantic service composition. This is an important technology for shifting the Internet of Things to the Web of Things. Semantic services are composed by connecting their inputs and outputs with compatible semantics. The connections between input and output of services could be implemented based on publish-subscribe mechanisms. The benefit of semantic service composition is that it makes automation compose services possible, and allows adaption to resource changes.

Acknowledgement. This work was carried out in the Mammoth project funded by Tekes — the Finnish Funding Agency for Technology and Innovation.

References

1. Gruber, T.R.: A Translation Approach to Portable Ontologies. Knowledge Acquisition 5(2), 199–220 (1993)
2. Zhou, J.: Pervasive Service Computing: Community Coordinated Multimedia, Context Awareness, and Service Composition. Dissertation, Acta Universitatis Ouluensis. Series C 399, University of Oulu, Finland (2011)
3. Russomanno, D.J., Kothari, C.R., Thomas, O.A.: Building a Sensor Ontology: A Practical Approach Leveraging ISO and OGC Models. In: The 2005 International Conference on Artificial Intelligence, Las Vegas, NV, pp. 637–643 (2005)
4. Avancha, S., Patel, C., Joshi, A.: Ontology-Driven Adaptive Sensor Networks. Mobile and Ubiquitous Systems: Networking and Services. In: The First Annual International Conference on MOBIQUITOUS 2004, pp. 194–202 (2004)

5. Neuhaus, H., Compton, M.: The Semantic Sensor Network Ontology: A Generic Language to Describe Sensor Assets. In: AGILE Workshop: Challenges in Geospatial Data Harmonisation (2009)
6. Jurdak, R., Lopes, C.V., Baldi, P.: A Framework for Modeling Sensor Networks. In: Workshop on Building Software for Pervasive Computing, OOPSLA (2004)
7. Jie, L., Feng, Z.: Towards Semantic Services for Sensor-Rich Information Systems. Broadband Networks. In: 2nd International Conference on BroadNets 2005, vol. 2, pp. 967–974 (2005)
8. Alamri, A., Eid, M., El Saddik, A.: Classification of the State-of-the-Art Dynamic Web Services Composition Techniques. Int. J. of Web and Grid Services 2(2), 148–166 (2006)
9. Matheus, C.J., Tribble, D., Kokar, M.M., Ceruti, M.G., Mcgirr, S.C.: Towards a Formal Pedigree Ontology for Level-One Sensor Fusion. In: 10th International Command & Control Research and Technology Symposium (2005)
10. CESN Sensor Ontology (2008), http://www.cesn.umb.edu/sensor/cesn.owl
11. Horan, B.: The Use of Capability Descriptions in a Wireless Transducer Network. SMLI Technical Report (2005)
12. Zhou, J., Gilman, E., Riekki, J., Rautiainen, M., Ylianttila, M.: Ontology-Driven Pervasive Service Composition for Everyday Life. In: Denko, M., Obaidat, M.S. (eds.) Pervasive Computing and Networking. Wiley (2010)
13. Sheth, A., Henson, C., Sahoo, S.S.: Semantic Sensor Web. IEEE Internet Computing 12(4), 78–83 (2008)
14. W3C, http://www.w3.org/2005/Incubator/ssn/ssnx/ssn
15. Sensor Modeling Language, http://www.opengeospatial.org/standards/sensorml
16. Efficient XML Interchange, http://www.w3.org/TR/exi/
17. Moritz, G., Golatowski, F., Timmermann, D., Lerche, C.: Beyond 6LoWPAN: Web Services in Wireless Sensor Networks. IEEE Transactions Industrial Informatics 99, 1–1 (2012)
18. Bui, N., Zorzi, M.: Health Care Applications: A Solution Based on the Internet of Things. In: Proceedings of the 4th International Symposium on Applied Sciences in Biomedical and Communication Technologies, pp. 131:1–131:5. ACM, New York (2011)
19. Käbisch, S., Peintner, D., Heuer, J., Kosch, H.: Efficient and Flexible XML-Based Data-Exchange in Microcontroller-Based Sensor Actor Networks. In: IEEE 24th International Conference on Advanced Information Networking and Applications Workshops (WAINA), pp. 508–513. IEEE Press, New York (2010)
20. DPWS, http://docs.oasis-open.org/ws-dd/ns/dpws/2009/01
21. Cucinotta, T., Mancina, A., Anastasi, G.F., Lipari, G., Mangeruca, L., Checcozzo, R., Rusina, F.: A Real-Time Service-Oriented Architecture for Industrial Automation. IEEE Transactions on Industrial Informatics 5(3), 267–277 (2009)
22. Calder, M., Morris, R.A., Peri, F.: Machine Reasoning about Anomalous Sensor Data. Ecological Informatics 5(1), 9 (2010)
23. Composite Capability/Preference Profiles. Composite Capability/Preference Profiles, W3C Working Draft (July 28, 2003), http://www.w3.org/TR/CCPP-struct-vocab
24. IEEE Standard for a Smart Transducer Interface for Sensors and Actuators Transducer to Microprocessor Communications Protocols and Transducer Electronic Data Sheet (TEDS) Formats. [IEEE 1451.1] (approved September 16, 1997)
25. National Marine Electronics Association (USA): Standard 0183, Standard for Interfacing Marine Electronic Devices, Version 3.01 (January 1, 2002)
26. TinyOS TinySchema: Managing Attributes, Commands and Events in TinyOS, Version 1.1 (September 2003), http://telegraph.cs.berkeley.edu/tinydb/tinyschema_doc/index.html

Modeling Decision Structures and Dependencies

Feng Wu, Laura Priscilla, Mingji Gao, Filip Caron,
Willem De Roover, and Jan Vanthienen[*]

Department of Decision Sciences & Information Management,
KU Leuven, Belgium
`jan.vanthienen@kuleuven.be`

Abstract. Decisions are often not adequately modeled. They are hardcoded in process models or other representations, but not always modeled in a systematic way. Because of this hardcoding or inclusion in other models, organizations often lack the necessary flexibility, maintainability and traceability in their business operations.

The aim of this paper is to propose a decision structuring methodology, named Decision Dependency Design (D3). This methodology addresses the above problems by structuring decisions and indicating underlying dependencies. From the decision structure, different execution mechanisms could be designed.

Keywords: Decision structuring, Decision dependencies, Decision modeling.

1 Introduction

Managing business decisions separately, and not only hidden in processes and procedures, is important for agility and traceability [1]. Moreover, not explicitly modeling decisions would result in insufficient documentation of the decision, which leads to problems during optimizing and redesigning operations [2].

This paper extends the concept of a decision goal tree, as presented in our earlier research [3] with the following contributions:

- Proposing a methodology that differentiates between different kinds of decision dependencies (information and combination dependencies), each with a distinct notation. The notation aims at distinguishing general decision structure from the more detailed decision logic expressed in business rule notations.
- Designing a mechanism to incorporate the decision dependencies into the execution mechanism using transformations.

The structure of this paper is as follows. Section 2 discusses related work. Section 3 states the overall scope of the Decision Dependency Design (D3) methodology. Sections 4 and 5 introduce the concepts and notation to structure decisions, and describe how to translate the models with a preliminary pattern language. We evaluate and conclude our proposed methodology in section 6.

---

[*] Corresponding author.

P. Herrero et al. (Eds.): OTM 2012 Workshops, LNCS 7567, pp. 525–533, 2012.

2   Related Work

In [4], Lars Braubach et al. presented a goal-oriented process modeling approach, which extends concepts from goal-driven process design [5]. Yet, concerning the decision making processes, especially those decisions that span across several business processes, the goals elicited for individual process are not necessarily aligned together to represent the characteristics of the final decision.

An alternative method, namely Product Based Workflow Design (PBWD) is presented in [6]. Similarities can be found between PBWD and case handling workflow management systems [7, 8], as they focus on the data elements rather than on the control flow of the process. Our approach is related, but focuses more on the decisions than on the data, and builds upon our earlier research in this area [3].

3   Scope of Decision Dependency Design (D3)

3.1   D3 Related Business Rules

A business rule is a statement that defines or constrains some aspect of the business [9]. While many types and forms of business rules exist, in the methodology we only focus on rules and dependencies for decision making. In the D3 model we distinguish the following dependency types:

- **Input dependencies** elicit all the possible elements to be used as inputs for the decision under consideration. These data elements can be information collected from business activities or the result of other (sub-)decisions. Input dependencies are used to construct the *input dependency model*. The goal of constructing such a model is to visualize the relations between the decision and its constituting elements in a top down approach, the most important decision at the top.
- **Input combination dependencies** determine the set of inputs that is valid in different decision situations. The set (or subset) of inputs is used for the decision situation, but the exact nature of the outcome is not known yet, as it belongs to the business logic. A subset of the inputs might suffice to draw a conclusion about the decision without knowing the other inputs. Input combination dependencies are represented in the *input combination dependency model*. An example of input combination dependencies can be "To decide whether to play tennis or not, we sometimes only consider weather and the schedule of the player, but some other time we only consider weather and time of the day instead".

The real constellation for deciding the outcome of a decision, based on some inputs, is called the business logic. For a decision, a set of business logics are associated with it, that react on the inputs and assign the output, expressed in the form of rules, tables or trees. Nevertheless, we do not embed detailed business logics in any of the artifacts produced by D3, because this logic can be managed separately so that the agility of the decision model can be enhanced. An example of business logic can be "IF the schedule of the player is busy and the weather is bad, THEN do not play tennis".

Other types of rules and constraints can exist. Process constraints, e.g., are rules controlling and managing the sequence of tasks appearing in business processes. They are embedded in the business process models produced by D3, but not in the input dependency model or the input combination dependency model. In contrast to the conventional business process design where the decision related rules are hardcoded, such that the ordering of tasks may indicate an input dependency rule or a process constraint, our approach manages them separately. An example of a process constraint can be "Always check weather condition first before checking other conditions".

Of course input dependencies and input combination dependencies can be derived from the business logic, but they can also exist on their own if the business logic is not fully known yet or often changes. For instance, a business rule stating that "IF the schedule of the player is busy and the weather is bad, THEN do not play tennis." can be categorized as business logic, since it tells what decision should be made under the given conditions. However, it also contains information about what inputs are needed for making this decision.

The reason for this distinction is that the dependencies might influence the structure of the business process, but business logics normally have no impact on business process execution, so that they can be managed elsewhere. Hardcoding business logics may cause maintenance problems in both process and decision management.

3.2 D3 Phases

Four major phases can be distinguished during a D3 project:

- Stage 1: Gathering requirements.
- Stage 2: Eliciting input dependencies and building the input dependency model.
- Stage 3: Eliciting input combination dependencies and building the input combination dependency model.
- Stage 4: Eliciting process constraints and transforming the input combination model to a process execution model.

The D3 model can be used to build one or more process models that comply with the input and input combination dependencies. Changes in dependencies will lead to other process model designs. Nevertheless, we cannot draw a clear line between each phase. Normally the project will be implemented in a cyclical manner. Evaluation of current deliverables will occur in every phase of D3. Business decisions and related business rules are not always well documented and tracked. They hide in process models, code, and texts. However, techniques exist to identify and model decisions from business routines [10].

4   D3 Notation

4.1   A Running Example: Unemployment Benefits

Suppose a government labor department has the obligation to give unemployment benefits to citizens (see also [2]). Everyday a lot of applicants apply to it each asking for approval. The approval decision is based on one or more of the following criteria: the nationality, the employment period, the employment type, the validation of the ID card, the physical test result, and also the health condition of the applicant. The health condition itself is determined by physical and psychological tests. Data inputs for each (sub-)decision can be collected from applicants or systems. Some of the data are always required (e.g. nationality), some are not, depending on the situation.

4.2   Input Dependency Model (IDM)

Notation:

	Decision input: Except for the top decision, all other sub-decisions shown in the model serve as inputs for their upper level decision(s).
	Input path: Showing the dependency relationship between input elements and decisions.
	Optional decision input: The result of this decision may be considered as input for upper level decisions under certain situations.
	Reusable sub-decision input: A sub-decision that will be used as repetitive input for multiple decisions. Reusable sub-decision input helps to increase efficiency by avoiding redundant data collection.
	Data input: Data elements which are not output from any sub-decisions.

The IDM reflects the relationship between lower and upper decisions and stays unchanged unless the most fundamental business rules change. The IDM for the unemployment example is presented in figure 1. In this model, there is no information on which input combinations exactly lead to certain decisions, but it already lists required and optional data inputs and sub-decisions. Therefore the model is not subject to minor policy changes and is stable enough to serve as a foundation for the process.

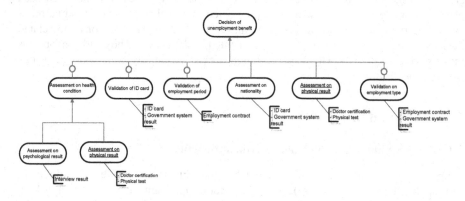

Fig. 1. Input dependency model

4.3   Input Combination Dependency Model (ICDM)

Notation:

Only notations different from the previous model will be presented.

(rounded double-oval symbol)	**Indispensable decision input:** A decision that will always be required to serve as input(s) for its upper level decision.
(joint input symbol)	**Joint decision input:** Showing a combination of inputs which is sufficient in certain situation for making the decision.
(disjoint input symbol)	**Disjoint decision input:** Indicating a combination of only one input which is sufficient in certain situation for making the decision.

Derived from the IDM and input combination dependencies, this model indicates decision paths leading to upper decisions. The ICDM for the unemployment example is presented in figure 2. This model shows all the combination of inputs from which the upper level decision can be made. Such combinations can be expressed as mathematical sets. The following example illustrates three combinations, one of which is <Validation of employment period, Assessment on nationality, Assessment on physical result, Decision of unemployment benefit>. In real life, the combinations can also be demonstrated with different colors for better interpretation. Since input combination rules are less stable because they convey more detailed decision logic than input dependency rules, the ICDM is less stable than the IDM.

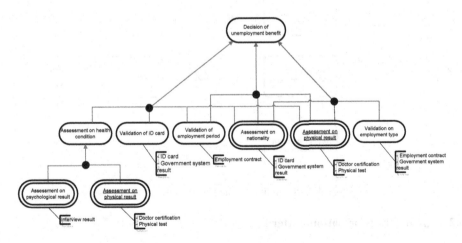

Fig. 2. Input combination dependency model

5   Transformation Patterns

A pattern is the description of a proven solution to common problems to achieve efficient and effective problem solving [11]. In this section, two transformation patterns are introduced to give guidance for transforming the decision structure into a process execution model: the disjoint transformation pattern and the joint transformation pattern. More transformation patterns satisfying other criteria will be a topic for future research.

5.1   Disjoint Transformation Pattern

This pattern will be applied to all cases that have a disjoint decision input symbol in the ICDM. We propose only one pattern here for transforming the disjoint decision input symbol into a process model: the exclusive gateway. A simple algorithm can be defined for the transformation:

```
If there is a disjoint decision input symbol
    If there is a joint decision symbol below
        Then group all the joint decision nodes as a sub-process con-
            taining mutually inclusive tasks
        Else put the disjoint decision nodes as tasks within exclusive
            gateways;
```

For the unemployment example, the process is derived from the IDCM and shown in figure 3. Three decision paths are derived to reach the decision and one of those paths will be chosen during execution.

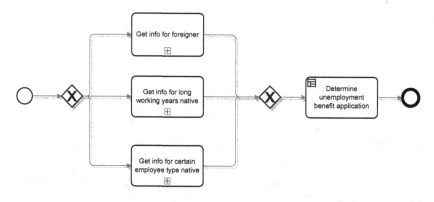

Fig. 3. Exclusive gateway process

5.2   Joint Transformation Pattern

This pattern applies to all cases that have a joint decision input symbol in the ICDM. We propose two general types of joint transformation pattern: the parallel pattern and the sequential pattern. Time and cost are the criteria to determine the selection of these patterns, but there can be more criteria for selecting the appropriate business process, such as desired flexibility, data constraints, etc. [12].

Parallel Pattern

When the criterion is to achieve minimal throughput time, the parallel pattern is best suited to build the process [12]. The algorithm is as follows:

```
If there is a joint decision input symbol
    If the joint decision has a group of lower decisions
        Then put the joint decision node as a sub-process task
        Else put the joint decision node as a task;
```

For the activity "Get info for foreigner" in figure 3 e.g., the sub-process to be built is shown in figure 4. This parallel process can be time efficient, because all tasks for the same case can start at the same time. However if the outcome is negative, a lot of unnecessary work may have been performed, so the cost will not always be minimal.

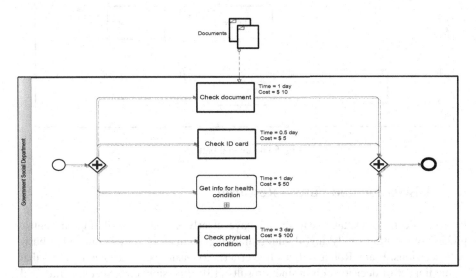

Fig. 4. Parallel pattern

Sequential Pattern

When the criterion is to minimize execution cost, the sequential pattern is best suited to build the process [12]. To transform an ICDM containing a joint decision input symbol into a sequential business process, a simple algorithm is defined:

```
If there is a joint decision input symbol
    If the joint decision has a group of lower decisions
        Then put the joint decision node as a sub-process task in se-
            quential order
        Else put the joint decision node as a task in sequential order;
```

Based on the algorithm above, a sequential process to get information for a foreigner in case of unemployment is presented in figure 5. On average, a sequential process has the advantage of reducing cost because during the execution, a decision process can be terminated if some preconditions are not met, therefore, it saves the cost of carrying out the remaining tasks [12].

The ordering of tasks within the process is still flexible. If there are process constraints applying to certain tasks, the ordering is determined accordingly. Otherwise multiple process models could exist with different orderings, each of which reflects particular business preferences and concerns. Normally it will be good practice to start with the simple (inexpensive) checks.

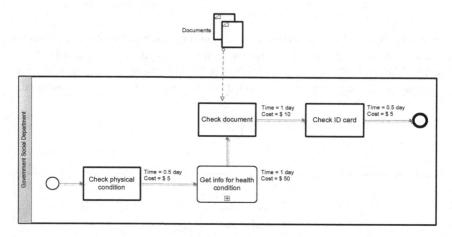

Fig. 5. Sequential pattern

6   Discussion and Future Research

Business decision management should have clearly stated goals during the entire process of eliciting, analyzing, defining, tracking, evaluating, and documenting business decisions. Frank Rohde defines five criteria to ensure better decision yield – that is, the impact of decisions on business results [13]: Precision, cost, speed, agility and consistency. The proposed D3 method results in a better separation between business decisions and execution processes, which makes it easier and clearer to achieve the above objectives. Business decisions that have been properly modeled can be better evaluated and improved throughout their lifecycle. Moreover, the transformation patterns allow for added operational agility when the characteristics (e.g. time and cost) for obtaining lower level elements change. Future research must focus on additional transformation patterns that take into account different characteristics (e.g. the organizational aspect where the goal would be to limit the number of handovers) or a combination of characteristics.

As stated in section 5, there can be more patterns for specific business circumstances to guide transforming decision models to business process models. The pattern language can incorporate best practices from industry. Furthermore, using existing systems and standards to support the modeling and implementation of D3 will be a topic for further investigation. Finally, the effectiveness and the complexity of this methodology will be tested in real life situations.

7 Conclusion

D3 enables better decision management by separating decisions from processes. It introduces models illustrating the relationships between decisions, and provides ways to derive business processes to facilitate corresponding decision making. This approach will increase the flexibility, traceability and maintainability of the underlying decision making processes, while at the same time, it minimizes the impact from changes caused by modification of specific decision logic.

References

1. Taylor, J.: Smart (enough) systems: how to deliver competitive advantage by automating the decisions hidden in your business. In: Taylor, J., Raden, N. (eds.) Prentice Hall, Upper Saddle River (2007)
2. Reijers, H.A., Limam, S., van der Aalst, W.M.P.: Product-based workflow design. J. Manage. Inform. Syst. 20(1), 229–262 (2003)
3. De Roover, W., Vanthienen, J.: On the Relation between Decision Structures, Tables and Processes. In: Meersman, R., Dillon, T., Herrero, P. (eds.) OTM-WS 2011. LNCS, vol. 7046, pp. 591–598. Springer, Heidelberg (2011)
4. Braubach, L., Pokahr, A., Jander, K., Lamersdorf, W., Burmeister, B.: Go4Flex: Goal-Oriented Process Modelling. In: Essaaidi, M., Malgeri, M., Badica, C. (eds.) Intelligent Distributed Computing IV. SCI, vol. 315, pp. 77–87. Springer, Heidelberg (2010)
5. Jacobs, S., Holten, R.: Goal driven business modelling: supporting decision making within information systems development. In: Proceedings of Conference on Organizational Computing Systems 1995, pp. 96–105. ACM, Milpitas (1995)
6. van der Aalst, W.M.P.: On the automatic generation of workflow processes based on product structures. Comput. Ind. 39(2), 97–111 (1999)
7. Vanderfeesten, I., Reijers, H.A., Aalst, W.M.P.: Case Handling Systems as Product Based Workflow Design Support. In: Enterprise Information Systems, pp. 187–198 (2008)
8. Vanderfeesten, I., Reijers, H.A., van der Aalst, W.M.P.: An evaluation of case handling systems for product based workflow design. In: International Conference on Enterprise Information Systems, ICEIS 2007 (2007)
9. Hay, D.A.H., Anderson, K., Hall, J., Bachman, C., Breal, J., Funk, J., Healy, J., Mcbride, D., Mckee, R., Moriarty, T., et al.: Defining Business Rules What Are They Really? The Business Rules Group (2000)
10. Taylor, J.: Decision management systems: a practical guide to using business rules and predictive analytics, vol. xxviii, p. 284. IBM Press/Pearson plc., Upper Saddle River (2012)
11. Alexander, C.: A pattern language: towns, buildings, construction (1977)
12. Reijers, H.A.: Best practices in business process redesign: an overview and qualitative evaluation of successful redesign heuristics. Omega: The International Journal of Management Science 33(4), 283 (2005)
13. Rohde, F.: Little decisions add up. Harvard Business Review 83(6), 24–+ (2005)

Knowledge Mining Approach for Optimization of Inference Processes in Rule Knowledge Bases

Agnieszka Nowak-Brzezińska and Roman Simiński

University of Silesia, Institute of Computer Science
ul. Będzińska 39, 41-200 Sosnowiec, Poland
{agnieszka.nowak,roman.siminski}@us.edu.pl

Abstract. The main aim of the article is to present modifications of inference algorithms based on information extracted from large sets of rules. The conception of cluster analysis and decision units will be used for discovering knowledge from such data.

Keywords: knowledge bases, inference, decision units, cluster analysis.

1 Introduction

Methods of inference dedicated for rule bases have a long history and are fairly well known, but no significant changes in the inference processes since RETE algorithm were made. The purpose of this study is to present a new approach to inference optimization in rule-based systems and evaluate the effectiveness of the proposed approach. The thesis of this work is that using information discovered in a rule base we transform that rule base into a net of decision units or clusters of rules, which in result improves the efficiency of inference algorithms.

2 Towards a New Modular Structure of a Knowledge Base

The decision units are simple and intuitive models describing relations in a knowledge base (KB), thus, the decision units can be considered as a simple tool for modelling rule bases. The concept of a decision unit is described in the [4,5]. The idea of decision units allows the division of a rule set into subsets called *elementary decision units*, *ordinal decision units* and *general decision units*. An example of using the decision units' properties in the inference optimization task is presented in [1]. Similar issues concering rule base modelling are shown in [5]. By organizing data into clusters, additional information about the analyzed data is acquired. The groups of rules can be further analyzed in order to observe the additional patterns which can be used to simplify the structure of a KB either by simplifying the rules or by reducing their number. Having the set of rules from a KB, in each step the two most similar rules or clusters of rules are found and linked into a cluster. The created structure is similar to a binary tree and the time efficiency of searching such trees is $O(\log_2 n)$. What is more

P. Herrero et al. (Eds.): OTM 2012 Workshops, LNCS 7567, pp. 534–537, 2012.

the clustering algorithm has to be executed only once [3] and though the time complexity of a typical hierarchical algorithm varies, it is often a member of the $O(n^2)$ class.

3   Modifications of Classical Versions of Inference Algorithms

The proposed approach assumes that we reorganize any attributive rule KB from a set of not related rules to groups of similar rules using cluster analysis [1,2] or decision units [5,4]. Thus, we can decompose a rule set into a hierarchical structure. This structure will be a source for extracting interesting information for used in the inference process.

The modification of the backward inference algorithm consists of initializing only promising recursive calls of the classical backward algorithm. The decision units' net provides information which allow a preliminary assessment of whether the call could potentially confirm the nominated subgoal of inference. The classic version of the algorithm doesn't known whether the call is promising — ie, it is unknown whether there is a rule that fits the new goal of inference. Indeed, in real cases very often there is no such rule and the recursive call is unnecessary. In figure 1 we present the backward inference algorithm, which uses the information from the decision unit's net described earlier. Input data for the backward inference algorith consists of: D — set of decition units, F — set of facts, g — goal of inference. The output data of the algorithm is: a set of facts with new facts obtained through inference, and a boolean value - true if the goal g is in the set of facts ($g \in F$), or false otherwise. The modification of the forward inference algorithm includes two steps: finding the relevant rule first, and then confirmating all premises of this selected rule. The first step means that we search the created structure ($Tree$, (T)) by comparring at each level of the tree the similarity between the set of facts (F) and the representatives of the left and right branch of a given node (($node.c$)). Having this we choose a higher value of such similarity. Finally, we get the level of rules (instead of rule clusters) and we start to confirm all premises of a given rule. If all premises are true a conclusion of a given rule is added to the set of facts ($F = F \cup \{node.d\}$). Input data for the forward inference algorithm consists of: T — set of rule clusters, F — set of facts. The output data of the algorithm is: a set of facts with new facts obtained through inference, and a boolean value - true if the re is at least one rule in a given KB, which premises are included in the set of facts, or false otherwise. In figure 2 we present the pseudocode of the forward inference algorithm.

4   Experiments

The goal of the experiments is to analyze the level of optimization brought by the proposed methods. For each KB the results of using a a classical version of inference algorithms and those based on rule clusters or decision units are

```
function bckInfDU( D, g, var F ) :
boolean
begin
  if g ∈ F then return true
  else
    A ← ∅
    select d ∈ D where g ∈ O(d)
    truePremise ← false
    while  ¬truePremise ∧ {R(d) −
A} ≠ ∅ do
      select r ∈ {R(d) − A}
      forall w ∈ cond(r) do
        truePremise ← ( w ∈ F )
        if ¬truePremise ∧ w ∈ IC(d)
then
          truePremise ← bckInfDU(
D, w, F )
          if ¬truePremise then
            truePremise ← environ-
mentConfirmsFact( w )
            if ¬truePremise then
              break
      endfor
      if ¬truePremise then
        A = A ∪ {r}
    endwhile
  endif
  if truePremise then
    F = F ∪ {g}
  return truePremise
end
```

Fig. 1. Backward Inference Algorithm

```
function forwardInferenceCA( T, F ) : boolean
begin
  node ← T[2n − 1]
  FactsConfirmation ← false
  while ¬ FactsConfirmation ∧ node.level >
0 do
    leftBranch ← T[node.i]
    rightBranch ← T[node.j]
    if  similarity(leftBranch.c,F) >
similarity(rightBranch.c,F) then
      node ← leftBranch
    else
      node ← rightBranch
    endif
  endhile
  check ← 1
  forall cond ∈ node.c do
    if truePremise(cond) then
      check ← check * 1
    else
      check ← check * 0
    endif
  endfor
  if check == 1 then
    FactsConfirmation ← true
    F = F ∪ {node.d}
  else
    FactsConfirmation ← false
  endif
  return FactsConfirmation
end
```

Fig. 2. Forward Inference Algorithm

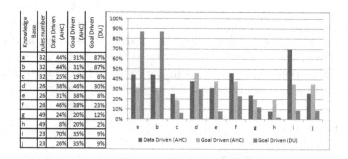

Fig. 3. Results of the experiments with inference optimization

presented. In figure 3 the results of experiments performed on four different KBs are presented. Instead of searching through the whole KB, we need to analyze only a small procentage of all rules to find the proper rule and finish the inference process successfully. There were also cases when during the searching process algorithms based on clustering rules did not find a suitable rule to activate, despite of the fact that it exists in a given KB. That is because, the procedure of creating good descriptions for rule clusters does not always give expected results.

5   Conclusions

In the presented work we propose modifications of inference algorithms based on information discovered in a rule base. We introduce a technique which uses the „knowledge maning aproach" — the main goal of this approach is to discover useful, potentially implicit and directly unreadable information from large rule sets. In this paper we combined two approaches — the hierarchical decomposition of large rule bases using cluster analysis and the decision units' conception. The proposed models of a KB allow us to analyze only a small procentage of all rules during the inference process. Only promising decision units are selected for further processing and only a selected subset of the whole rule set is processed in each iteration. Eventually only promising recursive calls are made. The modification of the forward inference algorithm is based on the rule clusters' tree, which is used to find the most relevant rule with a $O(\log 2n - 1)$ time complexity. We also plain to extend proposed algorithm for nondeterministic rules [6].

References

1. Nowak, A., Simiński, R., Wakulicz-Deja, A.: Towards modular representation of knowledge base. In: Intelligent Information Processing and Web Mining. AISC, pp. 421–428. Physica-Verlag, Springer Verlag Company (2006)
2. Nowak, A., Wakulicz-Deja, A.: The Way of Rules Representation in Composited Knowledge Bases. In: Cyran, K.A., Kozielski, S., Peters, J.F., Stańczyk, U., Wakulicz-Deja, A. (eds.) Man-Machine Interactions. AISC, vol. 59, pp. 175–182. Springer, Heidelberg (2009)
3. Nowak-Brzezińska, A., Simiński, R., Jach, T., Xięski, T.: Towards a Practical Approach to Discover Internal Dependencies in Rule-Based Knowledge Bases. In: Yao, J., Ramanna, S., Wang, G., Suraj, Z. (eds.) RSKT 2011. LNCS, vol. 6954, pp. 232–237. Springer, Heidelberg (2011)
4. Simiński, R., Wakulicz-Deja, A.: Verification of Rule Knowledge Bases Using Decision Units. In: Intelligent Information Systems. AISC, pp. 185–192. Physica Verlag, Springer Verlag Company (2000)
5. Simiński, R.: Decision units approach in knowledge base modeling. In: Recent Advances in Intelligent Information Systems, pp. 597–606. Academic Publishing House EXIT (2009)
6. Delimata, P., Marszał-Paszek, B., Moshkov, M., Paszek, P., Skowron, A., Suraj, Z.: Comparison of Some Classification Algorithms Based on Deterministic and Nondeterministic Decision Rules. In: Peters, J.F., Skowron, A., Słowiński, R., Lingras, P., Miao, D., Tsumoto, S. (eds.) Transactions on Rough Sets XII. LNCS, vol. 6190, pp. 90–105. Springer, Heidelberg (2010)

On Semantics in Onto-DIY

Yan Tang Demey[1] and Zhenzhen Zhao[2]

[1] Semantic Technology and Application Research Laboratory (STARLab),
Department of Computer Science,
Vrije Universiteit Brussel, Pleinlaan 2 B-1050 Brussels, Belgium
yan.tang@vub.ac.be
[2] Institut Mines-Télécom, Télécom SudParis
Service RS2M (Département Réseaux et Services Mutimédia Mobiles) – salle D 108 02
9, Rue Charles Fourier, 91000 Evry, France
zhenzhen.zhao@it-sudparis.eu

Abstract. This paper illustrates how semantics is modeled and used in the flexible and idea inspiring ontology-based Do-It-Yourself architecture (Onto-DIY). The semantics part contains three divisions - 1) semantics from the domain ontologies, which are used as the semantically rich knowledge for describing Internet of Things (IoT) components, 2) semantics stored in semantic decision tables, which contain decision rules on top of domain ontologies, and, 3) semantics from user-centric services, which define the software composition for the deployment.

Keywords: ontology, semantic decision table, decision table, user-centric service, Do-It-Yourself, description logic.

1   Introduction

In the past EU ITEA2 Do-it-Yourself Smart Experiences Project[1], we have developed a use case scenario as follows. Mary has a naughty boy called James. He treats Mary's iPhone as his favorite toy. Mary wants to create a small tool called "naughty boy protector" (NBP) using a smart rabbit (e.g., a Nabaztag rabbit[2]), which takes web feeds and speaks. What NBP does is as follows. When James shakes Mary's iPhone, iPhone will send a signal to NBP. When NBP gets this signal, it checks the rules stored in its rule base and fires the relevant rules. As the action of this rule, NBP sends a message to the server of this smart rabbit. After the rabbit gets the web feed, it speaks out loudly. At the end, Mary will reset the rabbit and take back her iPhone.

This use case has been used to design an architecture called Ontology-based Do-it-Yourself architecture (Onto-DIY[3]), which allows end users to create their own

---

[1] http://dyse.org:8080. The authors' work is also supported by OSCB (www.oscb.be)
[2] http://www.nabaztag.com; its APIs can be found at
http://api.nabaztag.com
[3] As a result, the demo can be viewed at
http://www.youtube.com/watch?v=OOhbB162HIY

P. Herrero et al. (Eds.): OTM 2012 Workshops, LNCS 7567, pp. 538–542, 2012.
© Springer-Verlag Berlin Heidelberg 2012

applications using their own evolving semantics. In this paper, we want to focus on how semantics is modeled and used in Onto-DIY.

2   Semantics in Onto-DIY

There are mainly three semantic divisions while designing Onto-DIY. The first one is the domain ontologies, which are used as the knowledge base for describing Internet-of-Things components, such as iPhone and smart rabbit. Fig. 1 shows how we model the concepts "iPhone" and "Smart Rabbit" in Semantic Decision Rule Language (SDRule-L, [3]), which is an extension to Object Role Modeling language (ORM/ORM2, [1]).

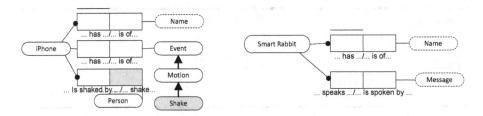

Fig. 1. The concepts defined in the IoT domain ontologies

Following the methodology called "an information analysis method" (NIAM, [5]), the ancestor of ORM, we use the idea of identifying an object type as a LOT (lexical object type) or a NOLOT (non-lexical object type). A LOT, modeled graphically in an eclipse with a dotted line, e.g. "Name" in Fig. 1, is an object that can be uttered and represented in a certain reality or context. A NOLOT, modeled graphically in an eclipse with a solid line, e.g. "iPhone" Fig. 1, is an object that cannot be represented. A NOLOT must be named, presented or referred to using a LOT. A binary fact type containing both a LOT and a NOLOT is called a "bridge type". An example of bridge type is <iPhone, has, is of, Name> (see Fig. 1). Furthermore, we call "has/is of" is the role pair that the objects "iPhone" and "Name" can play with each other.

Note that in Fig. 1, the role "shake" and the object "Shake" are shaded. When we highlight a role and an object in a same color, we call this object is an *objectification* of a role. It means that their meanings have a certain similarity. We use this mechanism to identify and discover tasks and events of a physical object for context-aware computing.

SDRule-L models can be translated into a text that is easy to read. This process is called "verbalization" in [1]. The verbalization of Fig. 1 is shown as follows.

Each iPhone has exactly one Name. An iPhone has an Event, a subtype of which is Motion. Shake is a subtype of Motion. Each iPhone is shaked by at least one Person. Each Smart Rabbit has exactly one Name. Each Smart Rabbit speaks at least one Message.

Fig. 1 is formalized in $\mathcal{SOIQ}$ – a Description Logic (DL [1]) dialect – as follows.

$$IPhone \sqsubseteq \leq 1has.Name \sqcap \exists has.Name$$
$$IPhone \sqsubseteq has.Event$$
$$Shake \sqsubseteq Motion \sqsubseteq Event$$

$$People \sqsubseteq shake.IPhone$$
$$SmartRabbit \sqsubseteq \leq 1has.Name \sqcap \exists has.Name$$
$$SmartRabbit \sqsubseteq \exists speaks.Message$$

The second semantic division is stored in semantic decision tables (SDT, [1]), with which we model decision rules using the semantics defined and formalized in domain ontologies. Table 1 is an example. The semantics from an SDT is considered as ontological commitments viewed by a particular business application. In this example, the semantics comes from the annotation using the domain ontologies (see the model in Fig. 1) and instantiation (see C1~6 in Table 1).

Table 1. An SDT of deciding on activate a smart rabbit

Condition	1		2	
People shake iPhone	Yes		No	...
...				
Action			...	
Bunny speaks	Message1		...	
...				
C1	$People \equiv \{james, mary\}$	C4	$shake(james, marysiPhone)$	
C2	$IPhone \equiv \{marysiPhone\}$	C5	$Message \equiv \{message1\}$	
C3	$SmartRabbit \equiv \{marysRabbit\}$	C6	$speak(marysRabbit, message1)$	

A non-technical user uses SDTs to model business/application rules that are consistent, complete and ontology-based.

The third semantic division is from user-centric services. User centric service is to apply user-centered design (UCD) process in designing a useful and easy-to-use service, which takes into account user motivation, user requirements, user behaviors, user interactions etc. End-user driven service creation aims to foster the evolution from the absolutely successful user-generated content (UGC) to the user-generated service (UGS) area, to empower end-users' creativity in service generation to achieve better service personalization [6]. The metrics, often termed service composition (back-end) and service mashups (front-end), allow users to play with various service building blocks to create enhanced services. To achieve a better UGS, an intuitive and easy-to-use platform, a use scenario which can promote greater user's motivation, and a sustainable service database, are desired. In return, the semantics, which is extracted from user-centric services, allows end-user to do goal-driven service creation in a technology-agnostic way. Separating technology of a service from its meaning could improve the process of assembling new services.

In order to deploy the SDT illustrated in Table 1, we propose to develop a semantic service creation assistant, e.g., whenever the user picks an existing service, the system should be able to suggest a set of syntactically or semantically related services that can be connected to the existing service (a kind of inter-service communication); or the user can locate a specific service based on a description of all (or part of) its functionality with a near natural language request. For example, we can use it to discover the web service of asking a smart rabbit to speak as shown in Fig. 2.

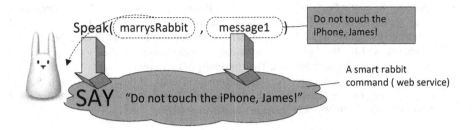

Fig. 2. The concepts defined in the IoT domain ontologies

3   Discussion, Conclusion and Future Work

We use SDRule-L and DL to formalize the semantics in Onto-DIY in this paper. Although we do not use other languages, readers should keep in mind that, for IoT applications, it is recommended to use any kinds of conceptual modeling means, as long as they meet the request and technically/conceptually sound.

With regard to the user-centric service creation in this paper, it is interesting to study the following aspects in the future:

- *Context-aware service creation* – tracing end-users' behaviors and help them to organize and filter information in order to provide personalized service
- *Service creation with trust* – assisting end-users to control privacy policies to protect their sensitive data in a nonintrusive manner
- *Social service co-creation* – allowing users to share their existing "Do-It-Yourself" solutions with others in order to "Do-It-Together"
- *Social service venue sharing* – bringing a business concern to Onto-DIY in order to promote software innovation and encourage users to create their solutions and provide to the market

A future refinement could also be done is the aspect of creating an automatic mapping between the semantics in the three semantic divisions illustrated in this paper.

References

[1] Baader, F., Calvanese, D., McGuinness, D., Nardi, D., Patel-Schneider, P. (eds.): The Description Logic Handbook: Theory, Implementation, and Applications, 2nd edn. Cambridge University Press (2007)
[2] Halpin, T., Morgan, T.: Information Modeling and Relational Databases. The Morgan Kaufmann Series in Data Management Systems (2008) ISBN-10: 0123735688
[3] Tang, Y., Meersman, R.: SDRule Markup Language: Towards Modeling and Interchanging Ontological Commitments for Semantic Decision Making. In: Handbook of Research on Emerging Rule-Based Languages and Technologies: Open Solutions and Approaches, USA, ch. V (sec. I). IGI Publishing (2009) ISBN: 1-60566-402-2

[4] Tang, Y.: Semantic Decision Tables - A New, Promising and Practical Way of Organizing Your Business Semantics with Existing Decision Making Tools. LAP LAMBERT Academic Publishing AG & Co. KG, Saarbrücken (2010) ISBN 978-3-8383-3791-3

[5] Wintraecken, J.J.V.R.: The NIAM information analysis method: theory and practice, p. 469. Kluwer Academic Publishers, The University of California (1990)

[6] Zhao, Z., Laga, N., Crespi, N.: The Incoming Trends of End-User Driven Service Creation. In: Telesca, L., Stanoevska-Slabeva, K., Rakocevic, V. (eds.) DigiBiz 2009. LNICST, vol. 21, pp. 98–108. Springer, Heidelberg (2010)

SINCOM 2012 PC Co-chairs Message

Welcome to the 1st International Workshop on Socially Intelligent Computing (SINCOM 2012). SINCOM focuses on the study, design, development and evaluation of emergent Socially Intelligent Computing systems. The workshop addresses all aspects of socially intelligent computing, that span a variety of issues ranging from the modeling of social behavior in social computational systems, the architectures and design issues of such systems, social media analytics and monitoring, stream processing of social data and social activities, semantic web and Linked Data approaches, the discovery, collection, and extraction of social networks, as well as information retrieval and machine learning methods for socially intelligent computing.

SINCOM 2012 was held in conjunction with the On The Move Federated Conferences and Workshops (OTM 2012) during September 10-14 in Rome, Italy. The workshop had the privilege of counting on a high-quality Program Committee which, including the Co-chairs, comprised more than 20 researchers. After peer reviews with each paper receiving three or more reviews, we accepted the 5 papers (out of the 11 original submissions) that appear in these proceedings. The papers were judged according to their originality, significance to theory and practice, readability and relevance to the workshop topics. The papers finally accepted present new approaches in socially intelligent computing with respect to simulation, social media use analysis, network of things, ontologies and social P2P.

Putting together a workshop like SINCOM is a team effort and many different contributions need to be acknowledged. First of all we would like to gratefully acknowledge the work of all the authors who submitted their papers to SINCOM, whether or not their paper was accepted. Thank you for choosing SINCOM to present your research work! Secondly, we are grateful to the dedicated work of the leading experts from all over the world who served on the Program Committee and whose names appear in the proceedings. Thanks for helping us in putting together an excellent program. Finally, we would like to thank the OTM Organizing Committee for its support and guidance in the smooth running of all the operational issues of the workshop.

We hope that the papers and discussions during SINCOM 2012 will further inspire research in socially intelligent computing and be the stimulus for addressing new challenging research issues in the future.

July 2012

Gregoris Mentzas
Wolgang Prinz

P. Herrero et al. (Eds.): OTM 2012 Workshops, LNCS 7567, p. 543, 2012.
© Springer-Verlag Berlin Heidelberg 2012

A Simulation Framework
for Socially Enhanced Applications

Mirela Riveni, Hong-Linh Truong, and Schahram Dustdar

Distributed Systems Group, Vienna University of Technology
1040 Vienna, Austria
{m.riveni,truong,dustdar}@infosys.tuwien.ac.at

Abstract. The emergence of complex computational problems, which cannot be solved solely by software and require human contribution, have brought the need of designing systems that efficiently manage a mix of software-based and human-based computational resources. Simulations are very appropriate for research on these systems, because they enable testing different scenarios, while avoiding the cost and time limitations of research in real systems. In this paper, we present a framework that enables the simulation of socially-enhanced applications utilizing both software and human based resources. Our framework addresses challenges in human-software environments, such as identifying relevant comparable metrics for mixed resources, mixed-resource selection, composition and scheduling algorithms, performance monitoring and analysis etc. We show the framework's usefulness and usability through a use case.

Keywords: Simulation, socially-enhanced applications, mixed systems.

1 Introduction

With technology advancement and the ever-evolving inter-business collaborations there is a growing need and opportunity to include humans as compute units in addition to software. There is an emergence of new types of complex and unconventional problems, which cannot be (accurately) solved solely by software and thus require human contributions. Examples of such problems are language translation, object recognition in images, common-sense reasoning [10], deciphering handwriting, and incident response management. The term Human Computation [10] was coined to describe the phenomena of using people for solving these type of problems. In our work, we are interested in socially-enhanced applications which use human computation to enhance software-based services (SBS)[1]. For example, a software-based language translation application may also utilize individual human-based services (HBS) or even a crowd [2] to evaluate the results translated from SBS and/or to edit and improve the translation.

Socially-enhanced applications bring a variety of research challenges due to the inclusion of HBS. Examples of such challenges are how to select and compose mixed HBS and SBS, when and how to include HBS in a process or a workflow

---

[1] In this paper we use the terms service and resource interchangeably.

P. Herrero et al. (Eds.): OTM 2012 Workshops, LNCS 7567, pp. 544–553, 2012.

(human in the loop), how to monitor the performance of HBS/SBS or mixed services, and how to schedule hybrid resources. To address these issues we need to provide test environments that support applications empowered with HBS.

Although there is already a considerable body of work regarding the characterization of services provided by humans as types of services which can be used comparably and along with software based services [7,8,2], there is a lack of tools supporting the design and testing of socially-enhanced applications on hybrid environments. Most of the tools are intended only for machine based resource environments (e.g., Grids and Clouds) or only for human-based resources (e.g., crowdsourcing platforms). Moreover, unlike tools for software-based applications, it is very challenging to design those intended for testing socially-enhanced applications in a real environment. We argue that simulations are very appropriate for testing hybrid environments, because as much as conducting research on frameworks with real data by using real HBS gives solid results, it also brings difficulties such as:

- high resource cost (e.g. humans based services and usage of machines on clouds need to be paid),
- long experimentation time,
- geographical distribution of resources, and
- difficulty in getting the same results when repeating experiments.

Simulations can provide controllable environments, with which we can experiment in a fast way and free of cost. In addition, they enable reproducible results providing for selection of (near) optimal solutions and analysing a variety of cases, e.g.,enabling process composers to change their process structure,such as modifying activitites and control flows.

In this paper, we propose a simulation framework that enables the integration of human-based computing resources with software-based ones. The purpose of the framework is to provide means for addressing the above-mentioned challenges in the development and testing socially-enhanced applications. In this paper, we provide a detailed requirement analysis for the need of a simulation framework for hybrid systems, present a conceptual design of the framework, discuss implementation issues of the framework, and provide a concrete case to illustrate the usefulness of the framework.

The rest of this paper is organized as follows: Section 2 presents related work. Section 3 details requirement analysis. We describe our framework in Section 4. Section 5 discusses an example to demonstrate the framework's usability and usefulness. Section 6 concludes the paper and outlines our future work.

2   Related Work

Human Computation Related Frameworks. A framework that allows to model human capabilities under the concept of Web services is presented in [7]. This framework includes an interface editor where "job requesters" can specify the tasks that need to be solved and a middleware which among others holds a layer responsible for dispatching requests and routing them to the selected human based service. A more specialized framework is presented in [5]. The framework presented is exclusively intended to be used for human computation. It is not aimed for hybrid-resource problem solving but for applications of crowdsourced multimedia processing and querying. Work in [8] presents a mixed system model evaluated for a language translation application. The model includes a planner which assigns resources to tasks based on requirements; it has a component that first estimates the resources to be chosen and an execution component that does coordination. A toolkit for quality management of human provided services was presented by Brenbach et al. in [1]. The toolkit enables qualification test creation and task result evaluation. The toolkit provides a simulation mode as well. All of the above-mentioned works relate to enabling human computation either in general for SOA environments or for specialized problem solving. However, we are interested in simulations which can enable controllable experiments and research on different types of socially-enhanced use cases.

Cloud/Grid Simulation Toolkits. CloudSim [4], is a framework that enables the simulation of cloud environments and application services. It provides the simulation of large scale datacenters and federated clouds as well. Entities such as cloud users, resources, virtual machines and their behavior based on different scheduling policies can be simulated and experimented with.GridSim [3] is an event-driven simulation tool for developing and testing Grid related simulations, such as grid resource management and scheduling. Both CloudSim and GridSim do not simulate HBS. However, the richness of features, with which the GridSim toolkit provides ways of specifying different types of machine-based resources and different ways of resource scheduling and management, was the motivating factor for us to integrate it into our simulation framework.

Research Based on Industry Solutions. Amazon Mechanical Turk (MTurk) is a good example for discussing research with *real* HBS enabled platforms. MTurk, apart from being used as a human-service marketplace for micro-tasks, is also being excessively used for crowdsourcing related research. Paolacci et al. [6] have made a study of the demographics of workers on MTurk and have discussed the advantages and difficulties of running experiments on this platform. What is important for us in this work is that the authors point to concerns about the validity of results in MTurk experiments, since the workers are payed little and there are no guarantees that the quality of data is the desired one. MTurk can be a good experiment tool for certain test cases related to human computation, precisely for questions such as how payments effect the quality/quantity of work. However, MTurk is not designed for running complex tasks. For instance, we can not experiment on metrics and algorithms of matching task requirements to worker capabilities. Thus, MTurk is a good example of why crowdsourced-enabled environments are difficult to experiment with, especially in relation to socially-enhanced applications: they are limited to only human computation environments, and there are cost and time related disadvantages as humans need to be paid and real work has to be carried through.

3 Requirements for Supporting Socially-Enhanced Application Simulations

There are fundamental requirements that a simulation framework for analyzing socially-enhanced applications (SEA) needs to fulfill. We identify the following ones:

Req.1 – *Support for different ways of specifying tasks*: SEAs need both SBS and HBS-related tasks but in many cases the developer should be able to indicate whether a task is designed specifically for SBS or HBS or the simulation framework should automatically select SBS or HBS for a task, depending on constraints, e.g., availability, price, response time, and quality of data. For example, depending on the price and quality, a translation task can be mapped to Google translation service or to a human based translaton service. Furthermore, depending on constraints, tasks can be mapped to individual or composite (mixed) units.

Req.2 – *Support for soft-constraint based parameter description and storage for HBS*: the developer of SEA should not deal with complex and large numbers of SBS and HBS in task assignments. For this, selecting and mapping HBS to tasks in SEA should be done automatically via controlled parameters. Therefore, various HBS related metrics should be supported, such as skill type, skill level, and trust. These metrics can be utilized not only for HBS selection and ranking algorithms but also for the development and analysis of different voting schemes in detecting adversary HBS's for example.

Req.3 – *Support for description of SBS and HBS in a unified way*: if SBS and HBS for SEA are described in a different way, the composition and inter-exchange of SBS and HBS for tasksis difficult. Therefore, the framework should provide a unifying model of describing non-functional parameters (NFPs), which can be similarly defined for both resource types, such as: availability, location, quality of results, and pricing models. This unifying model is crucial for enabling: (i) the comparison between SBS and HBS (e.g., when running task-to-resource matching algorithms, in adaptation techniques when replacing human by software or vice versa, and managing trust between HBS and SBS), and (ii) the characterization of mixed units (e.g., analyzing the performance of a mixed unit and resource interaction efficiency within a unit).

Req.4 – *Support a rich set of scheduling algorithms suitable for mixed units*: potentially there will be different ways of using SBS and HBS. In order to support the developer to find the best way to schedule tasks, various algorithms should be provided, based on, for example, client priority, task priority, workload concerns, injecting HBS (e.g. when and where to put an HBS for evaluation of SBS output). In particular, scheduling algorithms for mixed units are crucial because they have not been well developed.

Req.5 – *Support for analysis of NFPs:* several NFPs, such as price, response time, quality of data, and reliability must be monitored and analyzed in order to support (i) performance tradeoff analysis (e.g., price and response time), (ii) structural analysis (e.g., which mixed-unit topology is best for a case, which task routing/delegation algorithms are more efficient, bottlenecks due to dependency relations, resource unit elasticity: unit expansion and shrinkage, etc), failure/misbehavior analysis (e.g. testing of different adaptation algorithms). Such analyses are crucial for the developers of SEA in evaluating the cost of their applications and in decision-making on how to use resources and how to adapt the applications.

4   The Hybrid Simulation Framework

4.1   Architectural Overview

Figure 1 shows our proposed framework. *The Resource Unit Information Manager* acts like a repository for all existing resources. This component is utilized by the *Broker* for selecting the most appropriate resource/s for a given task. *The Broker* contains (hybrid) task-to-resource matching algorithms and ranking algorithms that are utilized for resource selection and/or composition. Thus, *The Broker* is associated with Req.1 discussed in section 3, because appropriate task specification is a prerequisite for developing matching algorithms to select (and/or rank) individual resources or hybrid-resource composite units for job execution. The output of the Broker can be a single resource, a (ranked) list of individual resources, a composite unit or a (ranked) list of composite units.

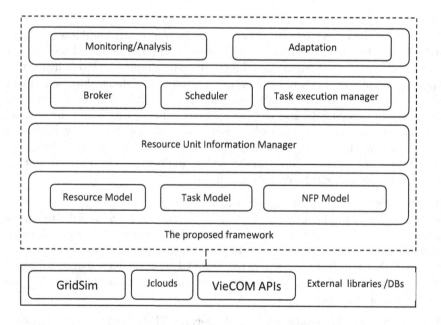

Fig. 1. The conceptual model of the proposed simulation framework

The Broker gives the *Scheduler* the list of appropriate resources for each client's tasks. The Scheduler's purpose is to enable running different scheduling algorithms (centralized/decentralized) and investigating which of them perform better for individual or composite compute units. It is our component for fulfilling Req.4. The *Execution Manager* maintains and manages the state of the application's tasks and their status. It may also be used to aggregate subtask results. The *Monitoring and Analysis* component monitors and stores information in a knowledge base about individual and composite resource performance, based on different NFPs. This component is responsible for Req.5, namely the support for NFP analysis. The *Adaptation* component utilizes information from the *Monitoring and Analysis* component, for optimization purposes. It runs adaptation and optimization functions which are used to communicate with the broker to instruct it to select new resource/s if needed, e.g., for reconfiguring the composite unit, and/or with the scheduler, to instruct it to reschedule the failed tasks. Figure 2 describes interactions among components in our framework.

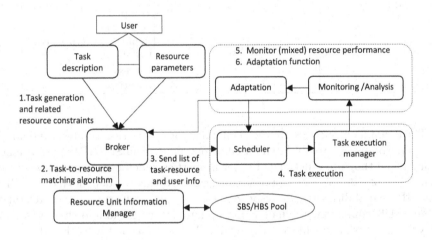

Fig. 2. Component interaction overview

4.2   Implementation

For the implementation of our framework we use the Java based GridSim toolkit[3] and build our own HBS features. Even though GridSim is primarily intended for simulation of Grid environments, several features of GridSim can be reused for modeling and executing SBS and for the development of HBS scheduling and description. Furthermore, we are integrating existing Cloud APIs, such as JClouds[2] to allow us to obtain real-world machine-based resources in different clouds. In addition, we are also integrating VieCOM APIs which are developed for accessing hybrid SBS and HBS [9].

---

[2] http://www.jclouds.org

4.3   Task and SBS/HBS Models

Preliminarily, we model both SBS and HBS task object types with the following properties: task input length, output length, price, start time, finish time, status. We model a resource by associating it with NFPs. NFPs can be static and dynamic. Table 1 describes the main NFPs in our model.

Table 1. Main NFPs for SBS and HBS

Resource Type	Static properties	Dynamic properties
SBS	Name Service Type/Architecture/OS Price Location	Availability Workload Rank Reliability Success Rate
HBS	Name Price	Availability Skill Competency Workload Reputation/Trust Score Reliability Success Rate Location

The dynamic properties are those intended for monitoring, analysis and adaptation purposes and are updated based on outcomes from SBS/HBS performance monitoring; they are functions of other properties which can be both static and dynamic. For example, the response time, can be defined as depended on the SBS and HBS capabilities respectively (e.g.,underlying resource architecture-static, human skill/competency-dynamic and updatable) workload and the tasks complexity (e.g., task input file length); availability depends on the workload and the resource's response time; the SBS/HBS success rate is defined as the number of successfully completed tasks over all assigned tasks etc. Properties such as skill, competency/skill level for HBS are responsible for satisfying Req.2, namely the soft constraints for HBS.

4.4   Scheduling Tasks

Tasks can be scheduled using a set of available algorithms (each as a plugin) for individual and composite compute units. Scheduling would take into account two-level priorities: task based and user based. This is an additional reason why the scheduler is separated from the broker. A matching algorithm can return a list of users and their associated tasks and appropriate resources, while the scheduling algorithms can be developed to take into account task and user priorities (among other factors). The design of our framework allows the integration of SBS-related, HBS-related and mixed-units related scheduling algorithms.

Appart from resource lock-in task scheduling algorithms, we are interested in developing algorithms which could enable SBS/HBS task delegation and routing capabilities even after a task is already assigned to them, e.g., task stealing algorithms.

4.5 Monitoring

When tasks are executed, monitoring events will be captured from the *Task Execution Manager* in order to determine NFPs, such as response time and failure. The Task Execution Manager will store the Task ID, their requirements, the resources to which the tasks are assigned and periodically record the task state. This state information will be sent to the Monitor. The monitoring algorithm will periodically check resource states so that if a resource has failed it can send this information to an adaptation algorithm. In addition, output from monitoring events can be used for storing feedback information from both clients and resources. Some usage examples of this feedback information include scenarios of rating and trust-based analysis. The knowledge base can be additionally used for building refined resource-selection algorithms, so they include not only resource properties but also historical performance data. For example, if there is a composite task executed by a composite unit, after job completion, a voting strategy can be implemented so that each HBS in the composition can give feedback, about the cooperation efficiency within it. This data, that shows the motivation of an individual unit to work within the same composition again, can be used as an additional efficiency or team-based trust metric for a composite-unit selection algorithm.

5   Discussion on the Framework's Usefulness

In this section, we describe a scenario that illustrates the usefulness of the simulation framework we propose. Figure 3 describes a case that shows the use of simulation to create and analyze what-if scenarios of injecting humans for evaluating quality of data (QoD) in different steps of a scientific-simulation workflow. Some of the reasons why we need HBS in long-running large resource-consuming scientific-simulation workflows are: 1) intermediate quality of result (QoR) evaluation and analysis, so as to assess if the output of SBS in a certain step is correct and appropriate to be used as input for the next step; 2) QoR enhancement by editing intermediate results (depending on the type of the simulation); 3) final QoR evaluation and analysis to check if the simulation result makes sense or not. These types of human computation are needed for enhancing the workflow execution and for optimizing the cost of compute resources, storage and people spent in long-running simulations. For example depending on the HBS evaluation, tasks in the workflow can be restarted on the same resource, stopped altogether to be rescheduled to a different resource, and the simulation can be set to restart from a few-tasks back. Thus, the simulation framework could support the developer to plan and optimize resources for real scientific simulation

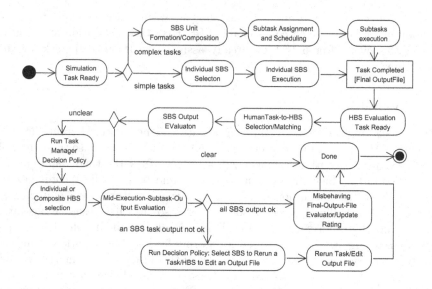

Fig. 3. Human-in-the-loop scenario

workflows. Figure 3 shows a specific case where an HBS is selected to evaluate the final QoR only after all tasks of the simulation are executed. In the case this HBS evaluates a bad result, a notification is sent to the task manager which can run a decision-policy about which task's output within the workflow should be chosen for QoR evaluation. For each of the chosen tasks an appropriate HBS is selected to inspect task results. If a task result within the workflow is evaluated as wrong the task manager is notified,so it can decide whether to reschedule the specific task on the same SBS, select another SBS and assign the task to it or select an HBS to edit the output file. If all the selected HBS for evaluating QoR of intermediary results indicate that task results are correct it means that the initial HBS selected for the final SBS QoR output evaluation is misbehaving and malicious, hence its trustworthiness and rating scores are updated.

Some of the capabilities, specific to this scenario, that our simulation framework design supports, are:

- Creating human tasks, the input data of which is the SBS output;
- Providing decision-making algorithms for injecting HBS to conduct result analysis or editing;
- Selecting the most appropriate resource for QoR evaluation;
- Monitoring and testing with updating HBS profile and performance based information.

More specifically, the framework could support different factors influencing decision-making, e.g., results from conducting tradeoff analysis of cost/QoD versus time, depending on the requirements of the tasks. Social choice theory research results could be integrated into the framework to support the selection of voting schemes which should be employed when intermediate HBS evaluators are used to evaluate and correct SBS output, to decide on the correctness of a final QoR evaluators assessment (e.g., to simulate the case when a final QoR HBS evaluator has assessed the final result to be incorrect and thus other HBS evaluators are injected after each SBS task when the same workflow is simulated anew).

6 Conclusions and Future Work

In this paper we present a simulation framework to support research on the development of socially-enhanced applications that need both software-based and human-based services. We have described an overview of the conceptual design of our framework discussing the need and use of each component. Thus, we have shown the need to have a hybrid simulation framework and the requirements that the framework needs to fulfill. As we are in the early stages of development, our future work concentrates on further implementation of the simulation framework with a particular focus on both centralized and decentralized mixed resource scheduling algorithms.

References

1. Bermbach, D., Kern, R., Wichmann, P., Rath, S., Zirpins, C.: An extendable toolkit for managing quality of human-based electronic services. In: Human Computation. Volume WS-11-11 of AAAI Workshops. AAAI (2011)
2. Bernstein, M.S., Little, G., Miller, R.C., Hartmann, B., Ackerman, M.S., Karger, D.R., Crowell, D., Panovich, K., Ma, C.: Soylent: A word processor with a crowd inside. In: Proc. UIST 2010 (2010)
3. Buyya, R., Murshed, M.: Gridsim: A toolkit for the modeling and simulation of distributed resource management and scheduling for grid computing. Concurrency and Computation: Practice and Experience (CCPE) 14(13), 1175–1220 (2002)
4. Calheiros, R.N., Ranjan, R., Rose, C.A.F.D., Buyya, R.: Cloudsim: A novel framework for modeling and simulation of cloud computing infrastructures and services. CoRR abs/0903.2525 (2009)
5. Chen, K.T., Wu, C.C., Chang, Y.C., Lei, C.L.: A crowdsourceable qoe evaluation framework for multimedia content. In: Proceedings of the 17th ACM International Conference on Multimedia, MM 2009, pp. 491–500. ACM, New York (2009)
6. Paolacci, G., Chandler, J., Ipeirotis, P.G.: Running experiments on amazon mechanical turk. Judgment and Decision Making 5(5), 411–419 (2010)
7. Schall, D., Truong, H.L., Dustdar, S.: Unifying human and software services in web-scale collaborations. IEEE Internet Computing 12, 62–68 (2008)
8. Shahaf, D., Horvitz, E.: Generalized task markets for human and machine computation. In: Fox, M., Poole, D. (eds.) AAAI. AAAI Press (2010)
9. Truong, H.L., Dustdar, S., Bhattacharya, K.: Programming hybrid services in the cloud. In: 10th International Conference on Service-oriented Computing (ICSOC 2012), Shanghai, China, Novemebr 12-16 (2012)
10. von Ahn, L.: Human Computation. PhD thesis, School of Computer Science, Carnegie Mellon University (2005)

Analyzing Tie-Strength across Different Media

Nils Jeners[1], Petru Nicolaescu[1], and Wolfgang Prinz[2]

[1] RWTH Aachen University, Informatik V, Aachen, Germany
{nils.jeners,petru.nicolaescu}@rwth-aachen.de
[2] Fraunhofer FIT, Sankt Augustin, Germany
wolfgang.prinz@fit.fraunhofer.de

Abstract. Human interactions are becoming more and more important in computer systems. The interactions can be classified according to predefined rules, based on the assumption that relations between humans differ greatly. The tie-strength notion is used throughout the social sciences literature in order to denote this classification. The present paper researches how the tie-strength between two persons can be computed automatically by applying structural data from different sources, e.g. email, shared workspaces. This data can provide a virtual copy of the ego-centric network of a user and therefore be utilized for social intelligent computing.

Keywords: Social media, social networks, email, shared workspaces, relationship modeling, tie-strength, sns.

1   Introduction

The basis for social intelligent computing is to understand human interactions, how communication and collaboration works. With the emergence and spreading of IT systems, the communication channels evolved rapidly. There are different types of communication mechanisms and many applications that support the communication, collaboration and coordination between people. Different channels such as telephone, email, social applications, shared workspaces, blogs, and forums are used nowadays to exchange professional and personal information. The user base for many of these systems is very large and is still growing rapidly.

There is a lot research in particular systems (such as social networking: Facebook [1], Twitter [2]; email [3], [4]; instant messaging and chat systems [5]; and shared workspace applications [6]) that are specialized in offering stable and well-designed functionalities (e.g., feeds, handling emails, instant messaging, handling video and image media, etc.). Providing unification of those different services have now started. However, there are still gaps containing important and useful aspects that should be considered in this regard.

Relationships between humans are the core of social systems. Their type differs across environments and depending on the people involved in a relationship. In the technical comprehension of this paper, two people have a relationship if they are exchanging information. Measuring the relationship intensity leads to the tie-strength

P. Herrero et al. (Eds.): OTM 2012 Workshops, LNCS 7567, pp. 554–563, 2012.

[7], the term that describes the mutual closeness between two people. Many different applications are used for communication or collaboration, but they all share some similarities, such as a sender, receiver and a message. Such applications allow humans to build relationships implicitly by communication or explicitly by asking for friendship. With the exchange of information or emotions, we build our own egocentric social network, embedded within other bigger networks.

The various channels used for social interactions contain much more data than the actual sender, receiver and the message, e.g. structural information (tags, priority). By managing this data and connecting it to a user interface in order to visualize it, it would be possible to support users in their communication and cooperation and increase the productivity. Our approach helps to understand the social environment of a user to form social intelligent user interfaces. The presented prototype monitors different communication channels, such as email and a shared workspace system, mines the gathered data and presents the results in an understandable and intuitive format.

The benefits that result from measuring the relation between persons (tie-strength) are multiple, such as:

1. Provide social intelligent user interfaces
2. Assessing personal or work relations
3. Identifying communication weaknesses between persons.
4. Identifying communities of practice.
5. Improving the media selection based on the media related tie-strength.

Considering the above mentioned facts, we build an ego-centric social network by identifying and weighting the most important communication factors of the media channels used by a person. The resulted information can be analyzed and the results containing the communication actors relevant to the person can be displayed in a simple and meaningful way. In order to better explore users' preferences and opinions on this particular topic, a questionnaire and user interviews were conducted. Moreover, for proving and evaluating the ideas described, a user-oriented software system has been designed and implemented.

2   Background and Related Work

The definition of a relation can be seen as an exchange of information between two people. A relation is grounded on communication and can have a certain quality [7]. Tie-strength can be defined as the tightness (intensity) of that relation. Examples of strong ties are close friends and examples of weak ties are acquaintances or coworkers which do not work on the same project.

The measuring of relations or the quantification of tie-strength is a question that has already attracted much research [8] [9] [10] [11] [12] [13] [14]. Hanneman and Riddle [15] presented scales of relation measurement: Binary measures, multiple-category nominal measures (e.g., colleague, business relation, husband, friend, etc.), grouped ordinal measures (which can be encoded as 1, -1 and 0), full-rank ordinal measures, interval measures.

Choosing an interval measure appears to be appropriate for a scenario, based on computers and multiple media channels. Granovetter [7] proposed four dimensions of tie-strength: amount of time, intimacy, intensity and reciprocal services. He later extended the list by factors such as network topology, emotional support, education, race, and gender, etc. [16]. Gilbert and Karahalios [1] give a strong indication that in practice the interaction frequency, recentness of communication and communication reciprocity can accurately determine the tie-strength. The *frequency* of contacts is the number of the interactions between two people in a specific period of time. Granovetter proposes a scale from "often" as being at least twice a week, to "rarely", representing less than once per year. "Occasionally" is meant to be between the two. A high degree of *frequency* leads to a higher tie-strength. *Reciprocity* refers to the direction of the communication. This can be a one-way communication with one sender and one receiver, or a two-way communication where the sender and receiver alternate mutually. A high degree of *reciprocity* leads to a higher tie-strength. *Recentness* means the age of the last exchanged message. A high degree of *recentness* leads to a higher tie-strength.

Shared workspaces research concerning social network data analysis is mostly dealing with the objects present in one's workspace and with people collaborating on the objects. Such an approach is presented in the paper of Nasirifard et al. [6], treating the extraction of an object-centric and a user-centric social network using the log files of a shared workspace system. The user-centric social network is computed by pairing the contacts which interact upon the same object. After building the network, the edges are weighted in order to determine the *CooperationIndex* between the users.

The background and related work of this field shows us how versatile the dimensions of tie-strength are. With the help of previous research we could apply the compatible dimensions to our given scenario. *Frequency*, *recentness* and *reciprocity* appear in every communication and cooperation media, so that a model can easily be adapted to heterogeneous media channels. Furthermore we have seen how networks are extracted from the various communication channels and how to overcome technical drawbacks. Therefore we could learn from existing research to go further and develop a new model.

3   Conceptual Model

In order to compute the interaction strength, a formalization of the notions involved was needed to establish the most determinant factors and to ease data handling. The mathematical framework can be used by integrated new media channels that might be added to the model to compute tie-strength.

In the following we will describe the final model with its components:

- $C = \{c_1, c_2, ..., c_n\}$ is denoted as the set of contacts that will be assigned to a user u.
- $M = \{m_1, m_2, m_3\}$ is denoted as the set of media channels.
- Each media channel is characterized by one or more objects. The objects are part of media channels.

- $O_{m_i} = \{o_1, o_2, \ldots, o_p\}$ is denoted as the set of objects of medium $m_i \in M$.
- Objects are the result of actions of persons. These actions determine the properties characteristic to each object and can be seen as events. Examples of different types of events are: incoming emails, uploaded documents etc.
- $E_{m_i} = \{e_1, e_2, \ldots, e_r\}$ is denoted as the set of events of medium $m_i \in M$. The importance of an event has been considered to be time dependent. Therefore, the impact value v of one event from medium m at time t can be described as:

$$v_m(t) = \lfloor v_m(0) * f(t) \rfloor,$$

where $v_m(0)$ is the initial value of the event on medium m and $f(t)$ is the aging function which results an aging factor at a given time t.
- Based upon the events occurring between two or more contacts on the same object, relations can be described. Relations are characterized by attributes such as strength (which we want to determine). Two contacts $(p_1; p_2)$ are considered to be in a relation if at any time t, at least one event took place on the same object, involving p_1 and p_2.

The tie-strength (which is also referred to the interaction or relation strength), is considered to be a combination of various measurable properties of the events and objects exchanged using different electronic media channels and which defines the intensity of a certain type of relation between two persons. In this context, we study the various types of relations in daily life by analyzing the available electronic actions that a person initiates with one or more of his contacts. As we could see in the theoretical notions exposed, the tie-strength can be predicted in some extent. The questions which need to be answered are: How can the analysis of online interactions and their environment influence the tie-strength? Which are the major indices to measure the tie-strength and how are the indices mapped to the features of depicted media channel? The properties considered in this computation, as well as more information about the procedures used for each media channel that was taken into consideration will be detailed in the following.

Because computing the tie-strength is the main focus of this paper, the relations component plays a very important role in the overall architecture of the AMICIS system. Analysis has been performed in order to identify the best way in which the overall strength can be computed. The final approach, taken after analyzing different options (i.e., linear vs. non-linear equations), was chosen in the form of a linear equation, the overall tie-strength being the sum of the individual tie-strengths computed for each media channel. The individual tie-strength components are then computed as the weighted sum of the relevant attributes specific to each media channel. Moreover, as it can be observed in the equation below, the tie-strength is a function dependent on time, its value decreasing with the time passing. Therefore, the overall tie-strength is considered to be the sum of the calculated tie-strength of each media with a certain aging effect.

3.1   Email

The computation of the individual tie-strength for email was done by identifying the influential properties of emails and applying them as factors of the tie-strength model. In order to compute a value which represents the tie-strength between two people, the first step is to identify the communication partners and then calculate the tie-strength between them. The relations in email can directly be deduced from the fields *from, to, cc* (and *bcc*). This makes eight possible (not-directed) relation types: *from*-{*to, cc, bcc*}, *to*-{*to, cc, bcc*}, and *cc*-{*cc, bcc*}.

For the calculation of the tie-strength, we assume that:

- Recent emails have a greater significance than older emails (*date*).
- The *direction* of email communication can be unidirectional (one-way) or bidirectional (two-way). Bidirectional emails reflect a higher importance. Unidirectional emails might be noise, e.g. newsletters and notification mails.
- Email *threads* are emails between two or more people with the same subject. Longer *threads* reflect a higher degree of interest.
- The total *number of emails* exchanged between two people in a certain period of time may reflect a strong relation between the two people.
- The lack of communication between two people for a longer period of time hint to a weakening of the relation or to a weak tie in general.

3.2   Shared Workspace

For our analysis we used a shared workspace system. It contains of different types of information such as documents, calendar, URLs, threaded discussions, and member profiles. The content is organized in a folder hierarchy, which can be used to grant access to a specific group of people. A typical example for such a shared workspace is the BSCW system [17].

The relations of a shared workspace system can be deduced by transforming the document-centric network in a people-centric one [6]. The three roles are depending on events respectively activities (*write, read*) on a certain object. *Creator, modifier,* and *reader* perform activities with an object and thus they have a relation to the other actors of this object.

For the calculation of tie-strength for the BSCW system, we assume that:

- A recent interaction on an object has greater significance than older ones (*date*).
- The *direction* indicator can range from non-directional (*read-read*), over unidirectional (*write-read*) to bidirectional (*write-write*). Bidirectional interactions lead to collaboration and reflect a higher degree of involvement, e.g. a direct work relation such as colleague-colleague relation within a team or a supervisor-subordinate relation.
- The *frequency* is the total number of events in a certain period of time of a certain document. A high frequency reflects a strong relation between the users.

- The lack of events respectively actions on an object for a longer period of time may hint that the object has become obsolete, i.e. the collaboration has stopped or rather paused. Therefore it points to a weak tie between the collaborators.

The data used in order to unify different media channels has been analyzed in order to find a model that would correspond to unifying social relationship data from various sources.

The main sources are represented each by an entity with the main attributes relevant to the tie-strength extraction. The objects belonging to each of the sources (e.g., email, BSCW document, etc.) determine an event. An event involves a relation between two contacts and it is characterized by a strength (which we have to determine). The relation between the contacts is directed, having an emitter and a receiver, depending on the initiator of the event and on its target. Events between other contacts are also computed, for a good overview of the relation network which is linked to the user. The contacts are extracted from the event's receiver/emitter address.

4   Prototype

The prototype (AMICIS – A Multisource social Interaction and Communication analysIStool) was implemented as a local browser-based application. The system imports the data from the provided user accounts (i.e., email and BSCW) and stores all occurred events after a specific date (which was chosen by the user as a starting point) for the data retrieval. The contacts of the user and the egocentric social network associated are computed during this process. When the data retrieval is completed, the tie-strength between each contact and the user of the application is computed. The initial import is only required at the first start of the application. The system updates after a certain time interval: New events are gathered, and the tie-strength values are updated. If no new events appear, the tie-strength values are also automatically updated, in order to reflect the time decay feature of the events.

The data can be visualized in several ways. A table containing the contacts ordered decreasingly according to the tie-strength is displayed on the top of the main page. The user is able to analyze the topmost contacts in terms of tie-strength. The tie-strength is also presented in a unified view for all the contacts from the different sources, separate views for each data source being also available. The social network can be visualized in a concentric circle view, the user being represented in the center and its contacts being spread around the user as bubbles in circles with the distance to the center and distinct diameter proportional to the tie-strength value (cf. [18]).

The tie-strength can be also presented without the time decay influence, such that the users can better differentiate between the contacts presented in the two settings and thus obtain more accurate results when evaluating the system.

The tie-strength between the user and its individual contacts is represented using a timeline feature, in which the events with the respective contact are represented with their value on a time axis. The value which is displayed is the current value at the time of the visualization, therefore both the event importance and the time decay of the events can be observed. Also, more than one contact can be added to the timeline at the same time, making it easy to compare the tie-strength between contacts as it can be seen in Figure 1.

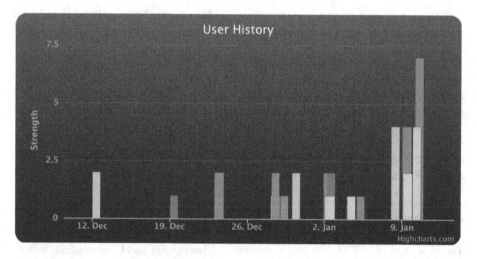

Fig. 1. Screenshot of the tie-strength of certain contacts (one color stands for one person; five people belonging to a group)

5   Evaluation

The user evaluation has been conducted during several days, with different users, the majority being students and researchers. A total number of eleven users have participated in the final evaluation, half of them having completed also the user studies performed in earlier stages of the project.

The objectives of the user evaluation were to test the usability of the AMICIS system, to find out how accurate the discovered relations are. Further we wanted to find out the benefits of such a tool, gather missing features and test the percentage of noise in the discovered relations. It was important to establish whether this tool could help, respectively assist the collaboration and communication.

In order to cover all the above mentioned aspects, the user evaluation was performed using a semi-structured interview performed in two stages. The first part was conducted before the actual usage of the tool. The second part was performed after the tool has been used. A questionnaire with open as well as closed questions regarding different objectives of the project was used. In the first part of the interview, we requested information about the general usage of the source channels in the social context, i.e. number of messages received per day, estimation of the number of contacts in the network, etc. After this step, the users were given a set of instructions to use the system. After the users accomplished the given tasks, they were free to use the tool without any specific tasks.

The relations discovered were considered accurate by 60% and very accurate by 40% of the users. The computation of the results with the time decay feature considered, were as expected for 50% of the users. This corresponds to the requirement study that indicated difficulties in finding a good decay function. The other 50% of the users, found the presented relations relevant, but they expected a bigger amount of relations to be present with contacts to whom they felt very close, but with whom they did not talk for a longer period of time. In general, the closest relations were accurate, but the older relations were harder to classify by the users. The users for which an exact match was not found used some other communication channels in their daily interactions (instant messaging, communication features from social network applications). 90% of the users considered that the decay of the relations with the time passing feature is relevant. 90% of the users appreciated the recommendation which helps them to see which relations need reinforcement. The recommended contacts initially had a relatively strong tie, but a lower value recently.

80% of the users appreciated the automatic discovery of the relation strength with their contacts as well as the unified view of all their relations in one place. 60% of the users would use the AMICIS system for a longer period of time and 50% of the users would use the AMICIS system in order to help them organize their contacts.

Some of the users considered that the relations presented initially had a high level of noise. Most of them considered that the blacklist feature is very good and appropriate in removing the noise, but they also wanted a feature for the automatic removal of only incoming edges from the relation graph. Therefore a modification was made to the AMICIS system and a button has been added for the automatic removal of just incoming links. This feature was appreciated by the users from the next evaluation sessions; however it also blacklisted relevant contacts, for which the events initiated by the user were not present in the history, because they were outside the considered time interval for the initial import.

All in all, we consider that based on the model presented, such a tool can successfully identify and compute the tie strength with a high degree of accuracy and with real benefits to the users. Some possible improvements, the conclusions of this work and the research issues which we consider remaining open, are presented in the section below.

6   Conclusion and Outlook

The present paper addresses questions regarding the methods which can be used in order to determine the tie-strength for individual users across different media. The unification of different media channels in influencing the social context in which the users interact has been studied, as well as the indicators and the practices which can influence the relation strength. Based on those attributes or indicators, the tie-strength has been finally computed.

As the evaluation results have shown, more sources should be analyzed for obtaining better approximations of the tie-strength for individual users. Because the users have very different behaviors when coming to the use of online applications for interacting with other people, resulting from differences in taste, habit, environment, popularity, needs, etc., the more data sources are integrated into the system, the more interactions may be analyzed. Therefore, by applying this, a more accurate computation of the relation strength and a better coverage of the relations may be achieved.

Another important point which should be further developed is that even though the system proposes to investigate the relation strength as its results from the online interactions of an individual user, the emotional intensity should be also considered in measuring the tie-strength. The time variable and the relation frequency may determine an important part of the relation strength, but the affective component has also a big influence in the user perception. A semantic analysis of the contents of the events exchanged, through tag extraction and language pattern analysis would be an important step in the direction of measuring the affective importance of events.

The users have hinted in the evaluation process that detection of groups and contextual computations of relation intensity (e.g., the relations and their strength in university groups, between the participants at a workshop or conference, between friends, etc.) would also improve the user experience and the quality of recommendations the system can provide.

This paper contributes a new model which incorporates two heterogeneous media channels. One communication system (email) and one cooperation system (BSCW) are harmonized in terms of tie-strength. Surprisingly for the users the two systems lead to two different egocentric networks which intersect in only single contacts. From this fact we can deduce that it is necessary to consider all used media to cover the whole network of one person. Therefore we are planning to incorporate two more classes of applications such as social networking sites and instant messaging systems. From our user study we learned that these two classes cover mainly private and leisure communication. But nevertheless they are important for the user.

We have tried to bridge the existing research gaps conducted for studying interpersonal relations in daily life (offline) and the studies on the relations which are established and/or maintained using online systems. After studying the attributes considered in measuring the relation strength in the literature, which proved to be quite different across different studies, the paper presents a series of attributes which proved to be most relevant in on-line tie-strength analysis. Here, the approach was to consider individual indicators suitable for each media channel and to provide the general model capable of unifying the values coming from the individual systems, in order to obtain one value for the relation strength.

Acknowledgments. This work is partly supported by the European Commission through the Seventh Framework Programme for Research and Technological Development (GRANATUM project).

References

1. Gilbert, E., Karahalios, K.: Predicting tie-strength with social media. In: Proceedings of the 27th International Conference on Human Factors in Computing Systems (CHI 2009), pp. 211–220. ACM, New York (2009)
2. Gilbert, E.: Predicting tie-strength in a new medium. In: Proceedings of the ACM 2012 Conference on Computer Supported Cooperative Work (CSCW 2012), pp. 1047–1056. ACM, New York (2012)
3. Bird, C., Gourley, A., Devanbu, P.T., Gertz, M., Swaminathan, A.: Mining email social networks. In: Proceedings of the International Workshop on Mining Software Repositories, Shanghai (2006)
4. Culotta, A., Bekkerman, R., McCallum, A.: Extracting Social Networks and Contact Information from Email and the Web. In: Proceedings of CEAS-1 (2004)
5. Resig, J., Dawara, S., Homan, C.M., Teredesai, A.: Extracting social networks from instant messaging populations. In: Proc. of the 7th ACM SIGKDD Workshop on Link KDD (2004)
6. Nasirifard, P., Peristeras, V., Hayes, C., Decker, S.: Extracting and Utilizing Social Networks from Log Files of Shared Workspaces. In: Camarinha-Matos, L.M., Paraskakis, I., Afsarmanesh, H. (eds.) PRO-VE 2009. IFIP AICT, vol. 307, pp. 643–650. Springer, Heidelberg (2009)
7. Granovetter, M.: The Strength of Weak Ties. American Journal of Sociology 78(6), 1360–1380 (1973)
8. Feld, S.: The Focused Organization of Social Ties. American Journal of Sociology 86(5), 1015–1035 (1981)
9. Marsden, P.V., Campbell, K.E.: Measuring Tie-strength. Social Forces 63(2), 482–501 (1984)
10. Cummings, J., Kiesler, S.: Who Works with Whom? Collaborative Tie-strength in Distributed Interdisciplinary Projects. In: Proceedings of the 3rd International e-Social Science Conference, Ann Arbor, Michigan, October 7-9 (2007)
11. Burt, R.: Structural Holes: The Social Structure of Competition. Harvard University Press (1995)
12. Roth, M., Flysher, G., Matias, Y., Leichtberg, A., Merom, R.: Suggesting Friends Using the Implicit Social Graph Categories and Subject Descriptors. Human Factors 371(9620), 233–241 (2010)
13. Ting, I.-H., Wu, H.-J., Chang, P.-S.: Analyzing Multi-source Social Data for Extracting and Mining Social Networks. In: 2009 International Conference on Computational Science and Engineering, vol. 4, pp. 815–820. IEEE (2009)
14. Haythornthwaite, C.: The strength and the impact of new media. In: Proceedings of the 34th Annual Hawaii International Conference on System Sciences, January 3-6, p. 10 (2001)
15. Hanneman, R.A., Riddle, M.: Introduction to Social Network Methods. Network, University of California, vol. 46, pp. 2890–2896 (2005)
16. Granovetter, M.: The Strength of Weak Ties: A Network Theory Revisited. In: Marsden, P.V., Lin, N. (eds.) Sociological Theory, vol. 1, pp. 201–233. John Wiley & Sons (1983)
17. Appelt, W.: WWW Based Collaboration with the BSCW System. In: Bartosek, M., Tel, G., Pavelka, J. (eds.) SOFSEM 1999. LNCS, vol. 1725, p. 66. Springer, Heidelberg (1999)
18. Erickson, T., Smith, D.N., Kellogg, W.A., Laff, M.R., Richards, J.T., Bradner, E.: Socially translucent systems: Social proxies, persistent conversation and the design of 'Babble.' In: Human Factors in Computing Systems: The Proceedings of CHI 1999. ACM Press (1999)

Internet of Future Enabling Social Network of Things

Moacyr Martucci Junior and Erica de Paula Dutra

Department of Computer and Digital Systems Engineering (PCS),
Escola Politécnica, Universidade de São Paulo,
Av. Prof. Luciano Gualberto, trav 3, no 158, São Paulo, SP, Brasil
moacyr.martucci@poli.usp.br, epdutra@usp.br

Abstract. Advances in the areas of embedded systems, computing, and networking are leading to an infrastructure composed of millions of heterogeneous devices and services. These devices will not simply convey information but process it in transit, connect peer to peer, and form advanced collaborations. This "Internet of Things" infrastructure must have the interoperability of solution at the communication level, as well as at the service level, has to be ensured across various platforms [1].In this paper we investigate on the potential of combining social and technical networks to collaboratively provide services to both human users and technical systems supported by the Internet of Future (IoF). In the Internet of Things (IoT), things talk and exchange information to realize the vision of future pervasive computing environments. The common physical and social space emerges by the objects' ability to interconnect, not only amongst themselves, but also with the human beings living and working in them. This paper intends to present an architecture and its application.

Keywords: internet of future, pervasive systems and computing, social networks, Internet of Things, ubiquitous communtication.

1   Introduction

Social networks are one of the most discussed topic in any kind of media. Many believe that the subject began with the advent of Facebook [2] and its creator Mark Zuckerberg. But the subject matter and his own records since1954 when J. A. Barnes began using the term systematically to show the patterns of ties, incorporating the concepts traditionally used either by society or by social scientists, well-defined groups (e.g., tribes, families) and social categories (e.g.: gender, ethnic group) .

The "social need" or the necessity to provide event information that we are active or alive, causes, according to a survey [3], 60% of Brazilian Internet interviewed users spend time on the Internet on social networks. Facebook reached the mark of 28 million Brazilian users and 753 million of global users [4].

This social interaction could also integrate elements of our surroundings, which we nominated as things. This would make the elements of everyday life, like our car or house, in members of our social network. It is possible to imagine our car as a virtual entity in our social network, "blogging" a bad humor declaration because its oil needs to be changed.

P. Herrero et al. (Eds.): OTM 2012 Workshops, LNCS 7567, pp. 564–573, 2012.
© Springer-Verlag Berlin Heidelberg 2012

This concept is possible if we consider the emerging Internet of Things. There are a great pool of products and things that are able to inform their status and also its functionality. As example, we have already washing machines twittering when it has done its job or if there is any kind of problem.

The Internet of Things (IoT) is a technological phenomenon originating from innovative developments concepts in information and communication technology associated with, ubiquitous communication, pervasive computing and ambient intelligence[5].

These concepts have a strong impact on the development the IoT. Ubiquitous communication means general ability of objects to communicate (anywhere anytime); pervasive computing means the enhancement of objects with processing power (the environment around becomes the computer); ambient intelligence means objects capability to register changes in the environment and thus actively interact in a typically internal network. Objects that fulfill these requirements are smart objects.

The IoT is defined as the smart objects ability to communicate among each other building networks of things, building the Internet of Things. But it is necessary to address scalability and interoperability requirements of a future IoT. Hence it is particularly important to understand the complete IoT domain model.

This paper aims to demonstrate architecture based on internet of future to fit the concept of IoT, social networks and human interaction. The paper is structured as follows. In Sec. 2, is presented a social networks overview. We introduce, in sec. 3, the discussion about Internet of Future. In sec. 4, we present the conceptual reference model and architecture for IoT based on IoT-A [13]. In Sec. 5 our motivation and idea for combined social networks and IoT is described. We conclude the paper by summarizing the contributions and limitations from the social networks and IoT architecture association and give an outlook on future research in Sec. 6.

2   Social Networks Concepts and Terminologies

To better understand how social networks (SNs) can be integrated with the physical world we need to understand the services provided by current social network platforms. The primary services are as follows: Identity and authorization services; APIs to access and manipulate the social network graph and publish and receive updates; container facilities for hosting third party applications.

All social networks store identity information about their users. This typically includes profile information, privacy settings, and connections with family, friends, colleagues or followers. SNs store content such as messages to each other, updates (e.g. to their "wall" or "tweets"), photos, videos, events, fan pages and other objects. All social networks support authentication to prove user identity. In some cases third party sites can use a SN authentication service as an identity provider. In the structure of SNs, social actors are characterized more by their relationships than by their attributes (gender, age, social class). These relationships have a variable density and some actors can occupy more central positions than others. In the market there are several tools available for development and social networking intersection. But one of the most interesting is Google's OpenSocial [18] [19].

OpenSocial is a set of APIs for building social applications that run on the web. OpenSocial's goal is to make more apps available to more users, by providing a common API that can be used in many different contexts. Developers can create applications, using standard JavaScript and HTML, that run on social websites that have implemented the OpenSocial APIs. These websites, known as OpenSocial containers, allow developers to access their social information; in return they receive a large suite of applications for their users.

The OpenSocial APIs expose methods for accessing information about people, their friends, and their data, within the context of a container. This means that when running an application on Orkut, we will be interacting with your Orkut friends, while running the same application on MySpace lets you interact with your MySpace friends. In figure 1 shows an example to see how to connect the OpenSocial APIs to an application layer.

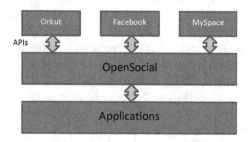

Fig. 1. Social Network connecting application

3   Internet of Future and Associations

The Internet, as we know, connects people, data and services, was conceived about 40 years ago. Since then has constantly evolved in transformation [7]. According to O'REILLY [8], was observed a sea transition from the "information sharing", known as Web 1.0, to the model of "contribution"- known as Web 2.0. For example, the users (people) in Web 2.0 can generate content across networks social. In the coming years, we have the expectation of a transition to a new collaborative model, called Web 3.0. In this model people, machines and objects can collaborate.

We can call this new environment as the Internet of the Future (IoF). In this environment, software solutions must adapt to the needs of their users, within the open, decentralized and dynamic without losing scalability and performance.

According to Papadimitrou [10], the IoF will support four key pillars, as well as physical infrastructure network: Through the Internet and people (Internet By and For People); Internet Content and Knowledge (Internet and Knowledge of Contents); IoT (Internet of Things); IoS (Internet of Services).

The term "Internet By and For the People" refers to the fact that the Internet of Future seeks to meet the growing demand from its main users, e.g., people. It will consolidate the collaborative model of Web 2.0, eliminating current barriers between suppliers and consumers of information.

The term "Internet Content and Knowledge" refers to the dissemination of local and global knowledge, through the generation of content that can be read or processed by people and mostly by machines. On the Web 3.0 generation, storage and process are made by machines. They use semantic annotations on all content generated. Machines or/and people will allow the exploration of a large volume of data, transforming it into useful information to the end user.

4   IoT Abstraction and Architecture Reference Model

According with the European Future Internet Portal [12], IoT has to ensure the interoperability of solutions at the communication level across various platforms. This motivates the creation of a reference model to IoT domain in order to promote a common understanding and businesses that want to create their own compliant IoT solutions. It also should be supported by a reference architecture that describes essential building blocks defining security, privacy, performance, and similar needs. Interfaces should be standardized and best practices (in terms of functionality and information) usage need to be provided.

The IoT-A project [13] is an architectural reference model for the interoperability of IoT systems, outlining principles and guidelines for technical design of its protocols, interfaces, and algorithms. This architectural reference model promotes a common understanding of the IoT domain as a top-level description and will be used to the basis architecture of this work. This model starts with a discourse that identifies abstract quality concepts that have to be taken into account for the realization of IoT systems. The domain model addresses to the discussion about heterogeneity, interoperability, scalability, manageability, mobility, security, reliability and ways to guarantee evolution.

The information model specifies the data semantics of the domain model and the communication model addresses high level communication paradigms pertinent to the IoT domain.

To add electronic devices to an IoT architecture and give them "life", we must carefully control and set all the requirements to transform them in a virtual entity (VE). But to do that, at first, is necessary to set all device connectivity and the communication, adjust the service orchestration and prepare the application layer to the interface with the world.

The associated middleware is still an open issue for complex, heterogeneous, distributed sensor-actor systems in the field of pervasive computing. The IoT-A presents [12][13] a poll of protocols, and techniques where is possible to detail the communication and interactions machine to machine (M2M). But the focus of this document is to present the reference architecture to the proposed problem.

In figure 2 we have the functional requirements of the reference architecture described in seven functionality groups as follow:

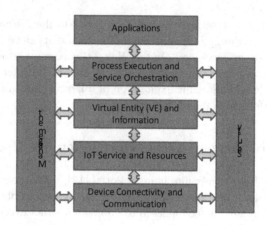

Fig. 2. Detailed view view of the IoT reference architecture [1]

- Applications – describes the functionalities provided by applications built on the top of the architecture.
- Process Execution and service orchestration – organizes the IoT resources. It is common to use APIs which works with the application layer.
- Virtual entity (VE) and information - organize the information exchanged by the physical entities, transforming in services all the output that those entities are plugged on.
- IoT service and resource – in this group is possible to manage all the IoT service resolution, understand and access its history and set the controls to manage the device.
- Device connectivity and communication – provides a set of methods and primitives for device connectivity and communication. It is possible to trace the device and associate its tag. This group also has a communication trigger and a unified communication layer to guarantee the device input/output.
- Management – all the groups above must have an external intervention which includes QoS, rules and device sets.
- Security – is one of the critical issues from the proposed architecture. There are a great heterogeneity of communication technologies, including security protocols and solutions. To guarantee the security of the device and user it must be addressed the problem by separation of high heterogeneity and demanding constraints from the more homogeneous domain. It includes authority sets (certification, authentication, and trust).

5   IoT Internet of Future to Enable the IoT Social Network

The Internet of future has its principle based on three macro dimensions. One of this dimensions is the Functional dimension which describes a static internet with unstructured information or web services working into two ways of requesting information with a defined protocol. The other is the Social dimension which includes service communities and on line communities characterizing the Web 2.0. Finally we have the Semantic dimension with machines processing information including an intelligent service discovery with interoperation. Indeed it leads to the Web 3.0 principle [20].

Simple mechanisms like OpenSocial, people can co-operate in building online communities around services. Simultaneously, such services could interoperate with one another to offer more sophisticated functionalities to the users in a largely automated way.

In a future vision, services will be combined in increasingly complex mash-ups that offer functions to support users both at home and work, helping them to perform their daily activities, transforming de devices in entities capable to interact at the social network layer.

By incorporating human interaction and cooperation into a comprehensive fashion, tasks such as service ranking and mediation, that would otherwise be computationally expensive or even infeasible, can be addressed.

When we connect both architectures, IoT to the SN OpenSocial architecture, we assembly a new architecture. The architecture presented in figure 3 unifies provides the abstraction for the Social Network of Things (SNoT)

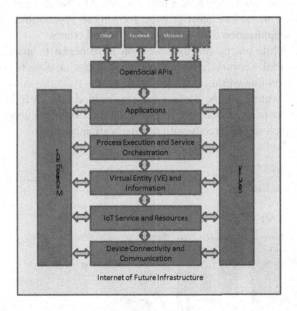

Fig. 3. SNoT Architecture

SNoT architecture must provide a stronger convergence of the real world with SNs will enable new applications and opportunities for social interaction between places and their owners, end users and the devices they control. For this to occur, stronger integration and continued convergence of the real world into SNs is necessary. However, to fully unify these worlds, there are several challenges that need to be addressed.

5.1   How the SNoT Works

Figure 4 depicts the relationship between services, resources, and devices and shows several deployment options. Network-based resources are not shown, as they can be regarded as being hidden behind cloud-based services.

We need to look at how things will interact with the online social world. How will a broad set of devices and objects ranging from passive objects like books or products on a shelf to sensors, actuators and home appliances both identify themselves and interact with SNs.

Extending SN APIs and Models for the SNoT. Second we need to consider how social network applications and the SN itself manifest things and objects in their APIs and data models to enable strong integration.

As we show in chapter II, Open Social is a set of APIs for building social applications on the web. It is an open specification with reference implementations available allowing anyone to create not only applications but also their own social network containers. Using these open APIs social application developers can write applications that "live" within any Open Social container. This allows Open Social containers to supply only the capabilities that their users need while maintaining compatibility with others at the same compliance level. Social API Server specification defines the services that a social site must provide for remote applications such as people, groups, activities, application data, albums, content and others.

In particular, while places and user location have begun to manifest themselves within on line social networks, is not clear how things or objects should manifest themselves in the on-line world.

On SNoT architecture, all the devices were embedded into a VE and they are controlled by the process execution and service orchestration. This control is generally made by APIs which works directly with the application layer.

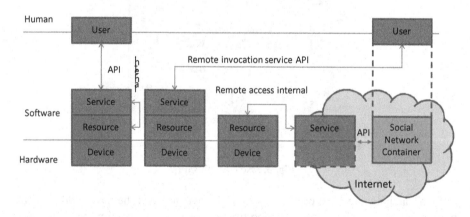

Fig. 4. SNoT working

We should consider how users interact on line with SNs that include places and things to how the real world exposes the on line social connections.

5.2   Applications Based on SNoT

Give "life" with social interaction and interoperability for a device is a concept still very advanced. But we can take advantage of the proposed architecture for various applications like e-health IoT, smart home, environment control, smart factory, among others.

A practical application extensively researched is e-health area. It is possible to have a social network composed by a doctor, nurse / medical assistant and patients, as shown in Figure 5. We could think of a community of patients with "problems" or interests, or even a direct doctor-patient relationship.

Inside the community, the patients can interact with each other about drug information and diagnoses. We can include a virtual community composed by virtual entities with the data from the medical devices or elements of health control (glucose meters, blood pressure analyzers).

In this direct relationship, the operating proceeding is executed by the technologies of IoT. The control signals can be transmitted through the Internet and it is the equipments' responsibility in IoT to connect the health and the Internet. As the result, the commands of the controller can be sent to the equipments through the Internet and IoT.

If there is any problem with one individual, automatically the IoT can send information to the other individuals from the community, thus a near neighborhood can help or give de correct assistance to the patient.

Since there is a spreading mechanism in the social network, other individuals in the community can get this information from the recommend information. This e-health interaction shows a typical application based on the SNoT. Social network can spread the related information through the relations in it. Obviously all the character of security and private can be set and managed to not expose particular information.

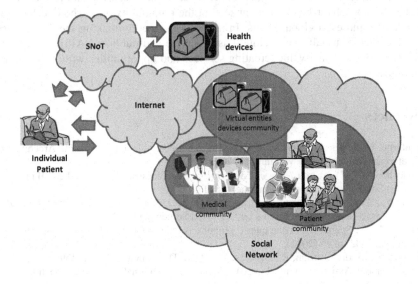

Fig. 5. SNoT E-health application

6   Conclusion and Future Work

As said before, the IoT supports different kinds of intelligent applications about devices, smart homes and etc. It can also feedback signals from different applications and provide the real time factors for real time decisions. With the information from social network, different people can be distributed into many groups with similar characteristics including the electronic devices [21].

Although many technologies and system providers label their solutions as Internet of Things technologies, in reality form a disjoint intra-nets of things. Furthermore, the existing solutions do not address the scalability requirements of a future IoT [22], both in terms of communication between and the manageability of devices. Additionally, many of these solutions area based on inappropriate models of governance and fundamentally neglect privacy and security in their design. The SNoT must address the integration between virtual and real world with the interoperability of solutions at the communication level, as well as at the service level, has to be ensured across various platforms with security, privacy and performance as show on the chapter II.

For future work, it is possible to include fuzzy logic or incertitude at the proposed SNoT to make not only the human brains as the major "component" for dealing with complexity. In the Internet of Things, objects will be duly identified (in most cases it will be either serialized or unique) and will be capable to act as autonomous media, either directly for those having active IDs with embedded software code, or indirectly throughout the network and application layers. This could potentially spread, over the existing Internet, new independent actors, capable to react and to influence the whole system.

Also at a public service level, the automatic collection of environmental data from connected sensors supports the creation of a "smart grid" — providing more accurate and timely information with which to make better decisions that optimize resource use, minimize environmental impact, improve safety and security, and provide a host of services that deliver beneficial impacts on the community as a whole at local, urban, national and even global levels. In many cases, merely making the data accessible and available (usually via a cloud-based service and published API) will spawn a wide range of additional value, creating services and opportunities within the broader community.

References

[1] Internet of things Architecture IOT-A. Project Delverable D1.2 – Initial Arcchitectural Reference Model for IoT V6 (June 16, 2001)
[2] Facebook (2011), http://www.facebook.com (acessed September 12, 2011)
[3] Redes Sociais – os números da internet (2011), http://www.osnumerosdainternet.com.br/internautas-passam-60-do-tempo-em-redes-sociais/ (acessed September 04, 2011)
[4] Pavão Jr., J., Sparai, R.: O que quer o senhor das redes – Geração F. Veja Magazine, 2237 edn., year 44, no. 40 (2011)
[5] Dohr, A., Modre-Osprian, R., Drobics, M., Hayn, D., Schreier, G.: The Internet of Things for Ambient Assisted Living. In: 2010 Seventh International Conference on Information Technology. IEEE (2010)

[6] Linked Data and the Semantic Web the way to Web 3.0? (2011), http://www.upvery.com/4162-linked-data-and-the-semantic-web-the-way-to-web-3-0.html (acessed, August 09, 2011)

[7] EFII, The European Future Internet Initiative, White paper on the Future Internet PPP Definition. [S.l.], p. 14 (2010)

[8] O'Reilly, T. (2009), http://www.oreillynet.com/pub/a/oreilly/tim/news/2005/09/30/what-is-web-20 (acessed, January 15, 2009)

[9] Ding, L., Shi, P., Liu, B.: The Clusterin g of Internet, Internet of Thin g s and Social Network. In: 2010 3rd International Symposium on Knowledge Acquisition and Modeling. IEEE (2010)

[10] Papadimitrou, D., et al.: Future Internet. The cross-ETP vision document. Version 1.0. Nessi Project resources (2009)

[11] Corner, M.: Sensors empower the "Internet of Things", pp. 32–38, ISSN 0012-7515

[12] IOT-A Europe (2011), http://www.iot-a.eu/public (acessed, September 24, 2011)

[13] Internet of things Architecture IOT-A, Project Deliverable D1.1 - SOTA report on existing integration frameworks/architectures for WSN, RFID and other emerging IoT related Technologies, V0.9 (2011) (acctual delivered date March 4, 2011)

[14] Kranz, M., Roalter, L., Michahelles, F.: Things That Twitter: Social Networks and the Internet of Things. In: ETH Department of Management, Technology, and Economics (D-MTEC), What can the Internet of Things do for the Citizen (CIoT) Workshop at The Eighth International Conference on Pervasive Computing (Pervasive 2010), Helsinki, Finland (May 2010)

[15] Williams, B.C., Nayak, P.P.: Immobile robots ai in the new millennium. AI Magazine 17(3), 16–35 (1996)

[16] Jara, A.J., Zamora, M.A., Skarmeta, A.F.G.: An architecture based on Internet of Things to support mobility and security in medical environments. In: IEEE Communications Society Subject Matter Experts for Publication in the IEEE CCNC 2010 Proceedings (2010)

[17] MacManus, R.: Social Networks for Things (February 2, 2010), http://www.readwriteweb.com/archives/social_networks_for_things.php (acessed August 28, 2011)

[18] Google OpenSocial (2011), http://code.google.com/apis/opensocial (acessed January 12, 2011)

[19] Malik, O.: OpenSocial, Google's Open Answer to Facebook (October 30, 2007), http://gigaom.com/2007/10/30/opensocial (acessed August 28, 2011)

[20] MacManus, R.: Top 10 Internet of Things Developments of 2010 (December 15, 2010), http://www.readwriteweb.com/archives/top_10_internet_of_thin gs_developments_of_2010.php (acessed August 28, 2011)

[21] Domingue, J., Fensel, D., Davies, J., Cabero, R., Pedrinaci, C.: The Service Web: a Web of Billions of Services, Towards the Future Internet. In: Tselentis, G., et al. (eds.), IOS Press (2009); © 2009 The authors and IOS Press, doi:10.3233/978-1-60750-007-0-203

[22] Zhu, Q., Wang, R., Chen, Q., Liu, Y., Qin, W.: IOT Gateway: Bridging Wireless Sensor Networks into Internet of Things. In: 2010 IEEE/IFIP International Conference on Embedded and Ubiquitous Computing (2010)

[23] Open Social strcuture (2012), http://opensocialresources.googlecode.com/svn/spec/2.0/OpenSocial-Specification.xml (acessed April, 2012)

SocIoS: A Social Media Application Ontology

Konstantinos Tserpes[1], George Papadakis[2], Magdalini Kardara[2],
Athanasios Papaoikonomou[2], Fotis Aisopos[2],
Emmanuel Sardis[2], and Theodora Varvarigou[2]

[1] Department of Informatics and Telematics, Harokopio University of Athens,
70 Eleftheriou Venizelou Str, 17676 Athens, Greece
tserpes@hua.gr
[2] Department of Electrical and Computer Engineering,
National Technical University of Athens,
9, Heroon Polytechniou Str, 15773 Athens, Greece
{gpapadis,nkardara,tpap,fotais,sardis,doravarv}@mail.ntua.gr

Abstract. The value that social web is adding is undeniable. However, social web is coming at a cost: the so-called "closed" web. Slowly but steadily, a growing portion of internet activity is confined within the spaces of social networking sites (SNS) or platforms that encompass social networking capabilities by default. Furthermore, due to their competitive stance between one another, conceptually common content and functionality are accessed through different mechanisms in SNSs. This work deals with the issue of semantic equivalence between the prevalent notions used in SNSs in order to device a common object model that will enable the integration of social platform APIs. The result is the proposal for an ontology for the implementation of cross-platform social applications. Two particular applications are considered as a guide for this reference model.

Keywords: Social Media, Semantic Web, Ontology, Application Programming Interface.

1 Introduction

Social media platforms are currently concentrating a great portion of web activity. Internet users are generating content and social graphs that carve the paths through which social information is shared. SNSs are exposing functionality and data not only through their usable GUIs but also through web APIs so as to ensure re-usability and interoperability. This enables them to support third party applications that add value to their platform and bring users in, without significant costs.

However, the competitive environment to which the SNSs are operating leads to the adoption of a multitude of data models that describe essentially similar notions, e.g. "friends" or shared "media items". Taking advantage of the conceptual similarity between these core SNS entities implies that the aggregation of the social functionality and data can provide the basis for a unique platform on top of which third parties can deploy new added value services, seamlessly using the underlying SNSs APIs.

P. Herrero et al. (Eds.): OTM 2012 Workshops, LNCS 7567, pp. 574–584, 2012.

In order to achieve that, the proposed solution attempts to develop an SNS-like API that will manage to aggregate data and functionality from underlying SNSs that deliver their functionality through web APIs. We call this API "SocIoS API" and it is the core component of the SocIoS integrated solution[1]. SocIoS aims at providing the tools to build applications that leverage on the dynamics and content that reside in the SNSs. These tools are a collection of services that make use of SNS metadata in order to organize information hosted in SNSs, each service for its own purpose. SocIoS platform allows the creative "mix-and-match" of these services to application workflows which are ready to be consumed.

This approach needs to be attacked on two sides: Firstly, by defining a new object model that captures all the conceptually similar notions, one can actually define the SNS API space. Each new SNS API that is added under this formal specification, needs to comply with the new object model. That is, a subset of the new SNS object model needs to be able to wrap into the common objects mentioned above. Such attempts have been undertaken by projects like GNIP® [1], hootsuite® [2] and Stroodle® [3], however, the most complete approach has been provided by OpenSocial [4].

Secondly, each time a new application service is created by combining available ones based on their specification, a new domain is created, extending the existing. This means that the specification has to be flexible so as to incorporate any possible new definition. Such generic-purpose modeling can be served by the Web Service Modeling Ontology (WSMO) [5] and the Semantic Annotation of Web Resources (SA-REST) [6].

Our method fosters ideas from both approaches: it defines the core objects of the SocIoS API domain through an ontology which helps to model these objects to the underlying SNS APIs using software wrappers (formally called SocIoS adaptors). To build this ontology we start with the conceptual analysis of proof of concept application scenarios in order to capture the main domain concepts. Next, we study a number of SNSs in order to identify the API objects that are semantically equivalent to the domain concepts. This helps us to place the domain concepts in the SNS context and examine their relationships and position in the object model hierarchy. The combination of these approaches leads to a conceptualization of the application domain that is formally captured in the presented SocIoS ontology.

The objective of this ontology is to provide the necessary flexibility of the SocIoS object model so as to be extended as necessary when new SNS APIs or application domains are to be included later in its lifetime. The model is captured using the ontology specification language (OWL) [7] that only includes the information that is necessary for an object model. We directly derive the initial SocIoS object model from this ontology.

The document is structured as such: Section 2 provides the related work in specifications and APIs that have similar goals as ours as well as ontologies from which our approach can adopt concepts so as to be extendible. Section 3 presents the domain concepts of proof of concept applications. In Section 4 the derived domain concepts

---

[1] www.sociosproject.eu

are projected to existing objects of a group of an appropriate selection of SNS APIs. Section 5 gives the proposed ontology as a result of this analysis and connects the classes to existing semantic web entities. Finally, Section 6, summarizes the key points that yield from this work.

2   Related Work

There have been a number of approaches to build a meta-API so as to implement functionality federation and data marshaling from numerous SNSs. However, as stated above, the majority comprise proprietary solutions which limits the extensibility of the platforms to non-supported APIs. Such examples are GNIP®, hootsuite® and Stroodle®.

Even though we study a number of SNS APIs so as to identify the dominant objects that they commonly use, our solution uses mainly OpenSocial as a reference specification. OpenSocial defines a common API for social applications across multiple websites. As it is a product of collaboration of a broad set of members of the web community it naturally encompasses the most dominant SNS concepts. However, OpenSocial is not meant to be used as a meta-API or an aggregator.

By defining the universe of discourse of the proof of concept applications, we assume that we will manage to capture the common denominator of the core SNS applications. This universe can be used at a higher layer by any service. However, here, we need to make a clear separation. With this work we do not want to model the real world concepts that appear in the SNS as a result of their use. Various efforts have been put on that aspect with the most prominent work being the one of Mika, 2007 [8]. Instead we are focusing on conceptual entities that are manifested in the object models of the existing SNSs. By using agreed-upon Semantic Web formats to describe people, content objects, and the connections that bind them together, SNSs can interoperate by appealing to common semantics [9].

To this end we analyze the existing work in the area of formal specifications of the SNS domain so as to investigate if and how there are ontologies that already capture notions that our approach would like to define.

2.1   Friend of a Friend (FOAF)

The Friend of a Friend (FOAF) project [10] is creating a Web of machine-readable pages describing people, the links between them and the things they create and do. FOAF is a descriptive vocabulary expressed using the Resource Description Framework (RDF) and the Web Ontology Language (OWL). Its purpose is to allow people define their profile, content and relationship to other people and contents so as to interconnect all web resources in a distributed manner.

FOAF's data specification is close to what our approach wants to achieve as it manages to capture basic abstract notions of a social network manifested using web resources, such as a "Person" and its defining properties. However, this proximity in the objectives could be characterized as coincidental given that the concept is rather different. FOAF is not meant to capture concepts that stem from the technical nature of SNS APIs that SocIoS attempts to unify. In other words, FOAF is meant to capture even intangible concepts, something that is not allowed in SocIoS. Our approach needs a representation that depicts tangible (even in digital format) entities.

2.2 Semantically-Interlinked Online Communities (SIOC)

The SIOC (Semantically-Interlinked Online Communities) Core Ontology [12] provides the main concepts and properties required to describe information from online communities (e.g., message boards, wikis, weblogs, etc.) on the Semantic Web [13]. As with FOAF, SIOC is very close to meeting SocIoS requirements in terms of data specification compatility. The major difference is that SIOC revolves around web communities emphasizing on forums missing some of the SNS concepts.

2.3 Linking Open Descriptions of Events (LODE)

Linking Open Descriptions of Events (LODE) is an ontology for publishing descriptions of historical events as Linked Data, and for mapping between other event-related vocabularies and ontologies [14]. Thus, the compatibility to SocIoS revolves around the notion of Event and the interplay between real world and SNS world events. As in the majority of the SNSs, the event depicts a calendar item that is planned to take place, in SocIoS we are interested in real-world events that generate intense and unusual in-world activity.

3   Application Domain Concepts

As a starting point to our analysis, we employ three application scenarios that stem from real end-user requirements. One scenario is related to journalism and the use of SNS users as a source of information to a multimedia dossier article and two are related to TV commercial production and particularly to the use of social media for location scouting and casting extras. The requirements of these applications are defined by leading companies in this line of business, and in particular, a news broadcasting agency and a TV production company. More details about these applications can be found on the website: www.sociosprject.eu.

All three applications relate to the exploitation of abstract social networks created on the fly based on demographic and social criteria (e.g. credibility, influences, etc), for finding and retrieving information in a reliable, timely and cost-efficient manner. These applications were analyzed so as to define the SocIoS domain of discourse and to have a reference conceptual classification of our universe.

The conceptual analysis of the abovementioned scenarios leads to the following conclusions:

The SNS **users** form a central concept. Their **activity** is important to the end-users who want to monitor it. From that activity the news broadcaster can collect details about events or the producers find locations or people of interest at any particular moment they are desire. For that reason, SNS users can be classified in **groups** so as to allow the end-users better monitor their activity. Typically, the problem of all social web applications is **reliability**. Reliability must be measured somehow and hints be provided to the end-users. Furthermore, the basic functionality has to support journalists or producers to look for **multimedia items** which are owned by SNS users. Multimedia items can steer end-users' interest if they directly fit to their criteria or if they emerge as central objects in occasions of intense and unusual activity, i.e. an **event**. Typically, an event is taking place at a **location** and this affects greatly the definition of events of interest of the end-users. Finally, communication between SNS users and end-users is achieved through the basic communication channel, which is the **message**.

Based on this short summary, we conclude to the a small number of common domain concepts, i.e: User, Activity, Group, Reliability, Multimedia item, Event, Location and Message.

In what follows, we explain how we formally capture and extend these notions based on the actual vocabulary used by the object models of the underlying SNSs.

4   SNSs API Analysis

Conceptually, the SNS universe as part of the social web, can be seen as a single social network, in which people are socially connected to each other and the basic social interaction is the sharing of content (text, visual and audio). In practice, this is achieved, if we consider the section of the groups of all the common basic entities of the underlying SNS. This task by itself is rather complex given the highly diverse nature of SNS applications: Communication, Collaboration/authority building, Multimedia, Reviews and opinions, Entertainment and Brand monitoring [15]. The entities "living" in them are generally different with the exception of few basic ones (like the notion of people).

This Section explains in a practical way what the main objects in the SNS API domain are which fit to the descriptions of the domain concepts as they generated from the two scenarios of Section 3. This analysis is pivotal in the definition of the intermediate ontology that will enable the SNS APIs integration and cross-platform application support.

For the analysis we used a set of social media platforms selected based on criteria such as: SNS Popularity, API Popularity, Scope, Openness and Maturity. Following these criteria, the following APIs were studied: OpenSocial, Facebook, Twitter, FlickR and Youtube. A summary of the results of this study are presented on Table 1.

A number of conclusions can be extracted from Table 1. Firstly, these notions differ in the naming as well as in the hierarchy in the formal description (others are first-class objects, while others are mere object properties). Therefore the relationship is not always one-to-one, nor the objects are the exact semantic match.

Table 1. Domain concepts and semantically equivalent objects in selected SNS API (N/S stands for "not supported")

Concept	Social Networking Site API objects				
	OpenSocial	Facebook	Twitter	FlickR	Youtube
User	Person	User	Users	people	users
Group	Group	Group and Friendslist	Lists	groups: members	N/S
MediaItem	MediaItems	Photo and Video	Tweets	photos	media
Message	Message	Message	Tweets and direct_ messages	activity: userComments	gd: comments
Activity	Activity	N/S	Timeline	activity	activity
Event	N/S	N/S	Trends	N/S	N/S
Reputation	N/S	Review: Rating	Users: suggestions	stats	ratings
Location	Person/ MediaItem: Location	Album: Location	geo	places	yt: location

Furthermore, not all the concepts are supported by all the SNS APIs (marked as "N/S"). Thirdly, some objects are implicitly related to the concepts, e.g. a Tweet object is semantically equivalent to a Message. Another conclusion is that not all conceptually similar objects are of the same class (Location is second-class in OpenSocial, Facebook and Youtube and first-class in all the rest). Finally, the notion of Events in the way it is defined in this document is only existent in Twitter.

Having defined and examined the domain concepts under an SNS context we can move to the designing of the SocIoS Core Ontology.

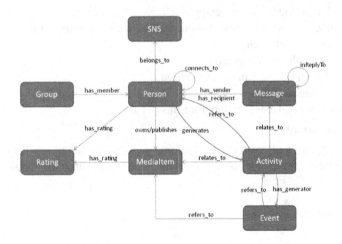

Fig. 1. Overview of simplified SocIoS ontology

5   SocIoS Core Ontology

From the abovementioned analysis, it is clear that the method to conceptually model the domain, is a combination of two efforts: map the underlying SNS object models into a single point of reference and model the SocIoS scenarios universe. As seen in Section 4, other domain concepts can be promoted to classes, whereas others remain as properties. Furthermore, the analysis of the objects and their members also assisted in the identification of the most prevalent data properties.

Given the above we drafted an ontology that captures the basic context and rules behind the SocIoS domain that we attempted to record. The ontology starts by putting Person and MediaItem as the central entities. Then, it analyzes the relationship that bind these two entities with the rest of the core entities. For practical reasons, a new entity is introduced so as to record the SNS in which a Person is active, publishing and sharing MediaItems. The overview of this ontology is presented in **Fig. 1**.

In what follows we present the classes depicted above along with their properties and relevant definitions that exist in the ontology projects analyzed in Section 4. The latter aims to help the reader who is familiar with these initiatives, better digest the semantics of the SocIoS Core Concepts.

5.1   Person

Properties

- connects_to: Other person entities with whom the person in question shares some kind of relationship (is a friend, follows, etc).
- owns: Photos that are published and owned by this person.
- has_rating: A person has a rating assigned by other people
- belongs_to: The SNS in which the Person exists
- birthday: The birthday of this person.
- displayName: The name of this Person, suitable for display to end-users.
- ethnicity: Person's ethnicity.
- gender: The gender of this person.
- location: Description of a person's location.
- name: The complete person's real name.
- tags: A user-defined category label for this person.

Relevant Definitions

Class: foaf:Person The Person class represents people. Something is a Person if it is a person. The Person class is a sub-class of the Agent class, since all people are considered 'agents' in FOAF.

5.2   MediaItems

Properties

- has_rating: Average rating of the media item on a scale of 0-10.
- created: Creation datetime associated with the media item.

- description: Description of the media item.
- duration: For audio/video clips - playtime length.
- last_updated: Update datetime associated with the media item.
- location: Location corresponding to the media item.
- num_comments: Number of comments on the media item.
- num_views: Number of views for the media item.
- num_votes: Number of votes received for voting.
- start_time: For streaming/live content, datetime when the content is available.
- tagged_people: Array of string (IDs) of people tagged in the media item.
- tags: Tags associated with this media item.
- title: Describing the media item.
- type: The type of media.

Relevant Definitions

Propery:foaf:depiction The basic notion of 'depiction' could also be extended to deal with multimedia content (video clips, audio), or refined to deal with corner cases, such as pictures of pictures etc.

5.3   Activity

Properties

- relates_to: MediaItem that may accompany the activity
- has_generator: An activity may be generated or related to an event
- refers_to: The person who triggered the activity
- body: Specifying an optional expanded version of an activity.
- publishes: Any photos, videos, or images that should be associated with the activity.
- postedTime: Specifying the time at which this activity took place.
- title: Specifying the primary text of an activity.

Relevant Definitions

No equivalent notions in other ontologies.

5.4   Events

Properties

- refers_to: a (physical, social, or mental) object involved in an event. In SocIoS this is related to MediaItems or Activity.
- atPlace: a named or relatively specified place that is where an event happened.
- atTime: an abstract instant or interval of time that is when an event happened.
- circa: an interval of time that can be precisely described using calendar dates and clock times.
- illustrates: an event illustrated by some thing (typically a MediaItem object)
- location: an abstract region of space (e.g. a geospatial point or region) that is where an event happened.

Relevant Definitions

Class: LODE: Event "Something that happened," as might be reported in a news article or explained by a historian. An event consists of some temporal and spatial boundaries subjectively imposed on the flux of reality or imagination, that we wish to treat as an entity for the purposes of making statements about it. In particular, we may wish to make statements that relate people, places, or things to an event.

5.5   Messages

Properties

- has_recipients: Person entities who receive the message.
- has_sender: The person who sent the message.
- body: The main text of the message.
- collections: Identifies the messages collection this message is contained in.
- inReplyTo: Use for threaded comments/messages.
- status: Status of the message. (NEW, READ, DELETED)
- timeSent: The time that the message was sent.
- subject: The subject of the message.

Relevant Definitions

Class: sioc: Post A Post is an article or message posted by a UserAccount to a Forum.

The SIOC Types Ontology Module describes some additional, more specific subclasses of sioc:Post.

5.6   Rating

Properties

- score: The score that depicts the rating
- range: The score range (min, max).

Relevant Definitions

No equivalent notions in other ontologies.

5.7   Group

Properties

- has_member: Person entities who are members of the group.
- title: Title of the group.
- description: Description of group.

Relevant Definitions

Class: sioc:Usergroup A set of UserAccounts whose owners have a common purpose or interest. Can be used for access control purposes. A Usergroup is a set of members or UserAccounts of a community who have a common Role, purpose or interest.

5.8   SNS

The SNS concept captures the notion of the container in which a typical social network is manifested for a person and the mediaitems are shared. Typical examples are Facebook, Twitter, MySpace, YouTube, FlickR.

Properties

• container: The platform SNS, e.g. Facebook, Twitter, etc.

Relevant Definitions

No equivalent notions in other ontologies.

6   Conclusions

This document summarizes the procedure and the results of the conceptualization of the SocIoS domain as an intermediate step to define the SocIoS Object Model (API). The analysis starts from the domain concepts defined by the SocIoS scenarios and continues with the identification of conceptually common data specifications from various APIs that semantically fit to the domain concepts. The result of this work is captured in the SocIoS core ontology that is expected to assist the developers to better comprehend the notions behind the SocIoS object model and extend it as appropriate.

The ontology permits the extension of the SocIoS API towards any direction, either for including new applications or for supporting further SNS APIs. This flexibility is also crucial in cases of strong dependence on third parties because it allows for quick cope with possible changes. Furthermore, we present how the ontology is linked to semantic web specifications, a fact that adds to the extendibility of our proposed solution.

Acknowledgments. This work has been supported by the SocIoS project and has been partly funded by the European Commission's 7th Framework Programme through theme ICT-2009.1.2: Internet of Services, Software and Virtualisation under contract no.257774.

References

1. Gnip, The Social Media API, http://gnip.com/
2. Hootsuit, Social Media Dashboard, http://hootsuite.com/
3. Stroodle, Your Social Pulse, http://stroodle.it/
4. OpenSocial Social Data Specification 1.1, http://opensocial-resources.googlecode.com/svn/spec/1.1/Social-Data.xml
5. Web Service Modeling Ontology (WSMO), http://www.wsmo.org/
6. W3C SA-REST: Semantic Annotation of Web Resources, http://www.w3.org/Submission/SA-REST/
7. McGuinness, D.L., van Harmelen, F. (eds.): OWL Web Ontology Language Overview. World Wide Web Consortium (W3C) recommendation (February 2004), http://www.w3.org/TR/owl-features

8. Mika, P.: Ontologies are us: A unified model of social networks and semantics. Journal of Web Semantics 5(1), 5–15 (2007)
9. Breslin, J., Decker, S.: The Future of Social Networks on the Internet: The Need for Semantics. IEEE Internet Computing 11(6), 86–90 (2007)
10. The Friend of a Friend (FOAF) project, http://www.foaf-project.org/
11. Brickley, D., Miller, L.: FOAF Vocabulary Specification v0.98 (August 9, 2010), http://xmlns.com/foaf/spec
12. The SIOC project, http://sioc-project.org
13. Berrueta, D., Brickley, D., Decker, S., Fernández, S., Görn, C., Harth, A., Heath, T., Idehen, K., Kjernsmo, K., Miles, A., Passant, A., Polleres, A., Polo, L.: SIOC Core Ontology Specification. In: Bojārs, U., Breslin, J.G. (eds.) March 25 (2010), http://sioc-project.org/ontology#term_Item
14. Ryan Shaw with contributions from Raphaël Troncy and Lynda Hardman, LODE: An ontology for Linking Open Descriptions of Events (July 7, 2010), http://linkedevents.org/ontology
15. From Wikipedia, Article available at, http://en.wikipedia.org/wiki/Social_media

A Social P2P Approach for Personal Knowledge Management in the Cloud[*]

Rebeca P. Díaz Redondo, Ana Fernández Vilas,
Jose J. Pazos Arias, and Sandra Servia Rodríguez

SSI Group. Department of Telematic Engineering,
University of Vigo. 36301 Vigo, Spain
{rebeca,avilas,jose,sandra}@det.uvigo.es

Abstract. The massive access to the Cloud poses new challenges for the cloud citizens to use services overcoming the risks of a new form of digital divide. What we envision is a socially orchestrated cloud, i.e. an ecosystem where the users put their experience and know-how (their personal knowledge) at the service of the social cloud, where social networks articulate the assistance to users. With his scenario in mind, this paper introduces a peer-to-peer solution to the problem of sharing personal knowledge for social search. We propose a routing mechanism in a peers' network, which uses both information about the social relation among peers and their personal knowledge. Finally, we deploy the proposal over Facebook as a support network.

Keywords: Social P2P, Knowledge Management, collaborative tagging, clustering, folksonomy, tag cloud.

1 Introduction

The Social Web has erupted accompanied by a growing wave of decentralization at all levels of Web value chain: content production, service provision, decision making, tagging, etc. This decentralization trend reaches its highest expression in the main idea underlying cloud computing, the conception of the Web as a cloud of services, resources and infrastructures fully interoperable. Unfortunately, the massive availability of services in the cloud poses challenges and opportunities comparable to those of the massive availability of information in the Internet. In fact, the full realization of the cloud computing vision could worsen the well-known digital divide born with the advent of the Information Society: a citizen with no access to the cloud, or without the ability to take advantage of it, could have lessened opportunities in society. What we

[*] This work was supported in part by the Ministerio de Educación y Ciencia (Gobierno de España) research project TIN2010-20797 (partly financed with FEDER funds); by the Consellería de Educación e Ordenación Universitaria (Xunta de Galicia) incentives file CN 2011/023 (partly financed with FEDER funds) and by Research supported by the European Regional Development Fund (ERDF) and the Galician Regional Government under project "Consolidation of Research Units: AtlantTIC 2012-2013.

P. Herrero et al. (Eds.): OTM 2012 Workshops, LNCS 7567, pp. 585–594, 2012.
© Springer-Verlag Berlin Heidelberg 2012

propose for this new sign of digital divide is a socially orchestrated cloudm a Social Cloud. This, taking advantage of the popularity of social networks to assist their subscribers to fulfill needs and offer opportunities in the cloud.

For this ecosystem to be developed, several aspects have to be solved: user modelling, services discovery, service description, modelling of relationships, social data mining, etc. One of the more essential ones is how we can maintain the collective intelligence in a scenario of global dimensions. Apart from the global nature of the data, changes in Web habits linked to cloud computing rule out the possibility of having a centralized architecture in which data is stored about users' consumption, tastes, assessments, etc. Deployment solutions should focus on models where the knowledge about users and services in the cloud (profiles and metadata) are owned by users and no more by providers or intermediaries, at least not only by them. This user-oriented conception (as opposed to product-oriented) comes to the aid of growing concern in the privacy of data. Then, Social Cloud can be aligned with *Personal Knowledge Management* (PKM) which, according to Higgison's definition [1], entails *"managing and supporting personal knowledge and information so that it is accessible, meaningful and valuable to the individual; maintaining networks, contacts and communities; making life easier and more enjoyable, and exploiting personal capital."* Collective intelligence of users takes the form of knowledge disseminated all over the cloud, which does not fit properly with closed solutions to decision assistance. Quite the contrary, it comes to reconciling decision-making in the cloud with P2P-related approaches so that it can take advantage of the knowledge residing in other peers.

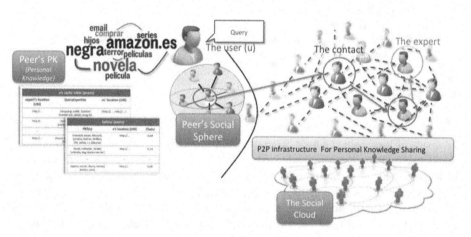

Fig. 1. The scenario por PKM in social P2P network

Taking all this reality in mind, the proposal in this paper is a Social approach to the problem of PKM whose intend is (a) to support the knowledge modeling by mining interactions in social networks; and (b) to articulate the processes in PKM by applying social P2P approaches for knowledge dissemination, retrieving, etc., i.e. P2P approaches which rely on users' relationships (social context) of cloud citizens to establish the peers architecture.

According the scenario we introduce in Fig. 1, the user u is a citizen of the cloud who shares his life and experiences in different Social Networks Sites (SNS). The u's contacts on these SNS build his social sphere: all of them have some kind of relationship with u, varying the strength and the context of these relationships. Besides, u uses SNSs as spaces of personal knowledge sharing. Depending on the privacy politics of the SNSs, the information could be confined to u's the social sphere, restricting the possibility for other users outside the social sphere to access to his knowledge. What we propose is that the user u takes advantadge of his contacts in order to access to knowledge outside his sphere. We see contacts as social peers and, as other social P2P approaches, we build an overlay network based on the peers' social characteristics. What is a novelty in our contribution is that we propose a solution that respects the privacity and construct the overlay network only with information that is accessible in SNSs throught their publics APIs.

Under these premises, the user u firstly tries to find an expert on a specific matter, and so raise the query message to his social peers, which is automatically routed on the overly network until the experts is found. After that, u raises the question to the expert. Although it is possible a direct contact between them, we provide a mechanism based on a chain of intermediate peers who participate in propagating the questions to the expert, with the aim of guarantying that all the communications take place between two peers that share, at least, a link in one social network site and so, ensuring the communication is possible.

2   Social Spheres

According to our approach, users have a biased and egocentric vision of the world, and consequently of the social networks structure. This perspective is focused on (a) the colleagues to whom the user interacts (links or ties) and (b) the subjects about they talk about (content). With this information we define the Social Sphere from the perspective of the user u, as a set of 3-tuplas: $S_{ph}(u) = \{v, TS_u(v), PKS(v)\}$, where (a) v is a colleague of u in the cloud; (b) $TS_u(v)$ represent the tie strength of their relationship (a measure of the closeness and level of activity of the interactions between them) and (c) $PKS(v)$ is the v's personal knowledge summary, i.e. the subjects or themes in which v shows a certain kind of expertise.

The concept of tie strength was firstly introduced by Granovetter [2] as a function of duration, emotional intensity, intimacy and exchange of services and recently these measures of closeness have been used to improve a wide range of applications in social and in computer sciences. In our previous works [3, 4], we have taken advantage of the public APIs that every social network sites offer and we have automatically and dynamically obtained, having the users' consent, information about the tie strength of the users' relationships. However, and from the information about the users' activity in these sites (tie signs), we can obtain not only the tie strength (second component of the social spheres) but also the information about the context of the interaction (ways and content description), used to build the third component of the social spheres.

Tie Strength. Measuring the closeness of the relationship between a user u and another colleague v (a colleague of user u at least in one social site) is the objective of the tie strength index, $TS_u(v)$. Our proposal [3, 4] briefly consists of (a) classifying the tie signs according to their level of intimacy (direct interactions vs. indirect interactions, public interactions vs. private interactions), and (b) normalizing this values with respect to the rhythm of interaction of the user u.

$$TS_u(v) = \sum_{c \in \{d,i,pb,pr\}} \alpha_c \cdot f\left(\left|Signs_{ulc}(v)\right|\right)$$

where α_c denotes the desired weight for the signs in the category direct (d), indirect (i), public (pb) and private (pr); f is the normalization function and $|Signs_{ulc}(v)|$ is the number of tie signs for the category c associated to the interaction between u and v. Weak ties entail values close to 0, whereas strong ties entail values close to 1. Additionally, this tie strength index is not reflexive and so $TS_v(u)$ may be higher, equal or lower, i. e. since it is u-centered only shows the u's perspective.

Personal Knowledge Characterization. We extend the mining process to extract not only the kind and number of interactions in social sites (tie signs), but also their textual description or content (knowledge signs), obtained from the social site APIs. From each knowledge sign, we obtain a set of representative or relevant tags that describe the interaction nature. This extraction is done using a natural language processor; concretely, we use the *Stanford CoreNLP* (http://nlp.stanford.edu) that allows us to generate the word lemmas for the tags and natural language in the matter of the interaction. After that, we remove the common words (*stop words*) that have little value in helping to characterize personal knowledge. Despite *CoreNLP* incorporates some form of stopping; we have utilized a larger list which include specific stop words of the domain of social interaction. The nature of the interactions any user u has allows us to model the personal knowledge of u ($PK(u)$) as a set of tag-weight pairs (tag cloud) denoted as: $PK(u) = \{t, w_u(t)\}$, where t is any representative tag involved in any interaction and $w_u(t)$ is the weight (relevance) of t in the u's tag cloud.

This tag cloud is progressively built by adding every relevant tag t extracted from the knowledge signs. Being $Tags(u)$ the set of tags in $PK(u)$, then we denote (a) its size as $\#Tags(u)$, i.e. the number of tags, and denote (b) the multiplicity of tag t as $m(t,Tags(u))$, i.e. the number of times tag t was extracted as a relevant tag from a interaction description. Consequently, $w_u(t)$ is obtained as follows:

$$w_u(t) = \frac{m(t,Tags(u))}{\#Tags(u)}.$$

Therefore, $PK(u)$ represents those matters or topics about the users u talks about in the social network sites. Our starting hypothesis is that $PK(u)$ constitutes an accurately representative set of terms about user u is interested in and so: (a) or user u knows about these matters or (b) has in his social sphere other colleagues with knowledge on these topics. We define u as an expert on the topics in PK(u): someone who talks about these matters and, consequently, is interested in them. Therefore, an expert is a key person because he probably knows the answer of questions related to the topics in his knowledge or because he knows someone who can give them to us.

Personal Knowledge Summary. *PK(u)* is an extensive characterization for personal knowledge and therefore, it exhibits a great potential of reasoning. However, when storing information about the peers in order to route a query, we propose that *u* stores only a brief summary of the knowledge of his peers. This *Personal Knowledge Summary (PKS)* is computed from *PK* by applying a clustering algorithm which partitions *PK* into a set of clusters of weighhted tags so that points in the same cluster are close together according to some distance meaure among tags. We have implemented our first trials by using *k*-means algorithm and NGD (*Normalized Google Distance*) [5]. Once we have identified *k* clusters in *PK*, we use the set of cluster centroids as *PKS*. So, in this implementation, *PKS* is a set of k vectors where each vector that contains the most representative tags in the cluster.

3   The Problem to Solve

The *leit motiv* of this paper is providing a P2P architecture based on social relationships that allows any user *u* to find an expert (or experts) on a specific matter or topic, according to the expert definition given in the previous section. The search starts by user *u* asking a specific query in natural language, for instance, *"Which is the dog vaccination schedule?"*, which is processed by using the aforementioned natural language processor *Stanford CoreNLP* to extract a set of relevant tags: a query tag cloud, denoted *QTC*, that constitutes the starting point of the search.

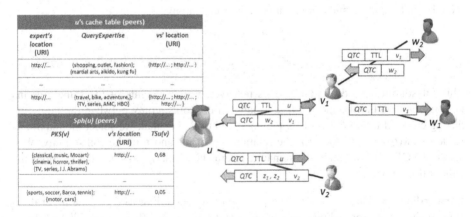

Fig. 2. *u*'s information for the distributed search

Since we have defined a user-centered knowledge model, each user in the cloud maintains his own information coming from two different sources (Fig. 2): (a) his own social sphere, $S_{ph}(u)$; and (b) a cache table keeping the information about experts out of his sphere (second table in Fig. 2), as consequence of the P2P search algorithm.

The social shere, $S_{ph}(u)$ stores the description, location information and tie strength of each user *v* to whom *u* is related in any social network site. The *u*'s table cache stores information about each expert that *u* has found as result of the execution of the

P2P search algorithm: his location information, the tag cloud of the queries on which is supposed to be expert on, and a list of the colleagues in the u's social sphere through whom the expert was located (see Sect. 4).

4   The Intelligent Seach Algorithm

The search algorithm starts trying to find at least one expert among the peers user u has knowledge about (tables in Fig. 2). If this attempt fails, it is time to forward the query to other peers to find this information out of the u's scope. Finally, whenever a user v has a set of experts for the target query, he returns this information to the user u, so he can address the question directly or indirectly to one of them.

Peers Ranking. In order to find those peers in the u's peer set (social sphere and cache table) whose expertise is close to the target matter, the algorithm firstly computes a peers ranking: (a) by comparing the query tag cloud (QTC) to the personal knowledge summary (PKS) of each colleague in the u's social sphere and (b) by comparing the QTC to the $QueryExpertise$ of each expert in the cache table.

With this aim, we have proposed a similarity measure between two elements e_i and e_j (which might be any tag cloud previously defined: PK, PKS, QTC or $QueryExpertise$). This comparison takes into account not only direct tag matching but also relations among tags in a folksonomy (see our previous work [6]). This folksonomy-based similarity $FolkSim(e_i, e_j)$ takes into account those terms that, although not being included in both tag clouds, are related in the folksonomy:

$$FolkSim(e_i,e_j)=\frac{\sum_{t_k\in TC(e_i)}w(t_k,e_i)\cdot \max\{w(t_l,e_j)\cdot r_{kl}|\forall t_l\in TC(e_i)\}}{\sqrt{\sum_{t_k\in TC(e_i)}w^2(t_k,e_i)}\cdot \sqrt{\sum_{t_l\in TC(e_j)}\max^2\{w(t_l,e_j)\cdot r_{kl}|\forall t_l\in TC(e_i)\}}} \quad (1)$$

This folksonomy-based similarity does not average the weights of the same tags in both tag clouds, but the more relevant paths in the folksonomy between the tag t_k in the tag cloud of e_i and the tag t_l in the tag cloud of e_j. For that, we select the maximal value of $\{w(t_k, e).\ r_{kl}\}$, been r_{kl} the relationship of t_k and t_l in the folksonomy. We also use NGD [16] to obtain the semantic relatioships among tags, i.e. the relations in a the folksonomy.

Forwarding the Query. Having the peers ranking according to QTC, the algorithm stops if there are users whose comparison results are higher than an established threshold Th_{pks}. Otherwise, u has to forward the query (together with the time-to-live, TTL, and the u's URI) to a subset of his peers (see Fig. 2), which is selected according to the following 3 criteria:

a) All those peers having comparison values higher than Th_{approx_pks}. Thus, they are not experts in the query, but their knowledge is close enough to the required one. So, they constitute a target group of peers who talk about related topics to the query.

b) Those peers in the u's social sphere having the highest tie strength indexes; under the premise that the more active a user is, the more possibilities there are of finding an expert among his peers.

c) A set of randomly selected peers in the u's social sphere having low tie strength indexes; with the aim of broadening the search and increase the possibility of finding experts out of the u's social range of action.

So, the whole procedure is as follows. Whenever a peer v receives the query message starts checking if himself is an expert by obtaining the similarity between $PK(v)$ and the QTC, using Eq. (1). If this value is higher than Th_{pks}, v is identified as an expert and, consequently, the search ends (like w_2 in Fig.2). Otherwise, v checks the degree of expertise of his peers (table cache and social sphere) on the query's subject, if this comparison results on a set of peers having a higher value than the established threshold Th_{pks} then the search ends because a list of experts has been found (like v_2 in Fig.2). If the comparison does not succeed, v forwards the query according to the previous criteria replacing in the query message the u's URI by his own identification (URI) until the query TTL expires (like v_1 in Fig.2).

5 After Finding the Expert

Once the routing algorithm has been explained, the process is completed with mechanisms to (1) propagate back experts' location; (2) update information stored by peers; and (3) formulate the question to the selected experts by using some publishing mechanisms in SNS.

Answer Propagation Throughout the Peers Network. Once a peer v has a list of potential experts to return (himself or a subset of their peers in his social sphere or his table cache), the answer message is created, including the following information: the QTC, the set of the URIs of the potential experts, and the v's URI (like v_2 in Fig.2). This message is propagated throughout the peers network following the same path that the query has done, but in the other way round. So, the answer message is always sent to the colleague who forwarded the query to v, who replaces the v's URI by his own URI (like v_1 in Fig.2) and proceeds in the same way starting a chain that ends with the user who forwarded the query in the first place: user u. Therefore, u has the list of potential experts and now he is ready to make the question.

Updating Both Social Spheres and Table Caches. Information in cache table is updated each time a user v receives a list of potential experts from any colleague in his social sphere: he checks one by one if the experts are already in his cache table or no and updates the data, i.e. the query the peer is supposed to be expert on, his location information and the colleague who sent the information. Finally, and with the aim of maintaining a reasonable cache table size, we introduce a forgetting mechanism to remove those entries that have not been used for a long time. Data in social spheres is also updated using the answer propagation mechanism: whenever a user v sends a response message to one of his colleagues, he also sends his updated personal knowledge summary, $PKS(v)$.

Formulating the Question to the Experts. The whole procedure ends by user u asking the query, or any other question about a related issue, to one or more of the experts he has located. We have two main issues here: (a) how u selects the most appropriate expert to ask the question, and (b) how the question is sent to the expert. Regarding the former, having a list of experts to address the questions, user u has the opportunity of selecting a specific subset. Although in the current solution, the question is sent to all of them, we are working in incorporating some mechanism of reputation management that can aid the user in selecting the expert. Regarding formulating the question, there are two different ways to proceed. User u might contact directly with the expert by using one of the mechanism supported by a social network site or by using other communication strategies (e-mail, phone, etc.). Althougt this solution is efficient, it may not be the most adequate: (a) because u is trying to contact to a total stranger who could be reluctant to give him an answer; and (b) because some social network sites not allow direct communication with users out of our social circle. The other option is propaging the specific queries or questions throughout the overly peers network using the same peers-path used to locate the expert, by in the other way round. This is the reason why we propose to store the information about the colleagues who have forwarded the query message. Using this solution, we avoid the two aforementioned problems of communication in the social network site and/or cooperation from the expert.

6   Deployment

For the deployment of our proposal, we provide a SaaS (Software as a Service) solution for both social mining and knowledge sharing. Regarding the process of social mining, we have developed a crawler service in charge of monitoring and processing Facebook evidences or signs of relationship and knowledge in this social network site. This service, called *mySocialSphere*, acts on behalf of the user and queries the Facebook public API in order to extract evidences and to build up a model of his social sphere and personal knowledge. At the same time, *mySocialSphere* made this information available to other services in the cloud through a REST API (provided that these services have users' permission). In the architectonic scenarios, several socially-enhanced services can be deployed which make use of this information without the need of gathering it.

Despite the statistics analysis of precision and recall of our proposal is part of our future work, we have deployed a Facebook application to validate our proposal. This application improves the functionality of Facebook Questions, which let users get recommendations from his friends and other people. Our application SQ (*Smart Questions*) allows the user to make a question and automatically routes it according to the relevant tags in the question and the personal knowledge and tie strength of social peers according to the routing scheme in this paper. For this purpose, the application asks the user for his permission to use the service *mySocialSphere* on his behalf. SQ posts the question to the wall of the social peers selected by the routing algorithm. We recruit users among (under)graduate students from the University of Vigo to use the application and to give feedback about the perceived utility of the responses and the willingness to rely on a response to take some decision. We compare the students' scores in the Facebook Questions case and in the SQ case. The perceived utility of the responses improves twice in the case of SQ, although the number of responses is approximately 1/3 less in the SQ case. Unfortunaltely, the second parameter (willingness to rely on the response) worsens when the expert is outside the social sphere of the user. As we developed the trials with Facebbok, we can say that students were reluctant to take decisions according to the expert's response when the expert is neither a "friend" nor a "friend of a friend". This observation poses the need to incorporate some form of reputation management in our proposal.   Besides, students have expressed a significative disappointment with the fact that some selected experts take some days to give a response in the Facebook wall. In some cases, the response is decreasingly useful when times go. That observation has motivated a modification of the search algoritm as it is described in the discussion.

7   Discussion and Further Work

In this research, we propose a social P2P approach to knowledge management based on the idea that people build social relationships which may help them in finding appropriate information or services more effectively. Social networks and P2P networks have been integrated in several previous proposals: peers in a P2P network can be viewed as subscribers to a social network and, consequently, the edges in the P2P network as the social ties in the social network. Firstly, there are some works that tackle the management of social data in a P2P architecture, i.e. a decentralized social network which does not depend on a Internet connection to access to the social network – PeerSoN [7] Safebook [8] and LifeSocial.KOM [9]. Other works [10, 11, 12] directly use the social relationships among users to construct social overlays in a P2P network that improve content location, preserve anonymity, reduce delays, etc.

More directly related with our work, in [13, 14, 15] peers are organized into social P2P networks based on similarity among users. Using the peers' knowledge and social spheres we define a dynamic overlay networks adapted on the fly to the requested matter. Besides, and because of the random factor in peers selection, deadlocks or endogamy issues are avoid. Unlike other proposals [13,14,15], our approach does not need to build social groups according to users' preferences and similarities. Unlike other proposals in the literature, we are not interested in obtaining a complete interaction network. On the contrary, we provide a social sphere centered in the user, which makes up the accessible network in the social P2P approach to knowledge sharing in the cloud. Apart from that, this social spehere is computed only by taking into account the information available in the cloud through public APIs.

Several open works are going on both in evaluating and extending our proposal in differente ways. On the one hand, after the promising subjective evaluation of undergraduate students in resolving queries, we are preparing a simulated scenario for an objective evaluation of precision and recall. On the other hand, we are defining a new scenario and a modified version of the algorithm to maximize the possibility of obtaining an inmediate response. For this new scenario the routing mechanism has to take into account the availability of the peers or, in other words, the peers that are online in the social network.

References

1. Higgison, S.: Your say: Personal Knowledge Management. Knowledge Management Magazine 7 (2004)
2. Granovetter, M.S.: The strength of weak ties: A network theory revisited. Sociological Theory 1(1), 201–233 (1983)
3. Servia-Rodríguez, S., Díaz-Redondo, R., Fernández-Vilas, A., Pazos-Arias, J.: Using Facebook activity to infer social ties. In: 2nd International Conference on Cloud Computing and Services Science, CLOSER (2012)
4. Servia-Rodríguez, S., Fernández-Vilas, A., Díaz-Redondo, R., Pazos-Arias, J.: Inferring Ties for Social-aware Ambient Intelligence: the Facebook Case. In: 3rd International Symposium on Ambient Intelligence, ISAmI (2012)
5. Cilibrasi, R., Vitanyi, P.: The Google Similarity Distance. IEEE Trans. Knowledge and Data Engineering 19(3), 370–383 (2007)
6. Fernández-Vilas, A., Díaz-Redondo, R., Pazos-Arias, J., Ramos-Cabrer, M., Gil-Solla, A.: A Social Approach to Parental Monitoring Over DVB-IPTV. In: International Conference on Consumer Electronics, ICCE (2102)
7. Buchegger, S., Schiöberg, D., Vu, L., Datta, A.: PeerSoN: P2P social networking: early experiences and insights. In: SNS 2009: Proceedings of the Second ACM EuroSys Workshop on Social Network Systems, pp. 46–52. ACM, New York (2009)
8. Cutillo, L.A., Molva, R., Strufe, T.: Safebook: a Privacy Preserving Online Social Network Leveraging on Real-Life Trust. IEEE Communications Magazine 47(12) (2009); Consumer Communications and Networking Series
9. Graffi, K., Gross, C., Stingl, D., Hartung, D., Kovacevic, A., Steinmetz, R.: LifeSocial.KOM: A Secure and P2P-based Solution for Online Social Networks. In: Proc. of the IEEE Consumer Communications and Networking Conference, IEEE CCNC (2011)
10. Gong, Y., Yang, F., Su, S., Zhang, G.: Improve Peer Cooperation Using Social Peer-to-Peer Networks. In: Proc. 1st IEEE Intl. Conf. on Information Science and Engineering, ICISE (2009)
11. Pouwelse, P., Garbacki, J., Wang, A., Bakker, J., Yang, A., Iosup, D.H.J., Epema, M., Reinders, M., van Steen, Spis, H.: Tribler: A social-based peer-to-peer system. Concurrency and Computation: Practice and Experience 20, 127–138 (2008)
12. Marti, S., Ganesan, P., Garcia-Molina, K.: SPROUT: P2P Routing with Social Networks. In: Lindner, W., Fischer, F., Türker, C., Tzitzikas, Y., Vakali, A.I. (eds.) EDBT 2004. LNCS, vol. 3268, pp. 425–435. Springer, Heidelberg (2004)
13. Yang, S., Zhang, J., Lin, L., Tsai, J.: Improving peer-to-peer search performance through intelligent social search. Expert Syst. Appl. 36(7) (2009)
14. Lin, C.J., Chang, Y.T., Tsai, S.C., Chou, C.F.: Distributed social-based overlay adaptation for unstructured P2P networks. In: IEEE Global Internet Symposium (2007)
15. Wang, F., Sun, Y.: Self-organizing peer-to-peer social networks. Computational Intelligence 24(3) (2008)

SOMOCO 2012 PC Co-chairs Message

The rapid progress of the Internet as new platform for social and collaborative interactions and the widespread usage of social online applications in mobile contexts have led the research areas of social and mobile computing to receive an increasing interest from academic and research institutions as well as from private and public companies.

Social computing deals with the design and application of information and communication technologies (ICT) in social contexts, analyzing the relationships between ICT and the pervasiveness of new devices and embedded sensors, which enable a wide access of data and information by people and an effective use of new services. In this scenario, the emerging technologies are stimulated and stimulate social evolution, considering that they will be used by very heterogeneous people according to their social, cultural and technological features. Social computing addresses many challenges, such as increasing interactive collaboration, understanding social dynamics of people, socially constructing and sharing knowledge, helping people to find relevant information more quickly.

Mobile computing plays an important role in many social and collaborative activities, predominantly in those activities where having the right data at the right time is a mission critical issue. Mobile services and technologies serve groups of people on the move, sharing activities and/or interests; in particular, mobile technologies enable geographically distributed users to access information and services anytime and everywhere. Challenging activities that have been conducted in mobile computing include wireless mobile networks, ad-hoc networks, smart user devices, mobile computing platforms, and location-based and context-aware mobile services.

To discuss such research activities, challenges and solutions, the International Workshop on SOcial and MObile COmputing for collaborative environments (SOMOCO'12) was organized in conjunction with the OTM Federated Conferences. The workshop, held in September 2012 in Rome, Italy, provides a forum for discussing about artificial social systems, mobile computing, social computing, networking technologies, human-computer interaction, and collaborative environments.

This year, after a rigorous review process, five papers were accepted for inclusion in the workshop proceedings. Each of these submissions was rigorously peer reviewed by at least three experts. The papers were judged according to their originality, significance to theory and practice, readability, and relevance to workshop topics. The selected papers investigated the use of Social Network approaches for evaluating the performance of virtual teams, for marketing strategies and their evolution within Social networks and mobile devices wide usage, and for studying the effectiveness of movie recommendations algorithms. Moreover, they investigated the adoption of some Bluetooth based functionalities for a public digital display in a high school, and methods for improving naturalness

P. Herrero et al. (Eds.): OTM 2012 Workshops, LNCS 7567, pp. 595–596, 2012.
© Springer-Verlag Berlin Heidelberg 2012

of human machine interaction, making multimodal interaction evolutionary over time.

The success of the SOMOCO 2012 workshop would not have been possible without the contribution of the OTM 2012 organizers, PC members and authors of papers, all of whom we would like to sincerely thank.

July 2012

Fernando Ferri
Patrizia Grifoni
Arianna D'Ulizia
Maria Chiara Caschera
Irina Kondratova

An SNA-Based Evaluation Framework for Virtual Teams

Lamia Ben Hiba and Mohammed Abdou Janati Idrissi

Equipe TIME (Technologies d'Information et Management d'Entreprise),
ENSIAS University of Souissi, Rabat, Morocco
benhiba.lamia@gmail.com, janati@ensias.ma

Abstract. Organizations are increasingly aware of the underlying forces of social networks and their impact on information and knowledge dissemination within virtual teams. However, assessing these networks is a challenge for team managers who need more complete toolkits in order to master team metrics. Social Network Analysis (SNA) is a descriptive, empirical research method for mapping and measuring relationships and flows between people, groups, organizations and other connected information/knowledge entities. In this article we establish a framework based on SNA to evaluate virtual teams.

Keywords: virtual teams, team performance, team evaluation framework, social networks, social network analysis.

1   Introduction

Globalization, the rise of the knowledge worker, the need for innovation, and the increasing use of information and communication technology (ICT) have given birth to virtual teams as a new form of organizational structure [1]. While virtual teams enable many organizations to enhance the productivity of their employees and tap into a global pool of talent, their implementation often faces significant organizational, technological, personal, and cultural barriers.

Research has thus closely examined how virtual teams are organized. And though teams are considered knowledge processing units [2], the literature around the subject tends to ignore the details of what knowledge was shared how, where, when, and for whom. There has also been little research conducted in the area of social interactions and their consequences on the functioning of virtual teams [3]. In fact, the interactions between team members are considered the logistics through which knowledge is accessed, transferred, and absorbed into new knowledge, ideas and insights [2]. It is thus important to understand the dynamics of social interactions within teams and their impact on team's performance. The study of these interactions is at the heart of Social Network Analysis (SNA). SNA is a discipline that draws concepts and techniques from network theory in order to examine the impact that social networks have on people's behavior [4]. While SNA has provided important measures to evaluate networks, choosing the most pertinent ones to use in a given context is a confusing process.

In this paper we examine the different network metrics that can be used to analyze virtual teams. The next section will make the case of using a network perspective for evaluating virtual teams. In the third section we will delve into Social Network

P. Herrero et al. (Eds.): OTM 2012 Workshops, LNCS 7567, pp. 597–607, 2012.

Analysis metrics used to evaluate teams. The fourth section will present the framework for the assessment of virtual teams and give an overview on the application of the framework. We conclude by discussing the implications of the framework and future research directions.

2   Evaluating Virtual Teams: A Network Perspective

As organizations are becoming more information-based, more team-based and collaborative, more reliant on technological competence, more mobile and less dependant on geography, [5] their structuring is undergoing a major shift. Many organizations are evolving from the hierarchical, top down structure into a more fluid one, based on relentlessly changing templates, quick improvisation and ad hoc responses [6].

The new form of organizations enables them to innovate by continuously creating new (combinations of) resources. As a result, the functional and matrix team structures are being transformed into temporary virtual project teams and the top-down communication is flowing in a more democratized way. Virtual teams are actually defined as teams that have these key features [2]: (a) Members interact through interdependent tasks guided by common purposes, (b) They use ICT substantially more than face-to-face communication and (c) They are geographically dispersed from each other (a key feature of a virtual team's configuration but not a defining characteristic [1]).

Although these changes have offered speed and agility to organizations, they have also triggered many challenges mainly relative to communication and information flow. In fact, relying on information and communication technologies is thought to restrict the communication process [7] and to limit conveying non-verbal information, which is important for building trust among stakeholders [8].

Managing projects successfully in the midst of autonomous participants, diverse motives, interests and cultures relies on stakeholders sharing a common vision, on building and maintaining trust and on resolving conflicts effectively. Thereby the institution of effective communication and knowledge processes is crucial. While frequency of communication in virtual projects is significantly superior to traditional projects [9], the isolation of team members can decrease motivation and exacerbate distrust [1] causing information hoarding. Therefore the efficiency of the communication process –and thus of teams- needs constant monitoring, as it is easy to fall in the information overload or isolation traps.

Communication is a dynamic network phenomenon. During a project, (organizational or/and unofficial) ties among stakeholders are built to allow knowledge and information dissemination. As the project progresses, links are developed and some disappear, conflicts create barriers while familiarity between members produce enhanced communication channels. Given these dynamics, a "network perspective" can be a viable approach to understanding the underlying forces of project's communication and knowledge dissemination. Therefore techniques from Social Network Analysis (SNA) can provide an effective toolbox to help make sense of these flow patterns and examine the ties between the project's stakeholders under a network perspective. In the next section we present some of the concepts from SNA that would be included in our evaluation framework.

3   SNA on the Team Level

This section aims to define Social Network Analysis and position it in the team context by introducing the key measures used to assess networks in the team level.

3.1   Introducing Social Network Analysis

Social Network Analysis (SNA) is the discipline that studies networks as a mathematical representation of complex systems by expressing them in terms of relational patterns among actors. It is a descriptive, empirical research method for mapping and measuring relationships and flows between people, groups, organizations and other connected information/knowledge entities. SNA has four features [10]: 1) It is motivated by a structural intuition based on ties linking social actors, 2) It is grounded in systematic empirical data, 3) It draws heavily on graphic imagery, and 4) It relies on the use of mathematical and/or computational models.

SNA models complex systems as sets of networks. Networks are composed of "nodes" that represent agents (team stakeholders for instance) and "links" that show the interactions between these nodes.

SNA also provides a collection of measurements that supply specifications in term of patterns of relations, characterizing a group or social system as a whole [11]. These measurements, called structural variables, help validate theories made about group relational structure. Below, we overview key SNA measures that will help understand the framework we're presenting in section 4.

3.2   The Principal SNA Measures for Teams

Empirical literature on the subject of social networks in the team level identified a very diverse set of metrics that describe the structure of networks [3]. We have classified these metrics into three dimensions. Each dimension describes a different aspect of the network structure through a range of measures.

Network Density. Marsden [12] defines network density as "the mean strength of connections among units in a network". It is assessed in the literature of teams through two measures: density and cohesion. Density, according to [11], is the actual number of edges in the graph as a proportion of the total number of possible edges. Leenders et al. [13] define it as the overall level of interactions among the team members, analogous to the number of ties between them. Luo [14] introduced the notion of group viscosity, which is the number of arcs divided by the number of nodes. Density is considered a good estimator of the physical cost of a network (for example: the resources requirements). Cohesion is used by Kratzer et al. [15] as the mean number of contacts per team member. Shrader et al. [16] define it as connectedness, which is the degree to which group members are linked.

Centrality. Centrality is measured on three different levels. The centrality of a node measures how many of the shortest paths between all other node pairs in the network pass through it [17]. This is equivalent to the degree to which an individual is close to all other actors in the network, either directly or indirectly [18]. Kratzer et al. [15] look at centrality as the number of units directly connected to the unit under scrutiny and introduces Peripheral positions as low degree centrality. Mote [19] identifies three measures: *Closeness centrality*, which is the potential independence of an actor in the flow of communication; *Betweeness centrality*, the extent to which a node is between two other nodes and eigenvector centrality which takes into account not only how many actors you know, but how many they know. *Group centrality or centralization* contrasts the gap between the largest actor centrality and the other values [17]. It ranges from 0 to 1, reaching the maximum when all others choose only one central actor (star) and the minimum when all actors have identical centralities (circle). For [13] it is the extent to which interactions are concentrated in one or a small number of team members rather than distributed equally among all of them. And for Luo [14], it is the variance owned by each group member. When the variance is low no group member is more important than another.

Network centralization is the dispersion of or variance in individual actors' in-degree centrality indices across the group [20]. According to Sparrowe et al. [21] it can be measured as the sum of differences between the largest individual centrality score and the scores of all other individuals in the network divided by the maximum possible sum of differences.

Disconnected Cliques and Bridges. Disconnected cliques and bridges have been measured in different ways through the literature of teams.

When the nearest neighbors of a node are also directly connected to each other they form a cluster. A cluster, also called clique or partition, is a subset of a signed graph where each positive line joins two nodes in the same subset and each negative line joins two nodes in different subsets [11]. Lin et al. [22] identify two members of the same cluster as members who belong to the same block or are structurally equivalent.

The absence of ties between two parts of a network creates structural holes. Balkundi et al. [23] define structural holes as the number of intransitive triads (sets of three connected notes) and vacuously transitive triads divided by the number of triads of all kinds.

Bridging structural holes is called Brokerage. Gluckler and Simon [24] measured a brokerage score based on two parameters: a) the extent to which communication relations are committed to non-redundant contacts and b) The frequency to which a person is on the shortest path connecting any other pair of actors in the network.

And finally, the heterogeneity of a network is measured as the number of distinct external groups upon which the group relies for knowledge. Yang and Tang [25] called this external network range. Oh et al. [26] define heterogeneity, or intergroup vertical bridging conduit, as the group member's informal socializing relationships with the formal leaders of different groups.

Now that we listed the most pertinent metrics related to teams in general, the next section will present a draft framework for the assessment of virtual teams. The framework will use, in addition to SNA metrics, other more commonly used measures that take into account the intrinsic features of the network nodes (team members) and the general outcome of the team (performance and satisfaction).

4   Towards an SNA-Based Framework for Evaluating Virtual Teams

We present in this section a framework for assessing virtual teams on six different dimensions using a three-factors-based model.

4.1   Assessing the Network

A network representing a virtual team is comprised of a set of nodes (team stakeholders) and links that embody the interactions between them. These interactions reflect information and knowledge dissemination among team members and can be collected from the mailing system or the collaborative platform the team is using for the project at hand. We propose that the built network will be assessed on three different aspects:

1) Structural aspect: the structure of a network plays an important role in its outcome.
2) Intrinsic aspect: Looking at the network-intrinsic features. Trust is one of the key factors influencing the performance of virtual teams [27]. Its existence or lack of it reflects the "health of the network".
3) Functional aspect: It evaluates the outcome of the network on two different dimensions: Performance and satisfaction.

Structural Aspect. Identifying the structure of the network is an important first step to examining a network. The table below summarizes the main metrics related to the structure of the network that were stated in the previous section. We utilize those same metrics in order to assess the structure of virtual team.

Table 1. Measures of the network structure

Assessment aspect	Dimension	Metrics
Network structure	Density	Density
		Cohesion
	Group Centrality	Centrality
		Group centralization
		Network centralization
	Disconnected cliques and bridges	Structural holes
		Brokerage score
		Partition/clique/clusters
		Heterogeneity

Intrinsic Aspect. While focusing on the structure of the network, we tend to view the relationships contained in the network as having positive connotations. But in most network settings, interactions between people or groups are regularly beset by controversy, disagreement, and sometimes, outright conflict [28]. It has also been proved that interpersonal trust has direct effect on important organizational processes such as communication, conflict management, satisfaction, and performance (both on the individual and unit level) [29]. Trust is thought to be one of the major challenges virtual teams must face [30]. It is therefore a good indicator of the health of relationships within the network and hence of the overall health of the network.

C. Li [31] introduced three elements that define the level of trust in a social group: Sincerity (are you saying what you genuinely feel or believe?) Competency (Do you have the ability to do what you say you can do successfully or efficiently?) and Reliability (can people depend on you?). Zhi-Ping F. et al. considered trust in the case of virtual teams and provided a more detailed model for trust estimation with two dimensions: Reputation and Collaboration. Reputation represents the trustworthiness of members in the team and collaboration represents the cooperation situations between members [27]. For each dimension, Zhi-Ping F. et al. identified a range of attributes as described in the table below.

Table 2. Attributes for trust estimation on reputation and collaboration [27]

Dimensions	Attributes	Description
Reputation (R)	Integrity (R1)	Integrity is the member's quality of being honest and morally upright. It is also the normal rule of behavior towards other members
	Competence (R2)	Competence is the required personal qualification to fulfill the task. It reflects as the aptitude, knowledge and skills of Members
	Professionalism (R3)	Professionalism is an authoritative representation in certain fields. It shapes after a long period of learning, instruction and social contact in team cooperation
	Loyalty (R4)	Loyalty is the attitude that makes a member being faithful and endeavor hard to the team cooperation
	Benevolence (R5)	Benevolence is the assessment on how a member concerned about other members' welfare, or either advance other members' interests, or at least not impede them. It reflects as the accommodating behavior towards other members
Collaboration (C)	Cooperative outcomes (C1)	Cooperative outcomes are the work outcomes that one member collaborates with other members through information and resource share
	Collaboration satisfaction (C2)	Collaboration satisfaction is the mutual satisfaction between members in the process of cooperation

With a network perspective, we can argue that reputation attributes (R1, R2, R3, R4, R5) are mostly intrinsic features that characterize the nodes of the network. The cooperative outcomes (C1) and Collaboration satisfaction (C2) on the other hand can be considered as part of the third dimension of our framework that we will discuss in the next section.

Studying trust means thus studying the nodes, i.e. team members, examining how they view themselves and other members of the team and rating it on a 1 to 5 scale. Conducting a survey on egocentric networks can help collect these data. It is worth mentioning though that handling this type of surveys represents a big challenge, as it is difficult to design a rating system and survey questions that wouldn't generate biased final results.

Functional Aspect. Overviewing the literature on the outcome measurements of virtual teams showed that there are two different dimensions to evaluate network outcome: Performance and Satisfaction.

Team performance is defined as the extent to which a team accomplishes its goals or mission [32]. Glückler and Schrott [24] indentified 5 criteria for evaluating team performance: Cooperation, Quality of work, Reliability, Communication and flexibility.

Satisfaction is seen as the extent of the members' perception of decision and agreements with the eventual outcomes [33]. It can be evaluated on different levels: Members satisfaction measures to which extent members liked working in the groups.

Stakeholders' satisfaction measures their contentment with respect to team's achievements. There are two main aspects of satisfaction: "satisfaction with the process" (satisfaction with the interaction process, perceived quality of discussion, and level of teamwork) [34] and "satisfaction with the outcomes" (is related, in part, to the attitudes of the group members towards one another) [35].

Evaluating the outcome of the network can be done regardless of the network perspective.   Performance can be measured using three types of methods: grader/ranking (members/supervisors rate team performance related criterions), discussion board/videotape (data is collected and discussions are analyzed), and questionnaires [36]. Satisfaction on the other hand is as intrinsic as trust and can only be examined through surveys destined to gauge team stakeholders' contentment with the final results or with each other.

4.2   Evaluating Virtual Teams

The framework we propose aims to provide an overview of network metrics that can be used to assess virtual teams. The framework is a three-factors-based model that assesses teams on the structural, intrinsic and functional aspects. Assessing virtual teams using this framework means evaluating them on six dimensions. These dimensions can be measured on multiple levels and each level can be evaluated using different metrics (cf. Table 3).

Table 3. Summary of the framework metrics

Assessment aspect	Dimension	Metrics
Network structure	Density	Density
		Cohesion
	Group Centrality	Centrality
		Group centralization
		Network centralization
	Disconnected cliques and bridges	Structural holes
		Brokerage score
		Partition/clique/clusters
		Heterogeneity
Health of the network	Trust	Integrity
		Competence
		Professionalism
		Loyalty
		Benevolence
Outcome of the network	Performance	Cooperation
		Quality of work
		Reliability
		Communication
		Flexibility
	Satisfaction	Satisfaction with the process
		Satisfaction with the outcomes

We have graphically summarized the six dimensions in figure 1. Of the six axes in the polar graph, Trust, performance and satisfaction are positively correlated with teams' well-being. For example, the more trust there is among team members, the better their relationships are and the more effective the team is.

The density axis reflects the level of interaction among the team members and can give an idea on the extent of information dissemination and knowledge exchange within the team. According to [20], [37], internal network density is positively related to team effectiveness. [26] affirms that density has an inversed U-shaped relationship with team effectiveness.

The centrality axis describes the distribution of links in the overall network. Centrality is often a good indicator of the availability of information and the effectiveness of the decision-making process. Studies [38], [39], [40], [20] that examined teams' centrality showed that decentralized networks are more efficient than centralized networks even when solving moderately complex problems. Another set of research [13], [14] on the other hand, found that team centrality is negatively related to its creativity and that only modest centralization has positive impact on team performance.

Finally, the disconnected cliques and bridges axis describes the clusters, structural holes and weak ties existing in the network. Weak ties are used to assess creativity, innovation and inter-units information dissemination. External range has been considered to have a positive impact on team performance [20] [37], [41]. [42] and [43] state that this is not always the case as weak inter-unit ties speed up projects only when the knowledge transferred is not complex. [23] affirm that moderate proportions of structural holes are positively related to team performance.

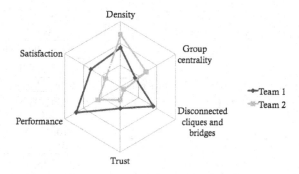

Fig. 1. The six metrics to assess virtual teams

Asserting the correlation between the last three axes and team well-being is hence still waiting to be confirmed by more experimental research. The most recent studies defend an inversed U-shaped relationship where an optimal value has to be reached. This middle value is however very context-based and depends on the nature of the project, the team and the organization. An estimation of this value can still be calculated based on a history of similar projects but wouldn't necessarily be accurate due to the multiple factors that come into play.

The virtual team is rated along each of the six axes and can thereby be visually evaluated. The closer from the periphery the ratings of the three first axes are, the more positive the team well-being can be. If the ratings of the last three axes are neither near the center nor at the periphery, there are more chances they can hit the optimal values.

Assessing virtual teams using this SNA based framework suggests that the evaluator uses the six dimensions mentioned above. It is important though that he chooses the right metrics for his objectives.

5   Conclusion and Future Work

The fundamental goal of this paper is to propose an SNA-based framework to evaluate virtual teams. The framework is a three-factors-based model that assesses teams on six dimensions. A range of metrics is available for every dimension. This suggests that it is up to the evaluator to choose the most adequate indicators to assess his team. A decision support system needs to be built to assist the evaluator in the process of choosing the metrics and weighting them based on their priority. The same system will have to determine how to calculate the metrics and restitute the global results for interpretation. This requires building the network using data collected from a collaborative platform. Further research will need to examine the process of building the network in more details and seek to improve visualization and therefore interpretation [46]. An experimental study will also have to be conducted to refine the framework by applying it on different teams and comparing the final results.

References

1. Pauleen, D.J.: Virtual Teams: Projects, Protocols and Processes. Idea Group Publishing, London (2004)
2. Brauner, E., Scholl, W.: The information processing approach as perspective for group research. Grp Proc. Int. Rel. 3, 115–122 (2000)
3. Henttonen, K.: Exploring social networks on the team level - A review of empirical literature. J. Eng. Tech. Mgt. 27, 74–109 (2010)
4. Kilduff, M., Tsai, W.: Social Networks and Organizations. Sage Publications: Athenaeum Press Limited, Gateshead (2007)
5. Tapscott, D., Williams, A.D.: Wikinomics: How mass collaboration changes everything. Portfolio – Penguin Edition, USA (2010)
6. Schreyögg, G., Sydow, J.: Organizing for fluidity? Dilemmas of New Organizational Forms. Organization 21(6), 1251–1262 (2010)
7. Sproull, L., Kiesler, S.: Reducing Social Context Cues: Electronic Mail in Organizational Communication. Mgt. Sc. 32(11), 1492–1512 (1986)
8. Ernø-Kjølhede, E.: Project Management Theory and the Management of Research Projects. Politics and Philosophy Copenhagen Business School (2000)
9. Galegher, J., Kraut, R.E.: Computer-mediated Communication for Intellectual Teamwork: An Experiment in Group Writing. Info. Sys. Research 5(2), 110–138 (1994)

10. Freeman, L.C.: The development of social network analysis: A study in the sociology of science. ΣP Empirical Press, Vancouver (2004)
11. Wasserman, S., Faust, C.: Social network analysis methods and applications. Cambridge University Press, Cambridge (1994)
12. Marsden, P.V.: Network data and measurement. An. Rev. Soc. 16, 435–463 (1990)
13. Leenders, R., Van Engelen, J., Kratzer, J.: Virtuality, communication, and new product team creativity: social network perspective. J. Eng. and Tech. Mgt. 20(1), 69–92 (2003)
14. Luo, J.-D.: Social network structure and performance of improvement teams. Int. J. Bus. Perf. Mgt. 7(2), 208–223 (2005)
15. Kratzer, J., Leenders, R., Van Engelen, J.: Informal contacts and performance in innovation teams. Int. J. Manpower 26(6), 513–528 (2005)
16. Shrader, C.B., Dellva, W.L., McElroy, J.C.: Social networks and group performance: A partial test of the Pearce and David hypotheses. Int. J. Small Grp. Res. 5, 145–162 (1989)
17. Freeman, L.C.: A set of measures of centrality based on betweenness. Sociometry 40, 35–41 (1977)
18. Baldwin, T.T., Bedell, M.D., Johnson, J.L.: The social fabric of a team-based M.B.A. program: network effects on student satisfaction and performance. Ac. Mgt. 40(6), 1369–1397 (1997)
19. Mote, J.E.: R&D ecology; using 2-mode network analysis to explore complexity in R&D environments. J. Eng. Tech. Mgt. 22(1-2), 93–111 (2005)
20. Wong, S.: Task knowledge overlap and knowledge variety: the role of advice network structures and impact on group effectiveness. J. Org. Beh. 29(5), 591–614 (2008)
21. Sparrowe, R.T., Liden, R.C., Wayne, S.J., Kraimer, M.L.: Social networks and the performance of individuals and groups. Ac. Mgt. J. 44(2), 316–325 (2001)
22. Lin, Z., Yang, H., Arya, B., Huang, Z., Li, D.: Structural versus individual perspectives on the dynamics of group performance: theoretical exploration and empirical investigation. J. Mgt. 31(3), 354–380 (2005)
23. Balkundi, P., Kilduff, M., Barsness, Z.I., Michael, J.H.: Demographic antecedents and performance consequences of structural holes in work teams. J. Org. Beh. 28, 241–260 (2006)
24. Glückler, J., Schrott, G.: Leadership and performance in virtual teams: exploring brokerage in electronic communication. Int. J. e-Collab. 3(3), 31–52 (2007)
25. Yang, H.-L., Tang, J.-H.: Team structure and team performance in IS development: a social network perspective. Inf. Mgt. 41, 335–349 (2004)
26. Oh, H., Chung, M.-H., Labianca, G.: Group social capital and group effectiveness: The role of informal socializing ties. Ac. Mgt. J. 47(6), 860–875 (2004)
27. Fan, Z.-P., Suo, W.-L., Feng, B., Liu, Y.: Trust estimation in a virtual team: A decision support method. Exp. Sys. W. App. 38(8), 10240–10251 (2004)
28. Easley, D., Kleinberg, J.: Networks, Crowds, and Markets: Reasoning About a Highly Connected World. Cambridge University Press, New York (2010)
29. McEvily, B., Perrone, V., Zaheer, A.: Trust as an Organizing Principle. Org. Sc. 14(1), 91–103 (2003)
30. DeRosa, M.D., Lepsinger, R.: Virtual team success: a practical guide for working and leading from a distance. Jossey-Bass, San Francisco (2010)
31. Li, C.: Open leadership: how social technology can transform the way you lead. Jossey-Bass, San Francisco (2010)
32. Bell, S.T.: Deep-level composition variables as predictors of team performance: a meta-analysis. J. App. Psy. 92(3), 595–615 (2007)

33. Chidambaram, L.: Relational development in computer-supported groups. MIS Qtly. 20(2), 143–165 (1996)
34. Ocker, R.J.: The mediating effect of group development on satisfaction in a virtual and mixed-mode environment. Paper Presented at the Proceedings of the 35th Hawaii International Conference on System Sciences (2002)
35. Warkentin, M.E., Sayeed, L., Hightower, R.: Virtual teams versus face-to-face teams: an exploratory study of a web-based conference system. Dec. Sc. 28(4), 975–996 (1997)
36. Lin, C., Standing, C., Liu, Y.-C.: A model to develop effective virtual teams. Dec. Supp. Sys. 45, 1031–1045 (2008)
37. Reagans, R., Zuckerman, E., McEvily, B.: How to make the team: Social networks vs. demography as criteria for designing effective teams. Adm. Sc. Qtly. 49, 101–133 (2004)
38. Leavitt, H.J.: Some effects of certain communication patterns on group performance. J. Ab. Soc. Psy. 46(1), 38–50 (1951)
39. Macy, J., Christie, L.S., Luce, R.D.: Coding noise in a task-oriented group. J. Ab. Soc. Psy. 48, 401–409 (1953)
40. Mulder, M.: Communication structure. Decision structure and group performance. Sociometry 23, 1–14 (1960)
41. Reagans, R., Zuckerman, E.W.: Networks, diversity, and productivity, the social capital of corporate R&D teams. Org. Sc. 12(4), 502–517 (2001)
42. Hansen, M.T.: The search-transfer problem, the role of weak ties in sharing knowledge across organisational subunits. Adm. Sc. Qtly. 44(1), 82–111 (1999)
43. Aral, S., Alstyne, M.V.: The Diversity-Bandwidth Trade-off. Am. J. Soc. 117(1), 90–171 (2011)
44. Hoppe, B., Reinelt, C.: Social network analysis and the evaluation of leadership networks. Lead. Qtly. 21(4), 600–619 (2010)
45. Bonchi, F., Castillo, C., Gionis, A., Jaimes, A.: Social Network Analysis and Mining for Business Applications. ACM Tran. Intel. Sys. Tech. 2(3), Article 22 (April 2011)
46. Bode, S., Spekowius, K., Thomas, H., Brecht, R., Markscheffel, B.: TMchartis – a Tool Set for Designing Multiple Problem-oriented Visualizations for Topic Maps. In: Scaling Topic Maps: 3rd International Conference on Topic Maps Research and Applications, Leipzig, Germany (2007)

Towards Evolutionary Multimodal Interaction

Maria Chiara Caschera, Arianna D'Ulizia, Fernando Ferri, and Patrizia Grifoni

Institute of Research on Population and Social Policies (IRPPS) –
National Research Council (CNR)
00185, Rome (Italy)
{mc.caschera,arianna.dulizia,fernando.ferri,
patrizia.grifoni}@irpps.cnr.it

Abstract. One of the main challenges of Human Computer Interaction researches is to improve naturalness of the user's interaction process. Currently two widely investigated directions are the adaptivity and the multimodality of interaction. Starting from the adaptivity concept, the paper provides an analysis of methods that make multimodal interaction adaptive respect to the final users and evolutionary over time. A comparative analysis between the concepts of adaptivity and evolution, given in literature, is provided, highlighting their similarities and differences and an original definition of evolutionary multimodal interaction is provided. Moreover, artificial intelligence techniques, quantum computing concepts and evolutionary computation applied to multimodal interaction are discussed.

Keywords: Multimodal interaction, Evolutionary computation, Adaptivity.

1 Introduction

In the next years, human-computer interaction will go towards a flexible and natural human-like interaction. Multimodality allows flexible interaction between users and systems because users have the freedom of using the modality of interaction of their choice (such as speech, handwriting, gestures, and gaze), and they have a sense of naturalness that derives from the use of interaction modes similar to the ones used in everyday human-human interactions.

One main challenge in multimodal interaction design lies in the adaptation of the interaction process to the users. In detail, the challenge is in selecting the optimal set of modal inputs combination that users will find easy and intuitive to produce, and that the system will be able to interpret in order to improve the degrees of flexibility and naturalness. The concept of adaptivity implies to decide on the appropriate devices, the appropriate interaction modalities according to user's profile information. User profiles include information about: user's preferences, rules, and settings (like name, address, birth date, or credit-card number); device and service profiles (like audio volume and text display properties); situation-dependent profiles (such as the context types such as environment and relevant changes within the current situation) [1]. User profiles contain dynamic information due to the fact that properties can be added, refined or deleted either manually/explicitly by the user or automatically/ implicitly by the system analysing the user's interaction process. This implies that,

P. Herrero et al. (Eds.): OTM 2012 Workshops, LNCS 7567, pp. 608–616, 2012.

during the interaction process, it is not sufficient to consider only issues related to adaptation but also evolutionary aspects. In fact, the user's profile evolves, and its evolution is due to the improvement, refinement and adaptation to changing of the user's preferences.

Although the naturalness and flexibility of human communication is hard to achieve, interactive systems will aim to these two main characteristics in a threefold way: through multimodality, adaptation, and evolution.

The naturalness and flexibility of multimodal interaction is motivated by the fact that humans communicate multimodally with their five senses. Human brain, indeed, processes multiple streams of information to assess the state of the world. The synergistic processing of these streams results in better performance and less cognitive load for the user compared to a situation in which s/he uses a single modality.

Analogously, the naturalness and flexibility of adaptive interaction is motivated by the fact that it supports heterogeneous user groups with variable and different needs, abilities and preferences by representing, reasoning, and acting on models of the user, domain, task, discourse, and media (e.g. graphics, natural language, gesture) [2].

Finally, the naturalness and flexibility of evolutionary interaction is motivated by the fact that human interaction is evolutionary by its nature, since all signs used during dialogues (language, gestures, eye movements, etc.) change and evolve over time.

Starting from the concepts of multimodality, adaptation, and evolution, the paper provides an analysis of methods applied for multimodal, adaptive and evolutionary interaction. In particular, the proposed work aims to investigate how artificial intelligence techniques, and in particular evolutionary computation, can be applied to make multimodal interaction evolutionary.

The remainder of the paper is structured as follows. The state of the art on multimodal interaction is presented in Section 2. Section 3 provides some notions and literature approaches on adaptive interaction. A comparative analysis between adaptivity and evolution is provided in Section 4, along with evolutionary algorithms applied in the human-computer interaction literature. Section 5 offers a discussion about research goals towards an evolutionary multimodal interaction. Finally, conclusions are presented in Section 6.

2   Multimodal Interaction

Multimodal interaction has emerged as the future paradigm of human computer interaction (HCI). This fact is gathered also by the increasing application of the multimodal paradigm to computer interfaces in order to make computer behaviour closer to human communication.

Communication among people is often multimodal as it is obtained combining different modalities, such as speech, gesture, facial expression, sketch, and so on. Multimodal interfaces allow several modalities of communication (see Fig.1) to be harmoniously integrated, making the system communication characteristics more and more similar to the human communication approach. The main features of multimodal interaction, such as the different classes of cooperation between different modes, the time relationships among the involved modalities and the relationships between chunks of information connected with these modalities, are described in [3].

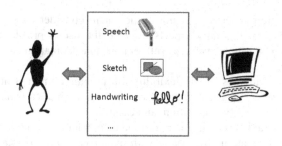

Fig. 1. Multimodal interaction

One of the main problems fundamental to the design of multimodal interfaces is the multimodal data fusion, i.e. the process of combining information from different modalities in order to have a comprehensive representation of the user's message. In the literature, three main different approaches to the fusion process have been proposed, according to the main architectural levels (recognition and decision) at which the fusion of the input signals can be performed: recognition-based (named also early or feature-based fusion), decision-based (named also late or semantic fusion), and hybrid multi-level fusion [4]. A more extensive discussion about multimodal input fusion strategies can be found in [5].

Analogously to the fusion process, another critical issue in multimodal interaction systems is the multimodal fission, i.e. the process of combining different outputs from modal channels in order to provide the user with consistent feedback. Foster [6] defines fission as *"the process of realising an abstract message through output on some combination of the available channels"*. A discussion about multimodal fission approaches can be found in [7].

The interpretation process is one important unit for building multimodal systems. The interpretation of user input is strictly connected to different features, such as available interaction modalities, conversation focus, and context of interaction. A correct interpretation can be reached by simultaneously considering semantic, temporal and contextual constraints. For example, in multimodal system based on video and audio input [8], the interpretation defines a multimodal corpus of digital and temporally synchronized video and audio recordings of human monologues and dialogues. An overview of methods for interpreting multimodal input is provided in [9].

3   Adaptive Interaction

Interaction techniques are defined as methods that allow a user to accomplish a given task via the user interface [10]. During the interaction process, every user has a certain physical ability level. An adaptation to the user's specific attributes implies to change certain parameters of the user interfaces and to adjusting its sensitivity according to the user's need. To adapt to user diversity, during interaction process, user models becomes crucial to provide adaptation and personalization for users.

In [11] three types of adaptation are presented: switching between interaction techniques; enhancing the interaction technique with modalities; and adapting the interaction technique itself.

During the interaction process, users may encounter different situations (e.g. environment condition, position of the user) that might influence the performance of executing the task. Switching between interaction techniques enables user to perform a task fitting the different environmental conditions.

The interaction process can be adapted by enhancing it with the use of multimodal feedback such as visual, audio or haptic [12].

Finally, adapting the interaction technique itself implies constructing, maintain and exploiting explicit representations of user. These models contain information and assumptions about users that system believes to be true, such as users' interaction patterns, preferences, interests, goals and characteristics. In detail, a user model combines the information provided by the user, direct inferences from the user's actions, and predictions made by stereotypes or user group models that are believed to be appropriate for this user [13].

Information for building the user model can be obtained simply asking the user for her/his preferences, or automatically inferring user habits, by learning user profile data. An example of automatic inference of user behaviours is proposed in [14] where users' knowledge and goals are used to automatically discover user profiles by analysing the tags users associate with available content. Moreover, contextual aspects, such as location and device constraints, are used in [13] where context-aware user profiles are proposed, in which the profile definitions are associated with particular situations encountered by the users.

Methods, those directly ask the user for her/his preferences, allows simply gather information for a user model. However, those methods are not always a trustworthy source of information about users because people tend to give socially acceptable or desirable answers or they may not be able to answer.

On the other hand, methods, those automatically infer user habits, allow constructing user models by making direct inferences from a user's behaviour to a model of the user. Disadvantages of those methods are: the difficulties to make inferences based on the available input; scarcity of data that is available; the difficulty to monitor user interactions; and the short-term knowledge that becomes outdated [12].

The limits of adaptive systems depend on some systems are targeted on user, others on task, others on system or environment and so these dependencies limit their extensibility and reusability [15].

4   From Adaptivity to Evolutionary

The concept of adaptive interaction, introduced in Section 3, is fundamental for designing interactive systems that are able to dynamically adapt the interaction to the user and context's features. This adaptation occurs for short-term changes, as the system reacts to situational changes, such as, for example, in context-aware systems.

However, the needs and conditions in which the interaction occurs can change over time due to various factors (for example, environmental or temporal). Therefore, this requires that the interactive system adapts and evolves the interaction process to these long-term changing circumstances.

In the literature the concept of "interaction evolution" has been introduced for representing the ability of interactive systems to evolve and tailor interaction in long-term changing situations. Interaction evolution is defined by McBryan et al. [16] as "multiple related instances of interaction configuration (customisation or personalisation) over time that have a goal to change some aspect of the systems interaction behavior". For interaction configuration the authors mean a combination of devices, interaction techniques, modalities used and supporting components required to instantiate a new configuration of the system.

In order to better specify the concepts of adaptive interaction and evolutionary interaction this work aims to make evident differences in terms of responses that the systems returns when unexpected stimuli are provided. For this purpose these definitions are provided.

Definition 1. *Adaptive Interaction* is characterized by an adaptive behavior of the system, i.e., the system reacts without producing a modification of its default functioning when it receives unexpected stimuli, but producing specific responses according to the different users or situations.   ∎

Definition 2. *Evolutionary Interaction* is characterized by an evolutionary behavior of the system, i.e. the system changes the default behavior when the same kinds of unexpected stimuli are frequent and repeated for a long time period, so that they become expected independently from the single user or situations features.   ∎

Fig. 2 shows the differences between adaptive (Fig. 2.a) and evolutionary interaction (Fig. 2.b). In the adaptive interaction, the system reacts in a twofold way, according to the kind of stimuli: for unexpected stimuli, it reacts with specific responses according to the user's features; for standard stimuli, it reacts with its default behavior (never changing). In the evolutionary interaction, the system reacts both to standard and unexpected stimuli with a default behavior (ever changing).

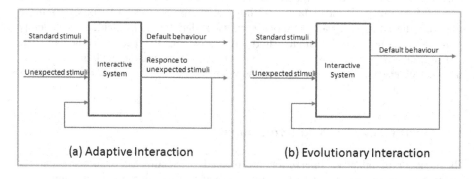

(a) Adaptive Interaction   (b) Evolutionary Interaction

Fig. 2. Adaptive (a) and Evolutionary (b) Interaction

Interaction evolution is the result of the efforts made to endow interactive systems with a flexible human-like interaction. Human interaction, indeed, is evolutionary by its nature, since all interaction abilities and features involved in dialogues (language, gestures, eye movements, etc.) change and evolve over time generation by generation.

Therefore, in recent years many works have focused on assuring flexibility and naturalness to human-system communication through the exploitation of the interaction evolution. In particular, McBryan et al. [16] proposed a model for representing the interaction evolution process, which is composed of one or more potentially linked interaction configurations, each of which consists of four sequential stages: identify opportunity, reflect, decide and implement. Goldin and Keil [17] provided some considerations about the relationships among interaction, evolution and intelligence. In particular, the authors stated that the paradigm shift from algorithmic computation towards evolutionary and interaction computing can contribute to establish the unified foundations of interactive systems, overcoming the limits of the algorithmic approaches in terms of intelligence.

Evolutionary computation is a field closely related to adaptation and evolution. Evolutionary algorithms, indeed, were proposed initially by Holland [18] to drive the adaptation of complex systems to changing and uncertain environments. They use nature inspired concepts, like mutation, recombination, and selection, applied to a population of individuals containing candidate solutions in order to evolve iteratively better and better solutions.

Therefore, evolutionary algorithms have been widely used for addressing adaptivity respect to users and contexts uncertainness and variations, and for optimizing adaptivity processes. According to the concept "evolutionary interaction", previously introduced, the different algorithms, proposed in the literature, can act on two levels, both at the level of adaptability and, at the level of default operation of the interaction producing its evolution on the base of unexpected configurations. The reference population and the evolution are then considered respect to the default interaction. This perspective considers communication and interaction between humans changing with the influence of context (e.g. cultural and socio-economic) and individual.

Hence, evolutionary algorithms have been successfully applied in the human-computer interaction literature to facilitate user personalisation without the need for time consuming explicit knowledge-acquisition process. Pauplin et al. [19] proposed an interactive evolution approach for developing rapidly reconfigurable systems in which the users' tacit knowledge and requirements can be elicited and used for finding the appropriate parameters to achieve the required image segmentation. Toney [20] applied an evolutionary-based reinforcement learning algorithm for automatically generating spoken strategies in a spoken dialogue system. Another evolutionary-based learning classifier algorithm was proposed in [21], which uses information from a user's environment for automatically personalizing desktop applications.

From the analysis of these evolutionary methods it is clear that they have been applied to specific domains for enabling a short-term adaptation to situational changes. However, considering the evolutionary nature of these methods, it is interesting to investigate the opportunity to apply them for modeling the interaction evolution in long-term changing situations.

5   Evolutionary Multimodal Interaction

Technology is changing, people are changing, society is changing, and HCI has to intervene and adapt itself to these changings. HCI needs to extend its methods and approaches in order to fit on human changing.

Considering human interaction, it changes and evolves through repeated use in order to adapt the features of interaction between people with differences in communication. The repetition of communication and the re-adaptation lead to evolution of the interaction process. The evolutionary nature of the human interaction has been investigated in [22] analyzing the repetition of miscommunication and the successful communication.

As well as human communication evolves, so the interaction between human and system evolves. Similarly to the natural world where genetic algorithms are used to analyze the evolution of species, so the evolutionary computation may be applied to multimodal interaction in order to observe the evolution of interaction.

As proof of this consideration, similarly to humans, the interaction between robots has been investigated and modeled in [23] using Recurrent Neural Networks (RNN) in order to obtain a mutual adaptation between agent robots. Moreover, adaptive statistical methods have been applied in [24] to optimize the combination of multimodal user input.

Researches on evolutionary computation integrated with multimodal and adaptive interaction will play a key role for designing interactive systems that enable a flexible natural human-like interaction. These researches will improve the current concepts, theories and models of evolutionary interaction given in the literature (e.g. [23], [24]). Starting from the Evolutionary Interaction concept provided in Definition 2, an effort in this direction will allow: (i) to define new interaction models and algorithms able to represent and manage the evolution over time of interaction processes, its interpretation; (ii) to define evaluation metrics for measuring interaction naturalness and the accuracy of models representing the evolution in long-term changing situations.

Considering new methodologies for the design of evolution of interaction models, different evolutionary algorithms and computational approaches can be used.

We believe that a view of particular interest may be genetic algorithms evolved in the perspective of quantum computing.

Quantum Genetic Algorithm (QGA) uses concepts of qubit, quantum superposition, quantum logic gate and other concepts [25] [26]. Qubit is the unit of quantum information; it is a two state system and it exists in all its potential states, but when it measured gives one only of the possible configurations (superposition).

In classical computing, the possible states of a system of n bits form a vector space of n dimensions while, in a quantum system of n qubits the state space has 2^n dimensions. An interesting example of QGA for multisensors image registration has been proposed in [27], but their use could be extended to the interaction and communication processes, and in particular to the multimodal interaction. In fact, these algorithms allow to represent the complexity of communication processes and, in particular, of multimodal input, even using populations having small size respect to the population for co-respective in traditional computing, providing an optimization in terms of computing time, and providing transformation and evolutions considering in a very efficient way and in parallel all coevolving communication issues.

6   Conclusion

This paper has discussed the roles of multimodality, adaptation and evolution in making interactive systems natural and flexible as human-human interaction.

In detail, the main features of multimodal interaction have been presented in order to underline how the naturalness can be achieved in HCI, emphasizing the importance of the adaptivity issue.

The paper presents the concept of adaptivity underlining how adaptation occurs for short-term changes. It underlines the necessity for interactive systems to consider the human changing in long time period and how they can be reflected in the interaction processes.

For this reason, the paper focuses on the evolutionary nature that the HCI has to consider in order to fit the changing and the uncertainties of human interaction.

Starting from the investigation on the application of evolutionary algorithms to users and contexts uncertainness and variations in short term adaptation, this paper addresses of using genetic algorithms evolved in the perspective of quantum computing to provide an evolutionary HCI.

References

1. Thomsen, J., Vanrompay, Y., Berbers, Y.: Evolution of context-aware user profiles. In: ICUMT 2009, vol. 1(6) (2009)
2. Maybury, M., Wahlster, W.: Intelligent User Interfaces: An Introduction. In: Readings in Intelligent User Interfaces, pp. 1–13. Morgan Kaufmann, San Francisco (1998)
3. Caschera, M.C., Ferri, F., Grifoni, P.: Multimodal interaction systems: information and time features. International Journal of Web and Grid Services (IJWGS) 3(1), 82–99 (2007)
4. D'Ulizia, A., Ferri, F., Grifoni, P.: Generating Multimodal Grammars for Multimodal Dialogue Processing. IEEE Transactions on Systems, Man and Cybernetics, Part A: Systems and Humans 40(6), 1130–1145 (2010)
5. D'Ulizia, A.: Exploring Multimodal Input Fusion Strategies. In: The Handbook of Research on Multimodal Human Computer Interaction and Pervasive Services: Evolutionary Techniques for Improving Accessibility, pp. 34–57. IGI Publishing (2009)
6. Foster, M. E.: State of the art review: multimodal fission. Public deliverable 6.1, COMIC project (2002)
7. Grifoni, P.: Multimodal fission. In: The Handbook of Research on Multimodal Human Computer Interaction and Pervasive Services: Evolutionary Techniques for Improving Accessibility, pp. 103–120. IGI Publishing (2009)
8. Harper, M.P., Shriberg, E.: Multimodal model integration for sentence unit detection. In: ICMI 2004, pp. 121–128 (2004)
9. Caschera, M.C.: Interpretation methods and ambiguity management in multimodal systems. In: Grifoni, P. (ed.) Handbook of Research on Multimodal Human Computer Interaction and Pervasive Services: Evolutionary Techniques for Improving Accessibility, pp. 87–102. IGI Global, USA (2009)
10. Bowman, D.A., Kruijff, E., LaViola, J.J., Poupyrev, I.: 3D User Interfaces. In: Theory and Practice. Addison-Wesley (2005)
11. Renny Octavia, J., Raymaekers, C., Coninx, K.: Adaptation in virtual environments: conceptual framework and user models. Multimedia Tools Appl. 54(1), 121–142 (2011)

12. Ehlert P.A.M.: Intelligent user interfaces: introduction and survey. Research Report DKS03-01 / ICE 01 Data and Knowledge Systems group Faculty of Information Technology and Systems Delft University of Technology (2003)

13. Au Yeung, C.M., Gibbins, N., Shadbolt, N.: A Study of User Profile Generation from Folksonomies. In: Social Web and Knowledge Management, Social Web 2008 Workshop at WWW 2008, Beijing, China, April 21-25 (2008)

14. Carrillo-Ramos, A., Villanova-Oliver, M., Gensel, J., Martin, H.: Contextual User Profile for Adapting Information in Nomadic Environments. In: Weske, M., Hacid, M.-S., Godart, C. (eds.) WISE Workshops 2007. LNCS, vol. 4832, pp. 337–349. Springer, Heidelberg (2007)

15. Rousseau, C., Bellik, Y., Vernier, F.: Architecture Framework for Output Multimodal Systems Design. In: Proceedings of OZCHI 2004, November 22-24. ACM Press (2004)

16. McBryan, T., McGee-Lennon, M.R., Gray, P.: An integrated approach to supporting interaction evolution in home care systems. In: 1st International Conference on Pervasive Technologies Related to Assistive Environments, Athens, Greece, July 16-18, vol. 282, p. 1. ACM Press (2008)

17. Goldin, D., Keil, D.: Interaction, Evolution, and Intelligence. In: Proc. CEC 2001 (Congress on Evolutionary Computation), Seoul, Korea, vol. 2, pp. 805–814. IEEE Press, Seoul (2001)

18. Holland, J.H.: Adaptation in Natural and Artificial Systems. The Univ. of Michigan Press (1975)

19. Pauplin, O., Caleb-Solly, P., Smith, J.: User-centric image segmentation using an interactive parameter adaptation tool. Pattern Recognition 43(2), 519–529 (2010)

20. Toney, D.: Evolutionary Reinforcement Learning of Spoken Dialogue Strategies. PhD thesis (2007), http://hdl.handle.net/1842/1769 (retrieved)

21. Shankar, A., Louis, S.J.: XCS for Personalizing Desktop Interfaces. IEEE Transactions on Evolutionary Computation 14, 547–560 (2010)

22. Miwa, Y., Wesugi, S., Ishibiki, C., Itai, S.: Embodied interface for emergence and co-share of 'Ba', usability evaluation and interface design. In: Proceedings of HCI Int., pp. 248–252 (2001)

23. Hinoshita, W., Ogata, T., Kozima, H., Kanda, H., Takahashi, T., Okuno, H.G.: Emergence of Evolutionary Interaction with Voice and Motion between Two Robots using RNN. In: IROS 2009 Proceedings of the 2009 IEEE/RSJ International Conference on Intelligent Robots and Systems, pp. 4186–4192 (2009)

24. Althoff, F., Al-Hames, M., McGlaun, G., Lang, M.: Towards a New Approach for Integrating Multimodal User Input Based on Evolutionary Computation. In: Proceedings ICASSP 2002. IEEE Signal Processing Society, Orlando, USA (2002)

25. Meshoul, S., Batouche, M., Belhadj-moustefa, K.: An evolutionary framework for image data fusion based on the maximization of mutual information. In: Proceeding of the International Symposium on Software and Systems, I3S 2001 (2001)

26. Han, K., Kim, J.: Quantum-inspired evolutionary algorithm for a class of combinatorial optimization. IEEE Transactions on Evolutionary Computation 6(6) (2002)

27. Draa, A., Batouche, M., Talbi, H.: A quantum-inspired differential evolution algorithm for rigid image registration. Trans. Eng. Comput. Technol., 408–411 (2004)

Interactive Public Digital Displays:
Investigating Its Use in a High School Context

Nuno Otero[1,2], Rui José[1], and Bruno Silva[1]

[1] Centro Algoritmi, University of Minho, Campus de Azurém, Guimarães, Portugal
[2] Department of Media Technology, Linnæus University, Sweden
{nuno.otero,rui,bruno.silva}@dsi.uminho.pt

Abstract. This paper presents a longitudinal user study that investigated the adoption of some Bluetooth based functionalities for a public digital display in a high school. More specifically, the utilization of Bluetooth device naming extended beyond social identity representation and introduced the use of a simple interaction mechanism. The interaction mechanism involves recognizing parts of the Bluetooth device name as explicit instructions to trigger the generation of content on an interactive public display. Together with representatives of the teachers' community, the design team defined some social rules concerning usage in order to account for the specificities of the place. In the user study, three fully functional prototypes were deployed at the school hall of the high school. The functionalities introduced with the different prototypes were: the visualization on the display of the Bluetooth device names, the possibility to contribute to tag clouds and the possibility to choose icons from a given set for self-expression. The results suggest that people appropriated some but not all of the functionalities employed. Implications of our findings to the design of interactive digital displays are pointed out.

Keywords: Ubiquitous computing; digital public displays; bluetooth, user studies.

1 Introduction

Our on-going long-term research goal concerns the investigation of the digital displays' design space to support people's interactions through these artefacts in public spaces. People are taking advantage of new web, mobile and ubiquitous technologies to explore novel ways to interact in complex social situations [4, 9, 16]. Digital displays can be an important technology for many types of ubiquitous computing scenarios since it can provide a simple and effective way to bring digital information into our public spaces. Furthermore, providing interactivity in digital displays can be used to foster user-generated pervasive content back to the virtual world. However, research has highlighted that enticing people to participate and explore the potential of the systems is a major challenge [1, 5]. Furthermore, there are complex issues related with publication management [6]. For example, the design of situated displays is fundamentally affected by a trade-off on control sharing. On the one hand, the need to

P. Herrero et al. (Eds.): OTM 2012 Workshops, LNCS 7567, pp. 617–626, 2012.
© Springer-Verlag Berlin Heidelberg 2012

support a wide range of practices and social settings around the display suggests approaches that build strongly on active user participation and high levels of appropriation. On the other hand, the expected convergence towards the social practices of the community as a whole, suggests approaches such as mediation and explicit user permissions that define more rigidly the purpose of the system.

The prototypes presented in this paper involve the scanning and depiction of Bluetooth device names in digital displays situated in public spaces. More specifically, using simple techniques involving the parsing of the device names, we were able to provide functionalities that not only served to communicate some sort of social identity but also to trigger particular types of interaction: influencing tag clouds and expressing preferences towards content.

This present work investigates how people sharing a particular place within a high school appropriated a set of Bluetooh based interactive mechanisms. Given the nature of the study we opted to consider research questions instead of fully-fledged hypotheses. The research questions are:

- Did people change the name of their device and created an individual public presence on the display?
- Did people use the tag clouds and icons functionalities (corresponding to the functionalities introduced with prototype 2 and 3 - see below the descriptions)?
- Did some of the features of the prototypes related to the display of content influence organizational practices?

The remainder of the paper goes as follows. Section two provides an overview of related work, focusing on situated public displays. Section three describes the framing of the study, including the prototype deployed and its functionalities. Section four presents the results and section five the overall discussion. In section six we present the lessons learned and future developments.

2   Background

The display of Bluetooth presence in public or semi-public displays has been explored in a variety of systems. Some studies have investigated Bluetooth scanning as a mechanism for sensing presence and uncovering all sorts of social patterns, e.g. the familiarity of the surrounding environment [15], the social situation [13], and more general large-scale reality mining [3]. The Cityware project [10] looked at several ways of leveraging the capture of information regarding Bluetooth mobility, including a set of in-situ visualizations about current or recent Bluetooth presences. The system supports links between Bluetooth devices and the Facebook identities of their owners, as a way to create a link between physical presence and virtual presence. The system uses in-situ presence information as a way to generate content for the virtual world. More specifically, it provides data to a Facebook application that lets people associate physical co-presence information with their social network.

Another example of the use of presence as a driver for situated interaction around public displays is the Proactive displays system [11, 12]. The detection of nearby

RFID tags was used as a trigger for showing profile information about the owner of the tag, in an attempt to promote occasional encounters between people around the display. However, this approach requires a priori definition of individual profiles with associated data and assumes that everyone will be using a particular type of tag. Furthermore, people have a very limited role in the system, which is basically to move around and be detected. The Bluescreen project, in its turn, explores the use of Bluetooth presence to optimise the selection of adverts for display [8]. Content that has already been shown when a particular Bluetooth device was present is avoided if that device is present again, thus reducing the likelihood of the same content being shown again to the same person.

In relation to research that specifically address people's usage of Bluetooth functionality and their appropriation to extend their social everyday practices the following two examples are particularly relevant. O'Neill et al. [9] investigated the use of Bluetooth and the naming of devices through the scanning of device names in public spaces. In their study they were able to classify distinct types of device names and proposed that people's usage of Bluetooth can be seen as an example of the emergence of a specific culture around artifact utilization. Kindberg and Jones [9] went beyond the simple scanning of device names and, through 29 semi-structured interviews, tried to uncover the meaning behind the naming practices. Kindberg and Jones [9] study revealed that people tend to use Bluetooth mainly to share files. Sometimes, however, people also choose device names that reflected their presences in other social circles: adopting the same name as the online one or choosing the same name that identifies them in particular practices. Kindberg and Jones [9] also report that most of their interviewed participants did not tend to change their device name frequently. The use of Bluetooth names for conveying simple commands to public displays has been studied by Jose et al. as part of the instant places system [7] and also by Davies et al [2] as part of the Lancaster e-campus system. Even though the interaction approach is essentially the same as in our prototype, these studies were both focused on the ability to support spontaneous interaction with the displays, and did not addressed the issues of control sharing involved.

3   Methodology

The methodology followed for the study involved the deployment of fully functional prototypes in a real world context and the provision of information about the functionalities of the system without suggesting particular ways of usage. The study ran for approximately 24 weeks. The next sub-sections will describe the different prototypes deployed, the setting of the study and the methods utilized.

3.1   The Prototypes

The prototypes deployed at the school included a public display in which content was generated, directly or indirectly, from Bluetooth presence. Generally speaking, the system comprises a Bluetooth enabled computer connected to a public screen and linked to a central repository. Information about nearby devices is periodically collected by a Bluetooth scanner and fed to a situation data model that manages data about the place and present devices. The central repository maintains persistent information about previous sessions, and combines information from pervasively distributed data sources, allowing for multiple screens in a large space to share the same presence view. The system does not need any a priori information about people, their profiles, permissions or groups, as all the information in the repository is entirely created from the history of presences. All the prototypes also included some specific content suggested by the school team, the most relevant being the school news feeds.

The basic form of interaction with the *first prototype* of the system is to have a discoverable Bluetooth device with its name shown on the public display. This can be viewed as an implicit form of interaction where a person unexpectedly finds his or her name on the display. However, it can quickly turn into an explicit form of interaction when that person changes the device name for visualization on the screen. The visualization of the Bluetooth presences provides an element of situation awareness that we hoped would foster the use of Bluetooth naming as a way for self-expression. In order to explore further this latter functionality, the system supported the use of simple commands in the Bluetooth device names by parsing the device names in search for keywords that were recognised as commands ('t.*word*' for tag clouds and 'g.*word*' for icons) and then using them to trigger specific actions. For the *second prototype* the added functionality was the introduction of tag clouds. In the *third prototype* the users were also able to choose icons from a specific set and displayed it next to his/her device name as a way to express some sort of individual preference.

3.2   The Place

The user study took place at a high school. As most high schools, this place is a vibrant space full of activities, where students, teachers and other supporting personnel meet daily. The school is divided into several distinct pavilions with different purposes (classrooms, refectory, administration, students' common room etc). After initial consultations with the school representatives it was deemed appropriate to install the digital display at the entrance hall of the administrative pavilion. The administrative pavilion contains the school office, the teachers' common room, the school library and other administrative offices. Very different groups of people use this pavilion in distinct ways. Teachers utilize their common room between teaching periods, usually staying for short bursts of around ten minutes and longer during lunch break. Administrative personnel, however, tend to spend their working day within their office. Students and their parents can go to the teachers' common room and to the school office for specific meetings and dealings, varying a lot the amount of time they spent at this location. The library activities frequently involve longer stays. Regarding the particular location where the display was installed, the entrance, it seems reasonable to consider that people do not tend to stay there for long periods but is frequently accessed. This means that Bluetooth scanning will probably pick this constellation of parallel occurrences but the actual time people tend to spend in the visualization of the display is bound to some passers-by place specificities just described.

3.3   The Methods Followed in the Design/Development Cycle

Meetings with Teachers

Several meetings took place between the design team and representatives of the school. In the beginning of the intervention, a meeting with the school's Director was set and aimed at: (a) presenting the general ideas behind the project, including the envisioned system's functionalities, and defining the general scope of the users' studies; and (b) agreeing on a particular line of action that involved the creation of a teachers' team to follow the project, provide the necessary support and vouch the different activities to be pursued. After this initial step with the school's Director, a school teachers' team was appointed by the school's Director to follow the project. More specifically the teachers' team was in charge of:

- Discussing with the design team the specifics of the prototypes' functionalities, approving the deployment of the different prototypes and controlling the correct usage of the system.
- Ensuring that the different school's content channels to feed the display were updated with relevant information.
- Checking the appropriateness of the Bluetooth device names in order to approve the different identities that were being created within the system. More specifically, the teachers' team was responsible for checking lists of scanned device names and approve them for publication on the digital display.

Collecting System Logs

We collected system logs over 24 weeks. The logs collected MAC addresses of the different devices within the range of the Bluetooth scanner, as well as the corresponding device names. This means that the database created can keep track of the different sightings of devices and the possible change of device names that, in turn, can correspond to the use of some of the functionalities provided (or just a change of the way the owner of the device decides to present himself to the system).

The data collected can be divided into the following distinct periods:

- *Silent scanning* - to begin with we installed a Bluetooth scanner just to collect the usual activity regarding Bluetooth usage in order to understand better what would be the changes of introducing our system. This period corresponded to the first five weeks of the study.
- *First prototype* - On week 7 we deployed the first prototype (see description above).
- *Second prototype* - On week 17 the second prototype was made available.
- *Third prototype* - Finally, on week 21 the third prototype with the remaining of the functionalities developed was introduced.

4   Results

Table 1 shows the number of device names submitted for approval and its actual approval by the school's team. At the end of the silent scanning period the first list of device names collected was submitted for approval to the school's team (see subsection "Meeting with teachers"), so that the device names that would be displayed initially with the first prototype conformed to school's norms. From Table 1 we can see that most of the unapproved device names are found in lists two and three. This is expected since it is the period where people are trying out the system and see if they can "win" and display inappropriate terms. What such behaviour also suggests is that people are trying to take advantage of the relative anonymity provided by the system in order to stretch social rules. Nevertheless, the number of inappropriate device names drops sharply: in the 4th list only 3 device names are not approved.

Table 1. Number of device names sent and approved per period of the study

Period	Sent	Approved
Silent scanning	1st list: week 6 (232 device names submitted)	1st list: week 6 (231 device names approved - **99%**)
First prototype	2nd list: week 9 (202 device names submitted) 3rd list: week 13 (130 device names submitted)	2nd list: week 9 (181 device names approved - **90%**) 3rd list: week 13 (107 device names approved - **82%**)
Second prototype	4th list: week 18 (102 device names submitted)	4th list: week 18 (99 device names approved - **97%**)
Third prototype	5th list: week 23 (155 device names submitted)	5th list: no response

The data collected using the system logs and displayed in Table 2 allow the inspection of how many devices were detected and how many times people changed their device name in the different periods under investigation. In relation to the number of devices detected, Table 2 shows an increase from the silent scanning period to the period corresponding to the two first weeks of the first prototype's deployment. However, after this initial period of adoption one can see fluctuations of usage (note, however, that in some weeks the numbers of devices spotted drops probably due to school holidays). Regarding the device names the first two weeks after the deployment of the first prototype is also the particular time window that seems to show people "experimenting" with their Bluetooth presence on the display. Most of the device names chosen (and approved) correspond to first names or nicknames. None of the users tried to change their icon.

Table 3 shows some indicators regarding the use of the tag cloud functionality. In total it seems that 39 people tried to take advantage of the tag cloud. This number corresponds approximately to one fourth of the people using the system in the corresponding period (the second prototype). However, we did register some problems with the syntax for a correct utilization since there were 18 mistakes detected coming from 13 distinct devices.

Table 2. Number of unique devices and names collected during the silent scanning and deployments periods

Prototype	Week	Unique devices	Unique device names	Nr devices > 1 name
Silent Scanning	*2*	74	74	0
	3	95	96	1
	4	78	78	0
	5	98	98	0
	6	97	97	0
	7	90	93	3
	Total	259	267	8
First prototype	*7+8*	148	181	23
	9	169	196	16
	10	99	113	5
	11	110	125	7
	12	112	119	6
	13	102	104	2
	14	40	42	2
	15	21	21	0
	16	93	94	1
	17	97	98	1
	18	126	127	1
	Total	504	628	74
Second proto- type	*19*	112	114	2
	20+21	106	109	3
	Total	164	169	5
Third prototype	*22*	161	165	4
	23+24	131	135	4
	Total	219	229	9
	All Prototypes Total	655	818	101
	Total	763	955	121

Notes - (1) In column "Nr devices > 1" the difference between the sum of week's partial results and the period's total can be explained by considering that some users probably changed their device name between weeks and outside the rage detection of the Bluetooth scanner. Also to note that not always the difference between the total of unique devices and the total of unique device names is equal to the number of devices with more than one name. This is easily explained by users that changed their device name more than once. (2) Weeks 7+8, 20+21 and 23+24 show aggregated results due to some technical problems that occured.

The news feeds provided by the school to be shown in the public display can give us a glimpse of the acceptance of the new artefact among the school's more formal organizational units/structure. Several school departments initially agreed to contribute. However, in many cases their actual involvement was not consistent over the time. In fact, most of the updates of the content happened during the first two months after the deployment of the first prototype. This suggests some kind of novelty effect that faded as time went by.

Table 3. Number of tags used during the study. Valid and invalid tags correspond to tags with a well formed or incorrect system syntax.

Tags	Number of used tags	Devices
Valid tags	29	26
Invalid tags	18	13

5   Discussion

The results reported suggest that people sharing the place did adopt some of the functionalities provided but not all. This seems to be in line with the views by   Brignull et al. [1] and Huang et al [5] that enticing people to interact with public displays remains a challenge. The remaining of the discussion follows the research questions stated above.

Did people change the name of their device and created an individual public presence on the display?

The results regarding the change of device names strongly suggest that people did create a presence to be displayed since the comparison of the visible device names between the silent scanning period and the periods corresponding to the deployment of the first prototype clearly shows an increase. In a previous study José and Otero [7] reported a different pattern of usage of the device name functionality: users were able to utilize this functionality in order to use the display as a message board. However, in this present study we did not observe the same phenomena and we believe this is due to the approvals' procedure set. The lag between changing the device name and the actual approval, with its consequent appearance on the display, makes the exchange of messages on the spot impossible. Furthermore, we should also note that the possible messages would only be displayed if the devices were detected and so leaving messages for others to see asynchronously was not possible as well unless the device was detected once again. In fact, considering the policy implemented by the school team to approve device names it seems reasonable to assume that any messaging system would have to undergo a similar approval procedure.

These considerations seem to highlight the point made regarding the need to consider carefully the issue of control sharing. In this present case the control was clearly centralized but this does not seem to be the best option if one intends to create a highly dynamic display, content wise. More research is needed regarding the mechanisms that can be put into place to allow a satisfactory control of the content without jeopardizing people's creative appropriations of the display.

Did people use the tag clouds and icons functionalities?

Our results show that tag clouds were used but people did not adopt the icons as a way to express themselves. The tag cloud functionality was set as a way to people express their preferences regarding some types of affiliation (like football clubs and school classes). In some way this functionality is working at a group identity level and the symbols are clearly defined and shared. However, people probably assumed that the icons are related to a more individual level of identification and they might prefer to create their own icons instead of having to choose from a pre-defined set. If this is indeed the case then there is a need to construct a distinct procedure that allows a less restrictive self-expression. Once again, however, we are touching the problem of control sharing.

Did some of the features of the prototypes related to the display of content influence organizational practices?

In relation to the organizational practices, two issues seem to be particularly relevant: the procedure set for device names' approval and the actual provision of news feeds to be displayed. The procedure put in place to approve the device names is fairly centralized in the school's team. This, of course, puts some pressure on the team's members since it is an extra task they have to engage with on top of their usual school activities. In turn this provoked some delays on the approvals that might have a negative influence on people's experimentation with distinct displayed identities. Once again, the same content regarding control sharing is relevant.

In relation to the news feeds, the initial response was very promising but the fading of the updates once again reveal that extra work needs a perceived added value. In other words, it seems to us that the centralized model of control sharing assumed in the school influenced the way the display was thought to be useful and created mechanisms that were not particularly successful in terms of a more spontaneous adoption by the community sharing the place.

6 Conclusions

The results show that people can be enticed to interact through digital public displays and, maybe, contribute to the construction of an extended understanding of the place by reaching into the digital world. However, our study also suggests that not all interaction mechanisms and procedures to generate content are suitable to all types of places. In other words, it seems that one size fits all type of solution is clearly not effective or efficient. More research is needed in order to understand the specificities of a particular place and how to match these with the appropriate interaction mechanisms.

Acknowledgements. The research leading to these results has received funding from FCT under the Carnegie Mellon - Portugal agreement: WESP (Web Securityand Privacy (Grant CMU-PT/SE/028/2008).

References

1. Brignull, H., et al.: The introduction of a shared interactive surface into a communal space. In: Proceedings of the 2004 ACM Conference on Computer Supported Cooperative Work, 49–58 (2004)
2. Davies, N., et al.: Using bluetooth device names to support interaction in smart environments. In: Proceedings of the 7th International Conference on Mobile Systems, Applications, and Services, New York, NY, USA, pp. 151–164 (2009)

3. Eagle, N., Pentland, A.: Reality Mining: Sensing Complex Social Systems. Personal and Ubiquitous Computing 10(4) (2006)
4. Hardey, M.: Life Beyond the Screen: Embodiment and Identity Through the Internet. The Sociological Review 50(4), 570–585 (2002)
5. Huang, E.M., et al.: Secrets to Success and Fatal Flaws: The Design of Large-Display Group-ware. IEEE Computer Graphics and Applications 26(1), 37–45 (2006)
6. José, R., et al.: Beyond interaction: Tools and practices for situated publication in display networks, Porto, Portugal (2012)
7. José, R., et al.: Instant Places: Using Bluetooth for Situated Interaction in Public Displays. IEEE Pervasive Computing 7(4), 52–57 (2008)
8. Karam, M., et al.: Evaluating BluScreen: Usability for Intelligent Pervasive Displays. In: The Second IEEE International Conference on Pervasive Computing and Applications (ICPCA 2007), Birmingham, UK (2007)
9. Kindberg, T., Jones, T.: "Merolyn the Phone": A Study of Bluetooth Naming Practices (Nominated for the Best Paper Award). In: Krumm, J., Abowd, G.D., Seneviratne, A., Strang, T. (eds.) UbiComp 2007. LNCS, vol. 4717, pp. 318–335. Springer, Heidelberg (2007)
10. Kostakos, V., O'Neill, E.: Cityware: Urban computing to bridge online and real-world social networks. In: Handbook of Research on Urban Informatics: The Practice and Promise of the Real-Time City, pp. 195–204 (2008)
11. McCarthy, J.F., et al.: Proactive Displays & The Experience UbiComp Project. In: First International Workshop on Ubiquitous Systems for Supporting Social Interaction and Face-to-Face Communication in Public Places, Seattle, Washington, USA (2003)
12. McDonald, D.W., et al.: Proactive displays: Supporting awareness in fluid social environments. ACM Trans. Comput.-Hum. Interact. 14(4), 1–31 (2008)
13. Nicolai, T., et al.: Exploring Social Context with the Wireless Rope. In: 1st International Workshop on MObile and Networking Technologies for social applications, MONET 2006, Montpellier, France (2006)
14. O'Neill, E., Kostakos, V., Kindberg, T., Schiek, A.F.g., Penn, A., Fraser, D.S., Jones, T.: Instrumenting the City: Developing Methods for Observing and Understanding the Digital Cityscape. In: Dourish, P., Friday, A. (eds.) UbiComp 2006. LNCS, vol. 4206, pp. 315–332. Springer, Heidelberg (2006)
15. Paulos, E., Goodman, E.: The familiar stranger: anxiety, comfort, and play in public places. In: Proceedings of the SIGCHI Conference on Human Factors in Computing Systems, pp. 223–230 (2004)
16. Turkle, S.: Life on the Screen: Identity in the Age of the Internet. Simon and Schuster Trade (1995)

Evolution of Marketing Strategies:
From Internet Marketing to M-Marketing

Tiziana Guzzo, Alessia D'Andrea, Fernando Ferri, and Patrizia Grifoni

Institute of Reaserch on Population and Social Policies (IRPPS-CNR)
00198, Rome, Italy
{tiziana.guzzo,alessia.dandrea,fernando.ferri,
patrizia.grifoni}@irpps.cnr.it

Abstract. The paper describes the evolution of marketing strategies from the advent of the Web (Internet Marketing) through the advent of Social Networks (Marketing 2.0) to the evolution of Mobile Social Networks (M-marketing). Moreover the paper analyses the use that Italian people make of mobile devices and the user perception and acceptance of M-marketing on considering the characteristics that influence them. Finally a short discussion on viral marketing trend is given.

Keywords: Internet Marketing, Marketing 2.0, M-marketing, User perceptions, Users acceptance, Viral Marketing.

1 Introduction

Marketing is "the process which creates, communicates, delivers the value to the consumers, and maintains the relationship with consumers. It generates the strategy that underlies sales techniques, business communication, and business developments. It is "an integrated process through which companies build strong consumers relationships and create value for their consumers and for themselves" [1].

Marketing strategies have a long history and mainly interested economists and sociologists. The wide use of Internet, pervasiveness of social networks and the evolution of mobile devise are implying a wider involvement of interdisciplinary competences enlarging the interest toward ICT competences.

This paper is to describe the evolution of marketing strategies from the advent of the Web (Internet Marketing) - through the advent of Social Networks (Marketing 2.0) - to the evolution of Mobile Social Networks (M-marketing). In particular, the paper analyses the use that Italian people make of mobile devices and the user perception and acceptance of M-marketing.

The advent of the Web had a significant impact on the way marketers do their strategies; it provides opportunities for companies to enhance their business in a cost-effective and practical manner. That is, the Web can be used by marketers to distribute products faster, to reach new markets, to conduct marketing research, to serve customers better, to solve customer problems and also to communicate more

P. Herrero et al. (Eds.): OTM 2012 Workshops, LNCS 7567, pp. 627–636, 2012.

efficiently with marketing partners. This evolution of marketing is called "Internet Marketing".

The widespread advent of Social Networking stimulated a further development of marketing (Marketing 2.0) defining a new perspective connected to the symmetry of companies and consumers in their communication process. Indeed, consumers do not passively receive marketers' messages; they actively express their needs, preferences and choices. All these issues stimulated the emerging of new marketing models with different aspects for successful marketing strategies such as: user information sharing and interaction, brand & corporate identity, search engine optimization (SEO) etc.. In the new marketing on Social Networks, databases play an enormous role in allowing the use and the integration of online tools. In particular they make it possible for consumers and companies to login and to have their own profile on a Social Networking site etc.; this give consumers and companies the possibility to connect each other and to fulfill their specific needs for information sharing and interaction and companies the possibility to outline the core concept of identity that, in the case of marketing strategies, can be extended to the analysis of the way in which consumers and companies develop their online profiles. This process can stimulate the presence of small enterprises on the market.

However, a stronger change is connected to the popularity of Social Networks, combined with the widespread diffusion of mobile technologies, such as pocket PC, PDA and cell phone; it has given rise to the phenomenon of Mobile Social Networks. Mobile Social Networks are considered to be the natural evolution of Social Networks; they can be seen as Social Networks communities specialized with mobile services. Mobile devices offer to Social Networks new opportunities connected with real-time location-based services, communication on the move and the sharing of information and services anywhere, anytime. This phenomenon is having a great impact on marketing sector. Mobile marketing (M-marketing) is defined as "the use of the mobile medium as a means of marketing communication" [2]. More specifically, it is "using interactive wireless media to provide customers with time and location sensitive, personalized information that promotes goods, services and ideas, thereby generating value for all stakeholders" [3].

In order to marketers adopt best M-marketing strategies it is very important to understand the use that users make of mobile devices, their perceptions and acceptance in terms of benefits and costs in using Mobile Social Networks for marketing purpose.

The integration of Internet Marketing, Marketing 2.0 and M-marketing has led to the development of a new type of marketing: the Viral marketing.

The reminder of the paper is organised as follows. Section 2 describes the Internet Marketing by discussing the different marketing ways, their advantages and limitations. Section 3 introduces the Marketing 2.0 by analyzing the benefits for consumers and companies. In Section 4 the different forms of mobile marketing strategies are discussed. Section 5 analyses the use that Italian people make of mobile devices and the user perception and acceptance of M-marketing on considering the characteristics that influence them. Finally Section 6 discusses the viral marketing trend.

2   Internet Marketing: Marketing on the Web

Internet Marketing is also called online Marketing, Website Marketing or e-Marketing. It is generally referred to the promotion of products or services over the Internet. Among the advantages of Internet Marketing there is mainly its cheapness both for companies and for buyers. Companies can reach a wide audience with minor budget respect to the traditional advertising while consumers can research and purchase products and services conveniently and quickly.

There are different ways of Internet Marketing which are listed below:

- *Pay per Click:* is a model where advertisers pay the publisher when the ad is clicked.
- *Marketing with Affiliates:* A company hires one or more affiliates that are paid commission for each visitor that click on the banner or logo. Visitors are connected to the sponsor's site for which affiliates are paid a commission.
- *Search Engine Optimization (SEO):* It allow to types keywords in search engines related to ones product and to have the list of different sites related to that product. SEO maintains ones site to collocate on the first page of the most search engines to attract more traffic. This can give good Return on Investment (ROI) and increase profits.
- *Advertising through Banner:* Advertiser purchases banner to be displayed on the website. Usually, banner marketing is used to divert potential traffic to the site.
- *Auction through Internet:* In a n online auction takes place when items are kept for selling. A minimum price for items is fixed by seller and buyers that offer the highest price will receive that product.
- *Listing on Directories:* People can place their site on Hellometro.com or Citysearch.com which act as Yellow Pages on the internet. This is cheaper than the other ways of internet marketing, so also small-scale enterprise can use it.

3   Marketing 2.0: Marketing on Social Networks

The advent of Social Networking provides marketers with new potentialities, not available in traditional channels, in particular for the products and services diffusion.

The importance of Social Networks and the key aspect of the companies' interest on them are due to the wide number of consumers that can be reached using these tools.

Marketers start from building a loyal constituency of consumers through advertisement on discussion forums, providing links to experts in specific areas for free consultation, and use of knowledge from other forums to honestly counsel consumers. Marketers may also open discussion to specifically attract new members according to their profile of interest. The real advantages of Social Networks can be exploited when marketers use the interactive capabilities of this new medium and build a personal community environment for the consumers, on considering each consumer as an individual in addressing promotional messages, providing all related services at a unique point, and making the virtual community a truly worthwhile place for the consumer to visit. The possibility to individually and interactively address consumers, allows marketers to understand their target better and to provide new products and services in fulfilling the consumers needs. The importance of Social Networking is, moreover, connected to the symmetry between companies and consumers in their communication process. Indeed, consumers do not passively receive marketers' messages they actively express their needs, preferences and choices [4] [5]. All these features of Social Networks allowed the introduction of different benefits on marketing process; the benefits can be view on considering the consumers as well as the companies' point of view.

From consumers' point of view the key useful characteristics of a Social Network to consider are:

- inter-activity: a consumer who joins a Social Network can seek information, test the product and proceed to place order for products. Consumers can also have access to the feedback of other people to make better informed decisions.
- aggregation of services: a Social Network allows aggregation of different services, coordinated and hyper-linked by the seller of the products or services. This gives consumers access to all the necessary information to make a better purchase decision.
- deliverability: a Social Network is delivered in real time 24 hours a day, and 7 days a week.

These characteristic allow consumers to:

- gather information about products and services offered by companies;
- interact with other consumers without spatial and temporal constraints and with reduced search costs;
- provide information about the product, to the company and to other consumers;
- add "collective content" using discussion forums;
- have economic benefits deriving from special prices, customized offers and better service from the qualitative point of view;
- being part of a powerful bargaining group that can influence important marketing decisions.

From the companies point of view the most important benefit that a Social Network can offer is given by the possibility to reach out and build interactive relationships with consumers on a global basis. In the past companies have been constrained by the inadequacies of the traditional channels, particularly in the products and services diffusion. Social Networks have the potential to transform and enhance this activity. As said before the key element for the interest in the use of Social Network is the critical mass of consumers that can be reached. Companies usually start from building a loyal community of consumers through advertisement on discussion forums, providing links to experts in specific areas for free consultation. Companies may also open discussion forums to specifically attract new members according to their profiles of interest. These discussion forums are rich sources of information about companies and their products/services and, at the same time, should be closely monitored by the marketer to identify the needs of the consumers. Companies can also facilitate an immersive experience to consumers, for example, by using 3-D virtual communities such as Second Life, they can create customized graphical user interfaces and include tutorials (Avatar), which can better explain to consumers how to move around and interact with the environment. Many real-word companies are taking interest in this latest online trend. American Apparel is the first "real world" company that has opened a store in the virtual world of Second Life. Its ultra-modern clothing store is located on a beach resort and has quickly become a hot spot within Second Life. Second life provides companies with the opportunity to build a strong trademark. Some brand owners have established an online presence by building retail stores to sell products in the real world. Moreover they have the possibility to create an event in the largest world virtual 3-D environment to directly communicate with the wide audience of the community members. For example, the MacArthur Foundation uses events on Second Life to introduce the foundation to a new audience and to stimulate discussions about the real-world issues that it seeks to resolve; William Gibson, the influential author who coined the word "cyberspace", had a reading in Second Life to promote his novel "Spook Country"; the Royal Liverpool Philharmonic have built a replica of their concert hall where they will perform works by Rachmaninov.

4   M-Marketing: Marketing on Mobile Social Networks

Today we live in a mobile-devices-focused society. Mobile technologies, such as PDA, pocket PC and cell phone, transform interpersonal communications, which are independent from the fixed location, and result in the phenomenon of "situated nowhere," in which communication occurs everywhere. Several studies individuate and classify mobile devices properties. In particular Klopfer et al. in [6] classify the following five property classes, to characterise mobile devices:

- Connectivity.
- Social interactivity.
- Individuality.
- Context sensitivity.
- Portability.

These properties are strictly related to several key elements: the user device, the user, user communities, the Network and the context. In this scenario, connectivity represents the interaction between the user device and the Network, many devices are characterised by a high connectivity (smart phones) other by a limited capability (PDAs). The Social interactivity represents the interaction between the user device and user communities that satisfy user need to communicate, this property class is strongly related to the previous connectivity class. The Individuality represents the interaction between the user device and its user and allows adapting content according to the user's needs and characteristics. The Context sensitivity represents the interaction between the user device and the external environment and permits to adapt content according to the context characteristics. Finally Portability represents the property to establish interactions between the user device and all others actors every-where and every-time. Being mobile adds a new dimension also for marketing strategies on Social Networks because of the mobile devices properties that give advantages to Social Networks. The real advantage of Mobile Social Networks compared to Social Networking websites is that mobile devices enhance the freedom of movement [7]. Moreover, they allow data sharing in peer-to-peer (P2P) networks with communication links created in ad hoc manner [8].

The widespread diffusion of Mobile Social Networks have great impact on marketing strategies; from marketing 2.0 we move to M-marketing that is defined as "the transactions of commodities, services, or information over the Internet through the use of mobile handheld devices" [9]. M-marketing has generally been viewed as "an extension of marketing 2.0 beyond the static terminal of the PC/TV to anytime, anyplace, anywhere on mobile and other wireless devices" [10]. M-marketing on Social Networks are increasingly a vital component of brand marketers' strategies, creating a rush to develop content and advertising to consumers via on their mobile devices. There are many forms of M-marketing such as Short Message Service (SMS), Multimedia Message Service (MMS), Mobile Web Marketing, and Location-based Services:

- *Short Message Service (SMS)*: SMS messaging is going to be the new e-mail which aim is to collect phone numbers instead of email addresses. To take full advantage of SMS, companies have to invest in dedicated mobile texting platforms (like MobileStorm or MooText) to create and manage M-marketing campaigns. These platforms typically incorporate a mobile CRM to expand customer's insights and data into mobile devices.

- *Multimedia Message Service (MMS):* Multimedia can break down the faceless marketing-to-consumer sales flow and make companies appear friendlier. Thanks to the use of Mobile Social Networks consumers have the possibility to use the web to look for videos and pictures of products they considering buying everywhere and every time. It's easy for companies to taking photos of their products but also to invite consumers to events to highlight their culture and recruit new employees.

- *Mobile Web Marketing:* M-marketing is great for all kinds of companies, but particularly for companies that have brick-and-mortar locations. As marketers start to leverage more mobile social platforms they most deliver the same message over multiple platforms instead of tailoring communications for each individual Mobile Social Network. However every mobile social platform have an ecosystem of their own, so it is important to consider that each of them is different from another, for instance specific style of writing might spread on Facebook but fail on Twitter, it is indeed relevant to customize the marketing message in order to ensures the success of each respective social platform.

- *Location based Services:* Being visible to consumers looking for a business in their area is extremely important. Make sure Social Network is included in local business directories in order to help ensure that consumers find you when they need you. This is possible through location-based services (LBS) are powerful tools for engendering loyalty from customers; examples are Gowalla, Foursquare and Facebook Places that companies can to run mobile promotions. For instance, Chili's ran a promotion where everyone who "checked in" to their locations using Foursquare got free cheese dip.

5   M-Marketing: The Consumers' Perspective

This section analyses the use that Italian people make of mobile devices and the user' perception and acceptance of M-marketing on considering the characteristics that influence them.

5.1   Diffusion of Mobile Devices in the Italian Market

The mobile is the most widespread tool among Italian consumers as well as the most personal and with characteristics of immediacy, geolocation, and very strong interaction. The big changes in terms of diffusion of intelligent devices (smartphones), growth of mobile Internet browsing, the new paradigm of the Mobile Application Store, makes it a highly attractive channel for communication and marketing activities of companies.

The development of mobile opens important perspectives on the market field in the next year. In Italy, in fact, about 20 million users have a smartphone, with a 52% increase compared to 2010 [11]. From a research commissioned by Google to Ipsos MediaCT (July, 2011) 53% of the respondents use these tools every day to surf the Internet wherever they are. The 45% takes smartphones to find information quickly. On the rise also the proportion of people who start to use the smartphone to buy directly on the web 23% had in fact, already made a purchase via mobile and 72% of smartphone owners remember to have noticed an advertisement on the mobile.

This trend will grow in the near future. According to data reported by Google, the volume of searches through mobile of 2011 increase of 224% compared to those of 2010. In particular 53% of respondents said to use mobile devices for daily researches, while 29% use them only weekly. Moreover 78% use them to find local information, while 43% to search products and services. Finally 35% of respondents had visited a business website then has activated a service.

These data are confirmed also in tourism field, in fact a recent survey conducted by the GDS (Global Distribution System) Sabre Travel Network, detects a sharp increase in the sale of tourism services through mobile. The analysis was conducted on business travelers who travel 7 times a year for business. For these users is a great convenience can search, book and pay directly via mobile. The 2/3 of respondents said they would be able to search and book hotels in mobile. 63% is not opposed to receiving bids and proposals relating to the destinations by local businesses. 72% want to be able to see the hotel on the map.

These data show that investing in the mobile market is an emergent and great opportunity in Italy.

This phenomenon is changing radically the logic of relation and interaction between businesses and consumers and is an opportunity for significant growth for the economy of the country.

According to [11] Italy is the market where the owners of mobile devices are more likely to click on an advertisement and to seek more information about a product. In 2011, the Italian market of Mobile Advertising, the corporate investments in advertising on the mobile channel, has increased by 50%, from 38 to 56 million euros, equal to about 5% of the total market of Internet Advertising. (Osservatorio Mobile Marketing & Service della School of Management del Politecnico di Milano) (www.osservatori.net). Among the sectors that invest most in Mobile Advertising there are: at the first place the automotive sector (+81%), at the second place Finance and Insurance (+22%) and at the third place Entertainment and Publishing (+40%).

5.2   User Perception, Acceptance of Mobile Social Networks for Marketing Purposes

In order to marketers adopt best strategies it is very important understand which are perceptions by consumers in terms of benefits and costs to use Mobile Social Networks for this purpose.

The study presented in [12] individuated some characteristics that influence consumers' perception. Respect to benefits perceived, mobile convenience and service compatibility directly and positively influence mobile values. Respect to costs perceived instead, security risk and cognitive effort negatively influence mobile values.

- *Service compatibility*: is the consistency of products and value perceived by consumer [13]. In the case of the market, consumers use mobile data services to satisfy their demands for desired products. Compatibility of mobile services is the ability to use the functions provided on Social Networks on mobile phone [14].
- *Security risk*: users perceive some risks for shopping on line and these risks are more perceived when they buy on Social Networks [14, 15]. In particular, users are concerned when use mobile since they think that their personal information can be diverted while using wireless. According to [12], users think that using Mobile Social Networks can cause security problems like transparency of personal information.
- *Cognitive effort*: if users use much time and effort to access Mobile Social Networks the user's self-confidence decreases [16]. In this case the user's mood can be spoiled and he can stop to use services or products.

The study of [17] found that consumers prefer that marketers interact with consumers in bi-directional communication, through actions such as responding to consumer-generated content.

Consumer acceptance and attitudes towards receiving communications from brands via social media could be improved if it was relevant, interactive, non-intrusive, and permission-based advertising. Furthermore, in order to improve the brand credibility, it is necessary to create a dialogue with the consumer, rather than using the media as a promotional vehicle [17].

According to [11] about trends and consumption patterns on social media in the U.S. and other major markets, 70 percent of active online adult Social Networkers shop online, 12 percent more likely than the average adult Internet user. Although most internet sites can be browsed on a mobile, the best sites are those designed specifically for that purpose. Some Mobile Social Networking sites are investing to respond to their customers' demands.

As reported in http://thesocialskinny.com/100-social-media-mobile-and-internet-statistics-for-2012/ "20% would purchase products from their favorite brands within their social media sites (as opposed to normal websites); 34% would be more likely to share information about a purchase on a social media site than one on a traditional marketing site; 45% of social media users are at least 'somewhat' comfortable providing credit card details through social media channels". These data demonstrate that M-marketing is having a great success in terms of user's perception and acceptance and we can foresee a positive and growing trend of use of these tools for marketing purposes.

6   Discussion and Conclusion

The paper describes the evolution of marketing strategies from the advent of the Web (Internet Marketing) through the advent of Social Networks (Marketing 2.0) to the evolution of Mobile Social Networks (M-marketing).

The evolution of these marketing strategies has led to the development of a new type of marketing: the Viral marketing. The Viral marketing is a technique that allows implementing actions and strategies by self-replicating viral processes. The elements that characterize the "viral" aspect are both communicative and technological.

On considering the communicative issue, the marketing message to become viral will reach the target of potential customers by transforming them in active agents that involve other people by sharing the message.

With respect to the technological prospective it is necessary to have flexible, easily accessible, highly integrated technologies that allow a quickly sharing of the messages.

In this scenario, Internet Marketing, Marketing 2.0 and M-marketing provide the necessary integration to define marketing strategies that can exponentially increase the number of people involved in marketing strategies by opening new perspectives for the development of new business and marketing models. Viral marketing could allow a new marketing model for a sustainable economy. It will be a future work the study of features that this model should contain.

References

1. Kotler, P., Rackham, N., Krishnaswamy, S.: Ending the War Between Sales and Marketing. Harvard Business Review 84(7/8), 68–78 (2006)
2. Karjaluoto, H., Leppaniemi, M.: Factor influencing consumers' willingness to accept mobile advertising: A conceptual model. International Journal of Mobile Communication 3(3), 197–213 (2005)
3. Leppaniemi, M.: Mobile Marketing Communications in Consumer Markets (Academic Dissertation. The Faculty of Economics and Business Administration of the University of Oulu, Finland) (2008)
4. Garton, L., Haythornthwaite, C., Wellman, B.: Studying Online Social Networks. Journal of Computer Mediated Communication 3 (June 1997)

5. Hale, R., Whitlam, P.: Towards the Virtual Organization. McGraw-Hill, London 1997 (2010); The official blog for Marketing 2.0, http://newmarketingera.blogspot.com

6. Klopfer, E., Squire, K., Jenkins, H.: Environmental Detectives: PDAs as a Window into a Virtual Simulated World. In: Kerres, M., Kalz, M., Stratmann, J., de Witt, C, eds. (2004)

7. Rana, J., Kristiansson, J., Hallberg, J., Synnes, K.: An Architecture for Social Mobile Networking Applications (2009)

8. Ioannidis, S., Chaintreau, A.: On the Strength of Weak Ties in Mobile Social Networks (2009)

9. Matthew, J., Sarker, S., Varshney, U.: M-Commerce Services: Promises and Challenges. Communications of AIS 2004(14), 1–11 (2004)

10. Clarke, I.: Emerging value propositions for m-commerce. Journal of Business Strategies 18(2), 133–148 (2001)

11. Nielsen, State of the Media: The Social Media Report (2011)

12. Lin, K.-Y., Lu, H.-P.: Understanding user intention to use mobile social networking sites: utilitarian and hedonic value perspectives. In: International Conference on Business and Information BAI 2011 (2011)

13. Meuter, M.L., Bitner, M.J., Ostrom, A.L., Brown, S.W.: Choosing among alternative service delivery modes: An investigation of customer trial of self-service technologies. Journal of Marketing 26(2), 61–83 (2005)

14. Powell, J.: 33 Million people in the room: How to create, influence, and run a successful business with social networking. FT Press, NJ (2009)

15. Tapscott, D.: Grown up digital: how the net generation is changing your world. McGraw-Hill, New York (2008)

16. Kim, H.W., Chan, H.C., Gupta, S.: Value-based adoption of mobile internet: An empirical investigation. Decision Support Systems 43(1), 111–126 (2007)

17. Bond, C., Ferraro, C., Luxton, S., Sands, S.: Social Media Advertising: An Investigation of Consumer Perceptions, Attitudes, and Preferences for Engagement. In: ANZMAC (2010)

Toward a Social Graph Recommendation Algorithm:
Do We Trust Our Friends in Movie Recommendations?[*]

Ali Adabi and Luca de Alfaro[**]

University of California Santa Cruz, Computer Science Department
Santa Cruz, CA, USA, 95065
{aadabi,luca}@soe.ucsc.edu

Abstract. Social networks provide users with information about their friends, their activities, and their preferences. In this paper we study the effectiveness of movie recommendations computed from such communicated preferences. We present a set of social movie recommendation algorithms, which we implemented on top of the Facebook social network, and we compare their effectiveness in influencing user decisions. We also study the effect of showing users a justification for the recommendations, in the form of the profile pictures of the friends that caused the recommendation.

We show that social movie recommendations are generally accurate. Furthermore, 80% of the users that are undecided on whether to accept a recommendation are able to reach a decision upon learning of the identities of the users behind the recommendation. However, in 27% of the cases, they decide *against* watching the recommended movies, showing that revealing identities can have a negative effect on recommendation acceptance.

Keywords: Social Recommendation, Friend Network.

1   Introduction

Web 2.0 is about joining communities, and connecting people to each other through social networks. Web 2.0 is making available in computational form a throve of information about the preferences and behavior of users, as well as their social connections. Recommender systems leverage this information to provide personalized recommendations for users, helping them to discover content that they might find of interest [2,4].

Taste in movies is both sophisticated and personal: the reaction of a user to a movie is a complex outcome of movie features, user preferences, previous movies seen, and so forth, that is difficult to summarize in a few simple criteria.

---

[*] This Work was supported in Part by a Gift from Google, Inc.
[**] This author has a financial interest in Google, Inc.

P. Herrero et al. (Eds.): OTM 2012 Workshops, LNCS 7567, pp. 637–647, 2012.
© Springer-Verlag Berlin Heidelberg 2012

For instance, one might like *Usual Suspects* and dislike *Seven* even though both movies belong to the crime-thrillers. In order to provide users with meaningful recommendations, some algorithms rely on collaborative filtering and user reviews [9,18], while others rely on content-tags [6,22].

We analyze the problem of generating movie recommendation and investigate ways to leverage the social graph in producing relevant recommendations for users. In the past approaches (*e.g.* Netflix), the item recommendations are computed based on the taste similarity. We will explore in this work *social* recommendations that are a function also of what the friends of a user like or dislike. We believe social recommendations are particularly effective for movies since most people like to watch movies in company: thus, suggestions based on a user's friend network may also facilitate the task of finding friends with whom to watch recommended movies.

We have built a social movie recommendation site on top of the Facebook social network, and we have compared the efficacy of several social recommendation algorithms. Our study was motivated by the following two hypotheses:

- The knowledge of the social graph of the user and the preference of their friends will enable us to make precise predictions.
- Communicating to a user, in addition to the recommendation, also the list of friends on which the recommendation is based, increases the trust of the user in the recommendations, and increases the likelihood that the recommendations are followed.

The first hypothesis was first put forward in [3], and validated in experiments in [5], among others. We find that, for movies as well, the use of social information leads to high-quality recommendations. As for the second hypothesis, the results were somewhat surprising. On the one hand, we found that providing information on the friends that were the source of the recommendations leads users to place increased trust in the recommendations themselves, in line with [8]. Indeed, in 80% of instances, users who were undecided on whether to accept a movie recommendation were able to make up their minds once they learned the identities of the friends who liked the movies. Surprisingly, we found that in 27% of instances, undecided users actually decided *against* watching recommended movies upon learning the identities of the friends who liked them, showing how identity information can have also an adverse effect on recommendation acceptance. This indicates that "friends" in social network are well aware of their (real or perceived) difference in content tastes, and modeling such "acceptance similarity" explicitly could lead to better recommendations.

2   Collaborative Filtering

One approach in designing recommendation systems is Collaborative Filtering (CF). In CF, users are compared according to their similarity in past preferences, and recommendations for new items are built on the basis of the preferences of similar users [12,18,21].

We rely on CF algorithms that perform these two steps:

1. Calculate the similarity $sim(u,v)$ between two users u and v, on the basis of preferences expressed by u and v.
2. Produce a prediction value p_u for user u on the basis of the preferences expressed by users similar to u.

Several approaches have been used to compute similarity between users. One of the most common approaches is *cosine-similarity*: the two users u and v are treated as two vectors in n-dimensional space, and the cosine of the angle across the two vectors is computed:

$$sim(u,v) = \frac{\sum_{i \in I} r_{u,i}\, r_{v,i}}{\sqrt{\sum_{i \in I} r_{u,i}^2}\,\sqrt{\sum_{i \in I} r_{v,i}^2}}. \tag{1}$$

where I is the set of items, $r_{u,i}$ is the rating of user u for item i, and $r_{v,i}$ is the rating of user v for item i.

Once user-to-user similarities are computed, recommendations are obtained by analyzing the preferences of users similar to the target user. We use neighborhood-based CF algorithms, where a subset of nearest neighbors (in the cosine-similarity metric) of a user is chosen, and a weighed average of the preferences of these nearest-neighbour users is used. Precisely, to make a prediction $p_{u,i}$ for user u on a certain item i, we take a weighted average of all the nearest-neighbour ratings on that item according to the following formula [13,18] :

$$p_{u,i} = \bar{r}_u + \frac{\sum_{v \in U_i} sim(u,v) \cdot (r_{v,i} - \bar{r}_v)}{\sum_{v \in U} sim(u,v)}. \tag{2}$$

where $\bar{r}_u$ and $\bar{r}_v$ are the average ratings for the user u and user v on all other rated items, and where $sim(u,v)$ is the similarity between the user u and user v. The summations are over all the users U_i who have rated the item i.

3 Recommendation via Friends

Social networking websites such as Facebook have became a prominent source of information sharing recently: for instance, Facebook had 901 million users in March 2012, and users shared over 3.2 billion "likes" per day on the site [7].

In this work, we rely on the Facebook API to get information on the social network of users, and on the movie preferences of the individual users (via the "likes" that users have expressed for the movies). On the basis of these expressed social connection and movie preferences, we compute personalized movie recommendations for users. We compare several algorithms for computing personalized preferences, as described below.

Algorithm 1. Basic Social Recommendation (BSR):

1: **Input:** A user $u \in U$.
2: For all movies $i \in I$, set $c(i) = 0$.
3: **for all** $v \in F_u$ **do**
4:     **for all** $i \in L(v)$ **do**
5:         $c(i) := c(i) + 1$
6:     **end for**
7: **end for**
8: Sort the movies list I in decreasing order of $c(i)$, $i \in I$.
9: **return** Top movies in the ordering.

3.1   Friends Network Algorithms

Basic Social Recommendation (BSR) BSR finds the most frequent recommended movies by friends. For a user $u \in U$, denote by F_u the set of friends of u in the social network, and let $L(u)$ be the set of movies that u has liked.

BSR scans all movies users' friends liked, and generates a list of highly recommended movies among each user's social network.

General Stranger Recommendation (GSR). In this algorithm, we compute movie recommendations by tallying likes across all users. In our experimental setting, however, the total number of users is small, and for many users u we have that $U \setminus F_u$ is not much larger than F_u: that is, the friendship neighborhood of a user comprises a significant portion of the overall user base. In order to minimize the effect of a user's friends neighborhood on the recommendation and better model the behavior of a true friendship-independent algorithm in the large scale, we exclude from the recommendation the friends of each user. Thus, the GSR algorithm is identical to the BSR algorithm above, except that in Step 2, we consider all $v \in U \setminus F_u$ rather than $v \in F_u$.

Explanation Social Recommendation (ESR). Many recommender systems are providing no transparency into the working of the recommendation. Explanations provide that transparency, exposing the reasoning and data behind a recommendation. The ESR algorithm explains to the user the origin of the social recommendations by displaying the faces and names of the friends that caused a recommendation next to the recommendation itself.

Clustering Social Recommendation (CSR). The CSR algorithm identifies in the social network of a user other friends who are similar in their movie tastes, and uses the preferences of such similar friends to generate recommendations for the target user. Given a target user u and a friend v, we compute their similarity simply as:

$$sim(u, v) = \frac{|L(u) \cap L(v)|}{|L(v)|} .$$

CSR calculates $sim(u, v)$ for all friends v of u, and sorts these friends in order of decreasing similarity. CSR then recommends to u the movies that these friends have liked, but u has not seen yet.

Algorithm 2. Explanation Based Recommendation (ESR) using BSR:

1: **Input:** A user $u \in U$.
2: For all movies $i \in I$, set $c(i) = 0$.
3: **for all** $v \in F_u$ **do**
4:    **for all** $i \in L(v)$ **do**
5:       $c(i) := c(i) + 1$
6:    **end for**
7: **end for**
8: Let M be the list of movies in I, sorted in decreasing order of $c(i)$, for $i \in I$.
9: For each movie $i \in I$, consider the friends $F_i = \{v \in U \mid i \in L(v)\}$ that liked i.
10: **return** The list M, with the pictures and names of the friends in F_i for each movie $i \in M$.

Algorithm 3. Clustering Social Recommendation (CSR):

1: **Input:** A user $u \in U$
2: **for all** $v \in F(u)$ **do**
3:    Compute $sim(u, v)$
4: **end for**
5: Sort F_u in decreasing order of $sim(u, v), v \in F_u$, obtaining F'.
6: $M =$ empty list.
7: **for** $v \in F'$ **do**
8:    Append the movies that v liked, and u has not seen, to M.
9: **end for**
10: **return** M

Clustering Based Recommendation (CBR). CBR is a generic form of CSR: instead of going through user friends, CBR goes through all strangers (not-user-friends), similarly to how GSR relates to BSR. In particular, CBR differs from CSR in Line 2, where $v \in F_u$ is replaced by $v \in U \setminus F_u$. The CBR serves as a base case for CSR in identifying the benefits or shortcomings of social network recommendations.

4 Experiments on the Effectiveness of Social Algorithms: BSR, GSR, ESR, CSR, and CBR

A series of experiments have been implemented on the social algorithms BSR, GSR, ESR, CSR, and CBR. The test subjects were 20 college students ages between 20 to 28. The size of the movie database in this study was 5000 titles. Users were asked to login into a Facebook application using their credentials. Upon successful authentication, the Facebook application was able to extract user and his or her friends' movie information. Users were shown a series of recommendations (BSR, GSR, etc.) and their answers were recorded.

4.1   BSR vs. GSR

In this experiment, 5 GSR movies were combined randomly with 5 BSR movies and have been offered to the users. Users were asked to pick if they like or dislike any of the 10 recommendations provided(so the results are not skewed). The displayed results gave users equal chances of choosing BSR or GSR movies. This study tested if users liked BSR or GSR movie recommendations without prior knowledge of their friends movie preferences.

As figure 1 shows, a majority of users (83%) liked either BSR or GSR movies, with BSR edging GSR. It is notable to consider that 17% of the recommended movies were disliked by the users (or users found them irrelevant). The reason that the values of BSR and GSR in figure 1 are similar could be due to the fact that the user sample is uniformly chosen from college students (age 20-28) and perhaps a non-uniform sample could change the results toward the BSR recommendations.

The overall BSR vs. GSR results showed that since a user's friend are generally similar in terms of age, culture, and geographical location, an overlap in interests is visible. Although these interests are not uniform since friends are not uniform, the integration of all friends' interest can be generally used as the user's preference as well.

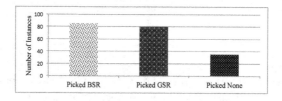

Fig. 1. BSR vs. GSR

Gender Attribute Applying a gender classification filter to the recommendations can lead to more personalized results. The gender filter was applied to the recommended movies which eliminated opposite sex recommendation and resulted figure 2.

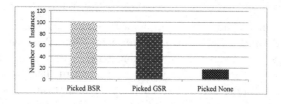

Fig. 2. BSR vs. GSR after applying a gender filter (Number of total instances was 200)

Figure 2 shows that adding a gender classifier can enhance the recommendations performance however anomalies can also be created. One of the visible issue was the elimination of some independent and not mainstream movies, which have been discarded, in the recommended movies specifically in the male participants results.

4.2 CSR vs. CBR

CSR finds people with similar taste within the friends' network. The experimentation was conducted to compare the effectiveness of recommendations of similar users between two distinct groups: Friends of a users (CSR) and strangers (CBR). Figure 3 shows the CSR and CBR recommendation comparison among users.

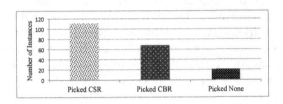

Fig. 3. CSR vs. CBR for 200 instances

Users preferred CSR results 21% more than CBR. This is because if a user u has a friend v, u already has some similarities to v, which may be cultural, geographical, or age-related. Searching the global network for similar users with CBR resulted in quality outcome as well. In our experiment, the overall number of users is small, but in large user bases, there is a higher probability of finding good matches for users (at the cost of an increased amount of computation).

4.3 ESR

In a separate experiment, the ESR algorithm was compared with BSR. ESR is similar to BSR, except that it also shows the recommenders' faces along with the results. This experiment measures the effect on movie recommendation acceptance of showing the identities of the friends on which the recommendations are based. We performed two experiments, termed A and B:

- In Experiment A, we studied the effect of adding, below the recommendations, the identities of 5 friends that contributed to the recommendations. When more than 5 friends supported a recommendation, we selected 5 such friends at random. Movies with less than 5 supporting friends were excluded from the experiment.
- In Experiment B, we proceeded as in experiment A, but we also we studied the effect of varying the number of faces displayed alongside the recommendations.

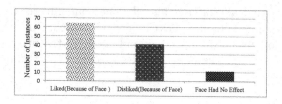

Fig. 4. ESR with constant face count effect calculated for 200 intances

Experiment A: Fixed Number of Recommenders. Figure 4 clearly illustrates that showing the identities of friends supporting a recommendation had a strong effect on people's decision to watch a movie. However, to our surprise, the effect was not all in the positive direction: in many cases, users were actually put off from the recommendation upon learning the identities of the friends on which the recommendation was based. Evidently, the trust that people may feel for their Facebook friends does not blankly extend to their taste for movies! Participants in our study valued a group of friends they recognized as individuals with great taste, or "tastemakers". When users saw the selected group of tastemakers recommended a specific movie, they instantly wanted to follow other movies they suggested.

Experiment B: Variable Number of Recommenders. In Experiment B, we varied the number of friends displayed next to the recommended movies from 1 to 10. We asked users if they would like to watch a movie they have not watched because a number of their friends recommended it.

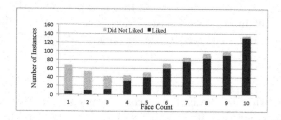

Fig. 5. ESR Face Count Effect

As figure 5 shows, recommender numbers has a direct effect on the user decision. This could be because the majority of the movies that have been liked by users, are in fact popular movies among users social network and therefore are relevant to the users. In recommendations with lower number of recommenders (ex. for 3 recommenders), when some of the users saw a specific friend watched the movie they disliked it. This is in par with the assumption made in Experiment A. However once the face count of the recommenders increase and pass a threshold, users tend to prefer the movies with higher count of friends faces.

5   ESR vs. BSR

For this experiment, the target user is given 10 BSR movie recommendations. Once the user has examined the recommendations, the user is showed the faces of the users that contributed to the recommendations, and is asked whether she is able to make a decision in the cases where she was undecided.

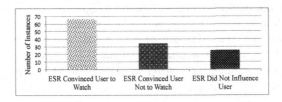

Fig. 6. *ESR* influence for 200 instances

As figure 6 shows, 80% of the users that were undecided on whether to watch a movie were able to reach a conclusion upon learning the identities of the users that were at the root of the recommendation. This means the explanation based recommendation has an important effect on users decision. However, as figure 6 illustrates, in 27% of total of cases, users decided not watch a movie after knowing some of their friends watched a movie. This exposes a new side of social recommendation, which is their negative effect on user's decision. We remarked that this negative effect is more significant for movies below a certain threshold of popularity. For little-known movies, if the user is doubtful, the user has roughly a one-in-three chance of deciding not to watch the movie when made aware of the identities of friends who liked the movie.

6   Conclusion

Our results show that social movie recommendations are effective in helping users decide which movies to watch — and, if the friend identities underlying the recommendations are revealed, also in helping users decide which movies *not* to watch. These results were partially expected, based on previous work by Suri and Watts [17]. This can be explained by the fact that users trust or distrust in some of their friends' taste as suggested by Jøsang, et al. [11] (correlation between taste and trust).

One of the problems with the current methodology of collaborative filtering is that when a new movie comes out, there is not sufficient rating data about the movie. A particular movie that a friend likes has a higher chance of being recognized by similar users. Abdul-Rahman and Hailes [1] showed that in a pre-defined context, such as movies, users develop social connections with people who have similar preferences. Ziegler and Lausen[23] extended these results in work that showed a correlation exists between trust and user similarity in an empirical study of a real online community. Clearly, recommendations only make sense when obtained from like-minded people [23].

Social recommendations used in the studies above show that the overall advantage of this method is relevancy of the result and trust that user have established with the recommender through their social network. As *Papagelis et al.* [20] states, retrieving data from the user and his social graph intrinsically alleviates the sparsity problem. Another advantage of social recommendation algorithms, over general collaborative filtering, is that these algorithms need to examine only the social neighbourhood of a user to produce recommendations for that user. Under the assumption that the size of such social neighbourhood is constant (very few users have over a few hundred friends), this leads to a computationally more tractable problem, compared to algorithms that scour the global set of users for users with similar tastes. Nevertheless, social movie recommendations face challenges regarding insufficiency of data, data normalization, and cold start:

- Insufficiency of data: Some users may be part of a sparse social networks, or they may be unwilling to disclose movie preferences, making it difficult to compute recommendations.
- Data normalization: Some users might not declare their interests in their profile, while others might overly exaggerate about their interest, creating anomalies.
- Cold Start: Users might not initially like a lot of movies this problem can be resolved if the user inputs movies they liked into their Facebook profile.

Future Work

The approaches outlined in this paper can be extended in several directions. The collaborative-filtering approach taken in this paper could be combined with a content-based approach, where movies are represented by feature vectors, and movie similarity is considered alongside user similarity. To alleviate the cold-start and data-insufficiency problems, a learning algorithm could be developed to identify the movie tastemakes among groups of friends, since tastemakers have a huge effect on decision of users.

References

1. Abdul-Rahman, A., Hailes, S.: Supporting trust in virtual communities. In: Hawaii International Conference on System Sciences. Maui (2000)
2. Adomavicius, G., Tuzhili, A.: Towards the Next Gen. of Recommender Systems. IEEE Transactions on Knowledge and Data Engineering 17, 634–749 (2005)
3. Asch, S.E.: Opinions and social pressure. Scientific American 193, 31–35 (1955)
4. Burke, R.: Hybrid Recommender Systems. User Mod. and User-Adap 12, 331–370 (2002)
5. Centola, D.: The Spread of Behavior in an Online Social Network Experiment. Science 329, 1194–1197 (2010)

6. Durao, F., Dolog, P.: A Personalized Tag-Based Recommendation in Social Web Systems. In: Intelligent Web and Information Systems.CoRR (2012)
7. Key Facts Statistics, http://newsroom.fb.com/content/default.aspx?NewsAreaId=22
8. Golbeck, J.:Generating Predictive Movie Recommendations from Trust in Social Networks, iTrust (2006)
9. Herlocker, J.L., Konstan, J.A., Riedl, J.: Explaining collaborative filtering recommendations. In: ACM Conference on Computer Supported Cooperative Work, pp. 241–250. ACM, New York (2000)
10. Huang, Z., Zeng, D., Chen, H.: A Link Analysis Approach to Recommendation under Sparse Data. In: Americas Conference on Information Systems (2004)
11. Jøsang, A., Quattrociocchi, W., Karabeg, D.: Taste and Trust. In: Wakeman, I., Gudes, E., Jensen, C.D., Crampton, J. (eds.) Trust Management V. IFIP AICT, vol. 358, pp. 312–322. Springer, Heidelberg (2011)
12. Resnick, P., Lacovou, N., Suchak, M., Bergstrom, P., Riedl, J.: Grouplens: An Open Architecture for Collaborative Filtering. In: ACM Conference on Computer Supported Cooperative Work, New York (1994)
13. Ricci, F., Rokach L.: Recommender Systems Handbook. Springer, New York (2011)
14. Sarwar, B.M., Karypis, G., Onstan, J.A., Riedl, J.: Recommender Systems for Large-scale E-Commerce. In: ICCIT (2002)
15. Social Recommender Systems Methods and User Issues, http://hci.epfl.ch/teaching/advanced-hci/slides/2011.5.23_Yu.pdf
16. Smith, B., Briggs, P., Coyle, M., O'Mahony, M.: Google Shared.A Case-Study in Social Search. In: International Conference, UMAP, 17 (2009)
17. Suri, A., Watts, D.J.: Cooperation and Contagion in Web-Based, Networked Public Goods Experiments. PLoS ONE, 6 e16836 (2011).
18. Su, X., Khoshgoftaar, T.: A Survey of Collaborative Filtering Techniques. In: Advances in Artificial Intelligence, 17 (2009)
19. Pazzani, M.J.: A Framework for Collaborative, Content-Based and Demographic Filtering. Artificial Intelligence Review, 393–408 (1999)
20. Papagelis, M., Plexousakis, D., Kutsuras, T.: Alleviating the Sparsity Problem of Collaborative Filtering Using Trust Inferences. iTrust, Heraklion (2005)
21. Melville, P., Sindhwani, V.: Recommender Systems. Encyclopedia of Machine Learning, New York (2010)
22. Vatturi, P.K., Geyer, W., Dugan, C., Muller, B.B.: Tag-based ltering for personalized bookmark recommendations. In: 17th ACM Conference on Information and Knowledge Mining, pp. 1395–1396. ACM, New York (2008)
23. Ziegler, C., Lausen, G.: Analyzing Correlation Between Trust and User Similarity in Online Communities. In: International Conference on Trust Management, vol.(2) (2004)

CoopIS 2012 PC Co-chairs Message

Welcome to the proceedings of CoopIS 2012. It was the 20th conference in the CoopIS conference series and took place in Rome, Italy, in September 2012. This conference series has established itself as a major international forum for exchanging ideas and results on scientific research for practitioners in fields such as computer supported cooperative work (CSCW), middleware, Internet & Web data management, electronic commerce, business process management, agent technologies, and software architectures, to name a few. In addition, the 2012 edition of CoopIS aims at highlighting the increasing need for data- and knowledge-intensive processes. As in previous years, CoopIS'12 was again part of a joint event with other conferences, in the context of the OTM ("OnTheMove") federated conferences, covering different aspects of distributed information systems.

Thanks to the many high-quality submissions we were able to put a strong program together. The selection process was very competitive which resulted in quite a few good papers to be rejected. Each paper received at least three, in a number of cases even four, independent peer reviews. From the 100 submissions we were able to accept only 22 papers as full papers and eight papers as short papers.

We are very grateful to the reviewers who worked hard to meet the tight deadline. We thank also the staff of the OTM secretariat, especially Jan Demey, Daniel Meersman, and Carlos Madariaga and the OTM General Chairs Robert Meersman, Tharam Dillon, and Pilar Herrero for their support.

July 2012

Stefanie Rinderle-Ma
Xiaofang Zhou
Peter Dadam

P. Herrero et al. (Eds.): OTM 2012 Workshops, LNCS 7567, p. 648, 2012.
© Springer-Verlag Berlin Heidelberg 2012

Operational Semantics of Aspects in Business Process Management

Amin Jalali[1], Petia Wohed[1], and Chun Ouyang[2]

[1] Stockholm University, Sweden
[2] Queensland University of Technology, and NICTA, Australia
{aj,petia}@dsv.su.se, c.ouyang@qut.edu.au

Abstract. Aspect orientation is an important approach to address complexity of cross-cutting concerns in Information Systems. This approach encapsulates these concerns separately and compose them to the main module when needed. Although there are different works which shows how this separation should be performed in process models, the composition of them is an open area. In this paper, we demonstrate the semantics of a service which enables this composition. The result can also be used as a blueprint to implement the service to support aspect orientation in Business Process Management area.

Keywords: Business Process Management, Workflow Management Systems, Aspect Oriented, Coloured Petri Nets, Weaving.

1 Introduction

Reducing complexity in Information Systems is a main concern in both research and industry. One strategy for reducing complexity is separation of concerns. This strategy advocates separating various concerns, like security and privacy, from the main concern. It results in less complex, easily maintainable, and more reusable Information Systems. Separation of concerns is addressed through the Aspect Oriented paradigm. This paradigm has been well researched and implemented in programming, where languages such as AspectJ have been developed. However, the research on aspect orientation for Business Process Management is still at its beginning. While some efforts have been made proposing Aspect Oriented Business Process Modelling (e.g. [3,4,5]), it has not yet been investigated how to enact such process models in a Workflow Management System. We create a Coloured Petri Net (CPN) specification for the semantics of a so-called Aspect Service that extends the capability of a Workflow Management System with support for execution of aspect oriented business process models. The design specification of the Aspect Service has been inspected through state space analysis. In this paper, we briefly present the ideas of the CPN solution.

2 Running Example

For explaining the Aspect Service, we use an abstract example (see Figure 1). The example contains a main process with three aspects X,Y and Z, which are

P. Herrero et al. (Eds.): OTM 2012 Workshops, LNCS 7567, pp. 649–653, 2012.
© Springer-Verlag Berlin Heidelberg 2012

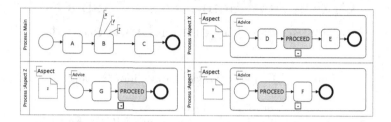

Fig. 1. An abstract example of an aspect oriented process model based on AO4BPMN

defined for one of its activities, activity B. The enactment of the business processes is managed through a WfMS. It results in four different process instances. The Aspect Service takes care of the weaving of the aspects to the main process. This means that the advices are executed in parallel, and a synchronisation towards the main process is made at the Proceed placeholder as well as at the end of the execution of the advices. In this particular example, the execution sequence of the activities will be A, followed by D and G in parallel, then B, followed by E and F in parallel, and finally C. This is written as regular expression $A(D\|G)B(E\|F)C$. In aspect oriented terminology, the activity B is called an advised joint point. An advised joint point contains a so called pointcut condition. If the condition is satisfied the associated advice is triggered. An aspect can contain several advice processes.

3   Overview of the Solution

We define the Aspect Service as a sub-service of the Worklet Service [2]. The Worklet Service is designed to support flexibility in business process management and has certain built-in functions, e.g. suspension of an work item, which are useful for the Aspect Service. The Worklet Specifications repository is used to store the advices. The communication between the Worklet Service and the Workflow engine occurs through a number of message exchanges. These are visualised in the right hand side of Figure 2.

The Aspect Service gets enabled upon receiving a message, which can be one of the following, *ItemPreConstraint, ItemPostConstraint* and *CasePostConstraint*. ItemPreConstraint and ItemPostConstraint represent the beginning and ending of a work item while CasePostConstraint represent the ending of a case. When a work item gets enabled, i.e. a constraint of the type ItemPreConstraint is raised by the WfMS, the Aspect Service performs two checks: a check on whether the workitem has a pointcut associated to it and if so, if the pointcut condition is met. If the workitem is not related to a pointcut, or if a pointcut condition is not met, the execution of the workitem is proceed as usual. Otherwise, the Aspect Service starts the weaving of the corresponding aspect(s). The CPN model in Figure 3 captures the behaviour of the service associated with these checks. The weaving is performed in four steps. These are visualized in the left hand side of Figure 2 and described below.

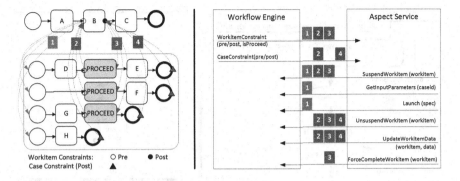

Fig. 2. Weaving steps and corresponding messages

1 *Launching*: When the Aspect Service is activated, it sends a message to the WfMS to suspend the main process. When the suspension is confirmed by the WfMS, the Aspect Service sends messages to the WfMS for launching the relevant advices.

2 *Pausing*: When an advice reaches the Proceed placeholder, the Aspect Service sends a message to the WfMS to suspend the advice. However, advices that do not have a Proceed placeholder will reach to their End. Once the relevant advices have been suspended or ended, the Aspect Service orders un-suspension of the advised join point.

3 *Resuming*: After the advised join point has been completed, the WfMS raises an ItemPostconstraint. The Aspect Service sends messages for suspension of the advised join point and un-suspension of the corresponding advices. Then, it sends messages to force complete the Proceed placeholders, so the advices can be continued.

4 *Finalizing*: When all advices are ended (i.e. their *CasePostconstraints* have been raised), the Aspect Service sends message to the WfMS to un-suspend the advised join point. Hence, the weaving is completed, and the control of the main process is handed back to the WfMS.

During all this steps, the business data is synchronised between the main process and its aspects. In case several advices operate on the same data simultaneously (e.g. activities D and G in Figure 2) the last workitem to complete will overwrite the data stored by the workitems completed earlier.

4   Formal Semantics

The formalisation of the Aspect Service is specified throug a three-level CPN model. The top-level module captures the behaviour of the Initiation of the service, and the second level captures the weaving behaviour (see Figure 3). This model contains four modules capturing steps 1 to 4 described previously. It also contains a module for communicating with the WfMS and performing actions

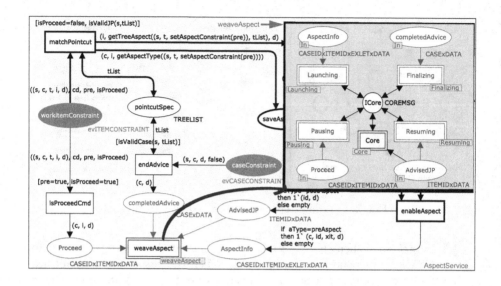

Fig. 3. Tow modules in Aspect Service CPN

for data persistence, which is needed for the weaving of the aspects to the main process. These five modules constitute the third level of the CPN Model.

The model defines 57 colour sets and 33 functions. Full details of the model with definition of the colour sets, variables and functions can be downloaded from [1]. We re-used some of the colour sets, variables and functions from the Worklet Service CPN model [2].

5   Conclusions and Future Work

In this paper, we presented a generic solution for the execution semantics for the weaving of aspects to business processes. The solution is designed based on AO4BPMN and is formalised with CPNs. We have verified the soundness of the design using state space analysis [1].

A direction for future work includes the implementation of the solution in a WfMS. The solution is currently limited to weaving advices in which the Proceed placeholder is only enabled once. This means that the Proceed placeholder can not be included in loops and that in case several Proceed placeholders are defined within the same advice, only one of them should be enabled during the execution of the advice (e.g. as a result of an XOR split). The impact of these limitations, i.e. how frequent such scenarios occur in real life, needs to be further investigated. Moreover, we do not capture the precedence requirement of aspects in this work, which is defined in [5].

References

1. Aspect-Oriented Business Process Management, http://aobpm.blogs.dsv.su.se/
2. Adams, M.J.: Facilitating Dynamic Flexibility and Exception Handling for Work-flows. PhD thesis, Faculty of IT, QUT (November 2007)
3. Charfi, A.: Aspect-oriented workflow languages: AO4BPEL and applications. PhD thesis, Dr.-Ing. thesis, der Technischen Universitat Darmstadt, Darmstadt (2007)
4. Cappelli, C., et al.: Reflections on the modularity of business process models: The case for introducing the aspect-oriented paradigm. Business Process Management Journal 16, 662–687 (1995)
5. Jalali, A., Wohed, P., Ouyang, C.: Aspect Oriented Business Process Modelling with Precedence. To appear in Proc. 4th Int. Workshop on BPMN (2012)

Multi-objective Resources Allocation Approaches for Workflow Applications in Cloud Environments

Kahina Bessai[1], Samir Youcef[2], Ammar Oulamara[2],
Claude Godart[2], and Selmin Nurcan[1]

[1] University of Paris1-Panthéon- Sorbonne, Centre de Recherche en Informatique
90, rue de Tolbiac 75634 Paris, France
{kahina.bessai,selmin.nurcan}@malix.univ-paris1.fr
[2] University of Lorraine, LORIA-INRIA-UMR 7503
BP 239, Vandoeuvre-les-Nancy, France
{youcef,oulamara,godart}@loria.fr

Abstract. Resources allocation and scheduling has been recognised as an important topic for business process execution. However, despite the proven benefits of using Cloud to run business process, users lack guidance for choosing between multiple offering while taking into account several objectives which are often conflicting. Moreover, when running business processes it is difficult to automate all tasks. In this paper, we propose three complementary approaches for Cloud computing platform taking into account these specifications.

1 Introduction

The Cloud computing has quickly changed the way that compute resources can be used and allow users to access compute on the fly according to the application's need. For example, to run any desired software Amazon's EC2 provide a Web service through which users can boot an Amazon Machine Image. However, despite the proven benefits of using Cloud to execute business processes, users lack guidance for choosing between different offering while taking into account several objectives often conflicting.

Moreover, most existing workflow matching and scheduling algorithms consider only an environment in which the number of resources is assumed to be bounded. However, in distributed systems such as Cloud computing this assumption is in opposition to the usefulness of such systems. Indeed, the "illusion of infinite resources" is the most important feature of Clouds [2][3], which means that users can request, and are likely to obtain, sufficient resources for their need at any time. Additionally to this characteristic, a Cloud computing environment can provide several advantages that are distinct from other computing environments [3]. Moreover, unlike scientific workflows, where generally their processing are fully automated, when executing workflow processes it is difficult to automate all theirs tasks. Indeed, certain tasks require validations that cannot be automated because they are subject to human intervention.

P. Herrero et al. (Eds.): OTM 2012 Workshops, LNCS 7567, pp. 654–657, 2012.
© Springer-Verlag Berlin Heidelberg 2012

To overcome the limitations of existing approaches for workflow process optimization, we propose an extension of our recent study [1].

2   Problem Formulation

Definition 1 (Business process). *A business process application is represented as a directed acyclic graph (DAG) denoted $G = (T, E)$, where:*

1. *$T = \{t_1, ..., t_n\}$ is a finite set of tasks.*
2. *E represents the set of directed edges. An edge (t_i, t_j) of graph G corresponds to the data dependencies between these tasks (the data generated by t_i is consumed by t_j).*
3. *Task t_i is called the immediate parent of t_j which is the immediate child task of t_i.*

Let $Data$ be a $n \times n$ matrix of communication data, where $data[i, j]$ is the amount of data required to be transmitted from task t_i to task t_j.

Definition 2 (Resource graph). *The resources are represented as a directed graph denoted RG. Formally, a resources graph is represented by $RG = (R, V)$, where:*

1. *$R = \{VM_1, ..., VM_m, HR_1, ..., HR_{m'}\}$ is a finite set of virtual machines types and human resources.*
2. *V represents the set of directed edges. Each edge is denoted (VM_i, VM_j) corresponding to the link between these virtual machines.*

Let B be a $m \times m$ matrix, in which $B[i, j]$ is the bandwidth between virtual machine types VM_i and VM_j, where $B[i, i] \longrightarrow \infty$ means that there is no transfer data.

Let $r(t_j)$ denotes the resource (virtual machine or human resource) that executes task t_j. The transfer time $TT(r(t_i), r(t_j))$, which is for transferring data from task t_i (executed by $r(t_i)$) to task t_j (executed by $r(t_j)$) is defined by:

$$TT(r(t_i), r(t_j)) = \frac{data[i, j]}{B[r(t_i), r(t_j)]}$$

Let ET be a $n \times m$ execution time matrix in which $ET(t_i, r_j)$ gives the execution time estimation to complete task t_i by resource r_j.

Let UEC be a $(m + m')$−dimensional unit execution cost vector, where $UEC(r_j)$ represents the cost per time unit incurred by using the resource r_j. Let EC be a $n \times m + m'$ execution cost matrix in which $EC(t_i, r_j)$ gives the execution cost to complete task t_i by resource r_j defined by:

$$EC(t_i, r_j) = ET(t_i, r_j) \times UEC(r_j)$$

The data transfer cost $TC(r(t_i), r(t_j))$, which is the cost incurred due to the transfer of data from task t_i (executed by $r(t_i)$) to task t_j (executed by $r(t_j)$), is defined by: $TC(r(t_i), r(t_j)) = data[i, j] \times (C_{out}(r(t_i)) + C_{in}(r(t_j)))$

where $C_{out}(r(t_i))$ and $C_{in}(r(t_j))$ represent respectively the cost of transferring data from $r(t_i)$ and the cost of receiving data on $r(t_j)$.

3 The Objective Functions

a. Time Objective Function. Let EST (earliest start time) and EFT (earliest finish time) attributes that characterize the set of resources (virtual machine types and human resources). These attributes are derived from a given partial matching and scheduling (i.e. a task t_i is assigned to virtual machine $VM(t_i)$ or human resource $HM(t_i)$). The partial schedule refers to the fact that for each task the earliest start time and the earliest finish time values are obtained using only the tasks that must be performed before it. $EST(t_i, r_j)$ and $EFT(t_i, r_j)$ are the earliest execution start time and the earliest execution finish time of task t_i on resource r_j, respectively. For the input task t_{input}, the earliest execution start time and the earliest execution finish time are given by Equation 1 and Equation 2, respectively:

$$EST(t_{input}, r_j) = 0 \tag{1}$$

$$EFT(t_{input}, r_j) = ET(t_i, r_j) \tag{2}$$

For the other tasks in the graph, the EST and the EFT values are computed recursively, starting from the initial task, as shown in Equation 3 and Equation 4. In order to compute the EFT of a task t_j, all immediate predecessor tasks of t_j must have been assigned and scheduled with the consideration of the transfer time.

$$EFT(t_i, r_j) = EST(t_i, r_j) + ET(t_i, r_j) \tag{3}$$

$$EST(t_i, r_j) = \max \left\{ avail[j], \max_{t_p \in pred(t_j)} [AFT(t_p) + TT(r(t_p), r(t_i))] \right\} \tag{4}$$

where $pred(t_i)$ is the set of immediate predecessors of task t_i. $avail[j]$ is the earliest time at which resource r_j is ready for task execution. As the number of virtual machines is assumed to be infinite, then $avail[j] = 0$ for all the used virtual machines. In other words, if task t_i is performed by resource r_j which is a virtual machine then $EST(t_i, r_j)$ is computed as follows:

$$EST(t_i, r_j) = \max_{t_p \in pred(t_j)} \{ AFT(t_p) + TT(r(t_p), r(t_i)) \} \tag{5}$$

The $avail[j]$ is the time that resource r_j completed the execution of the task t_i and it is ready to execute another task. The inner max block in the EST equation returns the ready time, i.e. the time when all required data by t_i has arrived at resource r_j.

After a task t_i is scheduled on a resource r_j, the earliest start time and the earliest finish time of t_i on resource r_j is equal to the actual start time, denoted $AST(t_i)$, and the actual finish time, denoted $AFT(t_i)$, of task t_i, respectively.

After all tasks in a graph are scheduled, the schedule length (i.e., the overall completion time) will be the actual finish time of the exit task (i.e. $AFT(t_{exit})$). The schedule length, also called *makespan*, is defined as:

$$makespan = AFT(t_{exit}) \tag{6}$$

Predictive Heuristic for Human Resource Availabilities. The actual finish time as computed previously does not take into account the fact that human resources can perform other tasks that do not belong to the same process. More precisely, the work list of a given human resource may contain work items of different processes. The realism of this assumption can be disputed as a human resources are "shared" by more than one process. Thus, it is might be desirable to design a procedure in order to predict the human resources availabilities. Concretely, we propose to estimate this availability values taking into account the previous observation. Let $availability[j]_{k+1}$ is the estimation of resource j availability and t_i the next task that can be performed by this resource. Instead of simply adapting to the computed availability using equation 4, one can try to forecast and estimate what $availability[j]_{k+1}$ will be using the historical data.

b. Cost Objective Function. The cost function is a structure independent criterion defined as the sum of the costs of executing all workflow tasks, given by:

$$cost = \sum_{j=1}^{n} \left\{ EC(r(t_j)) + \sum_{p \in pred(t_j)} TC(r(t_j), r(t_p)) \right\} \tag{7}$$

Thus, the *cost objective function* is to determinate the assignment of tasks of a given workflow application such that its overall execution cost is minimized.

To take into account these objectives simultaneously, we propose to use the proposed approaches in our study [1] by replacing the execution time and the execution cost by respectively Equations 4 and 7.

4 Conclusion

In this paper, we have proposed a model for business processes execution in Cloud computing environments. The proposed approaches extend our previous algorithms. More precisely, three complementary approaches are designed to deal with the problem of matching and scheduling business process tasks in Cloud context taking into account two objectives (execution time and cost incurred using a set of resources). We plan to extend the proposed work to take into account others criteria like carbon emission and energy cost.

References

1. Bessai, K., Youcef, S., Oulamara, A., Godart, C., Nurcan, S.: Bi-criteria workflow tasks allocation and scheduling in Cloud computing environments. In: Cloud Computing 2012, pp. 638–645 (2012)
2. Workflow Management Coalition: Terminology & Glossary, WfMC-TC-1011 (1999)
3. Buyya, R., Pandey, S., Vecchiola, C.: Cloudbus Toolkit for Market-Oriented Cloud Computing. In: Jaatun, M.G., Zhao, G., Rong, C. (eds.) Cloud Computing. LNCS, vol. 5931, pp. 24–44. Springer, Heidelberg (2009)

SeGA: A Mediator
for Artifact-Centric Business Processes[*]

Yutian Sun[1], Wei Xu[2,**], Jianwen Su[1], and Jian Yang[3]

[1] Department of Computer Science, UC Santa Barbara, USA
[2] School of Computer Science, Fudan University, China
[3] Department of Computing, Maquaire University, Australia

Abstract. Business processes (BPs) can be designed using a variety of modeling languages and executed in different systems. In most BPM applications, the semantics of BPs needed for runtime management is often *scattered* across BP models, execution engines, and auxiliary stores of workflow systems. The inability to capture such semantics in BP models is the root cause for many BPM challenges. In this paper, an automated tool SeGA for wrapping BPs is developed. We demonstrate that SeGA provides a simple yet general framework for runtime querying and monitoring BP executions cross different BP management systems.

1 Introduction

In today's economic market, different Business Processes (BPs) need to engage with each other to achieve competitiveness. Enabling collaboration between different BPs continues to pose a fundamental challenge. A standard BP management system (BPMS) is typically used in internal BP management in a business unit. Such systems are inadequate for business collaboration that involves different independently executing processes, and under different business process models. Therefore, interoperation between BPMSs remains in huge demand and an extremely hard problem.

BP interoperation needs to address two fundamental issues: (1) transformation between different BP model, and (2) runtime BP status and behavior monitoring, The former can smooth the communication, and the latter is critical for execution analysis and management. Web service standards such as WSDL, BPEL, WSCDL provide primitive interoperation support specified in terms of flow of activities, messages to be exchanged, roles and relationships. But they still lack satisfactory support in runtime monitoring, analysis, and process change.

Among emerging data-centric approaches to BPs is artifact-centric BPs initiated in [10]. This approach centers around *business artifacts* (or simply *artifacts*), which are business objects augmented with lifecycle information. Lifecycle information reflects the anticipated status changes of artifacts. However, to support BP mediation and runtime execution monitoring and analysis, we need business data in artifacts as well as process models and execution status information. Unfortunately, the existing artifact

---

[*] Supported in part by NSF grant IIS-0812578 and grants from IBM and Bosch.
[**] Part of work done while visiting UCSB.

P. Herrero et al. (Eds.): OTM 2012 Workshops, LNCS 7567, pp. 658–661, 2012.

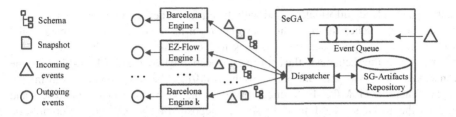

Fig. 1. SeGA Engine

BP modeling formalisms and systems [5,11] are still unable to capture BP semantics in this level of detail, though they provide a good starting point.

In data integration frameworks, wrappers and mediators are frequently used to facilitate interoperation between autonomous data management systems with heterogeneous database schemas. In this short note, we initiate a step towards BP mediation support. We look into two representative artifact BP models: GSM [5] and EZ-Flow [11]. A software tool SeGA is developed to automatically generate BP wrappers for GSM and EZ-Flow BP models. In addition, we demonstrate that SeGA can effectively support runtime management including query, constraints checking, and dynamic modifications.

This paper is organized as follows. §2 reviews GSM and EZ-Flow as well as outlines the SeGA prototype. §3 illustrates support for execution status queries and dynamic model modification. §4 discusses related work.

2   SeGA: Automated Generator for BP Wrappers

This section introduces two existing artifact-centric BP engines. Based on these two engines, a tool "SeGA" is developed to mediate the BPs that run across them.

One artifact-centric BP engine is "Barcelona" [4] that is based on GSM semantics [2]. The communication between the environment and Barcelona is accomplished through events. When an incoming event (sent by a task or a user) arrives, an update to the correlated GSM artifact instance stored in a DB2 database will be performed according to the schema. Some depending GSM artifacts may also change during the same "B-step". Once it is done, the engine will process next event if any arrives.

EZ-Flow [11] is the other artifact-centric BP engine. A step of execution in EZ-Flow moves from one snapshot to another by performing a *transition* on an EZ-Flow artifact instance. A transition is associated with execution of a task. In EZ-Flow, a task (execution) is triggered by an event. During the execution, correlated artifact instances are fetched and modified by the task. When it completes, all the affected artifact instances are stored back to repositories.

Based on the GSM and EZ-Flow artifacts, we develop a tool SeGA (Self-Guided Artifact wrapper) that can serve both as a manager of BP and execution data, and as an automated generator for process wrappers that dispatch execution of individual BPs.

Fig. 1 shows the architecture of a SeGA wrapper (or simply SeGA). Once an engine (GSM or EZ-Flow) is connected to SeGA (through a configure file), all stored artifacts will be automatically transformed to "self-guided artifacts" and stored in a repository. A *self-guided artifact* (or *sg-artifact*) is a GSM/EZ artifact augmented with state and runtime dependency information, and with the artifact schema. When an external event comes, SeGA fetches the relevant sg-artifact from its local repository, separates the schema from the sg-artifact, maps it back to the original form (GSM or EZ-Flow), deposits the artifact schema in the appropriate location where the GSM/EZ-Flow engine can access, and passes the control over to the GSM/EZ-Flow engine via forwarding the event. When the GSM/EZ-Flow engine receives the incoming event, it processes and updates the artifacts according to the schema deposited by SeGA. Once it completes, SeGA is notified and subsequently fetches all updated artifacts, maps them back to sg-artifacts and stores into its own repository. With SeGA the GSM/EZ-Flow engines can focus on execution and have no need for maintaining data, states, dependencies, and even schemas before and after execution.

Based on the design in Fig. 1, a prototype was developed to generate wrappers for GSM and EZ-Flow. The Dispatcher is written in JAVA, implementation of Event Queue and SG-Artifact Repository uses MySQL. A RESTful interface is used for accepting incoming events to SeGA, while SeGA interacts with Barcelona and EZ-Flow through their RESTful interfaces.

3   Runtime Management: Queries, Constraints, and Modifications

In this section, we demonstrate how SeGA can support BP execution querying, constraints checking, and dynamic modifications in a simple manner.

Querying and monitoring
In SeGA, all sg-artifact instances are stored in the form of relations in MySQL system. This can easily facilitate the support for querying (both current and completed) BP execution through the standard query language SQL. However, SQL does not provide constructs/vocabulary for BPs and artifacts. In order to allow BP stakeholders to query and understand BP executions, we develop a query language SGA-Q that incorporates artifact and BP concepts into an OQL-like syntax (Object Query Language [1]).

Checking choreography constraints
In collaborative BPs, choreography constraints are used to restrict how one BP should execute in a collaboration with other BPs to prevent undesirable behaviors by one process. SeGA framework provides a uniformed approach for specifying and maintaining constraints at runtime.

SeGA uses a state machine to model constraints for a BP and monitor running instances. Each BP instance is created with its associated state machine. SeGA maintains a *state table* that records sg-artifact IDs and the current states of the corresponding state machines. The constraints are based on ECA (event-condition-action) rules, i.e., when an event is received (or sent) by a running instance, if the corresponding condition is satisfied, a transition of the associated state machine is made, and this change is recorded in the *state table*. At the end of the lifecycle of the running instance, if the state machine reaches a final state, the constraints are satisfied.

Dynamic modification
BP models often change. In the literature and current practice in BPM and workflow systems, the specification of a BP model is shared by *all* running instances of the model.

Thus modification of the model presents many difficult situations, for example the instance migration problem of deciding a running instance should follow the old model or the new model. By associating each instance with its own schema, SeGA restricts the impact of a schema change to only one running instance, and thus avoids the instance migration problem.

4 Related Work

Process views have been used as an abstraction of BPs to support BP collaboration in [7,3]. Their approach supports design time BP coordination, it does not tackle the hard issue of run time management. [6] proposed a centralized artifact hub in coordinating business processes. It mainly deals with access restrictions that can be placed on stakeholders when they can view the artifacts differently.

Various techniques and formal models are proposed for BP verification [8,9]. They are only performed at the model level. Their applications to runtime analysis therefore are very limited.

Providing process flexibility to support foreseen and unforeseen changes is a very active research area. [11] presented a novel and functional mechanism to handle ad hoc and just-in-time changes at runtime.

References

1. Cattell, R., Barry, D.: The Object Data Standard: ODMG 3.0. Morgan Kaufmann (2000)
2. Damaggio, E., Hull, R., Vaculín, R.: On the Equivalence of Incremental and Fixpoint Semantics for Business Artifacts with Guard-Stage-Milestone Lifecycles. In: Rinderle-Ma, S., Toumani, F., Wolf, K. (eds.) BPM 2011. LNCS, vol. 6896, pp. 396–412. Springer, Heidelberg (2011)
3. Eshuis, R., Grefen, P.: Constructing customized process views. Data Knowl. Eng. 64(2), 419–438 (2008)
4. Heath, T., Vaculin, R., Hull, R.: Barcelona: A design and runtime environment for modeling and execution of artifact-centric business processes (demo paper). In: BPM 2011 (2011)
5. Hull, R., Damaggio, E., et al.: Business artifacts with guard-stage-milestone lifecycles: managing artifact interactions with conditions and events. In: Proc. of the 5th ACM International Conference on Distributed Event-Based System, DEBS 2011, pp. 51–62 (2011)
6. Hull, R., Narendra, N.C., Nigam, A.: Facilitating Workflow Interoperation Using Artifact-Centric Hubs. In: Baresi, L., Chi, C.-H., Suzuki, J. (eds.) ICSOC-ServiceWave 2009. LNCS, vol. 5900, pp. 1–18. Springer, Heidelberg (2009)
7. Liu, D.-R., Shen, M.: Business-to-business workflow interoperation based on process-views. Decision Support Systems 38(3), 399–419 (2004)
8. Lohmann, N., Massuthe, P., Stahl, C., Weinberg, D.: Analyzing interacting ws-bpel processes using flexible model generation. Data Knowl. Eng. 64(1), 38–54 (2008)
9. Nakajima, S.: Model-checking behavioral specification of bpel applications. Electr. Notes Theor. Comput. Sci. 151(2), 89–105 (2006)
10. Nigam, A., Caswell, N.S.: Business artifacts: An approach to operational specification. IBM Syst. J. 42, 428–445 (2003)
11. Xu, W., Su, J., Yan, Z., Yang, J., Zhang, L.: An Artifact-Centric Approach to Dynamic Modification of Workflow Execution. In: Meersman, R., Dillon, T., Herrero, P., Kumar, A., Reichert, M., Qing, L., Ooi, B.-C., Damiani, E., Schmidt, D.C., White, J., Hauswirth, M., Hitzler, P., Mohania, M. (eds.) OTM 2011, Part I. LNCS, vol. 7044, pp. 256–273. Springer, Heidelberg (2011)

An Approach to Recommend Resources for Business Processes

Hedong Yang[1,2], Lijie Wen[2], Yingbo Liu[2], and Jianmin Wang[2]

[1] Department of Computer Science & Technology, Tsinghua University
yanghd06@mails.tsinghua.edu.cn
[2] School of Software, Tsinghua University
{wenlj00,lyb01}@mails.tsinghua.edu.cn, jimwang@tsinghua.edu.cn

Abstract. Workflow management is an important technology of business process management that links tasks and qualified resources as a bridge. Researches have been carried out to improve the resource allocation of workflow that is often performed manually and empirically either by mining resource allocation rules or by optimizing the resource allocation for tasks to achieve certain goals such as minimal cost or duration. None of these approaches can guarantee to give the suitable solution to resource allocators because of the dynamic natures of business process executions. In this paper we propose an approach, $BNRR$ (Bayesian Network-based Resource Recommendation), to recommend the most proficient sets of resources for a business process based on event logs, which gives the allocators chances to find the most suitable solution. Our approach considers both the information about the resource dependency and the information about the resource capability. The approach can be applied to recommend resources either for a whole workflow or for an individual task. The approach is validated by experiments on real life data.

Keywords: Resource recommendation, staff assignment, Bayesian Network, business process management.

1 Introduction

Workflow management is such a business process technology that links tasks and resources as a bridge [2]. Human beings, as the kind of resource that we focus on in the paper, play an important role in workflow management systems because human beings cannot be replaced entirely by computers or machines in many business processes. Hence resource allocation of workflow, namely allocating right persons for right tasks at right time, becomes the basis of a successful business process. Researches have been carried out to loosen the dependence on personal experiences for resource allocation, e.g. mining resource allocation rules (e.g.[3]), finding suitable resources for tasks iteratively(e.g.[5]), and analyzing resource patterns [7]. New directions are emerging on these work. One is that more types of information available, more precise resources recommended. The other is that allocating resources for a whole workflow is better than that for individual tasks in most occasions [6]. Till now resource allocation is still a challenging topic in process mining [8].

P. Herrero et al. (Eds.): OTM 2012 Workshops, LNCS 7567, pp. 662–665, 2012.
© Springer-Verlag Berlin Heidelberg 2012

Following the second direction, we extend our work [9] to deal with general workflow models and propose an approach, *BNRR* (Bayesian Network-based Resource Recommendation), to recommend the most suitable sets of employees for a business process based on its event logs. The *BNRR* works like a search engine. The *BNRR* will recommend suitable sets of employees according to a submitted workflow model or a workflow instance, and rank these employees sets by their proficiency values. All information required for the allocation has to be mined out of event logs which record execution history of business processes concerned. Event logs are chosen as the input of the approach because they are widely available in information systems. Furthermore, a ranked list of candidates rather than the optimal one are recommended for allocators because of the dynamic natures of business process execution. The results of experiment on real world workflow event logs show that *BNRR* works as expected.

The *BNRR* can work either as a filter of the resource allocation mechanism available in a legacy PAIS to propose the most efficient sets of candidates for tasks, or as a framework of resource allocation which can deal conveniently with additional staff assignment rules, with employees joining in or leaving dynamically, and with new tasks, by changing the abundant parameters of *BNRR*. Since event logs are easily obtained, the *BNRR* would have widespread applications.

2   Preliminaries

We extend the Workflow Net by adding information about task performers. Figure 1(A) graphically describes an extended workflow as an example. The grey part of the figure depicts the control flow of the workflow, where places are denoted with cycles and tasks with squares. A dashed line links a task and its candidate employees.

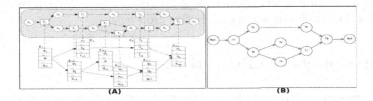

Fig. 1. (A)An extended workflow model (B)A Bayesian Network model

Bayesian Network (BN) is a tool for solving inference problems in which thousands of random variables are linked in complex ways. BN has been widely used in fields such as bioinformatics and speech processing [4]. Figure 1(B) is a graphical BN model. A node depicts a random variable, and an edge from a *parent node* to a *child node* indicates assignment of the child node depending on the value of the parent node. These dependence relationships are described mathematically by conditional probability distribution functions, which are referred to as *potential functions*. These functions are parameters of a BN model.

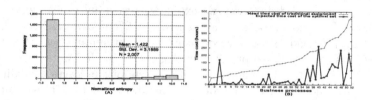

Fig. 2. (A)The normalized Shannon's entropy distribution of cooperative proficiency of employees (B)Time costs of 52 business processes

3   Bayesian Network-Based Resource Recommendation

The first step of the $BNRR$ is converting a given extended workflow model W into a bayesian network model B by means of the proposed algorithm $W2B$, which works similarly to a breadth first traversal of a graph. The principles of conversion include 1) a discrete random variable whose values are IDs of candidate employees for the task, and 2) each pair of tasks in W are connected by a directed edge in B if they were executed consecutively at least once. Figure 1(B) depicts a BN model converted from the workflow model shown in Fig. 1(A) by means of the W2B.

The second step of the $BNRR$ is calculating the parameters. $BNRR$ requires two kinds of parameters, i.e. the individual proficiency of an employee for a task and the cooperative proficiency among employees. Since proficiency is skillfulness deriving from practice, the two kinds of parameters can be approximated naturally by execution frequency of the task by the employee and by co-occurrence frequency of the employees for consecutive tasks respectively.

The last step is calculating the optimal sets. The Bucket Elimination (BE) algorithm [1] is extended for $BNRR$, by calculating the top N proficient sets rather than the optimal set of employees at each iterative step, and by considering both individual proficiency and cooperative proficiency.

4   Experiments and Evaluations

The data used in experiments are real life workflow event logs generated during last three years by PAIS systems running respectively in three vehicle manufacturing companies in China. These logs contain 7158 successful executions of 52 workflow models and 691 different tasks performed by 484 different employees. Each model has at least five executions.

Figure 2(A) depicts the impact of staff assignment of an antecedent task on that of the subsequent task. Given a task and its performer, 81.86% of performers for the subsequent tasks are determined(the leftmost bar), and only 5.38% of performers are allocated randomly(the rightmost bar). Namely 94.62% of assignments of tasks depend on those of the parent tasks in these companies.

Figure 2(B) depicts that the expected time cost of a process with the optimal set is less than the mean value apparently. This complies with the common sense that proficient person costs less for a task, so does the optimal set for a business process. It is important to note that we cannot guarantee that $BNRR$ would find out a set of employees with the minimum expected time cost of a process.

5 Conclusion and Future Work

In this paper, we propose an approach, $BNRR$, which offers a novel way of aiding to allocate employees for a business process in whole rather than only for individual tasks based on workflow event logs. A BN model is adopted as a tool to describe dependency relationships among employees. We present an algorithm to derive structure of a BN model from a workflow model, describe how to extract information from logs, and extend the BE algorithm to calculate the most proficient sets of employees for a business process. Experiment results reveal the existence of dependency relationships among employees, and validate the feasibility of the approach.

Acknowledgements. This research was partially supported by grants from Project 61003099 and Project 61073005 supported by NSFC, Project 2009CB320700 supported by National Basic Research Program (973 Plan), Project Project 2010ZX01042-002-002 by National HGJ program.

References

1. Dechter, R.: Bucket elimination: A unifying framework for probabilistic inference. In: Proc. Twelth Conf. on Uncertainty in Artificial Intelligence, Portland, Oregon, pp. 211–219 (1996)
2. Dumas, M., van der Aalst, W.M.P., ter Hofstede, A.H.M. (eds.): Process-Aware Information Systems: Bridging People and Software through Process Technology. Wiley-Interscience, Hoboken (2005)
3. Huang, Z., Lu, X., Duan, H.: Mining association rules to support resource allocation in business process management. Expert Syst. Appl. 38(8), 9483–9490 (2011)
4. Jordan, M.I.: Graphical models. Statistical Science 19(1), 140–155 (2004)
5. Liu, Y., Wang, J., Yang, Y., Sun, J.: A semi-automatic approach for workflow staff assignment. Computers in Industry 59(5), 463–476 (2008)
6. Niedermann, F., Pavel, A., Mitschang, B.: Beyond Roles: Prediction Model-Based Process Resource Management. In: Abramowicz, W., Maciaszek, L., Węcel, K. (eds.) BIS Workshops 2011 and BIS 2011. LNBIP, vol. 97, pp. 5–17. Springer, Heidelberg (2011)
7. Russell, N., van der Aalst, W.M.P., ter Hofstede, A.H.M., Edmond, D.: Workflow Resource Patterns: Identification, Representation and Tool Support. In: Pastor, Ó., Falcão e Cunha, J. (eds.) CAiSE 2005. LNCS, vol. 3520, pp. 216–232. Springer, Heidelberg (2005)
8. van der Aalst, W.M.P., et al.: Process Mining Manifesto. In: Daniel, F., Barkaoui, K., Dustdar, S. (eds.) BPM Workshops 2011, Part I. LNBIP, vol. 99, pp. 169–194. Springer, Heidelberg (2012)
9. Yang, H., Wang, C., Liu, Y., Wang, J.: An Optimal Approach for Workflow Staff Assignment Based on Hidden Markov Models. In: Meersman, R., Tari, Z., Herrero, P. (eds.) OTM-WS 2008. LNCS, vol. 5333, pp. 24–26. Springer, Heidelberg (2008)

ODBASE 2012 PC Co-chairs Message

We are happy to present the papers of the 11th International Conference on Ontologies, DataBases, and Applications of Semantics (ODBASE) held in Rome (Italy) on September 11th and 12th, 2012. The ODBASE Conference series provides a forum for research on the use of ontologies and data semantics in novel applications, and continues to draw a highly diverse body of researchers and practitioners. ODBASE is part of On the Move to Meaningful Internet Systems (OnTheMove) that co-locates three conferences: ODBASE, DOA-SVI (International Symposium on Secure Virtual Infrastructures), and CoopIS (International Conference on Cooperative Information Systems). Of particular interest in the 2012 edition of the ODBASE Conference are the research and practical experience papers that bridge across traditional boundaries between disciplines such as databases, networking, mobile systems, artificial intelligence, information retrieval, and computational linguistics. In this edition, we received 52 paper submissions and had a program committee of 82 people, which included researchers and practitioners from diverse research areas. Special arrangements were made during the review process to ensure that each paper was reviewed by members of different research areas. The result of this effort is the selection of high quality papers: fifteen as regular papers (29%), six as short papers (12%), and three as posters (15%). Their themes included studies and solutions to a number of modern challenges such as search and management of linked data and RDF documents, modeling, management, alignment and storing of ontologies, application of mining techniques, semantics discovery, and data uncertainty management.

We would like to thank all the members of the Program Committee for their hard work in selecting the papers and for helping to make this conference a success. We would also like to thank all the researchers who submitted their work. Last but not least, special thanks go to the members of the OTM team for their support and guidance.

We hope that you enjoyed ODBASE 2012 and had a wonderful time in Rome!

July 2012

Sonia Bergamaschi
Isabel Cruz

P. Herrero et al. (Eds.): OTM 2012 Workshops, LNCS 7567, p. 666, 2012.

MASTRO: Ontology-Based Data Access at Work (Extended Abstract)

Giuseppe De Giacomo, Domenico Lembo, Maurizio Lenzerini, Antonella Poggi, Riccardo Rosati, Marco Ruzzi, and Domenico Fabio Savo

Sapienza Università di Roma – Dip. di Ing. Informatica, Automatica e Sistemistica
`lastname@dis.uniroma1.it`

In this paper we present the current version of MASTRO, a system for ontology-based data access (OBDA) developed at Sapienza Università di Roma. MASTRO allows users for accessing external data sources by querying an ontology expressed in a fragment of the W3C Web Ontology Language (OWL). As in data integration [5], mappings are used in OBDA to specify the correspondence between a unified view of the domain (called global schema in data integration terminology) and the data stored at the sources. The distinguishing feature of the OBDA approach, however, is the fact that the global schema is specified using an ontology language, which typically allows to provide a rich conceptualization of the domain of interest, independently from the source representation.

In the current version of MASTRO, ontologies are specified in $DL\text{-}Lite_{A,id,den}$, a logic of the $DL\text{-}Lite$ family of tractable Description Logics, which is specifically tailored for OBDA and is at the basis of OWL 2 QL, one of the profiles of OWL 2, the current W3C standard language for specifying ontologies. $DL\text{-}Lite_{A,id,den}$ captures the main modeling features of a variety of representation languages, such as basic ontology languages and conceptual data models [6]. Furthermore, it allows for specifying advanced forms of identification and denial assertions [4], which are not part of OWL 2, but are very useful in practice.

Answering unions of conjunctive queries (UCQs) in MASTRO can be done through a technique that reduces this task to standard SQL query evaluation. The technique is purely intensional and is performed in three steps:

1. *TBox rewriting:* The first step rewrites the input UCQ according to the ontology. The rewriting, performed using the Presto algorithm [7], produces as output a non-recursive Datalog program, which encodes the intensional knowledge expressed by the ontology and the user query. The output Datalog program contains the definition of auxiliary predicates, not belonging to the alphabet of the ontology.

2. *Datalog Unfolding:* The output of the first step is then unfolded into a new UCQ by means of the *Datalog Unfolding* algorithm. It consists of a classic rule unfolding technique which eliminates all the auxiliary predicate symbols introduced by the Presto algorithm and produces a final UCQ expressed in terms of ontology concepts, roles, and attributes.

3. *Mapping Unfolding:* The last step takes the unfolded UCQ and the mapping assertions as input and produces an SQL query which can be directly evaluated over the data sources. In particular, the mapping assertions are first *split* into assertions of a simpler form, in which the head of every mapping

P. Herrero et al. (Eds.): OTM 2012 Workshops, LNCS 7567, pp. 667–668, 2012.

assertion contains only a single ontology predicate; then, the final reformulation is produced through a mapping unfolding step, as described in [6].

Notice that the use of Presto is one of the key features of the current version of MASTRO wrt previous ones [1]. Presto is an optimization of the well-known PerfectRef [2] algorithm. The latter may indeed produce rewritings consisting of a lot of UCQs, many of which are possibly redundant. Presto instead rewrites the user query into a Datalog program whose rules encode only necessary rewriting steps, thus preventing the generation of useless rules.

The usefulness of OBDA and the efficiency of the MASTRO system are showed by several industrial applications in which it has been experimented [3], e.g. in collaboration with SELEX Sistemi Integrati, Banca Monte dei Paschi di Siena and Accenture. As an example, we briefly report on the experiments carried out with the Italian Ministry of Economy and Finance (MEF). The main objectives of the project have been: the design and specification in $DL\text{-}Lite_{A,id,den}$ of an ontology for the domain of the Italian public debt; the realization of the mapping between the ontology and relational data sources that are part of the management accounting system currently in use at the ministry; the definition and execution of queries over the ontology aimed at extracting data of core interest for MEF users. In particular, the information returned by such queries relates to sales of bonds issued by the Italian government and is at the basis of various reports on the overall trend of the national public debt. The Italian public dept ontology is over an alphabet containing 164 atomic concepts, 47 atomic roles, 86 attributes, and comprises around 1440 ontology assertions. The 300 mapping assertions involve around 60 relational tables managed by Microsoft SQLServer. We tested a very high number of queries and produced through MASTRO several reports of interest for the ministry.

An extended version of this abstract can be found in [3].

References

1. Calvanese, D., De Giacomo, G., Lembo, D., Lenzerini, M., Poggi, A., Rodriguez-Muro, M., Rosati, R., Ruzzi, M., Savo, D.F.: The Mastro system for ontology-based data access. Semantic Web J. 2(1), 43–53 (2011)
2. Calvanese, D., De Giacomo, G., Lembo, D., Lenzerini, M., Rosati, R.: Tractable reasoning and efficient query answering in description logics: The *DL-Lite* family. J. of Automated Reasoning 39(3), 385–429 (2007)
3. De Giacomo, G., Lembo, D., Lenzerini, M., Poggi, A., Rosati, R., Ruzzi, M., Savo, D.F.: Mastro: A reasoner for effective ontology-based data access. In: Proc. of ORE 2012. CEUR, vol. 858 (2012), ceur-ws.org
4. Lembo, D., Lenzerini, M., Rosati, R., Ruzzi, M., Savo, D.F.: Inconsistency-tolerant first-order rewritability of DL-Lite with identification and denial assertions. In: Proc. of DL 2012. CEUR, vol. 846 (2012), ceur-ws.org
5. Lenzerini, M.: Data integration: A theoretical perspective. In: Proc. of PODS 2002, pp. 233–246 (2002)
6. Poggi, A., Lembo, D., Calvanese, D., De Giacomo, G., Lenzerini, M., Rosati, R.: Linking Data to Ontologies. In: Spaccapietra, S. (ed.) Journal on Data Semantics X. LNCS, vol. 4900, pp. 133–173. Springer, Heidelberg (2008)
7. Rosati, R., Almatelli, A.: Improving query answering over *DL-Lite* ontologies. In: Proc. of KR 2010, pp. 290–300 (2010)

A XPath Debugger
Based on Fuzzy Chance Degrees

Jesús M. Almendros-Jiménez[1], Alejandro Luna[2], and Ginés Moreno[2]

[1] Dept. of Languages and Computation, University of Almería, Spain
jalmen@ual.es
[2] Dept. of Computing Systems, University of Castilla-La Mancha, Spain
Alejandro.Luna@alu.uclm.es, Gines.Moreno@uclm.es

Abstract. We describe how we can manipulate an XPath expression in order to obtain a set of alternative XPath expressions that match to a given XML document. For each alternative XPath expression we will give a chance degree that represents the degree in which the expression deviates from the initial expression. Thus, our work is focused on providing the programmer a repertoire of paths that (s)he can use to retrieve answers. The approach has been implemented and tested.

The eXtensible Markup Language (XML) provides a very simple language to represent the structure of data, using tags to label pieces of textual content, and a tree structure to describe the hierarchical content. The XPath language [2] was designed as a query language for XML in which the path of the tree is used to describe the query. This work is motivated by the evidence that users frequently omit some tags on paths, add more than necessary, or employ wrong tags, in order to help them when formulating XPath queries.

XPath debugging has to take into account the previous considerations. Particularly, there is an underlying notion of *chance degree*. When the programmer makes mistakes, the number of bugs can be higher or lower, and the chance degree is proportional to them. Moreover, there are several ways on which each bug can be solved, and therefore the chance degree is also dependent from the number of solutions for each bug.

Our debugging method acts on a given initial XPath query Q preceded by the [DEBUG $= r$] command, where r is a real number in the unit interval used at debugging time for labeling *swapping* [1], *deletion* and *jumping* actions. So, assume that we plan to process "[DEBUG=0.5]/bib/book/title" with respect to the following XML document:

```
<bib>
    <name>Classic Literature</name>
    <book year="2001" price="45.95">
        <title>Don Quijote de la Mancha</title>
        <author>Miguel de Cervantes Saavedra</author>
        <references>
```

---

[1] We are nowadays equipping our tool with techniques for automatically extracting *similarity degrees* between tags from standard internet resources such as WordNet.

P. Herrero et al. (Eds.): OTM 2012 Workshops, LNCS 7567, pp. 669–672, 2012.
© Springer-Verlag Berlin Heidelberg 2012

```
            <novel year="1997" price="35.99">
                <name>La Galatea</name>
                <author>Miguel de Cervantes Saavedra</author>
                <references>
                    <book year="1994" price="25.99">
                        <title>Los trabajos de Persiles y Sigismunda</title
                        >
                        <author>Miguel de Cervantes Saavedra</author>
                    </book>
                </references>
            </novel>
        </references>
    </book>
    <novel year="1999" price="25.65">
        <title>La Celestina</title>
        <author>Fernando de Rojas</author>
    </novel>
</bib>
```

Our technique produces a set of alternative queries $Q_1, ..., Q_n$, packed into an output XML document, each one adorned with attributes about the changes that deviates Q_i from Q. The set of proposals is sorted with respect to a *CD* key meaning that, as much changes are performed on Q_i and as more *traumatic* they are w.r.t to Q, then its *"Chance Degree"* becomes lower according a policy based on the *product fuzzy logic*.

```
<result>
    <query cd="1.0">/bib/book/title</query>
    <query cd="0.8" book="novel">/bib/[SWAP=0.8]novel/title</query>
    <query cd="0.5" bib="//">/[JUMP=0.5]//book/title</query>
    <query cd="0.45" book=""  title="name">
        /bib/[DELETE=0.5][SWAP=0.9]name
    </query>
    <query cd="0.225" bib="" book="//" title="name">
        /[DELETE=0.5][JUMP=0.5]//[SWAP=0.9]name
    </query>
    ...
</result>
```

So, executing the first alternative -which coincides with the original query-, we can retrieve "Don Quijote de La Mancha", the second query returns "La Celestina", the third one adds "Los trabajos de Persiles y Sigismunda" to "Don Quijote", whereas the case with commands DELETE, JUMP and SWAP of lowest CD value (i.e., 0.225) is even able to produce "Classic Literature", as shown in Figure 2. The *RSV* key -*Retrieval Status Value*- means the satisfaction degree of each solution with respect to the considered query.

In order to explain how our technique works, let us consider a path P of the form "/tag_1/.../tag_i/tag_{i+1}/...", where $P[i]$ references tag_i in P: this notation is used in the following sketched algorithm where symbols Q and B refers to the original Xpath query and any *branch* of the input XML document, respectively.

```
For each branch B in the input document
  For each tag Q[i] in the input query
    If Q[i] and B[i] are ''syntactically'' different tags then
      Add a new query with SWAP if Q[i] and B[i] are ''similar'' tags
      Add a new query with JUMP if Q[i] coincides with B[j], being j>i
      Add a new query with DELETE if Q[i] coincides with B[i+1]
```

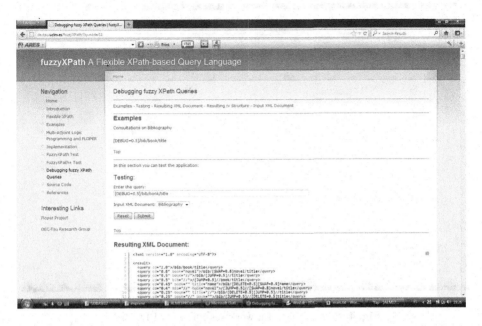

Fig. 1. Screen-shot of an on-line work session with the XPath debugger

```
<result>
  <name rsv="0.225">Classic Literature</name>
  <name rsv="0.028125">La Galatea</name>
</result>
```

Fig. 2. Execution of query "/[DELETE=0.5][JUMP=0.5]//[SWAP=0.9]name"

```
<result>
    <query cd="0.54" classic="" cost="price">
        /bib/[DELETE=0.6]//book
                [(@year < 2000) avg{3,1} ([SWAP=0.9]@price < 50)]/title
    </query>
    <query cd="0.54" classic="//" cost="price">
        /bib/[JUMP=0.6]//book
                [(@year < 2000) avg{3,1} ([SWAP=0.9]@price <50)]/title
    </query>
    <query cd="0.432" classic="" book="novel" cost="price">
        /bib/[DELETE=0.6]//[SWAP=0.8] novel
                [(@year < 2000) avg{3,1} ([SWAP=0.9]@price < 50)]/title
    </query>
    .........
    ......
    ..
</result>
```

Fig. 3. Debugging effects on XPath conditions
[DEBUG=0.6]/bib/classic//book[@year < 2000 avg{3,1} @cost < 50]/title

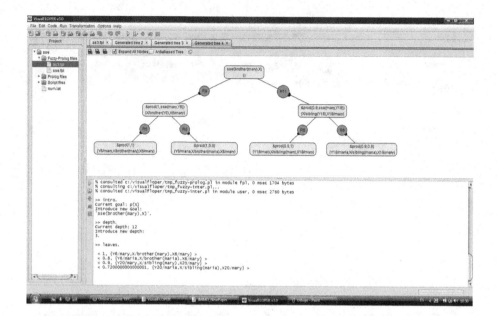

Fig. 4. Screen-shot of a work session with FLOPER

We would like to remark that even when we have worked with a very simple query with three tags in our examples, our technique works with more complex queries with larger paths and connectives in conditions. For instance, in Figure 3 we debug a query which needs to SWAP the wrong occurrence of *"cost"* by the similar word *"price"*. The first alternative deletes the tag *"classic"*, but our debugger achieves also more changes based on JUMP and SWAP commands.

To finish, we would like to mention that both the interpreter and the debugger of the fuzzy XPath dialect considered in this paper have been implemented with a fuzzy logic language (see [1] for more details) called FLOPER (see Figure 4 and visit http://dectau.uclm.es/floper/) and an on-line session is available from http://dectau.uclm.es/fuzzyXPath/.

Acknowledgements. Work partially supported by the EU, under FEDER, and the Spanish Science and Innovation Ministry (MICINN) under grant TIN2008-06622-C03-03, as well as by Ingenieros Alborada IDI under grant TRA2009-0309, and the JUNTA ANDALUCIA administration under grant TIC-6114.

References

1. Almendros-Jiménez, J.M., Luna Tedesqui, A., Moreno, G.: A Flexible XPath-based Query Language Implemented with Fuzzy Logic Programming. In: Pasche, A. (ed.) RuleML 2011 - Europe. LNCS, vol. 6826, pp. 186–193. Springer, Heidelberg (2011)
2. Berglund, A., Boag, S., Chamberlin, D., Fernandez, M.F., Kay, M., Robie, J., Siméon, J.: XML path language (XPath) 2.0. W3C (2007)

Efficiently Producing the K Nearest Neighbors in the Skyline for Multidimensional Datasets

Marlene Goncalves and Maria-Esther Vidal

Universidad Simón Bolívar, Venezuela
{mgoncalves,mvidal}@ldc.usb.ve

Abstract. We propose a hybrid approach that combines Skyline and Top-k solutions, and develop an algorithm named k-NNSkyline. The proposed algorithm exploits properties of monotonic distance metrics, and identifies among the skyline tuples, the k ones with the lowest values of the distance metric, i.e., the k nearest incomparable neighbors. Empirically, we study the behavior of k-NNSkyline in both synthetic and real-world datasets; our results suggest that k-NNSkyline outperforms existing solutions by up to three orders of magnitude.

1 Introduction

Nowadays, Web based infrastructures have been developed and allow large datasets to be published and accessed from any node of the Internet. Although the democratization of the information provides the basis to manage large volumes of data, there are still applications where it is important to efficiently identify only the best tuples that satisfy a user requirement. Based on related work, we devised a solution to this ranking problem and developed techniques able to identify the nearest neighbors to a user query which are non-dominated by any other element in the dataset. The set of non-dominated points is known as a skyline, i.e., set of points such that, none of them is better than the rest [1–4]. We developed an algorithm named k-NNSkyline to decide which of the skyline points are the nearest points to the input query; properties of a distance metric are exploited by the algorithm to avoid the computation of the whole skyline and minimize execution time as well as the number of probes required to output the k-nearest neighbors. k-NNSkyline assumes that elements or points in a dataset are characterized by multidimensions. Points are stored following the vertical partition approach; points are maintained ordered and indexed. Additionally, the algorithm maintains information about the worst values seen so far; furthermore, the multidimensional values of the k-th best points seen so far are registered. These registered values are used to stop traversing the tables while completeness and correctness are ensured, and the number of probes and executing time are minimized. We empirically studied the properties of k-NNSkyline with respect to existing approaches; results suggest that k-NNSkyline may reduce execution time by up to three orders of magnitude in both real-world and correlated synthetic data.

P. Herrero et al. (Eds.): OTM 2012 Workshops, LNCS 7567, pp. 673–676, 2012.
© Springer-Verlag Berlin Heidelberg 2012

This paper is composed of three additional sections. Section 2 summarizes our approach and section 3 reports the results of the empirical evaluation. Finally, we conclude in section 4 with an outlook to future work.

2   Our Approach

A *database* is a set of multidimensional points which are univocally identified. A *query* is comprised of: *i*) a *bound condition* or list of bounds on attributes of the multidimensional dataset, *ii*) a monotonic distance metric ρ, and *iii*) a natural number k. The *answer of a query q* corresponds to the k points in the multidimensional dataset D that are incomparable and that have the minimal values of the distance metric to the query bound condition. The set of incomparable points is known as *skyline*, and it is composed of all the points p, such that: *i*) there is not other point p' in D with values better or equal than p in all the attributes of p, and *ii*) other points in the skyline are better than p in at least one attribute.

Finally, the k *nearest incomparable neighbors* of a query q in D, correspond to a list L of k points in D, where: *i*) points in L are incomparable, i.e., they are part of the skyline, *ii*) there is no point p'' in the skyline, such that, p'' is not in L and the values of the distance metric ρ of p'' is lower or equal than at least one point in L, i.e., there is not point p''' in L and $\rho(p'') \geq \rho(p''')$.

To illustrate our approach suppose a customer is interested in selecting touristic packages for visiting the best museums and gardens in Rome; museums and gardens are both equally important for her. Further, she just wants to see a limited number of places, so a touristic package is preferred for her, if the number of museums and the number of gardens that can be visited are both lower than 10, i.e., the query bound condition establishes that (Museums $\leq$ 10, Gardens $\leq$ 10). Following these criteria a package with numbers of both museums and gardens lower than 10 will be preferred, if there is no other package with a greater number of museums and gardens. This set of packages will compose the skyline. In order to have a good selection of packages for taking a decision, the customer wants to check the 3 packages that best meet her conditions, i.e., she wants 3 nearest incomparable neighbors computed in terms of the Euclidean distance metric. The answer to this query corresponds to the 3 nearest incomparable neighbors such that, there is no package that dominates them, and there is no package with lower values of the Euclidean distance metric to the bound condition of the query.

We propose the k-NNSkyline algorithm to compute the k nearest incomparable neighbors of a query q in a multidimensional dataset D. k-NNSkyline exploits the properties of the query monotonic distance metric, and identifies among the set of skyline of points, the ones with the lowest values of this metric. The result of executing k-NNSkyline is the top-k incomparable points that satisfy the query bound condition, and with the lowest values of the distance metric, i.e., the k nearest incomparable neighbors with respect to q. k-NNSkyline assumes that data are stored following a vertically partitioned table representation, i.e., for each dimension a, there exists a relation aR composed of two attributes, *PointId* and *aValue*, that correspond to the point identifier and the value of the dimension a. Each table is indexed by two indices, one on the attribute *PointId* and the other on *aValue*; points are ordered in aR based on the values of a. k-NNSkyline implements an index based algorithm to minimize the number of probes between data dimensions to compute the skyline as well as the number of evaluations of the monotonic distance metric. k-NNSkyline relies on the indices of the vertically partitioned tables to perform an index scan; also, the ordered scan operator is implemented to retrieve the points. k-NNSkyline iterates over the different vertically partitioned tables to identify the points that have the best values, i.e., there is no other point that dominates these points. The algorithm records in a structure named *WVSF*: *i*) the *worst values* seen so far for each dimension, *ii*) the *points associated with* these values, and *iii*) the k best points seen so far. k-NNSkyline works in iterations, where the best entry(ries) in each of the vertical tables is(are) considered in one iteration. *WVSF* is updated whenever: *i*) values of a seen point are worse than the values registered in *WVSF*, *ii*) new associated points are added to the structure, or *iii*) a point with lowest values of ρ is found. The algorithm stops when a fixed-point on *WVSF* is reached.

3 Experimental Study

We empirically analyze and report on the performance of the k-NNSkyline with respect to the Top-k Skyline algorithm TKSI [3]. We considered both synthetic and real-world data. A data generator was used to build 2 synthetic datasets with 1,000,000 and 5,000,000 of points, respectively. Points are univocally identified and have ten dimensions whose values range from 0.0 to 1.0. Five of the dimensions are highly correlated to the other five, i.e., the correlation between the i-th and (i+5)-th dimensions is higher than 90%. A point dimension may have duplicated values. Furthermore, real-world datasets are composed of 1,061,664 authors and their publications were available at the DBLP site in January 2012 [1]. Queries have 10 dimensions, and k varies from 1 to 10.

Figures 1(a) and (b) report on the execution time and Figures 1(c) and (d) show the number of probes. In both cases, k-NNSkyline is compared to TKSI. In general, we can observe that k-NNSkyline outperforms TKSI in the number of probes and execution time by up to three orders of magnitude. Based on information recorded in WVSF, the k-NNSkyline algorithm is able to reach a fixed-point by checking in average 50% of the Skyline points. Contrary, TKSI is not able to detect the top-k skyline points until the whole skyline is scanned. Additionally, in presence of small skylines and large number of dominated points, TKSI may probe a point with the others to detect if this is a dominated point; this increased the number of probes. Furthermore, TKSI requires to pre-compute the distance metric values for all data which represents up to 60% of the total

---

[1] http://www.informatik.uni-trier.de/~ley/db/

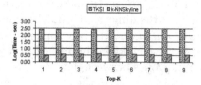

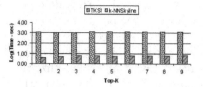

(a) Execution Time for Synthetic Dataset (log-scale)-1 Million Points

(b) Execution Time for Synthetic Dataset (log-scale)-5 Million Points

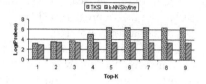

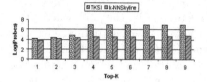

(c) Number of Probes for Synthetic Dataset (log-scale)-1 Million Points

(d) Number of Probes for Synthetic Dataset(log-scale)- 5 Million Points

Fig. 1. Execution Time and Number of Probes (log-scale)-Synthetic Data

execution time. We also evaluate these algorithms on research publications available from the DBLP website; our results confirm that k-NNSkyline outperforms TKSI algorithm by at least two orders of magnitude.

4   Conclusions and Future Work

We have casted the problem of locating the k nearest incomparable neighbors into Top-k Skyline, and proposed a ranking algorithm that provides an efficient solution to this problem. Empirically we studied the performance of our solution on real-world and synthetic data. Experimental results suggest that our algorithm may overcome existing approaches by up to three orders of magnitude. In the future we plan to exploit properties of variations of R-trees to improve the performance of our approach.

References

1. Chen, L., Lian, X.: Dynamic skyline queries in metric spaces. In: EDBT, pp. 333–343 (2008)
2. Fuhry, D., Jin, R., Zhang, D.: Efficient skyline computation in metric space. In: EDBT, pp. 1042–1051 (2009)
3. Goncalves, M., Vidal, M.-E.: Reaching the Top of the Skyline: An Efficient Indexed Algorithm for Top-k Skyline Queries. In: Bhowmick, S.S., Küng, J., Wagner, R. (eds.) DEXA 2009. LNCS, vol. 5690, pp. 471–485. Springer, Heidelberg (2009)
4. Skopal, T., Lokoc, J.: Answering metric skyline queries by pm-tree. In: DATESO, pp. 22–37 (2010)

Evaluating Semantic Technology: Towards a Decisional Framework

Roberto Armenise, Daniele Caso, and Cosimo Birtolo

Poste Italiane S.p.A.
TI - RS - Centro Ricerca e Sviluppo - 80133 Napoli, Italy
{armenis5,casodan2,birtoloc}@posteitaliane.it

Abstract. Time required to access data and query knowledge base is one of the most important parameter in designing information system. When the size increases, the complexity of an ontology makes reasoning and querying processes less efficient and very time consuming. Although performances are crucial, other features, such as the type of license, the availability of a related community support or the ease of adoption of a particular technology are often key elements in a decision-process of an industrial designer. This paper proposes an evaluation of main semantic technologies in terms of different metrics at varying ontology sizes. The evaluation aims at building a concrete framework for supporting industrial designers of ontology-based software systems to make proper decisions, taking into account the scale of their knowledge base and the main metrics.

Keywords: benchmark, ontology, OWL, semantic, reasoning.

1 Related Works

In spite of their usefulness for automatic reasoning in complex software systems, ontology-based technologies still have a limited adoption in industrial contexts where performance plays a crucial role among non-functional attributes. Performance is considered the real Achilles' heel of ontologies, especially when their size grows. Indeed, the larger the ontology size, the higher the complexity that makes less efficient both reasoning and querying activities. Nevertheless, ontology-based semantic technologies could have a wider diffusion if their performances would be related to the application contexts where they are proposed.

In literature, many benchmarks have been developed in order to test performance of semantic technologies and different metrics arise. A widely used benchmark for comparing the performance, completeness and soundness of OWL reasoning engines is the Lehigh University Benchmark (LUBM), proposed by Guo et al. [1,2]. LUBM consists of a university domain ontology, customizable and repeatable synthetic data, a set of test queries, and several performance metrics developed to facilitate the evaluation of Semantic Web repositories and to evaluate the performance of those repositories over a large data set. Garcia et al. [3] denote the importance of evaluation of quality parameters as a guide to

P. Herrero et al. (Eds.): OTM 2012 Workshops, LNCS 7567, pp. 677–680, 2012.

choose an ontological tool. They considered usability, defined as the measure of the ease of use of the ontology tools including aesthetic factors and compliance with usability and accessibility guidelines. In the current state-of-the-art, several implementations of semantic technologies are available either from opensource communities or from commercial vendors. Among them, the main opensource semantic projects can be represented by: Apache Jena, openRDF Sesame and Minerva; while in the commercial offer we can find: Oracle semantic technology, openLink Virtuoso and Ontotex OWLIM.

2 Comparing Semantic Technologies

The aim of this work is to build a complete and exhaustive decisional framework able to guide designers of industrial information systems into the huge plethora of semantic technologies. For this reason, we decide to evaluate the leading semantic technologies (choosing among commercial and opensource offer) on the basis of a set of qualitative and performance metrics. In particular, we tested

The adopted benchmark model is univ-bench LUBM [1,2]. We use Data Generator tool (UBA tool) in order to create three different ontologies: (i) LUBM(1,0) consisting of 15 departments and 1 university, (ii) LUBM(5,0) consisting of 5 universities and 93 departments, and (iii) LUBM(10,0) with 10 universities and 189 departments. In order to evaluate the inference capability and scalability of ontology systems under test, we use a set of 13 queries, defined by Guo et al.[1] and we take into account the following metrics: (i) **Specifications** which is a set of qualitative non-functional characteristic supplied by each technology, (ii) **Load Time** which measures the elapsed time to load the ontology model into storage repository, (iii) **Query Response Time** which is the time elapsed to issue the query, to obtain the result set and to traverse that set sequentially, and (iv) **Query Completeness** which is the degree of completeness of each query answer and is evaluated by the ratio between the number of the provided answers and the expected ones.

Results: We investigate[1] the different technologies by means of three directions: (i) Specifications, (ii) Load Time, (iii) Query Response Time and Completeness. Collecting together results of the qualitative and quantitative evaluations, we will define a decisional tool that gives a general overview of each technology.

Specifications are introduced to investigate some important qualitative features non-related to the performance requirements. We take into account: (i) the type of license, (ii) the documentation supporting the deployment phase, (iii) the existence of a support community, (iv) the ease of installation and (v) the ease of use of the technology itself. We express a rating for each metric according to our experience in adopting, installing and testing these technologies. The ratings

---

[1] Experiments were carried out on Intel Xeon E5650 QuadCore 2.67GHz machine with 32 GB of RAM running Windows Server 2003 R2 Enterprise x64 Edition Service Pack 2 with Java 1.6 update 26 64-bit. We performed all the execution with Java VM's heap space set between 2GB and 24GB.

are integer numbers on a -1("poor")-to-1("good") scale. Collecting the scores of different feature, we obtain that: Jena reaches a total score of 4, Sesame 3, Minerva −3, Oracle 2 (good in Documentation and Ease of use), Virtuoso 2 (good in Ease of installation and Ease of use), and OWLIM 3.

Investigating load time for the different semantic technologies, we prove that the larger the dataset size, the higher the load time. This kind of analysis lets us to make a choice of one technology rather than another one depending on the frequency of loading tasks expected in our software design.

In order to investigate query response time and completeness, we define a fitness function of a technology x: $fitness(x) = \frac{1}{Q} \cdot \sum_{q=1}^{Q} \sqrt{\left(1 - \frac{t_q(x)}{T_q}\right) \cdot C_q(x)}$ where q is the query, $t_q(x)$ is the average time (10 different runs) requested by the technology x to answer the query q, T_q is the maximum time requested for the execution of a target query q, $C_q(x)$ is the completeness of the answer provided by the technology x after the question q, and Q is the number of queries. Investigating the fitness value per technology, we can state that Minerva and OWLIM outperform in the three case studies. Indeed, these two technologies guarantee a completeness equal to 100% thus entails that they are able to provide all the expected answers in a shorter response time.

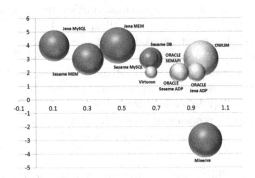

Fig. 1. Decisional framework: Investigating fitness (x axis), load time (dimensions of the bubbles), qualitative features (y axis) and license type (opensource (dark-grey bubbles), proprietary (light-grey bubbles))

The various analysis performed are able to support the choice of a semantic technology. Indeed, industrial designers of ontology-based software systems have to take into account different requirements that arise from the application they need to design.

In order to provide a decisional framework, Fig. 1 depicts our findings[2]. Each bubble refers to a semantic technology. Load time is represented by the dimension d of the bubbles (where $d = 1 - \frac{loadTime}{maxAllowedTime}$). In detail, the largest

---

[2] *MEM* refers to memory-based approach; while *DB* and *MySQL* are two different database-based approaches; *SEMAPI*, *Sesame ADP* and *Jena ADP* are different adapters of Oracle technology.

bubbles represent the technologies with the shortest loading time. X axis represents the average fitness value, while y axis represents the sum of qualitative ratings ranging in the [-4;4] interval. Fig. 1 is able to support industrial designers of ontology-based software systems in the selection process of a semantic technology. The proper choice is strongly related to the expected performance requirements, available budgets in terms of licence costs and seniority of available developers. Indeed, qualitative features which include well-supported technology and extremely comprehensive, detailed and up to date documentation can be a key element in some decisional processes. For instance, if a designer is looking for a higher level of performance and good qualitative features, he can choose OWLIM; instead, if qualitative features are not so crucial but he needs higher performances, he can choose Minerva.

3   Conclusion and Future Work

In this paper we investigate different knowledge management technologies: (i) Jena, (ii) Oracle with different adapters, (iii) SESAME, (iv) Virtuoso, (v) Minerva and (vi) OWLIM. Performance and completeness are key metrics in some decisional processes, but qualitative features such as the license, the provided documentation, the support of related communities are very important at the same time. Moreover, the easiness in installation and use play a relevant role too. Experimental results investigated different directions: (i) Specifications, (ii) Load Time, (iii) Query Response Time and Completeness. The different criteria address the problem of the selection of the proper technology according to desired characteristic of the target application. As next steps, we plan to investigate semantic technology behavior increasing dataset size and examining the relative strengths and weaknesses of these different technologies when different ontology-based software systems have to be designed.

Acknowledgments. This work was partially supported by MIUR under the MODERN Project PON01-01949. The authors would like to thank Eugenio Zimeo, whose contributions made this work possible.

References

1. Guo, Y., Pan, Z., Heflin, J.: LUBM: A benchmark for OWL knowledge base systems. Web Semantics: Science, Services and Agents on the World Wide Web 3(2-3), 158–182 (2005)
2. Guo, Y., Qasem, A., Pan, Z., Heflin, J.: A requirements driven framework for benchmarking semantic web knowledge base systems. IEEE Transactions on Knowledge and Data Engineering 19(2), 297–309 (2007)
3. García-Castro, R., Gómez-Pérez, A.: Guidelines for Benchmarking the Performance of Ontology Management APIs. In: Gil, Y., Motta, E., Benjamins, V.R., Musen, M.A. (eds.) ISWC 2005. LNCS, vol. 3729, pp. 277–292. Springer, Heidelberg (2005)

About the Performance of Fuzzy Querying Systems

Ana Aguilera[2,3], José Tomás Cadenas[1,2], and Leonid Tineo[1,2]

[1] Departamento de Computación, Universidad Simón Bolívar
Caracas, Venezuela
`jtcadenas@usb.ve, leonid@usb.ve`
[2] Centro de Análisis, Modelado y Tratamiento de Datos, CAMYTD
Facultad de Ciencias y Tecnología, Universidad de Carabobo, Venezuela
[3] Departamento de Computación, Universidad de Carabobo
Valencia, Venezuela
`aaguilef@uc.edu.ve`

Abstract. Traditional database systems suffer of rigidity. Use of fuzzy sets has been proposed for solving it. Nevertheless, there is certain resistance to adopt this, due the presumption that it adds undesired costs that worsen the performance and scalability of software systems. RDBMS are rather complex by themselves. Extensions for providing higher facilities, with a permissible performance and good scalability would be appreciated. In this paper, we achieve a formal statistics study of fuzzy querying performance. We considered two querying systems: SQLfi (loose coupling) and PostgreSQLf (tight coupling). Observed times for the later are very reasonable. It shows that it is possible to build high performance fuzzy querying systems.

Keywords: Fuzzy Query Processing, PostgreSQL, SQLf, Performance Analysis.

1 Introduction

Emerging applications require DBMS with uncertainty capabilities. SQLf [1] is a fuzzy query language that allows the use of a fuzzy condition anywhere SQL allows a Boolean. SQLf definition was updated till standard SQL:2003 [5]. High performance is a necessary precondition for the acceptance of such systems by end users. However, performance issues have been quite neglected in research on fuzzy database so far. In this paper we deal just with SQLf basic block queries using conjunctive fuzzy conditions, interpreting AND connector by the t-norm minimum. We prove that an implementation with tight-coupling strategy has better performance than one with loose-coupling. Section 2 is devoted to the Performance Analysis and section 3 points out Concluding Remarks and Future Works

2 Performance Analysis

Fuzzy querying systems may be built as extension of existing RDBMS using one of three possible extension methods: loose, middle, and tight-coupling strategies [6].

P. Herrero et al. (Eds.): OTM 2012 Workshops, LNCS 7567, pp. 681–684, 2012.

Loose-coupling consists in implement a logic layer on top of a RDBMS, processing fuzzy queries over the result of regular ones. That's the case of SQLfi [4] where, in order to keep low the extra added cost of external processing, we apply the Derivation Principle [2]. Main advantage of loose-coupling is portability. Open source RDBMS allow tight-coupling. We have made an extension of PostgreSQL for fuzzy query processing, called PostgreSQLf [3]. Fuzzy predicates definitions are stored in a catalogue table. Dynamic structures parse tree, query tree and plan tree were extended for fuzzy queries. The Planner/Optimizer derives Boolean condition from the fuzzy one. The optimization is done with the basis of the derived condition; nevertheless the evaluation is made with the fuzzy one. Evaluator's physical access mechanisms and operators were extended for computing membership degrees.

We have made an experimental performance study using formal model statistic method. The idea is to explain the influence of several factors in the observed values from experiments [7]. The importance of a factor is measured by the proportion of the total variation in the response that is explained by the factor. We designed a multi-factorial experiment of five factors with two levels for each: X1 coupling strategy (loose–tight), X2 volume (low–high), X3 number of tables (single–multiple), X4 number of monotonous fuzzy predicates (single–multiple) and X5 number of unimodal fuzzy predicates (single–multiple). It gives 2^5 combinations of levels, but we replicate, thus we did 64 runs. We took as observed variable of this experiment, the total spent time. This design supposes the value of the answer variable to be a linear combination of the factors and theirs interactions

An experimental database was created with STUDENT - ENROLL – COURSE tables. We populated them with Universidad Simón Bolívar graduate students real data from 1969 to 2007; 20,102 students; 6,640 courses and 1,759,819 enroll rows. We take this population as the low level volume. Remark we use real life data provided by the students control office. We projected a high level data volume with: 100,510 student rows; 6,640 course rows and 5,243,292 enroll rows. To guarantee the same conditions we restart the PostgreSQL server before each experiment. We compute the analysis of variance ANOVA for the model with experiment result. Obtaining that proposed model fits very well. Interaction between volume (X2) and number of unimodal predicates (X5) results been the less significant. On the other hand, experiment shows that factor coupling strategy (X1) an its interactions have very important influence in observed run times. It verifies our working hypothesis. Formal model statistic method experimentally confirms the influence of coupling strategy in run time for fuzzy query processing. In Fig. 1 we may observe the interaction plots between factor coupling strategy and others. Difference between loose-coupling and tight-coupling is evident. Query processing times for loose-coupling strategy is considerably greater than that of tight-coupling. Furthermore, this later seems to rest near to be constant. The run time is inversely proportional to the number of predicates. This is because, we experimented with fuzzy conjunctive queries. Use of more predicates reduces the number of resulting rows, so that also declines the efforts due to computation of membership degrees. Result is as expected.

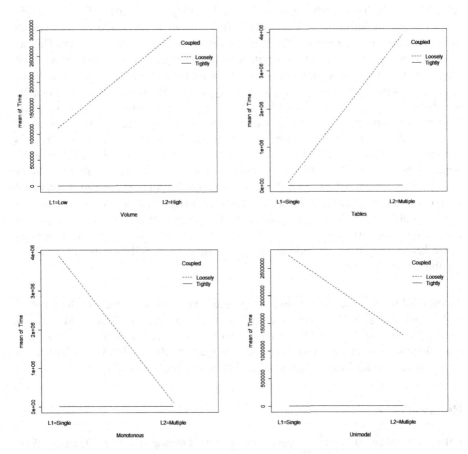

Fig. 1. Interaction Plots for factor Strategy vs: Volume (top-left). Number of Tables (top-right), Monotonous Fuzzy Predicates (bottom-left) and Unimodal Fuzzy Predicates (Bottom- right).

3   Concluding Remarks and Future Works

There is an increasing interest in the problem of dealing with vagueness and uncertainty in data and querying. These systems promises to have much applications. Therefore is very important to provide fuzzy database systems with reasonable performance. In this sense, SQLfi and PostgreSQLf were conceived. The first uses a loose-coupling strategy architecture while the later uses tight-coupling. Experiment shows that factor coupling strategy has very important influence in query processing time. In general, the results indicate that the behavior in run time of tight-coupling is significantly better. We show that between two approaches, the run time difference increases in the extent that database volume does. Moreover, this difference increases in the extent that the volume of rows rises. Observed times for tight-coupling strategy are very reasonable. They are on the order of magnitude between 10^{-1} and 10^{0} in the scale of seconds. It shows that it is possible to build high performance fuzzy querying systems. In a loose-coupling strategy, the fuzzy query is processed by an external layer. This tier obtains form the RDBMS the result set of a traditional query. This set of rows is rescanned in order to compute satisfaction degree of fuzzy conditions. This increases the query processing cost in terms of total spent time. On the other hand, with tight-coupling strategy, we implement physical access mechanisms that compute membership degrees of fuzzy conditions in the fly. That is while rows are retrieved. Also physical operators are programmed to take into account the fact that row might be provided of membership degree. These operators might combine such degrees according to fuzzy logic conditions involved in the query. It is worth the effort in the implementation of an RDBMS kernel to improve performance and scalability in fuzzy queries. This adds flexibility to SQL improving significantly the run times compared to loose-coupling strategy. In future works, it would be important to analyze how to provide SQLf affects the cost model of the RDBMS optimizer. As current version of PostgreSQLf supports a subset of SQLf, it is recommended to continue the extension in the kernel in order to provide all features form current SQLf definition, which is feasible and promising.

Acknowledgment. We give thanks all people who worked in the development of SQLfi and PortgreSQLf fuzzy querying systems, as well as Venezuela national founds for sciences FONACIT that has supported these developments. This work is done for the glory of the Lord "The horse is made ready for the day of battle, but victory rests with the Lord." Proverbs 21:31 New International Version (NIV).

References

1. Bosc, P., Pivert, O.: SQLf: A Relational Database Language for Fuzzy Quering. IEEE Transactions on Fuzzy Systems 3(1) (February1995)
2. Bosc, P., Pivert, O.: SQLf query functionality on top of a regular relational DBMS. In: Pons, O., Vila, M.A., Kacprzyk, J. (eds.) Knowledge Management in Fuzzy Databases (2000)
3. Aguilera, A., Cadenas, J., Tineo, L.: Fuzzy Querying Capability at Core of a RDBMS. In: Yan, L., Ma, Z. (eds.) Advanced Database Query Systems: Techniques, Applications and Technologies, pp. 160–184. IGI Global, New York (2011)
4. Goncalves, M., Tineo, L.: SQLfi and its Applications. Avances en Sistemas e Informática, vol. 5(2) (2008); Medellin, ISSN 1657-7663
5. Goncalves, M., González, C., Tineo, L.: A New Upgrade to SQLf: Towards a Standard in Fuzzy Databases. In: Proc of DEXA 2009 Workshops (2009)
6. Timarán, R.: Arquitecturas de Integración del Proceso de Descubrimiento de Conocimiento con Sistemas de Gestión de Bases de Datos: un Estado del Arte. Ingeniería y Competitividad 3(2) (2001)
7. Raj, J.: The Art of Computer Systems Performance. John Wiley/Sons, Inc. (1991)

Author Index